SIR PHILIP SIDNEY

The Countess of Pembroke's
Arcadia

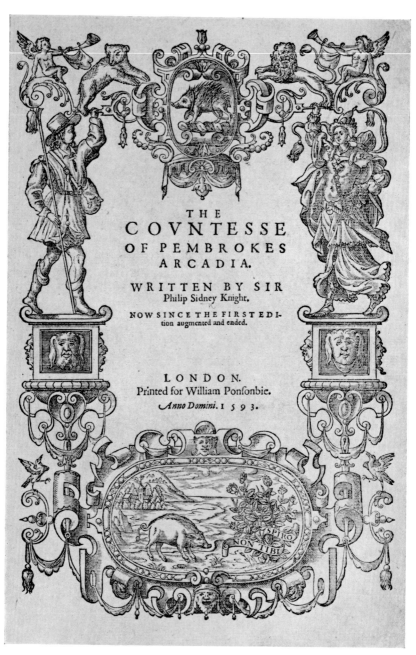

THE
COVNTESSE
OF PEMBROKES
ARCADIA.

WRITTEN BY SIR
Philip Sidney Knight.

NOW SINCE THE FIRST EDI-
tion augmented and ended.

LONDON.
Printed for William Ponsonbie.
Anno Domini. 1 5 9 3.

SPIRO
NON TIBI

Title-page of *The Countess of Pembroke's Arcadia* (1593)

SIR PHILIP SIDNEY

The Countess of Pembroke's Arcadia

(THE OLD ARCADIA)

EDITED WITH
INTRODUCTION AND COMMENTARY
BY
JEAN ROBERTSON

OXFORD
AT THE CLARENDON PRESS
1973

Oxford University Press, Ely House, London W. 1

GLASGOW NEW YORK TORONTO MELBOURNE WELLINGTON
CAPE TOWN IBADAN NAIROBI DAR ES SALAAM LUSAKA ADDIS ABABA
DELHI BOMBAY CALCUTTA MADRAS KARACHI LAHORE DACCA
KUALA LUMPUR SINGAPORE HONG KONG TOKYO

*Printed in Great Britain
at the University Press, Oxford
by Vivian Ridler
Printer to the University*

PREFACE

THIS is the first attempt to establish an accurate text for the whole of Sidney's *Old Arcadia*. Professor William A. Ringler, Jr., has already done this in his edition of *The Poems of Sir Philip Sidney* (Oxford: Clarendon Press, 1962) for the poems in the *Old Arcadia*, and his analysis of the relationships of the surviving texts has provided the groundplan for this undertaking. Sidney scholars have had reason to be grateful to the late Professor Albert Feuillerat and the Cambridge University Press for the fact that the *Old Arcadia* has been available in print since 1926 as Volume IV of *The Complete Works of Sir Philip Sidney* (*The Prose Works* were reprinted in 1962). But as early as 1929 Professor Zandvoort's comparison of the two versions of the *Arcadia* revealed how far short of representing Sidney's text this edition fell. It is an extremely accurate transcript (I have noted less than 100 errors), with a few corrections, of the Clifford MS.; but this is a rather inaccurate copy made by a scribe much prone to eyeskip from the scribal manuscript (now lost) that Sidney used as his working copy, and from which all the extant manuscripts of the *Old Arcadia* ultimately derive. Moreover, the Clifford MS. was copied before Sidney had made his fourth set of revisions in his working copy. Nor was more than minimal reference made in this edition to the other four manuscripts known to Feuillerat; and since 1926 another four have turned up, as well as one containing most of the poems and one passage of prose. Not much was done to correct obvious errors from the version of Books III–V of the *Old Arcadia* that was added to the *New Arcadia* in the edition of 1593. Again, the passages from the *Old Arcadia* that Sidney incorporated in Books I and II of the *New Arcadia*, first published in 1590, were not consulted for the light they can throw on the readings in the *Old Arcadia* manuscripts (the manuscript copy of the *New Arcadia* in the Cambridge University Library was not known to Feuillerat).

The manuscripts in the Bodleian Library, Oxford, and in the Library of St. John's College, Cambridge, both incorporate later revisions than do the other surviving manuscripts of the *Old Arcadia*. The St. John's College MS. is the more accurate of the two, and it has therefore been used as the copy-text for this edition. The other

witnesses to the text have all been collated and misreadings in the
copy-text have been corrected. The variant readings reveal Sidney's
successive revisions. The textual complexities are discussed, and the
editorial procedure adopted to deal with them is explained, in the
Textual Introduction.

Feuillerat's transcript reproduces all the peculiarities of ortho-
graphy and punctuation, as well as the endless succession of
unparagraphed pages, found in the Clifford MS. The result is a
daunting obstacle to the enjoyment of Sidney's work. In the absence
of Sidney's holograph, there seems little point in preserving the
idiosyncrasies of one particular scribe. In this edition, therefore,
spelling and punctuation have been normalized, and paragraphs and
inverted commas for speeches have been supplied. In general,
quotations taken from Sidney's other works, and also from the
works of other writers, are given in modern spelling.

The General Introduction places the *Old Arcadia* in the context
of Sidney's life and thought and of the development of prose fiction.
His principal sources and his innovations are indicated; but little is
said about his metrical experiments, because Professor Ringler has
already dealt so thoroughly with the poems. However, Sidney's
prose style and diction are discussed.

In the Commentary the important textual variants are considered,
and the meaning of ambiguous or tangled sentences is elucidated.
Possible sources for particular passages are indicated. There are
notes on words that call for more comment than the brief definitions
in the Glossary; and attention is drawn, often by reference to
Abraham Fraunce's *The Arcadian Rhetoric*, to the principal rhetorical
figures used by Sidney. Proverbs are identified by Tilley's numbers,
and where dates are given for his earliest citations, it may be
assumed that no earlier examples are to be found in the third
edition of the *Oxford Dictionary of English Proverbs*, unless there is
a statement to the contrary. The list of references and abbreviations
indicate which works I have found most useful. Professor Ringler's
notes on the poems are frequently either quoted or summarized.
Books and articles bearing on particular passages only are cited in
the relevant place in the Commentary. I have tried to read every-
thing that has been published on the *Arcadia*, and have been much
aided in this endeavour by the kindness of authors in sending me
copies of their publications. I hope that those scholars who do not
find their views and interpretations reported in what can only be a

brief guide to the *Old Arcadia* will forgive me. There is a 'Bibliography of Sidney Studies since 1935', prepared by W. L. Godshalk, in the second edition of K. Myrick, *Sir Philip Sidney as a Literary Craftsman* (University of Nebraska Press, 1965);[1] and there is a Supplement to S. A. Tannenbaum, *Sir Philip Sidney: a Concise Bibliography* (New York, 1941), compiled by G. R. Guffey, in *Samuel Daniel, 1942–65; Michael Drayton, 1941–65; Sir Philip Sidney, 1941–65* (London: Nether Press, 1967). The Arcadian literature is surveyed in F. Marenco, '"Une apothéose de genres": Sidney e l'*Arcadia* nella critica letteraria', *Filologia e letteratura*, xii, fasc. iv (1966), 337–76. Professor Ringler is preparing the section on Sidney for *The New Cambridge Bibliography of English Literature*.

I am grateful to the Leverhulme Trust and to the Folger Shakespeare Library for Fellowships that enabled me to work for uninterrupted periods on this edition, and to the University of Southampton for a term's leave of absence during the final stage of its preparation. On two occasions the hospitality of the Principal and Vice-Principal of Lady Margaret Hall enabled me to work in Oxford under ideal conditions.

I have received much help and kindness from the staff of the libraries in which I have worked; in particular, I would name the Bodleian Library, Oxford, the British Museum Reading, Manuscript, and Map Rooms, the University of Southampton Library, the Folger Shakespeare Library, the H. E. Huntington Library, and the Newberry Library, Chicago.

I am indebted to the Council of St. John's College, Cambridge, for permission to use their manuscript of the *Old Arcadia* as the copytext for this edition, and to the governing bodies of the following institutions and libraries for permission to cite variants from the manuscripts and prints in their possession: the Bodleian Library, Oxford; the British Museum; the Cambridge University Library; Jesus College, Oxford; Queen's College, Oxford; the Folger Shakespeare Library; the H. E. Huntington Library. To this list must be added the name of one individual: Mr. Arthur A. Houghton, Jr., who kindly sent me a microfilm of the Helmingham Hall MS. soon after he had purchased it.

I have incurred numerous obligations to individuals, and thank all those who have helped me with advice and answers to queries;

[1] See also *English Literary Renaissance*, No. 4 (1972).

among them are Mr. John Buxton, Professor Norman Davis, Dr. J. A. van Dorsten, Professor Ephim G. Fogel, Dr. Bent Juel-Jensen, Dr. C. S. Levy, and Professor F. T. Prince. Dr. Ethel Seaton came to my rescue in early days, when Volume IV of *The Complete Works of Sir Philip Sidney* was out of print, with the loan of her own annotated copy. Miss Katherine Duncan-Jones has dealt frequently, patiently, and rapidly with my inquiries, which often involved the consultation of material in the Bodleian Library, Oxford.

My attention was first drawn to the need for a critical edition of both versions of the *Arcadia* by Professor D. J. Gordon, when he invited me to read a paper on 'The Editorial Problem in Sidney's *Arcadia*' at a Symposium on Sir Philip Sidney held at the University of Reading in 1954. I should not have had the temerity to take up the challenge without my early training at the University of Liverpool under Professor L. C. Martin, and its continuation over many years, terminated only by their deaths, by Mr. John Crow and Professor F. P. Wilson. Even so, I should never have got started had not the main work on the textual problems already been done by Professor William A. Ringler, Jr. The almost-wearisome iteration of the word *Ringler* throughout the Introduction and Commentary falls far short of covering the full extent of my indebtedness to him. Whenever we have met, he has given generously of his time and advice, and a sense of my obligation to him has sustained me over the years. Latterly, I have had much help from Mr. Victor Skretkowicz, Jr., particularly in making available to me his collations of the manuscript in the Cambridge University Library with the printed editions that he has examined for his forthcoming edition of the *New Arcadia*. I owe a special debt of gratitude to Professor Dame Helen Gardner for finding the time to scrutinize my early drafts of the Introduction and Commentary, and for making so many equally valuable constructive and destructive suggestions. The faults that remain are mine; they would have been far more numerous without her help. Finally, my husband, Professor J. S. Bromley, deserves a place in the story for his forbearance during my long sojourn in Arcadia.

J. R.

University of Southampton
October 1970

CONTENTS

REFERENCES AND ABBREVIATIONS

The following abbreviations are used for titles of Sidney's works:

AS *Astrophil and Stella*
CS *Certain Sonnets*
LM *Lady of May*
NA *New Arcadia*
OA *Old Arcadia*
OP 'Other Poems'

References to particular poems are made on Ringler's system: AS 4 denotes the fourth sonnet of *Astrophil and Stella*; AS 4. 9 denotes the ninth line of the fourth sonnet. Ringler's numbers for the *Old Arcadia* poems are given in the Commentary, and again in the first-line index.

The abbreviations used for extant manuscripts will be found in the List of Sigla on p. lxxii. The following abbreviations are used for lost manuscripts:

G The *New Arcadia* MS. that Sidney left with Greville
P The *Old Arcadia* MS. that Sidney gave to his sister
T Scribal transcript of Sidney's *Old Arcadia* foul papers (also lost)
   T was used by Sidney as his working copy, and T¹–T⁵ indicate successive revisions of T
X The *Old Arcadia* MS. that was copied from T¹, the original of Je and Hm
Y The *Old Arcadia* MS. that was copied from T², the original of Ph

The following abbreviations are used for editions of Sidney's works:

Pears   *The Correspondence of Sir Philip Sidney and Hubert Languet*, ed. S. A. Pears (London, 1845)
Ringler *The Poems of Sir Philip Sidney*, ed. W. A. Ringler, Jr. (Oxford, 1962)
Shepherd *Sir Philip Sidney: 'An Apology for Poetry, or The Defence of Poesy'*, ed. G. Shepherd (London, 1965)
Works *The Complete Works of Sir Philip Sidney*, ed. A. Feuillerat, 4 vols. (Cambridge, 1912–26)

Other references:

Arundel Harington MS. *The Arundel Harington Manuscript of Tudor Poetry*, ed. R. Hughey, 2 vols. (Columbus, Ohio, 1960)
W. Blount   Contemporary annotations by W. Blount in the Folger Shakespeare Library copy of *The Countess of Pembroke's Arcadia* (1593)
Brewer   *A Dictionary of Phrase and Fable*, by E. C. Brewer
Brie   *Sidneys Arcadia*, by F. Brie (Strasburg, 1918)
Buxton   *Sir Philip Sidney and the English Renaissance*, by J. Buxton, 2nd edn. (London, 1964)
Davis, *Map* *A Map of Arcadia: Sidney's Romance in its Tradition*, by W. R. Davis (New Haven, Conn., 1965)

Dent   *John Webster's Borrowing*, by R. W. Dent (Berkeley:
                        University of California Press, 1960)
Diana, ed. Kennedy   *Yong's Translation of George of Montemayor's
                        'Diana' and Gil Polo's 'Enamoured Diana'*, a
                        critical edn. by J. M. Kennedy (Oxford, 1968)
Dorsten, *Poets*   *Poets, Patrons, and Professors: Sir Philip Sidney,
                        Daniel Rogers, and the Leiden Humanists*, by J. A.
                        van Dorsten (Leiden and Oxford, 1962)
K. Duncan-Jones   'Sidney's Pictorial Imagination', by K. Duncan-
                        Jones (Oxford B.Litt. Thesis, 1964)
England's Helicon   *England's Helicon*, ed. H. E. Rollins, 2 vols. (Cam-
                        bridge, Mass.: Harvard University Press, 1935)
England's Parnassus   *England's Parnassus*, ed. C. Crawford (London, 1913)
Fellowes, 3rd edn.   *English Madrigal Verse, 1588–1632*, ed. E. H.
                        Fellowes, revised and enlarged by F. W. Sternfeld
                        and D. Greer (Oxford, 1967)
Fogel   'The Personal References in the Fiction and Poetry
                        of Sir Philip Sidney', by E. G. Fogel (Ohio State
                        University Doctoral Thesis, 1958)
Fraunce   *'The Arcadian Rhetoric'*, by Abraham Fraunce, ed.
                        E. Seaton (Luttrell Society ix, Oxford, 1950)
Goldman   *Sir Philip Sidney and the 'Arcadia'*, by M. S. Gold-
                        man (Urbana, Ill., 1934)
Greville, *Life*   *The Life of the Renowned Sir Philip Sidney*, by Fulke
                        Greville, ed. Nowell Smith (London, 1907)
Harington   *'Orlando Furioso' in English Heroical Verse*, translated
                        by Sir John Harington (1591)
Heliodorus   *Heliodorus's 'An Aethiopian History'*, translated by
                        T. Underdowne, ed. C. Whibley (London, 1895)
Hoskyns   *'Directions for Speech and Style'*, by John Hoskyns,
                        ed. H. H. Hudson (Princeton, N.J., 1935)
Juel-Jensen   'Check-List of Editions of *Arcadia* to 1739', by B. E.
                        Juel-Jensen, *The Book Collector*, xi (1962), 468–
                        79.
Kalstone   *Sidney's Poetry: Contexts and Interpretations*, by D.
                        Kalstone (Cambridge, Mass.: Harvard University
                        Press, 1965)
Lanham   *'The Old Arcadia'*, by R. A. Lanham (New Haven,
                        Conn., 1965)
Myrick   *Sir Philip Sidney as a Literary Craftsman*, by K. O.
                        Myrick (Harvard University Press, 1935; 2nd edn.,
                        Lincoln: University of Nebraska Press, 1965)
Puttenham   *The Art of English Poesy* [by George Puttenham], ed.
                        G. D. Willcock and A. Walker (London, 1936)
Rubel   *Poetic Diction in the English Renaissance*, by V. L.
                        Rubel (New York, 1941)
Rudenstine   *Sidney's Poetic Development*, by N. L. Rudenstine
                        (Cambridge, Mass.: Harvard University Press, 1967)

Sargent	*At the Court of Queen Elizabeth: Life and Lyrics of Sir Edward Dyer*, by R. M. Sargent (London, 1935)
Scott	*Les Sonnets élisabéthains*, by J. G. Scott (Paris, 1929)
Tilley	*Dictionary of Proverbs in English in the Sixteenth and Seventeenth Centuries*, by M. P. Tilley (Ann Arbor, Mich., 1950)
Wallace	*The Life of Sir Philip Sidney*, by M. W. Wallace (Cambridge, 1915)
Wilson	*Sir Philip Sidney*, by M. Wilson, 2nd edn. (London, 1950)
Wolff	*Greek Romances in Elizabethan Prose Fiction*, by S. L. Wolff (New York, 1912)
Zandvoort	*Sidney's 'Arcadia': a Comparison between the Two Versions* (Amsterdam, 1929)
Comp. Lit.	*Comparative Literature*
H.L.Q.	*Huntington Library Quarterly*
J.E.G.P.	*Journal of English and Germanic Philology*
M.L.N.	*Modern Language Notes*
M.L.R.	*Modern Language Review*
M.P.	*Modern Philology*
N. & Q.	*Notes and Queries*
O.D.E.P.	*Oxford Dictionary of English Proverbs*, 3rd edn. (1970)
O.E.D.	*Oxford English Dictionary*
P.M.L.A.	*Publications of the Modern Language Association of America*
Ph.Q.	*Philological Quarterly*
R.E.S.	*Review of English Studies*
S.P.	*Studies in Philology*

GENERAL INTRODUCTION

DATE

EDMUND MOLYNEUX, secretary to Sidney's father, stated that Sidney began to write his *Arcadia* soon after his return from his embassy to Germany in June 1577: 'not long after his return from that journey, and before his further employment by her majesty,[1] at his vacant and spare times of leisure (for he could endure at no time to be idle and void of action), he made his book which he named his *Arcadia*'.[2] Sidney's dedicatory letter makes it abundantly clear that the *Old Arcadia* was very much the Countess of Pembroke's book, 'done only for you, only to you'; and 'being done in loose sheets of paper, most of it in your presence, the rest by sheets sent unto you as fast as they were done' strongly suggests that most of it was written whilst he was staying with his sister at Wilton. George Carleton was the only one of the contemporary elegists who refer to the *Arcadia* to mention that it was written at Wilton.[3] Much of John Aubrey's gossip about Sidney and his sister is doubtless unreliable, but there was probably some truth behind the anecdote told him by his great-uncle, Thomas Browne: 'he was often wont, as he was hunting on our pleasant plains, to take his table-book out of his pocket, and write down his notions as they came into his head, when he was writing his Arcadia (which was never finished

[1] Presumably Molyneux refers to Sidney's appointment as Governor of Flushing in 1585; and his statement may be taken to cover both versions of the *Arcadia*—he does not mention, if he knew, that Sidney began to rewrite his book.

[2] Note contributed to Stow's continuation of Holinshed's *Chronicles* (1587, uncensored version), iii. 1554ᵃ. As was noted by Zandvoort, 5, Molyneux may be inaccurate, for he said that Sidney was 'not above one and twenty years old' at the time of the German embassy, whereas he was in fact twenty-two.

[3]
> Arcades o saltem, soli cantare periti
> Arcades, o, vestras inter si carmina siluas
> Maiore insonuit calamo: secumque canentem
> Si summo valuit deducere Pana Lycaeo:
> Et quae Maenalio ludebant vertice, Nymphas
> Pembrochia potuit si sistere primus in aula:
> Montibus haec vestris cantabitis Arcades; imis
> Vallibus haec: siluae vobis vallesque loquentes.

Exequiae (1587), L1ᵛ–L2.) The poem was reprinted in Carleton's *Heroici Characteres* (1603).

by him).'¹ Sidney was at Wilton in August, September, and December 1577, and he might have begun his *Arcadia* during these visits: but the evidence points to the composition of the bulk of the story when he was at Wilton and Ivy Church from March to August 1580. Neither Thomas Moffet's attempt to suggest that all Sidney's imaginative works were *adolescentia*,² nor Thomas Howell's complaint in his *Devises* (1581), in a rather cryptic poem 'Written to a most excellent book, full of rare invention', that 'all too long thou hid'st so perfect work',³ need be taken to imply that the *Old Arcadia* was completed in the 1570s. Howell's general hyperbole is consonant with the interpretation that to keep the work from circulation for a moment after its completion was an unjust deprivation of the reader. There must have been some authority for the statement in the title of the Phillipps MS. (though this copy of the *Old Arcadia* was made after Sidney's death) that the work was 'made in the year 1580'.⁴ When Sidney was back at Leicester House, he wrote to his brother Robert on 18 October 1580: 'My toyful book(s) I will send with God's help by February.'⁵ Whether Sidney wrote book or books,⁶ the reference must surely be to the *Old Arcadia*, written in five books or acts. David Hume of Godscroft, a member

---

¹ *Brief Lives*, ed. Clark, ii. 248. In the expanded version in *The Natural History of Wiltshire*, i. 262, 311, Aubrey simply states that Sidney wrote down the dictates of the Muses 'in his table-book, though on horseback'. Either version is compatible with Sidney's known dislike of hunting; see Sir John Harington, *Metamorphosis of Ajax*, ed. Donno, p. 108, and Spenser's 'Astrophil', 79–82.

² *Nobilis*, ed. and trans. V. B. Heltzel and H. H. Hudson (1940), pp. 73–4. Moffet was anxious to hold up Sidney as an example to his evidently already rakishly inclined nephew, William Herbert. He reports that Sidney favoured burning *Astrophil and Stella*, and smothering the *Arcadia* at birth.

³ Ed. W. Raleigh (1906), pp. 44–5. We learn from the rest of the poem that the author is young, the book is learned, and full of pleasant tunes, and though it contains

> Discourse of lovers, and such as fold sheep,
> Whose saws well mixed, shrouds mysteries deep

readers will also learn how useless it is

> To shun high powers that sway our states below

and its circulation would maintain the Countess of Pembroke's name. *Devises* is dedicated to her. Howell was an old Pembroke servant who had gone with Lady Anne Herbert, daughter of William, Earl of Pembroke, when she married Francis, Lord Talbot, and had returned to Wilton with Lady Katherine Talbot, the previous wife of Henry, Earl of Pembroke. Vague as the poem is, the details fit the *Arcadia* well enough.

⁴ What evidence there is suggests that the other extant *Old Arcadia* manuscripts were not copied before 1580–2.

⁵ *Works*, iii. 132.

⁶ The letter at Penshurst is not holograph; it is impossible to say whether the transcriber intended -*e* or the abbreviation for -*es* at the end of *book*.

of the Earl of Angus's train, records that after the death of his uncle Morton, Angus retired to England, where he was

honourably entertained by the bountiful liberality of that worthy queen Elizabeth . . . [and received] love and favour both from her Majesty's self, and her Councillors and Courtiers that then guided the state; such as Sir Robert Dudley (Earl of Leicester), Sir Francis Walsingham, Secretary; and more especially, he procured the liking of him who is ever to be remembered with honour, Sir Philip Sidney I mean; like disposition, in courtesy, of nature, equality of age and years, did so knit their hearts together, that Sir Philip failed not (as often as his affairs would permit him) to visit him, in so much that he did scarce suffer any one day to slip, whereof he did not spend the most part in his company. He was then in travail, or had brought forth rather (though not polished and refined it as now it is) that his so beautiful and universally accepted birth, his *Arcadia*. He delighted much to impart it to Angus, and Angus took as much pleasure to be partaker thereof.[1]

Morton was brought to the scaffold at Edinburgh on 2 June 1581, and Angus left London in August 1582.[2] When, therefore, Fulke Greville wrote to Walsingham in November 1586 about the proposal to print 'S*ir* philip sydneys old arcadia': 'I haue sent my lady yor daughter at her request, a correction of that old one don 4 or 5 years since which he left in trust with me . . .',[3] it seems clear that 'don 4 or 5 years since' must refer to the date of the completion of the *Old Arcadia*. If we bear in mind the successive revisions revealed by the extant *Old Arcadia* manuscripts, the evidence suggests that the first draft was more or less completed by the spring of 1581, and that Sidney continued to tinker with his transcript during 1581–2, before starting to rework his story as the *New Arcadia*.

It is impossible to say when Sidney began to write poetry,[4] but some of the poems included in the *Old Arcadia* may well have been

---

[1] David Hume of Godscroft, *The History of the Houses of Douglas and Angus* (Edinburgh, 1644), pp. 361–2.

[2] Ibid., pp. 356–7, 367. Sidney again entertained Angus in 1585; Walsingham wrote on 4 September: 'The poor Earl of Angus and Earl of Mar receive here little comfort otherwise than from poor Sir Philip Sidney, so as our course is to alienate all the world from us'; and again on 10 September: 'The burden of the charges of entertaining the Scottish lords will light upon Sir Philip Sidney' (*Hamilton Papers*, cited by Wallace, 321–2).

[3] P.R.O., S.P. 12/195/33, from Ringler's transcript, 530.

[4] After surveying the meagre evidence for the years 1572–5, Ringler, xxiii, concludes that 'If he had any interest in vernacular poetry, he kept it to himself. . . . The men who knew him best on the Continent thought of him as a young man interested in learning and religion; they did not think of him as a future poet.'

written before the story took shape. The earliest reference to his
interest in poetry is in the opening line of the poem addressed to him
by Melissus (Paul Schede, librarian to the Elector Palatine) after
Sidney's visit to Heidelberg in 1577:

Sydnee Musarum inclite cultibus.[1]

Melissus may have encouraged Sidney's interest in experimental
verse forms, including quantitative metres;[2] but he had obtained
some rules on the application of quantity to English verse drawn up
by Thomas Drant, who died in 1578.[3] These rules are first mentioned
in October 1579 by Spenser in his letter to Harvey,[4] and it is only in
this year that there is any firm evidence of Sidney's own poetic
activity.[5] On 14 January 1579, when he was with Hubert Languet at
Ghent, Daniel Rogers addressed a long Latin poem to Sidney,
beginning with an elaborate tribute to Queen Elizabeth and the
ladies of the Court, which leads to the suggestion that Sidney's and
Dyer's poetic gifts were more fitted to celebrate them than his own.[6]
Later in the same poem Rogers refers to the discussions on law,

---

[1] The poem was not printed until 1586. Dorsten, *Poets*, 51, takes this line as a tribute
to Sidney as a poet, but Buxton, 91, as a reference to his reputation as a patron; *cultus*
will bear either interpretation. Nor should Gabriel Harvey's address to Sidney as one
'In quibus ipsae habitent Musae, dominetur Apollo' (*Gratulationum Valdinensium
Libri Quatuor* (1578), K3ᵛ) necessarily be taken literally, 'since he also gave him the
attributes of all the other deities of the pantheon' (Ringler, lxi n.).

[2] The two men kept in touch for several years (Ringler, xxv).

[3] Thomas Drant had addressed adulatory remarks to Sidney in *Praesul* (1576), and
presumably gave him his rules sometime thereafter.

[4] Spenser referred to them again in April 1580: *Poetical Works of Edmund Spenser*,
ed. de Selincourt, pp. 612, 635.

[5] The *Lady of May* was composed for the entertainment of Queen Elizabeth when
she visited Sidney's uncle, the Earl of Leicester, at Wanstead. She was there during
6–16 May 1578, and again in 1–2 May 1579. 'Lady of the whole month of May', and
'Lady of this Dame Maia's month', might be thought to cover the fact that the enter-
tainment took place after 1 May, as it did in 1578, and Ringler prefers the earlier date,
as the jog-trot rhythms and nature of the characters suggest that the *Old Arcadia* had
not yet assumed definite form; but this argument could apply equally well to May
1579. Furthermore, the additional final speech of Rombus in the Helmingham/Houghton
MS. states that Master Robert of Wanstead 'is foully commaculated with the papistical
enormity'. This is more appropriate to 1579, the year of the French marriage negotia-
tions, opposed by Walsingham, Leicester, and Sidney. In May the English Catholics'
hopes were high, and attacks on Leicester intensified. Simier had arrived early in
January as Alençon's agent, and though he did not inform Elizabeth of Leicester's
secret marriage in October 1578 to Lettice Knollys, widow of the Earl of Essex, until
July, the intensity of her wrath would be accounted for if she had but recently been
offered the homage of the *Lady of May*. I therefore incline to 1579 as the date of this
pastoral entertainment.

[6] Lines 51–64; the poem is printed in Dorsten, *Poets*, 176 ff.

religion, and moral philosophy that Sidney was sharing with Dyer
and Greville. He does not say so, but the 'happy blessed Trinity'[1]
may well have been writing verse as well. By the spring of 1579
Spenser had probably entered the service of Leicester; and between
April and December 1579 he was writing, or at any rate revising,
some of the eclogues of *The Shepherds' Calendar*.[2] It is true that
pastoral was the recognized form in which a young poet should try
his wings; and, despite the eye-catching references to the 'famili-
arity' in which Dyer and Sidney were good enough to hold Spenser
in the Spenser/Harvey correspondence, it may also be true that
Sidney and Spenser 'never became well acquainted and never had
any really serious discussions of the technicalities of their craft'.[3]
Yet it surely seems likely that the experiments of the two poets
in using continental verse forms and rustic or archaic words for
pastoral eclogues were not made in entire ignorance of each other's
labours, seeing that they were both resident in Leicester House in
1579. When Sidney retired to Wilton in the spring of 1580, he may
already have had the nucleus of his four sets of Eclogues with their
prose links; for by the end of the year he had nearly completed the
first draft of his story.

SOURCES

The Spenser/Harvey correspondence makes it abundantly clear that
in the matter of writing English verses in classical metres Spenser
was the rather inefficient pupil; nor does he show Sidney's under-
standing of such continental forms as the sestina. On the other hand,
his pervasive and continued use of an 'old rustic language' may
have encouraged Sidney in his few experiments of this kind;[4] and

---

[1] OP 6. Greville left England on 14 February (Wallace, 204–7). The claim on the
title-page of Greville's posthumously published *Works* (1633) that they were 'Written
in his Youth and familiar Exercise with Sir Philip Sidney' is untenable for the plays
and treatises, which were written after Sidney's death; but may be true of some of the
poems in *Caelica*.

[2] It was entered in the Stationers' Register on 1 December 1579. Ringler in *Renais-
sance News*, xiv (1961), 159–61, has shown that Spenser first intended to dedicate the
work to Leicester, but by October he was asking Harvey whether it were not 'too base
for his excellent Lordship', and the title-page finally bore a Dedication 'To the most
noble and virtuous gentleman most worthy of all titles both of learning and chivalry
M. Philip Sidney'. Although E. K.'s prefatory epistle to Gabriel Harvey is dated
10 April 1579, he draws attention in it to this post-October Dedication to 'Ma. Phi.
Sidney, a special favourer and maintainer of all kind of learning'.

[3] Ringler, xxxiii–xxxiv.

[4] Ringler, xxix, would allow that Spenser influenced the vocabulary of OA 66;

his qualification to his tribute to the unnamed author of *The Shepherds' Calendar* may be thought to be somewhat disingenuous: 'That same framing of his style to an old rustic language I dare not allow; since neither Theocritus in Greek, Virgil in Latin, nor Sannazaro in Italian, did affect it.'[1]

Its title alone indicates that Sidney's work has some relation to Sannazaro's *Arcadia*; and this collection of eclogues with short prose links is clearly the model for Sidney's four sets of Eclogues that 'mingled prose and verse'.[2] But for the story that he wrote for his sister, in which these Eclogues are interludes, he turned to another imitation of Sannazaro, the *Diana* of Montemayor, a prose romance with songs inserted. Sidney's debt was widely recognized and frequently acknowledged by readers of the *New Arcadia*. It is seen also in the *Old Arcadia*, where, however, the structure seems to reflect the influence of Gil Polo's continuation rather than Montemayor's work, not only in the division into five books, but also in the didactic opening of each book, and in the grouping and function of the poems.[3]

The *Old Arcadia*, in 'Five Books or Acts', is a tragicomedy, with a serious double plot and a comic underplot, based on a Terentian structure of exposition, action, complication, reversal, and catastrophe (with an unexpected anagnorisis and peripeteia at the end).[4] In Book I Sidney sets the action in motion with Basilius's retirement to the country in order to avoid the disasters foretold by the oracle; the princes arrive in Arcadia, and adopt their disguise in order to get access to Basilius's daughters, with whom they have fallen in

I would add OA 29, 64, and 10 (where Sidney, like Spenser on occasion, seems to have turned also to Chaucer). He considers that 'The personal acquaintances most likely to have influenced him as a poet were Thomas Drant, Daniel Rogers, Fulke Greville, Edward Dyer, and Edmund Spenser'. He had not seen Rogers's poems, since printed in Dorsten, *Poets*; but, as he opined, these Latin commendatory verses can scarcely have influenced Sidney as an English poet. In the case of Greville, it appears that it was he who was influenced by Sidney. Dyer's name was far more regularly linked with Sidney's as a poet; but what little survives of his rather old-fashioned verse makes the praise of Dyer, by Sidney himself, and by others, a matter for surprise.

[1] *Defence of Poesy (Works*, iii. 37).

[2] Sidney's words referring to Sannazaro in the *Defence of Poesy (Works*, iii. 22). Examples of specific imitation of Sannazaro's *Arcadia* in Sidney's Eclogues are the double sestina (OA 71), the singing match with its triple rhymes (OA 7), and the fictionalized portrait of Philisides (pp. 334–5), which is clearly modelled on Sannazaro's self-portrait as Sincero. See also Kalstone, 9–101, and Davis, *Map*, 7–22.

[3] See Mrs. Kennedy's edition of Yong's translation, pp. xxiii–xxxix, the most recent and thorough treatment of Sidney's debt to Montemayor and Gil Polo.

[4] Ringler, xxxvii–xxxviii.

love. In Book II the action develops, Gynecia and Basilius both falling in love with Pyrocles, disguised as the Amazon Cleophila. In Book III the complication consists of Musidorus's stratagem to get rid of Dametas and family, so that he can elope with Pamela, and Pyrocles's stratagem to get Gynecia and Basilius into bed with each other, whilst he enjoys a night with his beloved Philoclea. Book IV contains the complete reversal of the fortunes of the princes: Pyrocles and Philoclea are discovered by Dametas; Basilius is apparently dead; and Pamela and Musidorus are captured. Book V presents the catastrophe in Euarchus's condemnation of Gynecia and the princes to death, with the denouement and consequent happy ending in the restoration to life of Basilius.

In addition to having this classical five-act structure, the Italian plays of the early sixteenth century frequently contained *intermezzi* between the acts. This may have encouraged Sidney to include eclogues in his tragicomedy; but he integrated them far more firmly into his main structure.[1] Ringler concludes that 'Sidney produced in prose a pastoral tragi-comedy before the earliest examples of the genre, the *Aminta* and *Pastor Fido* of Tasso and Guarini, were available in print'.[2]

Into this pastoral world Sidney introduced, though with a good deal of refinement, some of the themes of the chivalric romances. For his central situation he went to the *Amadis de Gaule*,[3] and based the adventures of Pyrocles and Musidorus in Arcadia on those of

[1] The first three sets of 'pastoral pastimes' are attended by the ducal party as spectators, and on occasion Musidorus and Pyrocles take part in the proceedings; their past exploits are recounted in Eclogues I and II. As Ringler has shown, the first two sets are carefully matched in number and kinds of poems, and each set is related in theme to the book it concludes: the first tells of unrequited love; the second of the struggle between reason and passion; the third, following the consummation of the love of Pyrocles and Philoclea outside wedlock, celebrates the marriage of the honest shepherds Lalus and Kala 'with the consent of both parents'; and the fourth combines elegies for the supposedly dead Basilius with the laments of unrequited lovers.

[2] *Il Pastor Fido* was composed between 1580 and 1590, when it was first printed; but the first performance of the *Aminta* was given on 31 July 1573 at the Este residence on the Isola Belvedere by the Gelosi Company, who gave a performance of this play in Pesaro in 1574. They were in Venice in February, and again in July, 1574. Sidney was in Venice on both these occasions, and K. M. Lea, *Italian Popular Comedy* (Oxford, 1934), i. 262, has suggested that he may have seen the Gelosi Company perform; it may even be that he saw them act *Aminta*. The mythological *intermezzi* were not included in the early performances; nor, it must be said, does the simple surface tale of Aminta's love for Sylvia have much in common with Sidney's *Old Arcadia*.

[3] This is the form in which he cites the title in the *Defence of Poesy*, and we can assume that he used one of the editions of the French version.

Agesilan and his cousin Arlanges in Book XI of the *Amadis*. Agesilan falls in love with a picture of Diane, and Arlanges later falls in love with Cléophile; they go to the court of Diane disguised as female minstrels called Daraïde and Garaye. Agesilan, still disguised as Daraïde, arrives at the court of Galdap, where both King Galinides and Queen Salderne fall in love with him, just as Basilius and Gynecia fall in love with Pyrocles disguised as the Amazon Cleophila. Sidney drew also on the story in Book VIII concerning Amadis de Grèce, who, disguised as the Amazon Néreïde, woos Niquée; she, because of a prophecy, has been immured by her father, Soudan Basilique, who falls in love with Néreïde. Musidorus's disguise as the shepherd Dorus, in order to be near Pamela, may be compared with that of Florisel, who becomes a shepherd in order to woo Silvie in Book IX. The stratagem of Pyrocles, whereby Basilius spends the night with his own wife, is a variation of a stock theme;[1] and many of the reported adventures of Sidney's heroes that occurred before they set foot in Arcadia are common romance material, found in Malory and Ariosto, whom Sidney would seem to bracket together: 'I dare undertake Orlando Furioso, or honest King Arthur, will never displease a soldier.'[2]

Like Ariosto, Sidney interjects addresses to the audience,[3] and uses the technique of breaking off his narrative—in fact Sir John Harington invokes Sidney's practice in the *Old Arcadia* in his rebuttal of the censures of Ariosto:

> One, that he breaks off narrations very abruptly, so as indeed a loose unattentive reader will hardly carry away any part of the story: but this doubtless is a point of great art, to draw a man with a continual thirst to read out the whole work, and toward the end of the book to close up the

---

[1] In Book IX of the *Amadis* Arlande, princess of Thrace, visits Florisel in the garments of his beloved Silvie; but here Sidney is much closer to Heliodorus, I. ix–xvii, where a wife expecting a gallant is visited by her own husband. The most recent account of Sidney's indebtedness to the *Amadis* is John J. O'Connor's *Amadis de Gaule and its Influence on Elizabethan Literature* (New Brunswick, N.J.: Rutgers University Press, 1970), pp. 183–201; he adds the parallel in Book VIII to those long recognized in Book XI. A. W. Osborn, *Sir Philip Sidney en France* (Paris, 1932) should also be consulted.

[2] *Defence of Poesy* (*Works*, iii. 32). Drummond of Hawthornden reported, rather improbably, that Ben Jonson said that 'Sir Philip Sidney had ane intention to have transformed all his *Arcadia* to the stories of King Arthur'.

[3] This was fairly common form; compare, for example, Sidney's apostrophes to the 'fair ladies' with the addresses to the 'right courteous gentlewomen' in Rich's *Farewell to the Military Profession* (1581).

diverse matters briefly and cleanly. If Sir Philip Sidney had counted this a fault, he would not have done so himself in his *Arcadia*.[1]

Doubtless Ariosto's two pairs of lovers became the model for the later prose romances, and perhaps we should note *Orlando Furioso*, Canto XXII, where two men disguise themselves as women to get access to their ladies; but, with *Amadis de Gaule* in front of him, Sidney had no cause to collect these details from Ariosto.[2]

Both the later books of *Amadis de Gaule* and the *Diana* drew material from Heliodorus's *An Aethiopian History*. In the *New Arcadia* Sidney not only added episodes from this source, but also recast his narrative on Heliodorus's interlocking pattern; but even in the *Old Arcadia* there is some direct influence. The story of Amasis and his stepmother in the Second Eclogues runs on the same lines as Cnemon's tale of the wicked devices of his stepmother Demaenete and her maid Thisbe in *An Aethiopian History*; but because the tale is linked with a sleeping potion and a trial,[3] it seems highly probable that Sidney drew also on Apuleius's tale, in Book X of *The Golden Ass*, of a stepmother who tries to seduce her stepson, who attempts to flee; the frustrated stepmother turns against him, and prepares poison; her own son drinks it and dies. She complains to her husband that the stepson had tried to seduce her, and that when he failed, he poisoned her own son. The father begs the justices to condemn his son to be stoned to death; but the truth emerges at the trial, where the poison turns out to have been a sleeping potion, much as the effect of Gynecia's potion wears off, and Basilius is restored to life after sentence of death has been passed on Gynecia and the princes.[4]

[1] Sir John Harington, 'Preface to the translation of *Orlando Furioso*', *Elizabethan Critical Essays*, ed. G. Gregory Smith, ii. 216–17.

[2] F. L. Townsend, 'Sidney and Ariosto', *P.M.L.A.* lxi (1946), 97–108, concludes that any influence Ariosto had on Sidney was in structure rather than narrative material.

[3] There is a rather feeble trial scene in Achilles Tatius's *Clitophon and Leucippe*, another Greek prose romance that Sidney almost certainly knew. F. A. Yates, 'Elizabethan Chivalry: The Romance of the Accession Day Tilts', *Journal of the Warburg and Courtauld Institutes*, xx (1957), 4–25, has suggested that Sidney may have been present at Woodstock (Dyer and Mary Sidney were certainly there) in September 1575, when 'The Tale of Hemetes the Hermit', an early example in English of a story combining chivalric and pastoral elements, was presented for the entertainment of Queen Elizabeth by Sir Henry Lee, who may have been the author. C. T. Prouty, *George Gascoigne* (New York, 1942), p. 228 n., points to the possible influence of Heliodorus on this tale.

[4] Some of Sidney's proper names occur also in *The Golden Ass*, and there, too, he may have read the tale of Psyche and Cupid. Ringler (xxiv n.) first drew attention

The Golden Ass may also have been Sidney's model for the way in which he switches from the serious troubles of his main personages to the farce of the deceptions practised by Musidorus on Dametas, Miso, and Mopsa, so that he can elope with Pamela. After his complaints in the *Defence of Poesy* against the lack of decorum in tragicomedies, Sidney goes out of his way to justify Apuleius's practice:

But besides these gross absurdities, how all their plays be neither right tragedies, nor right comedies, mingling kings and clowns, not because the matter so carrieth it, but thrust in the clown by head and shoulders to play a part in majestical matters, with neither decency nor discretion; so as neither the admiration and commiseration, nor the right sportfulness is by their mongrel tragicomedy obtained. I know Apuleius did somewhat so, but that is a thing recounted with space of time, not represented in one moment.[1]

In spite of the moral benefits that Sidney claimed could be derived from reading *Amadis de Gaule*,[2] neither it nor the Greek romances had any real ethos behind the sentiment and the emotion.[3] Nevertheless, the faithful loves of Theagenes and Chariclea provided Sidney with an example of the edifying nature of imaginative literature, and he regarded *An Aethiopian History* as a heroic poem, though written in prose: '. . . For Xenophon who did imitate so excellently as to give us *effigiem justi imperii*, the portraiture of a just empire under the name of Cyrus, as Cicero saith of him, made therein an absolute heroical poem. So did Heliodorus in his sugared invention of that picture of love in *Theagenes and Chariclea*, and yet both these wrote in prose'.[4] Here it is bracketed with Xenophon's *Cyropaedia*, which Sidney goes on to praise for giving a 'feigned example' that has more force to teach than the true Cyrus in Justin.[5]

to Sidney's indebtedness to *The Golden Ass*. The English translation by William Adlington, first printed in ?1569, was dedicated to the Earl of Sussex, Sidney's uncle by marriage.

[1] *Works*, iii. 39–40.

[2] 'Truly I have known men that, even with reading *Amadis de Gaule*, which, God knoweth, wanteth much of a perfect poesy, have found their hearts moved to the exercise of courtesy, liberality, and especially courage' (*Defence of Poesy*, *Works*, iii. 20).

[3] With the possible exception of Longus's *Daphnis and Chloe*, which is both the only truly *pastoral* Greek romance and also the only one to combine a love story with the theme of good government; but it had no detectable influence on the *Old Arcadia*.

[4] *Defence of Poesy* (*Works*, iii. 10).

[5] Ibid. 16–18. Sidney is much indebted to Cornelius Agrippa in the *Defence of Poesy*, and this example could have come from him; cf. '. . . Such an example hath Xenophon

The description of the upbringing and education of Pyrocles and
Musidorus would seem to owe something to Xenophon's account of
the early training of Cyrus; and it is possible that the idea of intro-
ducing a political theme into his romance derived from his early
reading of Xenophon.[1]

The basis, however, for the moral and political ideas in the *Old
Arcadia* is to be found in the *Ethics* and *Politics* of Aristotle. Sidney's
education in statecraft can be traced in the correspondence with
Languet; and its Aristotelian foundation is apparent. On 22 January
1574 Languet advised him next after the sacred scriptures, 'to
study that branch of moral philosophy which treats of justice and
injustice'.[2] Sidney replied on 4 February 1574 that he only wished
to learn as much Greek

as shall suffice for the perfect understanding of Aristotle. For though
translations are made almost daily, still I suspect they do not declare the
meaning of the author plainly or aptly enough; and besides, I am utterly
ashamed to be following the stream, as Cicero says, and not go to the
fountain head. Of the works of Aristotle, I consider the politics to be the
most worth reading; and I mention this in reference to your advice that
I should apply myself to moral philosophy.[3]

Later, he is able to hand on the torch to his brother:

I think you have read Aristotle's Ethics; if you have, you know it is the
beginning and foundation of all his works, the good end [to] which every
man doth and ought to bend his greatest actions, . . .[4]

Aristotle may be the foundation of Sidney's moral and political
philosophy, as he feigns notable images of virtues and vices, or what
else, with delightful teaching, in order to show the consequences of
Basilius's foolish relinquishment of his duties to his dukedom, and
the civil dissensions that arise from his supposed death; but it must
never be forgotten that he set out to produce a story rather than a
treatise. The events recounted in the *Old Arcadia* are the 'imagina-
tive groundplot of a profitable invention', and the moral and political
reflections arise from them. As Bacon remarked in another context:

set out of a Cyrus, not as it was, but as it ought to be, as a resemblance and pattern
of a singular good prince' (*Of the vanity and uncertainty of arts and sciences*, trans.
James Sanford (1569)).

[1] The *Cyropaedia* was the principal Greek text in the school curriculum at Shrews-
bury. Sidney refers to it in his letter to Languet of 15 April 1574, and in his letter
to his brother Robert of 18 October 1580, and mentions it no less than eight times in
the *Defence of Poesy*.

[2] Pears, 26.   [3] Pears, 28.   [4] *Works*, iii. 124.

'Nevertheless in many the like encounters, I do rather think that the fable was first and the exposition devised than that the moral was first and thereupon the fable framed.'[1] However, John Hoskyns attributed the fact that 'Men are described most excellently' in the *New Arcadia* in the first place to Sidney's study of Aristotle:

... he that will truly set down a man in a figured story must first learn truly to set down a humour, a passion, a virtue, a vice, and therein keeping decent proportion, add but names and knit together the accidents and encounters. The perfect expressing of all qualities is learned out of Aristotle's ten books of moral philosophy, but because, as Machiavelli saith, 'Perfect virtue or perfect vice is not seen in our time', which altogether is humorous and spirting, therefore the understanding of Aristotle's *Rhetoric* is the directest means of skill to describe, to move, to appease, or to prevent any motion whatsoever; whereunto whosoever can fit his speech shall be truly eloquent. This was my opinion ever, and Sir Philip Sidney betrayed his knowledge in this book of Aristotle to me, before ever I knew that he had translated any part of it, for I found the two first books Englished by him in the hands of the noble, studious Henry Wotton, but lately; I think also that he had much help out of Theophrastus's *Imagines*.[2]

Hoskyns goes on to praise Sidney's method of portraying characters with 'ever a steadfast decency and uniform difference of manners observed'. In the *Defence of Poesy* Homer, Virgil, Xenophon, Heliodorus, Terence, and others, are praised for their creation of characters in similar terms; and I think we can accept Hoskyns's suggestion that Sidney was using the rhetorical figure of *effictio* (a branch of *energia*) in order to portray such minor exemplary personages as Philanax, Timautus, and even Euarchus, whose very names indicate that they represent particular qualities. We may even concede that Mopsa remains bounded by 'proud, ill-favoured, sluttish simplicity', and Dametas by 'fear and rudeness with ill-affected civility'; but the six main characters in the *Old Arcadia* are not constructed on such a frigid pattern.[3]

[1] *The Advancement of Learning* (J. E. Spingarn, *Critical Essays of the Seventeenth Century*, i. 8).

[2] Hoskyns, 41–2. Sidney's translation of Aristotle's *Rhetoric* is lost. It is unlikely that Sidney read Theophrastus's *Characters*, for Casaubon's Latin translation was not published until 1592, and Sidney was not encouraged by Languet to continue his study of Greek. The popularity of character-books in the seventeenth century led other readers besides Hoskyns to approach the *Arcadia* from this angle; see John Buxton, *Elizabethan Taste* (London, 1963), pp. 260–1.

[3] It was perhaps, in recognition of this fact that Hoskyns added, 'Sir Philip Sidney's

Sidney may have turned from Aristotle to Plato's *Symposium* and *Phaedrus* for his reflections on virtue and reason, beauty and love;[1] and the conception of justice and harmony in Book V of the *Old Arcadia* may ultimately derive from the *Republic*;[2] but much of Sidney's Platonism probably reached him through such works as Castiglione's *The Courtier* and Elyot's *The Governor*.

The exaltation of poetry over philosophy and history in the *Defence of Poesy* is in part special pleading, for Sidney advised his brother Robert, when reading such historians as Herodotus, Thucydides, and Xenophon, 'to note the examples of virtue or vice, with their good or evil successes, . . . the enterings and endings of wars, and therein the stratagems against the enemy . . .'. He goes on to advise his brother, especially when dealing with philosophers, who sometimes embark on religious or legal discussions in the middle of their ethical or political discourses, to classify his notes under different heads, 'And so, as in a table, be it witty word, of which Tacitus is full; sentences, of which Livy; or similitudes, whereof Plutarch, straight to lay it up in the right place of his storehouse'.[3] If Sidney kept such a table-book himself, it would account for the eclectic nature of the reflective comments and illustrations in the *Old Arcadia*.

In addition to Greek and Roman authors he also read the continental historians and political theorists. In Venice he obtained copies of Guicciardini's *La Historia d'Italia* (1569),[4] Contarini's and Donato Giannotti's treatises on the Republic of Venice;[5] but he told his brother that little wisdom could be gathered from the provinces of Italy, 'excepting Venice, whose good laws and customs we can hardly proportion to ourselves, because they are

---

course was (besides reading Aristotle and Theophrastus) to imagine the thing present in his own brain, that [h]is pen might the better present it to you.'

[1] Brie, 151 f.; Ringler, 468, has drawn attention to echoes of J. Serranus's Introductions to the *Symposium* and *Ion* in the *Defence of Poesy*, and it is possible that Sidney read the Introduction to the *Phaedo* before he wrote the account of the conversation of Musidorus and Pyrocles on immortality in Book V of the *Old Arcadia*. These Introductions were printed in H. Stephanus's edition of Plato's *Works*, a copy of which was sent to Sidney by Stephanus in June 1579.   [2] Davis, *Map*, 137 ff.

[3] Letter of 18 October 1580 (*Works*, iii. 130–1). Plutarch's *Moralia* was one of Sidney's favourite quarries; other illustrations came from Virgil; but for the bulk of his numerous similes and metaphors from classical mythology in the *Old Arcadia* Sidney went to Ovid's *Metamorphoses*, sometimes in Golding's translation.

[4] W. Godshalk, 'A Sidney Autograph', *The Book Collector*, xiii (1964), 65.

[5] *Works*, iii. 81. On 29 April 1574 he began a letter to Languet with a casual reference to Machiavelli (*Works*, iii. 90).

quite of a contrary government, there is little there but tyrannous oppression and servile yielding to them that have little or no rule over them.'[1] It is not, therefore, surprising to find that the views on monarchical government and 'mixed rule' expressed in the *Old Arcadia* are in line with the accepted Tudor doctrine on the hierarchy of government, as found in the works of such writers as Sir Thomas Elyot and Sir Thomas Smith.[2]

Sidney had, of course, ample opportunity for imbibing Languet's opinions, and some of this experienced statesman's reflections in his private letters found their way into the *Old Arcadia*.[3] As the doubt over the attribution of the *Vindiciae Contra Tyrannos* (1579)[4] indicates, many of Languet's convictions were shared by Duplessis-Mornay; and no doubt it was through Languet that he and his wife became close friends of Sidney when they came to England in April 1577 for eighteen months. Although Duplessis-Mornay's *Traité de la vérité de la religion chrestienne* was not published until 1581, Sidney may have seen it in manuscript, or discussed its contents-to-be with Duplessis-Mornay, before he wrote the final pages of the *Old Arcadia*.[5] In Chapter xi of his treatise Duplessis-Mornay opposes to the conception of fortune, chance, or destiny, the belief that 'God governeth the world and all things therein by providence'. In common with most Elizabethan authors, Sidney permits his characters to rail against the fickleness of fortune; but at the same time one is aware throughout the *Old Arcadia* of a contrary conviction, culminating in his final verdict that 'all has fallen out by the

---

[1] *Works*, iii. 127; cf. Languet's letter to Sidney of 11 June 1574; 'But nowadays, after your Italian school, we give to vices the names of virtues, and are not ashamed to call falsehood, treachery, and cruelty, by the names of wisdom and magnanimity' (Pears, 78).

[2] Although he knew Bodin's *Six livres de la République* (1576/7)—see *Works*, iii. 130, and Sargent, 49—there is no need to suppose that in the 'Ister Bank' poem Sidney set out to refute his arguments against 'mixed rule'. Further light is shed on Sidney's reading by his letter to Edward Denny of 22 May 1580 (Sotheby's *Catalogue of the Bibliotheca Phillippica*, New Series: Seventh Part (1971), No. 1660).

[3] Rudenstine devotes his first two chapters to the influence of Languet's letters on the *Old Arcadia*.

[4] Sidney probably read this work and George Buchanan's *De Jure Regni apud Scotos* (Edinburgh, 1579) whilst he was writing the *Old Arcadia*; see J. E. Phillips, 'George Buchanan and the Sidney Circle', *H.L.Q.* xii (1948), 39–45.

[5] Later Sidney started to translate Duplessis-Mornay's treatise into English, and then asked Arthur Golding to take it over when he went to the Low Countries (*A work concerning the trueness of the Christian religion* (1587), sig. 3ᵛ). E. M. Tenison, 'Philip Sidney and Arthur Golding's Translation of Duplessis', *De la vérité de la religion chrestienne*, *Elizabethan England*, vii (1940), 145–60, considers that Golding was responsible for the whole translation as printed.

highest providence', that human affairs are not governed by blind chance.[1] Here his phraseology is often close to Duplessis-Mornay's; but this does not mean that he was trying to turn his often light-hearted tale into a Calvinistic treatise.

PROSE STYLE AND DICTION

It has become increasingly clear that, for all the anti-Ciceronian utterances,[2] the model for most Elizabethan prose, including Sidney's, was the highly articulated Ciceronian period.[3] Whereas Lyly concentrated on achieving balance and antithesis, the most obvious feature of Sidney's style is parenthesis; sometimes, indeed, his long involved sentences trail off as invertebrates. He is at his best in descriptions and speeches, but his control of his medium tends to falter when it comes to narration. This may be because the seemingly simple art of the story-teller is something that anyone schooled, as Sidney evidently was, in the art of rhetoric (whether Aristotle's, Cicero's, the pseudo-Ciceronian *Rhetorica ad Herennium*, or Quintilian's) had little opportunity to acquire. Because rhetorical training was originally directed to the spoken, as opposed to the written, word, whenever speeches are required an author is likely to work with the greater assurance. Sidney's speeches are forensic and deliberative (persuasive), and not merely epideictic (ornamental). They are constructed in accordance with Aristotle's principles; and so the arguments Philanax uses to try to persuade Basilius not to retire to the country are adjusted to his hearer's inability to be reasonable, and Pyrocles' arguments to the mutinous mob are adapted to the self-interest of his ignorant hearers. In the trial scene Philanax's oration is built on the method and divisions prescribed for a classical oration, and he shows a self-conscious awareness of what he is doing, but he transgresses against the

[1] In writing of pre-Christian Greeks, Sidney availed himself of an accepted convention whereby, although Basilius pays his rites to Apollo, and 'the gods' are vaguely invoked, other references to the 'unsearchable wisdom' of the Almighty give a Christian tone to the theological orientation of his characters.

[2] These really belong to the debate on the proper use of imitation, particularly in writing Latin prose. On 1 January 1574 Languet, probably echoing Erasmus, having advised Sidney to improve his Latin style by retranslating Cicero, added 'But beware of falling into the heresy of those who think that the height of excellence consists in the imitation of Cicero, and pass their lives in labouring at it' (Pears, 20). Sidney's letter of 18 October 1580 to his brother Robert is couched in similar terms: 'So you can speak and write Latin not barbarously, I never require great study in Ciceronianism, the chief abuse of Oxford, *Qui dum verba sectantur, res ipsas negligunt*' (*Works*, iii. 132).

[3] See Wilson, 307–8.

Aristotelian principle that forensic oratory should not be directed to arousing the feelings of the audience, and there is a deliberate contrast with Euarchus who (affecting to despise the colours of rhetoric) reaches his verdict by logical reasoning and the application of general principles.[1] In these speeches Sidney does not attempt to reproduce the rhythms of colloquial speech; his is a carefully studied style, and his main concern is to accommodate it to the subject-matter. He also attempts to follow Aristotle's emphasis on thought and organization; to offer 'more weight than copy'.[2] Yet, although he inveighs against the abuse of eloquence 'apparelled, or rather disguised, in a courtesan-like affectation', Sidney does not write the plain style we might expect from such a theorist. Copiousness[3] and eloquence are in fact ever present, manifesting themselves in the use of a wide variety of tropes and figures.[4]

Hoskyns's *Directions on Speech and Style* (c. 1600) and Fraunce's *The Arcadian Rhetoric* (1588) testify to the profit and delight that a contemporary reader could get from the use of rhetorical figures in the *Arcadia*; and the two authors take their examples from both the poetry and the prose.[5] Hoskyns thought that metaphor was 'the best flower growing most plentifully in all *Arcadia*', and for the benefit of his young student of rhetoric, he marked the metaphors in his copy of the *New Arcadia* (1590) with an M in the margin. It was certainly one of the features of his style with which Sidney took considerable trouble.[6] Hoskyns also comments on Lyly's use of

---

[1] See L. Challis, 'The Use of Oratory in Sidney's *Arcadia*', *S.P.* lxii (1965), 561–76.

[2] P. A. Duhamel, 'Sidney's *Arcadia* and Elizabethan Rhetoric', *S.P.* xlv (1948), 134–50, has analysed a passage from Lyly's *Euphues* and another from the *Arcadia* on the method recommended by John Brinsley in *Ludus Literarius* (1612), placing in the left-hand column the themes (*inventio*), and in the right-hand column the figures. The result is that *Euphues* is shown to be short of argument, matter, and structure, and to be virtually all ornament; the *Arcadia* has far stronger arguments and greater structure; but fewer, though more varied, figures, and often of a more extended kind.

[3] Erasmus's *De Copia* was used in grammar schools for exercises in amplification, and once the habit was acquired it would have been difficult to shake off, even if a writer had wanted to—the figure suited the verbal exuberance of the Elizabethans. Sidney may also have been influenced by the ornate style of the Greek romances and the *Amadis*.

[4] Rubel, 156, finds that the figures most frequently used by Sidney are anadiplosis, anaphora, epizeuxis, ploce, prosonomasia, and traductio. I would add paroemia—the use of proverbs; here Erasmus's *Adagia* proved useful.

[5] Most of Fraunce's citations are indicated in the Commentary; but not those of Hoskyns, as he refers to the *New Arcadia*.

[6] For example, on p. 121, 22–3 the earlier OA manuscripts read 'Shall I *seek* [*labour* Cl, As] to lay colours over my *galled* thoughts'; this is altered in St and Bo to '*decayed* thoughts'; and finally in NA the metaphor from painting over woodwork to make it look like marble is made even more explicit: 'Shall I *labour* to lay *marble* colours over

agnominations and droves of similes that 'Sir Philip Sidney would not have his style be much beholding to this kind of garnish'.[1] There is no indication that Sidney had read *Euphues* before he wrote the *Old Arcadia*, and his use of one, or at the most two, illustrative similes was a matter of individual choice rather than a reaction against Lyly's proliferations. When he did read it, however, his reaction was unreservedly hostile:

Now for similitudes in certain printed discourses, I think all herbarists, all stories of beasts, fowls, and fishes, are rifled up that they may come in multitudes to wait upon any of our conceits, which certainly is as absurd a surfeit to the ears as is possible. For the force of a similitude not being to prove any thing to a contrary disputer, but only to explain to a willing hearer, when that is done, the rest is a most tedious prattling, rather overswaying the memory from the purpose whereto they were applied than any whit informing the judgement already either satisfied, or by similitudes not to be satisfied.[2]

Whereas most of Lyly's critics objected to the 'counterfeit' nature of his similes, it will be noted that Sidney's objection is to their superfluity. Unlike Lyly or Bacon, Sidney does not use similes to prove anything, but simply for illustration and explanation. This would seem to put him in the Ramist camp, where the function of figures of speech is relegated from persuasion or proof to decoration. However, despite the Dedication to him of de Banos's *Life of Ramus* (1577), his patronage of Abraham Fraunce and William Temple, and their testimony to his interest, it is to be doubted whether Sidney was really much impressed by the Ramist attempts to simplify the teaching of logic and rhetoric.[3] He did not need Ramus to tell him

my *ruinous* thoughts' (*Works*, i. 260). Cf. p. 93, 19–20, where the earlier OA manuscripts read 'as it were paint out the *sharpness* of the pain', and St, Bo, and 90 '*hideousness*', again removing the mixture of metaphors.

[1] Cf. Drayton's praise of Sidney in his 'Epistle to Henry Reynolds' because he
did first reduce
Our tongue from Lyly's writing then in use,
Talking of stones, stars, plants, of fishes, flies,
Playing with words and idle similes.
[2] *Defence of Poesy* (*Works*, iii. 42–3): cf. AS 3. 7–8:
Or with strange similes enrich each line,
Of herbs or beasts, which Ind or Afric hold.
G. K. Hunter (*John Lyly: The Humanist as Courtier* (1962), p. 287) regards the 'pathetic fallacy' as Sidney uses it as his equivalent for Lyly's simile from natural history. There is a good deal more of sympathetic nature in the *New* than in the *Old Arcadia*.
[3] See G. W. Hallam, 'Sidney's Supposed Ramism', in *Renaissance Papers* (1963), pp. 11–20; and Shepherd, 230.

that all discourse must be soundly based in dialectic. Thomas Wilson in his *Art of Rhetoric* (1553) had already warned English writers to have logic perfect before looking for profit from rhetoric; and Sidney could truthfully claim to be 'a piece of a logician'.

Some of the past comparisons between the style of the *Old* and the *New Arcadia* have been vitiated by the fact that the *Old Arcadia* passages were not taken from the two latest manuscripts. In practice, little time can have elapsed between the *Old Arcadia* revisions to which the St. John's College, Cambridge, and the Bodleian Library manuscripts bear witness, and the recasting of the work as the *New Arcadia*. The process of revision was a fairly constant one, and on small stylistic points sometimes involved the pruning of rhetorical excesses, and sometimes led to greater ornamentation. Broadly, the tendency was in the direction of elaboration, and the distaste and apologies for Arcadianism are generally based on some of the highly wrought passages in the *New Arcadia*; for one thing, the dramatic presentation of the *Old Arcadia* makes for more dialogue and less description.

Hoskyns took his examples from the *Arcadia* because he thought that it contained not only 'all the figures of rhetoric', but also 'the art of the best English'. I would like to think that the latter phrase was intended to embrace Sidney's word usage. Harington noted Sidney's use of triple rhymes; otherwise the only feature commented on by a near contemporary was his use of double epithets, praised by Joseph Hall:

> He knows the grace of that new elegance
> Which sweet Philisides fetch't of late from France,
> That well beseem'd his high-styl'd Arcady,
> Though others mar it with much liberty;
> In epithets to join two words in one,
> Forsooth, for adjectives cannot stand alone;[1]

Ringler[2] thinks that Sidney was following classical rather than continental writers, in that in the *Defence of Poesy* English is said to be 'particularly happy in compositions of two or three words

---

[1] *Virgidemiarum Sex Libri*, VI. i. 255-60 (*The Collected Poems of Joseph Hall*, ed. A. Davenport (Liverpool, 1948), p. 95). Although the 'elegance' appeared to be new to Hall, compound epithets are to be found in the works of many previous English poets, including Chaucer, and were used by most Elizabethan poets, and with notable success by Spenser and Shakespeare. See the 'Note on Compound Words' in *The Poems*, ed. J. C. Maxwell (New Cambridge Shakespeare), p. 155; and N. E. Osselton, *The Well-Languag'd Poet* (Leiden: University Press, 1970).   [2] Ringler, liii.

together, near the Greek, far beyond the Latin, which is one of the greatest beauties can be in a language';[1] but he must have been aware of the French precedents. Du Bellay and Ronsard acclaimed these words, and their use had a vast extension in *La Semaine* of Du Bartas, which Sidney translated.[2] Later, Dryden bracketed Sidney and Sylvester, the translator of Du Bartas, together in regretting the use of compound epithets in English:

'tis evident that the English does more nearly follow the strictness of [Latin] than the freedoms of [Greek]. Connection of epithets, or the conjunction of two words in one, are frequent and elegant in the Greek, which yet Sir Philip Sidney and the translator of Du Bartas have unluckily attempted in the English; though this, I confess, is not so proper an instance of poetic licence, as it is of variety of idiom in languages.[3]

Although it is mainly in his poems, where they achieve a welcome concision, that Sidney uses these compounds, there are a large number of attractive examples in the prose of the *Old Arcadia*[4]— though not enough to invite comment to the exclusion of other features. I have been struck in compiling even a rudimentary glossary to the *Old Arcadia* by the choiceness of his vocabulary. He avoids the frequent use of outlandish terms or Latinisms, but exercises a judicious balance between innovation and conservatism that embraces both 'old rustic' words and importations. The introducer of new verse forms had also to import words such as 'sestina', 'madrigal', 'stanza', to describe them; but Sidney also has a peculiarly happy way of handling the counters of the current sixteenth-century English so as to enlarge their scope or shift their

---

[1] *Works*, iii. 44.

[2] The translation is lost; see Ringler, 339. Du Bartas named Sidney, More, Sir Nicholas Bacon, and Queen Elizabeth as the four pillars of the English language in the *Second Semaine* (1584); see Ringler, lxi. Although King James VI was influenced by Du Bellay, and invited Du Bartas to Edinburgh for a visit which lasted six months, he preferred circumlocution ('Apollo, reular of the Sunne') to 'making a corruptit worde, composit of twa dyvers simple wordis, as Apollo gyde-Sunne' ('Ane Schort Treatise . . .' (1584), *Elizabethan Critical Essays*, ed. G. C. Moore Smith, i. 219).

[3] 'The Author's Apology for Heroic Poetry and Poetic Licence' (1677), *Essays of John Dryden*, ed. W. P. Ker (Oxford, 1926), i. 189.

[4] B. Groom, 'The Formation and Use of Compound Epithets in English Poetry from 1579', *S.P.E.* xlix (1937), 295–322, notes their presence in *Arcadia* as an expected feature of rhetorical prose. Sidney uses most of the grammatical combinations listed by Groom (p. 296). Some examples are : '*promise-breaking* attempt' (p. 306, 22); '*death-deserving* vice' (p. 290, 25); '*long-painful late-pleasant* affection' (p. 288, 28); '*long-exercised* virtue' (p. 91, 16); '*hang-worthy* necks' (p. 306, 31); '*yearly-used* hymn' (p. 134, 6).

meanings, and thus a word that has been used by Sidney may never be quite the same again. Many of his innovations have become assimilated into the English language. Dr. Johnson fixed Sidney's work as the boundary beyond which he made 'few excursions', and cited Sidney and Spenser as providing sufficient English words for 'the dialect of poetry and fiction'.[1]

THE NATURE OF THE OLD ARCADIA

Considering the wide range of sources from which Sidney drew his material, it is not surprising that the *Old Arcadia* does not readily fall into any one category. Although the Eclogues contain pastoral poems with short prose links in the manner of Sannazaro's *Arcadia*, and the main story is a prose narrative with interspersed lyrics in the manner of the *Diana* of Montemayor and Gil Polo, the *Old Arcadia* is not really a pastoral romance concerned with the celebration and examination of love in an ideal world to which the heroes have retired from the world of chivalry. Arcadia is very far from being such an ideal country; it contains no magic healing centre such as the cave in Sannazaro or the temple of Diana in Montemayor.[2] The lady Felicia, who resides in this temple, and to whom the lovers take their problems for resolution, and from whom they receive mysterious predictions of happiness to come, is a development of the benevolent oracle of the Greek romances,[3] which, instead of threatening disaster, has 'assumed an almost contrary character and become a symbol of the second chance';[4] whereas the oracle which has caused Basilius foolishly to dwell among shepherds, and to make the boorish Dametas guardian of his daughter Pamela, is an oracle of menace on the older pattern of the terrible Greek myths, and it is Basilius's attempts ('menaced by fortune') to evade the fate predicted that bring him and his to near disaster.[5] No reproaches whatever are levelled at those who consult the oracle in the Greek prose romances, or directed to the unhappy lovers who resort to the lady Felicia in the *Diana*, but Sidney makes his disapproval of Basilius's idle curiosity ('in vain to desire to know that of which in

---

[1] Preface to Johnson's *Dictionary* (see E. L. McAdam, Jr., and George Milne, *Johnson's Dictionary: A Modern Selection* (London, 1963), pp. 18–19).

[2] See Davis, *Map*, chap. 1.   [3] See, for example, Heliodorus, ii. 26 and 36.

[4] M. M. Lascelles, 'Shakespeare's Pastoral Comedy', in *More Talking of Shakespeare*, ed. John Garrett (1959), p. 75.

[5] As Miss Lascelles remarks, 'the point of these stories seems to be that it is a man's efforts to avert his fate which fasten it upon him'.

vain thou shalt be sorry after thou hast known it') abundantly clear, both in his own voice, and in the unavailing sage counsel of Philanax.[1]

Sidney, then, has availed himself of a pastoral setting for a story of a very different kind from the *Diana*. Even pastoral, the lowest of the eight kinds of poetry Sidney lists in the *Defence of Poesy*, is defended, not by reference to the ideal world portrayed in such works as the *Diana*,[2] but for its ability to comment on moral and political questions.[3] This emphasis was determined by Sidney's desire to prove that even the humble pastoral is superior to history and philosophy in its power to teach. As 'the best and most accomplished kind of poetry', the heroical poem carried out this function most efficaciously. Under this heading Sidney included not only the *Iliad*, the *Aeneid*, and *Orlando Furioso* but also such prose works as Xenophon's *Cyropaedia*, Heliodorus's *An Aethiopian History*,[4] and (with a note of apology) the *Amadis de Gaule*. Certainly the *Old Arcadia* is not behind *Amadis* in moving men's hearts 'to the exercise of courtesy, liberality, and especially courage'. In his discussion of heroic poetry Sidney emphasizes 'the functional rather than the formal aspects of the genre';[5] and Aeneas, Cyrus, 'honest King Arthur', and the rest are discussed in terms of the lessons that can be drawn from their noble actions. John Hoskyns's theory of Sidney's construction of characters according to ideal types and the strictest rules of decorum is in line with this emphasis, and it works well enough for some of the minor personages,[6] but even in the

---

[1] Sidney refers to the oracle as 'that impiety', and Philanax calls oracles 'these kinds of soothsaying sorceries', and suggests that the heavenly powers ought 'to be reverenced and not searched into, and their mercy rather by prayers to be sought than their hidden counsels by curiosity'.

[2] The *Diana* is one of the few sources for the *Old Arcadia* that is not even mentioned in the *Defence of Poesy*.

[3] Sidney refers to Virgil's Eclogue i and Mantuan's Eclogue ix; see *Works*, iii. 22.

[4] See p. xxiv.

[5] A. D. Isler, 'Heroic Poetry and Sidney's Two *Arcadias*', *P.M.L.A.* lxxxiii (1968), 368–79. The only indication that the Italian debate on the epic and the romance had attracted Sidney's attention is the remark that critics say 'that even to the heroical, Cupid hath ambitiously climbed' (*Works*, iii. 30). Harington quoted this phrase when answering objections to 'lightness and wantonness' in the *Orlando Furioso* (Preface, printed in G. Gregory Smith, *Elizabethan Critical Essays*, ii. 209).

[6] See p. xxvi. The phrases in inverted commas which follow are taken from Hoskyns. Dametas and his family fulfil the function of the servants in the comedies of Plautus and Terence. Sidney's broad humour in their delineation is quite foreign to the spirit of the Greek romances and of Sannazaro and Montemayor; it also lacks Shakespeare's sympathy for his humble characters.

Old Arcadia the delicate discriminations between Pamela and Philoclea go much further than embodying 'wise courage in Pamela, mild discretion in Philoclea'; and 'respective and restless dotage in Gynecia's love' does scant justice to the near-tragic portrayal of the struggle of this middle-aged wife with her illicit passion. Similarly, the behaviour of the two princes, perplexed by the conflict between reason and passion, falls somewhat short of the exemplary, and in so doing makes them that much more credible as persons.

Yet Sidney makes it quite clear that Basilius ought not to have neglected his duties as a duke; that the princes have done wrong; that Gynecia ought not to have yielded to her guilty passion—but here we should note Sidney's ironic comment when she emerges with an unscathed reputation at the end of the trial scene. Apart from this, and the overthrow of Euarchus's verdict at the end of Book V,[1] the *Old Arcadia* is very 'doctrinable'. Although we should be continually on the alert for his ironic tone, and never forget that he began his story to entertain his sister; and despite his references to the *Old Arcadia* as 'this idle work of mine', 'but a trifle and that triflingly handled', and 'my toyful book';[2] Sidney's discussion of the earlier prose fictions that had provided material for the *Old Arcadia* leaves little room for doubt that his own story was intended to fulfil the function of heroic poetry.[3] There is no need to deny the pastoral element, for Sidney himself allowed of mixed genres:

Now in his parts, kinds, or species, as you list to term them, it is to be noted that some poesies have coupled together two or three kinds, as the tragical and comical, whereupon is risen the tragicomical, some in the like manner have mingled prose and verse, as Sannazaro and Boethius; some have mingled matters heroical and pastoral; but that cometh all to one in this question, for if severed they be good, the conjunction cannot be hurtful.[4]

[1] For what I believe to be Sidney's attempt to remedy this flaw, see p. lxii.

[2] No doubt this is an example of *sprezzatura*, the courtly grace which conceals a sober purpose, and is indeed the mark of consummate artistry (see Myrick, 1–45); but these phrases from the Dedication of the *Old Arcadia* to his sister and from his letter to his brother of 18 October 1580 should also serve as a warning that Sidney did not set out to write a Calvinist treatise on the wretchedness of man, as one might gather from F. Marenco, *Arcadia Puritana* (Bari, 1968).

[3] Sir John Harington refers to the *Old Arcadia* as a work of exactly the same kind as the *Orlando Furioso*. Sidney's highly wrought rhetorical prose might be said to be the equivalent of the *ottava rima* of the *Orlando Furioso*; but Harington, like Sidney, is emphasizing the function rather than the style of epic.

[4] *Works*, iii. 22.

In the *Old Arcadia* we shall find all the three kinds of mingling described here. When he comes later to censure 'mongrel tragicomedy', 'mingling kings and clowns, not because the matter so carrieth it, but thrust in the clown by head and shoulders to play a part in majestical matters, with neither decency nor discretion', he exempts Apuleius because he separates his comic episodes temporally from his serious ones.[1] In the *Old Arcadia* the sub-plot of Dametas, Miso, and Mopsa is handled with consummate decency, and the scenes of high farce are always separated from the scenes of equally high tragedy. Its Terentian structure in five books or acts, with eclogues after the first four, perhaps in imitation of the *intermezzi* of the Italian dramas, but, unlike them, fully integrated into the main plot, underlines the affinities of the work with the mixed (but not mongrel) kind of tragicomedy. It is clear from the words of the oracle at the very beginning that Sidney had planned his five-act drama with extreme care; and he triumphantly carried out his intentions with unflagging execution right through to the final scene.[2] This firmness of structure was Sidney's most individual contribution to prose fiction, and had the *Old Arcadia* rather than the *New Arcadia* been printed in 1590, we might have been spared some of the long-winded imitations of the seventeenth century, and the criticisms of the *Arcadia* voiced in the eighteenth century.[3]

INFLUENCE

The *Arcadia* that had most influence on later writers was one that Sidney himself never designed: the hybrid version published in 1593, containing the *New Arcadia* (1590) and Books III–V of the *Old Arcadia* with some alterations and additions. Through this version much of the *Old Arcadia* material reached the public, but few had any knowledge of the story in its original and completed form. The only works of fiction that show any signs of their authors' having seen a manuscript of the *Old Arcadia* are the pastoral tales of Lodge and Greene, which are of modest length, fairly straightforward in structure, and interspersed with lyrics. They were working together in the 1580s, and Lodge's *Forbonius and Prisceria* was

[1] *Works*, iii. 39–40; see p. xxiv.
[2] Even such a feature as the sudden switching from one pair of lovers to another may not be youthful incompetence, but rather a deliberate imitation of the technique of Ariosto.
[3] This is even more true of the later editions containing not only, as in 1593, Books III–V of the *Old Arcadia*, but also the Supplement of Sir William Alexander, and the continuation of Sir Richard Bellings.

published with his *An Alarum against Usurers* (1584), which was
dedicated to Sidney. The resemblances to the *Arcadia* are rather
slight,[1] and as Prisceria is the granddaughter of Theagenes and
Chariclea, one may suspect that Lodge, like Greene, turned to
Heliodorus for his story material. *Menaphon* (1589) is Greene's most
Arcadian work.[2] It is true that some of the themes are also found in
Amadis de Gaule[3] and in the Greek romances;[4] but in the place of
the benevolent oracles of the latter, Greene, like Sidney, has an
ambiguous one, the explanation of which, and of the true identities
of the characters, by an old crone, narrowly averts the execution of
the principal personages. Furthermore, without having seen the
Old Arcadia, Greene would hardly have called his heroine Samela,
and his two male leads Democles and Doron. Stylistically, Greene
is a follower of Lyly, and it was only the posthumous editions,
published long after the *New Arcadia* was in print, that were
entitled *Greene's Arcadia or Menaphon*; the subtitle of the 1589
edition was 'Camilla's Alarm to the Slumbering Euphues'. Similarly,
Lodge's *Rosalynde* (1590) is subtitled 'Euphues' Golden Legacy',
and is written in a euphuistic style; although his central plot has
some similarity to that of the *Old Arcadia*,[5] and there are minor
incidents that recall Sidney's story.[6] Both the early dates of these
romances by Lodge and Greene, and the nature of the resemblances
in total effect and in detail, imply that any indebtedness there may
have been was to the *Old* rather than to the *New Arcadia*.

We have already seen that Sir John Harington found the *Old
Arcadia* useful in his defence of the *Orlando Furioso*.[7] The way that
Sidney's story kept coming into his mind whilst he was translating
Ariosto's poem may be illustrated by his comment (on Beatrice's
refusal to accept Rogero as a son-in-law until she heard that he had

---

[1] They are assembled in F. L. Beaty, 'Lodge's *Forbonius and Prisceria* and Sidney's
Arcadia', *English Studies*, xlix (1968), 38–45.

[2] See R. Pruvost, *Robert Greene et ses romans* (Paris, 1938), p. 349; and G. K. Hunter,
John Lyly (1962), p. 286. Other works of Greene sometimes cited as Arcadian imitations
are *Arbasto* (1584), *Pandosto* (1588), and *Ciceronis Amor* (1589).

[3] Book ix could have suggested the wife wooed by a husband under the delusion that
she was his mistress; Pruvost, p. 301, gives *Amadis* as the source of *Pandosto*.

[4] See Wolff, 422–45.

[5] E. Greenlaw, 'Shakespeare's Pastorals', *S.P.* xiii (1916), 122–54, sets out the
evidence for Lodge's indebtedness to the *Arcadia*.

[6] For example, the wound received by Rosader in rescuing his sleeping brother from
a lion, and the near-capture of Aliena by outlaws. The parallels are assembled in P. A.
Burnett, 'Thomas Lodge, *Rosalynde* (1590): An Annotated Critical Edition' (Oxford
B.Litt. Thesis, 1968), pp. lxxi–lxxxvi.   [7] See pp. xxii–xxiii.

been chosen king) that Sir Philip Sidney was well acquainted with this aspiring humour of women—

making in his *Arcadia* not only the stately Pamela to reject the naked virtue of Musidorus, till she found it well clothed with the title to a sceptre, but even Mistress Mopsa, when she sat hooded in the tree to beg a boon of Apollo, to ask nothing but to have a king to her husband, and a lusty one too; and when her pitiful father Dametas (for want of a better) played Apollo's part, and told her she should have husbands enough, she prayed devoutly they might be all kings: and thus much for the Moral.[1]

Harington had his own manuscript copy of the *Old Arcadia*, from which he transcribed two poems into the Arundel Harington MS.,[2] and he was well aware that the 1590 edition of the *New Arcadia* was a different work, distinguishing at one point between the 'first Arcadia' and the 'printed book'.

Abraham Fraunce had the advantage of access to the best of the surviving manuscripts for his numerous illustrations from the *Old Arcadia* in his *The Arcadian Rhetoric* (1588).[3] George Puttenham's *The Art of English Poesy* (1589) refers the reader to Sidney, Chaloner, and Spenser 'for eclogue and pastoral poesy'; and elsewhere mentions Sir Philip Sidney's description of his mistress 'in his book of Arcadia', indicating that the two quotations from poems in the *Old Arcadia* came from a manuscript of the whole work.

Some of the funeral elegies show awareness that Sidney wrote about Arcadia, but little familiarity with the contents of his book.[4] Angel Day has ten lines on the pastoral poems 'In sundry metres', with the marginal note 'A book by him penned, called the Countess of Pembroke's Arcadia';[5] and George Whetstone gets no further than a reference to

> His Arcadia, unmatched for sweet device,
> Where skill doth judge, is held in sovereign price.

---

[1] Harington, 404, Notes to Canto XLVI. The episode concerning Mopsa occurs at the beginning of Book IV of the *Old Arcadia*.

[2] It is not possible to determine the relationship of Harington's manuscript to the surviving *Old Arcadia* manuscripts.

[3] St. John's College, Cambridge, MS.; see p. xlv.

[4] Arcadia is mentioned several times in *Exequiae* (1587) and *Peplus* (1587). Ringler, lxii, comments on the ignorance of the contents of Sidney's story shown by Roydon in his 'Elegy . . . for his Astrophil'. The possible reference to *Arcadia* by Jan Dousa the younger (Dorsten, *Poets*, 101), and the specific reference by Gruterus (J. van Dorsten in *R.E.S.* xvi (1965), 174–7), which could have been made in Sidney's lifetime, are equally applicable to the *Old* or the *New Arcadia*.

[5] *Upon the Life and Death of . . . Sir Philip Sidney* (n.d., ent. 22 February 1587), A3ᵛ.

This is glossed in the margin 'His Arcadia a book most excellently written'.[1] However, Sidney's secretary, William Temple, refers to 'Arcadiae docuit fabrica texta novae',[2] thereby implying a knowledge of the existence of the older version. This confirms the impression given by Molyneux that only members of Sidney's immediate entourage had been allowed to see his *Arcadia*: 'few works of like subject hath been either of some more earnestly sought, choicely kept, nor placed in better place, amongst better jewels than that was; so that a special dear friend he should be that could have a sight, but much more dear that could once obtain a copy of it'.[3] Molyneux does not distinguish between the two versions of the *Arcadia*. No doubt Greville was inspired by a desire to emphasize the greater value of the *New Arcadia* when he wrote to Sir Francis Walsingham (who endorsed the letter 'november 1586'):

Sir this day one ponsonby a booke bynder in poles church yard, came to me, and told me that ther was one in hand to print, Sir philip sydneys old arcadia asking me yf it were done, with yor honors co[n]s[ent] or any other of his frends, I told him to m[y] knowledge no, then he advised me to give w[ar]ning of it, ether to the archebishope or doctor Cosen, who haue as he says a copy of it to pervse to that end / Sir I am lothe to reneu his memori vnto you, but yeat in this I might presume, for I haue sent my lady yor daughter [Sidney's widow] at her request, a correction of that old one don 4 or 5 years since which he left in trust with me wherof ther is no more copies, & fitter to be printed then that first which is so common, . . .[4]

The title of the Phillipps Manuscript contains the suggestion that copies of the *Old Arcadia* circulated more freely after Sidney's death: 'emparted to some few of his frends in his lyfe time and to more sence his vnfortunat deceasse'. Further copies besides this manuscript may have been made in the period 1586–90, but after the publication of the *New Arcadia* 'no incentive would have remained to justify the enormous labour of copying by hand some

---

[1] *Sir Philip Sidney* (n.d., ent. 15 June 1587), B2; see T. C. Izard, *George Whetstone* (New York, 1942), p. 287.

[2] *Academiae Cantabrigiensis Lachrymae* (1587), p. 85.

[3] Holinshed, *Chronicles* (1587, uncensored version), iii. 1554a; see also pp. xv ff. There are indications of possible associations with the Sidney or Pembroke family circles in some of the surviving manuscripts.

[4] P.R.O., S.P. 12/195/33, from Ringler's transcription (p. 530). That a copy had already been submitted for licensing indicates how narrowly the *Old Arcadia* escaped printing.

180,000 words'.[1] The editor of the 1613 edition of the *Arcadia* had access to an *Old Arcadia* manuscript, and referred to it in these terms: 'Thus far the worthy author had revised or enlarged that first written Arcadia of his, which only passed from hand to hand, and was never printed.' This statement was reprinted in all the subsequent folio editions; but thereafter the *Old Arcadia* itself disappeared from view,[2] until Bertram Dobell discovered and described three manuscripts.[3]

[1] Ringler, 367. We now know of nine copies of the complete *Old Arcadia*, and a study of the relationships of the surviving manuscripts indicates that at least four more copies existed in the sixteenth century.

[2] David Hume of Godscroft, *The History of the Houses of Douglas and Angus* (1644), mentions that the *Arcadia* was 'polished and refined' after 1581-2; see pp. xvi–xvii.

[3] The discovery was announced in *The Athenaeum*, 7 September 1907; and the manuscripts were described and discussed in 'New Light upon Sir Philip Sidney's *Arcadia*', *Quarterly Review*, ccxi (1909), 74-100.

TEXTUAL INTRODUCTION

(1) *Old Arcadia* manuscripts[1]

Group I

[Je] Jesus College, Oxford, MS. 150.

Quarto. 187 ff. (ff. 1–5, 12–16, 64–5, 75–7, 88–9, 124, and 147–87 now wanting).

Amongst the names written on the front cover are those of various members of the Thelwall family, including Edward, who was at one time tutor to Lord Herbert of Cherbury. He was the brother of Sir Eubule Thelwall (1562–1630), principal of Jesus College.

[Hm] Arthur A. Houghton, Jr. (Helmingham Hall MS.).

Folio. [i]+158+[i] ff. (ff. 25 and 33–44 now wanting).

ff. 1–152^v, *Old Arcadia*; ff. 153^v–154^r, blank; ff. 154^v–158^r, the *Lady of May* (with an additional final speech not in the 1598 edition).

The manuscript is written in a single late sixteenth-century hand on paper made by Nicolas Lebé of Troyes, and contains at least two variants of his signed watermark. The watermarks are similar to Briquet's Nos. 8077–82, which he dates 1561–1602. The binding is early seventeenth-century English brown calf gilt; the same corner-pieces are found on a Bible of 1608 with James I's arms.[2] As with a volume of *Statutes*, 1587 and 1589,[3] the initials SLT are tooled on the binding. They probably belonged to Sir Lionel Tollemache (1562–1612); but the 2nd baronet was also named Lionel, and a letter to him from William Herbert, Earl of Pembroke, dated 26 August 1619, ends 'Your very assured loving friend and kinsman'.[4]

[Qu] Queen's College, Oxford, MS. R 38/301.

Folio. vii+142+ii ff.

---

[1] Full descriptions and details of provenance, etc., will be found in Ringler, 525–38 with a brief account of Hm on p.x. Except in the case of this last manuscript, bare particulars only are given here, unless I have anything to add to Ringler's information.

[2] Sotheby's *Catalogue of Highly Important Manuscripts and Printed Books, the Property of the Rt. Hon. Lord Tollemache, M.C., T.D. . . .*, sold on 6 June 1961, Lot 21.

[3] Ibid., Lot 34.

[4] Folger Shakespeare Library; the letter is reproduced in *Elizabethan Handwriting*, by G. E. Dawson and L. Kennedy-Skipton (London, 1968), no. 37.

Group II

[Da] British Museum MS. Additional 41204 (Davies MS.).

Folio. ii+190 ff.

[Ph] British Museum MS. Additional 38892 (Phillipps MS.).

A treatis made by Sr Phillip Sydney Knyght of certeyn accidents in Arcadia, made in the yeer 1580 and emparted to some few of his frends. in his lyfe time and to more sence his vnfortunat deceasse.|

Quarto. i+202 ff.

Group III

[Cl] Folger Shakespeare Library MS. H.b.i [formerly 4009.03] (Clifford MS.).

Folio. [ii]+226+[i].

ff. 1–216^r, *Old Arcadia*; ff. 216^v–226^v, 'Dyuers and sondry Sonett*es*' (*Certain Sonnets*, 3–32).

This manuscript was published by Feuillerat as Volume IV of Sidney's *Works* in 1926 (reprinted 1962).

Amongst the names scribbled on the first and last leaves are 'Alexander Clifforde', 'Willm Clyforde', 'Mountgomrey', and 'Iohn lluid'. In his Preface Feuillerat draws attention to Anne Clifford, daughter of the 3rd Earl of Cumberland, who married as her second husband Philip Herbert, 4th Earl of Pembroke and Montgomery, 'But it would be dangerous to speculate too much on this coincidence'. With the manuscript is a typed letter from Dr. George Williamson of Guildford to Mr. W. A. White, dated 27 September 1926, giving particulars of John Lloyd (1558–1603), without mentioning that he edited, and dedicated to Henry Herbert, Earl of Pembroke, *Peplus* (1587), the New College volume of elegies for Sidney. He, rather than Gwinne (Hudson, in *H.L.Q.* ii (1938–9), 216), was the 'Lydus' referred to in Huntington Library MS. HM 1337, f. 28, as 'condus promusque Sydniadis elegantiarum'.

[Le] British Museum MS. Additional 41498 (Lee MS.).

Folio. 38 ff.

ff. 2–37^v, 66 poems in the order in which they appear in the *Old Arcadia*, and two short passages of prose from Book II. The poems omitted are OA 5, 6, 9, 10, 25, 26, 28, 29, 58, 68, and 77.

Upside down on the back parchment cover is written, 'Sir Henry

Lee delivered being champean to the qwene delivered to my lord cwmberla[n]d deli by willeam simons'. F.A. Yates, 'Elizabethan Chivalry: The Romance of the Accession Day Tilts', *Journal of the Warburg and Courtauld Institutes*, xx (1957), 4–25 points out that this parchment cover may not have enclosed this manuscript originally, and as it remained at Ditchley, neither it nor the manuscript were in fact sent to the Earl of Cumberland, who did not become Queen's champion until 1590. This article assembles the evidence for the close connection between Lee and Sidney (see also p. xxiii n.). Lee's portrayal in one of the *New Arcadia* tilts was first suggested by J. H. Hanford and S. R. Watson, 'Personal Allegory in the *Arcadia*: Philisides and Lelius', *M.P.* xxxii (1934), 1–10.

[As] Huntington Library MS. HM 162 (Ashburnham MS.).

Folio. 189 ff. (ff. 1–6 now wanting).

On f. 86ᵛ is written 'Robert Walker'. A man of this name was treasurer to Sir Henry Sidney from 1575 until about 1581, and he appears in the Sidney family records until 1583.

Group IV

[St] St. John's College, Cambridge, MS. I. 7.

Folio. [ii]+236+[iv].

ff. 1–236ᵛ, *Old Arcadia*. Some letters have disappeared on the first leaves, owing to the crumbling of the paper on the outer edges. On f. 160 the scribe inadvertently began to copy what he had already written on f. 159ᵛ, and continued on f. 160ᵛ before discovering his error and cancelling both sides.

The inscription on f. 236ᵛ (see below) indicates that when Walker bought the manuscript, that was the final leaf. The last four leaves are of different paper and the writing is in a different hand. They contain *Certain Sonnets* 19, 6, 5, 3, and 30, in that order, on ff. [ii]–[iii].

St has been used as the copy-text for this edition of the *Old Arcadia*.

In the margin of f. 1 is written: 'Tho: Baker dedit Coll: Jo: socius ejectus / liber olim Ornatiss: vir Thoma' Wagstaff.' Wagstaffe died in 1712, and Baker must have given the manuscript to St. John's not long after, as it was listed in their catalogue of *c.* 1717.[1]

---

[1] Baker also gave St. John's their copy of Fraunce's *The Arcadian Rhetoric*.

On f. 1 is a note 'Will Walker of Cheswick in Middlesex bought this Booke among other Manuscripts of the Executor of Sr Edmonde Scorie Knight And now possesses it A D 1633.'; and another on f. 236^v, 'This Manuscript wth many others were bought of Mr Busbie Executor to Sr Edmonde Scorie Knight by Will Walker Theol. Bac:'. Sir Edmund Scory's Will[1] was made on 4 May 1632, with codicils revoking some legacies added on 9 May and 23 June. Among the remaining legacies were:

Item I give and bequeath unto Giles Baker my servant who hath lived under the tyranny of my wife to the danger of his life during the space of two years the sum of twenty shillings of lawful English money.

Item I give and bequeath unto Dame Sylvester Scory my wife who I heartily forgive all her wicked attempts against me a prayer book called the *Practice of Piety*[2] desiring that she better love and affect the same than hitherto she hath done it.

The rest of his estate he bequeathed to 'his faithful servant Hugh Busby', whom he made his executor. Dame Sylvester protested that her husband was out of his mind at the time he made his Will; but Busby declared that his master was sane, and the Will was proved by him and the deceased's brother, Sylvanus Scory (who died a debtor in Wood St. Counter in 1641).

Of much more importance than Sir Edmund Scory's ownership of the manuscript in 1632 is the fact that, as Ringler has demonstrated, and as an examination of the prose confirms, the numerous quotations from the *Arcadia* in Abraham Fraunce's *The Arcadian Rhetoric* (1588) were almost certainly taken from St.[3] He suggested that Fraunce might have borrowed the manuscript whilst he was practising as a barrister at the Court of the Marches at Ludlow from Sir Edmund's father, Sylvanus Scory, who lived nearby in Herefordshire. But even if Fraunce went to Ludlow shortly after he was called to the Bar in February 1588,[4] this scarcely allows sufficient time to make his extracts from St for *The Arcadian Rhetoric*, which was entered on the Stationers' Register on 11 June 1588. Moreover, both Sylvanus and his father John Scory, Bishop of Hereford, had quarrelled with Sidney and his father,[5] and Sylvanus is not likely to have come within the category of 'a special dear friend' to whom a

---

[1] Somerset House, Awdelay 81, 'Sir Edmund Skory Knight Salop'.
[2] By Lewis Bayly, Bishop of Bangor.   [3] Ringler, 562.
[4] There is no record of his presence at Ludlow before the summer of 1590.
[5] *H.M.C., De L'Isle*, ii. 98.

copy of the *Old Arcadia* would have been given. Furthermore, there is no indication that Sylvanus had any interest in literature;[1] whereas William Walker says that he bought the manuscript St 'with many others' from Sir Edmund Scory's executor. We may assume, therefore, that Sir Edmund was something of a collector.[2]

Fraunce was a native of Shropshire who entered Shrewsbury School in January 1572, some three years after Sidney left. This may have served to bring him to Sidney's attention; for he was, he said 'bred up' at St. John's College, Cambridge, from 1576 until 1583, when he received his M.A., partly by the assistance of Sidney, whom he called his 'Master and Patron'. He 'first came into the presence of' Sidney in 1581, and between that year and 1583 he dedicated his manuscript treatises on logic and imprese, and the Latin comedy *Victoria*, to Sidney.[3] Ringler deduces that, since Fraunce did not mention in these Dedications that his patron was a man of letters, he did not gain access to his writings until after Sidney's death. But even if we accept the argument from Fraunce's silence, we need not deduce that he remained ignorant of Sidney's literary activity from 1583 until after his death. He could have obtained St at any time between 1583 and 1588.[4]

[Bo] Bodleian Library MS. e Museo 37.

Folio. i+247 ff.

ff. 1–236ᵛ, *Old Arcadia*; ff. 237–46, 'Certein lowse Sonnett*es* and songes' (27 of the *Certain Sonnets*).

ff. 1–96 have the same watermark (Briquet No. 11055) as a holograph letter of Sidney's to the Earl of Leicester written at Salisbury on 28 December 1581.

---

[1] Neither books nor manuscripts are mentioned in his Will (Somerset House, Weldon 127, proved in October 1617).

[2] Indications of a literary bent are some Latin verses with an anagram of Scory's name: 'E.Sc.Duris Decis omen', in Drayton's *Heroical Epistles* (1597); and 'The 21 and 45 Psalme paraphrased by Sʳ Ed: Scorey' listed in Warwick Castle MS. 2703, f. 4. This manuscript is an inventory of items no longer at Warwick Castle (information kindly supplied by the County Record Office, Warwick).

[3] E. Seaton, Introduction to *The Arcadian Rhetoric*.

[4] Fraunce was a member of Gray's Inn from 1583 until 1588; at Sidney's funeral he walked in the procession among his gentlemen and yeomen servants. After Sidney's death he sought and received the patronage of the Countess of Pembroke, dedicating *The Arcadian Rhetoric*, and subsequent works, to her. Ringler shows that the quotations from AS in *The Arcadian Rhetoric* come from the manuscript (X) used by the printer of 98, and that CS 3 also came from the manuscript used by the printer of 98. He assumes that Fraunce had obtained these manuscripts from the Countess of Pembroke herself by 1588.

(2) Manuscripts containing poems from the *Old Arcadia*[1]

[Dd] Cambridge University Library MS. Dd.5.75 (2).

OA 2, 3, 35, 41, 42 (lines 1–8), 48, 51, 62.

[Eg] British Museum MS. Egerton 2421.

OA 62 (the last 3 lines only).

[Fl] Folger Shakespeare Library MS. V. a. 339 [formerly 2071.7].

OA 17.

[Ha] British Museum MS. Harleian 6910.

OA 3, 15 (10 lines only), 64.

[Hn] Arundel Castle, His Grace the Duke of Norfolk, 'Harrington MS. Temp. Eliz.'.

Edited by Ruth Hughey, *The Arundel Harington Manuscript of Tudor Poetry*, 2 vols. (Columbus: Ohio State University Press, 1960).

OA 51, 74.

[Hy] British Museum MS. Harleian 7392(2).

OA 3, 45, 51, 60.

[Ma] Marsh's Library, Dublin MS. Z. 3. 5. 21.

OA 17.

[Ra] Bodleian Library MS. Rawlinson Poetical 85.

OA 7 (5 lines only), 13 (38 lines only), 21, 22, 33, 38, 41, 51, 71.

(3) Printed books containing poems from the *Old Arcadia*[2]

[Hn] Sir John Harington, *Orlando Furioso in English Heroical Verse* (1591).

OA 64 (4 lines only), 65.

[Pu] [George Puttenham], *The Art of English Poesy* (1589).

Edited by Gladys D. Willcock and Alice Walker (London, 1936).

OA 45 (lines 1–8, arranged as a 10-line song), 61 (2 lines only).

---

[1] Manuscripts containing substantive texts only are listed here. Ringler, 552–61, gives full descriptions of the manuscripts containing poems by Sidney; and on p. 366 n., is a short list of 'early texts [of poems from the *Arcadia*] deriving from other known manuscripts or printed editions, and therefore not substantive'; these copies are noted in my commentary on individual poems.

[2] Books containing substantive texts only are listed here. Ringler, 561 ff., gives details of all printed books containing poems by Sidney.

(4) *New Arcadia* texts

[Cm] Cambridge University Library MS. Kk.i.5(2).
Folio. 210 ff.

Written in a single elaborate Italian hand,[1] including the date 1584 in the upper left margin of f. 1.

[90] *The Countess of Pembroke's Arcadia, written by Sir Philip Sidney. For William Ponsonby*, 1590.

S.T.C. 22539[a]. Juel-Jensen 1*a*.[2]

[variant imprint] *John Windet for William Ponsonby*, 1590.

S.T.C. 22539. Juel-Jensen 1*b*.

Entered in the Stationers' Register on 23 August 1588.

Ringler, 532, assembles the evidence for Fulke Greville's general editorship, and Matthew Gwinne's involvement, but drops John Florio from the editorial team, despite the evidence for his close collaboration with Gwinne in other literary projects, and his attacks on Hugh Sanford and his editorial work in the 1593 edition of the *Arcadia*. The full story is told by F. A. Yates, *John Florio* (1934).

[93] *The Countess of Pembroke's Arcadia. Written by Sir Philip Sidney Knight. Now since the first edition augmented and ended. For William Ponsonby*, 1593.

S.T.C. 22540. Juel-Jensen 2.

Engraved title-page border, McKerrow and Ferguson, 212.

The title-page is reproduced as a frontispiece to this edition. The animal in the top central medallion is a compromise between the porcupine of the Sidney crest (reproduced on the title-page of 90) and the 'bristly Arcadian boar' (Lucretius, v. 25). The left supporter is the bear of the Dudley arms, but without a chain, to indicate that it is also the animal slain by Musidorus, who stands below it, disguised as the shepherd Dorus, on a plinth containing the head of a man and two profiles. The lion on the right is the sinister supporter of the Sidney arms, but without a crown, to

---

[1] Miss K. Duncan-Jones informs me that the Norwich MS. of the *Defence of Poesy* (identified by Miss M. R. Mahl; see *T.L.S.* 21. xii. 67) appears to be written by the same scribe; it offers a text of the same low standard of accuracy.

[2] References are to Dr. Bent Juel-Jensen's checklist in *The Book Collector*, xi (1962), 469–79. As he is preparing a Bibliography of Sidney's Printed Works, to be published by the Oxford Bibliographical Society, full descriptions are not included here; collations will be found in Ringler, 531–8.

indicate that it is also the animal slain by Pyrocles, who stands below
it, disguised as the Amazon Zelmane (Cleophila in the *Old Arcadia*),
on a plinth containing the head of a man and two profiles. A central
medallion at the foot of the design features a pig repelled by a bush
of sweet marjoram, bearing the motto *Non tibi spiro*.[1] That the
editor was responsible for this design is clear from his remark in the
Preface that 'the worthless reader can never worthily esteem of so
worthy a writing', and from the merriment it gave rise to.[2] The full
text of the Preface is as follows:

TO THE READER

The disfigured face, gentle reader, wherewith this work not long since
appeared to the common view, moved that noble lady, to whose honour
consecrated, to whose protection it was committed, to take in hand the
wiping away those spots wherewith the beauties thereof were unworthily
blemished. But, as often in repairing a ruinous house, the mending of
some old part occasioneth the making of some new; so here her honour-
able labour begun in correcting the faults, ended in supplying the defects;
by the view of what was ill done guided to the consideration of what was
not done. Which part with what advice entered into, with what success it
hath been passed through, most by her doing, all by her directing, if they
may be entreated not to define, which are unfurnished of means to discern,
the rest (it is hoped) will favourably censure. But this they shall, for their
better satisfaction, understand, that though they find not here what might

---

[1] R. L. Eagle, 'The *Arcadia* (1593) Title-Page Border', *The Library*, 5th Ser. iv
(1949), 68–71, points to the most likely source in Joachimus Camerarius the younger,
Symbolorum & Emblematum ex re herbaria desumtorum centuria (Nuremberg, 1590),
Emblem xciii (p. 103), which shows below the motto *Non tibi spiro* a pig repelled by
a bush in a pot, and underneath, the lines
Pravis est animis virus doctrina salubris:
Sic lutulens fugitat porcus amaracinum.
The emblem is reproduced in *Emblemata. Handbuch zur Sinnbildkunst des XVI. und
XVII. Jahrhunderts*, ed. Arthur Henkel and Albrecht Schöne (Stuttgart, 1967),
p. 549. To Eagle's references to Lucretius, vi. 973, and Aulus Gellius, *Noctes, praef.*
19 (where it is described as an old proverb), is added Erasmus, *Adagia*, i. 335. The
reference to roses in his Preface shows that the editor of 93 also knew the similar pro-
verb 'It is folly to strew roses among swine' (Tilley, F436, earliest citation is for 1616).
This is No. 50 in Camerarius's second volume of *Emblemata*. The connection with
Matthew 7: 6, 'Cast not pearls before swine' (Tilley, P165), is made by Florio in his
attack on 93 in the Preface to his translation of Montaigne's *Essays* (1603): 'Why but
pearls should not be cast to swine: yet are rings put in their noses; and a swine should
know his sty, and will know his meat and his medicine, and as much beside, as any
swine doth suppose it to be marjoram.'

[2] See Nashe, *Lenten Stuff* (1599), Dedication to Humphrey King (*Works*, ed.
McKerrow, iii. 147); and John Florio, *A World of Words* (1598), Preface, and
Montaigne's *Essays* (1603), Preface.

be expected, they may find nevertheless as much as was intended, the conclusion, not the perfection of *Arcadia*; and that no further than the author's own writings, or known determinations, could direct. Whereof who sees not the reason, must consider there may be reason which he sees not. Albeit I dare affirm he either sees, or from wiser judgements than his own may hear, that Sir Philip Sidney's writings can no more be perfected without Sir Philip Sidney than Apelles' pictures without Apelles. There are that think the contrary; and no wonder. Never was Arcadia free from the cumber of such cattle. To us, say they, the pastures are not pleasant; and as for the flowers, such as we light on we take no delight in, but the greater part grow not within our reach. Poor souls! What talk they of flowers? They are roses, not flowers, must do them good, which if they find not here, they shall do well to go feed elsewhere. Any place will better like them; for without Arcadia nothing grows in more plenty than lettuce suitable to their lips. If it be true that likeness is a great cause of liking, and that contraries infer contrary consequences, then is it true that the worthless reader can never worthily esteem of so worthy a writing; and as true that the noble, the wise, the virtuous, the courteous, as many as have had any acquaintance with true learning and knowledge, will with all love and dearness entertain it, as well for affinity with themselves, as being child to such a father. Whom albeit it do not exactly and in every lineament represent; yet considering the father's untimely death prevented the timely birth of the child, it may happily seem a thank-worthy labour, that the defects being so few, so small, and in no principal part, yet the greatest unlikeness is rather in defect than in deformity. But howsoever it is, it is now by more than one interest *The Countess of Pembroke's Arcadia*; done, as it was, for her; as it is, by her. Neither shall these pains be the last (if no unexpected accident cut off her determination) which the everlasting love of her excellent brother will make her consecrate to his memory.

H. S.

The identity of H. S. with Hugh Sanford, secretary to the Earl of Pembroke, has long been established;[1] and the replies of John Florio to the attack on 90 at the beginning of this Preface have frequently been noted.[2] Sanford makes it clear at the end of the Preface that the

[1] Godshalk in *Ph.Q.* xliii (1964), 179 ff., provides a useful summary of the evidence, and of what is known about Sanford and his fondness for 'pedantic inventions'. John Hoskyns, *Directions for Speech and Style* (c. 1599), first indicated his editorship of 93 when he stated that his quotations were 'taken out of Sir Philip Sidney's *Arcadia*, the first edition in quarto, without Samford's [*sic*] *Additions*'.

[2] The fullest account will be found in F. A. Yates, *John Florio*. In his Preface to *A World of Words* (1598) he combined mockery of the title-page with interpreting the initials 'H. S.' to stand for abusive names in Latin and Italian, as well as such English insults as 'Huff Snuff', 'Humfrey Swineshead', and 'Hodge Sowgelder'.

Countess of Pembroke had personally taken part in the preparation of 93; and Florio's use of his Dedication of Book II of his translation of Montaigne's *Essays* to Sidney's daughter, the Countess of Rutland, and to Lady Penelope Rich, to return to the attack on 93 suggests that the quarrel was not entirely confined to the editorial staff.

[98] *The Countess of Pembroke's Arcadia. Written by Sir Philip Sidney Knight. Now the third time published, with sundry new additions of the same author. For William Ponsonby,* 1598.

S.T.C. 22541 Juel-Jensen 3.[1]

This was the first collected edition of Sidney's works, and was issued with the approval of the family.

[05] *The Countess of Pembroke's Arcadia. Written by Sir Philip Sidney Knight. Now the fourth time published, with sundry new additions of the same author. For Simon Waterson,* 1605.

S.T.C. 22543. Juel-Jensen 5*a*.

[variant imprint] *For Mathew Lownes,* 1605.

S.T.C. 22543a. Juel-Jensen 5*b*.

[13] *The Countess of Pembroke's Arcadia. Written by Sir Philip Sidney Knight. Now the fourth time published, with some new additions.*

H.L. for Simon Waterson, 1613.

S.T.C. 22544. Juel-Jensen 6*a*.

[variant imprint] *H.L. for Mathew Lownes,* 1613.

S.T.C. 22544a. Juel-Jensen, 6*b*.

This is the only folio edition to omit Sanford's address 'To the Reader', but his remark that the editing of 93 had been 'most by her [the Countess of Pembroke's] doing, all by her directing' is used as the basis of the statement in the link passage on sig. Ee5 of 13 that the *Arcadia* was 'afterwards printed as now it is only by her noble care to whose dear hand they were first committed'. Ringler may still be right that the Countess of Pembroke had no hand in this edition. He is certainly right to dismiss the inscription 'This was the Countess of pembrokes owne booke given me by the Countess of Montgomery her daughter 1635' in the Harvard Widener copy of 13 as a forgery.[2]

---

[1] Juel-Jensen 4 is the Edinburgh pirated edition of 1599.

[2] Ringler, 537. He also concludes that the comments in the Harvard copy 14457.23.8.7 F* are not in the hand of Gabriel Harvey (see also W. Godshalk in *M.L.R.* lix (1964),

Juel-Jensen lists several copies of 13 containing the Supplement by Sir William Alexander; and he has now established that a copy of 13 with the Supplement was bought in 1618.[1] It was entered in the Stationers' Register to W. Barrett on 31 August 1616, and transferred to M. Lownes on 22 March 1619.

THE RELATIONSHIPS OF THE TEXTS[2]

In the Dedication to his sister, deprecating his work as 'but a trifle', Sidney says 'Your dear self can best witness the manner, being done in loose sheets of paper, most of it in your presence, the rest by sheets sent unto you as fast as they were done.' The matter is scarcely susceptible of proof, but on balance Ringler thinks that, despite the suggestion in this passage of an author scribbling away, the sheets sent to the Countess of Pembroke were in fact a scribal copy (P) made from the *Old Arcadia* foul papers. Something of the nature of P can be deduced from the 1593 edition, which will be dealt with later. The editor of the 1613 edition embroidered Sidney's remark in the Dedication as follows: 'So that all which followeth here of this work remained as it was done and sent away in several loose sheets (being never after reviewed, nor so much as seen all together by himself), without any certain disposition or perfect order.' It is quite true that Sidney never saw Books III–V of the *Old Arcadia* with the alterations and additions made to them in the 1593 edition; but, as Ringler says, 'variants in the texts of the surviving manuscripts show that Sidney retained in his own possession a transcript of his work which he afterwards revised on at least five different occasions' (p. 366). This transcript from the *Old Arcadia* foul papers is designated by T, and by the symbols T^1–T^5 to indicate the various revisions made by Sidney. As one would expect, these were more numerous in the poems, but such alterations as he did make

497–8). Dr. J. A. van Dorsten has drawn my attention to a copy of 13 in the University of Leiden Library with the Waterson imprint, an inscription 'Ex Bibliotheca Viri Illust. Isaaci Vossii', and numerous annotations in Latin, which may be by Vossius himself.

[1] *The Book Collector*, xi (1962), 473–4, and xii (1963), 201. Dr. Juel-Jensen informs me privately that he has found another copy without the Supplement which was purchased on 6 March 1617.

[2] My task has been greatly simplified by Professor Ringler's massive labours on the text of the *Old Arcadia* poems. His detailed evidence will be found on his pp. 364–70. It has seemed sufficient to summarize his conclusions here, with some additional evidence provided by the prose. The minor adjustments I would propose to his stemma have mostly been signalized in his Preface.

in the prose support Ringler's arrangement of the manuscripts in
the sequence I have indicated by the Groups I–IV.

The Group I manuscripts (Je–Hm–Qu) bear witness to the text
of T¹. When Ringler wrote his Preface (x–xi), he was able to place
Hm with Je–Qu; but I had not then obtained the evidence that Qu
is in fact a careless copy of Hm. They share numerous omissions;
but I have found no omissions in Hm of words or sentences found
in Qu, whereas Qu omits words and sentences found in Hm.¹
Finally, whereas all the errors found in Hm are also found in Qu,
Qu has errors not found in Hm. Qu is therefore only substantive for
the passages written on the now-missing folios (ff. 25 and 33–44) of
Hm. Group I then reduces to Je–Hm. Their agreements in error
are far too numerous (Ringler estimated those (in Je–Qu) in the
poems alone at several hundred) for Je and Hm to have been copied
independently from T. Therefore, with Ringler, I conclude that
they descend from T through a common intermediary X, which was
a rather careless copy.

Je–Hm (Qu) are the only manuscripts that contain the passage on
quantitative verse at the end of the First Eclogues (pp. 89–90),
with an early version of the final sentences. This is their most
striking difference from the manuscripts of Group II (Da–Ph)
which witness to T². Da is a fairly accurate copy, with some tendency
towards sophistication. As Ph was transcribed after 1586, but con-
tains the text in the T² state, it must derive from a lost transcript
of T², which I follow Ringler in calling Y. The errors, omissions,
and additions in Ph may derive, at any rate in part, from this lost
manuscript. When Ringler wrote his Preface (x), I had not signalized
my acceptance of his conclusion that some fifty additions or substi-
tutions in Ph were the result of scribal inventiveness and lively
participation. This is the only possible explanation.² Da–Ph offer
some shared readings, against all the other manuscripts, that must
be scribal; but they are neither numerous nor important enough to
warrant any suggestion of a common intermediary between T and Y.³

---

¹ The most significant are two omissions in Qu of words which form exactly one
line in Hm (p. 179, 8–9, *favour . . . any*; p. 366, 2–3, *the trying . . . because*). At
p. 399, 33 the word *vagabonding* is cut to *vagabon* at the end of the line in Hm, and the
scribe forgot to write the rest of the word at the beginning of the next line; in Qu it
appears medially as *vagabon*.

² I do not give these passages in the variants, but they will be found in the Commen-
tary; see, for example, the notes to pp. 52, 16–17; 122, 11; 202, 6; 299, 25.

³ The most striking example is p. 292, 20; *as though he had looked* in Da–Ph, for
as if he had hoped in the other manuscripts.

After Da and Y were copied from T², Sidney made some further changes, transforming it into T³. This state is represented by the Group III manuscripts (Cl–Le–As). Besides the revisions in the poems noted by Ringler, Cl–As (Le only contains one short passage of prose) reveal a scattering of minor revisions in the prose.[1] Cl–As contain a fairly large number of shared omissions[2] and errors.[3] Most of these can be explained by the fact that different scribes make the same mistakes independently, and that once one has explained how an error arose, it is easy to accept that it could happen again. For example, at p. 280, 28 the reading of all the other manuscripts is *climbing*, probably spelt *clyming* in T; Cl has misread as *glymīng* (i.e. 'glimmering' or 'gleaming'); and As reads *shining*, which looks like a synonym for the Cl reading, but it could just as well have derived from an independent misreading of T's *clyming* as *glyming*, and the substitution of a more familiar word. But p. 389, 28 *full graceless* for *O hopeless*, and p. 401, 28 *gallant speaker* for *copious* (*compendious* Hm) *talker* are harder to accept as independent happenings; and even more so is p. 273, 3 *divinely* for which Cl substituted *by fore appointment*; and this reading would seem to have given rise to As's *before appointment*. It seems to me that *contaminatio* is a more likely explanation than that Cl–As both derive from a lost copy of T³. For one thing, there are a few indications that As was copied from T³ slightly later than Cl. The As scribe knew of the existence of the Note on the rules for quantitative verse which appears in St only (pp. 80–1); for immediately after the poem 'Fortune, Nature, Love' As has 'Write these rules', followed by a blank page. Whereas the Cl ending to the First Eclogues (p. 88) still shows traces of the T¹ ending (hopelessly scamped in Da–Ph), As's version is tidied up and corresponds with St–Bo.[4] These indications of a forward relationship to T⁴ in As are more important for establishing the

[1] For example, see pp. 286, 3; 352, 19; 363, 10; 390, 12, 34; 392, 12; 393, 24; 394, 1, 9.

[2] For example, see pp. 94, 29; 130, 25; 283, 16–17; 299, 28; 316, 14–15; 319, 31–2; 324, 4; 351, 6; 359, 13–14; 376, 7; 378, 16; 379, 31; 380, 20; 381, 10; 384, 31; 389, 22.

[3] In the following examples the Cl–As shared substitutions are followed by the reading of the other manuscripts in brackets: pp. 153, 20–1 *indeed* (*in the end*); 159, 8 *discourse* (*narration*); 205, 31 *reverence* (*recompense*); 223, 33 *garment* (*apparel*); 374, 13 *heedful* (*curious*); 375, 8 *noble* (*principal*); 386, 30 *love* (*faith*); 389, 34; *garments* (*lodging*); 391, 21 *sadness* (*sorrow*).

[4] Minor alterations found in St, Bo, and As, but not in Cl, are on pp. 117, 32–3; 126, 35; and 169, 6.

development of Sidney's text than the Cl–As shared readings against all the other manuscripts, which cannot be correct.

The Group IV manuscripts (St–Bo) are the latest surviving *Old Arcadia* manuscripts, and show that Sidney made further changes in T³, transforming it into T⁴. In addition to the changes made in the poems,¹ evidently a decision was taken to build up the character of Agelastus (pp. 284, 2–7; 344, 22). Its absence in 90 (*Works*, i. 348) suggests that a sentence at p. 146, 14 n., omitted in St–Bo, had been deliberately cancelled in T⁴. On p. 37, 18, an inaccurate reflection, in the absence of a motto, on imprese is omitted; in 90 (*Works*, i. 90) there is a different device with a motto. On p. 47, 21–6 Pyrocles' wound is made a less serious affair. St is the only manuscript to have the Note giving the rules of syllabic quantities, written in the margin opposite OA 11 (pp. 80–1), though a space was left for it in As. It may have been on a loose sheet of paper, and so overlooked by the Bo scribe, who was a much more careless copyist than St's; for St and Bo must have been copied from T⁴ at about the same time.

There is even less evidence pointing to a common intermediary than in the case of Cl–As;² but one or two agreements in what I take to be error, rather than authorial emendation in T⁴, are a little hard to accept as independent coincidental readings. For example, at p. 26, 26 St–Bo have *trial* for *paragon*, and at p. 280, 2 *O foul fiend despair* for *O snaky despair*.³ But when one considers the numerous Je–Hm agreements in error against all the other manuscripts, clearly the St–Bo agreements in error are not in this category; and if coincidental error cannot be accepted, then they must be explained by *contaminatio*. It is a possibility that either the copyist of St or the copyist of Bo (whichever made his copy of T first) made some changes in readings in T.⁴ Finally, one or two changes were made in St. in a later hand, apparently by reference to 93 or a later print.⁵

¹ Further revisions were made to the poem OA 62 (pp. 238 ff.), and the name 'Cosma' was substituted for 'Hyppa' in OA 29 (p. 142).

² There is no difficulty over two scribes independently omitting a line (p. 63, 4), or a word (pp. 52, 11; 67, 3), or using the singular for the plural (p. 91, 11), or writing *threatens* for *threatenings* (p. 156, 20). The omission of a whole clause at p. 50, 32–4, can also be explained as a mere coincidence, and the reading 'his eyes *closed*', with the blank in As to indicate difficulty in deciphering *fixed*, is susceptible of the same explanation (p. 279, 2).

³ See Commentary for the evidence that the St–Bo readings are not authorial.

⁴ At p. 137, 2 the original reading *convoy*, if it were spelt *cõuoye* in T, could have given rise to *course* in St–Bo; but its presence also in 90 (the passage occurs in the Eclogues which the editors of 90 supplied from T) suggests that it had been altered in T by either the St or the Bo copyist to *course*. Authorial correction cannot be ruled out, but I do not think it likely. ⁵ See Ringler, 529.

The probable relationships of the surviving *Old Arcadia* manu-
scripts to the scribal transcript (T) of Sidney's foul papers can be
summarized in the following diagram:

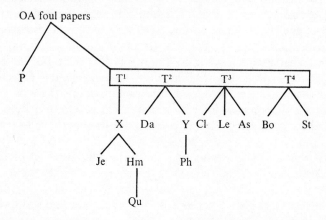

The surviving copies of T are not the only witnesses to the text
of the *Old Arcadia*. For when Sidney composed Books I and II of
the *New Arcadia*, he incorporated in them (using his own manu-
script, T) almost all of the corresponding books of the *Old Arcadia*,
and he transferred some of the poems in later books of the *Old
Arcadia* either to Books I and II of the *New Arcadia*, or to the
entirely new and unfinished Book III. And when the Countess of
Pembroke, with the assistance of Hugh Sanford, re-edited the *New
Arcadia* (90) in 1593, Books III–V of the *Old Arcadia* were added to
it, with sundry alterations and additions.

We must first consider the relation of Books I and II of the
principal *New Arcadia* texts (Cm, 90, 93) to Books I and II of the
Old Arcadia. Greville's lost manuscript (G) was used by his
editorial assistants, John Florio and Matthew Gwinne, as the basis
for their text of 90. Cm was an inaccurate copy of G. Comparison of
Cm and 90 reveals so many shared errors that there is a strong
presumption that their common original G was a scribal copy of the
New Arcadia foul papers. It also suggests that many of the con-
fusions which Cm took over from G were still in the manuscript
when Greville received it [1] In Cm a few poems only are given in full;

---

[1] Ringler accepted Greville's statement that there were 'no more copies' of the *New*

for others the first few lines only appear; and for some a blank space is left. This was evidently the case also in G, and the editors of 90 had therefore to get the full texts of the poems from T.[1] The texts of OA 2, 7, and 8 in 90 reveal that Sidney made some changes in these poems after St and Bo had been copied from T⁴, thereby producing the fifth state of his transcript, T⁵. These changes may have been intended for the *Old Arcadia*; since their earliest appearance is in 90, however, I have not incorporated them in my *Old Arcadia* text, but they are recorded in the textual apparatus. T⁵ was also used by Sidney when he altered and expanded the prose of the *Old Arcadia* Books I and II to form the corresponding Books in the *New Arcadia* foul papers. That some of the alterations in words and phraseology found in Books I and II of 90 were in reality alterations made for the *Old Arcadia* in T⁵, rather than alterations made in the process of transforming the *Old Arcadia* into the *New Arcadia*, is a possibility, but not one susceptible of proof. I have therefore only recorded in my textual apparatus those readings in 90 which help to establish the

Arcadia manuscript (G) which Sidney 'left in trust' with him, and concluded that the date 1584 on the first leaf of Cm must refer to the date of commencement of the composition of the *New Arcadia*, as the copy could not have been made until after Greville's letter was written (it is endorsed 'november 1586'). But 1584 is too late a date for the beginning of the revision; I think that the scribe is recording the date at which he began to make his transcript, and I assume that Greville did not know that Cm had been made. Cm breaks off in the middle of a sentence some fifteen pages before the 90 text comes to an end (also in the middle of a sentence), possibly because these pages had not yet been copied from the *New Arcadia* foul papers into G. The failure in Cm to fill in the blanks left for writing the proper names with a different pen, or the filling of them in incorrectly, was probably peculiar to this manuscript; but the mingling of *Old* and *New Arcadia* nomenclature must reflect confusion in G. Florio wrote, in his Dedication to the Countess of Rutland (Sidney's daughter) and to Lady Penelope Rich of Book II of his translation of Montaigne's *Essays* (1603): '. . . and though it were much easier to mend out of an original and well corrected copy, than to make up so much out of a most corrupt, yet see we more marring that was well than amending what was amiss.' I think that 'a most corrupt' refers to G, and not, as Joan Rees has suggested in *R.E.S.* xvi (1966), 57, to the Countess of Pembroke's *Old Arcadia* manuscript (P). Quite apart from the corruptness in G revealed by Cm, one would not expect Florio to make the point that he and Gwinne had had the easier row to hoe.

[1] See Ringler, 371, for a demonstration that the editors of 90 went direct to T for the text of OA 62. They also went to T for the Eclogues. Cm is a continuous text, without division into books or chapters, and there are no eclogues. That this was also the case in G is evident from the statement in 90 that 'The division and summing of the chapters was not of Sir Philip Sidney's doing, but adventured by the overseer of the print, for the more ease of the readers', and that the eclogues 'have been chosen and disposed as the overseer thought best' (A4ᵛ); and by the fact that the editors of 93 removed the chapter divisions and summaries (they also made some rearrangements in the eclogues on their own responsibility).

correct reading where the surviving *Old Arcadia* manuscripts leave
it in doubt.

Considering what the copy must have been like by the time the
editors had finished with it, the printing of 90 was done with reason-
able care by Elizabethan standards. There was some spasmodic
proof correction of the sheets throughout the work's progress
through the press,[1] but there inevitably remained some errors to
justify Sanford's remarks in his Preface to 93 about wiping away
spots and correcting faults.[2]

The editors of 93 reprinted 90, and added Books III–V of the *Old
Arcadia*. On balance, the printers of 93 introduced about as many
errors as they corrected, but the copy of 90 from which it was set had
some corrections. Cm sometimes agrees in readings with 90, and
sometimes with 93; this is most likely to be the result of independent
interpretations of the readings, insertions, and cancellations in G.[3]
Furthermore, 93 has passages, which occur in the narrative parts of
the *New Arcadia* that have no counterpart in the *Old Arcadia*, which
are not found in Cm or in 90.[4] These passages must have come from
G, which the Countess of Pembroke must have obtained from
Greville.[5] He was after all one of her brother's closest friends, and
initially relations must have been sufficiently cordial for her to have

---

[1] Cm readings indicate that in some cases what might have appeared to be com-
positors' errors were in fact present in G when it was sent to the printing house. For
example, *Works*, i. 403, uncorrected sheets of 90 have 'sorrow to *distress* itself in her
beauty', Cm has '*destres*', corrected sheets of 90 and the 93 text read '*dress*'; 465,
uncorrected sheets of 90 and Cm read 'her *iminate* humbleness', corrected sheets of
90 and the 93 text read '*innate*'; 470, uncorrected sheets of 90 and Cm read 'rather than
fact of conquest', corrected sheets of 90 and the 93 text read '*fail*'.

[2] Most of the misprints in 90 listed by Feuillerat (*Works*, i. 520–1) escaped detection
by the editors of 93.

[3] When Ringler wrote his Preface, I had suggested to him that the editors of 93
might have used another transcript of G rather than Cm. This now seems an unnecessary
hypothecation. The existence of Cm has to be accepted and explained, but one does
not want to have to suppose that there was yet another copy of a manuscript that
Greville claimed to be unique.

[4] At *Works*, i. 191, 90 and Cm read 'till now finding him able . . .'; 93 expands to
'till now, being both sent for by Euarchus, and finding Pyrocles able'. At i. 508, 93
inserts a clause, not found in 90 (Cm text ends before this point in the narrative), 'since
our own parents are content to be tyrants over us'. As the next clause reads 'since
our own kin are content traitorously to abuse us', the omission in 90 might have been
due to eyeskip, unless the clauses were intended to be alternatives, and the first was
imperfectly deleted by the scribe of G.

[5] John Powell's expenses incurred on Greville's behalf in 1590 include two payments
(of 2s. 6d. and 30s.) to a messenger from Lady Pembroke (B.M. Additional MS. 37482,
f. 68).

sent him the Dedication to the *Old Arcadia*, which was printed with 90, and they need not have become strained until after the publication of Sanford's attack on the editors of 90 in his Preface to 93. Some of the corrections to 90 in 93 restore the *Old Arcadia* readings.[1] These may simply be the correct *New Arcadia* readings taken from G, but they could have come from the Countess of Pembroke's own *Old Arcadia* manuscript (P).[2] P was used by the editors of 93 when they added Books III–V of the *Old Arcadia* to 90;[3] but there is evidence that they sometimes preferred to turn to T[5].[4] Since most of the poems in 90 were printed from T[5], it would have been natural for Greville to send this manuscript along with G to the Countess of Pembroke.

For Books I and II 93, like 90, can help to establish the correct *Old Arcadia* readings where the surviving manuscripts leave them in doubt. In these cases, and when the readings in 93 evidently come from P, and therefore represent the earliest version of the *Old Arcadia*, they are recorded in the textual apparatus.

When the editors of 93 added Books III–V of the *Old Arcadia* to the *New Arcadia*, Books I–III, they had to make many minor changes to bring such things as the nomenclature into conformity with the revised version;[5] and a few changes were made to take account of

---

[1] For example, *Works*, i. 80, 'an *ill* brain' 90 and Cm ('a *weak* brain' 93, OA); i. 78, 'there is no man suddenly excellently good, or extremely evil' 90 and Cm ('there is no man suddenly *either* excellently good, or extremely evil' 93, and OA); i. 83, 'the mighty passions' 90 and Cm ('the *two* mighty passions' 93, OA).

[2] Ringler has shown that, although the editors of 93 were for the most part content to reprint the poems as they appeared in 90, poems which were not included in 90 were printed in 93 from P. Thus lines 12 and 32 of OA 13 (p. 83, 6 and 27) appear in a version which seems to be earlier than that in any of the manuscripts deriving from T.

[3] At p. 284, 2–7 the sentence about Agelastus in the T[1–3] version is also in 93, and at p. 327, 5–6 93 again reads, with the manuscripts representing T[1–3], 'sorrow desires company', against T[4], 'sorrow refuseth not sorrowful company'; and 93 agrees with T[1–2] against T[3–4] at p. 390, 12 in omitting 'I hope but offered'; at p. 393, 24 in reading 'mercenary' for 'immodest'; at p. 394, 9 in reading 'treacherously' for 'injuriously'. These agreements with the earliest state of T indicate that 93 is following P.

[4] 93 agrees with the manuscripts representing T[3–4], and may therefore be following T[5], at p. 281, 17 'fantastical' (T[1–2], 'imaginative'); at p. 352, 19 'made him willing to protect' (T[1–2] 'made him to protect'); at p. 390, 34 'tiger' (T[1–2], 'pirate'); at p. 392, 12 'words' (T[1–2], 'words of this coward creature'); p. 392, 13–14 'unto him' (T[1–2] 'to handless and heartless people'); p. 394, 1 'throw down' (T[1–2], 'participate' [?precipitate]).

[5] The old names (Cleophila for Zelmane, Kerxenus for Kalander, Timopyrus for Daiphantus, duke and duchess for king and queen) had to be altered; the authorial intrusions and apostrophes to the 'fair ladies' had to be removed. The fact that this work was rather inefficiently done is not at all surprising in a sixteenth-century editor— even a scholar of Sanford's standing. The slips in revision are listed by Zandvoort,

events which took place in the 'captivity episode' (*New Arcadia*, Book III).[1] I do not think that Sidney had any hand in these changes. It is inconceivable that after the sufferings of the princesses in the 'captivity episode' Sidney would have attempted to return to the *Old Arcadia* story without very considerable changes.[2] As Florio remarked of the 93 composite version, 'this end we see of it, though at first above all, now is not answerable to the precedents'.[3]

There are, however, some important differences between the text of the *Old Arcadia* Books III–V in the manuscripts and the text of these Books in 93, where the new passages show no knowledge of the events in *New Arcadia* Book III, but have every appearance of being authorial. Sanford claimed in his Preface to 93 that in concluding the *Arcadia* he went 'no further than the author's own writings, or known determinations could direct'. I believe that in addition to P, Sanford is here referring to the 'direction' mentioned in Greville's letter to Walsingham;[4] and that this 'direction', containing a few redrafted passages and some notes indicating further changes that Sidney intended to make in the *Old Arcadia* Books III–V, was left

---

28. Examples of carelessness in nomenclature are pp. 412, 11 and 415, 10 'Kerxenus'; p. 415, 5 'duke's body'; p. 415, 13 'duke'; p. 416, 16 'Cleophila'; p. 417, 5 'dukedom' (some of these slips were corrected in 98). Whereas authorial intrusions were removed, at pp. 185, 20–9; 227, 34; 231, 10; 310, 32, there was a failure to remove one at p. 193, 8 and another at p. 202, 17–19.

[1] At p. 285, 26 f. the *Old Arcadia* reference to the Phagonian rebels of Book II is replaced by a more general reference to the late mutiny, and at p. 306, 29 a similar change is made; at p. 303, 24 Philoclea refers to the help that she gave Philanax when he was taken prisoner by Amphialus (*Works*, i. 399–402). These adjustments are such as any editor could have made. There are editorial failures: for example, the reference to recent eclogues at p. 213, 8 is not removed. Neither the princes' ages nor their age differential are increased as in the *New Arcadia* (*Works*, i. 190).

[2] Sidney inserted a second oracle near the end of the unfinished Book III of the *New Arcadia*, in which Basilius is told that his daughters will shortly be released from captivity, and he is to 'keep on his solitary course, till both Philanax and Basilius fully agreed in the understanding of the former prophecy' (*Works*, i. 510). But I do not think we should deduce from this that Sidney intended to conclude his story with the *Old Arcadia* ending as it stood.

[3] Dedication to Book II of his translation of Montaigne's *Essays*.

[4] '. . . I haue sent my lady yor daughter at her request, a correction of that old one don 4 or 5 years since which he left in trust with me wherof ther is no more copies, & fitter to be printed then that first which is so common, notwithstanding euen that to be amended by a direction sett doun vndre his own hand how & why, so as in many respects espetially ye care of printing it i[s] to be don with more deliberation, . . .' (S.P. 12/195/33, from Ringler's transcription, 530). 'notwithstanding euen that' would seem grammatically to refer to the *Old Arcadia*; but Greville's statement is consonant with the evidence that whilst Sidney was revising Books I and II for the *New Arcadia*, he made certain changes in Books III–V of the *Old Arcadia*.

by Sidney with his own working copy of the *Old Arcadia*, T⁵, and that Greville sent it to the Countess of Pembroke along with T⁵ and G.

The longest new passage is the revised account of the journey of Euarchus to Arcadia in Book V (pp. 355–7), which takes up the story of Plangus, Artaxia, and Plexirtus from the end of the *New Arcadia* Book II (*Works*, i. 337–8). Euarchus has heard nothing to contradict Plangus's report of the supposed deaths of the princes; nor of the captivity of Pamela and Philoclea at the instigation of Cecropia; nor of Basilius's attempts to besiege the island on which they are immured—nor is any remark made to explain his ignorance of these events. This suggests that the revised account of the journey in 93 was written after the *New Arcadia* Book II was completed, but before the *New Arcadia* Book III had been composed. Ringler has argued that the specific geographical details in this account, as also in the journey that Pyrocles planned to take with Philoclea at the end of the *Old Arcadia* Book III in 93 (in the *Old Arcadia* his plans went no further than spending the night with her), could only have been supplied by someone who had studied Mercator's maps, as he suggests Sidney had done for the *New*, but not for the *Old Arcadia*.[1]

Sidney is most likely to have started to redraft the end of the *Old Arcadia* Book III (pp. 236–7) when he removed from it the poem which Philisides is said to have written in praise of his mistress, and which came into Pyrocles's mind as he gazed at Philoclea lying on her bed,[2] and inserted it in the *New Arcadia* Book II, where Pyrocles sees Philoclea bathing in the river Ladon (*Works*, i. 218). If we can accept that he was responsible for Pyrocles' proposed journey in 93, then Sidney must also be held accountable for the change in his hero's behaviour that caused him to plan this journey. In the *Old Arcadia* Pyrocles visits Philoclea's chamber expressly for the purpose of spending the night with her, and they consummate their 'marriage'. In 93 Pyrocles visits Philoclea in order to persuade her to flee with him to his father's kingdom; but after a lover's quarrel and reconciliation, they fall asleep from exhaustion. A similar change was made in the conduct of his cousin. In the *Old Arcadia*, after Musidorus has persuaded Pamela to elope with him, they halt for rest and refreshment; Musidorus is about to break his

---

[1] Ringler, 376–8. He also points out that the two journeys are linked in 93 by the references in both of them to a second uprising of the Helots (pp. 217 and 357), which is not mentioned in either the *Old Arcadia* or in 90.

[2] OA 62, 'What tongue can her perfections tell'.

vow and rape Pamela whilst she is asleep, when he is interrupted by
the arrival of the Phagonian rebels. This incident is omitted from 93.[1]

These changes were not entirely a matter of greater maturity or
sterner morality;[2] but were, as Ringler notes, a consequence of
Sidney's incompletely carried-out intention to remedy a serious
flaw in the ending of the *Old Arcadia*. Euarchus condemns the
princes to death, in accordance with the Arcadian laws, for abduction
and seduction; when Basilius comes to life, he reprieves the princes
and they marry his daughters, thereby setting aside the just judge-
ment of the good ruler. Sidney saw that this could be avoided if the
charge against the princes were confined to the murder of Basilius;
then, like Gynecia, they would be seen to be guiltless when he
turned out to be alive. Three extra lines in the revised form of the
oracle in Book II of the *New Arcadia* point in this direction:

> Both they themselves [the princesses] unto such two shall wed,
> Who at thy bier, as at a bar, shall plead
> Why thee (a living man) they had made dead.[3]

Thus the major changes in Books III–V of the *Old Arcadia* as
printed in 93 are interrelated, and were probably either made or their
nature indicated by Sidney himself. They were probably intended,
not for the *Old Arcadia*, but for the *New Arcadia* as it stood before
the new Book III was written. Books III–V of the *Old Arcadia* as
printed in 93 also contain some readings derived from P, and also
many minor editorial changes necessitated by the addition of these
Books to the *New Arcadia*. All these changes are recorded in my
textual apparatus.

The later folios, with the exception of 13, need not detain us. In
98 the *Arcadia* was printed from 93 but a good many obvious errors

---

[1] These alterations in the love stories involved a good many minor textual changes,
some of which are clumsily handled, or imperfectly carried out, probably by the editors.
Although the princes were condemned for the same crime and given the same sentence
in the revised 93 version (pp. 405, 26; 406, 11), the two different punishments were
allowed to stand (p. 408, 2–3).

[2] I believe, however, that Sidney did come to wish his heroes and heroines to emulate
the chastity of Theagenes and Chariclea, and I discount the view that these changes
were the result of bowdlerization by the Countess of Pembroke. His constant references
in the *Old Arcadia* to the 'wise innocency' of Philoclea suggest that he was already
uneasy about her willingness, in common with most of the heroines in *Amadis de Gaule*,
to give herself to her lover before her wedding night. The judgement of Euarchus makes
the suggestion that 'passing the promise of marriage' was to be taken by the reader as
equivalent to a real marriage untenable.

[3] *Works*, i. 327. This hint was picked up neither by the editors of 93 nor by most
commentators on the alterations in 93 before Ringler.

were corrected (and as many new ones introduced); in 05 it was printed from 98, and again there are corrections of misprints, including some which were overlooked in 93 by 98. In 13 the *Arcadia* is a reprint of 98;[1] but the editor had access to an *Old Arcadia* manuscript. Ringler noted the evidence in the poems, and came to the conclusion that 13's *Old Arcadia* manuscript 'was similar to Cl, Le, and As; it could not have been St, Bo, Da, Ph, Je, or Qu'.[2] The rather slight evidence that I have found in the prose points to As, and I have therefore tentatively connected this manuscript with 13 in the stemma.[3]

Summary

Sidney had a copy of his *Old Arcadia* foul papers made for his sister (P), and another for himself (T); he made alterations, especially in the poems, in the latter fairly continuously. These are found in the surviving *Old Arcadia* manuscripts, which all derive directly, or through lost intermediaries, from T. When Sidney started to turn Books I and II of the *Old Arcadia* into the *New Arcadia*, the work was done by retranscribing; but not all the poems were copied out in full from T, either in the *New Arcadia* foul papers, or in the scribal copy (G). And so 90 was printed from G (prose and some poems) and from T^5 (poems). Cm, an inaccurate copy of G, bears witness to the process. Books I–III of the *New Arcadia* were reprinted in 93 from 90, with some correction from G and T^5, and on occasion from P. Books III–V of the *Old Arcadia* were printed in 93 from P, with some reference to T^5, and the addition of some new passages, and the adoption of the instructions for the amendment of the *Arcadia* in the 'direction set down under his own hand', both of which Sidney had left with T^5. The *Arcadia* was reprinted in 98

---

[1] Juel-Jensen, 473, says of 05, but none of the errors peculiar to this edition is present in 13; however, 13 referred once or twice to 90 or 93 (Ringler, 537).

[2] Ringler, 538. Three lines were added to 98's text of OA 67 (p. 263, 22–4) from a manuscript of the *Old Arcadia*.

[3] For example, on p. 206, 30 13 reads *others'* with the *Old Arcadia* manuscripts, against *our own* in Da, 93 and 98; on p. 208, 15 13 reads *pleasing* with the *Old Arcadia* manuscripts, against *pleasant* in Da, and *pleased* in Ph, 93 and 98; on p. 367, 31 13 agrees with Cl, As, Ph, and Hm in reading *assaulters* for *assaults*; and on p. 373, 33 with As and Ph in reading *only* for *owly*. Da and Ph would seem to be eliminated by the citations from pp. 206, 30 and 208, 15: that would appear to leave us with As. There is a small point on p. 377, 32 where the other *Old Arcadia* manuscripts and 93 read *on a boy*, Ph omits altogether, and As and 13 read *in a boy*. But these three last examples of As and 13 shared readings are agreements in error, and it must be stressed that they could easily have arisen independently.

from 93, and in 05 from 98. Finally 13 used an *Old Arcadia* manuscript, which may have been As, for one or two minor corrections to 98, from which it was printed.

These relationships may be expressed in the following diagram, which is substantially Ringler's, with one or two modifications:

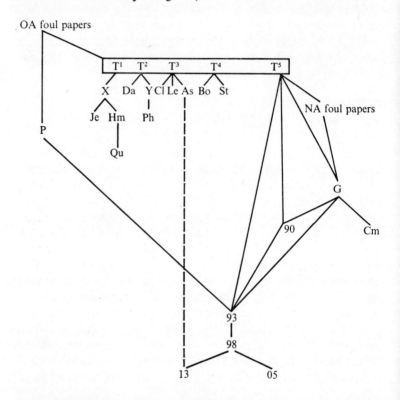

As the diagram shows, where readings are not demonstrably affected by Sidney's revisions in T, there is no reason why a later copy should be more accurate than an earlier one, and the correct reading has to be determined by weighing variants and by taking into account the habits of the different scribes. Thus Cl's copyist was not only careless and prone to eyeskip, but also, like the Da copyist, apt to alter the text in the interests of smoothness and clarity. In the case of Ph, lively participation has led to embellishment.

As Greg declared: 'To show that a reading is original, two main lines of argument are available: that the reading is itself satisfactory, and that it explains the origin of the erroneous alternative.'[1] For example, at p. 116, 13 *high thoughts* in Cl, Da, Ph can be identified as the original reading that gave rise to *by thoughts* in St, Bo, As, Je (Hm wanting, Qu omits); *h* and *b* are graphically similar, and the spelling in T was probably *hie* or *hy*. *Fair thoughts* 90 (also the reading of Cm and 93, and so of G) may have been a scribal substitution; but the whole passage was subjected to a good deal of authorial tinkering for the *New Arcadia*. At p. 102, 32 *which in* is the correct reading, preserved in Bo, Cl, Le, 90, that gave rise to the erroneous *within* in St, Da, Ph; *in* Je, Qu was probably an attempt to emend by leaving out the awkward *with*; As's *which is in* introduces a new error. On p. 26 there is an elaborate description of Pyrocles's hair, which 'lay upon the upper part of his forehead in locks, some curled and some, as it were, forgotten, with such a careless care, and with an art so hiding art, that he seemed he would lay them for a *paragon* whether nature simply, or nature helped by cunning, be the more excellent'. The collations are as follows: paragon Da, Ph, Je, Hm: trial St, Bo; pattern *corr. to* paragon Cl; pattern As, 90. Here I take *paragon* to be the original reading which, as Cl's correction indicates, gave rise to the erroneous *pattern* in As and 90 (it must have been in G as it is also the reading of Cm and 93). I take the weaker synonym *trial* to be scribal substitution. Although Sidney did make some changes in this description in 90, they do not begin until p. 26, 31. Nor can I believe that he would have altered *paragon* to *trial*, and then again to *pattern*, which is what the chronological sequence of the texts by itself might be thought to suggest. At p. 259, 11 it is immediately apparent that *gloire* is the original reading for which *glory* and *praise* are scribal substitutions; but it is not always possible to be so sure which is the more satisfactory reading that gave rise to the substitutions. For example, at p. 103, 3, 'There is no man in a burning fever feels so great contentment in cold water greedily received (which, as soon as the drink ceaseth, the *heat* reneweth)', possibly *heat* (St, Bo, Da, Ph, Je, Hm) is preferable with *burning* and *cold*, but *rage* (Cl, Le, As, 90) is perfectly good sense, and perhaps slightly less obvious.[2] Here, Sidney himself may have hesitated between the two words. For the *Old Arcadia*[3] the

---

[1] *The Calculus of Variants* (1929), p. 20, n. 1.

[2] Languet used this similitude twice in his letters to Sidney, but taken together his sentences favour either reading; see Commentary.

[3] For the *New Arcadia* 90 is supported by Cm and 93, and *rage* may be assumed to have been the reading in G.

support for *heat* is much stronger, and this is the reading I have adopted.[1]

Many of the agreements in error or omissions are random, cutting across the groupings of the manuscripts. It is disturbing to find As out of step in reading *second* with the earlier manuscripts Da, Ph, Je, Hm against 'The gods *make fortune to wait on* thy virtues', the reading in St, Bo, Cl, 93; but *second* was probably imperfectly deleted in T, and the As copyist overlooked the substitution in the margin of *make fortune to wait on*.[2] As Ringler is at pains to emphasize, 'Human minds and hands are prone to similar lapses, and two or more scribes copying the same original will from time to time make identical mistakes.'[3] In sum, scribal intervention is a constant source of corruption in a text like the *Old Arcadia* that survives in nine manuscripts, none of which is holograph.

THIS EDITION

The aim has been to produce a clean, readable text of the latest version available of Sidney's *Old Arcadia*, and to provide in the textual apparatus all the earlier passages that were later cancelled or altered. St has therefore been used as the copy-text for this edition. It is more accurate than Bo, the other manuscript which incorporates the revisions that Sidney made in T[4]. Apart from these authorial revisions shared with Bo, St has neither more nor less authority than

---

[1] Cf. George Kane, *The A-Text of Piers Plowman* (London: Athlone Press, 1960), p. 145, 'Where two variants leave nothing to choose between them the possibility of both being authorial may be allowed, however little it helps the editor'; and p. 148, 'The agreement of a considerable majority of manuscripts must, *in the absence of all other considerations*, be taken to indicate presumption of originality.'

[2] For evidence that this is the correct reading see note in the Commentary on pp. 175, 4–5 and 176, 10–11.

[3] See Ringler, 368 n. 1, where he advances the following explanation for the absence or presence of four sets of lines in OA 62, cutting across the groupings of the manuscripts: 'The explanation I offer, that the lines in question were added by Sidney in the margin of his working copy—or possibly on appended slips of paper—and that some transcribers copied them and others overlooked them, makes it possible to arrange the manuscripts in order in accordance with the other evidence. Some readers may consider this more a device for the editor's convenience than an explanation. But I can think of no other theory that will explain the facts, and must reiterate that Elizabethan scribes frequently *did* omit material in the margins of their copy.' Both errors arising from the failure to notice corrections and marginal additions, and from the substitution of one word for another, whether intentionally or inadvertently, are often perpetrated by two or more scribes independently. Cf. Sir Walter Greg, *The Calculus of Variants*, p. 20 n. 1, 'As a rule, the easier it is to explain how an error arose, the less valid the assumption that it only occurred once.'

any other *Old Arcadia* manuscript deriving at first-hand from T. Although the scribe was careful and seemingly anxious to follow his copy without embellishment, Ringler's 'an almost perfect reproduction of its original' may appear to need modification to anyone who studies the variants in the textual apparatus.[1] For I have recorded all departures from the copy-text, except for the habit of St's copyist of using the unemphatic form *the* for *they*, writing *virtues* for *virtuous*, and using some final ę clearly intended for singulars. This has made St the most accurate manuscript, appear less accurate than all the other manuscripts; for I have not in general given variants where they are peculiar to one *Old Arcadia* manuscript. In consequence, the many errors and omissions in Cl (the basis of Feuillerat's text) are not revealed. Variants which occur in Je–Hm and are neither supported by 93 (and so possibly derive from P), nor otherwise manifestly early authorial readings (the most important example of these is the ending of the First Eclogues), are treated as having the support of only one manuscript, because Je–Hm are in hypothetical descent from an exclusive common ancestor X. For the large stints where Je is wanting, Hm variants have been carefully considered, lest they should contain early authorial readings, but no readings unsupported by other texts were found that merited recording. Qu variants are only cited where Hm is wanting. The refusal to record the numerous errors and omissions made by one, or sometimes two, scribes has lightened the textual apparatus considerably.

When the manuscripts divide, and neither Sidney's revisions nor the sense dictate the reading, the reading of the majority of the manuscripts is adopted. Minority readings, other than T⁴ authorial revisions, have not been adopted, save in cases of absolute necessity.[2] When the manuscripts divide equally, in the absence of the other considerations mentioned, the reading supported by the copy-text is adopted.

For Books I and II no attempt has been made to give the variant

---

[1] Examples of unique errors in St are: p. 35, 14 *suspention* for *suspicion*; p. 393, 23 *match* for *mouth*, 24 *light* for *slight*; p. 406, 28 *particular* for *peculiar*.

[2] At p. 101, 18–19, 'O let not an excellent spirit do itself such wrong as *to think* where it is placed, embraced, and loved, there can be any unworthiness', *to think* is supplied from Cl, supported by 90 (Da reads '*once to imagine*')—these are doubtless scribal and editorial emendations (Cm omits *to think*), but necessary to the sense. At p. 228, 24 *pangs* is read on the authority of As and Hm (*pages* in the other texts is evidently a mistranscription of *pāges*).

readings caused by the revision for the *New Arcadia*; but when the *Old Arcadia* manuscripts diverge on individual words, Cm, 90, 93, 98, 05, and 13 readings are given where available, and have been weighed before adopting a reading in the text.[1] The revisions that Sidney made in T after St and Bo were copied in the poems OA 2, 7, and 8, and which are found in 90, are not incorporated in the text, as one cannot be sure that they were made for the *Old* rather than the *New Arcadia*; but they are recorded in the variants. The editorial changes in the Eclogue prose-links are ignored.

The unique readings (other than misprints) in Books III–V of the *Old Arcadia* in 93 have been recorded in the apparatus. Unless they are absolutely necessary to the meaning, they have not been adopted in the text, because editorial interference is always a possibility in 93,[2] and those most likely to be authorial were probably made for the *New Arcadia* at the time that Sidney was revising Books I and II, and before he had embarked on the new Book III. One or two emendations have been accepted from 93 where it may be presumed to preserve the correct reading in P and the scribe of T has made an error in transcription; some of the variants recorded for 93 also represent an earlier version in P.[3]

When one of the later folios corrects a reading in 93 which is recorded in the textual apparatus, this is noted. Particular care has been taken to record corrections in 13, because an *Old Arcadia* manuscript was referred to in preparing this edition.[4]

A textual apparatus that recorded only those variants which were manifestly the result of changes made by the author himself would have been attractive; but in the absence of holograph it would have

[1] I have used the copies of the printed texts in the Huntington Library: for 90, Hn 69442 (Juel-Jensen 1*b*: 2), and for 13 the copy with the Lownes imprint. I have collated the following copies of 90 in Juel-Jensen's checklist: 1*a*: 1, 2, 3, 4; 1*b*: 2; and have made some spot checks in 1*a*: 5, 6, 10, 11, 14; 1*b*: 1. Some of the variants are referred to on p. lvii n. 1; only a handful are of interest to an editor of the *Old Arcadia*, and these are recorded in the textual apparatus. At p. 8, 26 90's '*to* have been' has been accepted against *might* or *should* in the *Old Arcadia* manuscripts.

[2] Thus I have rejected the rather attractive readings of 93 at p. 168, 11, but have accepted *joy* for *joys* at p. 168, 22; p. 234, 13 *falsehood* for *fellowship* (*friendship* Hm); p. 266, 1 *so suddenly* (OA *suddenly*); p. 278, 13 *limit* (OA *limits*), 15 *striving* (OA *finding*); p. 287, 22 *so looking* (OA *looking*); p. 287, 35 *fortune, like* (OA *fortune but like*); and at p. 384, 1 I have accepted 93's placing of *so*.

[3] See Ringler, 374, for examples of both correct and also earlier readings from P in 93's versions of the poems OA 9 and 13.

[4] I have only once availed myself of a post-13 emendation: when, for the sake of the grammatical structure, I have accepted the reading of the edition of 1627 at p. 402, 20. The only emendation made on my own authority is the addition of *have* at p. 168, 29.

been misleading to leave the reader with the impression that Sidney's exact words were being printed from unanimous witnesses. Giving variants which occur in two or more manuscripts has, of course, loaded the apparatus with Greg's herd of dull commonplace readings (*to/into*; *on/upon*; *these/those*), most of which have little effect on the meaning. With some guidance from the Commentary, the reader should be able to pick out genuine authorial variants from those resulting simply from scribal indifference, carelessness, or interference.

As there is no holograph, there is little point in preserving the idiosyncrasies of one particular scribe. Spelling has therefore been normalized, but old grammatical forms such as *spake, gat, awaked, foen*, are retained. Old usage of singular and plural, for example *other* for *others*, is preserved, but I have regarded *Euarchus his kingdom* as a vulgarism, and print *Euarchus's kingdom*; for possessives are given their apostrophes, often involving editorial decisions on singulars and plurals. Dialect and obsolete words and word-forms are kept in the 'Ister Bank' poem, and elsewhere when they were clearly intended. Older forms such as *franzy, vilde, sprite*, are not preserved, unless used as rhyme words. I have kept *wrack* and *marchpane*, because these are the standard forms used throughout all the texts;[1] but because the scribes vary and are not consistent in their own preferences, I have used the modern forms (given last) in the following pairs: *ensample/example*; *gloze, glose/gloss*; *sound, swound/swoon*. Modern usage has determined which spelling has been adopted for the following pairs of words: *again/against*; *divers/diverse*; *estate/state*; *later/latter*; *metal/mettle*; *price/prize*; *then/than*; *travel/travail*; *troth/truth*; *whether/whither*. *Evil* and *ill* are used in accordance with modern practice, unless rhyme or scansion demand the less usual form. I have standardized to modern preferred forms (given last) in words containing *d* or *th*: *burthen/ burden*; *furder/further*; *murther/murder*; *quod/quoth*. I have preferred the following forms: *afterwards, besides, especially, sometimes, towards*.

In the poems I have indicated where elisions are necessary for the scansion; for example, I read *whisp'ring*, but not *follow'd* where *followed* will yield the correct pronunciation.

Punctuation runs from the heavy, if often mistaken, punctuation

---

[1] But it seemed unnecessarily pedantic to keep *alablaster* for *alabaster* or *arrant* for *errand*; and on the one occasion when all the manuscripts read *harrish* I have modernized to *harsh*, the form used for the word elsewhere.

of Cl and 93 to the almost non-existent punctuation of Bo. Commas (but few other punctuation marks) appear in St in accordance with sixteenth-century usage, but inappropriately placed to assist the reader of a normalized text. The use of parentheses in the manuscripts is more constant and often helpful, and I have found their use essential for dealing with Sidney's long sentences, loaded with subsidiary clauses and asides. It would be utterly impossible to record all the different ways the manuscripts punctuate a sentence. I have therefore supplied a fairly light punctuation throughout, and indicate in the Commentary where a different punctuation found in some texts would alter the meaning.

Incidentals, such as the use of capital letters, have been normalized. Paragraphs have been supplied where appropriate, and the speeches are enclosed in inverted commas.

The textual apparatus at the foot of each page gives variant readings on the principles outlined above. The lemma, closed by a square bracket, is followed by its variants. The authority for these is shown by the sigla following them, separated from each other by commas; when there is more than one variant for a lemma, the variants are separated by semicolons.[1] The variants are given in modern spelling, unless old spelling is important for demonstrating the transmission of the text. When the lemma is the reading of St, no sigla are shown in support of it; this means that the lemma is also the reading of any manuscript or print available for that particular stint[2] whose siglum does not appear after one of the variants. Where a manuscript omits the lemma, or a phrase or sentence containing the lemma, this is noted. When the text does not follow the reading of St, the lemma is followed by the sigla of all the manuscripts and prints supporting the reading, followed by a colon; and the St reading appears as a variant. When it is a case of the rest of the manuscripts versus St, I have used the siglum OA to represent all the other *Old Arcadia* manuscripts (minus any that are wanting at this point).

Scribes used various methods for deleting and altering words; in St a line is generally run through the word to be deleted; in Cl the

---

[1] This is a departure from Ringler's unpunctuated textual apparatus; but I think it is clearer, and as I do not record punctuation variants (as he does), there is no danger of confusion on this score.

[2] It is noted in the apparatus that, for example, 'Je *is missing from here*', or 'Hm *begins again*'. Apart from one passage of prose, Le contains poems only; it is noted when a poem is not in Le.

word is often underlined and the correction is written above it. I have therefore indicated alterations by *corr. to*. Whether or no the substituted word is in fact an improvement, the intention of the scribe was to correct what he had written.

I use Ringler's sigla for the manuscripts, and have added Hm for the Helmingham Hall/Houghton manuscript. I cite them in his order: St, Bo, Cl, Le, As, Da, Ph, Je, Hm (Qu), followed where available by the manuscripts and printed texts containing poems in substantive texts: Hn, Dd, Ra, Ha, Hy, Ma, Fl, Hn, Pu. But I cite the *New Arcadia* texts after instead of before the manuscripts, in the order: Cm, 90, 93, 98, 05, 13. '90' by itself indicates that this can be taken to be the *New Arcadia* reading, found in Cm and 93, etc., as well as in 90, but ignoring scribal errors in Cm, and printers' errors in 93 and later prints. '90 (*only*)' indicates that Cm and 93, etc., do not follow the reading of 90, but agree with the lemma. '90 (*ex.* Cm)' indicates that, with the exception of Cm, which agrees with the lemma, the *New Arcadia* texts follow the reading of 90. '90 (*corr.* 93)' indicates that Cm follows the reading of 90, but that 93 reverts to the *Old Arcadia* reading of the lemma. Where Cm, 90, and 93 are all available, and a variant reading is cited for 93 and/or Cm, this means that the reading of 90 is that of the lemma. Where a later print emends 93, this is indicated by, for example, '93 (*corr.* 98)'; this means that the correction is back to the reading of the lemma. At the beginning of each poem it is stated which manuscripts and prints (other than the *Old Arcadia* manuscripts) contain copies.

LIST OF SIGLA

(1) Old Arcadia *manuscripts*

As	Huntington Library MS. HM 162 (Ashburnham MS.)
Bo	Bodleian Library MS. e Museo 37
Cl	Folger Shakespeare Library MS. H. b.1 [formerly 4009.03] (Clifford MS.)
Da	British Museum Additional MS. 41204 (Davies MS.)
Hm	Arthur A. Houghton, Jr. (formerly Helmingham Hall MS.)
Je	Jesus College, Oxford, MS. 150
Le	British Museum Additional MS. 41498 (Lee MS.)
Ph	British Museum Additional MS. 38892 (Phillipps MS.)
Qu	The Queen's College, Oxford, MS. 301
St	St. John's College, Cambridge, MS. I. 7
OA	All the *Old Arcadia* MSS. other than any one indicated by its siglum

(2) *Manuscripts containing poems from the* Old Arcadia

Dd	Cambridge University Library MS. Dd. 5. 75 (2)
Eg	British Museum Egerton MS. 2421
Fl	Folger Shakespeare Library MS. V. a. 339 [formerly 2071.7]
Ha	British Museum Harleian MS. 6910
Hn	Duke of Norfolk, 'Arundel Harington' MS.
Hy	British Museum Harleian MS. 7392 (2)
Ma	Marsh's Library, Dublin, MS. Z. 3. 5. 21
Ra	Bodleian Library MS. Rawlinson Poetical 85.

(3) *Printed books containing poems from the* Old Arcadia

Hn	Ariosto's *Orlando Furioso*, translated by Sir John Harington (1591)
Pu	[George Puttenham], *The Art of English Poesy* (1589)

(4) New Arcadia *texts*

Cm	Cambridge University Library MS. Kk.i. 5 (2)
90	*The Countess of Pembroke's Arcadia* (1590)
93	*The Countess of Pembroke's Arcadia* (1593)
98	*The Countess of Pembroke's Arcadia . . . with sundry new additions* (1598)
05	*The Countess of Pembroke's Arcadia . . . with sundry new additions* (1605)
13	*The Countess of Pembroke's Arcadia . . . with some new additions* (1613)

THE COUNTESS OF PEMBROKE'S
ARCADIA

TO MY DEAR LADY AND SISTER
THE COUNTESS OF PEMBROKE

HERE now have you (most dear, and most worthy to be most dear, lady) this idle work of mine, which I fear (like the spider's web) will be thought fitter to be swept away than worn to any other purpose. For my part, in very truth (as the cruel fathers among the Greeks were wont to do to the babes they would not foster) I could well find in my heart to cast out in some desert of forgetfulness this child which I am loath to father. But you desired me to do it, and your desire to my heart is an absolute commandment. Now it is done only for you, only to you; if you keep it to yourself, or to such friends who will weigh errors in the balance of goodwill, I hope, for the father's sake, it will be pardoned, perchance made much of, though in itself it have deformities. For indeed, for severer eyes it is not, being but a trifle, and that triflingly handled. Your dear self can best witness the manner, being done in loose sheets of paper, most of it in your presence, the rest by sheets sent unto you as fast as they were done. In sum, a young head not so well stayed as I would it were (and shall be when God will) having many many fancies begotten in it, if it had not been in some way delivered, would have grown a monster, and more sorry might I be that they came in than that they gat out. But his chief safety shall be the not walking abroad; and his chief protection the bearing the livery of your name which (if much much goodwill do not deceive me) is worthy to be a sanctuary for a greater offender. This say I because I know the virtue so; and this say I because it may be ever so; or, to say better, because it will be ever so. Read it then at your idle times, and the follies your good judgement will find in it, blame not, but laugh at. And so, looking for no better stuff than, as in a haberdasher's shop, glasses or feathers, you will continue to love the writer who doth exceedingly love you, and most most heartily prays you may long live to be a principal ornament to the family of the Sidneys.

Your loving brother,

Philip Sidney

Text from 90.   29 in a 93: in an 90.

THE FIRST BOOK OR ACT OF
THE COUNTESS OF PEMBROKE'S ARCADIA

ARCADIA among all the provinces of Greece was ever had in singular reputation, partly for the sweetness of the air and other natural
5 benefits, but principally for the moderate and well tempered minds of the people who (finding how true a contentation is gotten by following the course of nature, and how the shining title of glory, so much affected by other nations, doth indeed help little to the happiness of life) were the only people which, as by their justice
10 and providence gave neither cause nor hope to their neighbours to annoy them, so were they not stirred with false praise to trouble others' quiet, thinking it a small reward for the wasting of their own lives in ravening that their posterity should long after say they had done so. Even the muses seemed to approve their good determina-
15 tion by choosing that country as their chiefest repairing place, and by bestowing their perfections so largely there that the very shepherds themselves had their fancies opened to so high conceits as the most learned of other nations have been long time since content both to borrow their names and imitate their cunning. In this place some
20 time there dwelled a mighty duke named Basilius, a prince of sufficient skill to govern so quiet a country where the good minds of the former princes had set down good laws, and the well bringing up of the people did serve as a most sure bond to keep them. He married Gynecia, the daughter of the king of Cyprus; a lady worthy
25 enough to have had her name in continual remembrance if her latter time had not blotted her well governed youth, although the wound fell more to her own conscience than to the knowledge of the world, fortune something supplying her want of virtue. Of her the duke had two fair daughters, the elder Pamela, the younger Philoclea,
30 both so excellent in all those gifts which are allotted to reasonable creatures as they seemed to be born for a sufficient proof that nature is no stepmother to that sex, how much soever the rugged disposition of some men, sharp-witted only in evil speaking, hath sought to

Text from St, *but the edges of the first folios are damaged, and missing letters have been silently supplied from* Bo. *The first folios of* As, Je *are missing.*   1–2 Da, Ph *have no heading for the Book or Act.*   11 were they not OA: were not they St; are they not 90.   15 chiefest] chief Ph, 90.   21 skill] virtue Bo, Ph. 24 daughter of] daughter to Ph, 90.   33 hath] have Cl, 90.

disgrace them. And thus grew they on in each good increase till
Pamela, a year older than Philoclea, came to the point of seventeen
years of age. At which time the duke Basilius—not so much stirred
with the care for his country and children as with the vanity which
possesseth many who, making a perpetual mansion of this poor 5
baiting place of man's life, are desirous to know the certainty of
things to come, wherein there is nothing so certain as our continual
uncertainty—Basilius, I say, would needs undertake a journey to
Delphos, there by the oracle to inform himself whether the rest of
his life should be continued in like tenor of happiness as thitherunto 10
it had been, accompanied with the wellbeing of his wife and children,
whereupon he had placed greatest part of his own felicity. Neither did
he long stay; but the woman appointed to that impiety, furiously
inspired, gave him in verse this answer:

> Thy elder care shall from thy careful face 15
> By princely mean be stolen and yet not lost;
> Thy younger shall with nature's bliss embrace
> An uncouth love, which nature hateth most.
> Thou with thy wife adult'ry shalt commit,
> And in thy throne a foreign state shall sit. 20
> All this on thee this fatal year shall hit.

Which, as in part it was more obscure than he could understand, so
did the whole bear such manifest threatenings, that his amazement
was greater than his fore curiosity—both passions proceeding out
of one weakness: in vain to desire to know that of which in vain thou 25
shalt be sorry after thou hast known it. But thus the duke answered
though not satisfied, he returned into his country with a countenance
well witnessing the dismayedness of his heart; which notwithstand-
ing upon good considerations he thought not good to disclose, but
only to one chosen friend of his named Philanax, whom he had ever 30
found a friend not only in affection but judgement, and no less of
the duke than dukedom—a rare temper, whilst most men either

---

12 greatest] the greatest Bo, Da, Ph.   15–21 90–93 *transfer to Book II, where* Cm
leaves a blank space for the poem.   19–21 90 *reads:*
> Both they themselves unto such two shall wed,
> Who at thy bier, as at a bar, shall plead
> Why thee (a living man) they had made dead.
> In thy own seat a foreign state shall sit.
> And ere that all these blows thy head do hit,
> Thou with thy wife adult'ry shall commit.

32 whilst] while Da, Ph, 90.

servilely yield to all appetites, or with an obstinate austerity, looking to that they fancy good, wholly neglect the prince's person. But such was this man; and in such a man had Basilius been happy if his mind, corrupted with a prince's fortune, had not resolved to
5 use a friend's secrecy rather for confirmation of fancies than correcting of errors, which in this weighty matter he well showed. For having with many words discovered unto him both the cause and success of his Delphos journey, in the end he told him that, to prevent all these inconveniences of the loss of his crown and children
10 (for as for the point of his wife, he could no way understand it), he was resolved for this fatal year to retire himself with his wife and daughters into a solitary place where, being two lodges built of purpose, he would in the one of them recommend his daughter Pamela to his principal herdman—a place in that world, not so far gone into
15 painted vanities, of some credit—by name Dametas, in whose blunt truth he had great confidence, thinking it a contrary salve against the destiny threatening her mishap by a prince to place her with a shepherd. In the other lodge he and his wife would keep their younger jewel, Philoclea; and because the oracle touched some
20 strange love of hers, have the more care of her, in especial keeping away her nearest kinsmen, whom he deemed chiefly understood, and therewithal all other likely to move any such humour. And so for himself, being so cruelly menaced by fortune, he would draw himself out of her way by this loneliness, which he thought was the
25 surest mean to avoid her blows; where for his pleasure he would be recreated with all those sports and eclogues wherein the shepherds of that country did much excel. As for the government of the country, and in especial manning of his frontiers (for that only way he thought a foreign prince might endanger his crown), he would leave
30 the charge to certain selected persons; the superintendence of all which he would commit to Philanax. And so ended he his speech, for fashion's sake asking him his counsel. But Philanax, having forthwith taken into the depth of his consideration both what the duke said and with what mind he spake it, with a true heart and
35 humble countenance in this sort answered:

'Most redoubted and beloved prince, if as well it had pleased you at your going to Delphos, as now, to have used my humble service, both I should in better season and to better purpose have spoken, and you perhaps at this time should have been, as no way more in danger, so undoubtedly much more in quietness. I would then have said unto you that wisdom and virtue be the only destinies appointed to man to follow, wherein one ought to place all his knowledge, since they be such guides as cannot fail which, besides their inward 5 comfort, do make a man see so direct a way of proceeding as prosperity must necessarily ensue. And, although the wickedness of the world should oppress it, yet could it not be said that evil happened to him who should fall accompanied with virtue; so that, either standing or falling with virtue, a man is never in evil case. I would 10 then have said the heavenly powers to be reverenced and not searched into, and their mercy rather by prayers to be sought than their hidden counsels by curiosity; these kinds of soothsaying sorceries (since the heavens have left us in ourselves sufficient guides) to be nothing but fancies wherein there must either be vanity or infallibleness, and 15 so either not to be respected or not to be prevented. But since it is weakness too much to remember what should have been done, and that your commandment stretcheth to know what shall be done, I do, most dear lord, with humble boldness say that the manner of your determination doth in no sort better please me than the cause of 20 your going. These thirty years past have you so governed this realm that neither your subjects have wanted justice in you, nor you obedience in them; and your neighbours have found you so hurtlessly strong that they thought it better to rest in your friendship than make new trial of your enmity. If this, then, have proceeded out of 25 the good constitution of your state, and out of a wise providence generally to prevent all those things which might encumber your happiness, why should you now seek new courses, since your own example comforts you to continue on, and that it is most certain no destiny nor influence whatsoever can bring man's wit to a higher 30 point than wisdom and goodness? Why should you deprive yourself of governing your dukedom for fear of losing your dukedom, like one that should kill himself for fear of death? Nay rather, if this oracle be to be accounted of, arm up your courage the more against it; for who will stick to him that abandons himself? Let your sub- 35 jects have you in their eyes, let them see the benefits of your justice

1 at . . . been] should have been at this time Da, 90.   2 then have OA, 90: have then St.   4 to man OA, 90: for man St.   6 direct OA, 90: directly St.   9 to him OA, 90: unto him St.   20 sort better OA, 90: sort no better St.

daily more and more; and so must they needs rather like of present sureties than uncertain changes. Lastly, whether your time call you to live or die, do both like a prince. And even the same mind hold I as touching my ladies, your daughters, in whom nature promiseth
5 nothing but goodness, and their education by your fatherly care hath been hitherto such as hath been most fit to restrain all evil, giving their minds virtuous delights, and not grieving them for want of well ruled liberty: now to fall to a sudden straitening them, what can it do but argue suspicion, the most venomous gall to virtue?
10 Leave women's minds, the most untamed that way of any; see whether any cage can please a bird, or whether a dog grow not fiercer with tying. What doth jealousy else but stir up the mind to think what it is from which they are restrained? For they are treasures or things of great delight which men use to hide for the aptness they
15 have to catch men's fancies; and the thoughts once awaked to that, harder sure it is to keep those thoughts from accomplishment than it had been before to have kept the mind (which, being the chief part, by this means is defiled) from thinking. Now, for the recommending so principal a charge of her, whose mind goes beyond the
20 governing of many hundreds of such, to such a person as Dametas is, besides that the thing in itself is strange, it comes of a very ill ground that ignorance should be the mother of faithfulness. O no, he cannot be good that knows not why he is good, but stands so far good as his fortune may keep him unassayed. But coming to that, his
25 rude simplicity is either easily changed or easily deceived; and so grows that to be the last excuse of his fault which seemed to have been the first foundation of his faith. Thus far hath your commandment and my zeal drawn me to speak; which I, like a man in a valley may discern hills, or like a poor passenger may spy a rock, so humbly
30 submit to your gracious consideration, beseeching you to stand wholly upon your own virtue as the surest way to maintain you in that you are, and to avoid any evil which may be imagined.'

Whilst Philanax used these words, a man might see in the duke's face that, as he was wholly wedded to his own opinion, so was he
35 grieved to have any man say that which he had not seen. Yet did the goodwill he bare to Philanax so far prevail with him that he passed

---

7 minds virtuous] minds to all virtuous Cl: minds to virtuous Da: minds in virtuous **Ph** (in *deleted* St).   10 women's OA, 90: woman's St.   26 which seemed to **have** 90: which seemed might have St, Cl, Da, Hm; which ⟨ ⟩ might have Bo; which should have Ph.

into no further choler, but with short manner asked him: 'And would you, then', said he, 'that in change of fortune I shall not change my determination, as we do our apparel according to the air, and as the ship doth her course with the wind?'

'Truly sir,' answered he, 'neither do I as yet see any change; and though I did, yet would I think a constant virtue, well settled, little subject unto it. And, as in great necessity I would allow a well proportioned change, so in the sight of an enemy to arm himself the lighter, or at every puff of wind to strike sail, is such a change as either will breed ill success or no success.'

'To give place to blows', said the duke, 'is thought no small wisdom.'

'That is true,' said Philanax, 'but to give place before they come takes away the occasion, when they come, to give place.'

'Yet the reeds stand with yielding', said the duke.

'And so are they but reeds, most worthy prince,' said Philanax, 'but the rocks stand still and are rocks.'

But the duke, having used thus much dukely sophistry to deceive himself, and making his will wisdom, told him resolutely he stood upon his own determination; and therefore willed him, with certain other he named, to take the government of the state, and especially to keep narrow watch of the frontiers. Philanax, acknowledging himself much honoured by so great trust, went with as much care to perform his commandment as before he had with faith yielded his counsel, which in the latter short disputations he had rather proportioned to Basilius's words than to any towardness of argument. And Basilius, according to his determination, retired himself into the solitary place of the two lodges, where he was daily delighted with the eclogues and pastimes of shepherds. In the one of which lodges he himself remained with his wife and the beauty of the world, Philoclea; in the other, near unto him, he placed his daughter Pamela with Dametas, whose wife was Miso and daughter Mopsa, unfit company for so excellent a creature, but to exercise her patience and to serve for a foil to her perfections.

Now, newly after that the duke had begun this solitary life, there came (following the train their virtues led them) into this country two young princes: the younger, but chiefer, named Pyrocles, only son to Euarchus, king of Macedon; the other his cousin german,

---

2 shall] should Cl, Ph.　　25 disputations OA: disputinges St.　　26 towardness] soundness Cl, Da, Hm (Ph *omits* 25-6 which . . . argument).

Musidorus, duke of Thessalia; both like in virtues, near in years, near in blood, but nearest of all in friendship. And because this matter runs principally of them, a few more words how they came hither will not be superfluous. Euarchus, king of Macedon, a prince
5 of such justice that he never thought himself privileged by being a prince, nor did measure greatness by anything but by goodness; as he did thereby root an awful love in his subjects towards him, so yet could he not avoid the assaults of envy—the enemy and yet the honour of virtue. For the kings of Thrace, Pannonia, and Epirus,
10 not being able to attain his perfections, thought in their base wickedness best to take away so odious a comparison, lest his virtues, joined now to the fame and force of the Macedonians, might in time both conquer the bodies and win the minds of their subjects. And thus conspiring together, they did three sundry ways enter into
15 his kingdom at one time. Which sudden and dangerous invasions, although they did nothing astonish Euarchus, who carried a heart prepared for all extremities (as a man that knew both what ill might happen to a man never so prosperous, and withal what the uttermost of that ill was), yet were they cause that Euarchus did send away
20 his young son Pyrocles, at that time but six years old, to his sister, the dowager and regent of Thessalia, there to be brought up with her son Musidorus. Which, though it proceeded of necessity, yet was not the counsel in itself unwise, the sweet emulation that grew being an excellent nurse of the good parts in these two princes, two
25 princes indeed born to the exercise of virtue. For they, accompanying the increase of their years with the increase of all good inward and outward qualities, and taking very timely into their minds that the divine part of man was not enclosed in this body for nothing, gave themselves wholly over to those knowledges which might in the
30 course of their life be ministers to well doing. And so grew they on till Pyrocles came to be seventeen and Musidorus eighteen years of age; at which time Euarchus, having after ten years' war conquered the kingdom of Thrace and brought the other two to be his tributaries, lived in the principal city of Thrace called at that time
35 Byzantium, whither he sent for his son and nephew to delight his aged eyes in them and to make them enjoy the fruits of his victories. But so pleased it God, who reserved them to greater traverses, both of good and evil fortune, that the sea, to which they committed

---

27 taking very timely into Bo, Cl, Da, Hm: taking very ^timely equity into St; (even
being children) to Ph.   37 greater traverses] travers Ph: great travises Hm.

themselves, stirred with terrible tempest, forced them to fall far from
their course upon the coast of Lydia where, what befell unto them,
what valiant acts they did, passing in one year's space through the
lesser Asia, Syria, and Egypt, how many ladies they defended from
wrongs, and disinherited persons restored to their rights, it is a work 5
for a higher style than mine. This only shall suffice: that their fame
returned so fast before them into Greece that the king of Macedon
received that as the comfort of their absence, although accompanied
with so much more longing as he found the manifestation of their
worthiness greater. But they, desirous more and more to exercise 10
their virtues and increase their experience, took their journey from
Egypt towards Greece. Which they did, they two alone, because,
that being their native country they might have the most perfect
knowledge of it; wherein they that hold the countenances of princes
have their eyes most dazzled. 15

And so, taking Arcadia in their way, for the fame of the country,
they came thither newly after that this strange solitariness had pos-
sessed Basilius. Now so fell it unto them that they, lodging in the
house of Kerxenus, a principal gentleman in Mantinea, so was the
city called, near to the solitary dwelling of the duke, it was Pyrocles' 20
either evil or good fortune walking with his host in a fair gallery that
he perceived a picture, newly made by an excellent artificer,
which contained the duke and duchess with their younger daughter
Philoclea, with such countenance and fashion as the manner of their
life held them in, both the parents' eyes cast with a loving care upon 25
their beautiful child, she drawn as well as it was possible art should
counterfeit so perfect a workmanship of nature. For therein, besides
the show of her beauties, a man might judge even the nature of her
countenance, full of bashfulness, love, and reverence—and all by
the cast of her eye—, mixed with a sweet grief to find her virtue 30
suspected. This moved Pyrocles to fall into questions of her; wherein
being answered by the gentleman as much as he understood, which
was of her strange kind of captivity; neither was it known how long
it should last; and there was a general opinion grown the duke would
grant his daughters in marriage to nobody. As the most noble heart 35
is most subject unto it, from questions grew to pity; and when with
pity once his heart was made tender, according to the aptness of the
humour, it received straight a cruel impression of that wonderful

18 lodging] lodged Cl, Ph.   19 of Kerxenus . . . Mantinea] of a principal gentleman
of Mantinea called Kerxenus Da, Ph, Hm.   36 is most subject OA : is subject St.

passion which to be defined is impossible, by reason no words reach near to the strange nature of it. They only know it which inwardly feel it. It is called love. Yet did not the poor youth at first know his disease, thinking it only such a kind of desire as he was wont to have

5 to see unwonted sights, and his pity to be no other but the fruits of his gentle nature. But even this arguing with himself came of a further thought; and the more he argued, the more his thought increased. Desirous he was to see the place where she remained, as though the architecture of the lodges would have been much for his

10 learning; but more desirous to see herself, to be judge, forsooth, of the painter's cunning—for thus at the first did he flatter himself, as though his wound had been no deeper. But when within short time he came to the degree of uncertain wishes, and that those wishes grew to unquiet longings; when he could fix his thoughts upon

15 nothing but that, within a little varying, they should end with Philoclea; when each thing he saw seemed to figure out some part of his passions, and that he heard no word spoken but that he imagined it carried the sound of Philoclea's name; then did poor Pyrocles yield to the burden, finding himself prisoner before he had

20 leisure to arm himself, and that he might well, like the spaniel, gnaw upon the chain that ties him, but he should sooner mar his teeth than procure liberty. Then was his chief delight secretly to draw his dear friend a-walking to the desert of the two lodges where he saw no grass upon which he thought Philoclea might hap to tread but that

25 he envied the happiness of it; and yet, with a contrary folly, would sometimes recommend his whole estate unto it. Till at length love, the refiner of invention, put in his head a way how to come to the sight of his Philoclea; for which he with great speed and secrecy prepared everything that was necessary for his purpose, but yet

30 would not put it in execution till he had disclosed it to Musidorus, both to perform the true laws of friendship and withal to have his counsel and allowance. And yet, out of the sweetness of his disposition, was bashfully afraid to break it with him to whom (besides other bonds), because he was his elder, he bare a kind of

35 reverence, until some fit opportunity might, as it were, draw it from him. Which occasion time shortly presented unto him.

12 his wound] the wound Cl, Da.   15 varying] *om.* Ph; wavering Hm.
21 ties] tyeth Ph; holds Hm.   23 friend a-walking Cl, Da, Hm: friend, and
walking St, Bo: friend abroad, and walking Ph.   26 at length] at the length
Cl, Ph.   30 disclosed it to] disclosed to Ph, Hm.

For Musidorus, having informed himself fully of the strength and riches of the country; of the nature of the people, and of the manner of their laws; and seeing the duke's court could not be visited, and that they came not without danger to that place, prohibited to all men but to certain shepherds, grew no less weary of his abode there than marvelled of the great delight Pyrocles took in that place. Whereupon one day, at Pyrocles' earnest request being walked thither again, began in this manner to say unto him:

'A mind well trained and long exercised in virtue, my sweet and worthy cousin, doth not easily change any course it once undertakes but upon well grounded and well weighed causes; for being witness to itself of his own inward good, it finds nothing without it of so high a price for which it should be altered. Even the very countenance and behaviour of such a man doth show forth images of the same constancy by maintaining a right harmony betwixt it and the inward good in yielding itself suitable to the virtuous resolutions of the mind. This speech I direct to you, noble friend Pyrocles, the excellency of whose mind and well chosen course in virtue, if I do not sufficiently know, having seen such rare demonstrations of it, it is my weakness and not your unworthiness. But as indeed I do know it, and knowing it, most dearly love both it and him that hath it, so must I needs say that since our late coming into this country I have marked in you, I will not say an alteration, but a relenting, truly, and slacking of the main career you had so notably begun and almost performed; and that, in such sort as I cannot find sufficient reasons in my great love towards you how to allow it. For, to leave off other secreter arguments which my acquaintance with you makes me easily find, this in effect to any man may be manifest: that, whereas you were wont, in all the places you came, to give yourself vehemently to knowledge of those things which might better your mind; to seek the familiarity of excellent men in learning and soldiery; and lastly, to put all these things in practice both by continual wise proceeding and worthy enterprises, as occasions fell for them; you now leave all these things undone; you let your mind fall asleep, besides your countenance troubled (which surely comes not out of virtue; for virtue, like the clear heaven, is without clouds);

16 resolutions] resolution Ph, 90 (*ex.* Cm).   17 to you] unto you Ph, Hm. 20–1 I do know] I know Cl, 90.   24 notably OA, 90: nobly St.   26 reasons] reason Ph, 90 (*ex.* Cm).   32 practice both by] practice by Bo, Hm.   33 proceeding] proceedings Cl, Da, Ph, Hm, Cm.   occasions] occasion Bo, Da, 90 (*ex* Cm); actions Ph.

and lastly, which seemeth strangest unto me, you haunt greatly this
place, wherein, besides the disgrace that might fall of it (which, that
it hath not already fallen upon you, is rather luck than providence,
this duke having sharply forbidden it), you subject yourself to
5 solitariness, the sly enemy that doth most separate a man from well
doing.'

These words, spoken vehemently and proceeding from so dearly
an esteemed friend as Musidorus, did so pierce poor Pyrocles that
his blushing cheeks did witness with him he rather could not help,
10 than did not know, his fault. Yet, desirous by degrees to bring his
friend to a gentler consideration of him, and beginning with two or
three broken sighs, answered him to this purpose:

'Excellent Musidorus, in the praises you gave me in the beginning
of your speech, I easily acknowledge the force of your goodwill unto
15 me; for neither could you have thought so well of me if extremity of
love had not something dazzled your eyes, nor you could have loved
me so entirely if you had not been apt to make so great, though
undeserved, judgement of me. And even so must I say of those
imperfections, to which though I have ever through weakness been
20 subject, yet you by the daily mending of your mind have of late
been able to look into them, which before you could not discern; so
that the change you spake of falls not out by my impairing but by
your bettering. And yet, under the leave of your better judgement,
I must needs say thus much, my dear cousin, that I find not myself
25 wholly to be condemned because I do not with a continual
vehemency follow those knowledges which you call the bettering of
my mind; for both the mind itself must, like other things, sometimes
be unbent, or else it will be either weakened or broken, and these
knowledges, as they are of good use, so are they not all the mind may
30 stretch itself unto. Who knows whether I feed not my mind with
higher thoughts? Truly, as I know not all the particularities, so yet
see I the bounds of all those knowledges; but the workings of the
mind, I find, much more infinite than can be led unto by the eye or
imagined by any that distract their thoughts without themselves.
35 And in such contemplations, or, as I think, more excellent, I enjoy

1 strangest] strange Cl, Hm.   7 dearly] dear Bo; deeply Ph.   17 to make]
As *begins here*.   18 judgement] judgements Cl, As, 90.   of those] to those Ph,
90 (*ex*. Cm).   22 spake of]speak of Bo, As, Da, Ph, Hm, 90.   my] *om*. Da, Cm.
26 bettering Bo, Da, Ph, Hm, 90: betterings St, Cl, As.   30 knows whether I
feed not my] knows whether I feed my Cl, Da; knows not whether I feed my Hm.
31 Truly] Je *begins here*.   32 those] these Ph, Cl, 90.

my solitariness; and my solitariness, perchance, is the nurse of these contemplations. Eagles, we see, fly alone; and they are but sheep which always herd together. Condemn not, therefore, my mind sometimes to enjoy itself, nor blame not the taking of such times as serve most fit for it!' 5

And here Pyrocles suddenly stopped, like a man unsatisfied in himself, though his wit might well have served to have satisfied another. And so, looking with a countenance as though he desired he should know his mind without hearing him speak, and yet desirous to speak to breathe out some part of his inward evil, sending again new 10 blood to his face, he continued his speech in this manner:

'And lord! dear cousin,' said he, 'doth not the pleasantness of this place carry in itself sufficient reward for any time lost in it, or for any such danger that might ensue? Do you not see how everything conspires together to make this place a heavenly dwelling? Do you 15 not see the grass, how in colour they excel the emeralds, everyone striving to pass his fellow—and yet they are all kept in an equal height? And see you not the rest of all these beautiful flowers, each of which would require a man's wit to know, and his life to express? Do not these stately trees seem to maintain their flourishing old age 20 with the only happiness of their seat, being clothed with a continual spring because no beauty here should ever fade? Doth not the air breathe health, which the birds, delightful both to the ear and eye, do daily solemnize with the sweet concent of their voices? Is not every echo here a perfect music? And these fresh and delightful 25 brooks, how slowly they slide away, as loath to leave the company of so many things united in perfection! And with how sweet a murmur they lament their forced departure! Certainly, certainly, cousin, it must needs be that some goddess this desert belongs unto, who is the soul of this soil; for neither is any less than a goddess worthy to 30 be shrined in such a heap of pleasures, nor any less than a goddess could have made it so perfect a model of the heavenly dwellings.'

And so he ended, with a deep sigh, ruefully casting his eye upon Musidorus, as more desirous of pity than pleading. But Musidorus had all this while held his look fixed upon Pyrocles' countenance, 35 and with no less loving attention marked how his words proceeded from him. But in both these he perceived such strange diversities

18 the rest of all] all the rest of As, Ph; the rest of 90.   27–8 sweet a murmur] sweet murmur As, Je.   33 eye upon] eye on Bo, Je.   34 more] rather Bo; now Hm (now rather Qu).   37 such] so Bo, Hm.

that they rather increased new doubts than gave him ground to settle any judgement; for, besides his eyes sometimes even great with tears, the oft changing of his colour, with a kind of shaking unstaidness over all his body, he might see in his countenance some
5 great determination mixed with fear, and might perceive in him store of thoughts rather stirred than digested, his words interrupted continually with sighs which served as a burden to each sentence, and the tenor of his speech (though of his wonted phrase) not knit together to one constant end but rather dissolved in itself, as the
10 vehemency of the inward passion prevailed: which made Musidorus frame his answer nearest to that humour which should soonest put out the secret. For, having in the beginning of Pyrocles' speech which defended his solitariness framed in his mind a reply against it in the praise of honourable action (in showing that such kind of
15 contemplation is but a glorious title to idleness; that in action a man did not only better himself but benefit others; that the gods would not have delivered a soul into the body which hath arms and legs (only instruments of doing) but that it were intended the mind should employ them; and that the mind should best know his own good or
20 evil by practice; which knowledge was the only way to increase the one and correct the other; besides many other better arguments which the plentifulness of the matter yielded to the sharpness of his wit), when he found Pyrocles leave that, and fall to such an affected praising of the place, he left it likewise, and joined therein with
25 him because he found him in that humour utter most store of passion. And even thus, kindly embracing him, he said:

'Your words are such, noble cousin, so sweetly and strongly handled in the praise of solitariness, as they would make me likewise yield myself up unto it, but that the same words make me know it is
30 more pleasant to enjoy the company of him that can speak such words than by such words to be persuaded to follow solitariness. And even so do I give you leave, sweet Pyrocles, ever to defend solitariness so long as, to defend it, you ever keep company. But I marvel at the excessive praises you give to this desert. In truth, it is not unpleasant;
35 but yet, if you would return into Macedon, you should see either many heavens or find this no more than earthly. And even Tempe,

4 unstaidness] unsteadfastness Cl, Je, Hm.   14 such kind] such a kind Bo, 90.
16 gods] heavens Bo; heaven Hm.   25 most store] more store Cl, Ph, 90.   26 passion] passions Da, Je, Hm.   28–9 make me likewise yield myself] likewise make me yield myself Bo, As, Je, Hm; make me yield myself likewise Cl.   30 that can] who can Bo; which can Da.   35 would] will Bo, Da.   into] to Bo, Da; unto Cl.

in my Thessalia, where you and I (to my great happiness) were brought up together, is nothing inferior unto it. But I think you will make me see that the vigour of your wit can show itself in any subject; or else you feed sometimes your solitariness with the conceits of the poets whose liberal pens can as easily travel over mountains 5 as molehills, and so (like well disposed men) set up everything to the highest note—especially when they put such words in the mouth of one of these fantastical mind-infected people that children and musicians call lovers.'

This word of lover did no less pierce poor Pyrocles than the right 10 tune of music toucheth him that is sick of the tarantula. There was not one part of his body that did not feel a sudden motion, the heart drawing unto itself the life of every part to help it, distressed with the sound of that word. Yet, after some pause, lifting up his eyes a little from the ground, and yet not daring to place them in the 15 face of Musidorus, armed with the very countenance of the poor prisoner at the bar whose answer is nothing but 'guilty', with much ado he brought forth this question:

'And alas,' said he, 'dear cousin, what if I be not so much the poet, the freedom of whose pen can exercise itself in anything, as 20 even that very miserable subject of his cunning whereof you speak?'

'Now the eternal gods forbid', mainly cried out Musidorus. But Pyrocles, having broken the ice, pursued on in this manner:

'And yet such a one am I,' said he, 'and in such extremity as no man can feel but myself, nor no man believe; since no man ever 25 could taste the hundredth part of that which lies in the inwardmost part of my soul. For since it was the fatal overthrow of all my liberty to see in the gallery of Mantinea the only Philoclea's picture, that beauty did pierce so through mine eyes to my heart that the impression of it doth not lie but live there, in such sort as the question is 30 not now whether I shall love or no, but whether loving, I shall live or die.'

Musidorus was no less astonished with these words of his friend

---

5 can as easily OA, 90: can easily St.   10 word of lover] word lover Cl, As, 90. 14–15 his eyes a little OA, 90: a little his eyes St.   18 ado he brought] ado brought Bo, Hm; ado brought he Je.   21 that very miserable] that miserable Cl, Ph, 90 (*ex.* Cm).   speak Bo, As, Ph, 90: speak of St, Da, Je, Hm; spake Cl, spake of Cm. 24 am I] as I Ph, Je.   25–6 ever could taste] could ever taste Bo, Da; could taste As; could ever trust Ph; ever did taste Je; ever did last Hm.   26 inwardmost] innermost Cl, As, Da, Ph, Hm; inwardest Je.   29 mine eyes] my eyes As, Da, Cl.   29–30 impression of it doth] impression doth Cl, As.

than if, thinking him in health, he had suddenly told him that he
felt the pangs of death oppress him. So that, amazedly looking upon
him (even as Apollo is painted when he saw Daphne suddenly turned
to a laurel), he was not able to say one word; but gave Pyrocles
5 occasion, having already made the breach, to pass on in this sort:

'And because I have laid open my wound, noble cousin,' said he,
'I will show you what my melancholy hath brought forth for the
preparation at least of a salve, if it be not in itself a medicine. I am
resolved, because all direct ways are barred me of opening my suit
10 to the duke, to take upon me the estate of an Amazon lady going
about the world to practise feats of chivalry and to seek myself a
worthy husband. I have already provided all furniture necessary
for it; and my face, you see, will not easily discover me. And here-
about will I haunt till, by the help of this disguising, I may come to
15 the presence of her whose imprisonment darkens the world, that
my own eyes may be witnesses to my heart it is great reason why he
should be thus captived. And then, as I shall have attained to the
first degree of my happiness, so will fortune, occasion, and mine own
industry put forward the rest. For the principal point is to set in a
20 good way the thing we desire; for then will time itself daily discover
new secret helps. As for my name, it shall be Cleophila, turning
Philoclea to myself, as my mind is wholly turned and transformed
into her. Now therefore do I submit myself to your counsel, dear
cousin, and crave your help.'

25   And thus he ended, as who should say, 'I have told you all, have
pity on me.' But Musidorus had by this time gathered his spirits
together, dismayed to see him he loved more than himself plunged
in such a course of misery. And so, when Pyrocles had ended, casting
a ghastful countenance upon him, as if he would conjure some
30 strange spirit he saw possess him, with great vehemency uttered
these words:

'And is it possible that this is Pyrocles, the only young prince in the
world, formed by nature and framed by education to the true exer-
cise of virtue? Or is it, indeed, some Amazon Cleophila that hath
35 counterfeited the face of my friend in this sort to vex me? For
likelier, sure, I would have thought it that any outward face might

---

2 felt] had felt Bo, Hm.   4 to a laurel] into a laurel Cl, As, Da, Ph, 90 (ex. Cm).
14 this disguising OA: these disguisings St.   16 my own] mine own Cl, Ph,
Hm.   witnesses OA: witness St.   great] good Cl, As.   16–17 he should be thus]
he should thus be Da; it is thus Je.   18 mine] my As, Da, Je.   27 together]
om. Cl, As.   him he] him whom he Cl, Je, Hm.

have been disguised than that the face of so excellent a mind could
have been thus blemished. O sweet Pyrocles, separate yourself a
little, if it be possible, from yourself, and let your own mind look
upon your own proceedings; so shall my words be needless, and you
best instructed. See with yourself how fit it will be for you in this 5
your tender youth (born so great a prince, of so rare, not only expec-
tation, but proof, desired of your old father, and wanted of your
native country, now so near your home) to divert your thoughts
from the way of goodness to lose, nay to abuse, your time; lastly, to
overthrow all the excellent things you have done, which have filled 10
the world with your fame (as if you should drown your ship in the
long-desired haven, or like an ill player should mar the last act of his
tragedy). Remember (for I know you know it) that, if we will be
men, the reasonable part of our soul is to have absolute command-
ment, against which if any sensual weakness arise, we are to yield 15
all our sound forces to the overthrowing of so unnatural a rebellion;
wherein, how can we want courage, since we are to deal against so
weak an adversary that in itself is nothing but weakness? Nay, we
are to resolve that if reason direct it, we must do it; and if we must
do it, we will do it; for to say I cannot is childish, and I will not 20
womanish. And see how extremely every way you endanger your
mind; for to take this woman's habit, without you frame your
behaviour accordingly, is wholly vain; your behaviour can never
come kindly from you but as the mind is proportioned unto it. So
that you must resolve, if you will play your part to any purpose, 25
whatsoever peevish imperfections are in that sex, to soften your
heart to receive them—the very first down step to all wickedness.
For do not deceive yourself, my dear cousin; there is no man sud-
denly either excellently good or extremely evil, but grows either as
he holds himself up in virtue or lets himself slide to viciousness. And 30
let us see what power is the author of all these troubles: forsooth,
love; love, a passion, and the basest and fruitlessest of all passions.
Fear breedeth wit; anger is the cradle of courage; joy openeth and
enableth the heart; sorrow, as it closeth it, so yet draweth it inward
to look to the correcting of itself. And so all of them generally have 35
power towards some good, by the direction of reason. But this
bastard love (for, indeed, the name of love is unworthily applied to

22 woman's] womanly Cl, Da, Je, Hm; womanish As, 90; *om.* Ph.   26 imperfections]
affections Je, 90 (*only*).   27 to receive] for to receive Bo, Cl, As, Ph, Je, Hm.
34 enableth] inhabiteth Ph, Je, Hm.   yet draweth] it draweth As, Da, 90.

so hateful a humour as it is, engendered betwixt lust and idleness),
as the matter it works upon is nothing but a certain base weakness,
which some gentle fools call a gentle heart; as his adjoined com-
panions be unquietness, longings, fond comforts, faint discomforts,
5 hopes, jealousies, ungrounded rages, causeless yieldings; so is the
highest end it aspires unto a little pleasure, with much pain before,
and great repentance after. But that end, how endlessly it runs to
infinite evils, were fit enough for the matter we speak of; but not for
your ears, in whom, indeed, there is so much true disposition to
10 virtue. Yet thus much of his worthy effects in yourself is to be seen:
that it utterly subverts the course of nature in making reason give
place to sense, and man to woman. And truly, I think, hereupon it
first gat the name of love. For, indeed, the true love hath that
excellent nature in it, that it doth transform the very essence of the
15 lover into the thing loved, uniting and, as it were, incorporating it
with a secret and inward working. And herein do these kinds of love
imitate the excellent; for, as the love of heaven makes one heavenly,
the love of virtue, virtuous, so doth the love of the world make one
become worldly. And this effeminate love of a woman doth so
20 womanize a man that, if you yield to it, it will not only make you a
famous Amazon, but a launder, a distaff-spinner, or whatsoever
other vile occupation their idle heads can imagine and their weak
hands perform. Therefore, to trouble you no longer with my tedious
but loving words, if either you remember what you are, what you
25 have been, or what you must be; if you consider what it is that moves
you, or for what kind of creature you are moved, you shall find the
cause so small, the effects so dangerous, yourself so unworthy to run
into the one or to be driven by the other, that I doubt not I shall
quickly have occasion rather to praise you for having conquered it
30 than to give you any further counsel how to do it.'
    Pyrocles' mind was all this while so fixed upon another devotion
that he no more attentively marked his friend's discourse than the
child that hath leave to play marks the last part of his lesson, or the

1 a humour Da, Qu, 90: an humour St, Bo, Cl, As, Ph, Je, Hm.   2 matter it]
matter that it Je, Hm (which Qu).   4 longings] longing Ph. Je, Hm.   7 end-
lessly] endless Cl, As, Je, Hm, 90.   10 thus much] this much Je, Hm, 13.
seen] found Cl, Da.   14 very] *om*. Da, Je.   16 kinds of love, Cl, Ph, Cm, 90:
kind of loves St, Bo, As, Je, Hm; kind of love Da.   18–19 one become worldly]
one worldly Bo, Je.   20 womanize Bo, Je, Hm, Cm, 93: womanish St, Cl, As, Da,
Ph, 90.   21 launder] launderer Ph, Je.   26 for] with Cl; by 90 (*ex*. Cm).
27 effects] effect Ph, Je, Hm, 90.   30 you any further] you further Cl, Hm, 90;
you any Je.

diligent pilot in a dangerous tempest doth attend to the unskilful
words of the passenger. Yet, the very sound having left the general
points of his speech in his mind, the respect he bare to his friend
brought forth this answer, having first paid up his late-accustomed
tribute of sighs: 5

'Dear and worthy friend, whatsoever good disposition nature hath
bestowed on me, or howsoever that disposition hath been by bring-
ing up confirmed, this must I confess: that I am not yet come to that
degree of wisdom to think lightly of the sex of whom I have my life;
since, if I be anything (which your friendship rather finds than I   10
acknowledge), I was to come to it born of a woman and nursed of a
woman. And certainly (for this point of your speech doth nearest
touch me) it is strange to see the unmanlike cruelty of mankind who,
not content with their tyrannous ambition to have brought the
others' virtuous patience under them, like childish masters, think   15
their masterhood nothing without doing injury to them who (if we
will argue by reason) are framed of nature with the same parts of
the mind for the exercise of virtue as we are. And, for example, even
this estate of Amazon's, which I now for my greatest honour do seek
to counterfeit, doth well witness that, if generally the sweetness of   20
their disposition did not make them see the vainness of these things
which we account glorious, they neither want valour of mind, nor
yet doth their fairness take away their force. And truly, we men and
praisers of men should remember that, if we have such excellencies,
it is reason to think them excellent creatures of whom we are, since   25
a kite never brought forth a good flying hawk. But to tell you true,
I do both disdain to use any more words of such a subject which is so
praised in itself as it needs no praises; and withal fear lest my conceit
(not able to reach unto them) bring forth words which for their un-
worthiness may be a disgrace to them I so inwardly honour. Let this   30
suffice: that they are capable of virtue. And virtue, you yourself say,
is to be loved; and I, too, truly. But this I willingly confess: that it
likes me much better when I find virtue in a fair lodging than when
I am bound to seek it in an ill-favoured creature, like a pearl in a
dunghill.'   35

And here Pyrocles stayed as to breathe himself, having been

1 attend to the] attend the As, 90.   22 words of the] *om.* Cl; words of a Je, 90.
3 bare] beare Ph; bore Hm.   4 late-] last- Bo, As, Da, Je, Hm.   7 on me]
upon me As, Ph, 90.   9 lightly] light Cl, As, 90; little Ph.   16 to them] unto
them Cl, Je.   27–8 is so praised] is praised As, Je.   28 praises] praise
As, Da.   30 to them] unto them Bo, Cl, Je, 90 (*corr.* 93).

transported with a little vehemency because it seemed him Musidorus had over bitterly glanced against the reputation of womankind. But then quieting his countenance, as well as out of an unquiet mind it might be, he thus proceeded on:

5 'And poor love,' said he, 'dear cousin, is little beholding unto you, since you are not contented to spoil it of the honour of the highest power of the mind (which notable men have attributed unto it), but you deject it below all other passions—in truth, something strangely since, if love receive any disgrace, it is by the company of those
10 passions you prefer unto it. For those kinds of bitter objections (as that lust, idleness, and a weak heart should be, as it were, the matter and form of love), rather touch me, dear Musidorus, than love. But I am good witness of mine own imperfections, and therefore will not defend myself. But herein, I must say, you deal contrary to
15 yourself; for, if I be so weak, then can you not with reason stir me up, as you did, by the remembrance of mine own virtue. Or if indeed I be virtuous, then must you confess that love hath his working in a virtuous heart. And so no doubt hath it, whatsoever I be. For, if we love virtue, in whom shall we love it but in virtuous creatures?—
20 Without your meaning be I should love this word of virtue when I see it written in a book. Those troublesome effects you say it breeds be not the fault of love, but of him that loves, as an unable vessel to bear such a power—like ill eyes, not able to look on the sun, or like a weak brain, soonest overthrown with the best wine. Even that
25 heavenly love you speak of is accompanied in some hearts with hopes, griefs, longings, and despairs. And in that heavenly love, since there are two parts (the one, the love itself; the other, the excellency of the thing loved), I (not able at the first leap to frame both in myself) do now, like a diligent workman, make ready the chief instrument
30 and first part of that great work, which is love itself. Which, when I have a while practised in this sort, then you shall see me turn it to greater matters. And thus gently you may, if it please you, think of me. Neither doubt you, because I wear a woman's apparel, I will be the more womanish; since, I assure you, for all my apparel, there is
35 nothing I desire more than fully to prove myself a man in this

8 deject it below] deject below As, Je, Hm.   something] somewhat Ph, 90; sometimes Je.   10 kinds Da, 90: kind St, Bo, Cl, As, Ph, Je, Hm.   13 mine own] my own Bo, Cl, As, Da, Je.   16 mine own] my own Bo, As, Da, Je, 90 (ex. 98, 13). 20 word of virtue] word virtue As, 90.   21 Those troublesome] These troublesome Bo, As, Hm.   22 be not Cl, 90: is not St, Bo, As, Da, Ph, Je, Hm.   fault] faults Cl, 90.   27 the one, the love] the one, love As, Ph.

enterprise. Much might be said in my defence, much more for love, and most of all for that divine creature which hath joined me and love together. But these disputations are fitter for quiet schools than my troubled brains, which are bent rather in deeds to perform, than in words to defend, the noble desire that possesseth me.' 5

'O lord,' said Musidorus, 'how sharp-witted you are to hurt yourself!'

'No,' answered he, 'but it is the hurt you speak of which makes me so sharp-witted.'

'Even so', said Musidorus, 'as every base occupation makes one 10 sharp in that practice and foolish in all the rest.'

'Nay rather', answered Pyrocles, 'as each excellent thing, once well learned, serves for a measure of all other knowledges.'

'And is that become', said Musidorus, 'a measure for other things, which never received measure in itself?' 15

'It is counted without measure', answered Pyrocles, 'because the workings of it are without measure; but otherwise in nature it hath measure, since it hath an end allotted unto it.'

'The beginning being so excellent, I would gladly know the end.'

'Enjoying', answered Pyrocles, with a deep sigh. 20

'O', said Musidorus, 'now set you forth the baseness of it since, if it end in enjoying, it shows all the rest was nothing.'

'You mistake me,' answered Pyrocles, 'I spake of the end to which it is directed; which end ends not no sooner than the life.'

'Alas! Let your own brain disenchant you', said Musidorus. 25

'My heart is too far possessed', said Pyrocles.

'But the head gives you direction.'

'And the heart gives me life', answered Pyrocles.

But Musidorus was so grieved to see his beloved friend obstinate, as he thought to his own destruction, that it forced him, with more 30 than accustomed vehemency, to speak these words:

'Well, well,' said he, 'you list to abuse yourself. It was a very white and red virtue which you could pick out by the sight of a picture. Confess the truth, and you shall find the uttermost was but beauty; a thing which, though it be in as great excellency in yourself 35 as may be in any, yet am I sure you make no further reckoning of it than of an outward fading benefit nature bestowed upon you. And

yet, such is your want of a true-grounded virtue (which must be like itself in all points) that what you wisely count a trifle in yourself, you fondly become a slave unto in another. For my part, I now protest I have left nothing unsaid which my wit could make me know, or my
5 most entire friendship to you requires of me. I do now beseech you, even for the love betwixt us (if this other love have left any in you towards me), and for the remembrance of your old careful father (if you can remember him, that forgets yourself), lastly, for Pyrocles' own sake (who is now upon the point of falling or rising), to purge
10 your head of this vile infection. Otherwise, give me leave rather in absence to bewail your mishap than to bide the continual pang of seeing your danger with mine eyes.'

The length of these speeches before had not so much cloyed Pyrocles (though he were very impatient of long deliberations) as
15 this last farewell of him he loved as his own life did wound his soul— as, indeed, they that think themselves afflicted are apt to conceive unkindness deeply—; insomuch that, shaking his head, and delivering some show of tears, he thus uttered his griefs:

'Alas,' said he, 'Prince Musidorus, how cruelly you deal with me!
20 If you seek the victory, take it; and if you list, triumph. Have you all the reason of the world, and with me remain all the imperfections; yet such as I can no more lay from me than the crow can be persuaded by the swan to cast off his blackness. But truly, you deal with me like a physician that, seeing his patient in a pestilent fever,
25 should chide him instead of ministering help, and bid him be sick no more; or rather, like such a friend that, visiting his friend condemned to perpetual prison and loaden with grievous fetters, should will him to shake off his fetters, or he would leave him. I am sick, and sick to the death. I am prisoner; neither is there any redress but
30 by her to whom I am slave. Now, if you list, leave him that loves you in the highest degree; but remember ever to carry this with you: that you abandon your friend in his greatest need.'

And herewith, the deep wound of his love being rubbed afresh with this new unkindness, began, as it were, to bleed again, in such
35 sort that he was unable to bear it any longer; but, gushing out abundance of tears and crossing his arms over his woeful heart, he sank down to the ground. Which sudden trance went so to the heart

11 bide] abide Cl, As, Ph, Je, Hm.   12 mine] my Cl, As.   14 impatient] unpatient Ph, 90 (only).   21 of the world] in the world Ph, Hm.   29 am prisoner] am a prisoner Cl, As, 90 (ex. 93).   30 am slave] am a slave Cl, As, Da, 98, 13.

of Musidorus that, falling down by him, and kissing the weeping eyes
of his friend, he besought him not to make account of his speech
which, if it had been over vehement, yet was it to be borne withal,
because it came out of a love much more vehement; that he had
never thought fancy could have received so deep a wound, but now 5
finding in him the force of it, he would no further contrary it, but
employ all his service to medicine it in such sort as the nature of it
required. But even this kindness made Pyrocles the more melt in the
former unkindness, which his manlike tears well showed, with a
silent look upon Musidorus, as who should say, 'and is it possible 10
that Musidorus should threaten to leave me?' And this strook
Musidorus's mind and senses so dumb, too, that for grief not being
able to say anything, they rested with their eyes placed one upon
another, in such sort as might well paint out the true passion of
unkindness, which is never aright but betwixt them that most dearly 15
love.

And thus remained they a time, till at length Musidorus, em-
bracing him, said, 'And will you thus shake off your friend?'

'It is you that shake off me,' said Pyrocles, 'being, for my un-
perfectness, unworthy of your friendship.'   20

'But this,' said Musidorus, 'shows you much more unperfect, to
be cruel to him that submits himself unto you. But since you are
unperfect,' said he, smiling, 'it is reason you be governed by us wise
and perfect men. And that authority will I begin to take upon me
with three absolute commandments: the first, that you increase not 25
your evil with further griefs; the second, that you love Philoclea with
all the powers of your mind; and the last commandment shall be
that you command me to do you what service I can towards the
attaining of your desires.'

Pyrocles' heart was not so oppressed with the two mighty passions 30
of love and unkindness but that it yielded to some mirth at this com-
mandment of Musidorus that he should love Philoclea. So that,
something clearing his face from his former shows of grief, 'Well',
said he, 'dear cousin, I see by the well choosing of your command-
ments that you are far fitter to be a prince than a councillor. And 35

2 besought Bo, Cl, Da, Ph, Je, Hm, 90: be thought St, As.   5 never thought
fancy could have] thought fancy could never have Bo, Ph, Je, Hm; not thought fancy
could have 90.   8–9 in the former] in his former Bo, Hm.   12 dumb] dump Bo;
down As.   21 you much more] you more Je, 90.   unperfect Bo, Cl, Da, Je, Hm,
90: imperfect St. As, Ph.   28 do you what] do what Bo, 90.   35 far fitter]
fitter As, 90 (ex. 93).

therefore I am resolved to employ all my endeavour to obey you, with this condition: that the commandments you command me to lay upon you shall only be that you continue to love me, and look upon my imperfections with more affection than judgement.'

5 'Love you,' said he, 'alas, how can my heart be separated from the true embracing of it without it burst by being too full of it? But,' said he, 'let us leave off these flowers of new-begun friendship; and since you have found out that way as your readiest remedy, let us go put on your transforming apparel. For my part, I will ever remain
10 hereabouts, either to help you in any necessity or, at least, to be partaker of any evil may fall unto you.'

Pyrocles, accepting this as a most notable testimony of his long-approved friendship, and returning to Mantinea where, having taken leave of their host (who, though he knew them not, was in love with
15 their virtue), and leaving with him some apparel and jewels, with opinion they would return after some time unto him, they departed thence to the place where he had left his womanish apparel which, with the help of his friend, he had quickly put on in such sort as it might seem love had not only sharpened his wits but nimbled his
20 hands in anything which might serve to his service. And to begin with his head, thus was he dressed: his hair (which the young men of Greece ware very long, accounting them most beautiful that had that in fairest quantity) lay upon the upper part of his forehead in locks, some curled and some, as it were, forgotten, with such a care-
25 less care, and with an art so hiding art, that he seemed he would lay them for a paragon whether nature simply, or nature helped by cunning, be the more excellent. The rest whereof was drawn into a coronet of gold, richly set with pearls, and so joined all over with gold wires, and covered with feathers of divers colours, that it was
30 not unlike to a helmet, such a glittering show it bare, and so bravely it was held up from the head. Upon his body he ware a kind of doublet of sky-colour satin, so plated over with plates of massy gold that he seemed armed in it; his sleeves of the same, instead of plates, was covered with purled lace. And such was the nether part of his

---

6 by being] with being Da, Je.   8–9 us go put] us put Da, Hm.   17 where he] where they As, Da, Hm.   20 which might] that might As, Da.   22–3 had that] had it Cl, As.   25 with an art] with such an art Cl, As.   26 paragon Cl, Da, Ph, Je, Hm: trial St, Bo; pattern As, 90 (pattern *corr. to* paragon Cl).   28 pearls] pearl As, Ph, Je, Hm, 90 (richly . . . gold *om.* Cl).   30 a helmet] an helmet Bo, As, Ph, 90.   32 sky-colour] sky-coloured Cl, As, Je; green Ph.   34 purled] purple As, Ph.   lace. And] lace of the same. And Ph, Je, Hm.

garment; but that made so full of stuff, and cut after such a fashion
that, though the length fell under his ankles, yet in his going one
might well perceive the small of the leg which, with the foot, was
covered with a little short pair of crimson velvet buskins, in some
places open (as the ancient manner was) to show the fairness of the 5
skin. Over all this he ware a certain mantle of like stuff, made in such
manner that, coming under his right arm, and covering most part of
that side, it touched not the left side but upon the top of the shoulder
where the two ends met, and were fastened together with a very rich
jewel, the device whereof was this: an eagle covered with the 10
feathers of a dove, and yet lying under another dove, in such sort
as it seemed the dove preyed upon the eagle, the eagle casting up
such a look as though the state he was in liked him, though the pain
grieved him. Upon the same side, upon his thigh he ware a sword
(such as we now call scimitars), the pommel whereof was so richly 15
set with precious stones as they were sufficient testimony it could be
no mean personage that bare it. Such was this Amazon's attire: and
thus did Pyrocles become Cleophila—which name for a time here-
after I will use, for I myself feel such compassion of his passion that
I find even part of his fear lest his name should be uttered before fit 20
time were for it; which you, fair ladies that vouchsafe to read this,
I doubt not will account excusable. But Musidorus, that had helped
to dress his friend, could not satisfy himself with looking upon him,
so did he find his excellent beauty set out with this new change, like
a diamond set in a more advantageous sort. Insomuch that he could 25
not choose, but smiling said unto him:

'Well,' said he, 'sweet cousin, since you are framed of such a
loving mettle, I pray you, take heed of looking yourself in a glass lest
Narcissus's fortune fall unto you. For my part, I promise you, if
I were not fully resolved never to submit my heart to these fancies, 30
I were like enough while I dressed you to become a young
Pygmalion.'

'Alas,' answered Cleophila, 'if my beauty be anything, then will it
help me to some part of my desires; otherwise I am no more to set
by it than the orator by his eloquence that persuades nobody.' 35

'She is a very invincible creature, then,' said he, 'for I doubt

3 the leg] his leg Cl, As, Je, Hm; his legs Ph; her leg 90 (*ex.* Cm).   5–6 the skin]
his skin Cl, Hm.   15 we now call] we call As, Je; we call now Da, Ph.
17 this] the Da, Je.   18–19 for a time hereafter] hereafter for a time Ph; for a time Je.
30 my heart] myself Da, Je.   these] those Cl, Da.

me much, under your patience, whether my mistress, your mistress, have a greater portion of beauty.'

'Speak not that blasphemy, dear friend,' said Cleophila, 'for if I have any beauty, it is the beauty which the imagination of her strikes
5 into my fancies, which in part shines through my face into your eyes.'

'Truly,' said Musidorus, 'you are grown a notable philosopher of fancies.'

'Astronomer,' answered Cleophila, 'for they are heavenly fancies.'

In such friendly speeches they returned again to the desert of the
10 two lodges, where Cleophila desired Musidorus he would hide himself in a little grove where he might see how she could play her part; for there, she said, she was resolved to remain till, by some good favour of fortune, she might obtain the sight of her whom she bare continually in the eyes of her mind. Musidorus obeyed her request,
15 full of extreme grief to see so worthy a mind thus infected; besides he could see no hope of success, but great appearance of danger. Yet, finding it so deeply grounded that striving against it did rather anger than heal the wound, and rather call his friendship in question than give place to any friendly counsel, he was content to yield to the
20 force of the present stream, with hope afterwards, as occasion fell out, to prevail better with him; or at least to adventure his life in preserving him from any injury might be offered him. And with the beating of those thoughts, remained he in the grove till, with a new fullness, he was emptied of them—as you shall after hear.

25 In the mean time, Cleophila walking up and down in that solitary place, with many intricate determinations, at last wearied both in mind and body, sat her down, and beginning to tune her voice, with many sobs and tears, sang this song which she had made since her first determination thus to change her estate:

30   Transformed in show, but more transformed in mind,
          I cease to strive, with double conquest foiled;
          For (woe is me) my powers all I find
          With outward force and inward treason spoiled.

          For from without came to mine eyes the blow,
35   Whereto mine inward thoughts did faintly yield;

1 me much OA: not much St.   18 than OA, 90: the St.   19 content OA, 90: contented St.   23 those] these Ph, Je, Hm.   27 sat her down] sat down As, Da.   30–p. 29, 8, *The poem is in* Dd, Cm., 90–93.   34 mine] my Bo, Le, Da, Ph.   35 mine] my Bo, Le, Da, Ph, Je.

Both these conspired poor reason's overthrow;
False in myself, thus have I lost the field.

And thus mine eyes are placed still in one sight,
And thus my thoughts can think but one thing still;
Thus reason to his servants gives his right;   5
Thus is my power transformed to your will.
 What marvel, then, I take a woman's hue,
 Since what I see, think, know, is all but you?

I might entertain you, fair ladies, a great while, if I should make
as many interruptions in the repeating as she did in the singing. For 10
no verse did pass out of her mouth but that it was waited on with
such abundance of sighs, and, as it were, witnessed with her flowing
tears, that, though the words were few, yet the time was long she
employed in uttering them; although her pauses chose so fit times
that they rather strengthened a sweeter passion than hindered the   15
harmony. Musidorus himself (that lay so as he might see and hear
these things) was yet more moved to pity by the manner of
Cleophila's singing than with anything he had ever seen—so lively
an action doth the mind, truly touched, bring forth. But so fell it out
that, as with her sweet voice she recorded once or twice the last verse 20
of her song, it awakened the shepherd Dametas, who at that time had
laid his sleepy back upon a sunny bank not far thence, gaping as far
as his jaws would suffer him. But being troubled out of his sleep (the
best thing his life could bring forth) his dull senses could not convey
the pleasure of the excellent music to his rude mind, but that he fell 25
into a notable rage. Insomuch that, taking a hedging bill lay by him,
he guided himself by the voice till he came to the place where he saw
Cleophila sitting, wringing her hands, and with some few words to
herself, breathing out part of the vehemency of that passion which
she had not fully declared in her song. But no more were his eyes   30
taken with her beauty than his ears with her music. But beginning
to swear by the pantable of Pallas, Venus's waistcoat, and such other
oaths as his rustical bravery could imagine, leaning his hands upon

3 mine] my Bo, Le, Da.
3–4 Thus are my eyes still captive to one sight:
 Thus all my thoughts are slaves to one thought still: 90. (Cm *reads* griefs *for* eyes.)
5 gives] yields 90. 8 what] that As, Da. 15 sweeter] suters Bo; sweet
As, Je, Hm. 16 see and hear] hear and see Bo, As. 17 these] those Bo, Da.
21 awakened] awaked As, Ph, Je. 22 sleepy] sheppe As; shepe Hm. 32 pant-
able Bo, Da, Hm, 90: pantople St; pantaple Cl; pantables As; pantoffle Ph; pantoble
Je; pantofle 13. 33 hands] hand As, Da.

his bill, and his chin upon his hands, he fell to mutter such railings and
cursings against her as a man might well see he had passed through
the discipline of an alehouse. And because you may take the better
into your fancies his mannerliness, the manner of the man shall in
5 few words be described. He was a short lean fellow, of black hair,
and notably backed for a burden, one of his eyes out, his nose turned
up to take more air, a seven or eight long black hairs upon his chin,
which he called his beard; his breast he ware always unbuttoned for
heat, and yet a stomacher before it for cold; ever untrussed, yet
10 points hanging down, because he might be trussed if he list; ill
gartered for a courtlike carelessness; only well shod for his father's
sake, who had upon his death bed charged him to take heed of going
wet. He had for love chosen his wife Miso, yet so handsome a bel-
dam that she was counted a witch only for her face and her splay
15 foot. Neither inwardly nor outwardly was there anything good in
her but that she observed decorum, having in a wretched body a
froward mind. Neither was there any humour in which her husband
and she could ever agree, but in disagreeing. Betwixt these two
issued forth mistress Mopsa, a fit woman to participate of both their
20 perfections. But because Alethes, an honest man of that time, did
her praises in verse, I will only repeat them and spare mine own pen,
because she bare the sex of a woman; and these they were:

What length of verse can serve brave Mopsa's good to show,
Whose virtues strange, and beauties such, as no man them may
25   know?
Thus shrewdly burdened then, how can my muse escape?
The gods must help and precious things must serve to show her
                                                                    shape.
Like great god Saturn fair, and like fair Venus chaste;
30 As smooth as Pan, as Juno mild, like goddess Iris fast.
With Cupid she foresees, and goes god Vulcan's pace;
And for a taste of all these gifts, she borrows Momus' grace.
Her forehead jacinth like, her cheeks of opal hue,
Her twinkling eyes bedecked with pearl, her lips of sapphire blue;

6 and notably backed] and notably back Bo; a notable back Ph, Je, Hm.   7 eight
long black] eight black As, Da.   12 to take heed] om. As, Hm.   14–15 splay foot
Bo, Cl, As, Ph, Je, Hm, 90: splay feet St, Da.   18 Betwixt] Between Da, 90.
21 mine] my Bo, As, Da, Cm.   23–p. 31, 4, *The poem is in* Dd, Ha, Hy, Cm, 90–
93.   24 beauties] beauty Bo, Je.   them may] may them Le, Dd; om. As.
26 Je *is missing from here.*   30 as Juno OA, 90: a Juno St, Dd.   32 borrows]
steals god 90.   33 cheeks] cheek Le, Ph.   34 of] as 90.

Her hair pure crapal stone; her mouth O heavn'ly wide;
Her skin like burnished gold, her hands like silver ore untried.
　As for those parts unknown, which hidden sure are best,
　Happy be they which will believe, and never seek the rest.

The beginning of this Dametas's credit with Basilius was by the 5
duke's straying out of his way one time a-hunting where, meeting
this fellow, and asking him the way, and so falling into other ques-
tions, he found some of his answers touching husbandry matters (as
a dog sure, if he could speak, had wit enough to describe his kennel)
not unsensible; and all uttered with such a rudeness, which the duke 10
interpreted plainness (although there be great difference betwixt
them), that the duke, conceiving a sudden delight in his entertain-
ment, took him to his court, with apparent show of his good opinion;
where the flattering courtier had no sooner taken the prince's mind
but that there were straight reasons to confirm the duke's doing, and 15
shadows of virtues found for Dametas. His silence grew wit, his
bluntness integrity, his beastly ignorance virtuous simplicity; and
the duke (according to the nature of great persons, in love with that
he had done himself) fancied that the weakness was in him, with his
presence, would grow wisdom. And so, like a creature of his own 20
making, he liked him more and more. And thus gave he him first the
office of principal herdman. And thus lastly did he put his life into
his hands—although he grounded upon a great error; for his quality
was not to make men, but to use men according as men were, no
more than an ass will be taught to manage, a horse to hunt, or a 25
hound to bear a saddle, but each to be used according to the force
of his own nature.

　But Dametas, as I said, suddenly awaked, remembering the duke's
commandment, and glad he might use his authority in chiding, came
swearing to the place where Cleophila was, with a voice like him that 30
plays Hercules in a play and, God knows, never had Hercules' fancy
in his head. The first word he spake, after his railing oaths, was 'Am
not I Dametas? Why, am not I Dametas?'

1 pure] like 90.　　　3 those] these As; the Le, Da; her 90.　　　4 be] are Le,
Ph, Dd.　　will] well Cl, Le, Da, Ph, Hm, Ha, Hy, 90.　　5 of this Dametas's] of
Dametas's Cl, Da, Hm; of his 90.　　6 his way] the way Hm, 90.　　10 such a
rudeness] such rudeness Ph, Hm, 90.　　11 betwixt] between Da, Ph, 90.　　14
taken the prince's OA: taken the the prince's St.　　16 wit] witty As, Ph.　　21 him
first] himself Cl; him thus Hm.　　　　22 of principal] of a principal Bo, As.
30 like him] like one As; of one 90.　　31 in a play Bo, Cl, Da, 90: in play St, As,
Hm; in the play Ph.

These words made Cleophila lift up her eyes upon him, and
seeing what manner of man he was, the height of her thoughts would
not suffer her to yield any answer to so base a creature; but casting
again down her eyes, leaning upon the ground, and putting her
5 cheek in the palm of her hand, fetched a great sigh, as if she had
answered him, 'my head is troubled with greater matters'. Which
Dametas (as all persons witnesses of their own unworthiness are apt
to think they are contemned) took in so heinous a chafe that, stand-
ing upon his tiptoes, and staring as if he would have had a mote
10 pulled out of his eye, 'Why,' said he, 'thou woman or boy, or both,
or whatsoever thou be, I tell thee, here is no place for thee; get thee
gone, I tell thee, it is the duke's pleasure. I tell thee, it is master
Dametas's pleasure.'

Cleophila could not choose but smile at him, and yet, taking herself
15 with the manner, spake these words to herself:

'O spirit', said she, 'of mine, how canst thou receive any mirth in
the midst of thine agonies? And thou, mirth, how darest thou enter
into a mind so grown of late thy professed enemy?'

'Thy spirit,' said Dametas, 'dost thou think me a spirit? I tell thee
20 I am the duke's officer, and have the charge of him and his daughters.'

'O pearl,' said sobbing Cleophila, 'that so vile an oyster should
keep thee!'

'By the combcase of Diana!' sware Dametas, 'this woman is mad;
oysters and pearls; dost thou think I will buy oysters? I tell thee,
25 get thee packing, or else I must needs be offended.'

'O sun,' said Cleophila, 'how long shall this cloud live to darken thee,
and the poor creatures that live only by thee be deprived of thee?'

These speeches to herself put Dametas out of all patience; so
that, hitting her upon the breast with the blunt end of his bill, 'Maid
30 Marian,' said he, 'am not I a personage to be answered?'

But Cleophila no sooner felt the blow but that, the fire sparkling
out of her eyes, and rising up with a right Pyrocles countenance in
a Cleophila face, 'Vile creature,' said she, laying her hand upon her
sword, 'force me not to defile this sword in thy base blood!'
35 Dametas, that from his childhood had ever feared the blade of a
sword, ran back backwards, with his hands above his head, at least
twenty paces, gaping and staring with the very countenance of those
clownish churls that by Latona's prayer were turned into frogs. At

2 manner of man OA: manner a man St.   17 thine] her Ph; your Hm.   30 personage] per-
son Cl, Ph.   33 Cleophila] Cleophila's As, Da, Ph, Hm.   36 back] om. Bo, Cl, As, Ph, 13.

length staying, he came a little nearer her again, but still without the compass of blows, holding one leg, as it were, ready to run away; and then fell to scolding and railing, swearing it was but a little bashfulness in him that had made him go back; and that if she stayed any longer he would make her see his blood came out of the 5 eldest shepherd's house in that country. But seeing her walk up and down without marking what he said, he went for more help to his own lodge where, knocking a good while, at length he cried to his wife Miso that in a whore's name she should come out to him. But instead of that, he might hear a hollow rotten voice that bid him 10 let her alone, like a knave as he was, for she was busy about my lady Pamela. This dashed poor Dametas more than anything, for old acquaintance had taught him to fear that place; and therefore, calling with a more pitiful voice to his daughter, he might see a face look out of a window, enough to have made any blind man in love. 15 It was mistress Mopsa that, instead of answer, asked him whether he were mad to forget his duty to her mother. Dametas shrunk down his shoulders, like the poor ass that lays down his ears when he must needs yield to the burden; and yet his tongue, the valiantest part of him, could not forbear to say these words: 'Here is foreign wars 20 abroad, and uncivil wars at home—and all with women. Now', said he, 'the black jaundice and the red flix take all the warbled kind of you!'

And with this prayer, he went to the other lodge where the duke lay at that time sleeping, as it was in the heat of the day. And there he whistled, and stamped, and knocked, crying 'Ho! my liege!' with 25 such faces as might well show what a deformity a passion can bring a man unto when it is not governed with reason; till at length the fair Philoclea came down in such loose apparel as was enough to have bound any man's fancies, and with a sweet look asking him what he would have. Dametas, without any reverence, commanded 30 her in the duke's name she should tell the duke he was to speak with the duke, for he forsooth had things to tell the duke that pertained to the duke's service. She answered him he should be obeyed, since such was the fortune of her and her sister. And so went she to tell her father of Dametas's being there, leaving him chafing at the door 35 and whetting his bill, swearing if he met her again neither she nor the tallest woman in the parish should make him run away any more.

3 swearing it] swearing that it Cl, Ph.   4 that had made] that made Ph, Hm.
5 came] come Cl, Ph, Hm.   10 bid] bad As; bed Hm.   18 his ears OA: her
ears St.   22 warbled] wrabbed Bo, Cl, Hm; crabbed Da, Ph.

But the duke, understanding by his jewel Philoclea that something there was which greatly troubled Dametas's conscience, came presently down unto him to know the matter; where he found Dametas, talking to himself, and making faces like an ape that had newly taken a purgation, pale, shaking, and foaming at the mouth. And a great while it was before the duke could get any word of him. At length, putting his leg before him (which was the manner of his curtsy), he told the duke that, saving the reverence of his duty, he should keep himself from thenceforward, he would take no more charge of him. The duke, accustomed to take all well at his hands, did but laugh to see his rage, and, stroking his head, desired him of fellowship to let him know the matter.

'I tell you', saith Dametas, 'it is not for me to be an officer without I may be obeyed.'

'But what troubles thee, my good Dametas?' said the duke.

'I tell you', said Dametas, 'I have been a man in my days, whatsoever I be now.'

'And reason,' answered the duke, 'but let me know that I may redress thy wrongs.'

'Nay,' says Dametas, 'no wrongs neither. But thus falls out the case, my liege; I met with such a mankind creature yonder, with her sword by her hip, and with such a visage as, if it had not been for me and this bill, God save it, she had come hither and killed you and all your house.'

'What, strike a woman!' said the duke.

'Indeed,' said Dametas, 'I made her but a little weep, and after I had pity of her.'

'It was well and wisely done,' said the duke, 'but I pray thee show me her.'

'I pray you,' said Dametas, 'first call for more company to hold me from hurting her; for my stomach riseth against her.'

'Let me but see the place', said the duke, 'and then you shall know whether my words or your bill be the better weapon.'

Dametas went stalking on before the duke as if he had been afraid to wake his child; and then, pointing with his bill towards her, was not hasty to make any nearer approaches. But the duke no sooner saw Cleophila but that he remained amazed at the goodliness of her stature and the stateliness of her march (for at that time she was

2 which] that Da, Ph.   13 saith] said Bo, Da, Ph, Hm.   20 says] said Cl, Da, Ph, Hm.   27 of] on Cl, Ph, Hm.   36 nearer] near Cl, Da.

walking with a countenance well setting forth an extreme distraction
of her mind), and, as he came nearer her, at the excellent perfection
of her beauty; insomuch that, forgetting any anger he conceived in
Dametas's behalf, and doing reverence to her, as to a lady in whom
he saw much worthy of great respect, 'Fair lady,' said he 'it is 5
nothing strange that such a solitary place as this should receive
solitary persons; but much do I marvel how such a beauty as yours
is could be suffered to be thus alone.'

She, looking with a grave majesty upon him, as if she found in
herself cause why she should be reverenced, 'They are never alone', 10
said she, 'that are accompanied with noble thoughts.'

'But those thoughts', said the duke (replying for the delight he
had to speak further with her), 'cannot in this your loneliness neither
warrant you from suspicion in others nor defend you from melan-
choly in yourself.' 15

Cleophila, looking upon him as though he pressed her further than
needed, 'I seek no better warrant', said she, 'than mine own con-
science, nor no greater pleasure than mine own contentation.'

'Yet virtue seeks to satisfy others', said Basilius.

'Those that be good,' answered Cleophila, 'and they will be satisfied 20
as long as they see no evil.'

'Yet will the best in this country', said the duke, 'suspect so
excellent a beauty, being so weakly guarded.'

'Then are the best but stark naught,' answered Cleophila, 'for
open suspecting others comes of secret condemning themselves. 25
But in my country,' said she, continuing her speech with a brave
vehemency, 'whose manners I am in all places to maintain and
reverence, the general goodness which is nourished in our hearts
makes everyone think that strength of virtue in another whereof they
find the assured foundation in themselves.' 30

But Basilius, who began to feel the sparkles of those flames which
shortly after burned all other thoughts out of his heart, felt such a
music, as he thought, in her voice, and such an eye-pleasing in her
face, that he thought his retiring into this solitary place was well
employed if it had been only to have met with such a guest. And 35
therefore, desirous to enter into nearer points with her, 'Excellent

12 those] these As, Hm.   13 loneliness] loveliness Cl, As, Ph, Hm.
14 suspicion Bo, Cl, Da, Ph, Hm, 90: suspention St; suspercion As.   17 mine]
my Bo, As, Da, 90.   18 mine] my Bo, Da.   25 condemning OA, 90: com-
mending St.   29 that] the As, 90.

lady,' said he, 'you praise so greatly, and yet so wisely, your country that I must needs desire to know what the nest is out of which such birds do fly.'

'You must first deserve that knowledge', said she, 'before you
5 obtain it.'

'And by what means', said Basilius, 'shall I deserve to know your estate?'

'By letting me first know yours', answered she.

'To obey you,' said he, 'I will do it; although it were so much
10 more reason yours should be known first, as you do deserve in all points to be preferred. Know you, fair lady,' said he, 'that my name is Basilius, unworthy duke of this country; the rest, either fame hath already brought to your ears, or, if it please you to make this place happy by your presence, at more leisure you shall understand of
15 me.'

Cleophila (who had from the beginning suspected it should be he, but would not seem she did so, to keep her majesty the better), making some reverence unto him, 'Mighty prince,' said she, 'let my not knowing of you serve for the excuse of my boldness, and the
20 little reverence I do you, impute it to the manner of my country, which is the invincible land of the Amazons, myself niece to Senicia, queen thereof, lineally descended of the famous Penthesilea, slain before Troy by the bloody hand of Pyrrhus. I, having in this my youth determined to make the world see the Amazons' excellencies,
25 as well in private as in public virtues, have passed many dangerous adventures in divers countries, till the unmerciful sea deprived me of all my company; so that shipwrack brought me to this realm, and uncertain wandering guided me to this place.'

Whoever saw a man to whom a beloved child long lost did, un-
30 looked for, return might easily figure unto his fancy the very fashion of Basilius's countenance—so far had love become his master. And so had this young siren charmed his old ears, insomuch that, with more vehement importunacy than any greedy host would use to well acquainted passengers, he fell to entreat her abode there for some
35 time. She, although nothing could come fitter to the very point of her desire, yet had she already learned that womanish quality to counterfeit backwardness in that she most wished; so that he, desirous to prove whether intercession coming out of fitter mouths

5 obtain] can obtain As; may obtain 90.   11 said he] *om.* Ph, 90.   12 un-
worthy] unworthily Bo, Cl, 90.   35 fitter] more fitting Bo; more fitter Hm.

might better prevail, called to Dametas, and commanded him to bring forth his wife and two daughters—three ladies, although of diverse, yet all of excellent beauty: the duchess Gynecia, in grave matronlike attire, with a countenance and behaviour far unlike to fall into those inconveniences she afterwards tasted of. The fair 5 Pamela, whose noble heart had long disdained to find the trust of her virtue reposed in the hands of a shepherd, had yet, to show an obedience, taken on a shepherdish apparel, which was of russet velvet, cut after their fashion, with a straight body, open breasted, the nether part full of pleats, with wide open sleeves, hanging down 10 very low; her hair at the full length, only wound about with gold lace—by the comparison to show how far her hair did excel in colour; betwixt her breasts, which sweetly rase up like two fair mountainets in the pleasant vale of Tempe, there hanged down a jewel which she had devised as a picture of her own estate. It was a 15 perfect white lamb tied at a stake with a great number of chains, as it had been feared lest the silly creature should do some great harm; neither had she added any word unto it, but even took silence as the word of the poor lamb, showing such humbleness as not to use her own voice for complaint of her misery.   20

But when the ornament of the earth, young Philoclea, appeared in her nymphlike apparel, so near nakedness as one might well discern part of her perfections, and yet so apparelled as did show she kept the best store of her beauties to herself; her excellent fair hair drawn up into a net made only of itself (a net indeed to have caught the 25 wildest disposition); her body covered with a light taffeta garment, so cut as the wrought smock came through it in many places (enough to have made a very restrained imagination have thought what was under it); with the sweet cast of her black eye which seemed to make a contention whether that in perfect blackness, or her skin in perfect 30 whiteness, were the most excellent; then, I say, the very clouds seemed to give place to make the heaven more fair. At least, the clouds of Cleophila's thoughts quite vanished, and so was her brain

---

3 yet all of] yet of Hm, 98, 13.   13 rase 90: rise OA ('rys' St); rose 98, 13. 14 mountainets Cl, As, 90 (*corr. sheets*), 93: mountains St, Bo, Da, Ph, Hm, Cm; mountaints 90 (*uncorr. sheets*).   15 a picture] an impresa Cl, As, Da, Ph; an impression Hm.   16–17 as it] as if it Da, Ph, Hm.   18 *after* unto it *insert*

(which is as it were the life of an impresa) Cl, As, Da, Ph;
(which is as it were the life of an impression) Hm.

32 At least] At the least Da, 90.

fixed withal that her sight seemed more forcible and clear than ever before or since she found it, with such strange delight unto her (for still, fair ladies, you remember that I use the she-title to Pyrocles, since so he would have it) that she stood like a well wrought
5 image, with show of life, but without all exercise of life, so forcibly had love transferred all her spirits into the present contemplation of the lovely Philoclea. And so had it been like enough she would have stayed long time but that by chance Gynecia stepped betwixt her sight and the lady Philoclea, and the change of the object made
10 her recover her senses; so that she could with good manner receive the salutation of the duchess and the princess Pamela, doing them yet no further reverence than one princess useth to another. But when she came to the lady Philoclea, she fell down on her knees, taking by force her fair hands and kissing them with great show of
15 extreme affection, and with a bowed-down countenance began this speech unto her: 'Divine lady,' said she, 'let not the world nor these great princes marvel to see me contrary to my manner do this especial honour unto you, since all, both men and women, owe this homage to the perfection of your beauty.'
20   Philoclea's blushing cheeks quickly witnessed how much she was abashed to see this singularity used to herself; and therefore, causing Cleophila to rise, 'Noble lady,' said she, 'it is no marvel to see your judgement much mistaken in my beauty, since you begin with so great an error as to do more honour unto me than to them to whom
25 I myself owe all service.'

'Rather', answered Cleophila, 'that shows the power of your beauty which hath forced me to fall into such an error, if it were an error.'

'You are so acquainted', said Philoclea, sweetly smiling, 'with
30 your own beauty that it makes you easily fall into the discourse of beauty.'

'Beauty in me!' said Cleophila, deeply sighing, 'Alas! if there be any, it is in mine eyes, which your happy presence hath imparted unto them.'

35   Basilius was even transported with delight to hear these speeches betwixt his well beloved daughter and his better loved lady; and so

6 present] pleasant As, Hm.   8 betwixt] between Bo, Hm, 90.   15 with a bowed] with bowed Da, Ph.   16 these] this Cl, As, Ph, Hm, 90: princess St, Cl; princesses Bo, 93.   24 to them] unto them Bo, Cl, Ph.   33 in] om. As, Da.   mine] your Bo; my Cl, As, 90.   35 even Cl, As, Ph, Hm: ever St, Bo, Da.

made a sign to Philoclea that she should entreat her to remain with them; which she willingly obeyed, for already she conceived delight in Cleophila's presence, and therefore said unto her: 'It is a great happiness, I must confess, to be praised of them that are themselves most praiseworthy. And well I find you are an invincible Amazon, since you will overcome in a wrong matter. But if my beauty be anything', said she, 'then let it obtain thus much of you: that you will remain in this company some time, to ease your own travail, and our solitariness.'

'First let me die', said Cleophila, 'before any word spoken by such a mouth should come in vain. I yield wholly to your commandment, fearing nothing but that you command that which may be troublesome to yourself.'

Thus, with some other words of entertaining, her staying was concluded, to the unspeakable joy of the duke—although, perchance, with some little envy in the other ladies, to see young Philoclea's beauty so greatly advanced. You ladies know best whether sometimes you feel impression of that passion; for my part, I would hardly think that the affection of a mother and the noble mind of Pamela could be overthrown with so base a thing as envy is—especially Pamela, to whom fortune had already framed another, who no less was dedicated to her excellencies than Cleophila was to Philoclea's perfections, as you shall shortly hear. For the duke going into the lodge with his wife and daughters, Cleophila desired them to excuse her for a while, for that she had thoughts to pass over with herself; and that shortly after she would come in to them—indeed meaning to find her friend Musidorus, and to glory with him of the happiness of her choice. But when she looked in the grove and could nowhere find him, marvelling something at it, she gave herself to feed those sweet thoughts which now had the full possession of her heart, sometimes thinking how far Philoclea herself passed her picture, sometimes fore-imagining with herself how happy she should be if she could obtain her desires; till, having spent thus an hour or two, she might perceive afar off one coming towards her, in the apparel of a shepherd, with his arms hanging down, going a kind of languishing pace, with his eyes sometimes cast up to heaven as though his fancies strave to mount up higher, sometimes thrown down to the

4–5 are themselves most] are most Hm, 90.   17 so greatly advanced] so advanced Cl, As.   23 perfections] perfection Cl, As.   26 in to] unto Bo, Cl, As. 29 feed] feed on Cl, Hm.   37 mount up higher] mount higher Bo, 90.

ground as if the earth could not bear the burden of his pains. At
length she heard him, with a lamentable tune, sing these few verses:

> Come shepherd's weeds, become your master's mind:
> Yield outward show, what inward change he tries:
> Nor be abashed, since such a guest you find,
> Whose strongest hope in your weak comfort lies.
>
> Come shepherd's weeds, attend my woeful cries:
> Disuse yourselves from sweet Menalcas' voice:
> For other be those tunes which sorrow ties
> From those clear notes which freely may rejoice.
>   Then pour out plaint, and in one word say this:
>   Helpless his plaint who spoils himself of bliss.

And having ended, she might see him strike himself upon the breast,
uttering these words: 'O miserable wretch, whither do thy destinies
guide thee?'

It seemed to Cleophila that she knew the voice; and therefore
drawing nearer, that her sight might receive a perfect discerning,
she saw plainly, to her great amazement, it was her dear friend
Musidorus. And now having named him, methinks it reason I should
tell you what chance brought him to this change. I left him lately,
if you remember, fair ladies, in the grove by the two lodges, there
to see what should befall to his dear new-transformed friend. There
heard he all the complaints (not without great compassion) that his
friend made to himself; and there (not without some laughter) did
he see what passed betwixt him and Dametas, and how stately he
played the part of Cleophila at the duke's first coming. And falling
into many kind fancies towards him, sometimes pitying his case,
sometimes praising his behaviour, he would often say to himself: 'O
sweet Pyrocles, how art thou bewitched! Where is thy virtue?
Where is the use of thy reason? Much am I inferior to thee in all the
powers of the mind; and yet know I that all the heavens cannot
bring me to such a thraldom.'

Scarcely, think I, he had spoken those words but that the duchess,

3–12 *The poem is in* Cm, 90, 93.   3 shepherd's Bo, Le, Da, Ph, Hm, 90: shep-
herd St, Cl, As.   4 change] chance Hm, 90 (*only*).   7 shepherd's Le, Da,
Ph, Hm, 90: shepherd St, Bo, Cl, As.   12 his Bo, Cl, Le, As, Da, Ph, 90:
is St, Hm.   14 thy] the As, Hm.   19 it reason] it is reason Bo, Da.
27 kind fancies] kind of fancies Cl, As, Da, Ph.   30 Much] How much Cl, As,
90.   to thee] unto thee Cl, Da, Hm.   33 those words] these words Cl, As,
Hm, Cm; this word 90 (*ex.* Cm).

being sent for to entertain Cleophila, came out with her two daughters; where the beams of the princess Pamela's beauty had no sooner stricken into his eyes but that he was wounded with more sudden violence of love than ever Pyrocles was. Whether indeed it were that this strange power would be bravely revenged of him for 5 the bitter words he had used, or that his very resisting made the wound the crueller (as we see the harquebus doth most endamage the stiffest metal), or rather that the continual healthfulness of his mind made this sudden ill the more incurable (as the soundest bodies, once infected, are most mortally endangered); but howsoever the 10 cause was, such was the effect that, not being able to bear the vehement pain, he ran away through the grove, like a madman, hoping perchance (as the fever-sick folks do) that the change of places might ease his grief. But therein was his luck indeed better than his providence; for he had not gone a little but that he met with 15 a shepherd (according to his estate, handsomely apparelled) who was as then going to meet with other shepherds (as upon certain days they had accustomed) to do exercises of activity and to play new-invented eclogues before the duke. Which, when Musidorus had learned of him (for love is full of desire, and desire is always inquisi- 20 tive), it came straight into his head that there were no better way for him to come by the often enjoying of the princess Pamela's sight than to take the apparel of this shepherd upon him. Which he quickly did, giving him his own much richer; and withal, lest the matter by him might be discovered, hired him to go without stay into Thessalia, 25 writing two or three words by him, in a pair of tables well closed up, to a servant of his that he should, upon the receipt, arrest and keep him in good order till he heard his further pleasure. Yet before Menalcas departed (for so was his name), he learned of him both his own estate and the manner of their pastimes and eclogues. And 30 thus furnished, he returned again to the place where his heart was pledged, so oppressed in mind that it seemed to him his legs were uneath able to bear him. Which grief he uttered in the doleful song I told you of before, and was cause that his dear he-she friend, Cleophila, came unto him; who, when she was assured it was he 35 (with wonted entireness embracing him), demanded of him what sudden thing had thus suddenly changed him; whether the goddess

5 of him] on him Bo, Cl, Hm.   21 into] unto Bo, As, Da.   24 much richer
OA: much richer worth St.   33 in the] with the Cl, As.   34 dear he-she]
dearest As, Ph.

8118554   H

of those woods had such a power to transform everybody; or
whether, indeed, as he had always in all enterprises most faithfully
accompanied her, so he would continue to match her in this new
metamorphosis. But Musidorus, looking dolefully upon her, wring-
5 ing his hands, and pouring out abundance of tears, began to recount
unto her all this I have already told you, but with such passionate
dilating of it that, for my part, I have not a feeling insight enough
into the matter to be able lively to express it. Sufficeth it that what-
soever a possessed heart with a good tongue, to a dear friend, could
10 utter was at that time largely set forth. The perfect friendship
Cleophila bare him, and the great pity she (by good experience) had
of his case could not keep her from smiling at him, remembering
how vehemently he had cried out against the folly of lovers; so that
she thought good a little to punish him, playing with him in this
15 manner: 'Why, how now, dear cousin,' said she, 'you that were even
now so high in the pulpit against love, are you now become so mean
an auditor? Remember that love is a passion, and that a worthy
man's reason must ever have the masterhood.'

'I recant, I recant!' cried Musidorus, and withal falling down
20 prostrate, 'O thou celestial, or infernal, spirit of love', said he, 'or
what other heavenly or hellish title thou list to have, for both those
effects I find in myself, have compassion of me, and let thy glory be
as great in pardoning them that be submitted to thee as in conquer-
ing those that were rebellious!'

25 'No, no!' said Cleophila, yet further to urge him, 'I see you well
enough; you make but an interlude of my mishaps, and do but coun-
terfeit thus to make me see the deformity of my passions. But take
heed,' said she, 'cousin, that this jest do not one day turn into
earnest.'

30 'Now I beseech thee,' said Musidorus, taking her fast by the hand,
'even by the truth of our friendship (of which, if I be not altogether
an unhappy man, thou hast some remembrance), and by those sacred
flames (which I know have likewise nearly touched thee), make no
jest of that which hath so earnestly pierced me through; nor let that
35 be light to thee which is to me so burdenous that I am not able
to bear it.'

Musidorus did so lively deliver out his inward griefs that

22 of me] on me Ph; upon me Hm.   28 into] to Cl, 90.   30 thee] ye Cl;
you Hm.   31 by] for Cl, As, 90.   our] your Ph, Cm.   32 sacred] secret
Cl, As, Ph, Cm, 93.

Cleophila's friendly heart felt a great impression of pity withal—as certainly all persons that find themselves afflicted easily fall to compassion of them who taste of like misery, partly led by the common course of humanity, but principally because, under the image of them, they lament their own mishaps; and so the complaints the others make seem to touch the right tune of their own woes. Which did mutually work so in these two young princes that, looking ruefully one upon the other, they made their speech a great while nothing but doleful sighs. Yet sometimes they would yield out suchlike lamentations: 'Alas! What further evil hath fortune reserved for us, or what shall be the end of this our tragical pilgrimage? Shipwracks, daily dangers, absence from our country, have at length brought forth this captiving of us within ourselves which hath transformed the one in sex, and the other in state, as much as the uttermost work of changeable fortune can be extended unto.'

And then would they kiss one another, vowing to continue partakers of all either good or evil fortune. And thus perchance would they have forgotten themselves some longer time, but that Basilius, whose heart was now set on fire with his new mistress, finding her absence long, sent out Dametas to her to know if she would command anything, and to invite her to go with his wife and daughters to a fair meadow thereby to see the sports and hear the eclogues of his country shepherds. Dametas came out with two or three swords about him, his hedging bill on his neck, and a chopping knife under his girdle, armed only behind, as fearing most the blows that might fall upon the reins of his back; for, indeed, Cleophila had put such a sudden fear into his head that from thenceforth he was resolved never to come out any more ill provided. Yet had his blunt brains perceived some favour the duke bare to this new-come lady; and so framing himself thereunto (as without doubt the most servile flattery is most easy to be lodged in the most gross capacity; for their ordinary conceit draws a yielding to their greatness, and then have they not wit to discern right degrees of goodness), he no sooner saw her but, with head and arms, he laid his reverence before her, enough to have made a man forswear all courtesy. And then, in the

5 complaints the] complaints that Cl, As, Hm.   6 others] other Bo, Ph.
8 fully one] fully the one As, Hm.   14 and] om. As, Ph.   26 upon] on Cl,
Hm.   29 this] his As, Ph, Hm.   lady] mistress As, Hm.   31 easy to
be] easily Bo, Cl, Hm; easily to be Da; easy As.   33 discern right] discern the
right Bo, Cl, As, Ph, Hm, 93; learn the right Cm, 90.   35 a man] a man corr. to
any Bo; any man Cl, 90.   forswear Da, 90: forsworn St, Bo, Cl, As, Ph, Hm.

duke's name, did he require her she would take pains to see their
pastorals (for so their sports were termed); but when he spied
Musidorus standing by her (for his eye had been placed all this while
upon her), not knowing him, he would fain have persuaded himself
5 to have been angry but that he durst not. Yet, muttering and champ-
ing as though his cud troubled him, he gave occasion to Musidorus
to come nearer him, and to feign a tale of his own life: that he was a
younger brother of the shepherd Menalcas, by name Dorus, sent by
his father in his tender age to Athens, there to learn some cunning
10 more than ordinary for to excel his fellow shepherds in their
eclogues; and that his brother Menalcas, lately gone thither to fetch
him home, was deceased; where, upon his deathbed, he had charged
him to seek the service of Dametas, and to be wholly and only guided
by his counsel, as one in whose judgement and integrity the duke
15 had singular confidence; for token whereof he gave him a sum of gold
in ready coin which Menalcas had bequeathed him upon condition
he should receive this poor Dorus into his service, that his mind and
manners might grow the better by his daily example. Dametas no
sooner saw the gold but that his heart was presently infected with
20 the self-conceit he took of it; which, being helped with the tickling
of Musidorus's praises, so turned the brain of good Dametas that he
became slave to that which he that would be his servant bestowed
on him, and gave in himself an example for ever that the fool can
never be honest since, not being able to balance what points virtue
25 stands upon, every present occasion catches his senses, and his
senses are masters of his silly mind. Yet, for countenance's sake, he
seemed very squeamish, in respect he had the charge of the princess
Pamela, to accept any new servant into his house. But such was the
secret operation of the gold, helped with the persuasions of the
30 Amazon Cleophila, who said it was pity so proper a young man
should be anywhere else than with so good a master, that in the end
he agreed to receive him for his servant, so as that day in their pas-
torals he proved himself active in mind and body.

   And thus went they to the lodge, with greater joy to Musidorus
35 (now only poor shepherd Dorus) than all his life before had ever
brought forth unto him—so manifest it is that the greatest point

13 service] Je *begins here.*   15 a sum] a good sum Da, Je, Hm; two talents Ph.
18 manners] manner Je, 90 (*corr.* 93).   23 on him Bo, Je, Hm: of him St; upon
him Cl, As, Da, Ph.   29 persuasions] persuasion Cl, As, Je, Hm, 90.   33 active
in] active both in Bo, Hm.   34 greater] great As, Da.

outward things can bring a man unto is the contentment of the mind, which once obtained, no state is miserable; and without that, no prince's seat restful. There found they Gynecia, with her two daughters, ready to go to the meadow; whither also they went. For, as for Basilius, he desired to stay behind them to debate a little with himself of this new guest that had entered and possessed his brains. There, it is said, the poor old Basilius, now alone (for, as I said, the rest were gone to see the pastorals), had a sufficient eclogue in his own head betwixt honour, with the long experience he had had of the world, on the one side, and this new assault of Cleophila's beauty on the other side. There hard by the lodge walked he, carrying this unquiet contention about him. But passion ere long had gotten the absolute masterhood, bringing with it the show of present pleasure, fortified with the authority of a prince whose power might easily satisfy his will against the far-fet (though true) reasons of the spirit— which, in a man not trained in the way of virtue, have but slender working. So that ere long he utterly gave himself over to the longing desire to enjoy Cleophila, which finding an old broken vessel of him, had the more power in him than, perchance, it would have had in a younger man. And so, as all vice is foolish, it wrought in him the more absurd follies. But thus, as I say, in a number of intermixed imaginations, he stayed solitary by the lodge, waiting for the return of his company from the pastorals, some good space of time, till he was suddenly stirred out of his deep muses by the hasty and fearful running unto him of most part of the shepherds who came flying from the pastoral sports, crying to one another to stay and save the duchess and young ladies. But even whilst they cried so they ran away as fast as they could; so that the one tumbled over the other, each one showing he would be glad his fellow should do valiantly, but his own heart served him not. The duke, amazed to see such extreme shows of fear, asked the matter of them. But fear had so possessed their inward parts that their breath would not serve to tell it him, but after such a broken manner that I think it best not to trouble you, fair ladies, with their panting speeches; but to make a full declaration of it myself. And thus it was: Gynecia, with her two daughters, Cleophila, the shepherds Dorus and Dametas, being parted from

the duke whom they left solitary at the lodge, came into the fair
meadow appointed for their shepherdish pastimes. It was, indeed, a
place of great delight, for through the midst of it there ran a sweet
brook which did both hold the eye open with her beautiful streams
5 and close the eye with the sweet purling noise it made upon the
pebble-stones it ran over; the meadow itself yielding so liberally
all sorts of flowers that it seemed to nourish a contention betwixt the
colour and the smell whether in his kind were the more delightful.
Round about the meadow, as if it had been to enclose a theatre, grew
10 all such sorts of trees as either excellency of fruit, stateliness of
growth, continual greenness, or poetical fancies have made at any
time famous. In most part of which trees there had been framed by
art such pleasant arbours that it became a gallery aloft, from one
tree to the other, almost round about, which below yielded a per-
15 fect shadow, in those hot countries counted a great pleasure.

In this place, under one of the trees, the ladies sat down, inquiring
many questions of young Dorus (now newly perceived of them),
whilst the other shepherds made them ready to the pastimes. Dorus,
keeping his eye still upon the princess Pamela, answered with such a
20 trembling voice and abashed countenance, and oftentimes so far
from the matter, that it was some sport to the ladies, thinking it had
been want of education which made him so discountenanced with
unwonted presence. But Cleophila (that saw in him the glass of
her own misery), taking the fair hand of Philoclea, and with more
25 than womanish ardency kissing it, began to say these words: 'O love,
since thou art so changeable in men's estates, how art thou so con-
stant in their torments?'—when suddenly there came out of the
wood a monstrous lion, with a she-bear of little less fierceness, which,
having been hunted in forests far off, had by chance come to this
30 place where such beasts had never before been seen. Which, when
the shepherds saw, like silly wretches that think all evil is ever next
themselves, ran away in such sort as I told you till they came to the
duke's presence. There might one have seen at one instant all sorts

4 her] their Da, Hm.   5 the sweet] her sweet Bo, Ph; a sweet Je.   6 pebble
Bo, Cl, Da, Je, Hm: pymple St; pyple As, Ph; pibble 90.   7 sorts Bo, Cl, Je:
sort St, As, Da; kind Ph; manner Hm.   contention Bo, Cl, As, Da, Ph, Je,
Hm: contentation St (contentation *corr. to* contention Da).   betwixt] between Bo, As.
8 were the more] were more As, Je, Hm.   10 sorts As, Da: sort St, Bo, Cl,
Ph, Je, Hm.   14 the other] another As, Ph, Hm.   16 the trees] these trees
Cl, Je.   18 pastimes] pastimes *corr. to* pastorals Cl; pastorals As.   21 to the
ladies] for the ladies Je, 13.   28 wood] woods As, Je.   31 is ever next] is
next Ph, Je.

of passions lively painted out in the young lovers' faces—an extremity of love shining in their eyes; fear for their mistresses; assured hope in their own virtue; anger against the beasts; joy that occasion employed their service; sorrow to see their ladies in agony. For, indeed, the sweet Philoclea no sooner espied the ravenous lion but 5 that, opening her arms, she fell so right upon the breast of Cleophila, sitting by her, that their faces at unawares closed together, which so transported all whatsoever Cleophila was that she gave leisure to the lion to come very near them before she rid herself from the dear arms of Philoclea. But necessity, the only overruler of affections, did 10 force her then gently to unfold herself from those sweet embracements; and so drawing her sword, waited the present assault of the lion who, seeing Philoclea fly away, suddenly turned after her. For, as soon as she had risen up with Cleophila, she ran as fast as her delicate legs would carry her towards the lodge after the fugitive 15 shepherds. But Cleophila, seeing how greedily the lion went after the prey she herself so much desired, it seemed all her spirits were kindled with an unwonted fire; so that, equalling the lion in swiftness, she overtook him as he was ready to have seized himself of his beautiful chase, and disdainfully saying 'are you become my com- 20 petitor?'—strake him so great a blow upon the shoulder that she almost cleaved him asunder. Yet the valiant beast turned withal so far upon the weapon, that with his paw he did hurt a little the left shoulder of Cleophila; and mortal it would have been had not the death wound Cleophila, with a new thrust, gave unto him taken away 25 the effect of his force. But therewithal he fell down, and gave Cleophila leisure to take off his head to carry it for a present to her lady Philoclea, who all this while, not knowing what was done behind her, kept on her course, as Arethusa when she ran from Alpheus, her light nymphlike apparel being carried up with the wind, that much 30 of those beauties she would at another time have willingly hidden were presented to the eye of the twice-wounded Cleophila; which made Cleophila not follow her over hastily lest she should too soon deprive

5 espied] spied, Bo, Da, Ph, Je, Hm.   15 would] could Je, Hm, 90.   20 and disdainfully] and so disdainfully As, Je.   21–2 strake . . . asunder] thrust the lion through the breast far into the body Cl, As, Da; thrust the lion far into the body through the breast Ph; thrust the lion through the breast far into the breast Je, Hm.   22 turned] came Cl, As, Da, Ph, Je, Hm.   23 did hurt a little] gave a sore wound to Cl, As, Ph, Je, Hm; gave a shrewd wound to Da.   25 Cleophila . . . unto him] he received already Cl, As, Da, Ph, Je, Hm.   26 the effect] the greatest effect Cl, As, Da, Ph, Hm.   31 have willingly hidden] willingly have hidden Bo; have hidden Je, Hm.

herself of that pleasure. But, carrying the lion's head in her hand, did not fully overtake her till they came both into the presence of Basilius, at that time examining the shepherds of what was passed, and preparing himself to come to their succour. Neither were they
5 long there but that Gynecia came to them; whose look had all this while been upon the combat, eyeing so fixedly Cleophila's manner of fighting that no fear did prevail over her but, as soon as Cleophila had cut off his head, and ran after Philoclea, she could not find in her heart but to run likewise after Cleophila. So that it was a new
10 sight fortune had prepared to those woods, to see these three great personages thus run one after the other, each carried away with the violence of an inward evil: the sweet Philoclea, with such fear that she thought she was still in the lion's mouth; Cleophila, with a painful delight she had to see without hope of enjoying; Gynecia,
15 not so much with the love she bare to her best beloved daughter as with a new wonderful passionate love had possessed her heart of the goodly Cleophila. For so the truth is that, at the first sight she had of Cleophila, her heart gave her she was a man thus for some strange cause disguised, which now this combat did in effect assure her of,
20 because she measured the possibility of all women's hearts out of her own. And this doubt framed in her a desire to know, and desire to know brought forth shortly such longing to enjoy that it reduced her whole mind to an extreme and unfortunate slavery—pitifully, truly, considering her beauty and estate; but for a perfect mark of
25 the triumph of love who could in one moment overthrow the heart of a wise lady, so that neither honour long maintained, nor love of husband and children, could withstand it. But of that you shall after hear; for now, they being come before the duke, and the fair Philoclea scarcely then stayed from her fear, Cleophila, kneeling down,
30 presented the head of the lion unto her with these words: 'Only lady,' said she, 'here see you the punishment of that unnatural beast which, contrary to his own kind, would have wronged prince's blood; neither were his eyes vanquished with the duty all eyes bear to your beauty.'

2 into Bo, Cl, As, Je, Hm: in St, Da; to Ph, 90.   3 shepherds of what] shepherds of that which Bo; shepherds of that Ph; shepherds what Je, Hm.   6 combat OA: accombat St.   9 but to run likewise after] but run likewise after Da, Ph; but to run after Je; but run after 90.   11 run one] run the one Ph, Hm. 12 with OA: in St.   13 thought she was still] thought still she was As, Je, Hm.   27-8 shall after hear] shall hereafter hear Ph; shall hear hereafter Je. 31 that] the As, Je.

'Happy am I and my beauty both', answered the fair Philoclea (the blood coming again to her cheeks, pale before for fear), 'that you, excellent Amazon, were there to teach him good manners.'

'And even thank that beauty,' said Cleophila, 'which forceth all noble swords to be ready to serve it.'   5

Having finished these words, the lady Philoclea perceived the blood that ran abundantly down upon Cleophila's shoulder; so that starting aside, with a countenance full of sweet pity, 'Alas,' said she, 'now perceive I my good hap is waited on with great misfortune, since my safety is wrought with the danger of a much more worthy   10 person.'

'Noble lady,' answered she, 'if your inward eyes could discern the wounds of my soul, you should have a plentifuller cause to exercise your compassion.'

But it was sport to see how in one instant both Basilius and Gynecia   15 (like a father and mother to a beloved child) came running to see the wound of Cleophila; into what rages Basilius grew, and what tears Gynecia spent—for so it seemed that love had purposed to make in those solitary woods a perfect demonstration of his unresistible force, to show that no desert place can avoid his dart. He must fly   20 from himself that will shun his evil. But so wonderful and in effect incredible was the passion which reigned as well in Gynecia as Basilius (and all for the poor Cleophila, dedicated another way) that it seems to myself I use not words enough to make you see how they could in one moment be so overtaken. But you, worthy ladies, that   25 have at any time feelingly known what it means, will easily believe the possibility of it. Let the ignorant sort of people give credit to them that have passed the doleful passage, and daily find that quickly is the infection gotten which in long time is hardly cured. Basilius sometimes would kiss her forehead, blessing the destinies   30 that had joined such beauty and valour together. Gynecia would kiss her more boldly, by the liberty of her womanish show, although her heart were set of nothing less; for already was she fallen into a jealous envy against her daughter Philoclea, because she found Cleophila showed such extraordinary dutiful favour unto her; and   35 even that settled her opinion the more of her manhood. And this doubtful jealousy served as a bellows to kindle the violent coals of

2 to her] into her As, Ph.   18 for so it] for it Cl, Da.   30 sometimes would]
would sometimes Ph, Je, Hm.   35 dutiful favour unto] dutifulness unto As, Hm;
duty to Je.

her passion. But as the over kind nurse may sometimes with kissing forget to give the child suck so had they, with too much kindness, unkindly forgotten the wound of Cleophila, had not Philoclea, whose heart had not yet gone beyond the limits of a right goodwill, advised
5 herself, and desired her mother to help her to dress the wound of Cleophila. For both those great ladies were excellently seen in that part of surgery—an art in that age greatly esteemed because it served as a minister to virtuous courage, which in those worthy days was even by ladies more beloved than any outward beauty. So to the
10 great comfort of Cleophila, more to feel the delicate hands of Philoclea than for the care she had of her wound, these two ladies had quickly dressed it, applying so precious a balm as all the heat and pain was presently assuaged, with apparent hope of soon amendment. In which doing, I know not whether Gynecia took some greater
15 conjectures of Cleophila's sex. But even then, and not before, did Cleophila remember herself of her dear friend Musidorus; for having only had care of the excellent Philoclea, she never missed neither her friend nor the princess Pamela—not so much to be marvelled at in her, since both the duke and duchess had forgotten their daughter,
20 so were all their thoughts plunged in one place. Besides Cleophila had not seen any danger was like to fall unto him, for her eye had been still fixed upon Philoclea, and that made her the more careless. But now, with a kind of rising in her heart, lest some evil should be fallen to her chosen friend, she hastily asked what was become of the
25 princess Pamela, with the two shepherds, Dametas and Dorus. And then the duke and Gynecia remembered their forgetfulness, and with great astonishment made like inquiry for her. But of all the company of the shepherds (so had the lion's sight put them from themselves), there was but one could say anything of her; and all he said was
30 this: that as he ran away he might perceive a great bear run directly towards her. Cleophila (whose courage was always ready without deliberation) took up the sword lying by her, with mind to bestow her life for the succour or revenge of her Musidorus and the gracious Pamela. But as she had run two or three steps, they might all see

7 surgery] chirurgery Je, 98, 13.   9 So to] So that to Cl, As; So that Ph, Hm.
11 her] the As, Je, Hm.   13 presently] om. Cl, As.   soon] some Bo, Cl, Da,
Je.   14 greater] great As, Je.   15–16 did Cleophila remember] Cleophila remem-
bered Ph; Cleophila remembers Je, Hm.   17 never missed neither] neither missed
Cl, Hm.   22 been still] still been Cl, As, Je.   23–4 be fallen to] befall unto Cl,
Da, Hm.   27 for her] of her Ph; after her Je.   29 one could] one that could Cl, Da.
32–4 with . . . Pamela OA: om. St, Bo.   34 had run] had gone Ph, Hm; was gone Je.

Pamela coming betwixt Dametas and Dorus, Pamela having in her
hand the paw of the bear which the shepherd Dorus had newly
presented unto her, desiring her to keep it, as of such a beast which,
though she was to be punished for her over great cruelty, yet was her
wit to be esteemed, since she could make so sweet a choice. Dametas 5
for his part came piping and dancing, the merriest man of a parish;
but when he came so near as he might be heard of the duke, he sang
this song for joy of their success:

> Now thanked be the great god Pan
> That thus preserves my loved life: 10
> Thanked be I that keep a man
> Who ended hath this fearful strife:
> > So if my man must praises have,
> > What then must I that keep the knave?
>
> For as the moon the eye doth please 15
> With gentle beams not hurting sight,
> Yet hath sir sun the greatest praise,
> Because from him doth come her light:
> > So if my man must praises have,
> > What then must I that keep the knave? 20

It were a very superfluous thing to tell you how glad each party
was of the happy returning from these dangers, and doubt you not,
fair ladies, there wanted no questioning how things had passed; but
because I will have the thanks myself, it shall be I you shall hear
it of. And thus the ancient records of Arcadia say it fell out: the 25
lion's presence had no sooner driven away the heartless shepherds,
and followed, as I told you, the excellent Philoclea, but that there
came out of the same woods a monstrous she-bear which, fearing to
deal with the lion's prey, came furiously towards the princess Pamela
who, whether it were she had heard that such was the best refuge 30
against that beast, or that fear (as it fell out most likely) brought
forth the effects of wisdom, she no sooner saw the bear coming
towards her but she fell down flat upon her face. Which when the
prince Musidorus saw (whom, because such was his pleasure, I am
bold to call the shepherd Dorus), with a true resolved magnanimity, 35

7 near as he] near he Da; near that he Hm.   9–20 Le *omits this poem; it is in* Cm,
90, 93.   10 That] Which 90.   11 keep OA, 90: keeps St, As.   12 fearful]
bloody Cm, 93.   13 So] For 90.   14 keep OA, 90: keeps St.   15 eye]
eyes 90 (*corr.* 93).   22 these] those Cl, As, Je; the Hm.   27 but that there OA:
but there St.   32 effects] effect Je, 90.

although he had no other weapon but a great shepherd's knife, he leaped before the head of his dear lady, and saying these words unto her, 'Receive here the sacrifice of that heart which is only vowed to your service', attended with a quiet courage the coming of the bear
5 which, according to the manner of that beast's fight, especially against a man that resists them, rase up upon her hinder feet, so to take him in her ugly paws. But, as she was ready to give him a mortal embracement, the shepherd Dorus, with a lusty strength and good fortune, thrust his knife so right into the heart of the beast that
10 she fell down dead without ever being able to touch him. Which being done, he turned to his lady Pamela (at that time in a swoon with extremity of fear), and softly taking her in his arms, he took the advantage to kiss and re-kiss her a hundred times, with such exceeding delight that he would often after say he thought the joy
15 would have carried his life from him, had not the grief he conceived to see her in such case something diminished it. But long in that delightful agony he was not; for the lady Pamela, being come out of her swoon, opened her fair eyes, and seeing herself in the hands of this new-come shepherd, with great disdain put him from her. But
20 when she saw the ugly bear lying hard by her, starting aside (for fear gave not reason leave to determine whether it were dead or no), she forgot her anger, and cried to Dorus to help her. Wherefore he, cutting off the forepaw of the bear, and showing unto her the bloody knife, told her she might well by this perceive that there was no
25 heart so base, nor weapon so feeble, but that the force of her beauty was well able to enable them for the performance of great matters. She, inquiring the manner, and whether himself were hurt, gave him great thanks for his pains, with promise of reward. But being ashamed to find herself so alone with this young shepherd, looked
30 round about if she could see anybody; and at length they both perceived the gentle Dametas, lying with his head and breast as far as he could thrust himself into a bush, drawing up his legs as close unto him as he could. For, indeed, as soon as he saw the bear coming towards him (like a man that was very apt to take pity of himself), he
35 ran headlong into this bush, with full resolution that, at the worst

4 attended] attending Cl, As, Je, Hm.   6 resists] resisteth Da, Hm.   rase] rose Cl; rise As; raised Da.   10 without ever being] without being Ph, Je.
11 at that Cl, As, Da, Ph, Je, Hm: that St, Bo.   19 this] the As, Hm.   25 of her beauty] of beauty As, Ph.   27 manner, and whether Cl, As, Da, Ph: manner, whether St, Bo, Je, Hm.   34 him] them Cl, As, Da, Ph, Je, Hm.   35 this OA: the St.

hand, he would not see his own death. And when Dorus pushed him, bidding him be of good courage, it was a great while before they could persuade him that Dorus was not the bear; so that he was fain to pull him out by the heels, and show him her as dead as he could wish her—which, you may believe me, was a very joyful sight unto him. And yet, like a man of a revengeful spirit, he gave the dead body many a wound, swearing by much it was pity such beasts should be suffered in a commonwealth. And then, with as immoderate joy as before with fear (for his heart was framed never to be without a passion), he went by his fair charge, dancing, piping, and singing; till they all came to the presence of the careful company, as before I told you. Thus now this little, but noble, company united again together, the first thing was done was the yielding of great thanks and praises of all sides to the virtuous Cleophila. The duke told with what a gallant grace she ran after Philoclea with the lion's head in her hand, like another Pallas with the spoils of Gorgon. Gynecia sware she saw the very face of young Hercules killing the Nemean lion; and all, with a grateful assent, confirmed the same praises. Only poor Dorus, though of equal desert, yet not proceeding from equal estate, should have been left forgotten, had not Cleophila (partly to put by the occasion of her own excessive praises, but principally for the true remembrance she had of her professed friend), with great admiration, spoken of his hazardous act, asking afresh (as if she had never before known him) what he was, and whether he had haunted that place before, protesting that, upon her conscience, she could not think but that he came of some very noble blood—so noble a countenance he bare, and so worthy an act he had performed. This Basilius took (as the lover's heart is apt to receive all sudden sorts of impression) as though his mistress had given him a secret reprehension that he had not showed more gratefulness to the valiant Dorus. And therefore, as nimbly as he could, began forthwith to inquire of his estate, adding promise of great rewards— among the rest offering to him that, if he would exercise his valour in soldiery, he would commit some charge unto him under Philanax, governor of his frontiers. But Dorus, whose ambition stretched a quite other way, having first answered (touching his estate) that he

2 courage] comfort As; cheer 90.   before they OA: before that they St.   5 believe me, was] believe, was Cl, As.   23 admiration, spoken of] admiration of As, Je. 24 she] he Cl, As.   29 impression] impressions Da, Je.   33 offering to him] offering him Cl, Ph.

was brother to the shepherd Menalcas whom the duke had well known, and excused his going to soldiery by the unaptness he found in himself that way, told the duke that his brother, in his last testament, had commanded him to dedicate his service to Dametas; and
5 therefore, as well for due obedience thereto as for the satisfaction of his own mind (which was wholly set upon pastoral affairs), he would think his service greatly rewarded if he might obtain by that means to live in the sight of the duke more than the rest of his fellows, and yet practise that his chosen vocation. The duke, liking well of his
10 modest manner, charged Dametas to receive him like a son in his house, telling him, because of his tried valour, he would have him be as a guard to his daughter Pamela, to whom likewise he recommended him, sticking not to say such men were to be cherished since she was in danger of some secret misadventure.
15   All this while Pamela said little of him, and even as little did Philoclea of Cleophila; although everybody else filled their mouths with their praises. Whereof seeking the cause that they which were most bound said least, I note this to myself, fair ladies, that even at this time they did begin to find they themselves could not tell what
20 kind of inclination towards them; whereof feeling a secret accusation in themselves, and in their simplicity not able to warrant it, closed up all such motion in secret, without daring scarcely to breathe out the names of them who already began to breed unwonted war in their spirits. For, indeed, fortune had framed a very stage-play of
25 love among these few folks, making the old age of Basilius, the virtue of Gynecia, and the simplicity of Philoclea, all affected to one; but by a three-headed kind of passion: Basilius assuring himself she was, as she pretended, a young lady, but greatly despairing for his own unworthiness's sake; Gynecia hoping her judgement to be right of his
30 disguising, but therein fearing a greater sore if already his heart were pledged to her daughter. But sweet Philoclea grew shortly after of all other into worst terms; for taking her to be such as she professed, desire she did, but she knew not what; and she longed to obtain that whereof she herself could not imagine the mean, but full of unquiet
35 imaginations rested only unhappy because she knew not her good hap. Cleophila hath (I think) said enough for herself to make you

3 in his last Cl, As, Da, Je, 90: in last St, Bo, Ph, Hm.   5 for due] for the due Cl, Da.   thereto] thereunto Hm, 90.   10 in his] into his As, Je, Hm, 90. 15 as little did] as little as did Ph, Je.   29 his] om. As; her Je, Hm.   30 already his heart Bo, As, Da, Ph, Je, Hm: his heart already St; his heart Cl.   34 mean] name Cl; means Je.

know, fair ladies, that she was not a little enchanted; and as for
Dorus, a shepherd's apparel upon a duke of Thessalia will answer
for him. Pamela was the only lady that would needs make open war
upon herself, and obtain the victory; for, indeed, even now find she
did a certain working of a new-come inclination to Dorus. But when 5
she found perfectly in herself whither it must draw her, she did
overmaster it with the consideration of his meanness. But how
therein Dorus sought to satisfy her you shall after hear; for now the
day being closed up in darkness the duke would fain have had
Cleophila gone to rest, because of her late-received wound. But she 10
(that found no better salve than Philoclea's presence) desired first that
by torchlight they might see some of the pastorals the lion's coming
had disordered. Which accordingly was done; whereof I will repeat
you a few to ease you, fair ladies, of the tediousness of this long
discourse.   15

Here ends the first book or act.

4-5 find she did] did she find Ph; found she Je.   16 Here . . . act] The End As;
Here endeth . . . act Ph, Je.

HERE BEGINS THE FIRST ECLOGUES

THE manner of the Arcadian shepherds was, when they met to-
gether, to pass their time, either in such music as their rural education
could afford them, or in exercise of their body and trying of
5 masteries. But, of all other things, they did especially delight in
eclogues; wherein sometimes they would contend for a prize of well
singing, sometimes lament the unhappy pursuit of their affections,
sometimes, again, under hidden forms utter such matters as other-
wise were not fit for their delivery. Neither is it to be marvelled that
10 they did so much excel other nations in that quality since, from their
childhood, they were brought up unto it, and were not such base
shepherds as we commonly make account of, but the very owners of
the sheep themselves, which in that thrifty world the substantiallest
men would employ their whole care upon. And when they had prac-
15 tised the goodness of their wit in such sports, then was it their
manner ever to have one who should write up the substance of that
they said; whose pen, having more leisure than their tongues, might
perchance polish a little the rudeness of an unthought-on song. But
the peace wherein they did so notably flourish, and especially the
20 sweet enjoying of their peace to so pleasant uses, drew divers
strangers, as well of great as of mean houses, especially such whom
inward melancholies made weary of the world's eyes, to come and
live among them, applying themselves to their trade: which likewise
was many times occasion to beautify more than otherwise it would
25 have been this pastoral exercise. But nothing lifted it up to so high
a key as the presence of their own duke who, not only by looking on
but by great courtesy and liberality, animated the shepherds the
more exquisitely to seek a worthy accomplishment of his good
liking, as this time after the valiant killing of the beasts by the
30 two disguised princes performed. The duke (because Cleophila
so would have it) used the artificial day of torches to lighten the
sports their inventions could minister. And yet, because many more
shepherds were newly come than at the first were, he did, with a

1 BEGINS] BEGINNETH Bo, Ph, Je.   4 could afford] would afford Je (would
corr. to could Cl); have found Ph.   15 wit] wits Cl, Je, Hm.   21 as of mean]
as mean Bo, As, Da, Ph.   29 as this time] at this time Ph; as at this time Je.
32, inventions] invention Bo Je.

gentle manner, chastise the cowardice of the fugitive shepherds
with making them for that night the torch bearers; and the others
later come, he willed, with all freedom of speech and behaviour, to
keep their accustomed method; which they prepared themselves to
do, while he sat himself down, having on the one side the duchess, 5
but of his heart side the fair Cleophila. To whom speaking in looks
(for as yet his tongue was not come to a thorough boldness), he
sought to send the first ambassade of his passions—little marked of
Cleophila whose eyes seemed to have changed sight with Philoclea's
eyes (whom Gynecia had of purpose placed by herself), so attentive 10
looks were mutually fixed between them, to the greatest corrosive
to Gynecia that can be imagined, whose love-open sight did more
and more pierce into the knowledge of Cleophila's counterfeiting,
which likewise more and more fortified her unlawful desires; yet
with so great and violent a combat with herself as the suppression 15
of a long-used virtue comes to. But another place shall serve to
manifest her agonies; this, being dedicated only to pastorals, shall
bend itself that way, and leave all those princely motions to their
considerations that, untold, can guess what love means—whereof
the princess Pamela, that sat next to Cleophila, was most free, 20
having in her mind used Dorus's baseness as a shield against his
worthiness. But they being set in order, Dametas, who much dis-
dained (since his late authority) all his old companions, brought his
servant Dorus in good acquaintance and allowance of them; and
himself stood like a director over them, with nodding, gaping, 25
winking or stamping, showing how he did like or mislike those things
he did not understand. The first sports the shepherds showed were
full of such leaps and gambols as (being accorded to the pipe which
they bare in their mouths even as they danced) made a right picture
of their chief god Pan and his companions, the satyrs. Then would 30
they cast away their pipes and, holding hand in hand, dance as it
were in a brawl by the only cadence of their voices, which they
would use in singing some short couplets; whereto the one half
beginning, the other half answered; as, the one half saying:

We love, and have our loves rewarded. 35

2 others] other As, Ph, Je, Hm.   6 of his heart] on his heart Bo, Ph; at his
other Je, Hm.   8 ambassade] heraldry Da, Hm; herald Je (6–9 To whom . . .
Cleophila *om.* Cl; 8 send . . . ambassade *blank left* Ph).   11 between] betwixt As,
Je.   corrosive] corosy Cl; corsie Ph, Je, Hm (corsie *corr. to* corrosive St).   15 a
combat OA: accombat St.   18 itself that OA: itself to that St.   30 their
chief god] their god As, Je.   35–p. 58, 14 Le *omits this poem; it is in* 90–93.

The others would answer:

    We love, and are no whit regarded.

The first again:

    We find most sweet affection's snare.

5 With like tune, it should be (as in a choir) sent back again:

    That sweet, but sour despairful care.

A third time likewise thus:

    Who can despair whom hope doth bear?

The answer:

10   And who can hope who feels despair?

Then, all joining their voices, and dancing a faster measure, they
would conclude with some such words:

    As without breath no pipe doth move,
    No music kindly without love.

15 Having thus varied both their songs and dances into diverse sorts
of inventions, their last sport was one of them to provoke another
to a more large expressing of his passions: which Lalus, a shepherd
accounted one of the best singers among them, having marked in
Dorus's dancing no less good grace and handsome behaviour than
20 extreme tokens of a troubled mind, he began first with his pipe,
and then with his voice, thus to challenge Dorus; and was by him
answered in the underwritten sort:

Lalus. Come, Dorus, come, let songs thy sorrows signify;
    And if, for want of use, thy mind ashamed is,
25   That very shame with love's high title dignify.
    No style is held for base where love well named is:
    Each ear sucks up the words a true love scattereth,
    And plain speech oft than quaint phrase better framed is.

Dorus. Nightingales seldom sing, the pie still chattereth;
30   The wood cries most before it throughly kindled be;
    Deadly wounds inward bleed, each slight sore mattereth;
    Hardly they herd which by good hunters singled be;
    Shallow brooks murmur most, deep silent slide away,
    Nor true love loves his loves with others mingled be.

5 tune] time Cl, As.   in a choir] in choir St, As, 90 (*only*).   10 who feels]
that feels Ph, Je, 90 (As *omits line*). 23–p. 64, 4 As *omits this poem; it is in* 90, 93.
23 *Lalus*] Thyrsis 93 (*and throughout poem*).   25 high OA, 90: by St.
30 throughly] thorough Le; *om.* Ph, Je.   34 his] those 90 (*only*). others] other Le, Je.

Lalus. If thou wilt not be seen, thy face go hide away,
 Be none of us, or else maintain our fashion:
 Who frowns at others' feasts doth better bide away.
But if thou hast a love, in that love's passion,
 I challenge thee, by show of her perfection,   5
 Which of us two deserveth most compassion.

Dorus. Thy challenge great, but greater my protection:
 Sing, then, and see (for now thou hast inflamed me)
 Thy health too mean a match for my infection.
No, though the heav'ns for high attempt have blamed me,   10
 Yet high is my attempt. O muse, historify
 Her praise, whose praise to learn your skill hath framed me.

Lalus. Muse, hold your peace! But thou, my god Pan, glorify
 My Kala's gifts, who with all good gifts filled is.
 Thy pipe, O Pan, shall help, though I sing sorrily.   15
A heap of sweets she is, where nothing spilled is,
 Who, though she be no bee, yet full of honey is:
 A lily field, with plough of rose, which tilled is.
Mild as a lamb, more dainty than a cony is:
 Her eyes my eyesight is, her conversation   20
 More glad to me than to a miser money is.
What coy account she makes of estimation!
 How nice to touch, how all her speeches peised be!
 A nymph thus turned, but mended in translation.

Dorus. Such Kala is; but ah, my fancies raised be   25
 In one whose name to name were high presumption,
 Since virtues all, to make her title, pleased be.
O happy gods, which by inward assumption
 Enjoy her soul, in body's fair possession,
 And keep it joined, fearing your seat's consumption.   30
How oft with rain of tears skies make confession
 Their dwellers rapt with sight of her perfection,
 From heav'nly throne to her heav'n use digression.
Of best things then what world can yield confection
 To liken her? Deck yours with your comparison: 35
 She is herself of best things the collection.

10 attempt] attempts 90.   11 my] mine Cl, Le, Je, Hm.   13 god Bo, Cl, Le, Ph,
Je, 90: good St, Da, Hm.   14 is] *om.* 93.   18 lily] little Cl, Le, Ph; silly Hm.
33 heav'n Bo, Cl, Le, Da, Ph, 90: heaunt St; heav'ns Je, Hm.

Lalus. How oft my doleful sire cried to me, 'tarry son',
    When first he spied my love? How oft he said to me,
    'Thou art no soldier fit for Cupid's garrison.
  My son, keep this that my long toil hath laid to me:
5   Love well thine own; methinks, wool's whiteness passeth all:
    I never found long love such wealth hath paid to me.'
  This wind he spent; but when my Kala glasseth all
    My sight in her fair limbs, I then assure myself,
    Not rotten sheep, but high crowns she surpasseth all.
10 Can I be poor, that her gold hair procure myself?
    Want I white wool, whose eyes her white skin garnished?
    Till I get her, shall I to keep inure myself?

Dorus. How oft, when reason saw love of her harnished
    With armour of my heart, he cried, 'O vanity,
15   To set a pearl in steel so meanly varnished!
  Look to thyself; reach not beyond humanity;
    Her mind, beams, state, far from thy weak wings banished;
    And love which lover hurts is inhumanity.'
  Thus reason said: but she came, reason vanished;
20   Her eyes so mast'ring me that such objection
    Seemed but to spoil the food of thoughts long famished.
  Her peerless height my mind to high erection
    Draws up; and if, hope failing, end life's pleasure,
    Of fairer death how can I make election?

25 *Lalus.* Once my well-waiting eyes espied my treasure,
    With sleeves turned up, loose hair, and breasts enlarged,
    Her father's corn (moving her fair limbs) measure.
  'O', cried I, 'of so mean work be discharged:
    Measure my case, how by thy beauty's filling
30   With seed of woes my heart brim-full is charged.
  Thy father bids thee save, and chides for spilling.
    Save then my soul, spill not my thoughts well heaped,
    No lovely praise was ever got with killing.'
  These bold words she did hear, this fruit I reaped,
35   That she, whose look alone might make me blessed,
    Did smile on me, and then away she leaped.

---

11 garnished] garnisheth Le, Ph, Je, Hm.   21 thoughts] thought Cl, Je.
26 breasts] breast Je, Hm, 90.   27 moving] mowing Le, Ph.   fair] fairs Cl, Da.
33 with] by Cl, Le, 90.   34 did hear] hard Ph; did bear 93.

Dorus. Once, O sweet once, I saw, with dread oppressed,
    Her whom I dread; so that with prostrate lying
    Her length the earth in love's chief clothing dressed.
I saw that richess fall, and fell a-crying:
    'Let not dead earth enjoy so dear a cover,   5
    But deck therewith my soul for your sake dying.
Lay all your fear upon your fearful lover:
    Shine eyes on me, that both our lives be guarded;
    So I your sight, you shall yourselves recover.'
I cried, and was with open rays rewarded;   10
    But straight they fled, summoned by cruel honour,
    Honour, the cause desert is not regarded.

Lalus. This maid, thus made for joys, O Pan, bemoan her,
    That without love she spends her years of love:
    So fair a field would well become an owner.   15
And if enchantment can a hard heart move,
    Teach me what circle may acquaint her sprite,
    Affection's charms in my behalf to prove.
The circle is my round-about-her sight:
    The power I will invoke dwells in her eyes: 20
    My charm should be she haunt me day and night.

Dorus. Far other care, O muse, my sorrow tries,
    Bent to such one, in whom, myself must say,
    Nothing can mend one point that in her lies.
What circle, then, in so rare force bears sway?   25
    Whose sprite all sprites can spoil, raise, damn, or save:
    No charm holds her, but well possess she may;
Possess she doth, and makes my soul her slave:
    My eyes the bands, my thoughts the fatal knot.
    No thralls like them that inward bondage have.   30

Lalus. Kala, at length, conclude my ling'ring lot:
    Disdain me not, although I be not fair.
    Who is an heir of many hundred sheep
Doth beauties keep, which never sun can burn,
    Nor storms do turn: fairness serves oft to wealth.   35

4 richess] richest Bo, Je, Hm.   5 dear] rich Le; fair Ph, Je, Hm.   10 open
Cl, Le, Ph, Je, Hm, 90: opened St, Bo, Da.   22 care] case Cl, Le, 93.
24 one] that 90 (*corr.* 98).   26 spoil] foil 93.   damn] down Le, Da.
30 thralls] thrall Je, Hm, 93.   34 never] neither Bo, Le, Da, Ph, Hm.

Yet all my health I place in your goodwill:
Which if you will (O do) bestow on me,
Such as you see, such still you shall me find:
Constant and kind. My sheep your food shall breed,
5   Their wool your weed: I will you music yield
In flow'ry field; and as the day begins
With twenty gins we will the small birds take,
And pastimes make, as nature things hath made.
But when in shade we meet of myrtle boughs,
10   Then love allows, our pleasures to enrich,
The thought of which doth pass all worldly pelf.

Dorus. Lady yourself, whom neither name I dare,
And titles are but spots to such a worth,
Hear plaints come forth from dungeon of my mind:
15   The noblest kind rejects not others' woes.
I have no shows of wealth: my wealth is you,
My beauty's hue your beams, my health your deeds;
My mind for weeds your virtue's liv'ry wears.
My food is tears; my tunes waymenting yield;
20   Despair my field; the flowers spirit's wars;
My day new cares; my gins my daily sight,
In which do light small birds of thoughts o'erthrown.
My pastimes none; time passeth on my fall.
Nature made all, but me of dolours made.
25   I find no shade, but where my sun doth burn;
No place to turn; without, within, it fries;
Nor help by life or death who living dies.

Lalus. But if my Kala this my suit denies,
Which so much reason bears,
30   Let crows pick out mine eyes which too much saw.
If she still hate love's law,
My earthy mould doth melt in wat'ry tears.

Dorus. My earthy mould doth melt in wat'ry tears,

11 doth] do Da, Hm.   14 Hear] Her Cl, Da, Ph.   18 virtue's] virtuous Cl, Ph, Je.
21 day] days Da, Je, Hm.   22 do light] I do delight Ph; delight Je, Hm.
28 this] thus 93.   30 mine] my Bo, Le.   30-1 90 (*only*):
                    Let crows pick out mine eyes, which saw too much:
                    If still her mind be such.
32 earthy Cl, Le, Hm, 90: earthly St, Bo, Da, Ph, Je.   doth] will 90 (*only*).
33 earthy Cl, Le, Da, Hm, 90: earthly St, Bo, Ph, Je, Ra.   doth] do Cl, Le, Ph, Hm.
33-p. 63, 4 *These lines are in* Ra.

And they again resolve
To air of sighs, sighs to the heart's fire turn,
Which doth to ashes burn;
Thus doth my life within itself dissolve.

Lalus. Thus doth my life within itself dissolve,   5
    That I grow like the beast
    Which bears the bit a weaker force doth guide,
    Yet patient must abide;
    Such weight it hath which once is full possessed.

Dorus. Such weight it hath which once is full possessed   10
    That I become a vision,
    Which hath in other's head his only being
    And lives in fancy's seeing.
    O wretched state of man in self-division!

Lalus. O wretched state of man in self-division!   15
    O well thou say'st! A feeling declaration
    Thy tongue hath made of Cupid's deep incision.
    But now hoarse voice doth fail this occupation,
    And others long to tell their loves' condition:
    Of singing thou hast got the reputation.   20

Dorus. Of singing thou hast got the reputation
    Good Lalus mine; I yield to thy ability:
    My heart doth seek another estimation.

2 heart's] heart Le, Ph.   4 *om.* St, Bo.   Thus] So 90 (*only*).   5 Thus]
So 90 (*only*).   8 patient] patience Cl, Da, Ph, Hm.   12 fancy's] fancy Da, 93.
6–17 90 (*only*):
    That I am like a flower
    New plucked from the place where it did breed,
    Life showing, dead indeed:
    Such force hath love above poor nature's power.
Dorus. Such force hath love above poor nature's power
    That I grow like a shade,
    Which being naught seems somewhat to the eyen,
    While that one body shine.
    Oh he is marred that is for others made!
Lalus. Oh he is marred that is for others made!
    Which thought doth mar my piping declaration,
    Thinking how it hath marred my shepherd's trade.
18 But now] Now my 90 (*only*).   20 thou hast got] take to thee 90 (*only*).
21 thou hast got] take to thee 90 (*only*).   22 Good Lalus mine] New friend of mine
90; Good Thyrsis mine 93.   23 heart] soul 90.

But ah, my muse, I would thou hadst facility
   To work my goddess so by thy invention
   On me to cast those eyes, where shine nobility:
Seen and unknown; heard, but without attention.

5   The eclogue betwixt Lalus and Dorus of every one of the be-
holders received great commendations, saving only of the two grave
shepherds, Geron and Dicus, who both plainly protested it was pity
wit should be employed about so very a toy as that they called love
was—Geron thereto the more inclined, as that age, having taken
10 from him both the thoughts and fruits of that passion, wished all
the world proportioned to himself. But Dicus, whether for certain
mischances of his own, or out of a better judgement, which saw the
bottom of things, did more detest and hate love than the most
envious man doth in himself cherish and love hate. Which, as he
15 did at all times publicly profess, so now he came, as a man should
say, armed to show his malice; for in the one hand he bare a whip,
in the other a naked Cupid, such as we commonly set him forth.
But on his breast he ware a painted table, wherein he had given
Cupid a quite new form, making him sit upon a pair of gallows,
20 like a hangman, about which there was a rope very handsomely
provided; he himself painted all ragged and torn, so that his skin
was bare in most places, where a man might perceive all his body full
of eyes, his head horned with the horns of a bull, with long ears
accordingly, his face old and wrinkled, and his feet cloven. In his
25 right hand, he was painted holding a crown of laurel, in his left a
purse of money; and out of his mouth hung a lace which held the
pictures of a goodly man and an excellent fair woman. And with
such a countenance he was drawn as if he had persuaded every man
by those enticements to come and be hanged there. The duke
30 laughed when he saw Dicus come out in such manner, and asked him
what he meant by such transforming the gentle Cupid. But Dicus,
as if it had been no jesting matter, told him plainly that long they
had done the heavens wrong to make Cupid a god, and much more
to the fair Venus to call him her son—indeed, the bastard of false
35 Argus, who, having the charge of the deflowered Io (what time she
was a cow), had traitorously in that shape begot him of her; and that

1 facility] agility 90 (only.)   6 commendations] commendation Bo, Cl, Hm.
10 and fruits] and the fruits Cl, As, Da, Ph.   22 all his] his Cl, As, Da.
25 left a] left hand a Ph, Hm, 90.   30 such] that Ph, Je.   34 to the fair] to
fair As, Ph.

the naughtiness of men's lust had given him so high a title. Everyone
of the company (except old Geron) began to stamp with their feet,
and hiss at him, as thinking he had spoken an unpardonable blas-
phemy. But Geron, well backing him in it, Dicus boldly stepped
forth and, after having railed at the name of Cupid as spitefully as 5
he could devise, calling to Pan to help his song in revenge of his
losing the fair Syrinx, he thus, tuning his voice to a rebeck, sang
against him:

> Poor painters oft with silly poets join
> To fill the world with strange but vain conceits: 10
> One brings the stuff, the other stamps the coin,
> Which breeds naught else but glosses of deceits.
> > Thus painters Cupid paint, thus poets do,
> > A naked god, blind, young, with arrows two.
>
> Is he a god, that ever flies the light? 15
> Or naked he, disguised in all untruth?
> If he be blind, how hitteth he so right?
> Or is he young, that tamed old Phoebus' youth?
> > But arrows two, and tipped with gold or lead:
> > Some hurt, accuse a third with horny head. 20
>
> No, nothing so; an old false knave he is,
> By Argus got on Io, then a cow,
> What time for her Juno her Jove did miss,
> And charge of her to Argus did allow.
> > Mercury killed his false sire for this act, 25
> > His dam, a beast, was pardoned beastly fact.
>
> With father's death, and mother's guilty shame,
> With Jove's disdain at such a rival's seed,
> The wretch compelled, a runagate became,
> And learned what ill a miser state doth breed; 30
> > To lie, to steal, to pry, and to accuse,
> > Naught in himself, each other to abuse.
>
> Yet bears he still his parents' stately gifts,
> A horned head, cloven foot, and thousand eyes,

1–2 Everyone of the company] *om.* Cl, As.   9–p. 66, 22 As *omits this poem*; 90, 93
transfer to Book II.   14 blind, young] young, blind 90 (*only*).   18 Or] How
90.   30 miser] wretched Bo; miser's Le, Da, Je, Hm.   31 to steal, to pry,
and to] feign, gloss, to steal, pry, and 90 (*only*).   34 foot] feet Cl, Le, Da, Ph, 93.

Some gazing still, some winking wily shifts,
With long large ears where never rumour dies.
His horned head doth seem the heav'n to spite:
His cloven foot doth never tread aright.

5   Thus half a man, with man he easily haunts,
Clothed in the shape which soonest may deceive:
Thus half a beast, each beastly vice he plants
In those weak hearts that his advice receive.
    He prowls each place still in new colours decked,
10   Sucking one's ill, another to infect.

To narrow breasts he comes all wrapped in gain:
To swelling hearts he shines in honour's fire:
To open eyes all beauties he doth rain;
Creeping to each with flatt'ring of desire.
15   But for that love is worst which rules the eyes,
    Thereon his name, there his chief triumph lies.

Millions of years this old drivel Cupid lives;
While still more wretch, more wicked he doth prove:
Till now at length that Jove him office gives
20   (At Juno's suit who much did Argus love),
    In this our world a hangman for to be
    Of all those fools that will have all they see.

He had not fully ended his last words of his invective song when
a young shepherd named Histor who, while Dicus was singing,
25 sometimes with his eyes up to heaven, sometimes seeming to stop
his ears, did show a fearful mislike of so unreverent reproaches, with
great vehemency desired all the hearers to take heed how they
seemed to allow any part of his speech against so revengeful a god
as Cupid was, who had even in his first magistracy showed against
30 Apollo the heat of his anger. 'But', said he, 'if you had heard or seen
such violence of his wrath as I even yesterday, and the other day,
have, you would tremble at the recital of his name.'
The duke and all the rest straight desired him to tell what it was;
and he (seeming loath, lest his words might disgrace the matter)

3 horned] horny Bo, Da.   4 foot] feet Cl, Le, Ph.   5 easily] daily 90.
15 love is worst which] love is worse which Le; love is most which Ph; love's desire
most 90 (only).   16 Thereon] Therein 90 (only).   26 so] such Cl; his Hm.
33 straight desired him] desired him As, Da; desired him straight Ph.

told them that, as he was two days before sitting in the shade of a
bush, he did hear the most wailful lamentation of an Iberian noble-
man called Plangus (uttered to the wise shepherd Boulon) that he
thought any words could express; and all touching a pitiful adven-
ture, the ground and maintenance whereof was only Cupid. 'And 5
that song', said he, 'for in a song I gathered it, would I let you hear
but that, for the better understanding, I must first repeat the subject
thereof. This Plangus, when no persuasion of the wise Boulon
could keep him from the pitiful complaining of his sorrows, yet
yielded so much to my request as to harbour with me these last days 10
in my simple cabin where, with much entreaty, he told me this
pitiful story:
   That of late there reigned a king of Lydia who had for the blessing
of his marriage his only daughter Erona, a princess worthy for her
beauty as much praise as beauty may be praised. This Erona being 15
fourteen years old, seeing the country of Lydia so much devoted to
Cupid as that in each place his naked pictures and images were
superstitiously adored, procured so much of her father (either
moved thereunto by the hate of that god, or the shamefast con-
sideration of such nakedness) utterly to deface and pull down all 20
those pictures of him; which how terribly he punished quickly after
appeared. For she had not lived a year longer when she was stricken
with most obstinate love to a young man, but of mean parentage,
in her father's court, named Antiphilus; so mean as that he was but
the son of her nurse, and by that means came known of her. And 25
so ill could she conceal this fire, and so wilfully persevered she in
it, that her father offering her the marriage of the great Otanes, king
of Persia (who desired her more than the joys of heaven), she, for
Antiphilus's sake, refused him. Many ways her father did seek to
withdraw her from it; sometimes persuasions, sometimes threaten- 30
ings, sometimes hiding Antiphilus and giving her to understand he
was fled the country; lastly making a solemn execution to be done
of another under the name of Antiphilus, whom he kept in prison.
But neither she liked persuasions, nor feared threatenings, nor
changed for absence; and when she thought him dead, it was 35
manifestly seen she sought all means, as well by poison as knife, to
follow him. This so brake the father's heart with grief that, leaving
things as he found them, he shortly after died. Then forthwith

3 wise shepherd Boulon Cl, As, Da, Ph, Je, Hm: wise Boulon St, Bo.   10 to my]
at my Cl, As.   25 known of] known to Cl, Da.   31 giving her to OA, 90: giving St.

Erona, being seized of the crown, sought to satisfy her mind with Antiphilus's marriage.

But before she could accomplish it, she was overtaken with a cruel war the king Otanes made upon her, only for her person, towards whom, for her ruin, love had kindled his cruel heart: indeed cruel and tyrannous; for being far too strong in the field, he spared not man, woman, nor child, but with miserable tortures slew them, although his fair sister Artaxia (who accompanied him in the army) sought all means to mollify his rage; till lastly he besieged Erona in her best city, vowing he would have her either by force or otherwise. And to the extremity he had brought her when there landed in Lydia, driven thither by tempest, two excellent young princes, as Plangus named them, Pyrocles, prince of Macedon, and Musidorus, duke of Thessalia (at these words, a man might easily have perceived a starting and blushing, both in Cleophila and Dorus; but being utterly unsuspected to be such, they were unmarked). Those two princes, as well to help the weaker as for the natural hate the Grecians bare the Persians, did so much with their incomparable valour as that they gat into the city, and by their presence much repelled Otanes' assaults. Which he understanding to be occasioned by them, made a challenge of three princes in his retinue against those two princes and Antiphilus; and that thereupon the matter should be decided, with compact that neither should help his fellows, but of whose side the more overcame, with him the victory should remain. Of his side was Barzanes, lord of Hyrcania, against Pyrocles; Nardes, satrapas of Mesopotamia, to fight with Musidorus; and against Antiphilus he placed this same Plangus, second son to the king of Iberia, who served him with dear estimation. And so it fell out that Pyrocles and Musidorus overcame both their adversaries, but of the other side Plangus took Antiphilus prisoner. Under which colour, as though the matter had been equal (though indeed it was not), Otanes continued his war; and to bring Erona to a compelled yielding, sent her one day word that the next morrow he would, before the walls of her town, strike off Antiphilus's head, if she yielded not to his desire.

Then, lo, was Cupid's work well seen; for he had brought this miserable princess to such a case as she had love against love. For

7 tortures] terrors Ph; torments Je, Hm.   11 the] the *corr. to* that Cl; this Je:
14 these] those Ph; whose Hm.   17 Those] These Da, Ph, 90.   18 the Persians OA:
to Persians St.   24 fellows] fellow Je, 90.   34 her] the Cl, As, Ph, 90.   37 case]
care Bo; cause Hm.

if she loved him (as unmeasurably she did), then could she con-
descend to no other; again, if she loved him, then must she save
his life; which two things were impossible to be joined together. But
the matchless courage of those two princes prevented him, and
preserved her; for the same night, with a desperate camisado, they 5
pierced into the midst of his army where Otanes, valiantly defend-
ing himself, was by Pyrocles slain, and Antiphilus by Musidorus
rescued. Plangus, seeing no other remedy, conveyed in safety to
her country the fair Artaxia, now queen of Persia, who, with the
extremest lamentations could issue out of a woman's mouth, testified 10
to the world her new greatness did no way comfort her in respect of
her brother's loss; whom she studied all means possible to revenge
upon every one of the occasioners.

But thus was Antiphilus redeemed, and (though against the con-
sent of all the Lydian nobility) married to Erona. In which case the 15
two Greek princes left them, being called away by one of the
notablest adventures in the world. But the vindicative Cupid, who had
given Erona only so much time of sweetness as to make the miseries
more cruel that should fall upon her, had turned Antiphilus's
heart while he was Otanes' prisoner quite from her to queen 20
Artaxia; insomuch that, longing to have the great crown of Persia
on his head and, like a base man suddenly advanced, having no
scope of his insolence, made Artaxia secretly understand (who, he
knew, mortally hated Erona) that, if she would reward his vehement
loving of her with marriage, he would either by poison or otherwise 25
make away the beautiful Erona, and so, with the might of Persia,
easily join those two kingdoms together. The wise Artaxia, that
had now a good entrance to her desires, finely handled the vile
Antiphilus and brought his heart to such a wicked paradise that one
day, under colour of hunting, he enticed abroad the excellent Erona to 30
a place where he had laid some of Artaxia's men in ambushment, and
there delivered both himself and her into their hands; who convey-
ing them to their mistress, Antiphilus was justly rewarded of his
expected marriage. For she presently gave him into the hands of
four valiant gentlemen, who dearly had loved their master Otanes, 35
to be slain with as many deaths as their wit and hate could find out.

1–2 condescend to no other Bo, Cl, Ph, Je, Hm: condescend to another St; not conde-
scend to another As; condescend to none other Da.   6–7 defending] defended As,
Je, Hm.   8 to] into Hm, 90.   12 studied all] studied by all As, Da.
17 notablest] noblest Cl, Ph.   20 to queen] to the queen Bo, Cl, Da, Je, Hm.
23 insolence] insolency Bo, Cl, As, Ph, Je, Hm.

Which accordingly was done, and he held a whole month together in continual wretchedness, till at last his life left him, rather with continuance of the miserable pain than any violent stroke added unto him. As for Erona, she put her in prison, swearing that, if by 5 that time two year she did not bring Pyrocles and Musidorus to fight with those four (who would prove upon them they had traitorously killed her brother Otanes), she should be publicly burned at a stake; which likewise she should be, if Pyrocles and his fellow were overcome. But if they would take the matter upon them, 10 then should they have a free camp granted them to try the matter in the court of the king of Parthia, because they might hold hers for suspected. This did she hoping that the courage of the two young princes would lead them to so unequal a match, wherein she rested assured their death, and so consequently her revenge, should be 15 fully performed. But Erona, because she might exceed even misery with misery, did not, for all the treachery of Antiphilus (able to make any love a mortal hatred), nor yet for his death (the breaker of all worldly fancies), leave to love Antiphilus and to hate herself since she had lost him. And in respect of his revenge upon those four his 20 murderers (not for her own life, which she was weary of), she desired that Pyrocles and Musidorus might against the day be brought thither, having such confidence in the notable proofs she had seen of their virtue that those four should not be able to withstand them, but suffer death for killing her (in spite of hate) beloved Antiphilus. 25 But whom to send for their search she knew not, when Cupid (I think for some greater mischief) offered this Plangus unto her, who from the day of her first imprisonment was so extremely enamoured of her that he had sought all means how to deliver her. But that being impossible, for the narrow watch was of her, he had (as well 30 he might, being greatly trusted of Artaxia) conference with Erona; and, although she would promise no affection in reward (which was finished absolutely in Antiphilus), yet he took upon him the quest of those two heroical princes who, in this mean time, had done such famous acts that all Asia was full of their histories. But he, having 35 travelled a whole year after them, and still hearing their doings

---

2 at last] at the last Da, Hm.   3 of the miserable Bo, Cl, As, Ph, Je, Hm: of miserable St; of this miserable Da.   6 them they] them that they Ph, Je. 14 assured their] assured by their Bo; assured of their Da, Ph, Hm.   death] deaths Ph, Je, Hm.   26 greater] great As, Ph.   29 impossible] unpossible Da, Hm.

notably recounted, yet could never (being stayed by many misad-
ventures) fully overtake them; but was newly come into Egypt after
they had shipped themselves thence for Greece; and into Greece
likewise followed, taking this country in his way because mariners
had told him such a ship had touched upon the south part of Pelo- 5
ponnesus, where it was my hap to hear him make the pitifullest
lamentation that ever before came into mine ears. Neither could the
wise Boulon (who had found him making the like doleful complaints,
as his mind otherwise occupied led him contrary to these woods)
anything mitigate his agonies; but, as he told us (having likewise at 10
our request recounted the full story of those two rare princes), his
purpose was to go into Thessalia and Macedon where, if he cannot
hear of them, he will return into Persia, and either find some way to
preserve Erona or burn at the stake with her.'

Great was the compassion Cleophila and Dorus conceived of the 15
queen Erona's danger—which was the first enterprise they had ever
entered into; and therefore (besides their ⌊noble humanity) they
were loath their own worthy work should be spoiled. Therefore,
considering they had almost a year of time to succour her, they
resolved as soon as this their present action (which had taken full 20
possession of all their desires) were brought to any good point they
would forthwith take in hand that journey; neither should they need
in the meantime anything reveal themselves to Plangus (who,
though unwittingly, had now done his errand). To which they
thought themselves in honour bound, since Artaxia laid treason 25
to their charge. But how that fancy was stopped shall be after told.

Now Dorus desired Histor to repeat the lamentable song he first
spake of; and Histor was ready to do it when out starts old Geron and
said it was very undecent a young man's tongue should possess so
much time, and that age should become an auditor. And therefore, 30
bending himself to another young shepherd named Philisides who
neither had danced nor sung with them, and had all this time lain
upon the ground at the foot of a cypress tree, leaning upon his elbow,
with so deep a melancholy that his senses carried to his mind no
delight from any of their objects, he strake him upon the shoulder 35

3 thence] *om.* Bo, As, Je, Hm.   for] from As, Ph, Hm.   7 ever] *om.* As, Je, Hm.
into] unto Da, Je; to Hm.   9 to] in Bo, Cl, As, Ph, Hm.   these] those Cl,
As; his Da.   woods] words Cl, As, Da, Ph (who . . . woods *om.* Je).   19 had
almost] had yet almost Cl, As, Da.   24 now] *om.* Bo (*inserted after* who *in line* 22),
Cl, As (*inserted above line* St).   26 after] hereafter Ph; afterward Je, Hm.
32 time] while Ph, 90.

with a right old man's grace that will seem livelier than his age will afford him; and thus began his eclogue unto him:

Geron   Philisides   Histor

Geron. Up, up, Philisides, let sorrows go,
5   Who yields to woe doth but increase his smart.
    Do not thy heart to plaintful custom bring,
    But let us sing, sweet tunes do passions ease,
    An old man hear, who would thy fancies raise.

Philisides. Who minds to please the mind drowned in annoys
10   With outward joys, which inly cannot sink,
    As well may think with oil to cool the fire;
    Or with desire to make such foe a friend,
    Who doth his soul to endless malice bend.

Geron. Yet sure an end to each thing time doth give,
15   Though woes now live, at length thy woes must die.
    Then virtue try, if she can work in thee
    That which we see in many time hath wrought,
    And weakest hearts to constant temper brought.

Philisides. Who ever taught a skill-less man to teach,
20   Or stop a breach, that never cannon saw?
    Sweet virtue's law bars not a causeful moan.
    Time shall in one my life and sorrows end,
    And me perchance your constant temper lend.

Geron. What can amend where physic is refused?
25   The wits abused with will no counsel take.
    Yet for my sake discover us thy grief.
    Oft comes relief when most we seem in trap.
    The stars thy state, fortune may change thy hap.

Philisides. If fortune's lap became my dwelling place,
30   And all the stars conspired to my good,
    Still were I one, this still should be my case,
    Ruin's relic, care's web, and sorrow's food;
    Since she, fair fierce, to such a state me calls,
    Whose wit the stars, whose fortune fortune thralls.

3–p. 76, 4 Le *and* 90 *omit this poem;* 93 *transfers it to the 2nd Eclogues.*   6 plaintful] painful As, Ph.   10 inly] inward Ph, Je.   21 causeful] causeless Bo, Hm. 25 no] in Ph; to Je, Hm.   33 a state] estate Cl, As, Je.

Geron. Alas, what falls are fall'n unto thy mind
    That there where thou confessed thy mischief lies
    Thy wit dost use still still more harms to find?
    Whom wit makes vain, or blinded with his eyes,
    What counsel can prevail, or light give light,   5
    Since all his force against himself he tries?
    Then each conceit that enters in by sight
    Is made forsooth a jurat of his woes:
    Earth, sea, air, fire, heav'n, hell, and ghastly sprite.
    Then cries to senseless things which neither knows   10
    What aileth thee, and if they knew thy mind
    Would scorn in man (their king) such feeble shows.
    Rebel, rebel, in golden fetters bind
    This tyrant love; or rather do suppress
    Those rebel thoughts which are thy slaves by kind.   15
    Let not a glitt'ring name thy fancy dress
    In painted clothes, because they call it love.
    There is no hate that can thee more oppress.
    Begin (and half the work is done) to prove
    By raising up, upon thyself to stand;   20
    And think she is a she that doth thee move.
    He water ploughs, and soweth in the sand,
    And hopes the flick'ring wind with net to hold,
    Who hath his hopes laid up in woman's hand.
    What man is he that hath his freedom sold?   25
    Is he a manlike man that doth not know man
    Hath power that sex with bridle to withhold?
    A fickle sex, and true in trust to no man;
    A servant sex, soon proud if they be coyed;
    And to conclude, thy mistress is a woman.   30

Histor. Those words did once the loveliest shepherd use
    That erst I knew, and with most plainful muse;
    Yet not of women judging, as he said,
    But forced with rage, his rage on them upbraid.

7 by] my Ph; his 93.   9 sprite] spirits Bo, Da, Je, Hm.   10 neither] never
As, Ph (never *corr. to* neither Da).   16 fancy Cl, As, Da, Hm, 93: fancies St, Bo,
Ph, Je.   18 Hm *has leaf missing* (*f. 25*) *from here.*   19 the] thy Da, Ph.
20 raising] rising Da, 93.   26 know man] know a man Cl, Qu.   27 sex] seeks
Da, Qu; sext Je.   31–4 *om.* 93.   31 Those] These Da, Ph, Je, Qu.
loveliest] lowliest Da, Je.   shepherd] shepherds Da, Qu.   32 plainful] painful
As, Je, Qu.

Philisides. O gods, how long this old fool hath annoyed
 My wearied ears! O gods, yet grant me this,
 That soon the world of his false tongue be void.
 O noble age who place their only bliss
5 In being heard until the hearer die,
 Utt'ring a serpent's mind with serpent's hiss!
 Then who will hear a well authorized lie
 (And patience hath), let him go learn of him
 What swarms of virtues did in his youth fly
10 Such hearts of brass, wise heads, and garments trim
 Were in his days: which heard, one nothing hears,
 If from his words the falsehood he do skim.
 And herein most their folly vain appears,
 That since they still allege, *When they were young*,
15 It shows they fetch their wit from youthful years.
 Like beast for sacrifice where, save the tongue
 And belly, naught is left; such sure is he,
 This 'live-dead man in this old dungeon flung.
 Old houses are thrown down for new we see;
20 The oldest rams are culled from the flock;
 No man doth wish his horse should aged be;
 The ancient oak well makes a fired block;
 Old men themselves do love young wives to choose;
 Only fond youth admires a rotten stock.
25 Who once a white long beard well handle does
 (As his beard him, not he his beard, did bear),
 Though cradle-witted, must not honour lose.
 O when will men leave off to judge by hair,
 And think them old that have the oldest mind,
30 With virtue fraught and full of holy fear?

Geron. If that thy face were hid, or I were blind,
 I yet should know a young man speaketh now,
 Such wand'ring reasons in thy speech I find.
 He is a beast that beast's use will allow
35 For proof of man who, sprung of heav'nly fire,
 Hath strongest soul when most his reins do bow.

2 gods] God Da, Je. 9 virtues] virtue Ph, Qu. 12 falsehood Bo, Da, Ph,
Je, Qu, 93: falsehoods St, Cl, As. do] doth Bo, Da, Je. 16 beast] beasts Da,
Ph; best Je. 20 culled] called Cl, As, Da, Qu. 29 oldest] eldest As, Je.
31 or] and Ph, Qu. 33 reasons] reason As, Da.

But fondlings fond know not your own desire,
Loath to die young, and then you must be old,
Fondly blame that to which yourselves aspire.
But this light choler that doth make you bold,
Rather to wrong than unto just defence,   5
Is passed with me, my blood is waxen cold.
Thy words, though full of malapert offence,
I weigh them not, but still will thee advise
How thou from foolish love mayst purge thy sense.
First, think they err that think them gaily wise   10
Who well can set a passion out to show;
Such sight have they that see with goggling eyes.
Passion bears high when puffing wit doth blow,
But is indeed a toy; if not a toy,
True cause of ills, and cause of causeless woe.   15
If once thou mayst that fancy gloss destroy
Within thyself, thou soon wilt be ashamed
To be a player of thine own annoy.
Then let thy mind with better books be tamed,
Seek to espy her faults as well as praise,   20
And let thine eyes to other sports be framed.
In hunting fearful beasts do spend some days,
Or catch the birds with pitfalls, or with lime,
Or train the fox that trains so crafty lays.
Lie but to sleep, and in the early prime   25
Seek skill of herbs in hills, haunt brooks near night,
And try with bait how fish will bite sometime.
Go graft again, and seek to graft them right,
Those pleasant plants, those sweet and fruitful trees,
Which both the palate and the eyes delight.   30
Cherish the hives of wisely painful bees;
Let special care upon thy flock be stayed;
Such active mind but seldom passion sees.

Philisides. Hath any man heard what this old man said?
    Truly, not I who did my thoughts engage   35
    Where all my pains one look of hers hath paid.

9 mayst] may Da, Je.   10 err] are Da, Je, Qu.   12 that] which Ph, Je.
16 fancy] fancies Bo, Cl; fancied Ph.   21 thine] thy Bo, Cl, Ph.   23 pitfalls
Ph, 93: pitfolds St, Bo, Cl, Da; pitfold As; pitfall Je, Qu.   25 early] earthly Cl,
Da.   34 Hm (*f. 26*) *begins again.*   any] my Bo, Da.   36 hers] her 93.

Histor. Thus may you see how youth esteemeth age,
  And never hath thereof arightly deemed,
  While hot desires do reign in fancy's rage,
  Till age itself do make itself esteemed.

5 Geron was even out of countenance, finding the words he thought
were so wise win so little reputation at this young man's hands; and
therefore, sometimes looking upon an old acquaintance of his called
Mastix, one of the repiningest fellows in the world, and that beheld
nobody but with a mind of mislike (saying still the world was amiss,
10 but how it should be amended he knew not), sometimes casting his
eyes to the ground, even ashamed to see his grey hairs despised, at
last he spied his two dogs, whereof the elder was called Melampus,
and the younger Lælaps (indeed the jewels he ever had with him),
one brawling with the other. Which occasion he took to restore
15 himself to his countenance, and rating Melampus, he began to
speak to his dogs as if in them a man should find more obedience
than in unbridled young men:

Geron   Mastix

Geron. Down, down, Melampus; what? your fellow bite?
20 I set you o'er the flock I dearly love
  Them to defend, not with yourselves to fight.
  Do you not think this will the wolves remove
  From former fear they had of your good minds,
  When they shall such divided weakness prove?
25 What if Lælaps a better morsel finds
  Than thou erst knew? Rather take part with him
  Than jarl: lo, lo, even these how envy blinds!
  And thou, Lælaps, let not pride make thee brim
  Because thou hast thy fellow overgone,
30 But thank the cause, thou seest, when he is dim.
  Here, Lælaps, here; indeed, against the foen
  Of my good sheep thou never truce-time took:

1–4 *om.* 93.   6 hands] hand Da, Je.   7 sometimes looking] looking Cl;
looking sometimes Ph.   called] named Bo, Cl, Je.   10 amended Cl, As, Ph, Je, Hm,
93: mended St, Bo, Da.   13 Lælaps 93: Lelanx St, Bo, Cl, As, Ph, Je, Hm;
Lenax Da.   14 the other] another Da, Je, Hm, 93.   18–p. 79, 12 90 *omits
this poem*; 93 *transfers to the 2nd Eclogues.*   25 Lælaps 93: Lelanx OA; Lenanx Da.
finds] find 93.   26 thou] you Da, 93.   28 thou] then Da, 93.   Lælaps 93:
Lelanx OA; Lenanx Da.   30 when] where 93,   31 Lælaps 93: Lelanx St, Bo
Cl, Le, As, Ph, Hm; Lenanx Da; Lilanx Je.   the] thy Cl, Da, Je, Hm.

Be as thou art, but be with mine at one.
For though Melampus like a wolf do look
(For age doth make him of a wolvish hue),
Yet have I seen when well a wolf he shook.
Fool that I am that with my dogs speak Grew. 5
Come nar, good Mastix, 'tis now full tway score
Of years (alas) since I good Mastix knew.
Thou heardst e'en now a young man sneb me sore
Because I red him as I would my son.
Youth will have will, age must to age therefore. 10

Mastix. What marvel if in youth such faults be done,
Since that we see our saddest shepherds out
Who have their lesson so long time begun?
Quickly secure, and easily in doubt,
Either asleep be all if naught assail, 15
Or all abroad if but a cub start out.
We shepherds are like them that under sail
Do speak high words when all the coast is clear,
Yet to a passenger will bonnet vail.
'I con thee thank' to whom thy dogs be dear, 20
But commonly like curs we them entreat,
Save when great need of them perforce appear,
Then him we kiss whom late before we beat
With such intemperance, that each way grows
Hate of the first, contempt of later feat. 25
And such discord 'twixt greatest shepherds flows,
That sport it is to see with how great art
By justice' work they their own faults disclose;
Like busy boys to win their tutor's heart,
One saith he mocks; the other saith he plays; 30
The third his lesson missed; till all do smart.
As for the rest, how shepherds spend their days
At blow point, hot cockles, or else at keels,
While, 'Let us pass our time', each shepherd says.
So small account of time the shepherd feels, 35
And doth not feel that life is naught but time,

2 do] doth Bo, Ph.   6 nar] near Cl, Ph, 93.   18 high] by Ph, Hm.
21 we them entreat] we do them entreat Cl; we do them treat Hm.   25 feat Bo,
Cl, Le, As, Ph, Je, Hm, 93: feats St, Da.   33 else at 93: *om.* OA.   34 While]
Why Ph, Je, Hm.

And when that time is past, death holds his heels.
To age thus do they draw their youthful prime,
Knowing no more than what poor trial shows,
As fish sure trial hath of muddy slime.

5   This pattern good unto our children goes,
For what they see their parents love or hate
Their first caught sense prefers to teacher's blows.
These cocklings cockered we bewail too late
When that we see our offspring gaily bent,
10 Women manwood, and men effeminate.

   Geron. Fie, man; fie, man; what words hath thy tongue lent?
Yet thou art mickle warse than ere was I,
Thy too much zeal I fear thy brain hath spent.
We oft are angrier with the feeble fly
15 For business where it pertains him not
Than with the pois'nous toads that quiet lie.
I pray thee what hath e'er the parrot got,
And yet they say he talks in great men's bow'rs?
A cage (gilded perchance) is all his lot.

20 Who off his tongue the liquor gladly pours
A good fool called with pain perhaps may be,
But e'en for that shall suffer mighty lours.
Let swan's example sicker serve for thee,
Who once all birds in sweetly singing passed,
25 But now to silence turned his minstrelsy.

For he would sing, but others were defaced:
The peacock's pride, the pie's pilled flattery,
Cormorant's glut, kite's spoil, kingfisher's waste,
The falcon's fierceness, sparrow's lechery,
30 The cuckoo's shame, the goose's good intent,
E'en turtle touched he with hypocrisy.
And worse of other more; till by assent
Of all the birds, but namely those were grieved,
Of fowls there called was a parliament.

35 There was the swan of dignity deprived,
And statute made he never should have voice,

---

10 manwood] manhood Da, Hm.   12 warse Bo, As, Da, Je, 93: worse St, Cl, Le,
Ph, Hm.   14 angrier] angry Ph, Je, Hm.   fly] flies Ph, Je.   16 toads]
toad Bo, Ph, Je.   quiet lie] still doth lie Bo; quietly Da; quiet lies Ph, Je.
28 kingfisher's] kings fishers Bo, Cl, As, Je; kings fisher Ph.   36 statute Bo, Le,
Je, Hm, 93: statutes St, Cl, As, Da, Ph.

Since when, I think, he hath in silence lived.
I warn thee therefore (since thou mayst have choice)
Let not thy tongue become a fiery match,
No sword so bites as that ill tool annoys.
Let our unpartial eyes a little watch   5
Our own demean, and soon we wonder shall
That, hunting faults, ourselves we did not catch.
Into our minds let us a little fall,
And we shall find more spots than leopard's skin.
Then who makes us such judges over all?   10
But farewell now, thy fault is no great sin,
Come, come, my curs, 'tis late, I will go in.

And away with his dogs straight he went, as if he would be sure
to have the last word, all the assembly laughing at the lustiness of
the old fellow, who departed muttering to himself he had seen more 15
in his days than twenty of them. But as he went out, Dorus seeing a
lute lying under the princess Pamela's feet, glad to have such an
errand to approach her, he came, but came with a dismayed grace,
all his blood stirred betwixt fear and desire; and playing upon it with
such sweetness as everybody wondered to see such skill in a shep-   20
herd, he sang unto it with a sorrowing voice these elegiac verses:

$$-\ -\ -\ -\ -\ \cup\ \cup\ -\ \cup\ \cup\ -\ \cup\ \cup\ -\ -$$

$$-\ -\ -\ \cup\ \cup\ -\ -\ \cup\ \cup\ -\ \cup\ \cup\ -$$

Dorus. Fortune, Nature, Love, long have contended about me,
    Which should most miseries cast on a worm that I am.   25
Fortune thus gan say: 'Misery and misfortune is all one,
    And of misfortune, Fortune hath only the gift.
With strong foes on land, on seas with contrary tempests,
    Still do I cross this wretch, what so he taketh in hand.'
'Tush, tush', said Nature, 'this is all but a trifle, a man's self   30
    Gives haps or mishaps, e'en as he ord'reth his heart.

---

4 tool] toil As; coal Ph.   9 more spots than leopard's] more faults than leopard's
Cl; more spots than leopard Da; moe than leopard's Ph; more than in leopard Je.
10 makes] make Ph, Je.   21 elegiac] elegial Bo, Je, Hm; elegian Cl.
22–p. 80, 12 90 *omits this poem; it is in* 93.   22–3 *Scansion in* St, Cl, As, Hm *only.*
22 St *strikes through first version, and in the second gives the first line as*

$$-\ -\ -\ -\ -\ \cup\ \cup\ -\ -\ \cup\ \cup\ -\ -$$

25 miseries] misery Cl, Le, As.   26 gan] can Bo, Cl, Le, Da.   30 self] life Cl,
Ph (life *corr. to* self Je).

But so his humour I frame, in a mould of choler adusted,
  That the delights of life shall be to him dolorous.'
Love smiled, and thus said: 'Want joined to desire is unhappy.
  But if he naught do desire, what can Heraclitus ail?
5 None but I works by desire; by desire have I kindled in his soul
  Infernal agonies unto a beauty divine,
Where thou, poor Nature, left'st all thy due glory to Fortune.
  Her virtue is sovereign, Fortune a vassal of hers.'
Nature abashed went back; Fortune blushed, yet she replied thus:
10 'And e'en in that love shall I reserve him a spite.'
Thus, thus, alas! woeful in nature, unhappy by fortune,
  But most wretched I am now love awakes my desire.

Nota

The rules observed in these English measured verses be these:
15 Consonant before consonant always long, except a mute and a liquid
(as *rĕfrain*), such indifferent.

Single consonants commonly short, but such as have a double sound (as
lăck, *wĭll*, *tĭll*) or such as the vowel before doth produce long (as *hāte*,
debāte).

20 Vowel before vowel or diphthong before vowel always short, except
such an exclamation as *ōh*; else the diphthongs always long and the single
vowels short.

Because our tongue being full of consonants and monosyllables, the
vowel slides away quicklier than in Greek or Latin, which be full of vowels
25 and long words. Yet are such vowels long as the pronunciation makes
long (as *glōry*, *lādy*), and such like as seem to have a diphthong sound (as
shōw, *blōw*, *dĭe*, *hĭgh*).

Elisions, when one vowel meets with another, used indifferently as the
advantage of the verse best serves; for so in our ordinary speech we do
30 (for as well we say *thou art* as *th'art*), and like scope doth Petrarch take
to himself sometimes to use apostrophe, sometimes not.

For the words derived out of Latin and other languages, they are
measured as they are denizened in English and not as before they came
over sea (for we say not *fortūnate* though the Latin say *fortūna*, nor *usūry*
35 but *ūsury* in the first); so our language hath a special gift in altering them
and making them our own.

Some words especially short.

Particles used now long, now short (as *bŭt*, *ŏr*, *nŏr*, *ŏn*, *tŏ*).

5 works] work Bo, As, Ph.   by desire; by desire OA, 93: by desire St.   7 left'st 93:
left OA; lefts Da.   9–11 *om.* Ph.   13–p. 81, 6 *This* Nota *is written in the
margin of* St *only. In* As *the scribe has written* Write these rules *and left a blank page.*

Some words, as they have diverse pronunciations, to be written diversely, (as some say *thōugh*, some pronounce it *thŏ*).

As for *wĕe*, *thĕe*, *shĕe*, though they may seem to be a double vowel by the wrong orthography, be here short, being indeed no other than the Greek iota; and the like of our *o*, which some write double in this word 5 *dŏo*.

Dorus, when he had sung this, having had all the while a free beholding of the fair Pamela (who could well have spared such honour, and defended the assault he gave unto her face with bringing a fair stain of shamefastness unto it), let fall his arms and remained 10 so fastened in his thoughts as if Pamela had grafted him there to grow in continual imagination. But Cleophila espying it, and fearing he should too much forget himself, she came to him and took out of his hand the lute; and laying fast hold of Philoclea's face with her eyes, she sang these sapphics, speaking as it were to her own hope: 15

$$\_ \cup \_ \_ \_ \cup \cup \_ \cup \_ \underline{\cup}$$

$$\_ \cup \_ \_ \_ \cup \cup \_ \cup \_ \_$$

$$\_ \cup \_ \_ \_ \cup \cup \_ \ \ \_ \underline{\cup}$$

$$\_ \cup \cup \_ \_$$

Cleophila.   If mine eyes can speak to do hearty errand, 20
      Or mine eyes' language she do hap to judge of,
      So that eyes' message be of her received,
          Hope, we do live yet.

      But if eyes fail then, when I most do need them,
      Or if eyes' language be not unto her known, 25
      So that eyes' message do return rejected,
          Hope, we do both die.

      Yet dying, and dead, do we sing her honour;
      So become our tombs monuments of her praise;
      So becomes our loss the triumph of her gain; 30
          Hers be the glory.

      If the senseless spheres do yet hold a music,
      If the swan's sweet voice be not heard, but at death,

7 sung this] sung this song, Ph, Je, Hm.   the while] this while As, Je, Hm. 14 hold of] hold on Ph, Je, 90 (*only*).   16–p. 82, 14 *The poem is in* 90–93. 16–19 *Scansion in* St, Cl, As, Hm, *only*; St *only gives alternate scansion of final syllable of first and third lines as short.*   20 Cleophila. Cl, Le: *om.* St, Bo, As, Da, Ph, Je, Hm, 90.   30 becomes] become Ph, Je.   loss Bo, Cl, Le, As, Da, Je, 90: losses St; lost Hm; minds Ph.   gain] game Bo, Cl, Je; mind Ph.   32 senseless spheres] spheres senseless 90.   33 at] a As, Ph.

If the mute timber when it hath the life lost,
    Yieldeth a lute's tune,
Are then human minds privileged so meanly
As that hateful death can abridge them of power
5   With the voice of truth to record to all worlds
    That we be her spoils?

Thus not ending, ends the due praise of her praise;
Fleshly veil consumes, but a soul hath his life,
Which is held in love; love it is that hath joined
10   Life to this our soul.

But if eyes can speak to do hearty errand,
Or mine eyes' language she do hap to judge of,
So that eyes' message be of her received,
    Hope we do live yet.

15   Great was the pleasure of Basilius, and greater would have been
Gynecia's but that she found too well it was intended to her
daughter. As for Philoclea, she was sweetly ravished withal; when
Dorus, desiring in a secret manner to speak so of their cases as per-
chance the parties intended might take some light of it, making low
20 reverence to Cleophila, he began this provoking song in hexameter
verse unto her. Whereunto she, soon finding whither his words were
directed (in like tune and like verse), answered as followeth:

Dorus   Cleophila

$$- \cup \cup - \cup \cup - \cup \cup - - \cup \cup - -$$

25 *Dorus.* Lady, reserved by the heav'ns to do pastors' company honour,
    Joining your sweet voice to the rural muse of a desert,
    Here you fully do find this strange operation of love,
    How to the woods love runs as well as rides to the palace,
    Neither he bears reverence to a prince nor pity to beggar,
30   But (like a point in midst of a circle) is still of a nearness,
    All to a lesson he draws, nor hills nor caves can avoid him.

1 If the mute Da, Ph, 90: If muett St; If mute Bo, Cl, Le, As, Je, Hm.   5 voice
OA: vow St, 90.   9 that hath joined] that buckles Ph; that joined Je, Hm.
18 to speak so] to speak Cl, 93; so to speak 13.   19 parties] party Cl, As.   light]
like As, Ph.   20 he] *om.* 13.   22 and like verse] and verse Cl, 93.
23–p. 88, 15 90 *omits this poem; it is in* 93, *which reads* Zelmane *for* Cleophila *through-*
out; Ra *has* p. 86, 16–p. 87, 13, p. 87, 15–18, *and* 20–8.   24 *Scansion in* St
and Hm (*omitting the first dactyl*) *only.*   28 rides Da, Je, 93: ride St, Bo, Cl.
Le, As, Ph, Hm.   29 to beggar] to a beggar Cl, Je, Hm.   31 nor
hills] neither hills 93.

Cleophila. Worthy shepherd, by my song to myself all favour is
 happened,
 That to the sacred muse my annoys somewhat be revealed,
 Sacred muse, who in one contains what nine do in all them.
 But O, happy be you which safe from fiery reflection   5
 Of Phoebus' violence in shade of stately cypress tree,
 Or pleasant myrtle, may teach th'unfortunate Echo
 In these woods to resound the renowned name of a goddess.
 Happy be you that may to the saint, your only Idea
 (Although simply attired), your manly affection utter.   10
 Happy be those mishaps which, justly proportion holding,
 Give right sound to the ears, and enter aright to the judgement;
 But wretched be the souls which, veiled in a contrary subject,
 How much more we do love, so the less our loves be believed.
 What skill serveth a sore of a wrong infirmity judged?   15
 What can justice avail to a man that tells not his own case?
 You, though fears do abash, in you still possible hopes be:
 Nature against we do seem to rebel, seem fools in a vain suit.
 But so unheard, condemned, kept thence we do seek to abide in,
 Self-lost and wand'ring, banished that place we do come from, 20
 What mean is there, alas, we can hope our loss to recover?
 What place is there left we may hope our woes to recomfort?
 Unto the heav'ns? our wings be too short, th'earth thinks us a
  burden;
 Air, we do still with sighs increase; to the fire? we do want none. 25
 And yet his outward heat our tears would quench, but an inward
 Fire no liquor can cool: Neptune's seat would be dried up there.
 Happy shepherd, with thanks to the gods, still think to be thankful,
 That to thy advancement their wisdoms have thee abased.

Dorus. Unto the gods with a thankful heart all thanks I do render, 30
 That to my advancement their wisdoms have me abased.

---

3 annoys] griefs Bo, Ph; *blank left* Le (2–3 *blank space left* As).   6 stately cypress
tree] cypress tree Je, Hm; sweet Cyparissus 93.   7 myrtle Bo, Cl, Le, As, Da,
Ph, 93: mirth St, Je, Hm. th'unfortunate 93: the unfortunate OA; unfortunate Da.
8 woods] words Da, Hm. 10 simply OA, 93: simple St. affection] affections
Cl, Da. 15 serveth] salveth 93. 17 in you] in your Bo, Cl, Ph. 20 and] in 93.
23 th'earth As: the earth St, Bo, Cl, Le, Ph, Je, Hm; that earth Da; earth 93. 27 can
cool Bo, Da, Ph, Je, Hm, 93: can cool *changed by another hand to* cools St; always Cl,
As; allays Le. Neptune's seat] the great seas Ph; Neptune's realm 93. would be
dried up there Bo, Cl, Le, As, Da, Ph, Je: quite would be dried up there St (*blank space
left before* would Da); would be dried up thereto Hm; would not avail us 93.

But yet, alas! O but yet, alas! our haps be but hard haps,
Which must frame contempt to the fittest purchase of honour.
Well may a pastor plain, but alas his plaints be not esteemed.
Silly shepherd's poor pipe, when his harsh sound testifies our
5   woes,
Into the fair looker-on, pastime, not passion, enters.
And to the woods or brooks, who do make such dreary recital
What be the pangs they bear, and whence those pangs be derived,
Pleased to receive that name by rebounding answer of Echo,
10 And hope thereby to ease their inward horrible anguish,
Then shall those things ease their inward horrible anguish
When trees dance to the pipe, and swift streams stay by the music,
Or when an echo begins unmoved to sing them a love song.
Say then what vantage do we get by the trade of a pastor?
15 (Since no estates be so base, but love vouchsafeth his arrow,
Since no refuge doth serve from wounds we do carry about us,
Since outward pleasures be but halting helps to decayed souls)
Save that daily we may discern what fire we do burn in.
Far more happy be you, whose greatness gets a free access,
20 Whose fair bodily gifts are framed most lovely to each eye.
Virtue you have, of virtue you have left proofs to the whole world,
And virtue is grateful with beauty and richess adorned,
Neither doubt you a whit, time will your passion utter.
Hardly remains fire hid where skill is bent to the hiding,
25 But in a mind that would his flames should not be repressed,
Nature worketh enough with a small help for the revealing.
Give therefore to the muse great praise in whose very likeness
You do approach to the fruit your only desires be to gather.

Cleophila. First shall fertile grounds not yield increase of a good seed;
30 First the rivers shall cease to repay their floods to the ocean;
First may a trusty greyhound transform himself to a tiger;
First shall virtue be vice, and beauty be counted a blemish,
Ere that I leave with song of praise her praise to solemnize,

4 shepherd's] shepherd Le, Je.   testifies Cl, Le, As, Da, Ph, Hm, 93: testify St, Bo,
Je.   our woes] our woe Bo; anguish 93.   6 passion] passions Le, Da.   enters] enter
Le; entices As.   7 make such dreary] make dreary Le; make a dreary Ph.
10 And] May 93.   11 *om.* Hm, 93.   12 swift] *om.* Ph; sweet Hm.   stay Cl,
Le, As, Je, 93: stayed St, Bo, Da, Ph; stays Hm.   18 Save] Since Cl, Le.
20 gifts are framed] gifts framed Bo, Je, Hm; gifts be framed Ph.   21 proofs] proof
Cl, 93.   22 richess Bo, Le, Da, Je, Hm: richenss St, Cl, As, Ph, 93.   25 repressed]
expressed Cl, Le.   28 fruit Cl, Le, As, Da, Ph, 93: fruits St, Bo, Je, Hm.

Her praise, whence to the world all praise had his only beginning:
But yet well I do find each man most wise in his own case.
None can speak of a wound with skill, if he have not a wound felt.
Great to thee my estate seems, thy estate is blest by my judge-
    ment: 5
And yet neither of us great or blest deemeth his own self.
For yet (weigh this, alas!) great is not great to a greater.
What judge you doth a hillock show by the lofty Olympus?
Such this small greatness doth seem compared to the greatest.
When cedars to the ground be oppressed by the weight of an   10
    emmet,
Or when a rich ruby's just price be the worth of a walnut,
Or to the sun for wonders seem small sparks of a candle:
Then by my high cedar, rich ruby, and only shining sun,
Virtue, richess, beauties of mine shall great be reputed.   15
O no, no, hardy shepherd, worth can never enter a title,
Where proofs justly do teach, thus matched, such worth to be
    naught worth.
Let not a puppet abuse thy sprite, kings' crowns do not help them
From the cruel headache, nor shoes of gold do the gout heal,   20
And precious couches full oft are shaked with a fever.
If then a bodily evil in a bodily gloss be not hidden,
Shall such morning dews be an ease to the heat of a love's fire?

Dorus. O glitt'ring miseries of man, if this be the fortune
    Of those fortune lulls, so small rest rests in a kingdom.   25
    What marvel though a prince transform himself to a pastor?
    Come from marble bowers, many times the gay harbour of anguish,
    Unto a silly cabin, though weak, yet stronger against woes.
    Now by thy words I begin, most famous lady, to gather
    Comfort into my soul. I do find, I do find, what a blessing   30
    Is chanced to my life, that from such muddy abundance
    Of carking agonies (to estates which still be adherent)

1 had] hath 93. only] *om.* Cl, As, Da.   4 my estate] in state Da, Ph; my state 93.
thy estate] thy state Da, 93: this state Ph.   6 great or blest] are blest Cl; greatly
blest Ph.   7 a] the Cl, Da, 93.   9 this small] this small *corr. to* my minute Cl;
my minute Da, Je, Hm, 93; my small Ph.   10 be oppressed] be pressed Ph;
fall down 93.   12 just] *om.* Le, As; due Ph.   14 rich ruby Cl, Le, 93: right
ruby St, Bo, As, Ph, Je, Hm; ruby right Da.   16 hardy] hardly Ph; worthy
93.   20 shoes Bo, Cl, As, Da, Je, Hm, 93: shows St. Le, Ph.   21 oft are],
of care Ph; soft are Je.   24 the] thy Da, Ph, Je, Hm.   32 estates] high states.
Ph; states 93.

Destiny keeps me aloof. For if all thy estate to thy virtue
Joined, by thy beauty adorned, be no means these griefs to
 abolish;
If neither by that help, thou canst climb up to thy fancy,
5 Nor yet, fancy so dressed, do receive more plausible hearing;
Then do I think, indeed, that better it is to be private
In sorrow's torments than, tied to the pomps of a palace,
Nurse inward maladies, which have not scope to be breathed out,
But perforce digest all bitter juices of horror
10 In silence, from a man's own self with company robbed.
Better yet do I live, that though by my thoughts I be plunged
Into my life's bondage, yet may disburden a passion
(Oppressed with ruinous conceits) by the help of an outcry:
Not limited to a whisp'ring note, the lament of a courtier,
15 But sometimes to the woods, sometimes to the heavens, do decipher,
With bold clamour unheard, unmarked, what I seek, what I suffer:
And when I meet these trees, in the earth's fair livery clothed,
Ease I do feel (such ease as falls to one wholly diseased)
For that I find in them part of my estate represented.

A Victory
B Lamenta-
 tion
C Quietness
D Love
E Refusal

F Death

A   B
Laurel shows what I seek, by the myrrh is showed how I seek it,
C
Olive paints me the peace that I must aspire to by conquest:
D   E
Myrtle makes my request, my request is crowned with a willow.
F
Cypress promiseth help, but a help where comes no recomfort.
Sweet juniper saith this, though I burn, yet I burn in a sweet fire.
25 Yew doth make me bethink what kind of bow the boy holdeth
Which shoots strongly without any noise and deadly without
 smart.
Fir trees great and green, fixed on a high hill but a barren,
Like to my noble thoughts, still new, well placed, to me fruitless.
30 Fig that yields most pleasant fruit, his shadow is hurtful,
Thus be her gifts most sweet, thus more danger to be near her,
But in a palm when I mark how he doth rise under a burden,

1 thy estate] this estate Cl; this state Da, 93; thy state Ph; thy estates Hm.
2 these] thy Bo, Ph; this Cl. griefs] grief Cl, Ph. 5 more] a Cl, Da, Hm.
15 heavens] heav'n Da, 93. do] to As, Da. 19 estate] state Da, Ph, Ra, 93.
20–3 *Marginal notes in* St, Je, Hm, Ra *only.* 21 by conquest] the conquest Cl;
my conquest Le; by the conquest 93. 23 recomfort Bo, Cl, Le, As, Da, Ph,
93: comfort St. Je, Hm, Ra. 25 bethink] think Bo, Ph, Hm, Ra, 93. 28 trees]
tree Ph; tree is Je, Hm. 32 But] Now 93.

And may I not (say I then) get up though griefs be so weighty?
Pine is a mast to a ship, to my ship shall hope for a mast serve?
Pine is high, hope is as high; sharp-leaved, sharp yet be my hope's
    buds.
Elm embraced by a vine, embracing fancy reviveth.   5
Poplar changeth his hue from a rising sun to a setting:
Thus to my sun do I yield, such looks her beams do afford me.
Old aged oak cut down, of new works serves to the building:
So my desires, by my fear cut down, be the frames of her honour.
Ash makes spears which shields do resist, her force no repulse takes: 10
Palms do rejoice to be joined by the match of a male to a female,
And shall sensive things be so senseless as to resist sense?
Thus be my thoughts dispersed, thus thinking nurseth a thinking,
Thus both trees and each thing else be the books of a fancy.
But to the cedar, queen of woods, when I lift my beteared eyes, 15
Then do I shape to myself that form which reigns so within me,
And think there she do dwell and hear what plaints I do utter:
When that noble top doth nod, I believe she salutes me;
When by the wind it maketh a noise, I do think she doth answer.
Then kneeling to the ground, oft thus do I speak to that image: 20
'Only jewel, O only jewel, which only deservest
That men's hearts be thy seat and endless fame be thy servant,
O descend for a while from this great height to behold me,
But naught else do behold (else is naught worth the beholding)
Save what a work by thyself is wrought: and since I am altered 25
Thus by thy work, disdain not that which is by thyself done.
In mean caves oft treasure abides, to an hostry a king comes.
And so behind foul clouds full oft fair stars do lie hidden.'

Cleophila. Hardy shepherd, such as thy merits, such may be her
    insight   30
Justly to grant thy reward, such envy I bear to thy fortune.
But to myself what wish can I make for a salve to my sorrows,
Whom both nature seems to debar from means to be helped,
And if a mean were found, fortune th'whole course of it hinders.
Thus plagued how can I frame to my sore any hope of amend- 35
    ment?

---

1 I not] not I Cl, Ra.   8 aged] age Bo, Da.   works] work Cl, Da; oaks Ph.
10 makes] make Le, Da.   15 lift] list As, Hm.   beteared] bleared Ph; betrayed
Hm.   17 do] doth Ph, Je, Hm.   plaints] plants 93.   20 do I] I do Ph, Ra.
31 thy reward] the reward Ph; thee reward 93.   35 Thus] This 93.

Whence may I show to my mind any light of a possible escape?
Bound, and bound by so noble bands as loath to be unbound,
Gaoler I am to myself, prison and prisoner to mine own self.
Yet be my hopes thus placed, here fixed lives my recomfort,
5   That that dear diamond, where wisdom holdeth a sure seat,
Whose force had such force so to transform, nay to reform me,
Will at length perceive these flames by her beams to be kindled,
And will pity the wound festered so strangely within me.
O be it so, grant such an event, O gods, that event give.
10   And for a sure sacrifice I do daily oblation offer
Of my own heart, where thoughts be the temple, sight is an altar.
But cease, worthy shepherd, now cease we to weary the hearers
With moanful melodies, for enough our griefs be revealed,
If by the parties meant our meanings rightly be marked,
15   And sorrows do require some respite unto the senses.

What exclaiming praises Basilius gave first to Cleophila's song,
and now to this eclogue, any man may guess that knows love is
better than a pair of spectacles to make everything seem greater
which is seen through it; and then is it never tongue-tied where fit
20 commendation (whereof womankind is so lickerous) is offered unto
it. But the wasting of the torches served as a watch unto them to
make them see the time's waste. And therefore the duke, though
unwilling, rase from his seat (which he thought excellently settled
of the one side), and considering Cleophila's late hurt, persuaded
25 her to take that far spent night's rest. And so of all sides they went
to recommend themselves to the elder brother of Death.

Here end the first eclogues of the
Countess of Pembroke's Arcadia.

1 a] *om.* Da, 93.   2 bands] bonds Da, Ph, Hm.   3 mine] my Bo, Cl, Le, Da, Je.
4 lives my] lives all my Cl, Da, 93.   7 these] their Bo; my Ph.   9 O gods]
O ye heavens Ph, Hm; O ye *followed by* heavens *crossed out* Je.   11 my] mine Da,
Ph, Je, Hm, 93.   an] the Ph; a 93.   12 the hearers] *illegible* St, *supplied from*
Bo *etc.*   22 time's Bo, As: time St.   23 settled] seated Bo.   24 hurt Bo,
As: hurts St.   27 end] ends Bo; endeth As.
19–28 and then . . . Arcadia] Cl *reads*: and then . . . is too lickerous) is offered unto it.
But the wasting of torches served for a watch unto them to make them know the night's
waste; and therefore Basilius, remembering Cleophila's hurt, though unwilling, rase up
from his seat (which he thought of the one side excellently seated), and persuaded her
to take her rest the like rest of that night. And so of all sides they went to recommend
themselves to the elder brother of Death.

Here ends the first eclogues of the Countess of
Pembroke's Arcadia.

Ph *reads*: And then is it never tongue-tied from the fit commendation.

Da *reads*: But the wasting of the torches made them find the night's waste; and therefore, remembering Cleophila's hurt, Basilius rose from his seat; and so the pastorals ended.

Je, Hm *read* (*text from* Je, *readings from* Hm):   5
and then is it never long tied as where fit commendations is so likewise offered unto it. But amongst the best singers of the shepherds, who had in their youth been brought up in some art, to help the natural benefits of the country muses, there grew a controversy whether these last kind of verses wherein every syllable is measured, or the other which are closed up in a rhyme, were the more commendable; Dicus liking the   10
measured, and Lalus the rhyming.

Dicus said that since verses had their chief ornament, if not end, in music, those which were just appropriated to music did best obtain their end, or at least were the most adorned; but those must needs most agree with music, since music standing principally upon the sound and the quantity, to answer the sound they brought words,   15
and to answer the quantity they brought measure. So that for every semibreve or minim, it had his syllable matched unto it with a long foot or a short foot, whereon they drew on certain names (as dactylus, spondeus, trocheus, etc.), and without wresting the word did as it were kindly accompany the time, so that either by the time a poet should straight know how every word should be measured unto it, or by the verse as soon find   20
out the full quantity of the music. Besides that it hath in itself a kind (as a man may well call it) of secret music, since by the measure one may perceive some verses running with a high note fit for great matters, some with a light foot fit for no greater than amorous conceits. 'Where', said he, 'those rhymes we commonly use, observing nothing but the number of syllables, as to make it of eight, ten, or twelve feet (saving perchance   25
that some have some care of the accent), the music, finding it confused, is forced sometimes to make a quaver of that which is rough and heavy in the mouth, and at another time to hold up in a long that which, being perchance but a light vowel, would be gone with a breath; and for all this comes at length a hink, tink, blirum and lirum, for a rhyming recompense, much like them that, having not skill to dance (proportioning   30
either slowly or swiftly his foot according to his ear), will yet for fellowship clap his feet together to make a noise. And this is the cause we have such hives full of rhyming poets, more than ever there were owls at Athens, where of the other there were but few in all ages come to our hands, but they dearly esteemed.'

Lalus on the other side would have denied his first proposition, and said that since   35
music brought a measured quantity with it, therefore the words less needed it, but as music brought time and measure, so these verses brought words and rhyme, which were four beauties for the other three. And yet to deny further the strength of his speech, he said Dicus did much abuse the dignity of poetry to apply it to music, since rather

---

6 and then . . . unto it Hm: *om*. Je.   7 amongst] among Hm.   singers of the Hm: *om*. Je.   8 of the: of y^t Je; of that Hm.   9 wherein Hm: where Je.
10 are Hm: were Je.   12 their] the Hm.   end] one Hm.   13–14 best . . . most] *om*. Hm.   15 quantity] quality Hm.   15–16 words, and] words Hm.   16 quantity] quality Hm.   17 syllable] syllables Hm.   unto it] accordingly Hm. or] and Hm.   17–18 they drew] drew they Hm.   18 on . . . as] divers names a Hm.
19 as it were] *om*. Hm.   by the time Hm: by time *corr. to* by tune Je.
20 straight] *om*. Hm.   measured] measuring Hm.   21–2 (as . . . it)] *om*. Hm.
22 secret] *om*. Hm.   24 those] these Hm.   25 saving] having Hm.   27 quaver] quality Hm.   at] *om*. Hm.   28 to hold] he would Hm.   29 tink Hm: Ink Je. blirum and lirum] lirum and blirum Hm.   31 according Hm: *om*. Je.
33 there] *om*. Hm.   35 on] of Hm.   proposition] proportion Hm.   38 his] the first Hm.

music is a servant to poetry, for by the one the ear only, by the other the mind, was pleased. And therefore what doth most adorn words, levelled within a proportion of number, to that music must be implied; which if it cannot do it well it is the musician's fault and not the poet's, since the poet is to look but to beautify his words to the most

5 delight, which no doubt is more had by the rhyme, especially to common ears to which the poet doth most direct his studies, and therefore is called the popular philosopher. And yet in this the finest judgement shall have more pleasure, since he that rhymes observes something the measure but much the rhyme, whereas the other attends only measure without all respect of rhyme; besides the accent which the rhymer regardeth,

10 of which the former hath little or none. 'And therefore', said Lalus, 'meseems rather those kind of poets are such manner dancers which, not binding them to return to one cadence, are ever kicking of their heels, and leave the pleasant observation of the chief cause. And where by the number of our kind you object too much facility, although easily no fault, yet they that will bind themselves to rhyme as the Tuscan and Arcadian

15 shepherds do, you shall not find them so thick. And for the few of the other kind, the cause is that many did write, but few wrote well, and therefore few lasted to the posterity; and the same no doubt will fall to a great number of rhymes, which die as soon as they are born, and few remain to come out of wardship.'

Dicus would have replied to have showed his evasions, but Basilius, after he had

20 moderated betwixt them, and said that in both kinds he wrote well that wrote wisely, and so both commendable, rose, remembering Cleophila's hurt, and therefore (though unwilling) persuaded her to take that far spent night's rest. And so of all sides they went to recommend themselves to the elder brother of Death.

Here endeth the first Eclogues.

---

1 the one Hm: *om.* Je.   was] is Hm.   2 within] with Hm.   3 implied] applied Hm.   4 to look but] but to look Hm.   8 whereas the other] whereas other Hm.   9 regardeth] doth especially regard Hm.   10 said] *om.* Hm. 11 such manner dancers Hm: such dancers Je.   13 cause] clause Hm.   where by: whereby Je; thereby Hm.   13–14 although . . . fault] *om.* Hm.   16 cause is Hm: cause is not Je.   17 great number] great many and number Hm.   21 rose Hm: rare Je.   22 unwilling Hm: unwillingly Je.   of Hm: on Je.   23 recommend] commend Hm.   24 endeth] ends Hm.

THE SECOND BOOK OR ACT

IN these pastoral pastimes a great number of days were sent to
follow their flying predecessors, while the cup of poison, which was
deeply tasted of all this noble company, had left no sinew of theirs
without mortally searching into it; yet never manifesting his 5
venomous work till once that, having drawn out the evening to his
longest line, no sooner had the night given place to the breaking out
of the morning's light and the sun bestowed his beams upon the tops
of the mountains but that the woeful Gynecia (to whom rest was no
ease) had left her loathed lodging and gotten herself into the 10
solitary places those deserts were full of, going up and down with
such unquiet motions as the grieved and hopeless mind is wont to
bring forth. There appeared unto the eyes of her judgement the
evils she was like to run into, with ugly infamy waiting upon them;
she saw the terrors of her own conscience; she was witness of her 15
long-exercised virtue, which made this vice the fuller of deformity.
The uttermost of the good she could aspire unto was but a fountain
of danger; and the least of her dangers was a mortal wound to her
vexed spirits; and lastly, no small part of her evils was that she was
wise to see her evils. Insomuch that, having a great while cast her 20
countenance ghastly about her, as if she had called all the powers of
the whole world to be witness of her wretched estate, at length
casting up her watery eyes to heaven: 'O sun,' said she, 'whose
unspotted light directs the steps of mortal mankind, art thou not
ashamed to impart the clearness of thy presence to such an over- 25
thrown worm as I am? O you heavens, which continually keep the
course allotted unto you, can none of your influences prevail so
much upon the miserable Gynecia as to make her preserve a course
so long embraced by her? O deserts, deserts, how fit a guest am I
for you, since my heart is fuller of wild ravenous beasts than ever 30
you were! O virtue, how well I see thou wert never but a vain name
and no essential thing, which hast thus left thy professed servant

2 pastoral] pastorals Da, Hm; pastorical Je.   sent] spent Cl, Da, Ph.   5 mortally]
mortality Je, Cm.   7–8 breaking out of the] *om.* Cl, Hm.   8 morning's] morning
As, Je, 90.   11 deserts Cl, As, Da, Ph, Je, Hm, 90: desert St, Bo.   were Da, Ph,
Je, Hm, 90: was St, Bo, As; *blank left* Cl.   12 hopeless] hapless Da, Je, Hm.
29 am I Cl, As, Da, Je, Hm, 90: I am St, Bo, Ph.   31 wert] art Ph; wast Je.

when she had most need of thy lovely presence! O imperfect proportion of reason, which can too much foresee, and so little prevent! Alas, alas,' said she, 'if there were but one hope for all my pains, or but one excuse for all my faultiness! But, wretch that I am,
5 my torment is beyond all succour, and my ill-deserving doth exceed my ill fortune. For nothing else did my husband take this strange resolution to live so solitary, for nothing else have the winds delivered this strange guest to my country, for nothing else have the destinies reserved my life to this time, but that only I, most wretched
10 I, should become a plague to myself, and a shame to womankind. Yet if my desire, how unjust so ever it be, might take effect, though a thousand deaths followed it, and every death were followed with a thousand shames, yet should not my sepulchre receive me without some contentment. But alas, sure I am not that Cleophila is such as
15 can answer my love. And if she be, how can I think she will, since this disguising must needs come for some foretaken conceit? And either way, wretched Gynecia, where canst thou find any small ground-plot for hope to dwell upon? No, no, it is Philoclea his heart is set upon (if he be a he); it is my daughter which I have borne to
20 supplant me. But if it be so, the life I have given thee, ungrateful Philoclea, I will sooner with these hands bereave thee of than my birth shall glory she hath bereaved me of my desires. In shame there is no comfort but to be beyond all bounds of shame.'

Having spoken this, she began to make a piteous war with her
25 fair hair when she might hear not far from her an extremely doleful voice, but so suppressed with a kind of whispering note that she could not conceive the words distinctly. But as a lamentable tune is the sweetest music to a woeful mind, she drew thither near away in hope to find some companion of her misery. And as she paced on,
30 she was stopped with a number of trees so thickly placed together that she was afraid she should with rushing through stop the speech of the lamentable party, which she was so desirous to understand. And therefore, sitting her down as softly as she could (for she was now in distance to hear), she might first perceive a lute, excellently

2 too] *om.* Da; so Je.   3 hope for] hope of Ph, Je (hope of *corr. to* hope for St).
7 solitary] solitarily Cl, 90.   have] did Cl; hath Ph.   19 if he] if it Da; if she
Je.   21 bereave thee of] bereave thereof Ph, Cm; bereaveth of Hm (St *could be read* thereof).   23 bounds] bonds Cl, Da, Hm.   25 an extremely doleful] an extreme doleful Bo; a piteous a doleful Cl; an extremity a doleful As; a doleful Da, Ph, Je, Hm.   26 suppressed] suspected Ph; oppressed Je.   29 companion] company Da, Je.   paced] passed Cl, Je, Hm, 90 (*corr.* 93).

well played upon, and then the same doleful voice accompanying it
with these few verses:

> In vain, mine eyes, you labour to amend
>   With flowing tears your fault of hasty sight;
> Since to my heart her shape you so did send   5
>   That her I see, though you did lose your light.
>
> In vain, my heart, now you with sight are burned,
>   With sighs you seek to cool your hot desire;
> Since sighs (into mine inward furnace turned)
>   For bellows serve to kindle more the fire.   10
>
> Reason in vain (now you have lost my heart)
>   My head you seek, as to your strongest fort;
> Since there mine eyes have played so false a part
>   That to your strength your foes have sure resort.
>   And since in vain I find were all my strife,   15
>   To this strange death I vainly yield my life.

The ending of the song served but for a beginning of new plaints;
as if the mind, oppressed with too heavy a burden of cares, was fain
to discharge itself in all manners, and as it were paint out the
hideousness of the pain in all sorts of colours. For the woeful   20
person, as if the lute had ill joined to the voice, threw it down to the
ground with suchlike words: 'Alas, poor lute, how much thou art
deceived to think that in my miseries thou couldst ease my woes, as
in my careless times thou wert wont to please my fancies! The time
is changed, my lute, the time is changed; and no more did my joyful 25
mind then receive everything to a joyful consideration than my
careful mind now makes each thing taste like the bitter juice of care.
The evil is inward, my lute, the evil is inward; which all thou dost
doth serve but to make me think more freely of; and the more I
think, the more cause I find of thinking, but less of hoping. The   30
discord of my thoughts, my lute, doth ill agree to the concord of thy
sweet strings; therefore, be not ashamed to leave thy master, since
he is not afraid to forsake himself.'

3–16 *The poem is in* Cm, 90–93.   4 fault] faint Cl; fate Je, Hm.   9 mine] my
Bo, Da, Je.   10 bellows OA, 90: bellow St.   15 And] All Hm; Then 90.
18 too heavy a burden] the heavy burden Cl; too heavy burden As.   20 hideous-
ness] sharpness Cl, As, Da, Ph, Je, Hm.   21 joined to] joined with Cl, As, 90.
down] *om.* As, 90.   22 thou art] art thou As, 90.   23 couldst Cl, Da, Je, Hm,
90: could St, Bo, Ph; *om.* As.   24 times] tunes Cl; time Ph; mind Hm.   wert]
were Ph; wast Hm; was 90 (*ex.* Cm).

And thus much spoken, instead of a conclusion, was closed up with so hearty a groaning that Gynecia could not refrain to show herself, thinking such griefs could serve fitly for nothing but her own fortune. But as she came into the little arbour of this sorrowful

5 music, her eyes met with the eyes of Cleophila (which was the party that thus had witnessed her sorrow), so that either of them remained confused with a sudden astonishment, Cleophila fearing lest she had heard some part of those sorrows which she had risen up that morning early of purpose to breathe out in secret to herself.

10 But Gynecia a great while stood still, with a kind of dull amazement, looking steadfastly upon her. At length returning to some use of herself, she began to say to Cleophila that she was sorry she would venture herself to leave her rest, being not altogether healed of her hurt. But as if the opening of her mouth to Cleophila had opened

15 some great flood-gap of sorrow, whereof her heart could not bear the violent issue, she sank to the ground with her hands over her face, crying vehemently: 'Cleophila, help me! O Cleophila, have pity of me!'

Cleophila ran to her, marvelling what sudden sickness had thus

20 possessed her; and beginning to ask her the cause of her sorrow, and offering her service to be employed by her, Gynecia opening her eyes wildly upon her, pricked with the flames of love and the torments of her own conscience: 'O Cleophila, Cleophila,' said she, 'dost thou offer me physic which art my only poison, or wilt

25 thou do me service which hast already brought me into eternal slavery?'

Cleophila yet more marvelling, and thinking some extreme pain did make her rave, 'Most excellent lady,' said she, 'you were best to retire yourself into your lodging that you the better may pass over

30 this sudden fit.'

'Retire myself,' said Gynecia, 'if I had retired myself into myself when thou (to me unfortunate guest) camest to draw me from myself, blessed had I been, and no need had I had of thy counsel. But now, alas, I am forced to fly to thee for succour whom I accuse of

3 her] Hm *missing from here* (ff. 33–45).   8 those] these Ph, Qu.   9 that morning early of purpose] early that morning of purpose Cl, Qu; that morning of purpose early Ph; that morning of purpose 90 (*only*).   15 great] *om*. As; greater Je. flood-gap] flood-gape Bo; flood-gates Je; flood-gate 90 (*ex*. Cm).   18 of] on Cl, Ph, Qu, 90.   20 sorrow] sorrows Je, Qu; pain 90.   28 to] *om*. Cl, As, 90. 29 the better may] may the better As, Da.   over] *om*. Cl, As, 90.   32 to me *om*. Da, Je.   camest 90: came OA, Cm.

all my hurt; and make thee judge of my cause who art the only author of my mischief.'

Cleophila, yet more astonished, 'Madam,' said she, 'whereof do you accuse me that I will not clear myself; or wherein may I stead you that you may not command me?' 5

'Alas,' answered Gynecia, 'what shall I say more? Take pity of me, O Cleophila, but not as Cleophila, and disguise not with me in words, as I know thou dost in apparel.'

Cleophila was stricken even dead with that word, finding herself discovered. But as she was amazedly thinking what to answer her, 10 they might see old Basilius pass hard by them, without ever seeing them, complaining likewise of love very freshly, and ending his complaint with this song, love having renewed both his invention and voice:

> Let not old age disgrace my high desire, 15
> O heav'nly soul in human shape contained.
> Old wood inflamed doth yield the bravest fire,
> When younger doth in smoke his virtue spend.

> Ne let white hairs (which on my face do grow)
> Seem to your eyes of a disgraceful hue; 20
> Since whiteness doth present the sweetest show,
> Which makes all eyes do honour unto you.

> Old age is wise and full of constant truth;
> Old age well stayed from ranging humour lives;
> Old age hath known whatever was in youth; 25
> Old age o'ercome, the greater honour gives.
> And to old age since you yourself aspire,
> Let not old age disgrace my high desire.

Which being done, he looked very curiously upon himself, sometimes fetching a little skip, as if he had said his strength had not 30 yet forsaken him. But Cleophila having in this time gotten some leisure to think for an answer, looking upon Gynecia as if she thought she did her some wrong, 'Madam,' said she, 'I am not acquainted with these words of disguising; neither is it the profession of an Amazon; neither are you a party with whom it is to be used. If my 35

10 amazedly] amazed Cl; advisedly Je; *om.* 90.   11 hard] *om.* Cl, Je.   15–28
The poem is in Ha (15–22 *only*), Cm, 90, 93.   19 do] doth Cl, Le, Da, Qu.
21 sweetest] bravest Je; clearest Ha.   22 honour] homage Cm, 93.   24 humour]
honour Cl, Le; humours Ph.   34 these] those Ph, 90.

service may please you, employ it, so long as you do me no wrong in misjudging of me.'

'Alas, Cleophila,' said Gynecia, 'I perceive you know full little how piercing the eyes are of a true lover. There is no one beam of
5 those thoughts you have planted in me but is able to discern a greater cloud than you do go in. Seek not to conceal yourself further from me, nor force not the passion of love into violent extremities!'

Now was Cleophila brought to an exigent, when the duke, turning his eye that way through the trees, perceived his wife and mistress
10 together; so that, framing the most lovely countenance he could, he came straightway towards them, and at the first word, thanking his wife for having entertained Cleophila, desired her she would now return into the lodge because he had certain matters of state to impart to the lady Cleophila. The duchess, being nothing troubled
15 with jealousy in that point, obeyed the duke's commandment, full of raging agonies, and determinately bent that, as she would seek all loving means to win Cleophila, so she would stir up terrible tragedies rather than fail of her intent.

But as soon as Basilius was rid of his wife's presence, falling down
20 on his knees, 'O lady,' said he, 'which have only had the power to stir up again those flames which had so long lain dead in me, see in me the power of your beauty which can make old age come to ask counsel of youth, and a prince unconquered to become a slave to a stranger. And when you see that power of yours, love that at least in
25 me, since it is yours, although of me you see nothing to be loved.'

'Worthy prince,' answered Cleophila, taking him up from his kneeling, 'both your manner and your speech are so strange unto me as I know not how to answer it better than with silence.'

'If silence please you', said the duke, 'it shall never displease me,
30 since my heart is wholly pledged to obey you. Otherwise, if you would vouchsafe mine ears such happiness as to hear you, they shall but convey your words to such a mind which is with the humblest degree of reverence to receive them.'

'I disdain not to speak to you, mighty prince,' said Cleophila,
35 'but I disdain to speak to any matter which may bring mine honour into question.'

5 those] the As; these Qu.   9 eye] eyes Je, 90.   20 on Cl, Da, Je, 90: of
St, Bo, As, Ph, Qu.   21 those] the As; these Je.   25 of] in Cl, Da, Je, Qu.
31 shall] should As, Je.   32 but] not Bo; *om.* 90.   35 mine] my Bo, Da,
Qu, 90.   36 into] in As, Qu.

And therewith, with a brave counterfeited scorn, she departed from the duke, leaving him not so sorry for this short answer as proud in himself that he had broken the matter. And thus did the duke, feeding his mind with these thoughts, pass great time in writing of verses, and making more of himself than he was wont to 5 do; that with a little help he would have grown into a pretty kind of dotage.

But Cleophila, being rid of this loving, but little loved, company, 'Alas,' said she, 'poor Pyrocles, was ever one but I that had received wrong, and could blame nobody; that, having more than I desire, 10 am still in want of that I would? Truly, Love, I must needs say thus much on thy behalf, thou hast employed my love there where all love is deserved; and for recompense hast sent me more love than ever I desired. Yet a child indeed thou showest thyself that thinkest to glut me with quantity, as though therein thou didst satisfy the 15 heart another way dedicated. But what wilt thou do, Pyrocles? Which way canst thou find to rid thee of these intricate troubles? To her whom I would be known to, I live in darkness; and to her am revealed from whom I would be most secret. What shield shall I find against the doting love of Basilius and the violent passion of 20 Gynecia? And if that be done, yet how am I the nearer to quench the fire that consumes me? Well, well, sweet Philoclea, my whole confidence must be builded in thy divine spirit, which cannot be ignorant of the cruel wound I have received by you.'

Thus did Cleophila wade betwixt small hopes and huge despairs, 25 whilst in the mean time the sweet Philoclea found strange unwonted motions in herself. And yet the poor soul could neither discern what it was, nor whither the vehemency of it tended. She found a burning affection towards Cleophila; an unquiet desire to be with her; and yet she found that the very presence kindled the desire. And examin- 30 ing in herself the same desire, yet could she not know to what the desire inclined. Sometimes she would compare the love she bare to Cleophila with the natural goodwill she bare to her sister; but she perceived it had another kind of working. Sometimes she would wish Cleophila had been a man, and her brother; and yet, in truth, 35 it was no brotherly love she desired of her. But thus, like a sweet

1 counterfeited] counterfeit As, Da.   2 this] his Cl, As, Da, Je, Qu, 90.   4 these] his Qu; those 90.   5 of] *om.* Bo, 90 (*ex.* Cm).   9 was ever] was there ever Je, 90. one] *om.* As; any Je.   13 hast As, Je, 90: hath St, Bo, Cl, Da; *om.* Ph, Qu. 17 these] *om.* As; thy 90.   18-19 am revealed] am I revealed Da, Je, Qu. 27 neither] never Ph, Qu; *om.* Je.

mind not much traversed in the cumbers of these griefs, she would even yield to the burden, rather suffering sorrow to take a full possession than exercising any way her mind how to redress it.

Thus in this one lodge was lodged each sort of grievous passions, 5 while in the other the worthy Dorus was no less tormented, even with the extremest anguish that love at any time can plague the mind withal. He omitted no occasion whereby he might make Pamela see how much extraordinary devotion he bare to her service, and daily withal strave to make himself seem more worthy in her sight; that 10 desert being joined to affection might prevail something in the wise princess. But too well he found that a shepherd's either service or affection was but considered of as from a shepherd, and the liking limited to that proportion. For indeed Pamela, having had no small stirring of her mind towards him, as well for the goodliness of his 15 shape as for the excellent trial of his courage, had notwithstanding, with a true-tempered virtue, sought all this while to overcome it; and a great mastery, although not without pain, she had wrought with herself. When Dorus saw of the one side that the highest point this service could bring him to should be but to be accounted a good 20 servant, and of the other that, for the suspiciousness of Dametas and Miso, with his young mistress Mopsa, he could never get any piece of time to give Pamela to understand the estate either of himself or affection—for Dametas, according to the right constitution of a dull head, thought no better way to show himself wise than by suspecting 25 everything in his way. Which suspicion Miso, for the shrewdness of her brain, and Mopsa, for a certain unlikely envy she had caught against Pamela's beauty, were very glad to execute. Insomuch that Dorus was ever kept off, and the fair Pamela restrained to a very unworthy servitude. Dorus, finding his service by this means lightly 30 regarded, his affection despised, and himself unknown, was a great while like them that in the midst of their leap know not where to light. Which in doleful manner, he would oftentimes utter, and make those desert places of counsel in his miseries. But in the end (seeing that nothing is achieved before it be attempted, and that lying still 35 doth never go forward), he resolved to take this mean for the manifesting of his mind—although it should have seemed to have

1 cumbers] combats Da; troubles Qu.   4 in this one] in one Cl, As, Da; in the one Ph, Je, Qu.   18–19 point this] point of this Ph, Je, Qu.   20 other that] other side that Ph, Je.   26 unlikely] unlike Cl; unliking Je, Qu.   29 Dorus] Le *begins here*.   32 make Bo, Cl, As, Ph, Je: making St, Da, Qu.

been a way the more to have darkened it: he began to counterfeit the extremest love towards Mopsa that might be; and as for the love, so lively indeed it was in him (although to another subject) that little he needed to counterfeit any notable demonstration of it. He would busily employ himself about her, giving her daily some country tokens, and making store of love songs unto her. Whereby, as he wan Dametas's heart, who had before borne him a certain rude envy for the favour the duke had lately showed unto him, so likewise did the same make Pamela begin to have the more consideration of him —for indeed so falls it often in the excellent women that even that which they disdain to themselves yet like they not that others should win it from them. But the more she marked the expressing of Dorus's affection towards Mopsa, the more she thought she found such phrases applied to Mopsa as must needs argue either great ignorance or a second meaning in Dorus; and so to this scanning of him was she now content to fall, whom before she was resolved to banish from her thoughts. As one time among the rest, Mopsa being alone with Pamela, Dorus with a face full of cloudy fancies came suddenly unto them, and taking a harp sang this passionated song:

> Since so mine eyes are subject to your sight,
> That in your sight they fixed have my brain;
> Since so my heart is filled with that light,
> That only light doth all my life maintain.
>
> Since in sweet you all goods so richly reign,
> That where you are no wished good can want;
> Since so your living image lives in me,
> That in myself yourself true love doth plant;
> How can you him unworthy then decree,
> In whose chief part your worths implanted be?

The song being ended, which he had oftentimes broken off in the midst with grievous sighs which overtook every verse he sang, he let fall his harp from him, and casting his eye sometimes upon Mopsa,

2 as] *om.* Ph, Je.   8 unto] *om.* Le, Je, Qu.   10 falls it often] falls it out often Le, Je.   11 to] unto Da, Qu.   12 expressing Cl, As, Da, Ph, Je, Qu: expressings St, Bo.   14 phrases] praises Ph; frenzies Qu.   19 unto OA: into St; in unto 90. this] a Da, Ph.   passionated] passionate Cl, As, Da, Ph, Je; passioned Qu; *om.* 90. 21–30 *The poem is in* Cm, 90–93.   30 part] plant Bo; parts As, Le, Ph, Qu. worths] worthies Le, Da, Je.   31 which he had] which had Cl, Le; which she had Da.   33 eye] eyes Je, Qu (eyes *corr. to* eye St).

but settling his sight principally upon Pamela: 'And is it only the fortune, most beautiful Mopsa,' said he, 'of wretched Dorus that fortune must be the measure of his mind? Am I only he that, because I am in misery, more misery must be laid upon me? Must that which should be cause of compassion become an argument of cruelty against me? Alas, excellent Mopsa, consider that a virtuous prince requires the life of his meanest subject, and the heavenly sun disdains not to give light to the smallest worm. O Mopsa, Mopsa, if my heart could be as manifest to you as it is uncomfortable to me, I doubt not the height of my thoughts should well countervail the lowness of my quality. Who hath not heard of the greatness of your estate? Who sees not that your estate is much excelled with that sweet uniting of all beauties which remaineth and dwelleth with you? Who knows not that all these are but ornaments of that divine spark within you which, being descended from heaven, could not elsewhere pick out so sweet a mansion? But if you will know what is the bond that ought to knit all these excellencies together, it is a kind mercifulness to such a one as is in soul devoted to those perfections.'

Mopsa (who already had had a certain smackering towards Dorus) stood all this while with her hand sometimes before her face, but most commonly with a certain special grace of her own, wagging her lips and grinning instead of smiling. But all the words he could get of her was (wrying her waist): 'In faith, you jest with me; you are a merry man indeed!'

But Pamela did not so much attend Mopsa's entertainment as she marked both the matter Dorus spake and the manner he used in uttering it. And she saw in them both a very unlikely proportion to mistress Mopsa, so that she was contented to urge a little further of him: 'Master Dorus,' said the fair Pamela, 'methinks you blame your fortune very wrongfully, since the fault is not in fortune but in you that cannot frame yourself to your fortune; and as wrongfully you do require Mopsa to so great a disparagement as to her

1 settling] setting Ph, Je, 90 (corr. 93).   only the] only Ph; the only Qu, 90. 9 to you] unto you Je, Cm.   10 lowness] lowliness Cl, Da.   12 excelled] extolled Da; excellent Je (excellent corr. to excelled St, Qu).   13 all] your Ph; om. Qu, Cm.   15 within] which is in As, Je.   17 bond] band Je, Qu, 90 (only).   17–18 kind mercifulness] kind of mercifulness Cl, Le, Je, 90 (corr. 93). 18 in soul] in his soul Le, 90 (his deleted St).   20 already had had] had had already Bo, Ph; already had Je.   smackering] smacking Le; smickering Je; smytering Qu. 24 wrying] om. Ph; wringing Je, Qu, 90 (corr. 93).   33 you do] do Le, 90; do you As, Je, Qu.

father's servant, since she is not worthy to be loved that hath not some feeling of her own worthiness.'

Dorus stayed a good while after her words in hope she would have continued her speech, so great a delight he received in hearing her. But seeing her say no further, with a quaking all over his body, he thus answered her: 'Lady most worthy of all duty, how falls it out that you in whom all virtue shines will take the patronage of fortune, the only rebellious handmaid against virtue—especially since before your eyes you have a pitiful spectacle of her wickedness, a forlorn creature which must remain not such as I am but such as she makes me, since she must be the balance of worthiness or disparagement? Yet alas, if the condemned man may even at his death have leave to speak, let my mortal wound purchase thus much consideration, since the perfections are such in the party I love as the feeling of them cannot come into any unnoble heart. Shall that heart, which doth not only feel them but hath all the workings of his life placed in them, shall that heart, I say, lifted up to such a height, be counted base? O let not an excellent spirit do itself such wrong as to think where it is placed, embraced, and loved, there can be any unworthiness; since the weakest mist is not easilier driven away by the sun than that is chased away with so high thoughts.'

'I will not deny,' answered the gracious Pamela, 'but that the love you bear to Mopsa hath brought you to the consideration of her virtues, and the consideration may have made you the more virtuous, and so the more worthy. But even that, then, you must confess you have received of her, and so are rather gratefully to thank her than to press any further till you bring something of your own by which to claim it. And truly, Dorus, I must in Mopsa's behalf say thus much to you: that if her beauties have so overtaken you, it becometh a true love to have your heart more set upon her good than your own, and to bear a tenderer respect to her honour than your satisfaction.'

'Now, by my halidom, madam,' said Mopsa, throwing a great

1 loved] beloved Ph, Qu.   4 hearing her] hearing of her Cl, Da.   5 But] And Le, As, Cm.   7 patronage Ph, 90: patrony St, Cl; patriconie Bo; pattern Le; patrocinie As, Je; patrimony Da; patronicy Qu.   13 thus] this Je, Cm. 15 unnoble] unmovable Da; humble Ph; immovable Je; unable Qu.   16 workings] working Je, 90.   19 as to think where Cl, 90: as where St, Bo, Le, As, Ph, Je, Cm; as once to imagine where Da; as when Qu.   20 unworthiness] worthiness Qu, Cm. 24 you the more] you more Bo, Le, Ph, Qu.   27 by which] whereby Le, As, 90. 29 becometh] becomes Cl, Le, As, 90.   31 a tenderer] a tender Le, Cm; a more tender Da.   than your] than to your Cl, Da.

number of sheep's eyes upon Dorus, 'you have even touched mine own mind to the quick, forsooth.'

Dorus, finding that the policy he had used had at leastwise procured thus much happiness unto him as that he might even in his lady's presence discover the sore which had deeply festered within him, and that she could better conceive his reasons applied to Mopsa than she would have vouchsafed them whilst herself was a party, thought good to pursue on his good beginning using this fit occasion of Pamela's wit and Mopsa's ignorance. Therefore with an humble but piercing eye, looking upon Pamela as if he had rather be condemned by her mouth than highly exalted by the other, turning himself to Mopsa, but keeping his eye where it was, 'Fair Mopsa', said he, 'well do I find by the wise knitting together of your answer that any disputation I can use is as much too weak as I unworthy. I find my love shall be proved no love, without I leave to love, being too unfit a vessel in whom so high thoughts should be engraved. Yet, since the love I bear you hath so joined itself to the best part of my life, as the one cannot depart but that the other will follow, before I seek to obey you in making my last passage, let me know which is my unworthiness, either of mind, estate, or both.'

Mopsa was about to say 'in neither', for her heart did even quab with overmuch kindness, when Pamela, with a more favourable countenance than before, finding how apt he was to fall into despair, told him he might therein have answered himself, for besides that it was granted him that the inward feeling of Mopsa's perfections had greatly beautified his mind, there was none could deny but that his mind and body of themselves deserved great allowance. 'But Dorus', said she, 'you must so far be master of your love as to consider that since the judgement of the world stands upon matter of fortune, and that the sex of womankind of all other is most bound to have regardful eye to men's judgements, it is not for us to play the philosophers in seeking out your hidden virtues, since that which in a wise prince would be counted wisdom, in us will be taken for a light-grounded affection; so is not one thing one, done by divers persons.'

1 mine] my Bo, As, Da.   6 could] would Cl, Le.   10 humble but piercing] humble piercing Cl, Le, As, 90.   11 be] been Cl, Ph, Je, 90.   15 no love] in love Cl, As, Ph.   20 my] mine Bo, Ph, Qu.   21 did even quab] did even quake Cl; I think tumbled 90.   27 of themselves] om. Le, 90.   30-1 have regardful] have a regardful As, Da, Je.   31 philosophers] philosopher Le, Je. 32 your] the As, Qu, Cm.   which in Bo, Cl, Le, 90: within St, Da, Ph; which is in As; in Je, Qu.

There is no man in a burning fever feels so great contentment in cold water greedily received (which, as soon as the drink ceaseth, the heat reneweth) as poor Dorus found his soul refreshed with her sweetly pronounced words, and newly and more violently again inflamed as soon as she had closed up her delightful speech with no less well graced silence. But remembering in himself that as well the soldier dies which stands still as he that gives the bravest onset, and seeing that to the making up of his fortune there wanted nothing so much as the making known of his estate, with a face well witnessing how deeply his soul was possessed, and with the most submissive behaviour that a thralled heart could express, even as if his words had been too thick for his mouth, at length spake to this purpose: 'Alas, most worthy princess,' said he, 'and do not then your own sweet words sufficiently testify that there was never man could have a juster action against filthy fortune than I, since all other things being granted me, her blindness is my only let? O heavenly gods, I would either she had such eyes as were able to discern my deserts, or I were blind not to see the daily cause of my misfortune! But yet,' said he, 'most honoured lady, if my miserable speeches have not already cloyed you, and that the very presence of such a wretch become not hateful in your eyes, let me reply thus much further against my mortal sentence by telling you a story which happened in this same country long since (for woes make the shortest time seem long), whereby you shall see that my estate is not so contemptible but that a prince hath been content to take the like upon him, and by that only hath aspired to enjoy a mighty princess.'

Pamela graciously hearkened, and he told his tale in this sort: 'In the country of Thessalia (alas, why name I that accursed country which brings forth nothing but matters for tragedies? But name it I must); in Thessalia, I say, there was—well may I say there was— a prince. No! no prince, whom bondage wholly possessed, but yet accounted a prince, and named Musidorus. O Musidorus! Musidorus! But to what serve exclamations where there are no ears to receive the sound? This Musidorus, being yet in the tenderest age,

3 heat] rage Cl, Le, As, 90.   7 which stands] with standing Je, Qu; which standeth 90.   12 thick] think Da, Ph; big Je.   16 gods] God Cl, Le, 90.
18 daily cause of my] cause of my daily Da; cause of my Je.   23 same] om. Da, Je.
24 my] mine Cl, Le.   29 for] of Cl, Ph, Je, Qu (of corr. to for St).   30 well may I say Cl, Le, Je, 90: well I may say St, Bo, As, Da, Ph; well I say Qu.
31 No! no] now no As; no Da.   33 serve Bo, Cl, Le, Je, 90: serves St, As, Da, Ph; service Qu.

his aged father paid up to nature her last duties, leaving his child to
the faith of friends and the proof of time. Death gave him not such
pangs as the foresightful care he had of his silly successor. And yet,
if in his foresight he could have seen so much, happy was that good
5 prince in his timely departure which barred him from the knowledge
of his son's miseries, which his knowledge could neither have
prevented nor relieved. The young Musidorus being thus (as for the
first pledge of the destinies' goodwill) deprived of his principal stay,
was yet for some years after (as if the stars would breathe themselves
10 for a greater mischief) lulled up in as much good luck as the heedful
love of his doleful mother and the flourishing estate of his country
could breed unto him. But when the time now came that misery
seemed to be ripe for him, because he had age to know misery, I
think there was a conspiracy in all heavenly and earthly things to
15 frame fit occasions to lead him unto it. His people (to whom all
foreign matters in foretime were odious) began now to wish in their
beloved prince experience by travel. His dear mother (whose eyes
were held open only with the joy of looking upon him) did now
dispense with the comfort of her widowed life, desiring the same her
20 subjects did, for the increase of her son's worthiness. And hereto
did Musidorus's own virtue (see how virtue can be a minister to
mischief) sufficiently provoke him. For, indeed, thus much I must
say for him (although the likeness of our mishaps makes me presume
to pattern myself unto him) that well doing was at that time his
25 scope, from which no faint pleasures could withhold him. But the
present occasion (which did knit all these together) was his uncle, the
king of Macedon, who (having lately before gotten such victories as
were beyond expectation) did at this time send both for the prince,
his son (brought up together, to avoid the wars, with Musidorus)
30 and for Musidorus himself, that his joy might be the more full having
such partakers of it. But, alas, to what a sea of miseries my plaintful
tongue doth lead me!'

And thus out of breath, rather with that he thought than with that
he said, Dorus stayed his speech till Pamela showing by countenance
35 that such was her pleasure, he thus continued it: 'These two young

1 her] his Ph, Cm.   6 neither] never Ph, Qu.   7 relieved] revealed Da, Je.
12 unto] into As; in Qu.   15 occasions] occasion Je, Qu, 90 (*corr.* 93).   16 in
foretime were] were As; were in foretime Qu.   now] *om.* Qu, 90.   19 widowed]
widowhood Cl, Ph, Qu; widowhead Le, As, 90.   22 I must] must I Cl, Le, Je
(*om.* For . . . him Ph).   26 these] those Ph; this 90 (*ex.* Cm).   33 than with
that] than that Je, 90.

princes, to satisfy the king, took their way by sea towards Byzantium, where at that time his court was. But when the conspired heavens had gotten this subject of their wrath upon so fit a place as the sea was, they straight began to breathe out in boisterous winds some part of their malice against him. So that, with the loss of all his navies, he 5 only with the prince, his cousin, were cast aland, far off from the place whither their desires would have guided them. O cruel winds in your unconsiderate rages, why either began you this fury, or why did you not end it in his end? But your cruelty was such as you would spare his life for many deathful torments. To tell you what 10 pitiful mishaps fell to the young prince of Macedon, his cousin, I should too much fill your ears with strange horrors; neither will I stay upon those laboursome adventures, nor loathsome mis-adventures, to which and through which his fortune and courage conducted him. My speech hasteth itself to come to the full point 15 of all Musidorus's infortunes. For as we find the most pestilent diseases do gather into themselves all the infirmities with which the body before was annoyed, so did his last misery embrace in the extremity of itself all his former mischiefs. Arcadia, Arcadia was the place prepared to be the stage of his endless overthrow; Arcadia 20 was (alas, well might I say it is) the charmed circle where all his spirits should for ever be enchanted. For here and nowhere else did his infected eyes make his mind know what power heavenly beauty hath to throw it down to hellish agonies. Here, here did he see the Arcadian duke's eldest daughter; in whom he forthwith placed so 25 all his hopes of joy and joyful parts of his heart, that he left in himself nothing but a maze of longing and a dungeon of sorrow. But alas, what can saying make them believe whom seeing cannot persuade? Those pains must be felt before they be understood; no outward utterance can command a conceit. Such was as then the 30 state of the duke as it was no time by direct means to seek her; and such was the state of his captived will as he could delay no time of seeking her. In this entangled case, he clothed himself in a shep-herd's weed, that under the baseness of that form he might at least have free access to feed his eyes with that which should at length eat 35

5 navies] navy Cl, As, 90; name Da. Qu; unconstant Ph; considerate Je. full point OA, 90: the point St. *deleted between* as *and* the) St. Arcadia OA, 90: Arcadia St. Cm); language Ph; lingering Qu.

8 unconsiderate] inconsiderate Bo, As, 13 stay] stand Ph; seem Qu.   15 the 16 as we find the most OA, 90: as the most (we 19 mischiefs] mischief Cl, Le, Je. Arcadia, 27 longing] lodging Cl (lodging *corr. to* longing 33 case] care Ph; sort Qu.

up his heart. In which doing, thus much without doubt he hath manifested: that this estate is not always to be rejected, since under that veil there may be hidden things to be esteemed. And that if he might, with taking on a shepherd's look, cast up his eyes to the
5 fairest princess nature in that time created, the like, nay the same, desire of mine need no more to be disdained or held for disgraceful. But now, alas, mine eyes wax dim, my tongue begins to falter, and my heart to want force to help either, with the feeling remembrance I have in what heap of miseries the caitiff prince lay at this time
10 buried. Pardon therefore, most excellent princess, if I cut off the course of my dolorous tale, since (if I be understood) I have said enough for the defence of my baseness. And for that which after might befall to that pattern of ill fortune, the matters are too monstrous for my capacity. His hateful destinies must best declare their
15 own workmanship.'

He ended thus his speech. But withal began to renew his accustomed plaints and humble intercessions to Mopsa, who (having no great battle in her spirit) was almost brought asleep with the sweet delivery of his lamentations. But Pamela (whom liking had made
20 willing to conceive, and natural wisdom able to judge) let no word slip without his due pondering; even love began to revive his flames, which the opinion she had of his meanness had before covered in her. She well found he meant the tale by himself, and that he did under that covert manner make her know the great
25 nobleness of his birth. But no music could with righter accords possess her senses than every passion he expressed had his mutual working in her. Full well she found the lively image of a vehement desire in herself, which ever is apt to receive belief, but hard to ground belief. For as desire is glad to embrace the first show of hope,
30 so by the same nature is desire desirous of a perfect assurance. She did immediately catch hold of his signifying himself to be a prince, and did glad her heart with having a reasonable ground to build her love upon. But straight the longing for assurance made suspicions arise and say unto herself, 'Pamela, take heed! The sinews of
35 wisdom is to be hard of belief. Who dare place his heart in so great places dare frame his head to as great feignings?' Dorus, that found his speeches had given alarum to her imaginations, to hold her the

3 that veil Bo, Cl, Le, Da, Je, Qu, 90: the veil St, As, Ph.   And that if] And if Le, As, 90.   13 to that] to the As, Ph, Qu.   pattern OA, 90: patron St.   32 a] *om.* Cl, Qu.   34 arise] rise Da, Je, Qu.   37 alarum] larum Ph; an allarum Je; a lantern Qu.

longer in them and bring her to a dull yielding-over her forces (as
the nature of music is to do), he took up his harp and sang these few
verses:

> My sheep are thoughts, which I both guide and serve:
> Their pasture is fair hills of fruitless love: 5
> On barren sweets they feed, and feeding starve:
> I wail their lot, but will not other prove.
> My sheephook is wanhope which all upholds:
> My weeds, desire, cut out in endless folds.
> What wool my sheep shall bear, while thus they live,   10
> In you it is, you must the judgement give.

The music added to the tale, and both fitted to such motions in her
as now began again to be awaked, did steal out of the fair eyes of
Pamela some drops of tears; although with great constancy she
would fain have overmastered at least the show of any such weakness. 15
At length, with a sigh come up even to her mouth and there stopped:
'But lord,' said she, 'if such were the prince's burning affection,
what could he hope by living here, if it were not to grow purer in the
fire like a salamander?'

'And even so too,' answered Dorus, 'but withal perchance (for 20
what cannot love hope?) he hoped to carry away the fire with him.'

'With him,' said she, 'now what could induce a princess to go
away with a shepherd?'

'Principally,' said he, 'the virtuous gratefulness for his affection;
then, knowing him to be a prince; and lastly, seeing herself in 25
unworthy bondage.'

Pamela found in her conscience such an accusing of secret consent
thereto that she thought it safest way to divert the speech, lest in
parley the castle might be given up. And therefore, with a gracious
closing up of her countenance towards Dorus, she willed Mopsa to 30
take good heed to herself, for her shepherd could speak well. 'But
truly Mopsa,' said she, 'if he can prove himself such as he saith (I
mean the honest shepherd Menalcas's brother and heir), I know no
reason why a better than you need think scorn of his affectionate
suit.'   35

4–11 *The poem is in* Ma, Fl, Cm, 90–93.   6 On Bo, 90: In St, Cl, Le, As, Ph,
Je, Qu, Ma, Fl; O Da.   10 while] whiles 90.   they] I Ma, Fl.   12 Le *does not
continue prose extract.*   15 would fain have] would have As, Ph; would have fain
Qu.   16 come] came Cl, Da.   up even] even up As, Da, Je.   27 of secret]
of a secret Bo, Cl, Da, Ph (found . . . that she *om.* Qu).   28 way] away Ph; *om.* Je.
divert] direct Cl, Ph; surcease Je.   31 good] *om.* Ph, 90.

Mopsa did not love comparisons, but yet, being far spent towards Dorus, she answered Pamela that, for all his quaint speeches, she would keep her honesty close enough. And that, as for the high way of matrimony, she would go never a furlong further till my master, 5 her father, did speak the whole word himself. But ever and anon turning her muzzle towards Dorus, she threw such a prospect upon him as might well have given a surfeit to any light lover's stomach. But Dorus, full of inward joy that he had wrought his matters to such a towardness, took out of his bag a very rich jewel, kept 10 among other of his precious things, which because of the device he thought fittest to give. It was an altar of gold, very full of the most esteemed stones, dedicated to Pollux who, because he was made a god for his brother Castor's virtue, all the honour men did to him seemed to have their final intent to the greater god Castor; about it 15 was written in Roman words, *Sic vos non vobis*. And kneeling down to the fair princess Pamela, he desired her she would in his behalf bestow it upon the cruel-hearted Mopsa who was as then benumbed with joy, seeing so fair a present. Pamela gave it to her, having received into her own mind a great testimony of the giver's worthiness.

20 But alas, sweet Philoclea, how hath my pen forgotten thee, since to thy memory principally all this long matter is intended. Pardon the slackness to come to those woes which thou didst cause in others and feel in thyself. The sweet-minded Philoclea was in their degree of well doing to whom the not knowing of evil serveth 25 for a ground of virtue, and hold their inward powers in better temper with an unspotted simplicity than many who rather cunningly seek to know what goodness is than willingly take into themselves the following of it. True it is that that sweet and simple breath of heavenly goodness is the easier to fall because it hath not passed 30 through the worldly wickedness, nor feelingly found the evil that evil carrieth with it. As now the amiable Philoclea, whose eyes and senses had received nothing but according as the natural course of each thing required, whose tender youth had obediently lived under her parents' behests without the framing (out of her own will) the

---

1 but] *om.* Cl; and As.   2 for all his quaint speeches OA: for his dainty speeches St; for all my quaint speeches 90.   4 would go never a] would go a Ph; could not go a Je; would not go a Qu; would step never a 90.   11 give. It OA: give it. It St.   14 greater] great Da, Qu.   15 *vos* Cl, As, Da, Je, Qu: *vobis* St, Bo, Ph.   21 long] *om.* Ph, Qu.   23 others Cl, As, Ph, Je Qu, 90: other St, Bo, Da.   24 their degree] the way As; the very degree Da; the degree Ph.   27 take] to take Cl, Qu.   30 nor feelingly] nor yet feelingly Cl, As.

forechoosing of anything, was suddenly (poor soul) surprised before
she was aware that any matter laid hold of her. Neither did she
consider that the least gap a sea wins is enough without gain-
striving industry to overflow a whole country; but finding a moun-
tain of burning desire to have overwhelmed her heart, and that the   5
fruits thereof, having new won the place, began to manifest them-
selves with horrible terrors of danger, dishonour and despair, she
did suffer her sweet spirits to languish under the heavy weight,
thinking it impossible to resist, as she found it deadly to yield. Thus
ignorant of her own disease, although (full well) she found herself   10
diseased, her greatest pleasure was to put herself into some lonely
place where she might freely feed the humour that did tyrannize
within her: as one night that, the moon being full did show herself
in her most perfect beauty, the unmatched Philoclea secretly stale
from her parents (whose eyes were now so bent upon another subject   15
that the easier she might get her desired advantage); and going with
uncertain paces to a little wood, where many times before she had
delighted to walk, her rolling eye lighted upon a tuft of trees, so
closely set together as with the shade the moon gave through it, it
bred a fearful devotion to look upon it. But well did she remember   20
the place, for there had she often defended her face from the sun's
rage, there had she enjoyed herself often while she was mistress of
herself and had no other thoughts but such as might arise out of
quiet senses. But the principal cause that made her remember it was
a fair white marble stone that should seem had been dedicated in   25
ancient time to the sylvan gods; which she finding there a few days
before Cleophila's coming, had written these words upon it as a
testimony of her mind against the suspicion she thought she lived in.
The writing was this:

> Ye living powers enclosed in stately shrine   30
> Of growing trees, ye rural gods that wield
> Your sceptres here, if to your ears divine
> A voice may come which troubled soul doth yield,
>   This vow receive, this vow O gods maintain:
>   My virgin life no spotted thought shall stain.   35

11 lonely] lovely Cl, As, Ph, Qu; lowly Da.   13 night that, the] night, the Da, Je.
22 while] whilst Ph; when Qu.   30–p. 110, 12 *The poem is in* 90–93; Cm *leaves*
a blank for it.   30 Ye] You 90.   31 ye] you Da, Je, 90; the Ph, Qu.   34 This
vow] This voice As, Ph.

Thou purest stone, whose pureness doth present
My purest mind; whose temper hard doth show
My tempered heart; by thee my promise sent
Unto myself let after-livers know.
5   No fancy mine, nor others' wrong suspect
Make me, O virtuous Shame, thy laws neglect.

O Chastity, the chief of heav'nly lights,
Which makes us most immortal shape to wear,
Hold thou my heart, establish thou my sprites;
10   To only thee my constant course I bear.
Till spotless soul unto thy bosom fly,
Such life to lead, such death I vow to die.

But now that her memory served as an accuser of her change, and
that her own hand-writing was there to bear testimony of her fall,
15 she went in among the few trees, so closed in the top together as they
seemed a little chapel; and there might she by the moonlight
perceive the goodly stone which served as an altar in that woody
devotion. But neither the light was enough to read the words, and
the ink was already foreworn and in many places blotted; which as
20 she perceived, 'Alas,' said she, 'fair marble, which never receivedst
spot but by my writing, well do these blots become a blotted writer;
but pardon her which did not dissemble then, although she have
changed since. Enjoy, and spare not, the glory of thy nature which
can so constantly bear the marks of my inconstancy!' And herewith
25 hiding her eyes awhile with her soft hands, there came into her
head certain verses which, if the light had suffered, she would fain
presently have adjoined as a retractation to the other. The verses
were to this effect:

My words, in hope to blaze my steadfast mind,
30   This marble chose, as of like temper known:
But lo, my words defaced, my fancies blind,
Blots to the stone, shame to myself I find;
And witness am, how ill agree in one,
A woman's hand with constant marble stone.

2 hard Cl, Le, As, Ph, Je, Qu, 90: heart St; hear Da.   8 makes] makest Le, 90.
15 top] tops Je, 90.   20 receivedst Da, Je, 90: received St, Bo, Cl, As, Ph;
receivest Qu.   22 have] hath Ph; had Je.   27 have Da, Je, Qu, 90: had St,
Bo, Cl, As, Ph.   retractation] retraction Cl, Ph, Je, Qu, Cm.   29–p. 111, 6 *The
poem is in* 90–93; Cm *leaves a blank for it.*   32 shame Bo, Cl, Da, Ph, 90: shames
St, As, Le, Je, 93; shame is Qu.

My words full weak, the marble full of might;
My words in store, the marble all alone;
My words black ink, the marble kindly white;
My words unseen, the marble still in sight,
    May witness bear, how ill agree in one,   5
    A woman's hand with constant marble stone.

But seeing she could not see so perfectly as to join this recantation
to the former vow, laying all her fair length under one of the trees,
for a while the poor soul did nothing but turn up and down and hide
her face, as if she had hoped to turn away the fancy that mastered 10
her, or could have hidden herself from her own thoughts. At length
with a whispering voice to herself, 'O me, unfortunate wretch,' said
she, 'what poisonous heats be these that thus possess me? How hath
the sight of this strange guest invaded my soul? Alas, what entrance
found this desire; or what strength had it thus to conquer me?' 15
Then looking to the stars, which had perfectly as then beautified the
clear sky, 'My parents', said she, 'have told me that in these fair
heavenly bodies there are great hidden deities which have their
working in the ebbing and flowing of our estates. If it be so, then,
O ye stars, judge rightly of me; and if I have willingly made myself 20
a prey to fancy, or if by any idle lusts I framed my heart fit for such
an impression, then let this plague daily increase in me till my name
be made odious to womankind. But if extreme and unresistible
violence have oppressed me, who will ever do any of you sacrifice,
O ye stars, if you do not succour me—no, no, you cannot help me; 25
my desire must needs be waited on with shame, and my attempt with
danger. And yet are these but childish objections. It is the impossi-
bility that doth torment me; for unlawful desires are punished after
the effect of enjoying, but impossible desires are plagued in the
desire itself.' Then would she wish to herself (for even to herself 30
she was ashamed to speak it out in words) that Cleophila might
become a young transformed Caeneus. 'For', said she, 'if she were a
man I might either obtain my desire, or have cause to hate for
refusal'—besides the many duties Cleophila did to her assured her
Cleophila might well want power, but not will, to please her. In this 35
depth of her muses there passed a cloud betwixt her sight and the
moon which took away the present beholding of it. 'O Diana,' said

20 ye Cl, Da, Qu: you St, Bo, As, Ph, Je, 90.   25 ye] you Ph, Qu, 90.   you]
ye Cl, Da.   26 desire OA: desires St.   attempt] attempts Ph, Je.

Philoclea, 'I would either the cloud that now hides the light of my virtue would as easily pass away as you will quickly overcome this let; or else that you were for ever thus darkened to serve for a better excuse of my outrageous folly.' In this diverse sort of strange dis-
5 courses would she ravingly have remained, but that she perceived by the high climbing of the moon the night was far spent. And there-fore, with stealing steps she returned to the lodge where, for all the lateness, she found her father and mother giving a tedious enter-tainment to Cleophila, oppressed with being loved almost as much
10 as with loving. Basilius, not so wise in covering his passion, would fall to those immoderate praises which the foolish lover ever thinks short of his mistress, although they reach far beyond the heavens; but Gynecia, whom womanly modesty did more outwardly bridle, yet did many times use the advantage of her sex in kissing Cleophila
15 (which did indeed but increase the rage of her inward fury)—both immoderately feeding their eyes with one intention, though by contrary means. But once Cleophila could not stir but that, as if they had been puppets whose motions stood only upon her pleasure, they would with forced steps and gazing looks follow her. Basilius's
20 mind Gynecia well perceived, and could well have found in her heart to laugh at—if her fortune might have endured mirth. But all Gynecia's actions were by Basilius interpreted as proceeding from jealousy; Cleophila betwixt both (like the poor child whose father while he beats him will make him believe it is for love, or as
25 the sick man to whom the physician swears the medicine he proffers is of a good taste), their love was hateful, their courtesy troublesome, their presence cause of her absence thence where her heart lived.

Philoclea coming among them made them all perceive it was time to rest their bodies, how little part soever their minds took of it.
30 And therefore, bringing Cleophila to her chamber, Basilius and Gynecia retired them to theirs, where Basilius being now asleep and all the lights (which naturally keep a cheerfulness in the mind) put out, Gynecia (kneeling up in her bed) began with a soft voice and swollen heart to renew the curses of her birth; and then in a
35 manner embracing her bed, 'Ah chastest bed of mine,' said she, 'which never heretofore couldst accuse me of one defiled thought,

4 sort] sorts Qu, 90 (ex. Cm).   5 ravingly have] have raveningly Ph; have (re deleted) raviningly Cm; have ravingly 90 (corr. 93).   11 ever] om. Qu, 90.   15 did indeed but] did but indeed Cl; did indeed Qu.   17 could] would Qu, Cm. 18 motions] motion Qu, 90.   her OA, 90: their St.   20 perceived] perceiving Ph; persuaded Qu; knew 90.   21 might] could Cl, As.

how canst thou now receive this disastered changeling? Happy,
happy be only they which be not, and thy blessedness only in this
respect: thou mayst feel that thou hast no feeling!' With that she
furiously tare off great part of her fair hair: 'Take here, O forgotten
virtue,' said she, 'this miserable sacrifice'—more she would have 5
said, but that Basilius, awaked with the noise, took her in his arms
and began to comfort her, the goodman thinking it was all for love
of him—which humour, if she would a little have maintained,
perchance it might have weakened his new-conceived heats. But he,
finding her answers wandering from the purpose, left her to herself, 10
glad the next day to take the advantage of her dead sleep (which her
overwatched sorrow had laid upon her) to have the more conference
with the afflicted Cleophila who, baited on this fashion by these two
lovers, and ever kept from any means to declare herself to Philoclea,
was in far harder estate than the pastor Dorus; for he had but to do, 15
in his pursuit, with shepherdish folks who troubled him with a
little envious care and affected diligence. But Cleophila was waited
on by princes, and watched by the two wakeful eyes of love and
jealousy.

But this morning of Gynecia's sleep, Basilius gave her occasion 20
to go beyond him in this sort. Cleophila thus at one instant both
besieged and banished, found in herself a daily increase of her
violent desires which, as a river, his current being stopped, doth
the more swell, so did her heart, the more impediments she met, the
more vehemently strive to overpass them. The only recreation she 25
could find in all her anguish was to visit sometimes that place where
first she was so happy as to see the cause of her unhap. There would
she kiss the ground, and thank the trees; bless the air, and do dutiful
reverence to everything that she thought did accompany her at the
first meeting. But as love, though it be a passion, hath in itself a 30
very active manner of working, so had she in her brain all sorts of
invention by which she might come to some satisfaction of it. But
still the cumbersome company of her two ill-matched lovers was a
cruel bar unto it; till this morning that Basilius, having combed and

---

1 disastered] disaltered Bo; disordered Da; *om.* Ph; distressed Qu; dastred Cm.
2 thy OA, 90: the St.   4 great] a great Cl, Ph, Qu.   8 maintained] seconded
Da, Ph, Je, Qu.   12 overwatched] overthwart Ph; overmatched Qu.   14 means]
mean Je, 90.   15–16 had but to . . .with] had to . . . with Cl, Qu; had to . . . but with
Ph; hast to . . . but with 90.   16 folks] flocks Da, Qu; *om.* Ph.   25 overpass]
pass Ph; overpress Je.   26 in all her] in her Bo, Ph, 90.   27 unhap] hap Da;
unhappiness Ph; mishap Je; unhappy Qu.   29 the] their Cl, 90; her Je, Qu.

tricked himself more curiously than any time forty winters before, did find her given over to her muses, which she did express in this song, to the great pleasure of the good old Basilius who retired himself behind a tree, while she with a most sweet voice did utter
5 these passionate verses:

> Loved I am, and yet complain of love;
> As loving not, accused, in love I die.
> When pity most I crave, I cruel prove;
> Still seeking love, love found as much I fly.

10
> Burnt in myself I muse at others' fire;
> What I call wrong, I do the same, and more;
> Barred of my will, I have beyond desire;
> I wail for want, and yet am choked with store.

> This is thy work, thou god for ever blind;
15
> Though thousands old, a boy entitled still.
> Thus children do the silly birds they find
> With stroking hurt, and too much cramming kill.
>   Yet thus much love, O love, I crave of thee:
>   Let me be loved, or else not loved be.

20 Basilius made no great haste from behind the tree till he perceived she had fully ended her music; but then, loath to lose the precious fruit of time, he presented himself unto her, falling down upon both his knees, and holding up his hands, as the old governess of Danae is painted, when she suddenly saw the golden shower: 'O heavenly
25 woman or earthly goddess,' said he, 'let not my presence be odious unto you, nor my humble suit seem of small weight in your ears. Vouchsafe your eyes to descend upon this miserable old man whose life hath hitherto been maintained but to serve as an increase of your beautiful triumphs. You only have overthrown me, and in my
30 bondage consists my glory. Suffer not your own work to be despised of you, but look upon him with pity whose life serves for your praise.'

Cleophila, keeping a countenance askances she understood him not, told him it became her ill to suffer such excessive reverence of
35 him, but that it worse became her to correct him to whom she owed

---

4 while] whilst Cl, Qu.   6–19 *The poem is in* Cm, 90–93.   9 fly]
die Cl, Qu.   28 hath hitherto OA, 90: hatherto St.   as] for Cl; *om.* Ph.
an] *om.* Da; one Ph.   33 askances] as though Ph; senses *altered to* seeming Je.

duty; that the opinion she had of his wisdom was such as made her esteem greatly of his words, but that the words themselves sounded so as she could not imagine what they might intend.

'Intend!', said Basilius (almost proud with being asked the question). 'Alas,' said he, 'what may they intend but a refreshing of 5 my soul, an assuaging of my heat, and enjoying those your excellencies wherein my life is upheld and my death threatened?'

Cleophila, lifting up her face as if she had received a mortal injury of him; 'And is this the devotion your ceremonies', said she, 'have been bent unto? Is it the disdain of my estate or the opinion 10 of my lightness that have emboldened such base fancies towards me? Enjoying, quoth you! Now little joy come to them that yield to such enjoying!'

Poor Basilius was so appalled that his legs bowed under him, his eyes waxed staring dead, and (his old blood going to his heart) a 15 general shaking all over his body possessed him. At length, with a wan mouth, he was about to give a stammering answer when Cleophila, seeing it was now time to make her profit of his folly, with something a relented countenance said unto him: 'Your words, mighty prince, were unfit either for you to speak or me to hear; but 20 yet the large testimony I see of your affection makes me willing to suppress a great number of errors. Only thus much I think good to say: that these same words in my lady Philoclea's mouth, as from one woman to another, might have had a better grace, and perchance have found a gentler receipt. Desire holds the senses open, and a 25 lover's conceit is very quick.'

Basilius no sooner received this answer but that, as if speedy flight might save his life, he turned without any ceremony away from Cleophila and ran with all speed his body would suffer him towards his fair daughter Philoclea, whom he found at that time watching 30 her mother Gynecia taking such rests as unquiet sleeps and fearful dreams would yield her. Basilius delayed no time, but with all those conjuring prayers which a father's authority may lay upon an humble child besought her she would preserve his life in whom her life was begun; she would save his grey hairs from rebuke, and his aged 35 mind from despair; that if she were not cloyed with his company,

6 an assuaging] and assuaging As, Cm; and an assuaging Je, Qu; and a swaging 90.
9–10 said she, 'have . . . unto] have . . . unto', said she Bo, Je, 90.   16 all over his]
over all his whole Bo; over all his Je.   19 something] somewhat Cl, Da.   relented]
relenting Ph Je.   23 these] om. Bo; the Cl, As, Da, 90.   25 gentler] gentlier
Da; gentle Qu.   31 rests] rest As, Qu.   32 yield] afford As; suffer Je, Qu.

and that she thought not the earth overburdened with him,
she would cool his fiery plague, which was to be done but with her
breath; that in fine whatsoever he was, he was nothing but what it
pleased Cleophila—he lived in her, and all the powers of his spirits
5 depended of her; that if she continued cruel he could no more
sustain himself than the earth remain fruitful in the sun's continual
absence. He concluded she should in one payment requite all his
deserts; and that she needed not disdain' v service, though never
so base, which was warranted by the sacred name of a father.

10 Philoclea more glad than ever she had known herself that she
might by this occasion enjoy the private conference of Cleophila, yet
had so sweet a feeling of virtue within her mind that she would not
suffer a vile colour to be cast over her high thoughts, but with an
humble look and obedient heart answered her father that there
15 needed neither promise nor persuasion unto her to make her do her
uttermost for her father's service; that, for Cleophila's favour in all
virtuous sort, she would seek it towards him; and that, as she would
not pierce further into his meaning than himself should declare, so
would she interpret all his doings to be accomplished in goodness.
20 And therefore desired, if otherwise it should be, he would not
impart it to her, who then should be forced to begin by true
obedience a show of disobedience, rather performing his general
commandment (which had ever been to embrace virtue) than any
new particular sprung out of passion and contrary to the former.

25 Basilius, that did but desire by her means to have the beginning
of a more free access unto Cleophila, allowed her reasons and
accepted her service, desiring but a speedy return of comfort. Away
departed the most excellent Philoclea with a new field of fancies in
her travailed mind; for well she saw her father was now grown her
30 adverse party, and yet her own fortune such as she must needs
favour her rival who might have show of hope where herself was out
of possibility of help. But as she walked a little on she saw at a river's
side a fair lady whose face was so bent over the river that her flowing
tears continually fell into the water, much like as we see in some
35 pleasant gardens costly images are set for fountains, which yield
abundance of waters to the delightful streams that run under them.

2 but] *om.* Da, Je.   with] by Cl, As, Da, 90.   5 of] in Bo, Je, Qu.   8 not
disdain] not to disdain Ph, Je, Qu.   12 within] in Cl, Je, 90.   13 high Cl,
Da, Ph: by St, Bo, As, Je; *om.* Qu; fair 90.   21 to her] unto her Cl, As, Da.
29 now] new Da; *om.* Qu, 90.   32 But] *om.* Cl, As, Da, Ph, Je, Qu.   34 into
OA, 90: unto St.

Newly was Philoclea departed out of the chamber when Gynecia, troubled with a fearful dream, frightfully awaked. The dream was this: it seemed unto her to be in a place full of thorns which so molested her as she could neither abide standing still nor tread safely going forward. In this case she thought Cleophila, being upon 5 a fair hill, delightful to the eye and easy in appearance, called her thither; but thither with much anguish being come, Cleophila was vanished, and she found nothing but a dead body which seeming at the first with a strange smell so to infect her as she was ready to die likewise, within a while the dead body (she thought) took her in 10 his arms and said: 'Gynecia, here is thy only rest.' With that she awaked, crying very loud: 'Cleophila! Cleophila!' But remembering herself, and seeing her husband by (as a guilty conscience doth more suspect than is suspected), she turned her call and called for Philoclea. Basilius (that God knows knew no reason why he might 15 spare to tell it) told her Philoclea was gone to entertain the lady Cleophila who had long remained in solitary muses. Gynecia, as if she had heard her last doom pronounced against her, with a side look and changing face: 'O my lord,' said she, 'what mean you to suffer these young folks together?' 20

Basilius smiling, took her in his arms: 'Sweet wife,' said he, 'I thank you for your care of your child, but they must be youths of other mettle than Cleophila that can endanger her.'

'O but'—cried out Gynecia; and therewith she stopped. For then indeed did her spirit suffer a right conflict betwixt the force of love 25 and the rage of jealousy. Many times was she about to satisfy the spite of her mind and tell Basilius what, and upon what reasons, she thought Cleophila to be far other than the outward appearance. But those many times were all put back by the manifold forces of her vehement love. Fain she would have barred her daughter's hap; but 30 loath she was to cut off her own hope. Often she offered to have risen to have broken that which her jealousy made her imagine, much more than so stolen a leisure could suffer. But Basilius, who had no less desire to taste of his daughter's labour, would never suffer it, swearing he saw sickness in his wife's face, and therefore would not the 35

3 be in a] be a Ph, Je, Qu, Cm (to be . . . molested her *om.* Da).   5 safely] safely *corr. to* softly Cl; softly As, Da, Je, Qu; fastly Ph.   8 seeming] seemed Bo, Qu; being Ph.   19 changing] changed Cl, As, 90.   20 these] those Cl, Ph, Je, Qu. 22 your care] the care As, Da, Je.   25 right] great Bo, Cl, Je.   27 spite] spirit Da, Ph, Je.   29 those] these Cl, Je.   32–3 much . . . suffer Cl, Da, Ph, Je, Qu: *om.* St, Bo, As.

air should have his power over her. Thus did Gynecia eat of her jealousy, pine in her love, and receive kindness nowhere but from the fountain of unkindness.

In the mean time Philoclea saw the doleful lady, and heard her
5 plaint which was uttered in this sort: 'Fair streams', said she, 'that do vouchsafe in your clearness to represent unto me my blubbered face, stay a little your course, and receive knowledge of my unfortunate fortune; or if the violence of your spring command you to haste away to pay your duties to your great mother the sea, yet carry
10 with you these few words, and let the uttermost ends of the world know them. A love as clear as yourselves, employed to a love (I fear) as cold as yourselves, makes me increase your flood with my tears and continue my tears in your presence.' With that she took a willow stick and wrote in a sandy bank these verses:

15   Over these brooks, trusting to ease mine eyes
       (Mine eyes e'en great in labour with their tears),
       I laid my face (my face wherein there lies
       Clusters of clouds which no sun ever clears).
          In wat'ry glass my watered eyes I see:
20   Sorrows ill eased, where sorrows painted be.

       My thoughts, imprisoned in my secret woes,
       With flamy breath do issue oft in sound:
       The sound to this strange air no sooner goes
       But that it doth with echo's force rebound
25   And make me hear the plaints I would refrain:
          Thus outward helps my inward griefs maintain.

       Now in this sand I would discharge my mind,
       And cast from me part of my burd'nous cares:
       But in the sands my pains foretold I find,
30   And see therein how well the writer fares.
          Since stream, air, sand, mine eyes and ears conspire:
          What hope to quench where each thing blows the fire?

15-32 *The poem is in* Ra, Cm, 90-93.   16 great in labour with] in great labour with Le; great with labour of Ph, Cm; great with Qu.   19 wat'ry] watered Le, Qu, Ra. watered] wat'ry Bo, Cl, 90 (*ex.* Cm).   22 breath] breaths 90 (*corr.* 13).   do] doth Cl, Le.   24 rebound] resound Ph, Je, Qu, Ra.   25 make] makes Cl, Da, Je.   26 Thus] That As, Cm.   griefs Le, As, Da, Ph, Je, Qu, Ra, 90: grief St, Bo, Cl, 93.   29 the] these Je, Qu, Ra.   sands] sand Le, As, 90.   pains] cares Bo; tales 90 (*ex.* Cm).

Philoclea at the first sight well knew this was Cleophila (for so indeed it was); but as there is nothing more agreeable than a beloved voice, she was well content to hear her words which she thought might with more cause have been spoken by her own mouth. But when Cleophila did both cease to speak and had ended her writing, 5 Philoclea gave herself to be seen unto her, with such a meeting of both their eyes together, with such a mutual astonishment to them both as it well showed each party had enough to do to maintain their vital powers in their due working. At length Philoclea, having a while mused how to wade betwixt her own hopeless affection and her 10 father's unbridled hope, with blushing cheeks and eyes cast down to the ground, began to say: 'My father, to whom I owe myself, and therefore must perform all duties unto—', when Cleophila straitly embracing her, and (warranted by a womanly habit) often kissing her, desired her to stay her sweet speech, for well she knew her 15 father's errand, and should soon receive a sufficient answer. But now she demanded leave, not to lose this long-sought-for commodity of time, to ease her heart thus far: that if in her agonies her destiny was to be condemned by Philoclea's mouth, at least Philoclea might know whom she had condemned. Philoclea easily yielded to this 20 request; and therefore, sitting down together upon the green bank hard by the river, Cleophila long in a deep doubt how to begin (though she had often before thought of it), with panting heart brought it forth in this manner: 'Most beloved lady, the incomparable worthiness of yourself, joined to the greatness of your estate, and 25 the importance of the thing whereon my life consisteth, doth require both length of time in the beginning and many ceremonies in the uttering my enforced speech. But the small opportunity of envious occasion, with the malicious eye hateful love doth cast upon me, and the extreme bent of my affection, which will either break out in 30 words or break my heart, compel me, not only to embrace the smallest time I may obtain, but to lay aside all respects due to yourself in respect of my own life, which is now or never to be preserved. I do therefore vow to you hereafter never more to omit all dutiful forms; do you now only vouchsafe to hear the matters of a most perplexed 35 mind. If ever the sound of love have come to your ears, or if ever you

6 unto] of Cl, Je, Qu (of *corr. to* unto Bo).   10 while] little As, 90.
13 straitly] strait Cl, Qu.   16 soon] *om.* Cl, Da.   27 both] *om.* Da, Qu.
28 my] of my Ph, Qu.   30 bent Bo, Cl, As, Da, Ph, Je, 90: bents St; beauty Qu.
34 forms] form As, 90.   35 now] *om.* As, Da.

have understood what force it hath had to conquer the strongest
hearts and change the most settled estates, receive here, not only an
example of those strange tragedies, but one that in himself hath
contained all the particularities of their misfortunes; and from
5 henceforth believe it may be, since you shall see it is. You shall see,
I say, a living image and a present story of the best pattern love hath
ever showed of his workmanship. But alas, whither goest thou, my
tongue; or how doth my heart consent to adventure the revealing
my nearest touching secrets? But spare not my speech; here is the
10 author of thy harms, the witness of thy words, and the judge of thy
life! Therefore again I say, I say, O only princess attend here a
miserable miracle of affection! Behold here before your eyes Pyrocles,
prince of Macedon, whom you only have brought to this fall of
fortune and unused metamorphosis; whom you only have made
15 neglect his country, forget his father, and lastly forsake himself!
My suit is to serve you, and my end to do you honour. Your fair
face hath many marks in it of amazement at my words; think then
what his amazement is from whence they come, since no words can
carry with them the life of the inward feeling. If the highest love in
20 no base person may bear place in your judgement, then may I hope
your beauty will not be without pity. If otherwise you be (alas, but
let it never be so) resolved, yet shall not my death be without com-
fort, receiving it by your sentence.'

   The joy which wrought into Pygmalion's mind while he found his
25 beloved image wax little and little both softer and warmer in his
folded arms, till at length it accomplished his gladness with a
perfect woman's shape, still beautified with the former perfections,
was even such as, by each degree of Cleophila's words, stealingly
entered into Philoclea's soul, till her pleasure was fully made up with
30 the manifesting of his being, which was such as in hope did overcome
hope. Yet did a certain spark of honour arise in her well disposed
mind, which bred a starting fear to be now in secret with him in
whose presence, notwithstanding, consisted her comfort—such

3 those] these Ph, Qu.   3-4 hath contained OA: hath continued St; containeth
90.   4 misfortunes] misfortune Cl, Da.   9 secrets] secret Qu, 90.   10 thy
harms] my harms Cl, As, Da.   11 again I say, I say] again I say, Je, Qu; I say, again
I say Cm; I say again 90.   16 and] om. Da, Ph, Je, Qu.   end to] end is to Cl, As.
honour. Your] honour, and my desire to deserve your favour. Your Da, Ph, Qu; honour
and my desire to do you favour. Your Je.   17 marks] works Je, Qu; tokens 90.
25 wax little] wax by little Cl, Ph, Je.   28 stealingly Bo, As, Da, Ph, Je, Qu:
stealing St, Cl; creepingly 90.   31 honour] humour As, Ph.

contradictions there must needs grow in those minds which neither absolutely embrace goodness nor freely yield to evil. But that spark soon gave place, or at least gave no more light in her mind than a candle doth in the sun's presence; but even astonished with a surfeit of joy, and fearful of she knew not what (as he that newly 5 finds much treasure is most subject to doubts), with a shrugging kind of tremor through all her principal parts, she gave these affectionate words for answer: 'Alas, how painful a thing it is to a divided mind to make a well joined answer; how hard it is to bring inward shame to outward confession; and how foolish, trow 10 you, must that answer be which is made one knows not to whom! Shall I say, "O Cleophila"? Alas, your words be against it! Shall I say, "prince Pyrocles"? Wretch that I am, your show is manifest against it. But this, this, I well may say: if I had continued as I ought Philoclea, you had either never been or ever been Cleophila; 15 you had either never attempted this change, fed with hope, or never discovered it, stopped with despair. But I fear me my behaviour ill governed gave you the first comfort. I fear me my affection ill hid hath given you this last assurance. If my castle had not seemed weak, you would never have brought these disguised forces. No, no; 20 I have betrayed myself. It was well seen I was glad to yield before I was assaulted. Alas, what then shall I do? Shall I seek far-fetched inventions? Shall I seek to lay colours over my decayed thoughts? Or rather, though the pureness of my virgin mind be stained, let me keep the true simplicity of my word. True it is (alas, too true it is), 25 O Cleophila (for so I love to call thee, since in that name my love first began, and in the shade of that name my love shall best lie hidden), that even while so thou wert (what eye bewitched me I know not) my passions were far fitter to desire than to be desired. Shall I say then I am sorry, or that my love must be turned to hate, 30 since thou art turned to Pyrocles? How may that well be; since, when thou wert Cleophila, the despair thou mightst not be thus did then most torment me? Thou hast then the victory; use it now with virtue, since from the steps of virtue my soul is witness to itself it

---

5 that] which Cl, Da.   6 much] great As (5–6 he . . . treasure] the richest man Ph); huge 90.   shrugging] shaking Ph; shrinking Je.   14 this, this,] this, Ph, Je, Qu.   well may] may well Cl, As, 90.   22 what then shall I do] then what shall I do Cl, Da; what shall I do then As, 90.   seek] labour Cl, As, 90. 23 decayed] galled Cl, As, Da, Ph, Je, Qu; ruinous 90. virgin] virgin's Ph, Qu. 26 I love] I do love Cl, Da.   27 lie] be Cl, Da, Ph.   28 wert] art As, Qu; were Ph. 29 far] om. Je, 90.   32–3 did then most] did most Cl, As, 90; did most then Da.

never hath, and pledge to itself it never shall decline no way to make me leave to love thee, but by making me think thy love unworthy of me.'

Pyrocles, so carried up with joy that he did not envy the gods' felicity, presented her with some jewels of inestimable price as tokens both of his love and quality, and for a conclusion of proof showed her letters from his father, king Euarchus, unto him; which hand she happily knew, as having kept divers which passed betwixt her father and him. There, with many such embracings as it seemed their souls desired to meet and their hearts to kiss as their mouths did, they passed the promise of marriage.

But Gynecia's restless affection and furious jealousy had by this time prevailed so much with her husband as to come to separate them. O jealousy, the frenzy of wise folks, the well wishing spite and unkind carefulness, the self-punishment for other's fault and self-misery in other's happiness, the sister of envy, daughter of love, and mother of hate, how couldst thou so quickly get thee a seat in the unquiet heart of Gynecia, a lady very fair in her strongest age, known wise and esteemed virtuous? It was thy breeder's power that planted thee there; it was the inflaming agonies of affection that drew on the fever of thy sickness in such sort that nature gave place. The growing of her daughter seemed the decay of herself. The blessings of a mother turned to the curses of a competitor, and the fair face of Philoclea appeared more horrible in her sight than the image of death. Possessed with these devils of love and jealousy, the great and wretched lady Gynecia had rid herself from her tedious husband (who thought now he might freely give her leave to go, hoping his daughter by that time had performed his message) and, as soon as she was alone, with looks strangely cast about her, she began to denounce war to all the works of earth and powers of heaven. But the envenomed heat which lay within her gave her not scope for many words, but (with as much rageful haste as the Trojan women went to burn Aeneas's ships) she ran headlongly towards the place where she guessed her daughter and Cleophila might be together. Yet by the way there came into her mind an old

8 betwixt] between Da, Qu.   9 embracings] embracements Qu, 90.   12 But] If Ph; *om.* Je, Qu.   15 for] of Ph, Je, Qu.   fault] faults Ph, Je, 90 (*corr.* 93). 16 daughter] the daughter Ph, Je.   17 quickly] quietly 90 (St *could be read* quietly). 20 inflaming] flaming Ph, 90 (*ex.* Cm); inflamed Da.   23 curses] cursings Ph, Qu. 28 hoping . . . had] hoping his daughter had by that time As; hoping by that time his daughter had Da; hoping his daughter had Qu.

song which she thought did well figure her fortune. The song was
this, though her leisure served her not as then to sing it:

> With two strange fires of equal heat possessed,
> The one of love, the other jealousy,
> Both still do work, in neither find I rest; 5
> For both, alas, their strengths together tie;
> The one aloft doth hold the other high.
>> Love wakes the jealous eye lest thence it moves;
>> The jealous eye, the more it looks, it loves.
>
> These fires increase, in these I daily burn: 10
> They feed on me, and with my wings do fly:
> My lively joys to doleful ashes turn:
> Their flames mount up, my powers prostrate lie:
> They live in force, I quite consumed die.
>> One wonder yet far passeth my conceit: 15
>> The fuel small, how be the fires so great?

Being come where they were, to the great astonishment of the sweet
Philoclea (whose conscience now began to know cause of blushing),
for first salutation she gave an eye to her daughter full of the same
disdainful scorn which Pallas showed to the poor Arachne that 20
durst contend with her for the prize of well weaving. Yet see, the
force of love did so much rule her that, though for Cleophila's sake
she did detest her, yet for Cleophila's sake she used no harder words
to her than to bid her go home and accompany her solitary father.

Then began she to display to Cleophila the storehouse of her 25
deadly desires, when suddenly the confused rumour of a mutinous
multitude gave just occasion to Cleophila to break off any such
conference (for well they found they were no friendly voices they
heard), and to retire with as much diligence as conveniently they
could towards the lodge. Yet before they could win the lodge by 30
twenty paces, they were overtaken by an unruly sort of clowns
which, like a violent flood, were carried they themselves knew not

2 as then] then Da; *om.* Qu.   3–16 *The poem is in* Ra, Cm, 90–93.   4 other
jealousy] other of jealousy Ph, Ra, 13 (of *deleted* St).   6 strengths] strength Da,
Ra.   tie] lie Cl, Qu; try Ra.   8 wakes] marks Ph, Ra; makes Je, Qu.   thence]
them As, Cm.   12 lively] lives Da; lovely 90 (*ex.* Cm).   16 fires] fire Le, Ph,
Qu.   19 the] *om.* Je, 90.   20 Arachne Bo, Cl, As, Da, Je, Qu, 90: Arkyve St;
Ariadne Ph.   24 to her] *om.* Bo; unto her Je, Qu.   26 a] *om.* Da; the Qu.
28 they found] she found Cl, 90.   30 towards] unto Bo, Je; to Qu.   31 sort]
company As, Je.

whither. But as soon as they came within the compass of blows, like enraged beasts, without respect of their estates or pity of their sex, they ran upon these fair ladies, to show the right nature of a villain, never thinking his estate happy but when he is able to do hurt. Yet
5 so many as they were, so many almost were the minds all knit together only in madness. Some cried 'take!', some 'kill!', some 'save!'; but even they that cried 'save!' ran for company with them that meant to kill. Everyone commanded, none obeyed. He only seemed to have most pre-eminence that was most rageful. Cleophila,
10 whose virtuous courage was ever awake in her, drawing out her sword, kept a while the villains at a bay while the ladies gat themselves into the lodge, out of which the good old Basilius, having put on an armour long before untried, came to prove his authority among his subjects, or at least to adventure his life with his dear
15 mistress. The ladies in the mean time tremblingly attended the issue of this dangerous adventure. But Cleophila did quickly make them perceive that one eagle is worth a great number of kites. No blow she strake that did not suffice for a full reward of him that received it. Yet at length the many hands would have prevailed against these
20 two, had not the noble shepherd Dorus heard this noise and come to their succour.

Dorus had been upon a fine little hill not far off, in the company of some other shepherds, defending him from the sun's heat with the shade of a few pleasant myrtle trees, feeding his master's sheep,
25 practising his new-learned shepherd's pipe, and singing with great joy for the long-pursued victory he had lately gotten of the gracious Pamela's favour—victory so far as the promising affection came unto, he having lately (keeping still his disguised manner) opened more plainly both his mind and estate. His song, as the shepherds
30 after recounted it, was this:

Feed on my sheep; my charge, my comfort, feed;
With sun's approach your pasture fertile grows,
O only sun that such a fruit can breed.

2 without] with Bo, Da.   3 villain] villainy Bo, Da; villains Qu.   5 the] their Cl, As, 90.   8 meant] went Da, Ph; cried Je.   commanded OA, 90: command St.   13 before] *om*, Je, 90.   15 tremblingly Bo, Cl, As, Da, 90: trembling St, Ph, Je Qu.   17 number of] many Da, Je.   24 few pleasant myrtle] few myrtle Cl, As, Ph, Je; few myrtle pleasant Qu.   feeding...sheep] *om*. Da, Je.   26 lately] *om*. Da, Je.   27 promising] promised Cl, As.   30 it] *om*. Bo, Je, Qu.   31-p. 125, 11 90-93 *omit this poem*.

Feed on my sheep, your fair sweet feeding flows,
Each flow'r, each herb, doth to your service yield,
O blessed sun whence all this blessing goes.

Feed on my sheep, possess your fruitful field,
No wolves dare howl, no murrain can prevail,   5
And from the storms our sweetest sun will shield.

Feed on my sheep, sorrow hath stricken sail,
Enjoy my joys, as you did taste my pain,
While our sun shines no cloudy griefs assail.

    Feed on my sheep, your native joys maintain,   10
    Your wool is rich; no tongue can tell my gain.

His song being ended, the young shepherd Philisides at that time in
his company, as if Dorus's joy had been a remembrance to his
sorrow, tuning his voice in doleful manner, thus made answer unto
him, using the burden of his own words: 15

    Leave off my sheep: it is no time to feed,
    My sun is gone, your pasture barren grows,
    O cruel sun, thy hate this harm doth breed.

    Leave off my sheep, my show'r of tears o'erflows,
    Your sweetest flow'rs, your herbs, no service yield,   20
    My sun, alas, from me for ever goes.

    Leave off my sheep, my sighs burn up your field,
    My plaints call wolves, my plagues in you prevail,
    My sun is gone, from storms what shall us shield?

    Leave off my sheep, sorrow hath hoised sail,   25
    Wail in my woes, taste of your master's pain,
    My sun is gone, now cloudy griefs assail.

    Leave leaving not my mourning to maintain,
    You bear no wool, and loss is all my gain.

Before Philisides had finished the last accent of his song, the   30
horrible cries of the mad multitude gave an untimely conclusion to
his passionate music. But Dorus had straight represented before the

---

1 flows] flowers Bo (flowers *corr. to* flows St).   3 blessing] blessings Ph, Qu.
goes] grows Da, Ph; go Qu.   10 native] nature Le, Qu.   13 to] of Ph, Qu.
14 tuning] turned As; turning Da, Ph, Qu.   16–29 90–93 *omit this poem.*
18 hate] heat Ph, Je (heat *corr. to* hate St).   20 yield] yields Le, Da, Je, Qu
(yields *corr. to* yield As).   24 what shall] that should Cl, Da; what should Ph.
28 mourning] mornings Da, Ph.   31 to] of Da, Je.   32 his] this Da, Ph.

eyes of his careful love the peril wherein his other soul might be.
Therefore, taking no other weapon than his sheephook (which he
thought sufficient because it had sufficed to bring him in a toward-
ness of his most redoubted conquest), he gave example to Philisides
and some other of the best-minded shepherds to follow him. First
he went to Pamela's lodge, where finding her already close in a
strong cave a little way from the lodge, not possible to be entered
into by force, with Miso, Mopsa, and Dametas (who would not that
time of day have opened the entry to his father), he led his little
troop to the other lodge, where he saw Cleophila, having three of
that rustic rout dead at her feet, and bathed in the blood of a great
number other; but both she and the duke so sore wearied with the
excessive number of them that they were but resolved to sell their
lives at a dear price, when Dorus coming in, and crying, 'courage,
here is Dorus!' to his dear friend Cleophila, felled one of them with
his sheephook, and taking his bill from him, valiantly seconded by
Philisides and the other honest shepherds, made so fair way among
them that he wan time for them all to recover the lodge, and to give
the rebels a face of wood of the outside. The joy Gynecia and
Philoclea felt in seeing them safely come in, whom both they loved,
and in whom their lives consisted, would have been unspeakable had
it not been much kept down with the savage howlings the rascals
made without; who now began to seek fire to burn the gates, seeing
otherwise they were unlikely to prevail.

But before I tell you what came thereof, methinks it reason you
know what raging motion was the beginning of this tumult. Bacchus,
they say, was begotten with thunder. I think that made him ever
since so full of stir and debate. Bacchus, indeed, it was which
sounded the first trumpet of this rude alarum, a manner the Arca-
dians had to solemnize their prince's birthdays with banqueting
together as largely as the quality of the company could suffer—a
barbarous opinion, to think with vice to do honour, or with activity
in beastliness to show abundance of love. This custom, being
general, was particularly this time of Basilius's nativity observed by
a town near the desert of the two lodges called Phagona. There,

1 other] *om.* Bo, Qu.   9 of day] of the day Cl, Ph, Je, Qu.   11 rustic]
rustical As, Ph.   12 number other] number of other Bo, Ph, Je.   13 but] both
Cl; *om.* As.   19 wood of] wood on Cl, As, Da.   22 howlings] howling Cl,
Ph, Je.   26 motion] motions Da, Qu.   28 which] that Da, Qu.   29 rude] *om.*
Bo, Je.   30 their] the Cl, As, Qu.   35 a town] a village Cl; a little town Da;
a little village Ph, Je, Qu.   There] They As, Qu.

being chafed with wine and emboldened with the duke's absented manner of living, there was no matter their ears had ever heard of that grew not to be a subject of their winy conference. Public affairs were mingled with private grudge; neither was any man thought of wit that did not pretend some cause of mislike. Railing 5 was counted the fruit of freedom, and saying nothing had his uttermost praise in ignorance. At the length the prince's person fell to be their table-talk; and to speak licentiously of that was a tickling point of courage to them. A proud word did swell in their stomachs, and disdainful reproaches to great persons had put on a shadow of 10 greatness in their base minds. Till at length, the very unbridled use of words having increased fire to their minds (which thought their knowledge notable because they had at all no knowledge to condemn their own want of knowledge), they descended to a direct mislike of the duke's living from among them. Whereupon it were tedious to 15 write their far-fetched constructions; but the sum was he disdained them, and what were the shows of his estate if their arms maintained him not? Who would call him duke if he had not a people? When certain of them of wretched estates (and worse minds), whose fortunes change could not impair, began to say a strange woman had 20 now possessed their prince and government; Arcadians were too plain-headed to give the prince counsel. What need from hence-forward to fear foreign enemies, since they were conquered without stroke striking, their secrets opened, their treasures abused, them-selves triumphed over, and never overthrown? If Arcadia grew 25 loathsome in the duke's sight, why did he not rid himself of the trouble? There would not want those should take so fair a cumber in good part. Since the country was theirs and that the government was an adherent to the country, why should they that needed not be partakers of the danger, be partakers with the cause of the danger? 30 'Nay rather', said they, 'let us begin that which all Arcadia will follow. Let us deliver our prince from foreign hands, and ourselves from the want of a prince. Let us be the first to do that which all the rest think. Let it be said the Phagonians are they which are not astonished with vain titles that have their forces but in our forces. 35 Lastly, to have said and heard so much was as punishable as to have

11 base] little Cl, As, 90.   12 to] in Qu, 90.   14 direct] great Ph, Je.
15–16 to write] Hm (f. 45) *begins with these words.*   18 duke] a prince Ph, 90.
27 those should] these that should As; those that would Je, 90.   29 not be] not
to be Cl, Je, Hm.   30 with] of As, Da, Hm.   33 from the want] from want
Bo, 90.   35 their forces] their force Cl, 90.

attempted; and to attempt they had the glorious show of common-
wealth with them.'

These words being spoken, like a furious storm presently took
hold of their well inclined brains. There needed no drum where
5 each man cried; each spake to other, that spake as fast to him; and
the disagreeing sound of so many voices was the only token of their
unmeet agreement. Thus was their banquet turned to a battle, their
winy mirths to bloody rages, and the happy prayers for the duke to
monstrous threatening his estate; the solemnizing his birthday
10 tended to the cause of his funerals. But as rage hath (besides his
wickedness) that folly that, the more it seeks to hurt, the less it
considers how to be able to hurt, they never weighed how to arm
themselves, but took up everything for a weapon that fury offered to
their hands: some swords and bills; there were other took pitchforks
15 and rakes, converting husbandry to soldiery. Some caught hold of
spits, things serviceable for the lives of men, to be the instruments
of their deaths; and there wanted not such which held the same pots
wherein they had drunk to the duke's health to use them (as they
could) to his mischief. Thus armed, thus governed, adding fury to
20 fury and increasing rage with running, they went headlong towards
the duke's lodge, no man in his own heart resolved what was the
uttermost he would do when he came thither. But as mischief is of
such nature that it cannot stand but with strengthening one evil by
another, and so multiply in itself till it come to the highest, and then
25 fall with his own weight, so to their minds once past the bounds of
obedience more and more wickedness opened itself, and they which
first pretended to succour him, then to reform him, now thought no
safety to themselves without killing him.

In this mad mood Cleophila's excellent valour, joined to Basilius,
30 and succoured by the worthy Dorus and his fellow shepherds, made
them feel the smart of their folly; till, for last extremity, they sought
for unmerciful fire to be their foregoer. Then did the ladies with
pitiful shrieks show the deadly fear they had of a present massacre,
especially the sweet Philoclea who ever caught hold of Cleophila, so
35 by the folly of love hindering the succour; which succour she desired.
But Cleophila, seeing no way of defence, nor time to deliberate,

1–2 of commonwealth] of a commonwealth Da, Je.   9 threatening] threatenings
Cl, Hm.   solemnizing his] solemnizing of his Bo, Ph, Je, Hm.   10 to the] to be the
Bo, Ph, Je; to have been the 90.   16 lives] life, Bo, 90.   18 had drunk]
drank Bo, 90.   21 his own heart] his heart As, Je.   25 bounds] bonds Cl, Da,
Ph, Je, Hm.

thought the only mean with extraordinary boldness to overcome
boldness, and with danger to avoid danger. And therefore, when
they were even ready to put fire, she caused the gate to be opened by
Dorus, who stood there ready to do his uttermost for her defence;
for all the rest cried to her she should not so adventure her life. 5
And so, with her sword by her side, ready but not drawn, she issued
among them. The blows she had dealt before (though all in general
were hasty) made each of them take breath before they brought
themselves suddenly over near her; so that she had time to get up to
the judgement seat of the duke which, according to the guise of that 10
country, was hard before the court gate. There she paused a while,
making sign with her hand unto them that she had something to say
would please them. Truly, outward graces are not without their
efficacies; the goodliness of her shape, with that quiet magnanimity
represented in her face in this uttermost peril, did even fix the eyes 15
of the barbarous people with admiration upon her. And the nature of
man is such that, as they leave no rageful violence unattempted
while their choler is nourished with resistance, so, when the very
subject of their wrath is unlooked-for offered to their hands, it makes
them at least take a pause before they determine cruelty. Cleophila 20
(whose wits were not dismayed) quickly spied her coming had bred
an alteration; and therefore, meaning to use the advantage of time,
and to speak determinately while she might be heard, with a brave
unbashed countenance, thus said: 'An unused thing it is, and I
think not heretofore seen, O Arcadians, that a woman should give 25
public counsel to men; a stranger to the country people; and that
lastly in such a presence a private person, as I am, should possess
the regal throne. But the strangeness of your action makes that used
for virtue which your violent necessity imposeth. For certainly a
woman may well speak to such men who have forgotten all manly 30
government; a stranger may with reason instruct such subjects that
neglect due points of subjection. And is it marvel this place is
entered into by another, since your own duke after thirty years'
government dare not show his face to his faithful people? Hear
therefore, O Arcadians, and be ashamed! Against whom hath this 35
zealous rage been stirred? Whither have you bent these manful
weapons of yours? In this quiet harmless lodge there are harboured

1 mean] way Da; means Je, Hm, 90 (*ex.* Cm).   16 the] this Cl, Ph; these Da.
20 at least] at last Ph, Hm.   24 unbashed] un͟a͟bashed Ph; unabashed 90.
30 manly] manner As; manlike 90.   37 harmless]*om.* Bo, Je.   are] be As, 93.

no Trojans, your ancient enemies; nor Persians, whom you have in present fear. Here lodge none but such as either you have great cause to love, or no cause to hate. But none other most sure it can be: is it I, O Arcadians, against whom your anger is armed? Am I the mark of your vehement quarrel? If it be so, that innocency shall not be a stop for fury; if it be so, that the law of hospitality may not defend a stranger fled to your arms for succour; if lastly it be so, that so many valiant men's courages can be inflamed to the mischief of one hurtless woman, I refuse not to make my life a sacrifice to your wrath. Exercise in me your indignation, so it go no further. I am content to pay the great favours I have received among you with the usury of my well deserving life. I present it here unto you, O Arcadians, if that may satisfy you, rather than you (called over the world the wise and quiet Arcadians) should be so vain as to attempt that alone which all your country will abhor; than you should show yourselves so ungrateful as to forget the fruit of so many years peaceable government, or so unnatural as not to have any fury overmastered with the holy name of your natural duke. For such a hellish madness, I know, will never enter into your hearts as to attempt anything against his person; which no successor, though never so hateful to him, will, for his own sake, ever leave unpunished. Neither can your wonted valour be turned to such a baseness as, instead of a duke delivered unto you by so many royal ancestors, to take the tyrannous yoke of your fellow subject, in whom the innate meanness will bring forth ravenous covetousness, and the newness of his estate suspectful cruelty. Imagine what would your enemies more wish unto you than to see you with your own hands overthrow your estate? O what would the first Arcadians, your worthy predecessors, say if they lived at this time and saw their offspring defacing such an excellent monarchy, which they with much labour and blood so wisely established? No, no, your honest hearts will neither so gratify your hateful neighbours, nor so degenerate from your famous ancestors. I see in your countenances, now virtuously settled, nothing but love and duty to him who

1 Trojans] traitors As; tyrants Ph; Argians 90.   2 but . . . have] but either such as you have As; but such as you have Ph, Je.   3-4 it can be] can it be Cl, Je, Hm. 4 is it I] It is I Ph, Cm (It is I *corr. to* is it I St); *om.* Je.   12 deserving] deserved As, Je, Hm.   it] *om.* Da, Je.   13 satisfy] suffice Cl, Je, Hm.   17 unnatural] unmerciful Cl, As.   25 innate] *blank left* Cl, As; mute Ph.   26 would] could Cl, As, Ph, 90; *om.* Da.   30-1 with much] with so much Bo, Ph, 90 (*corr.* 93).

for your only sakes doth embrace the government. The uncertainty of his estate made you take arms; now you see him well, with the same love lay them down. If now you end, as I know you will, he will take no other account of you but as of a vehement, I must confess over vehement, affection; the only continuance should prove a 5 wickedness. But it is not so; I see very well you began with zeal and will end with reverence.'

The action Cleophila used, with a sweet magnanimity and stately mildness, did so pierce into their hearts (whom the taking of breath had cooled, and leisure had taught doubts) that, instead of roaring 10 cries, there was now heard nothing but a confused muttering whether her saying was to be followed, betwixt doubt to pursue and fear to leave. Glad everyone would have been it had never been begun; but how to end it (each afraid of his companion) they knew not—so much easier it is to inflame than to quench, to tie than to loose knots. But 15 Cleophila, to take an assured possession of their minds which she found began to waver, 'Loyal Arcadians,' said she, 'now do I offer unto you the manifesting of your duties. All those that have taken arms for the duke's safety, let them turn their backs to the gate with their weapons bent against such as would hurt the sacred person of 20 the duke.'

O weak trust of the many-headed multitude, whom inconstancy only doth guide at any time to well doing! Let no man lay confidence there where company takes away shame, and each may lay the fault in his fellow. The word no sooner came from Cleophila but that 25 there were shouts of joy, with 'God save the duke!'; and they with much jollity grown to be the duke's guard that but then before meant to be his murderers. And, indeed, no ill way it is in such mutinies to give them some occasion of such service as they may think in their own judgements may countervail their trespass. Yet 30 was not this done with such an unity of hearts but that their faces well showed it was but a sheep's draught, and no thirst of goodwill: namely some of them who, as they were forwardest in the mischief, could least persuade a pardon to themselves, would fain have made a resistance to the rest. But their fellows, that were most glad to 35 have such a mean to show their loyalty, dispatched most of them with

1 for your only] for only your Cl, As; for your own Je.   5 continuance]
countenance Cl, As, Hm.   should] whereof shall As; whereof should Da; might 90.
8 magnanimity OA: imagination St.   25 in] on Da, Je, Cm, 93; of 90.   27 then]
a little Ph; little 90.   30 judgements] judgement Bo, 90.   31 an] om. As, Da,
Ph.   34 least Bo, Cl, As, Da, Ph: less St; best Hm.

a good rule: that to be leaders in disobedience teacheth ever dis-
obedience to the same leaders. So was this ungracious motion
converted into their own bowels, and they by a true judgement
grown their own punishers; till the duke, promising a general
5 pardon, most part with marks of their folly returned home, saving a
few to the number of a dozen, in whom their own naughtiness could
suffer no assurance, fled to certain woods not far off, where they
kept themselves to see how the pardon should be observed; where
feeding wildly upon grass and such other food, drinking only water,
10 they were well disciplined from their drunken riots.

To describe unto you the miserable fear Cleophila's lovers lived
in while she stood at the discretion of those undiscreet rebels, how
at every angry countenance any of them made they thought a knife
was laid upon their own throat, would require as many words as to
15 make you know how full they were now of unspeakable joy that they
saw, besides the safety of their own estates, the same wrought (and
safely wrought) by her mean in whom they had placed all their
delights. There wanted no embracements, no praises of her virtue,
no outward signs of their inward affection. But as they were in the
20 midst of those unfeigned ceremonies, a gittern ill played on, accom-
panied with a hoarse voice (who seemed to sing maugre the muses,
and to be merry in spite of fortune), made them look the way of the
ill-noised song. But the song was this:

A hateful cure with hate to heal:
25 A bloody help with blood to save:
A foolish thing with fools to deal:
Let him be bobbed that bobs will have.
But who by means of wisdom high
Hath saved his charge? It is e'en I.

30 Let others deck their pride with scars,
And of their wounds make brave lame shows:
First let them die, then pass the stars,
When rotten Fame will tell their blows.
But eye from blade, and ear from cry:
35 Who hath saved all? It is e'en I.

5 their folly] their follies Ph; their own folly Je; their own follies Hm.   9 upon] with
Cl, As.   12 those] these As, Je.   14 throat] throats Ph, 90.   24–35 Le *omits
this poem*; *it is in* Cm, 90, 93.   24 cure] cry Cl; cur Ph; care Cm.   27 bobbed]
bold, Bo, Cl, Da, Ph, 90 (*only*) (bold *corr. to* bobde St).   29 It is Bo, Cl, As, Da,
Je, Hm, 90: *It corr. to* 'Tis St; 'Tis Ph.   30 others] other Cl, 90 (*only*).   31 brave]
om. 93.

They had soon perceived it was master Dametas, who came with
no less lifted up countenance than if he had passed over the bellies
of all his enemies; so wise a point he thought he had performed in
using the natural strength of his cave. But never was it his doing to
come so soon thence till the coast were more assuredly clear; for it 5
was a rule with him that after great storms there ever fell a few
drops before they be fully finished. But Pamela (who had now
experienced how much care doth solicit a lover's heart) used this
occasion of going to her parents—indeed, unquiet till her eye might
assure her how her shepherd had gone through the danger. Basilius, 10
with the sight of Pamela, of whom almost his head (otherwise
occupied) had lost the wonted remembrance, was suddenly stricken
into a devout kind of admiration. And therefore presently commanded
his wife and daughters to assist him in a sacrifice he would make to
Apollo. 'For even now', said he, 'do I find the force of his oracle.' 15
He would not, for all that, reveal the secret thereof; for that no man
ever knew of him but his best trusted friend Philanax. But in his
mind thus he construed it:

That where the oracle said his elder care should by princely mean
be stolen away from him, and yet not lost, it was now performed, 20
since Cleophila had as it were robbed from him the care of his first
begotten child; yet was it not lost, since in his heart the ground of it
remained. His younger should with nature's bliss embrace the love
of Cleophila, because he had so commanded her for his service to
do; yet should it be with as much hate of nature, for being so 25
hateful an opposite to the jealousy he thought her mother had of
him. The third was it which most rejoiced him; for now he inter-
preted the meaning thereof that he should accomplish his unlawful
desires with Cleophila, and that after (by the death of Gynecia) she
should become his wife. And no less comfort received he of the last 30
point; for that he thought the threatening influence to his estate was
in this passed, in respect Cleophila had, as you have heard, possessed
his regal throne. Thus the fawning humour of false hope made him
take everything to his own best; and such is the selfness of affection
that, because his mind ran wholly upon Cleophila, he thought the 35

2–3 over . . . all] over all the bellies of Ph, Je, Hm.   5 coast Bo, As, Da, Ph, Je,
Hm, 90: coasts St, Cl.   6 fell] fall Bo, Ph, Hm, 93; falls As, Je.   10 assure
her] measure Bo: be assured Cl, As, 90.   14 daughters Cl, Da, Je, Hm: daughter
St, As, Ph.   15 do I find] I do find Ph, Hm.   24 service to] service so to Cl,
Da; sake to 90.   26 an] and Ph, Hm.   27 for now he] for he now Da; for
he Hm.   29 desires] desire Cl, As, Je, Hm.

gods in their oracles did mind nothing but her. These many good successes, as well essential as imaginative, made him grateful to Apollo; and therefore, excluding all the rest saving his wife and daughters (as their manner was when they privately made oblations
5 to their household gods), after sacrifice done, they sang together this their yearly-used hymn:

Apollo great, whose beams the greater world do light,
And in our little world dost clear our inward sight,
Which ever shines, though hid from earth by earthly shade,
10 Whose lights do ever live, but in our darkness fade;
Thou God, whose youth was decked with spoil of Python's skin
(So humble knowledge can throw down the snakish sin),
Latona's son, whose birth in pain and travail long
Doth teach to learn the good what travails do belong;
15 In travail of our life (a short but tedious space
While brickle hour-glass runs) guide thou our panting race:
Give us foresightful minds; give us minds to obey
What foresight tells; our thoughts upon thy knowledge stay.
Let so our fruits grow up that nature be maintained;
20 But so our hearts keep down, with vice they be not stained.
Let this assured hold our judgements ever take,
That nothing wins the heav'n but what doth earth forsake.

As soon as he had ended his devotion, the coming thither together of a great number of shepherds (which had followed Dorus to succour
25 him) remembered Basilius to call again for the pastorals; which in this sort was handled.

Here ends the second book or act.

1 oracles] oracle Ph, Je, Hm.   7–22 Le *omits this poem*; Cm *has The first four lines only*; *it is in* 90, 93.   8 dost Cl, As, Da, Je, Hm, Cm: does St, Bo: do Ph, 90.
9 shines] shine 90.   11 spoil] *om.* Je; spoils 90 (*only*).   12 sin] skin Je; kin 90 (*only*).   13 pain Da, Ph, 90: pains St, Bo, Cl, As, Je, Hm.   16 race] pace Da, 90.   21 judgements] judgement Da, Je.   ever take] overtake Je, 90.   23 his] their Bo, As, Da, Je.   27 ends] endeth Ph, Je.

HERE BEGIN THE SECOND ECLOGUES

THE rude tumult of the Phagonians gave occasion to the honest shepherds to begin their pastorals this day with a dance which they called the skirmish betwixt Reason and Passion. For seven shepherds, which were named the reasonable shepherds, joined themselves, 5 four of them making a square and the other two going a little wide of either side, like wings for the main battle, and the seventh man foremost, like the forlorn hope, to begin the skirmish. In like order came out the seven appassionate shepherds, all keeping the pace of their foot by their voice and sundry consorted instruments they 10 held in their arms. And first the foremost of the reasonable side began to sing:

> Thou rebel vile, come, to thy master yield.

And the other that met with him answered:

> No tyrant, no; mine, mine shall be the field. 15

Reason.   Can Reason then a tyrant counted be?
Passion.   If Reason will that Passions be not free.
R.   But Reason will that Reason govern most.
P.   And Passion will that Passion rule the roast.
R.   Your will is will; but Reason reason is. 20
P.   Will hath his will when Reason's will doth miss.
R.   Whom Passion leads unto his death is bent.
P.   And let him die, so that he die content.
R.   By nature you to Reason faith have sworn.
P.   Not so, but fellowlike together born. 25
R.   Who Passion doth ensue lives in annoy.
P.   Who Passion doth forsake lives void of joy.
R.   Passion is blind, and treads an unknown trace.
P.   Reason hath eyes to see his own ill case.

---

1 BEGIN] BEGINNETH Bo, Ph, Je; BEGINS As, Da, Hm.   7 for] of Cl, As, Da.   9 appassionate] passionate Cl, As, Ph, Hm; appassionated 90.   13–p. 136, 30 *The poem is in 90–93; the speech prefixes are not spelt out in lines 16 and 17 in all texts.*   24 have] hath Cl, Ph (hath *corr. to* have Le).

Then, as they approached nearer, the two of Reason's side, as if
they shot at the other, thus sang:

  R. Dare Passions then abide in Reason's light?
  P. And is not Reason dimmed with Passion's might?
5 *R.* O foolish thing which glory dost destroy!
  P. O glorious title of a foolish toy!
  R. Weakness you are, dare you with our strength fight?
  P. Because our weakness weak'neth all your might.
  R. O sacred Reason, help our virtuous toils!
10 *P.* O Passion, pass on feeble Reason's spoils!
  R. We with ourselves abide a daily strife.
  P. We gladly use the sweetness of our life.
  R. But yet our strife sure peace in end doth breed.
  P. We now have peace, your peace we do not need.

15 Then did the two square battles meet and, instead of fighting,
embrace one another, singing thus:

  R. We are too strong; but Reason seeks not blood.
  P. Who be too weak do feign they be too good.
  R. Though we cannot o'ercome, our cause is just.
20 *P.* Let us o'ercome, and let us be unjust.
  R. Yet Passion, yield at length to Reason's stroke.
  P. What shall we win by taking Reason's yoke?
  R. The joys you have shall be made permanent.
  P. But so we shall with grief learn to repent.
25 *R.* Repent indeed, but that shall be your bliss.
  P. How know we that, since present joys we miss?
  R. You know it not; of Reason therefore know it.
  P. No Reason yet had ever skill to show it.
  R.P. Then let us both to heav'nly rules give place,
30   Which Passions kill, and Reason do deface.

Then embraced they one another, and came to the duke who framed
his praises of them according to Cleophila's liking, that sat at that
time betwixt the duke and duchess, as if she had had her choice of

1 side Cl, As, Ph, Je, Hm, 93: sides St, Bo, Da, 90. 2 sang] saying Ph, Hm.
4 dimmed] dim Je, 93. 5 dost] doth Je, 90. 10 spoils] spoil Da, Je. 17 not]
no Ph, 90. 24 But] And Cl, Le, As. 29 *R.P.* 90: *Some mss. (includiug* St) *give to R.
alone, as does* 93, *but giving line 30 to P.*; Cl *has no speech prefix.* 30 kill Bo, As,
Da, Ph, 93: skill St, Cl, Le, Je, 90; bill Hm. Reason] Passions Cl; Reasons Le, As, Da.
do] to Ph, Hm; doth Je. 33 and duchess] and the duchess Cl, As, Je, Hm.

drowning or burning. But her two unrestrained parts, the mind and
eye, had their free convoy to the delicate Philoclea, whose look was
not short in well requiting it; although she knew it was a hateful
sight to the marking eye of her jealous mother. But Dicus, that
had in this time taken a great liking of Dorus for the good parts he 5
found above his age in him, had a delight to taste the fruits of
his wit—though in a subject which he himself most of all other
despised; and so entered into speech with him in the manner of
this following eclogue:

Dicus Dorus   10

Dicus. Dorus, tell me, where is thy wonted motion
    To make these woods resound thy lamentation?
    Thy saint is dead, or dead is thy devotion.
  For who doth hold his love in estimation,
    To witness that he thinks his thoughts delicious,   15
    Seeks to make each thing badge of his sweet passion.

Dorus. But what doth make thee, Dicus, so suspicious
    Of my due faith, which needs must be immutable?
    Who others' virtue doubt, themselves are vicious.
  Not so; although my metal were most mutable,   20
    Her beams have wrought therein most sure impression:
    To such a force soon change were nothing suitable.

Dicus. The heart well set doth never shun confession:
    If noble be thy bands, make them notorious:
    Silence doth seem the mask of base oppression.   25
  Who glories in his love doth make love glorious:
    But who doth fear, or bideth muett wilfully,
    Shows guilty heart doth deem his state opprobrious.
  Thou, then, that fram'st both words and voice most skilfully,
    Yield to our ears a sweet and sound relation,   30
    If love took thee by force, or caught thee guilefully.

---

2 eye] the eye Bo, Da, Ph, Hm; her eye Je.   convoy Cl, As, Je, Hm; course St,
Bo, 90; conveigh Da; convenience Ph.   4 marking] working Bo, Da; jealous Je.
8 into Bo, Cl, As, Ph, Je: to St, Da, Hm, 90.   10–p. 141, 15 Le omits this poem;
it is in 90–93.   16 Seeks] Thinks 90.   19 others' OA, 90: other St.   virtue]
virtues As, Da, Ph, Hm.   doubt 90: doubts OA.   20 metal] metals 93 (corr. 13).
21 sure] fair 90.   22 soon] some 90 (ex. 13); soon altered to some Je.
25 mask] mark Ph; mark corr. to mask Hm.   oppression] impression Ph, Hm.

Dorus. If sunny beams shame heav'nly habitation;
        If three-leaved grass seem to the sheep unsavoury,
        Then base and sour is love's most high vocation.
    Or if sheep's cries can help the sun's own bravery,
5   Then may I hope my pipe may have ability
        To help her praise, who decks me in her slavery.
    No, no; no words ennoble self-nobility.
        As for your doubts, her voice was it deceived me,
        Her eyes the force beyond my possibility.

10 *Dicus.* Thy words well voiced, well graced, had almost heaved me
        Quite from myself to love love's contemplation;
        Till of these thoughts thy sudden end bereaved me.
    Go on, therefore, and tell us by what fashion
        In thy own proof he gets so strange possession;
15   And how possessed, he strengthens his invasion?

Dorus. Sight is his root, in thought is his progression,
        His childhood wonder, prenticeship attention,
        His youth delight, his age the soul's oppression;
    Doubt is his sleep, he waketh in invention;
20   Fancy his food, his clothing is of carefulness;
        Beauty his book, his play lovers' dissension;
    His eyes are curious search, but veiled with warefulness;
        His wings desire oft clipped with desperation;
        Largess his hands could never skill of sparefulness.
25 But how he doth by might or by persuasion
        To conquer, and his conquest how to ratify,
        Experience doubts, and schools hold disputation.

Dicus. But so thy sheep may thy good wishes satisfy
        With large increase, and wool of fine perfection,
30   So she thy love, her eyes thy eyes may gratify,
        As thou wilt give our souls a dear refection,

---

9 eyes OA: eye St, 90.   my] all 90.   17 wonder] wander As; wanders Ph.
18 His means great shows of worth and intercession Da, Ph, Je, Hm.   20 clothing
is of 90: clothing as of St; clothing out of Bo; clothing all of Cl, As; cradle wracked
with Da; cradle rocked with Ph, Je, Hm.   21 To men most like, in him breeds
most dissension Da, Ph, Je, Hm (like] liked Da).   book Bo, Cl, As, 93: boot St, 90.
24 Friend to swollen hearts, and enemy of sparefulness Da, Ph, Je, Hm.

By telling how she was, how now she framed is
To help or hurt in thee her own infection.

Dorus. Blest be the name wherewith my mistress named is;
   Whose wounds are salves, whose yokes please more than
                         pleasure doth: 5
   Her stains are beams, virtue the fault she blamed is.
The heart, eye, ear here only find his treasure doth:
   All numb'ring arts her endless graces number not:
   Time, place, life, wit scarcely her rare gifts measure doth.
Is she in rage? So is the sun in summer hot,   10
   Yet harvest brings. Doth she, alas, absent herself?
   The sun is hid; his kindly shadows cumber not.
But when to give some grace she doth content herself,
   O then it shines; then are the heav'ns distributed,
   And Venus seems, to make up her, she spent herself.   15
Thus then (I say) my mischiefs have contributed
   A greater good by her divine reflection;
   My harms to me, my bliss to her attributed.
Thus she is framed: her eyes are my direction;
   Her love my life; her anger my instruction;   20
   Lastly, what so she be, that's my protection.

Dicus. Thy safety sure is wrapped in destruction;
   For that construction thy own words do bear.
   A man to fear a woman's moody eye,
Or reason lie a slave to servile sense,   25
   There seek defence where weakness is the force,
   Is late remorse in folly dearly bought.

Dorus. If I had thought to hear blasphemous words,
   My breast to swords, my soul to hell have sold
   I sooner would than thus my ears defile   30
   With words so vile, which viler breath doth breed.

---

2 or] our Cl; her Hm.   12 shadows cumber 90: shadow cumbers OA.]   20 in-
struction] destruction 90.   21 be] is 90.   that's 90: that is St, Bo, As, Da, Ph,
Hm; is Cl, Je.   23 thy] thine 90.   24 moody] muddy Cl, Da, Ph.
25 Or] Makes 90.   26 There seek] A weak 90.   the] thy Ph, 90.   27 Is late]
So is 90.   30 sooner] rather 90.   thus] have Da, Ph, Je, Hm.   my Bo, Cl, Da,
Ph: mine St, As, Je, Hm, 90.   defile] defiled Da, Ph, Je, Hm.   31 which . . .
breed] from viler mouth proceeding Da, Ph, Je, Hm.

O herds, take heed! for I a wolf have found
Who, hunting round the strongest for to kill,
His breast doth fill with earth of others' woe,
And loaden so, pulls down; pulled down, destroys.
5   O shepherd boys, eschew these tongues of venom
Which do envenom both the soul and senses!
Our best defences are to fly these adders.
O tongues, right ladders made to climb dishonour,
Who judge that honour which hath scope to slander!

10 *Dicus.* Dorus, you wander far in great reproaches,
So love encroaches on your charmed reason;
But it is season for to end our singing,
Such anger bringing; as for me, my fancy
In sick man's franzy rather takes compassion
15   Than rage for rage: rather my wish I send to thee,
Thou soon may have some help or change of passion.
She oft her looks, the stars her favour, bend to thee:
Fortune store, Nature health, Love grant persuasion.
A quiet mind none but thyself can lend to thee,
20   Thus I commend to thee all our former love.

Dorus. Well do I prove error lies oft in zeal;
Yet is it seal (though error) of true heart.
Naught could impart such heats to friendly mind.
But for to find thy words did her disgrace,
25   Whose only face the little heaven is,
Which who doth miss his eyes are but delusions,
Barred from their chiefest object of delightfulness,
Thrown on this earth the chaos of confusions.
As for thy wish to my enraged spitefulness,

1–5 Da, Ph, Je, Hm:
        But rotten bleeding argues ill complexion;
        A foul infection kills or breedeth botches;
        Men tongued like loaches (leaches Da), sucking others' sorrow
        Talking-time borrow for to spit their venom (sorrows Ph, Je)
3 breast] chest Cl, As.   woe Cl, As, 93: joys St, 90; *om.* Bo.   5 shepherd]
shepherds Bo, Cl, 90.   6 do] doth Da, Ph, Je, Hm.   7 fly Bo, As, Da, Ph,
Je, Hm, 90: flee St, Cl.   8 O tongues right] O tongues even Cl, As; O tongues
like 90; Whose cries are Da, Ph, Je, Hm.   11 on] in Cl, Da.   12 our] your
Da, Je, Hm.   13 me] *om.* Cl, As.   14 franzy] fancy Ph; frenzy 90.   18–19 *om.*
Ph.   22 is it] it is Je, 90.   seal] zeal Cl, Da, Ph, Je, 98, 13.   27 their]
his As, Da, Je, Hm (his *corr. to* their Cl); her Ph.   28 confusions] confusion Da,
Je.   29 my] mine Ph; thy Je.

The lovely blow with rare reward, my prayer is
Thou mayst love her that I may see thy sightfulness.
The quiet mind (whereof myself impairer is,
  As thou dost think) should most of all disquiet me
  Without her love than any mind who fairer is.   5
Her only cure from surfeit woes can diet me:
  She holds the balance of my contentation:
  Her cleared looks (naught else) in storms can quiet me.
Nay, rather than my ease discontentation
  Should breed to her, let me for ay dejected be   10
  From any joy which might her grief occasion.
With so sweet plagues my happy harms infected be:
  Pain wills me die, yet will of death I mortify;
  For though life irks, in life my loves protected be.
Thus for each change my changeless heart I fortify.   15

When they had ended to the good pleasing of the assistants,
especially of Cleophila who never forgat to give due commendation
to her friend Dorus, the more to advance him in his pursuit (although
therein he had brought his matters to a more wished conclusion
than yet she knew of), out starts a jolly younker (his name was Nico)   20
whose tongue had borne a very itching silence all this while; and
having spied one Pas (a mate of his as mad as himself—both indeed
lads to climb any tree in the world), he bestowed this manner of
salutation upon him, and was with like reverence requited:

Nico   Pas   Dicus   25

Nico. And are you there, old Pas? In truth I ever thought
  Among us all we should find out some thing of naught.
Pas. And I am here the same, so mote I thrive and thee,
  Despaired in all this flock to find a knave but thee.
Nico. Ah, now I see why thou art in thyself so blind;   30
  Thy grey hood hides the thing that thou despair'st to find.
Pas. My grey hood is mine own, all be it be but grey,
  Not as the scrip thou stal'st while Dorcas sleeping lay.

1 blow OA, 93: blowen *corr. to* blowme St; blowne 90.   6 cure] care Cl, Ph.
8 looks] eyes 90.   11 any] my Ph, Hm.   13 wills] bid Da; bids Je.   will] pain
Cl, Da, Ph.   17 commendation] commendations Ph, Je, 90.   18 to her] of her
Ph, Hm (of her *corr. to* to her Je).   25– p. 146, 12 Le, 93 *omit this poem; it is in* 90.
25 *Nico Pas Dicus*] *Nico Pas* Ph; *Nico Dorus* 90.   28 thrive and thee] thriving
be Cl, As; yet surely I Ph.   32 mine] my Bo, Da.   33 as] like 90.   stal'st]stol'st
Cl, Hm, 90.   Dorcas] Dorus Bo, Cl, Da, Ph, Je, Hm (Dicus *corr. to* Dorcas St).

Nico. Mine was the scrip; but thou, that seeming rayed with love,
　Didst snatch from Cosma's hand her green ywroughten glove.

Pas. Ah fool, so courtiers do. But who did lively skip
　When for a treen-dish stol'n thy father did thee whip?

5 *Nico.* Indeed the witch thy dam her crouch from shoulder spread,
　For pilf'ring Lalus' lamb, with crouch to bless thy head.

Pas. My voice the lamb did win, Menalcas was our judge
　Of singing match we made, whence he with shame did trudge.

Nico. Couldst thou make Lalus fly? so nightingales avoid
10　When with the cawing crows their music is annoyed.

Pas. Nay, like to nightingales the other birds give ear,
　My pipe and song made him both song and pipe forswear.

Nico. I think it well; such voice would make one music hate:
　But if I had been there, th'hadst met another mate.

15 *Pas.* Another sure, as is a gander from a goose;
　But still when thou dost sing methinks a colt is loose.

Nico. Well aimed, by my hat; for as thou sangst last day
　The neighbours all did cry, 'Alas, what ass doth bray?'

Pas. But here is Dicus old; let him then speak the word
20　To whether with best cause the nymphs fair flow'rs afford.

Nico. Content; but I will lay a wager hereunto,
　That profit may ensue to him that best can do.
　I have (and long shall have) a white great nimble cat,
　A king upon a mouse, a strong foe to a rat;
25　Fine ears, long tail he hath, with lion's curbed claw
　Which oft he lifteth up, and stays his lifted paw,
　Deep musing to himself, which after-mewing shows,
　Till with licked beard his eye of fire espy his foes.
　If thou (alas, poor if!) do win, then win thou this;
30　And if I better sing, let me thy Cosma kiss.

---

2 Didst Hm, 90: Did St, Bo, Cl, As, Da, Ph, Je.　　　Cosma's] Hyppa's Cl, As, Da,
Ph, Je, Hm (*and throughout rest of poem*).　　　green ywroughten] greeny wroughten
Cl, 90.　　7 our] the Cl, Ph.　　8 we] was 90.　　whence] when Cl, Da, Je, Hm.
9 fly] flee Cl, Da; fly in As.　　　12 song and pipe] pipe and song Bo, Da, 90.
20 whether] whither Cl, Ph.　　24 a rat Bo, Cl, Da, Ph, Je, Hm: the rat St, As, 90.
28 licked] like Cl; hooked Hm.　　espy] espies Cl, Je, Hm.　　29 thou . . . thou 90:
you . . . you OA.

Pas. Kiss her? Now mayst thou kiss. I have a fitter match:
  A pretty cur it is; his name iwis is Catch,
  No ear nor tail he hath, lest they should him disgrace,
  A ruddy hair his coat, with fine long speckled face:
  He never musing stands, but with himself will play,   5
  Leaping at every fly, and angry with a flea:
  He eft would kill a mouse, but he disdains the fight,
  And makes our home good sport with dancing bolt upright.
  This is my pawn; the prize let Dicus' judgement show:
  Such odds I willing lay; for him and you I know.   10

Dicus. Sing then my lads, but sing with better vein than yet,
  Or else who singeth worse, my skill will hardly hit.

Nico. Who doubts but Pas' fine pipe again will bring
  The ancient praise to Arcad shepherds' skill?
  Pan is not dead since Pas begins to sing.   15

Pas. Who evermore will love Apollo's quill,
  Since Nico doth to sing so widely gape?
  Nico his place far better furnish will.

Nico. Was this not he who, for Syringa's scape
  Raging in woes, first pastors taught to plain?   20
  Do you not hear his voice, and see his shape?

Pas. This is not he that failed her to gain,
  Which made a bay, made bay a holy tree;
  But this is one that doth his music stain.

Nico. O fauns, O fairies all, and do you see   25
  And suffer such a wrong? A wrong, I trow,
  That Nico must with Pas compared be.

Pas. O nymphs, I tell you news, for Pas you know;
  While I was warbling out your wonted praise,
  Nico would needs with Pas his bagpipe blow.   30

Nico. If never I did fail your holydays,
  With dances, carols, or with barleybreak,
  Let Pas now know how Nico maketh lays.

1 fitter] better 90.   7 eft] oft As, Ph, Je, Hm.   the] to 90.   11 but Da, Ph,
90: and St, Bo, Cl, As, Je, Hm.   12 worse] worst As, Ph, Je, 90.   will] may Cl,
As.   14 Arcad] Arcades Bo; Arcadia Cl; Arcadia's Ph; Arcady for Je.   17 widely]
wildly Ph; wild Hm.   19 this . . . Syringa's] not this he, who did for Syrinx 90.
20 first pastors taught] teach pastors first 90.   23 holy] holly Cl, As, Je, Hm; hollow
Ph.   33 maketh] makes the 90.

Pas. If each day hath been holy for your sake
   Unto my pipe, O nymphs, now help my pipe,
   For Pas well knows what lays can Nico make.

Nico. Alas, how oft I look on cherries ripe
5   Methinks I see the lips my Leuca hath,
   And wanting her, my weeping eyes I wipe.

Pas. Alas, when I in spring meet roses rathe,
   And think from Cosma's sweet red lips I live,
   I leave mine eyes unwiped, my cheeks to bathe.

10 *Nico.* As I of late near bushes used my sieve,
   I spied a thrush where she did make her nest;
   That will I take, and to my Leuca give.

Pas. But long have I a sparrow gaily dressed,
   As white as milk, and coming to the call,
15   To put it with my hand in Cosma's breast.

Nico. I oft do sue, and Leuca saith I shall;
   But when I did come near with heat and hope,
   She ran away and threw at me a ball.

Pas. Cosma once said she left the wicket ope
20   For me to come; and so she did. I came,
   But in the place found nothing but a rope.

Nico. When Leuca doth appear the sun for shame
   Doth hide himself; for to himself he says,
   If Leuca live, she darken will my fame.

25 *Pas.* When Cosma doth come forth the sun displays
   His utmost light; for well his wit doth know
   Cosma's fair beams emblemish much his rays.

Nico. Leuca to me did yestermorning show
   In perfect light, which could not me deceive,
30   Her naked leg, more white than whitest snow.

Pas. But yesternight by light I did receive
   From Cosma's eyes, which full in darkness shine,
   I saw her arm where purest lillies cleave.

Nico. She once stark nak'd did bathe a little tine;
 But still (methought), with beauties from her fell,
 She did the water wash, and make more fine.

Pas. She once, to cool herself, stood in a well;
 But ever since that well is well besought,   5
 And for rose-water sold of rarest smell.

Nico. To river's bank, being a-walking brought,
 She bid me spy her baby in the brook.
 Alas (said I) this babe doth nurse my thought.

Pas. As in a glass I held she once did look,   10
 I said my hands well paid her for mine eyes,
 Since in my hands self goodly sight she took.

Nico. O if I had a ladder for the skies,
 I would climb up, and bring a pretty star
 To wear upon her neck that open lies.   15

Pas. O if I had Apollo's golden car,
 I would come down and yield to her my place,
 That (shining now) she then might shine more far.

Nico. Nothing, O Leuca, shall thy fame deface,
 While shepherds' tunes be heard, or rhymes be read, 20
 Or while that shepherds love a lovely face.

Pas. Thy name, O Cosma, shall with praise be spread
 As far as any shepherds piping be,
 As far as love possesseth any head.

Nico. Thy monument is laid in many a tree,   25
 With name engraved; so though thy body die,
 The after-folks shall wonder still at thee.

Pas. So oft these woods have heard me 'Cosma' cry,
 That after death to heav'n in woods' resound,
 With echo's help, shall 'Cosma, Cosma' fly.   30

Nico. Peace, peace, good Pas, thou weariest e'en the ground
 With sluttish song; I pray thee learn to blea,
 For good thou mayst yet prove in sheepish sound.

---

1 tine] time Bo, Da, Ph, Je, Hm. 3 water] waters 90. 7 a-walking] to
walking Ph; a washing Hm; on walking 90. 8 bid] bed As; did Ph (did *corr. to*
bid St, Je); bad 90. 28 me] my Cl, Ph. 'Cosma'] Hyppa Cl, As, Da, Ph; happy
Je, Hm. 30 'Cosma, Cosma'] Hyppa, Hyppa Cl, As, Da, Ph; happy,
happy Je, Hm.

Pas. My father hath at home a pretty jay,
 Go win of him (for chatt'ring) praise or shame;
 For so yet of a conquest speak thou may.

Nico. Tell me (and be my Pan) the monster's name
5 That hath four legs, and with two only goes;
 That hath four eyes, and only two can frame.

Pas. Tell this (and Phoebus be): what monster grows
 With so strong lives that body cannot rest
 In ease until that body life forgoes?

10 *Dicus.* Enough, enough; so ill hath done the best
 That, since the having them to neither's due,
 Let cat and dog fight which shall have both you.

Some speech there straight grew among the hearers what they
should mean by the riddles of the two monsters. But Cleophila,
15 whose heart better delighted in wailful ditties as more according to
her fortune, she desired Histor he would repeat the lamentation
some days before he told them that he had heard of a stranger made
to the wise Boulon—indeed Cleophila desirous to hear of Plangus's
love, whose valour she had well seen (though against herself) in
20 the combat of the six princes. Basilius, as soon as he understood
Cleophila's pleasure, commanded Histor upon pain of his life (as
though everything were a matter of life and death that pertained to
his mistress's service) immediately to sing it; who, with great cun-
ning varying his voice according to the diversity of the persons,
25 thus performed his pleasure:

Histor

 As I behind a bush did sit
 I silent heard more words of wit
 Than erst I knew; but first did plain
30 The one, which tother would refrain.

7 this] me 90. 8 strong] strange Bo, Cl, As, Da, Ph, Je, Hm. 11 having them]
having of them Cl, Ph, Je, Hm. neither's 90: neither is OA. 14 monsters] Cl,
As, Da, Ph, Je, Hm *insert here*:
 But this eclogue of all other was counted the sportfullest they yet had heard; and
a greater question, whether indeed had won the wager: Dicus still demanding justice,
that since he had been lawfully appointed judge, the cat and dog might be sent for to
try the duello betwixt them.

other] others Da, Hm. yet had] had yet Ph, Je, Hm. greater] great Da, Je, Hm.
17 told] had told Cl, As (had *deleted* St, Je). 26–p. 152, 18 *The poem is trans-
ferred to Book II in* 90, 93; Cm *has* p. 147, 2–34 *only*. 26–30 *om*. Le, 90.
30 which] which *corr. to* whilst Cl; whiles Da. tother] th'other Bo, Ph; to ther
Cl; other Da.

Plangus   Boulon

Plangus. Alas, how long this pilgrimage doth last?
  What greater ills have now the heav'ns in store
  To couple coming harms with sorrows past?
Long since my voice is hoarse, and throat is sore,   5
  With cries to skies, and curses to the ground;
  But more I plain, I feel my woes the more.
Ah where was first that cruel cunning found
  To frame of earth a vessel of the mind,
  Where it should be to self-destruction bound?   10
What needed so high sprites such mansions blind?
  Or wrapped in flesh what do they here obtain,
  But glorious name of wretched human-kind?
Balls to the stars, and thralls to Fortune's reign;
  Turned from themselves, infected with their cage,   15
  Where death is feared, and life is held with pain.
Like players placed to fill a filthy stage,
  Where change of thoughts one fool to other shows,
  And all but jests, save only sorrow's rage.
The child feels that; the man that feeling knows,   20
  With cries first born, the presage of his life,
  Where wit but serves to have true taste of woes.
A shop of shame, a book where blots be rife
  This body is; this body so composed
  As in itself to nourish mortal strife.   25
So diverse be the elements disposed
  In this weak work that it can never be
  Made uniform to any state reposed.
Grief only makes his wretched state to see
  (E'en like a top which naught but whipping moves)   30
  This man, this talking beast, this walking tree.
Grief is the stone which finest judgement proves;
  For who grieves not hath but a blockish brain,
  Since cause of grief no cause from life removes.

1 *Boulon*] *Basilius* 90 (*and throughout*).   9 vessel of] vessel for Le; vessel to As.
10 to] the *corr. to* to Cl; the Le.   11 needed] need Ph, Hm.   mansions] mansion
Bo, Je.   15 cage Cl, Le, Da, Je, Hl 90: age St, Bo, Ph; rage As.   23 be] are
Cl; are *corr. to* be Cm.   34 from] of Bo, Ph.

Boulon. How long wilt thou with moanful music stain
    The cheerful notes these pleasant places yield,
    Where all good haps a perfect state maintain?

Plangus. Cursed be good haps, and cursed be they that build
5   Their hopes on haps, and do not make despair
    For all these certain blows the surest shield.
  Shall I that saw Erona's shining hair
    Torn with her hands, and those same hands of snow
    With loss of purest blood themselves to tear,
10   Shall I that saw those breasts where beauties flow,
    Swelling with sighs, made pale with mind's disease,
    And saw those eyes (those suns) such show'rs to show,
  Shall I whose ears her mournful words did seize
    (Her words in syrup laid of sweetest breath),
15   Relent those thoughts which then did so displease?
  No, no; despair my daily lesson saith,
    And saith, although I seek my life to fly,
    Plangus must live to see Erona's death.
  Plangus must live some help for her to try
20   Though in despair, for love so forceth me;
    Plangus doth live, and shall Erona die?
  Erona die? O heav'n (if heav'n there be)
    Hath all thy whirling course so small effect?
    Serve all thy starry eyes this shame to see?
25 Let dolts in haste some altars fair erect
    To those high pow'rs which idly sit above,
    And virtue do in greatest need neglect.

Boulon. O man, take heed how thou the gods do move
    To causeful wrath which thou canst not resist.
30   Blasphemous words the speaker vain do prove.
  Alas, while we are wrapped in foggy mist
    Of our self-love (so passions do deceive)
    We think they hurt when most they do assist.
  To harm us worms should that high justice leave

3 all] as Cl, Le.   6 these] those Bo, As; the Je, Hm.   12 show'rs] shows
Le, Da; shewers As, Je; shroud Ph.   13 did] do Cl, Le.   20 for love so
forceth] so love enforceth 90 (*only*).   21 shall] must 90 (*only*).   23 thy] the
Cl, Le.   29 causeful Cl, Le, As, Da, Ph, Je, 93: careful St; causeless Bo, Hm;
ireful 90.   30 do] doth Cl, Le.   34 high] by Cl, Le.

His nature? nay, himself? for so it is.
What glory from our loss can he receive?
But still our dazzled eyes their way do miss,
    While that we do at his sweet scourge repine,
    The kindly way to beat us on to bliss.   5
If she must die, then hath she passed the line
    Of loathsome days, whose loss how canst thou moan,
    That dost so well their miseries define?
But such we are, with inward tempest blown
    Of winds quite contrary in waves of will: 10
    We moan that lost, which had we did bemoan.

Plangus. And shall she die, shall cruel fire spill
    Those beams that set so many hearts on fire?
    Hath she not force e'en death with love to kill?
Nay, e'en cold death inflamed with hot desire   15
    Her to enjoy (where joy itself is thrall)
    Will spoil the earth of his most rich attire.
Thus death becomes a rival to us all,
    And hopes with foul embracements her to get,
    In whose decay virtue's fair shrine must fall.   20
O virtue weak, shall death his triumph set
    Upon thy spoils, which never should lie waste?
    Let death first die; be thou his worthy let.
By what eclipse shall that sun be defaced?
    What mine hath erst thrown down so fair a tower?   25
    What sacrilege hath such a saint disgraced?
The world the garden is, she is the flower
    That sweetens all the place; she is the guest
    Of rarest price, both heav'n and earth her bower.
And shall (O me) all this in ashes rest?   30
    Alas, if you a phoenix new will have
    Burnt by the sun, she first must build her nest.
But well you know the gentle sun would save
    Such beams so like his own, which might have might
    In him, the thoughts of Phaethon's dam to grave.   35
Therefore, alas, you use vile Vulcan's spite,

5 on to] to our 90 (*only*).   8 dost] durst Ph; doth Je, Hm.   10 winds] minds
90 (*only*).   quite] clean Cl, Le.   11 lost] loss Cl, Ph.   31 new] now Cl, Le,
Da.   have] save Je, Hm (save *corr. to* have St).

Which nothing spares, to melt that virgin wax
Which while it is, it is all Asia's light.
O Mars, for what doth serve thy armed axe?
To let that witold beast consume in flames
5   Thy Venus' child, whose beauty Venus lacks?
O Venus (if her praise no envy frames
In thy high mind) get her thy husband's grace.
Sweet speaking oft a currish heart reclaims.
O eyes of mine where once she saw her face
10   (Her face which was more lively in my heart),
O brain where thought of her hath only place,
O hand, which touched her hand when we did part;
O lips, that kissed that hand with my tears sprent;
O tongue, then dumb, not daring tell my smart;
15   O soul, whose love in her is only spent,
What e'er you see, think, touch, kiss, speak, or love,
Let all for her, and unto her be bent.

Boulon. Thy wailing words do much my spirits move,
They uttered are in such a feeling fashion
20   That sorrow's work against my will I prove.
Methinks I am partaker of thy passion,
And in thy case do glass mine own debility—
Self-guilty folk most prone to feel compassion.
Yet reason saith, reason should have ability
25   To hold these worldly things in such proportion
As let them come or go with e'en facility.
But our desire's tyrannical extortion
Doth force us there to set our chief delightfulness
Where but a baiting place is all our portion.
30   But still, although we fail of perfect rightfulness,
Seek we to tame these childish superfluities?
Let us not wink though void of purest sightfulness;
For what can breed more peevish incongruities

---

1 virgin Bo, Cl, Le, As, 90: virgin's St, Da, Ph, Je, Hm.   4 witold] withold Bo;
wi-told Da, 90; wit hold Hm.   flames] flame 90 (*only*).   5 Thy] The Ph, Hm.
child] shield Ph, Je, Hm.   12 we] she 90 (*only*).   13 that hand] her hand Je,
90 (*only*).   22 mine Cl, Le, Da, Ph, Je, Hm, 90: my St, Bo, As.   23 most
prone] must prove Bo, Cl, Le, As, Da, Ph, Je (most prove *corr. to* most prone St.).
25 worldly Bo, Cl, Le, As, Da, Je, Hm, 90: wordly St, Ph, 93 (*corr. 13*).   31 these]
those Je; the 90.   33 can breed] can yield Da, Je, Hm; yields Ph.

Than man to yield to female lamentations?
Let us some grammar learn of more congruities.

Plangus. If through mine ears pierce any consolations
    By wise discourse, sweet tunes, or poet's fiction;
    If aught I cease these hideous exclamations,   5
While that my soul, she, she lives in affliction;
    Then let my life long time on earth maintained be,
    To wretched me the last worst malediction.
Can I, that know her sacred parts, restrained be
    From any joy; know fortune's vile displacing her,   10
    In moral rules let raging woes contained be?
Can I forget, when they in prison placing her,
    With swelling heart in spite and due disdainfulness
    She lay for dead, till I helped with unlacing her?
Can I forget from how much mourning plainfulness   15
    With diamond in window glass she graved,
    'Erona die, and end this ugly painfulness'?
Can I forget in how strange phrase she craved
    That quickly they would her burn, drown, or smother,
    As if by death she only might be saved?   20
Then let me eke forget one hand from other;
    Let me forget that Plangus I am called;
    Let me forget I am son to my mother;
But if my memory thus must be thralled
    To that strange stroke which conquered all my senses,   25
    Can thoughts still thinking so rest unappalled?

Boulon. Who still doth seek against himself offences,
    What pardon can avail? Or who employs him
    To hurt himself, what shields can be defences?
Woe to poor man: each outward thing annoys him   30
    In diverse kinds; yet as he were not filled,
    He heaps in inward grief that most destroys him.

---

2 more] our Cl, Le.   3 mine] my Le, Da.   consolations Cl, Le, As, Da, Ph:
consolation St, Bo, Je, 90; consultations Hm.   5 hideous] odious Cl, Da.
6 she lives] liveth Da, Ph, Je.   7 long time on earth] on earth long time Cl, Le,
Ph, Je.   9 know] knew Cl, Le, Da.   sacred] secret Ph, Je, Hm.   10 From]
For Da, 90 (*only*).   11 moral] mortal Da, Ph, Je.   15 mourning] mournful
Bo, Je.   plainfulness] painfulness Le, Ph, Je.   17 this] thy 90 (*only*).
19 drown] down Cl, Hm.   24-6 *om.* Je.   24 thus must] must thus 90.
26 thoughts] thought Cl, Le.   29 shields] shield As, Ph.   32 inward] outward
Da, 93.   that] which 90 (*only*).

Thus is our thought with pain for thistles tilled:
Thus be our noblest parts dried up with sorrow:
Thus is our mind with too much minding spilled.
One day lays up stuff of grief for the morrow;
5   And whose good hap doth leave him unprovided,
Condoling cause of friendship he will borrow.
Betwixt the good and shade of good divided,
We pity deem that which but weakness is;
So are we from our high creation slided.
10   But Plangus, lest I may your sickness miss
Or rubbing, hurt the sore, I here do end.
The ass did hurt when he did think to kiss.

Histor. Thus did they say, and then away did wend;
High time for me, for scattered were my sheep
15   While I their speech in my rude rhyming penned.
Yet for that night my cabin did them keep
While Plangus did a story strange declare;
But hoarse and dry, my pipes I now must spare.

So well did Histor's voice express the passion of Plangus that all
20 the princely beholders were stricken into a silent consideration of it;
indeed everyone making that he heard of another the balance of his
own troubles. Pamela was the first that commanded her thoughts to
give place to some necessary words; and so, remembering herself
what Histor had said the other time of the pastorals touching
25 Musidorus (which as then she regarded not), she now desired him,
if he did bear it in memory, that he would tell what strange adven-
ture it was that had led away the two Greek princes from Erona,
after they had slain Otanes and settled her in her kingdom. And when
she had asked thus much, having had nothing but vehement desire
30 to her counsel, her sweet body did even tremble for fear lest she had
done amiss. But glad was her shepherd, not to have his doings
spoken of, but because any question of him proceeded out of that
mouth. Histor made answer that Plangus indeed had before his
departure towards Thessalia and Macedon, at his importunate desire,
35 made a brief declaration unto him thereof, but always with protesta-
tion that such things they were as many particularities of them had

1 Thus] This Bo, Le, Je.   5 hap doth] haps do 90.   13–18 Le, 90–93 *omit
these lines.*   25 she now] *om.* Cl, As.   33–4 his departure] he departed Bo, Cl,
Da, Je, Hm.

been full works to excellent historiographers; and that the first adventure was a man of monstrous bigness and force (and therefore commonly called a giant) who had wasted all the whole country of Paphlagonia by the help of a strong castle in the top of a high rock, where he kept a most terrible dragon which he had with such art 5 from youth trained up that it was much more at his commandment than the best reclaimed hawk; so that it would fly abroad and do incredible damage, and ever duly return again to the castle where the giant kept no living man but himself. This, besides his own force, forced the miserable people to come to what composition he 10 would: which was that monthly they should send him two maids not above sixteen years old, and two boys or young men under nineteen. The women he used at his beastly pleasure, and kept them imprisoned in his castle; the young men he was wont to sacrifice to an idol. This being come to the ears of those valiant young princes who (the 15 harder a thing were the more their hearts rase unto it) went to the desolate people, and there (after many horrible complaints of parents whose children by public force were taken from them) they offered themselves to pay the next month's wages, if better they could not do. Their beauty made all the people pity them, but in 20 the end self-respect prevailed over the pity, and the time being come, they armed themselves secretly under their long garments, and carrying short swords under their arms, were in that sort brought unto him by a man appointed to deliver them, for more the giant would not suffer to enter; who, when he saw their faces, was a 25 proud man of so goodly a sacrifice. But they were no sooner in but that, drawing out their swords, they made him look to his own life. Which he did, running to a horse-load of a mast he always used, and so weaponed (for armed he ever went) he let loose his trusty dragon. And so matched that ill-favoured couple with the matchless princes, 30 who (having an excellent strength, and courage to make that strength awake) had within small space dispatched the world of those monsters, Pyrocles having killed the dragon and Musidorus the giant. What honours were done unto them by that people (which they continually observe as towards their savers) were superfluous 35 to tell.

6 youth] his youth Cl, As.   9 This] Thus Da, Je.   13–14 imprisoned] in prison As, Da.   16 rase] rose Da, Ph; rise Je.   20–1 in the end Da, Je, Hm: in end St, Bo, Ph; in deed Cl, As.   28 mast] mase Bo, Cl, As, Da; mass Ph.   33 those monsters] these two monsters Cl, Hm.

But thence were they led by the fame of a great war betwixt two brethren, where the younger had rebelled against the elder (being king of Syria), forced thereunto because he had taken away from him the principality of Damascus which their father in partage had bestowed upon him. There did they show as much their wisdom as their valour; for the one putting himself of the one side, and the other of the other, they so behaved themselves that either part thought they had the bravest champion in the world, insomuch as both were content to let the matter be tried by them to save the blood of so many which of both sides were but one people. But they (having the matter without exception put into their hands) instead of fighting fell to arbitrage, and making the brothers see the shamefulness of their fault so to sever themselves whom nature in their very beginning had so nearly knit, and yet remembering that whosoever hath thoroughly offended a prince can never think himself in perfect safety under him, they did determine that the king, giving in riches to his brother as much as his principality came unto, should enjoy Damascus; and they, finding the younger a prince of great worthiness, did so much by their credit with the Paphlagonians that they married him to the inheritrix of that goodly province—leaving in this sort a perpetual monument of wit, liberality, and courage.

But after this the next notable chance fell unto them (for many hundred of their valiant acts Plangus said he neither could tell, nor much time would serve for the repeating) was by the great lady of Palestina's means (called Andromana) who, hearing of their singular valour, sent to beseech their aid against a young prince of Arabia who had promised her marriage, and upon that having gotten a child of her, had now left her. They, though they knew she should have done well to have been sure of the church before he had been sure of the bed, yet pitying womanhood and desiring to know what answer the Arabian could make for himself, they went to offer themselves unto her. But they had not been there a while, and made her see their activity in jousts and their valour in particular combats, but that she had quite forgotten her old fancy that had cost her so dear, and was grown into the miserablest and strangest passion of love

that can be imagined; for she loved them both with equal ardency.
The only odds was that when she saw Pyrocles she thought she
most desired him, and when she looked on Musidorus then was
Pyrocles overweighed. At these words a man might have seen the
eyes both of Pamela and Philoclea cast upon their servants to see 5
whether they had committed any trespass or no. But Histor pro-
ceeded on in declaring her divided desire. When she looked on
Musidorus then thought she a sweet brownness to be the most
delightful beauty; but when she marked Pyrocles' pure white and
red (for such difference Plangus said was betwixt them) then roses 10
and lilies were the fairest flowers. Musidorus as the elder and
stronger, Pyrocles as the younger and more delicate, contented her.
In fine, she would wish sometimes Musidorus to be Pyrocles,
another time Pyrocles to be Musidorus; but still she would have
both hers. But those two princes (that seemed to love anything 15
better than love) did so utterly discomfort her that she was forced to
fly to force and put them both (by a sleight she played) in prison,
where what allurements she used indifferently were long to tell.
But at length they obstinately so much more refusing her (as their
courages disdained to be compelled to anything), they had been like 20
enough to have tarried there a good number of days but that the
Arabian prince (hearing of their imprisonment) grew proud of his
strength, and entered into Palestina with hope to conquer it. Which
the people feeling (whether the lady would or no), delivered the
prisoners, who having likewise by their good conduct delivered 25
them of the Arabians, they themselves went into Egypt, as well to
fly such a heart-burning woman (who shortly after, as Plangus said,
had likewise forgotten them and, after divers changes, at last
married herself to an apple-monger) as because they heard great
fame of the king of Egypt's court, to be by reason of his magnificence 30
full of valiant knights, as also his country well policied with good
laws and customs, worthy to be learned.

But many notable accidents met with them as they passed the
desert way betwixt Palestina and Egypt, worthy to have whole books
written of them. But Plangus's appassionate mind could not brook 35
long discourses, and therefore hasted himself to let me know the

7 divided] devoted Ph; delivered Je.   8 to be] *om.* Cl, As.   14 another time]
and another time Cl, Ph; and other time Da; and other times Je, Hm.   15 those]
these Bo, Ph, Je, Hm.   21 enough] *om.* Cl, As, Da, Je.   29 great] a great As,
Da, Je.   31 policied] polished Da, Je, Hm; published Ph.   35 appassionate]
a passionate Cl, Hm; passionate Da; of a passionate Ph; passionated Je.

generality of their doings, which certainly were such as made me greatly delighted to hear them.

'But did he tell you no further', said the sweetest Philoclea, 'of those princes?'

5 'Yes', answered Histor, 'of a strange chance fell to them in Egypt, and that was this: riding together about six miles from the great city of Memphis they heard a pitiful cry as of one that either extreme grief or present fear had made his voice his best instrument of defence. They went the next way they thought should guide them

10 to the party, and there found they a young man, well apparelled and handsomely proportioned, in the hands of four murdering villains who were ready to slay him, having stayed for nothing but that he told them he knew a place where a great treasure was hid. The covetousness of that made them delay the killing of him till one of

15 the four, weary to follow him any longer, was ready to have given his mortal wound, at which he cried. But the other three stopped their fellow, when (in good time for him) came in these two princes who (seeing, how justly soever he had deserved death, that the manner was unjust by which they sought to lay it upon him) came

20 in among them with threatenings if they did not let him loose. But the four (better knowing their own number than the others' valour) scorned their commandment, till by the death of three of them the fourth was taught with running away to leave the prisoner to their discretion; who (falling on his knees unto them as to the bestowers

25 of a life upon him) told them the ground of his mischance, to this purpose: that he was a servant and of nearest credit to Amasis, son and heir to Sesostris, king of Egypt, and being of one age was also so like him as hardly (but by the great difference of their outward estates) the one could be known from the other; that the king

30 Sesostris, after the death of Amasis's mother, had married a young woman who had turned the ordinary course of stepmother's hate to so unbridled a love towards her husband's son Amasis that neither the name of a father in him, of a husband in her, nor of a mother and son between themselves, could keep her back from disorderly

35 seeking that of Amasis which is a wickedness to accept. But he (besides his duty to virtue) having his heart already pledged to

3 sweetest] sweet Da, Hm.   5 fell to] happened unto Bo; happened to Je.
17 when (in good Cl, As, Je: when good St, Bo, Da, Ph, Je, Hm.   20 threatenings
Cl, As, Da, Ph, Je, Hm: threatens St, Bo.   23 with running] by running Cl, As,
Ph, Je; to run Hm.   24 as to the] as to Ph; as the Je, Hm.   27-8 also so like]
also like Cl, Da.

Artaxia, queen of Persia, the more she loved him, the more detested
her; which finding her hot spirits to work upon, shame, disdain,
and lust converted all her affection to a most revengeful hatred,
insomuch that all her study was for some naughty policy to over-
throw him, whereof in the end this young man offered her occasion. 5
For considering the resemblance he bare to his master, she began to
make the poor youth believe she did extremely affect him in respect
of that likeness; which he, privy to all his master's counsels, well
knew she immoderately loved. Thermuthis (for so the young man
was called) thought himself advanced to the stars when he saw so 10
fair a queen bend her goodwill towards him, which she (so far was
she become a slave to sin) sealed unto him with the fruition of her
unchaste body. When she thus had angled Thermuthis then began
she to accuse Amasis to his father as having sought to defile his bed;
which opinion being something gotten in, though not fully imprinted 15
in Sesostris's head, she caused Thermuthis (who was fully at her
devotion) to come one night in his master's apparel he had that day
worn to her chamber with his sword ready to kill the king as he
slept, for so had she persuaded him to do. But as soon as he entered
into the chamber she awaked the king, and making him see him he 20
took to be his son (being deceived by candle-light and his raiment)
in that order coming to kill him, the poor Thermuthis astonished and
running away, she sent those four trusty servants after him, to whom
she had beforehand given charge to have eye of him, and as soon as
he should fly out of the chamber to follow him (under colour to help 25
him by her commandment) till they trained him into some secret place,
and there murder him. And thus much one of them appointed to kill
him (who was the man the queen of Egypt most trusted) had revealed
unto him, thinking his speedy death should keep it from being opened.
"And", said Thermuthis, "by this time I fear the king hath done 30
some hurt to my dear master, whom thus miserably I have ruined."

And indeed so the king meant to have done, and presently to have
killed him, whom she caused to be brought by force out of his
lodging, as though thither he had fled to shift himself, and so
escape—the poor prince newly being come out of his sleep, and with 35

1 more detested] more he detested Da, Ph, Je.   8 counsels] counsel Cl, Da.
12 sin Bo, Cl, As, Da, Ph, Je: him St; some Hm.   13 thus had] had thus Cl, As,
Je.   18 to kill] to have killed Cl, As, Je, Hm.   19 had she] she had Cl, As.
he entered] he had entered Bo, Je, Hm.   24 beforehand] before Cl, As, Hm.   of]
to Ph, Je; upon Hm.   26 into] to Bo, Ph; in Je.   35 newly being come]
being newly come Cl, Da; newly coming Hm (and so . . . himself om. Je).

his amazedness rather condemning himself than otherwise. But the king (neither taking pains to examine the matter to the uttermost, nor so much as to hear what Amasis could say in a matter by many circumstances easy enough to have been refelled), he presently 5 caused him to be carried to the Red Sea, there to be put in a ship without any man but himself in it, and so to be left to the wind's discretion. But the two princes, having understood the beginning of this matter by Thermuthis, taking him with them, they entered into Memphis as the poor prince was some few miles already carried 10 out towards his ship of death. Which they understanding, and fearing they should not have leisure to tell the king and save him, they first pursued after him and by force of arms, joined with the help of some of the country who were willing to help their prince, they rescued him out of their hands and, bringing him back to 15 the king, made him understand the whole circumstances by Thermuthis's confession; whose pardon they got, considering what a fault the king himself had done to run so hastily in the condemning his only son in a cause might both by Thermuthis's absence and many other ways have been proved contrary. As for his wife, she 20 was past either pardoning or punishing; for when she heard the matter was revealed, she killed herself. "Thence," Plangus said, "having left the father and son in unity, and Amasis acknowledging his life of them with great love (which notwithstanding he could not have done if he had known how Artaxia hated them), they 25 returned, as it was thought, to Greece-ward; whom he had still followed, and by many misfortunes could never find. And now his last hope is in one of their countries, being nevertheless in great doubt that they are already perished by sea.'"

Thus did Histor epitomise the worthy acts of those two worthies, 30 making (though unknown) their own ears witnesses of their glory; which in no respect rejoiced them so much as that their beloved ladies heard it, of whose esteeming them they had tenderest regard, and chiefly desired they might know it was no dishonour they sought unto them whose honour they held in more precious reckoning than 35 their own lives. But indeed unmeasurable was the contentment of the two ladies who, besides love had taught them to trust, might

---

4 easy . . . been] easy to be Bo, Je; easily Ph.   he] *om.* Da; who Je, Hm.   7 two] *om.* Bo, Je, Hm.   8 this] the Cl, As.   10 out] *om.* Cl, As.   15 circumstances] circumstance Cl, Je, Hm.   21 Thence] Then Bo, Ph, Je, Hm.   29 those] these Da, Ph, Hm.   34 honour Bo, As, Da, Ph, Je, Hm: *om.* St; honours Cl.

find by the circumstance of these things that these could be no other than their lovers, although either's heart was so deeply plunged in her own that she never pained herself to call in question her sister's case; so that neither Pamela ever took conceit of the Amazon, nor Philoclea of the shepherd. As for Gynecia, such an inward lordship Cleophila held in her that she saw only her, she heard nobody but her, and thought of nothing but of her; so that Histor's narration passed through her ears without any marking, judging (as commonly they do that are full of thoughts) by the beginning that it should nothing appertain to the party upon whom she knit all her imagining power. The duke would divers times very fain have broken off Histor's speech but that, finding Cleophila yield him acceptable audience, he was in doubt to displease her. But well afraid he was lest the great praises he gave to the famous Pyrocles might kindle Cleophila's heart unto him; for comparing their worthiness he was forced to confess in himself there would prove a noble match between them, which made him fear that Cleophila's young mind might be stirred that way. Therefore, as soon, or rather before, Histor had ended, lest he might renew again some mention of those two princes, he called to Philisides who (according to his custom) sat so melancholy as though his mind were banished from the place he loved to be, imprisoned in his body; and desired him he would begin some eclogue with some other of the shepherds according to the accustomed guise. Philisides (though very unwilling) at the duke's commandment offered to sing with Lalus; but Lalus directly refused him, saying he should within few days be married to the fair Kala and since he had gotten his desire, he would sing no more. Then the duke willed Philisides to declare the discourse of his own fortunes, unknown to them as being a stranger in that country. But he prayed the duke to pardon him, the time being far too joyful to suffer the rehearsal of his miseries. But to satisfy Basilius some way, he began an eclogue betwixt himself and the echo, framing his voice so in those desert places as what words

1 circumstance] circumstances Cl, Ph, Je.   2 other] others Cl, Ph.   4 neither] om. Bo, Je, Hm.   ever] neither Bo; om. Cl; either Da, Ph; never Je, Hm. 8 narration] discourse Cl, As.   11–12 divers . . . have] very fain divers times have Bo; very fain have divers times Je, Hm.   13 yield Bo, Cl, As, Je, Hm: yielded St; yielding Da, Ph (yielding corr. to yield Bo).   13–18 there is a small tear in St, and the following words have been supplied from Bo: audience/was/Pyrocles/comparing himself there/which made/stirred.   17 that] lest Cl; om. Ph.   18 young] om. Bo, Je.   26 Lalus] Thyrsis 93.   Lalus] he 93.   saying] said Je; seeing 93.

he would have the echo reply unto, those he would sing higher than the rest, and so kindly framed a disputation betwixt himself and it; which, with these hexameters in the following order, he uttered:

Philisides   Echo

5    $—\ —\ —\ \cup\ \cup\ —\ —\ —\ \cup\ \cup\ —\ \cup\ \cup\ —\ —$

Fair rocks, goodly rivers, sweet woods, when shall I
    see peace?   Peace.
Peace? What bars me my tongue? Who is it that
    comes me so nigh?   I.
10 Oh! I do know what guest I have met; it is echo.   'Tis echo.
Well met, echo, approach; then tell me thy will too.   I will too.
   Echo, what do I get yielding my sprite to my griefs? Griefs.
What medicine may I find for a pain that draws me to
    death?   Death.
15 O poisonous medicine! What worse to me can be than
    it?   It.
In what state was I then, when I took this deadly
    disease?   Ease.
And what manner a mind which had to that humour
20   a vein?   Vain.
Hath not reason enough vehemence the desire to
    reprove?   Prove.
Oft prove I; but what salve when reason seeks to be
    gone?   One.
25 Oh! What is it? What is it that may be a salve to my
    love?   Love.
What do lovers seek for, long seeking for to enjoy?   Joy.
What be the joys for which to enjoy they went to the
    pains?   Pains.
30 Then to an earnest love what doth best victory lend? End.

4–p. 162, 28 *The poem is in* 90, 93.   5 *The scansion appears before the first line in*
St *and* Hm, *and after the fourth line again in* St, *and also in* Cl, As; Je *and* Hm *leave a*
space after the fourth line.   8 What bars me] Who is it that bars Bo; Who bars me
Da; What answereth me Ph; What bars Je, Hm; Who debars me 90 (*only*).   10 have
met] do meet 90 (*only*). 'Tis 90: It is OA.   11 then] and 90 (*only*).   12–24
There is a small tear in St, *and the following words have been supplied from* Bo: Echo/
What/ O poisonous/ In what/ Hath not /Oft.   12 sprite] spirits Le, Ph,
13 pain] grief 93.   15 to me can be] can be to me Ph, Hm.   19 And what
manner a] And what manner of Bo, Hm; What manner of a Cl, Le, Ph.   humour]
honour Cl, Je.   21 vehemence] vehemency Cl, Da, Ph, Je, Hm.   27 seeking
for to] seeking to Da, Hm.   28 for which] which for 93.   went] want Cl, Le.

End? But I can never end; love will not give me the
    leave.   Leave.

How be the minds disposed that cannot taste thy
    physic?   Sick.

Yet say again thy advice for th'ills that I told thee.   I told thee. 5

Doth th'infected wretch of his ill th'extremity know? No.

But if he know not his harms what guides hath he
    whilst he be blind?   Blind.

What blind guides can he have that leans to a fancy? A fancy.

Can fancies want eyes, or he fall that steppeth aloft? Oft.   10

What causes first made these torments on me to light? Light.

Can then a cause be so light that forceth a man to go
    die?   Aye.

Yet tell what light thing I had in me to draw me to
    die?   Eye.   15

Eyesight made me to yield, but what first pierced to
    mine eyes?   Eyes.

Eyes' hurters, eyes' hurt, but what from them to me
    falls?   Falls.

But when I first did fall, what brought most fall to my   20
    heart?   Art.

Art? What can be that art which thou dost mean by
    thy speech?   Speech.

What be the fruits of speaking art? What grows by
    the words?   Words.   25

O much more than words: those words served more
    to me bless.   Less.

O when shall I be known where most to be known I
    do long?   Long.

Long be thy woes for such news, but how recks she   30
    my thoughts?   Oughts.

Then, then what do I gain, since unto her will I do
    wind?   Wind.

3 thy] the Da, 90 (only).   5 thy] th' 90 (only).   6 ill 90: evil
OA; harm 93.   8 whilst he be] while he is Cl, Le, Je.   9 leans] leads 90 (only).
10 want OA, 90: want corr. to be without St.   steppeth OA, 90: steppeth corr. to.
sleepeth St.   13 Aye] Die As; Eye Je, Hm; Yea 93.   14-15 om. Je, Hm.
14 tell]tell me Cl, Da, Ph.   16 pierced] pressed Cl; purest Je.   17 mine] my
Bo, 90.   22 which] whereof Ph; that 93.   25 the words] thy words Da, Ph, Je,
Hm.   26 served] seemed Cl, Le, As; sind Da.   27 to me] to my Je, Hm; me
to 90.   29 do] om. Da, Hm.   30 news, but] bad news: 90 (only).   recks Cl,
Le, As, Da, 90: rocks St, Bo, Ph, Hm; wrecks Je.

Wind, tempests, and storms; yet in end what gives
    she desire?   Ire.
Silly reward! Yet among women hath she of virtue
    the most.   Most.
5 What great name may I give to so heav'nly a woman?   A woe-man.
Woe, but seems to me joy that agrees to my thought
    so.   I thought so.
Think so, for of my desired bliss it is only the course.   Curse.
Cursed be thyself for cursing that which leads me to
10   joys.   Toys.
What be the sweet creatures where lowly demands be
    not heard?   Hard.
Hard to be got, but got constant, to be held like
    steels.   Eels.
15 How can they be unkind? Speak for th'hast narrowly
    pried.   Pride.
Whence can pride come there, since springs of beauty
    be thence?   Thence.
Horrible is this blasphemy unto the most holy.   O lie.
20 Thou li'st false echo, their minds as virtue be just.   Just.
Mock'st thou those diamonds which only be matched
    by the gods?   Odds.
Odds? What an odds is there since them to the
    heav'ns I prefer?   Err.
25 Tell yet again me the names of these fair formed to
    do ev'ls.   Dev'ls.
Dev'ls? If in hell such dev'ls do abide, to the hells I
    do go.   Go.

Philisides was commended for the placing of his echo, but little
30 did he regard their praises; who had set the foundation of his

3 among] above 90 (*only*).   3–4 of virtue the most. Most] a title. A tittle 90 (*only*).
6 my thought] my thoughts Bo, Cl, Le, Da, Ph.   8 Curse] Course As, Hm, 90
(*only*).   11 lowly] lovely Cl, Le, Je, Hm.   13–14 *om.* 93.   13 like]
very 90 (*only*).   15 How can they be] How be they held 90; What makes them be 93.
narrowly 90: nearly St, Bo, Cl, Le, As, Da, Je, Hm; newly Ph.   17 Whence]
How Je, 90 (*only*).   19 this] thy Cl, Le, As, Da.   25 Tell yet again, how
name ye the goodly made evil? A devil. 90 (*only*).   27 Devil? In hell where such
devil is, to that hell I do go. Go. 90 (*only*) *corrected formes*; Devil? where hell if such devil
is, to that hell I do go. Go. 90 (*only*) *uncorrected formes*.   29 was commended] was
singularly commended Da, Ph, Je, Hm.   the placing] the pretty placing Da, Ph,
Je, Hm.

honour there where he was most despised. And therefore returning
again to the train of his desolate pensiveness, Cleophila seeing
nobody offer to fill the stage, as if her long-restrained conceits did
now burst out of prison, she thus (desiring her voice should be
accorded to nothing but to Philoclea's ears) threw down the burden 5
of her mind in Anacreon's kind of verses:

ᴗ — ᴗ — ᴗ — —

My muse what ails this ardour
To blaze my only secrets?
Alas, it is no glory   10
To sing my own decayed state.
Alas, it is no comfort
To speak without an answer.
Alas, it is no wisdom
To show the wound without cure.   15

My muse what ails this ardour?
My eyes be dim, my limbs shake,
My voice is hoarse, my throat scorched,
My tongue to this my roof cleaves,
My fancy amazed, my thoughts dulled,   20
My heart doth ache, my life faints,
My soul begins to take leave.
So great a passion all feel,
To think a sore so deadly
I should so rashly rip up.   25

My muse what ails this ardour?
If that to sing thou art bent,
Go sing the fall of old Thebes,
The wars of ugly centaurs,
The life, the death of Hector,   30
So may thy song be famous;
Or if to love thou art bent,
Recount the rape of Europe,

4 desiring] desired Da, Ph, Je, Hm.   7–p.164, 30 90 *omits this poem*; 93 *restores it.*
7 *Scansion in* St, Bo, Cl, As, Hm *only.*   11 my Bo, Cl, Le, Da, Ph, Je, Hm, 93:
mine St, As, 90, 98.   15 wound] wounds Cl, Le, Hm.   17 My eyes] Mine
eyes Da, 93.   18 scorched] scorch Cl; is scorch Da.   20 thoughts] thought 93.
27 that to sing 93: unto sing St, Bo, Le, As, Je; unto song Cl, Da, Ph, Hm.   28 fall]
song Le, Hm.   31 thy] the 93.

Adonis' end, Venus' net,
The sleepy kiss the moon stale;
So may thy song be pleasant.

My muse what ails this ardour
5   To blaze my only secrets?
Wherein do only flourish
The sorry fruits of anguish,
The song thereof a last will,
The tunes be cries, the words plaints,
10   The singer is the song's theme
Wherein no ear can have joy,
Nor eye receives due object,
Ne pleasure here, ne fame got.

My muse what ails this ardour?
15   'Alas', she saith, 'I am thine,
So are thy pains my pains too.
Thy heated heart my seat is
Wherein I burn, thy breath is
My voice, too hot to keep in.
20   Besides, lo here the author
Of all thy harms; lo here she
That only can redress thee,
Of her I will demand help.'

My muse, I yield, my muse sing,
25   But all thy song herein knit:
The life we lead is all love,
The love we hold is all death,
Nor aught I crave to feed life,
Nor aught I seek to shun death,
30   But only that my goddess
My life, my death, do count hers.

Basilius, when she had fully ended her song, fell prostrate upon the
ground, and thanked the gods they had preserved his life so long as
to hear the very music they themselves used in an earthly body.

1-2 *blank left* Je.   2 moon stale] moon stall Bo, Le, As, Hm (stall *corr. to* stale
St); monastical Cl; moanful Ph.   8 a last] alas Cl, Le, Da, Ph; elect Je.
11 Wherein] When 93.   12 receives] revives Ph; receive Je, Hm, 93.   due] an Bo,
Cl.   13 ne fame] ne fancy Bo; in fame Cl; in fancy Le; no fame As; me fame Ph.
got] get Da, Hm, 93; gets Je.   20 lo here] to hear Bo, Le, Ph (to hear *corr. to* lo
here Cl).   21 thy] my Cl, Le, As, Je.   31 do] doth Cl, Le.

And then with like grace to Cleophila, never left entreating her till she had (taking a lyra Basilius held for her) sung these phaleuciacs:

— — — — ◡ ◡ — ◡ — ◡ — ◡

Reason, tell me thy mind, if here be reason
In this strange violence, to make resistance.   5
Where sweet graces erect the stately banner
Of virtue's regiment, shining in harness
Of fortune's diadems, by beauty mustered.
Say then, Reason, I say what is thy counsel?

Her loose hair be the shot, the breasts the pikes be,   10
Scouts each motion is, the hands the horsemen,
Her lips are the riches the wars to maintain,
Where well couched abides a coffer of pearl,
Her legs carriage is of all the sweet camp.
Say then, Reason, I say what is thy counsel?   15

Her cannons be her eyes, mine eyes the walls be,
Which at first volley gave too open entry,
Nor rampire did abide; my brain was up blown,
Undermined with a speech, the piercer of thoughts.
Thus weakened by myself, no help remaineth.   20
Say then, Reason, I say what is thy counsel?

And now fame, the herald of her true honour,
Doth proclaim (with a sound made all by men's mouths)
That nature, sovereign of earthly dwellers,
Commands all creatures to yield obeisance   25
Under this, this her own, her only darling.
Say then, Reason, I say what is thy counsel?

Reason sighs, but in end he thus doth answer:
'Naught can reason avail in heav'nly matters.'
Thus nature's diamond, receive thy conquest,   30

---

2 taking] taken Da, Hm.   3–p.166, 3 *The poem is in* Ra *and* 93; 90 *omits it.*
3 *Scansion in* St, Bo, Cl, As, Hm *only.*   4 here] this Da, Ra.   8 beauty]
virtue Hm, Ra.   10 breasts] breast Le, Hm, 93.   11 the horsemen] be horsemen
Da, Je, 93.   16 Je *is missing from here.*   17 at first] at the first Hm, Ra.   too
open Bo, Cl, Le, As, Da, Hm, 93: to open *corr. to* open St; an open Ph.   18 brain
Bo, Cl, Le, As, Da, Je, 93: train St, Ph.   20 remaineth] remained Da, Hm.
23 all by] by all As, Hm, Ra.   26 this, this] this Cl, Ra.   28 in end] in the
end Ph, Ra.   30 receive] receives 93.

Thus pure pearl, I do yield my senses and soul.
Thus sweet pain, I do yield what e'er I can yield.
Reason look to thyself, I serve a goddess.

Dorus had long, he thought, kept silence from saying somewhat
5 which might tend to the glory of her in whom all glory (to his
seeming) was included. But now he brake it, singing these verses,
called asclepiadics:

— — — ∪ ∪ — — ∪ ∪ — ∪ ∪

O sweet woods, the delight of solitariness!
10 O how much I do like your solitariness!
Where man's mind hath a freed consideration
Of goodness to receive lovely direction;
Where senses do behold th'order of heav'nly host,
And wise thoughts do behold what the creator is.
15 Contemplation here holdeth his only seat,
Bounded with no limits, borne with a wing of hope,
Climbs even unto the stars; nature is under it.
Naught disturbs thy quiet, all to thy service yield,
Each sight draws on a thought (thought mother of science),
20 Sweet birds kindly do grant harmony unto thee,
Fair trees' shade is enough fortification,
Nor danger to thyself, if be not in thyself.

O sweet woods, the delight of solitariness!
O how much I do like your solitariness!
25 Here no treason is hid, veiled in innocence,
Nor envy's snaky eye finds any harbour here,
Nor flatterers' venomous insinuations,
Nor cunning humorists' puddled opinions,
Nor courteous ruin of proffered usury,
30 Nor time prattled away, cradle of ignorance,
Nor causeless duty, nor cumber of arrogance,
Nor trifling title of vanity dazzleth us,
Nor golden manacles stand for a paradise,
Here wrong's name is unheard; slander a monster is.

8–p. 167, 16 90 *omits this poem*; 93 *restores it.*   8 *Scansion in* St, Bo, Cl, As, Hm
only.   13 th'] the Bo, Cl, Le, Da, Ph, Hm.   18 yield] yields Da, Hm, 93.
22 if be] if Cl; if it be Le, Da, Ph, Hm.   24 I do] do I Cl, Le, Da, Ph, Hm.
25 no] not Bo; nor 93.   innocence] innocency Cl, Le, Da, Ph, Hm.   28 cunning]
common Ph; coming 93 (*corr.* 13).   29 ruin] ruining Cl, Le.   31 *om.* Cl, Le.
arrogance] arrogancy Da, Hm.

Keep thy sprite from abuse, here no abuse doth haunt.
What man grafts in a tree dissimulation?

O sweet woods, the delight of solitariness!
O how well I do like your solitariness!
Yet dear soil, if a soul closed in a mansion   5
As sweet as violets, fair as a lily is,
Straight as cedar, a voice stains the canary birds,
Whose shade safety doth hold, danger avoideth her:
Such wisdom that in her lives speculation:
Such goodness that in her simplicity triumphs: 10
Where envy's snaky eye winketh or else dieth,
Slander wants a pretext, flattery gone beyond:
Oh! If such a one have bent to a lonely life,
Her steps glad we receive, glad we receive her eyes.
    And think not she doth hurt our solitariness,   15
    For such company decks such solitariness.

The other shepherds were offering themselves to have continued
the sports, but the night had so quietly spent most part of herself
among them that the duke, for that time, licensed them; and so
bringing Cleophila to her lodging (who would much rather have 20
done the same for Philoclea), of all sides they went to counterfeit a
sleep in their beds, for a true one their agonies could not afford them.
Yet there they lay (for so might they be most solitary for the food of
their thoughts) till it was near noon the next day. After which
Basilius was to continue his Apollo devotions, and the others to 25
meditate upon their private desires.

Here ends the second eclogues.

4 I do] do I Cl, Le, Da, Hm.   6 a] *om.* 93 (*corr.* 98).   7 as] as a Cl, Le, Da, Ph,
Hm.   8 safety Bo, Cl, Le, As, Ph, Hm, 13: safely St, Da, 93.   9 *om.* Le.
12 wants] wanteth Cl, Le; watches Ph.   13 lonely] lovely Bo, Cl, As, Da, Ph, Hm.
19 among Cl, As, Da: amoges St; amonges Bo; amongst Hm (Ph *substitutes* stolen upon
for spent . . . among).   22 beds Da, Hm, 90: bed St, Bo, Cl, As, Ph, 93.
24 near] nigh As; past Ph.   25 others: other OA, 90.   26 desires] cogitations
Ph; devices Hm.   27 ends] end Cl; endeth Ph.

THE THIRD BOOK OR ACT

THE next day, which followed a night full of passions, and yet brought in himself new matter to increase them (time upon time still adding growth to a well-rooted inclination), while the duke in 5 the afternoon time was busy about Apollo's rites, Cleophila (to whom the not-enjoying her dear friend Dorus had been one of her burdenous griefs) took hold of this opportunity, and calling her beloved cousin with her, went to the same place where first she had revealed unto him her enclosed passion and was by him (as you may 10 remember) with a friendly sharpness reprehended. There, sitting down among the sweet flowers (whereof that country was very plentiful) under the pleasant shade of a broad-leaved sycamore, they recounted one to another their strange pilgrimage of passions, omitting nothing which the open-hearted friendship is wont to lay 15 forth, where there is cause to communicate both joys and sorrows—for, indeed, there is no sweeter taste of friendship than the coupling of their souls in this mutuality either of condoling or comforting, where the oppressed mind finds itself not altogether miserable, since it is sure of one which is feelingly sorry for his misery; and the 20 joyful spends not his joy either alone or there where it may be envied, but may freely send it to such a well-grounded object, from whence he shall be sure to receive a sweet reflection of the same joy, and (as in a clear mirror of sincere goodwill) see a lively picture of his own gladness. Then would there arise betwixt them loving 25 debates of their ladies' beauties, of their own constancies; and sometimes gloriously strive whether had been the most wretched.

'O my Dorus, my Dorus,' said Cleophila, 'who would ever have thought so good a schoolmaster as you were to me could for lack of living have been driven to shepherdry?'

2-10 The next . . . There] 93 *substitutes* After that Basilius (according to the oracle's promise) had received home his daughters, and settled himself again in his solitary course and accustomed company, there passed not many days ere the now fully re-comforted Dorus, having waited a time of Zelmane's walking alone towards her little arbour, took leave of his master Dametas's husbandry to follow her. Near whereunto overtaking her, and   6 dear] *om.* Cl, As, Da.   9 unto OA: to St. 11 down among] down together among 93.   country] place 93.   12 of a OA, 93: of the St.   13 passions] passion Bo, Da.   17 their] *om.* 93. 22 joy 93: joys OA.   24-p. 172, 25 Then would . . . Mopsa so to do] *om.* 93. 29 living have been: living been OA.

'Even the same', said Dorus, 'that would have thought so true a chaste boy as you were could have become a counterfeit courtesan. But', said he, 'see whether you can show me so fair spoils of your victory'—and therewith he drew out a glove of Pamela's done with murrey silk and gold lace, and (not without tender tears kissing it) he put it again in his bosom, and sang these two stanzas:

Sweet glove, the witness of my secret bliss
(Which hiding didst preserve that beauty's light
That, opened forth, my seal of comfort is),
Be thou my star in this my darkest night,
Now that mine eyes their cheerful sun doth miss
Which dazzling still, doth still maintain my sight;
  Be thou, sweet glove, the anchor of my mind,
  Till my frail bark his hav'n again do find.

Sweet glove, the sweet despoils of sweetest hand,
Fair hand, the fairest pledge of fairer heart,
True heart, whose truth doth yield to truest band,
Chief band, I say, which ties my chiefest part,
My chiefest part, wherein do chiefly stand
Those secret joys, which heav'n to me impart,
  Unite in one, my state thus still to save;
  You have my thanks, let me your comfort have.

'Alas,' said Cleophila, when she had awhile paused after her friend's music, 'can you not joy sufficiently in your joys, but you must use your joys as if you would vauntingly march over your friend's miseries? Be happy still, my Dorus, but wish the same hap to him whom goodwill doth make to place much of his hap in you.'

'Not the same hap,' said Dorus smiling, 'Philoclea's hap I freely grant you; but I pray you let not your Amazon eyes be busy upon the lady Pamela, for her looks have an attractive power in them, and your heart is not of the hardest metal.'

'And are you afraid of that?' said Cleophila. 'From henceforward be not, for hardly are stars seen in daylight. But I would fain know

6 in] into Da, Ph, Hm. stanzas: stanses St, As; stances Bo; staves Cl, Da, Ph, Hm.
7–22 *The poem is in* Dd.   7 Sweet] O sweet Cl, Le, Ph.   8 didst] did Cl, Ph.
11 their Cl, Le, As: his St, Bo, Da, Hm, Dd (Ph *omits line*).   12 doth] dost Cl, Hm.
16 fairer] fairest Bo, Da.   17 to] the As, Dd.   truest] trusty Cl, Ph.
29 upon] about Bo, Hm.   30 her] your Cl, As.   31 not of] not made of Bo,
Cl, Da, Ph.   33 in daylight] in the daylight Bo, As, Hm.

what assurance you have of the changing favour of fortune. I have
heard of them that dreamed much of holding great treasures, and
when they waked found nothing in their hands but a bedstaff. Glad
would I be to be assured of your well-being, for methinks the gods
5 be too unequal to mankind if they suffer not good to come from one
kinsman to another by a secret infusion, as we find daily evil doth
by a manifest infection. Therefore, since your joy was such as you
could find in your heart to sing it, do now for my sake vouchsafe to
say it.'

10   'My joys are such', said Dorus, 'as neither suffer in themselves
uncertainty, nor are in danger by inconstancy. Let me, therefore,
do no wrong to my motherly destinies, which have woven me so
blessed a web, by ungrateful forgetting their favours; and since I
have often tired the muses with the hideous tune of my doleful
15 affects, I will now sauce those sorrows with some more pleasant
exercises.' And so took he his shepherd's pipe, and with the sounding
that, first seeming to invite the birds to mark his music, he after laid
down his pipe and sang these following:

>   The merchant man, whom gain doth teach the sea
> 20   Where rocks do wait for them the winds do chase,
>   Beaten with waves, no sooner kens the bay
>   Where he was bound to make his marting place,
>   But fear forgot, and pains all overpast,
>   Make present ease receive the better taste.

> 25   The labourer, which cursed earth up tears
>   With sweaty brows, sometimes with watered eyes,
>   Oft scorching sun, oft cloudy darkness fears,
>   While upon chance his fruit of labour lies;
>   But harvest come, and corn in fertile store,
> 30   More in his own he toiled, he glads the more.

>   Thus in my pilgrimage of mated mind,
>   Seeking the saint in whom all graces dwell,
>   What storms found me, what torments I did find,
>   Who seeks to know acquaints himself with hell;
> 35   But now success hath got above annoys,
>   That sorrow's weight doth balance up these joys.

3 waked] awaked Bo, Cl, As, Hm.   14 tired Cl, As, Da, Ph: tried St, Bo, Hm.
16 took he his] took his As, Hm.   24 better] bitter Da, Hm.   25 Je *begins
again*.   26 watered] wat'ry Bo, Cl, Le, Ph, Hm.

'Truly', said Cleophila, 'among so many qualities as all ages have
attributed to Cupid, I did never think him so good a minstrel that in
such short space could make his scholar so musical as you be. But
although, for my part, the stars have not held wholly an angry aspect
towards me, yet lest envious fortune should spite at the too much   5
boasting of your blessedness, I will mingle your comical tunes with
my long-used tragical notes, and will stain a little the fullness of
your hopes with the hanging on of my tedious fears.' Therewith
lying down with her face upward towards heaven, with her eye so
settled as one might well perceive it was nothing her eye could then   10
see which busied her common sense, with a fainting kind of voice
she thus sang:

> The merchant man, whom many seas have taught
> What horrors breed where wind dominion bears,
> Yet never rock, nor race, such terror brought   15
> As near his home when storm or shelf he fears;
>   For nature hath that never failing scope,
>   Most loath to lose, the most approaching hope.
>
> The labourer, whom tired body makes
> Hold dear his work, with sighs each change attends,   20
> But at no change so pinching care he takes
> As happy shows of corn when harvest sends;
>   For reason will, great sight of hoped bliss,
>   Make great the loss, so great the fear to miss.
>
> Thus tossed in my ship of huge desire,   25
> Thus toiled in my work of raging love,
> Now that I spy the hav'n my thoughts require,
> Now that some flow'r of fruit my pains do prove,
>   My dreads augment the more in passion's might,
>   Since love with care, and hope with fear do fight.   30

As she had ended the last word, she took Dorus in her arms: 'Ah!
my Dorus,' said she, 'these be as yet my harvests; these be as yet the
gains of my traffic! But I conjure thee by the inviolate name of our

10 then] there Cl, Hm.   13 have] hath Le, As, Ph, Hm.   14 breed] breeds Cl,
Le, Ph, Je.   19 tired] tried Ph (tried *corr. to* tired Cl).   20 sighs] sigh Cl, Le,
As.   21 at] as Le, Je, Hm.   26 toiled] toiling Da, Je, Hm.   27 hav'n]
heavens Ph; heavē Je.   28 fruit] fruits Cl, Da, Ph, Hm.

friendship, or (if your new flames have made that smoke) by the fair
hair of Pamela, that you tell me the story of your loving adventures,
that thus short of me, as I think, in affection, you have gotten so
much the fore-foot in affection's reward.'

5 'Alas,' said Dorus, with a changed countenance, 'the cruel
schoolmaster makes the silly child think a little play great sport, and
how much the more we need great help, small help seems the greater
unto us; for long beaten in miseries, it makes us measure our minds
by our powers and not by our wishes, and the heart stuffed up with
10 woefulness is glad greedily to suck the thinnest air of comfort. Far
am I (God knows) from the place where I hope to stop, but yet well
advanced am I from thence where I took my start.' Then did he
declare unto her the discourse of all that with which heretofore,
fair ladies, perchance I have troubled you: How Pamela, out of a
15 virtuous resolution in respect of his outward inequality, had wholly
disdained to speak with him, and misliked the shows he had made of
his love; the strait he was in to make himself known (he being
enviously looked upon, and she narrowly guarded); that in the end
he was forced to counterfeit a love to Mopsa, and tell her whatsoever
20 he would have Pamela understand; how in his tale he answered
Pamela's wit and abused Mopsa's ignorance—the manner whereof
you have before, fair ladies, understood. And further, since that time
having plainly found there wanted no liking in Pamela, if she might
have assurance of his worthiness, he had (still under the colour of
25 asking her whether it were not fit for Mopsa so to do) concluded with
her the stealing her away to the next seaport, under vehement oath
to offer no force unto her till he had invested her in the duchy of
Thessalia; that one of the greatest matters had won her to this was
the strange humours she saw her father lately fallen into, and
30 unreasonable restraint of her liberty (whereof she knew no cause but
light-grounded jealousies), added to the hate of that manner of life,

10 woefulness] joyfulness As, Da.   11 hope] mean As, Da, Je (mean *corr. to* hope
Bo).   12 am I] I am Cl, Da, Je, Hm.   20 his] this As, Ph.   he answered
OA: he had answered St.   25–9 concluded . . . into) 93 *resumes narrative with
new introductory sentence, followed by a re-working of this passage*: But after much dis-
course on either part, Dorus (his heart scarce serving him to come to the point whereunto
his then coming have been wholly directed, as loath in the kindest sort to discover to his
friend his own unkindness) at length, one word emboldening another, made known to
Zelmane how Pamela, upon his vehement oath to offer no force unto her till he had
invested her in the duchy of Thessalia, had condescended to his stealing her away to the
next seaport. That, besides the strange humours she saw her father more and more
falling into,   29 humours] humour Cl, Da, Ph.   31 jealousies] jealousy Cl, Da.

and confidence she had in his virtue; that now they waited for
nothing but some fit time by the absence of their three loathsome
companions in whom folly engendered suspicion. 'And therefore
now', said Dorus, 'my dear cousin (to whom nature began my
friendship, education confirmed it, and virtue hath made it eternal), 5
here have I discovered the very foundation whereupon my life is
built. Be you the judge betwixt me and my fortune. The violence
of love is not unknown unto you; and I know my case shall never
want pity in your consideration. How all the joys of my heart do
leave me in thinking I must for a time be absent from you! The 10
eternal truth is witness unto me, I know I should not so sensibly
feel the pangs of my last departure. But this enchantment of my
restless desire hath such authority in myself above myself that I am
become a slave unto it. I have no more freedom in mine own deter-
minations. My thoughts are now all bent how to carry away my 15
burdenous bliss. Yet, most beloved cousin, rather than you should
think I do herein violate that holy band of true friendship wherein
I unworthy am knit unto you, command my stay. Perchance the
force of your commandment may work such impression into my
heart, which no reason of mine own can imprint unto it. For the 20
gods forbid the foul word of abandoning Pyrocles might ever be
objected to the faithful Musidorus! But if you can spare my presence
(whose presence no way serves you, and by the division of these two
lodges is not oft with you); nay, if you can think my absence may
(as it shall) stand you in stead by bringing such an army hither as 25
shall make Basilius (willing or unwilling) to know his own hap in
granting you Philoclea, then I will cheerfully go about this my most
desired enterprise, and shall think the better half of it already
achieved, being begun in the fortunate hour of my friend's
contentment.' 30

These words, as they were not knit together with such a constant
course of flowing eloquence as Dorus was wont to use, so was his
voice interrupted with sighs and his countenance with interchanging

1-2 that . . . absence] the chiefest reason had won her to this was the late danger she
stood in of losing him, the like whereof (not unlike to fall if this course were continued)
she chose rather to die than again to undergo. That now they waited for nothing else
but some fit time for their escape by the absence 93.   3 folly] foully Bo, Hm;
fully Ph, Je.   7 you] thou Ph, Hm.   8 unto] to Hm, 93.   case] care Bo,
Ph.   13 am] _om._ As, Da.   14 mine] my Da, Ph, Hm.   15 how] _om._ As, Da.
16 you] I Da, 93 (_corr._ 98).   18 my] me As, Da, 93.   20 which] that As, Da, 93.
mine] my Cl, Da, Ph.   unto] into As, Je, Hm, 93.   24 can] _om._ Ph, Hm.   27 I
will] will I Ph, Je, Hm.   28 and shall 93: I shall OA ; and I shall Je.

colour dismayed—so much his own heart did find him faulty to unbend any way the continual use of their dear friendship. But, O feminine love, what power thou holdest in men's hearts! Many times he had been desirous to signify his happy success and final determina-
5 tion with Pamela, but his heart would never serve him to come to this point, till one word at this time emboldened another kindly to discover to his friend his own unkindness. Cleophila (who had before purposed to make the like declaration upon what slippery grounds her hopes stood, and yet how far her hopes in Philoclea
10 were advanced, how far by Gynecia they were hindered), when this last determination of Dorus strake her attentive ears, she stayed a great while oppressed with a dead amazement. There came straight before her mind, made tender with woes, the images of her own fortune; her tedious longings; her causes to despair; the cumbersome
15 folly of Basilius; the enraged jealousy of Gynecia; herself a prince without retinue, a man annoyed with the troubles of womankind, loathsomely loved, and dangerously loving; and now, for the perfecting of all, her friend to be taken away by himself, to make the loss the greater by the unkindness. But within a while she resolutely
20 passed over all inward objections; and therefore, preferring her friend's profit to her own desire, with a quiet but hearty look, she thus answered him:
'If I bare thee this love, virtuous Musidorus, for mine own sake, and that our friendship grew because I for my part might rejoice to
25 enjoy such a friend, I should now so thoroughly feel mine own loss that I should call the heavens and earth to witness how cruelly ye rob me of my greatest comfort, measuring the breach of friendship by mine own passion. But because indeed I love thee for thyself, and in my judgement judge of thy worthiness to be loved, I am
30 content to leave all that which might please myself. I am content to

2 unbend] unbind Cl, As, Da.   2–10 But . . . hindered] But Zelmane, who had all this while gladly hearkened to the other tidings of her friend's happy success 93.
5 him] om. Cl, As, Da.   7 to] unto As, Da, Hm.   8 declaration] determination Hm (determination corr. to declaration Bo).   9 grounds] ground Cl, Da, Hm; grant As. hopes stood] hope stood Cl, As, Da, Ph; haps stood Je.   11 attentive] om. Ph, Je.
13 images] image As, Je, Hm.   14 causes] cause As, Hm.   16 troubles] trouble Ph. Je.   19 by the unkindness] by unkindness Ph, Je.   20 therefore] om. 93.
23 mine] my Da, Ph, Je, Hm.   25 mine] my Da, Ph, Je.   26 heavens Bo, Cl, As, Da, Je, Hm, 93: havens St; heaven Ph.   ye] you Cl, As, Da, Ph, Je, Hm.
27 rob] robbed Ph, Hm; have robbed Je.   28 mine] my As, Da.   29 be loved] be beloved Cl, Ph, Je, Hm; beloved 93 (corr. to be loved 98).   29–30 I am . . . myself] om. As, Da, 93.   30 I OA, 93: and St.

build my pleasure upon thy comfort; and then will I deem my hap in friendship great when I shall see thee, whom I love, happy. Let me be only sure thou lovest me still—the only prize of true affection. Go therefore on, worthy Musidorus, with the guide of virtue and service of fortune. Let thy loves be loved, thy desires prosperous, thy escape safe, and thy journey easy. Let everything yield his help to thy desert. For my part, absence shall not take thee from mine eyes, nor afflictions shall bar me from gladding in thy good; nor a possessed heart shall keep thee from the place it hath forever allotted unto thee.'

Dorus would fain have replied again, to have made a liberal confession that Cleophila had of her side the advantage of well performing friendship; but partly his own grief of parting from one he loved so dearly, partly the kind care in what state he should leave Cleophila, bred such a conflict in his mind that many times he wished he had either never attempted, or never revealed, this secret enterprise.

But Cleophila, who had now looked to the uttermost of it, and established her mind upon an assured determination: 'My only friend,' said she, 'since to so good towardness your courteous destinies have conducted you, let not a ceremonial consideration of our mutual love be a bar unto it. I joy in your presence; but I joy more in your good. That friendship brings forth the fruits of enmity which prefers his own tenderness before his friend's damage. For my part, my greatest grief herein shall be I can be no further serviceable unto you.'

'O Cleophila,' said Dorus, with his eyes even covered with water, 'I did not think so soon to have displayed my determination unto you, but to have made my way first into your loving judgement. But, alas, as your sweet disposition drew me so far, so doth it now strengthen me in it. To you, therefore, be the due commendation given, who can conquer me in love, and love in wisdom. As for me, then shall goodness turn to evil, and ungratefulness be the token of a true heart, when Pyrocles shall not possess a principal seat in my soul, when the name of Pyrocles shall not be held of me in devout reverence.'

---

4 worthy] *om.* As, Hm.   5 loves] love Je, 93.   6 escape] estate Da, Je, Hm.
8 gladding] joying As, Da.   9 forever] ever As, Ph, Je.   10 thee 93: you OA.
12 Cleophila] Zelmane 93 (*and throughout*).   21 a] the As; *om.* Je, Hm.
22 fruits] fruit Da; root Hm.   23 damage] domage *corr. to* happiness Cl; well
doing Ph.   28 into] to Da; unto Ph, Hm; in 93.   30 commendation] com-
mendations Da Ph (commendations *corr. to* commendation St.)   32 ungrateful-
ness] ingratefulness Cl, Je, Hm.

I think they would never have come to the cruel instant of
parting, nor to the ill-faring word of farewell, had not Cleophila
seen afar off the old Basilius who had been everywhere to seek her
since he had ended his sacrifice; and now being come within compass
of discerning her, he began to frame the loveliest countenance he
could, stroking up his legs, setting his beard in due order, and
standing bolt upright.

'Alas,' said Cleophila, 'behold an evil foretoken of our sorrowful
departure! Yonder see I one of my furies which doth daily vex me.
Farewell, farewell, my Musidorus! The gods make fortune to wait on
thy virtues, and make me wade through this lake of wretchedness!'

Dorus burst out into a flood of tears, wringing her fast by the
hand: 'No, no,' said he, 'I go blindfold whither the course of my
ill-hap carries me; for now, too late, my heart gives me this our
separating can never be prosperous. But if I live, attend me here
shortly with an army.'

Thus both appalled with the grievous renting of their long
combination (having first resolved with themselves that, whatsoever
evil fell unto them, they should never upon no occasion utter their
names—for the conserving the honour of their royal parentage—but
took other names they agreed upon), they took diverse ways: Dorus
to the lodge-ward, where his heavy eyes might be something
refreshed; Cleophila towards Basilius, saying to herself with a
scornful smiling, 'yet hath not my friendly fortune wholly deprived
me of a pleasant companion.'

Basilius had inquired of his daughter Philoclea what receipt his
desires found in Cleophila, and had some comfort of her: that, by
her own good entertainment, she did imagine his cause was not
ungrateful unto her. And now, having with much search come to her
presence, doubt and desire bred a great quarrel in his mind; for late

---

1 I think] *om.* 93.   2 to] *om.* Bo, Cl, Da, Ph.   3–4 had . . . sacrifice] having per-
formed a sacrifice to Apollo for his daughters', but principally for his mistress's, happy
return, had since been everywhere to seek her 93.   5 loveliest] lowliest Da;
liveliest Ph.   8 our] your 93.   10 Farewell, farewell] Farewell Bo, Da.
make . . . on] second As, Da, Ph, Je, Hm.   19 evil] *om.* 93.   unto] on Da; *om.* Ph;
upon Je.   20 conserving] concerning Bo, Ph.   21 took . . . upon] keep the names
of Daiphantus and Palladius, as before had been agreed between them 93.   took other]
take other Da, Ph, Je.   names they agreed] names agreed As, Da.   22 something]
om. Cl; somewhat Ph.   24 scornful] sorrowful Ph, Je, Hm.   friendly] friend
Cl; freed Ph.   wholly] *om.* Cl, Da, 93.   26–9 Basilius . . . unto] *om.* 93.
29 ungrateful] so ungrateful As, Da.   And now] But he 93.   to] unto Ph, Je; into
Hm.   30 late] his former 93.

experience had taught him to doubt, and true feeling of love made
doubts dangerous. But the working of his desire had ere long won
the field; and therefore, with the most submissive manner his
behaviour could yield: 'O goddess', said he, 'towards whom I have
the greatest feeling of religion, be not displeased at some show of 5
devotion I have made to Apollo, since he (if he know anything)
knows that my heart bears far more awful reverence to yourself
than to any unseen deity.'

'You will ever be deceived in me,' answered Cleophila, 'I will
make myself no competitor with Apollo; neither can blasphemies to 10
him be duties to me.'

With that, Basilius took out of his bosom certain verses he had
written, and kneeling down, presented them to her. They contained
this:

>   Phoebus farewell, a sweeter saint I serve.   15
>   The high conceits thy heav'nly wisdoms breed
>   My thoughts forget: my thoughts which never swerve
>   From her in whom is sown their freedom's seed,
>   And in whose eyes my daily doom I read.
>
>   Phoebus farewell, a sweeter saint I serve.   20
>   Thou art far off, thy kingdom is above;
>   She heav'n on earth with beauties doth preserve.
>   Thy beams I like, but her clear rays I love;
>   Thy force I fear, her force I still do prove.
>
>   Phoebus yield up thy title in my mind.   25
>   She doth possess; thy image is defaced.
>   But if thy rage some brave revenge will find
>   On her, who hath in me thy temple razed,
>   Employ thy might, that she my fires may taste;
>   And how much more her worth surmounteth thee,   30
>   Make her as much more base by loving me.

'This is my hymn to you,' said he, 'not left me by my ancestors,
but begun in myself. The temple wherein it is daily sung is my soul,
and the sacrifice I offer to you withal is all whatsoever I am.'

2 desire] desires Da, Je, Hm.   6 know Bo, Hm, 93: knew St, Cl, As, Da, Ph, Je.
7 awful] and full Cl; joyful Hm.   8 any unseen] his, or any other the like 93.
15–31 *The poem is in* Ra *and* 93; Je *transcribes the lines in the order* 20–24, 15–19,
25–31.   16 wisdoms] wisdom Cl, Le, Da, Ph, Je, Ra.   17 which] will Da, Ra.
18 freedom's] freedom Bo, Je, Hm.   22 doth] do Cl; dost Ph.   23 clear] fair
Je, Ra.   28 On Bo, Cl, Le, Da, Ph, Je, Ra, 93: Or St (*might be* On), As; In Hm.

Cleophila (who ever thought she found in his speeches the ill taste
of a medicine, and the operation of a poison) would have suffered a
disdainful look to have been the only witness of her good accepta-
tion, but that Basilius began afresh to lay before her many pitiful
5 prayers; and in the end to conclude that he was fully of opinion the
hateful influence which had made him embrace this solitary life
was now passed over him, and withal living so weakly guarded, the
late tumult had taught him what dangers he might fall into. There-
fore he was now inclined to return to his palace in Mantinea, and
10 there he hoped he should be better able to show how much he
desired to make all he had hers—with many other such honey words
which my pen grows almost weary to set down.

This, indeed, nearly pierced Cleophila; for the good beginning
she had obtained of Philoclea made her desire to continue the same
15 trade till unto the more perfecting of her desires; and to come to
any public place she did deadly fear, lest her mask by many eyes
might the sooner be discovered, and so her hopes stopped, and the
state of her joys endangered. Therefore awhile she rested, musing at
the daily changing labyrinth of her own fortune; but in herself
20 determined it was her only best to keep him there, and with favours
to make him love the place where the favours were received, as
disgraces had made him apt to change the soil. Therefore, casting a
kind of corner look upon him, 'it is truly said', said she, 'that age
cooleth the blood. How soon, good man, you are terrified before you
25 receive any hurt! Do you not know that daintiness is kindly unto us,
and that hard obtaining is the excuse of women's granting? Yet
speak I not as though you were like to obtain, or I to grant; but
because I would not have you imagine I am to be won by courtly
vanities, or esteem a man the more because he hath handsome men
30 to wait on him when he is afraid to live without them.'

You might have seen Basilius humbly swell, and with a lowly look
stand upon his tiptoes—such diversity her words delivered unto him.

5 opinion] 93 *adds* it was only the unfortunateness of that place that hindered the pros-
perous course of his desires. And therefore since   7–8 and withal . . . fall into] (as
he doubted not the judgement of Philanax would agree with his), and his late mishaps
had taught him how perilous it was to commit a prince's state to a place so weakly
guarded; 93.   8 dangers] danger As, Da.   8–9 Therefore] *om.* 93.   14 had
obtained] had there obtained 93.   17 hopes] hope As, Je, Hm.   18 awhile]
while 93 (*corr.* 98).   19 labyrinth] labyrinths Ph, Je, Hm.   23 said she] saith
she Cl; *om.* Ph.   24 the] *om.* As, Da.   26 women's] woman's 93.
27 like] likely As, Da.   30 on As, Da, Ph, Hm: of St, 93; upon Bo, Cl, Je.
31 lowly] lovely As, Ph, Hm.

'O Hercules,' answered he, 'Basilius afraid! Or his blood cold,
that boils in such a furnace! Care I who is with me while I enjoy
your presence, or is any place good or bad to me but as it please you
to bless or curse it? O let me be but armed in your good grace, and I
defy whatsoever there is or can be against me! No, no! your love is 5
forcible, and my age is not without vigour.'

Cleophila thought it not good for his stomach to receive a surfeit
of too much favour; and therefore thinking he had enough for the
time to keep him from any sudden removing, with a certain gracious
bowing down of her head towards him, she turned away, saying she 10
would leave him at this time, to see how temperately he could use so
bountiful a measure of her kindness.

Basilius (that thought every drop a flood, that bred any refresh-
ment) durst not further press her, but, with an ancient modesty,
left her to the sweet repast of her own fancies.   15

Cleophila, as soon as he was departed, went towards Pamela's
lodge, in hope again to have seen her friend Dorus, to have pleased
herself with a new painful farewell. But being come even near the
lodge, she saw the mouth of a cave, made as it should seem by nature
in despite of art, so fitly did the rich growing marble serve to 20
beautify the vault of the first entry. Underfoot the ground seemed
mineral, yielding such a glistering show of gold in it as, they say,
the river Tagus carries in his sandy bed. The cave framed out into
many goodly spacious rooms, even such as the self-liking men have
with long and learned delicacy found out the most easeful. There 25
ran through it a little sweet river which had left the face of the
earth to drown herself for a small way in this dark, but pleasant,
mansion. The very first show of the place enticed the melancholy
mind of Cleophila to yield herself over there to the flood of her own
thoughts. And therefore, sitting down in the first entry of the cave's 30
mouth, with a song she had lately made she gave doleful way to her
bitter affects. She sang to this effect:

> Since that the stormy rage of passions dark
> (Of passions dark, made dark by beauty's light)

3 please] pleaseth Cl, Ph, 93.   5 whatsoever As, Da, Ph, Je, 93: whatever St,
Bo, Cl, Hm.   there] *om.* Bo, Je.   17 again] *om.* As, Da, 93.   18 a new]
another 93.   farewell. But] farewell, and further to have taken some advice with him
touching her own estate, whereof before sorrow had not suffered her to think. But 93.
even OA, 93: *om.* St.   20 fitly] little As; fit Hm.   23 into 93: to OA.
24 goodly] good Bo, Cl, Da, Ph.   even] *om.* 93.   33–p. 180, 12 *The poem is in* 93.
31 gave doleful] gave a doleful 93.   34 by] my Ph; of 93 (*corr.* 98).

With rebel force hath closed in dungeon dark
My mind ere now led forth by reason's light;

Since all the things which give mine eyes their light
Do foster still the fruit of fancies dark,
5   So that the windows of my inward light
Do serve to make my inward powers dark;

Since, as I say, both mind and senses dark
Are hurt, not helped, with piercing of the light;
While that the light may show the horrors dark,
10   But cannot make resolved darkness light;
    I like this place where, at the least, the dark
    May keep my thoughts from thought of wonted light.

Instead of an instrument, her song was accompanied with the
wringing of her hands, the closing of her weary eyes, and even
15 sometimes cut off with the swelling of her sighs, which did not
suffer the voice to have his free and native passage. But as she was
awhile musing upon her song, raising up her spirits, which were
something fallen into the weakness of lamentation, considering
solitary complaints do no good to him whose help stands without
20 himself, she might afar off first hear a whispering sound which
seemed to come from the inmost part of the cave, and being kept
together with the close hollowness of the place, had (as in a trunk)
the more liberal access to her ears. And by and by she might per-
ceive the same voice deliver itself into musical tunes, and with a
25 base lyre give forth this song:

Hark, plaintful ghosts! Infernal furies, hark
Unto my woes the hateful heav'ns do send—
The heav'ns conspired to make my vital spark
A wretched wrack, a glass of ruin's end!

30   Seeing, alas, so mighty powers bend
Their ireful shot against so weak a mark,
Come cave, become my grave; come death, and lend
Receipt to me within thy bosom dark!

3 give] gives Cl, Le, Hm.   mine] my Cl, As, Da, Ph, 13.   4 fruit] fruits Le, Ph,
Hm, 93.   11 where, at] whereat 93.   13–p.182, 10 Ph *omits leaving 2½ pages
blank*.   16 his] the Cl, 05 (*only*); *om.* Da.   18 something] somewhat Cl; sometime
As.   22 together OA, 93: altogether St.   23 to] unto Cl, Da.   25 lyre]
lyra Cl, As, 93.   give] gave Bo, Cl, Da, Je, Hm.   26–p. 181, 6 *The poem is in* 93.

For what is life to daily dying mind
Where, drawing breath, I suck the air of woe;
Where too much sight makes all the body blind,
And highest thoughts downward most headlong throw?
    Thus then my form, and thus my state I find: 5
    Death wrapped in flesh, to living grave assigned.

And pausing but a little, with moanful melody it continued this
octave:

Like those sick folks, in whom strange humours flow,
Can taste no sweets, the sour only please;   10
So to my mind, while passions daily grow,
Whose fiery chains upon his freedom seize,
    Joys strangers seem, I cannot bide their show,
    Nor brook aught else but well acquainted woe.
    Bitter grief tastes me best, pain is my ease,   15
    Sick to the death, still loving my disease.

'O Venus,' said Cleophila, 'who is this so well acquainted with me,
that can make so lively a portraiture of my miseries? It is surely the
spirit appointed to have care of me which doth now in this dark
place bear part with the complaints of his unhappy charge. For if it   20
be so, that the heavens have at all times a measure of their wrathful
harms, surely so many have come to my blissless lot that the rest of
the world hath too small a proportion to make with cause so wailful
a lamentation. But', said she, 'whatsoever thou be, I will seek thee
out; for thy music well assures me we are at least hand fellow   25
prentices to one ungracious master.' So rase she and went, guiding
herself by the still plaining voice, till she saw upon a stone a little
wax light set, and under it a piece of paper with these verses very
lately (as it should seem) written in it:

How is my sun, whose beams are shining bright,   30
Become the cause of my dark ugly night?
Or how do I, captived in this dark plight,
Bewail the case, and in the cause delight?

6 to living] to live in Da, Hm; living, my Je.   9–16 *The poem is in* Dd, Ra, *and*
93.   10 sweets] sweet Da, Je, Hm, Ra.   sour] sour doth Da, Dd, Ra.
13 strangers seem] strang:s seem Le; stranger seems As; stranges seems Hm.   15 grief
tastes] griefs taste As, Ra; grief taste Da.   21 their OA, 93: the St.   22 blissless
OA, 98: blisses St; blistless 93.   23 hath] have Bo, Cl, Je.   proportion] portion
As, Da, Je, Hm, 93.   27 plaining] playing Cl, As, Da, Je, Hm.   30–p. 182, 10
The poem is in Dd (30–p.182, 4 *only*), *and* 93.

My mangled mind huge horrors still do fright,
With sense possessed, and claimed by reason's right:
Betwixt which two in me I have this fight,
Where whoso wins, I put myself to flight.

5   Come, cloudy fears, close up my dazzled sight;
Sorrow, suck up the marrow of my might;
Due sighs, blow out all sparks of joyful light;
Tire on, despair, upon my tired sprite!
       An end, an end, my dulled pen cannot write,
10   Nor mazed head think, nor falt'ring tongue recite!

And hard underneath the sonnet were these words written:

This cave is dark, but it had never light.
This wax doth waste itself, yet painless dies.
These words are full of woes, yet feel they none.

15   I darkened am, who once had clearest sight.
I waste my heart, which still new torment tries.
I plain with cause, my woes are all mine own.

No cave, no wasting wax, no words of grief,
Can hold, show, tell, my pains without relief.

20   She did not long stay to read the words, for not far off from the
stone she might discern in a dark corner a lady lying with her face
so prostrate upon the ground as she could neither know nor be
known. But (as the general nature of man is desirous of knowledge,
and sorrow especially glad to find fellows) she went as softly as she
25   could convey her foot near unto her, where she heard these words
come, with vehement sobbings, from her:
      'O darkness,' said she, 'which doth lightsomely, methinks, make
me see the picture of my inward darkness, since I have chosen thee
to be the secret witness of my sorrows, let them receive a safe
30   receipt in thee, and esteem them not tedious! But, if it be possible,
let the uttering them be some discharge to my overladen breast.

6 Sorrow] Sorrows 93.   8 tired OA, 93: tired *altered to* tried St.   9 dulled]
dull As, Da, Je.   11 Ph *begins again.*   12–19 *The poem is in* 93.   13 yet]
it As, Da.   15 who] which Le, Je.   16 torment] torments Le, As, Ph, Je,
Hm.   17 are all] are still Cl; are Le; all are Ph.   mine] my Bo, Da, Ph, Hm.
20 off] *om.* As, Hm.   25 foot] feet Cl, As.   26 sobbings] sobbing Cl, Da, Je, Hm.
27 doth] dost Bo, 93.   28 my] mine Cl, Ph.   29 them] me Da, 93; him Hm.
31 uttering them] uttering of them Da, Ph.   overladen] overladed Hm; overloaden 93.

Alas, sorrow, now thou hast the full sack of my conquered spirits, rest thyself awhile, and set not still new fire to thy own spoils. O accursed reason, how many eyes thou hast to see thy evils, and how dim, nay blind, thou art in preventing them! Forlorn creature that I am, I would I might be freely wicked, since wickedness doth prevail; 5 but the footsteps of my overtrodden virtue lie still as bitter accusations unto me. I am divided in myself; how can I stand? I am overthrown in myself; who shall raise me? Vice is but a nurse of new agonies, and the virtue I am divorced from makes the hateful comparison the more manifest. No, no, virtue; either I never had 10 but a shadow of thee, or thou thyself art but a shadow, for how is my soul abandoned! How are all my powers laid waste! My desire is pained, because it cannot hope; and if hope came, his best should be but mischief. O strange mixture of human minds: only so much good left as to make us languish in our own evils! Ye infernal 15 furies—for it is too late for me to awake my dead virtue, or to place my comfort in the angry gods—ye infernal furies, I say, aid one that dedicates herself unto you! Let my rage be satisfied, since the effect of it is fit for your service; neither be afraid to make me too happy, since nothing can come to appease the smart of my guilty 20 conscience! I desire but to assuage the sweltering of my hellish longing. Dejected Gynecia!'

Cleophila no sooner heard the name of Gynecia but that, with a cold sweat all over her, as if she had been ready to tread upon a deadly stinging adder, she would have withdrawn herself, but her 25 own passion made her yield more unquiet motions than she had done in coming; so that she was perceived, and Gynecia suddenly risen up. For, indeed, it was Gynecia gotten into this cave (the same cave wherein Dametas had safely kept Pamela in the late uproar) to pass her pangs with change of places. And as her mind ran still upon 30 Cleophila, her piercing lover's eye had soon found it was she; and seeing in her a countenance to fly away, she fell down at her feet, and catching fast hold of her:

'Alas,' said she, 'whither or from whom dost thou fly away?

2 fire] fires Cl, Da, Ph.   thy] thine Bo, Cl; live Ph.   3 thou hast] hast thou Cl, As.   thy] thine Cl, Je.   3-4 how dim] thou dim 93 (*corr.* 98).   4 thou art] art thou Cl, As; *om.* Hm.   6-7 accusations] accusation Bo, As, Je; occasions Ph. 8 but a nurse] a nurse Ph; the nurse Je, Hm.   10 the more] more Da, Je, Hm. 16 virtue] virtues Bo, Da, Ph, Je, Hm.   place] please Cl, As (please *corr. to* plase St). 28 risen] rising Da; rose Hm.   32 fly Bo, As, Da, Ph, Je, Hm, 93: flee St, Cl. 34 fly Bo, As, Da, Ph, Je, Hm, 93: flee St, Cl.

The savagest beasts are won with service, and there is no flint but may be mollified. How is Gynecia so unworthy in thine eyes; or whom cannot abundance of love make worthy? O think not that cruelty or ungratefulness can flow from a good mind! O weigh, alas,
5 weigh with thyself the new effects of this mighty passion: that I, unfit for my state, uncomely for my sex, must become a suppliant at thy feet! By the happy woman that bare thee, by all the joys of thy heart and success of thy desire, I beseech thee turn thyself into some consideration of me, and rather show pity in now helping me
10 than in too late repenting my death, which hourly threatens me.'

Cleophila, imputing it to one of her continual mishaps thus to have met with this lady, with a full weary countenance: 'Without doubt, madam,' said she, 'where the desire is such as may be obtained, and the party well deserving as yourself, it must be a great excuse
15 that may well colour a denial; but when the first motion carries with it a direct impossibility, then must the only answer be comfort without help and sorrow to both parties: to you, not obtaining; to me, not able to grant.'

'O,' said Gynecia, 'how good leisure you have to frame these
20 scornful answers! Is Gynecia thus to be despised? Am I so vile a worm in your sight? No, no, trust to it, hard-hearted tiger, I will not be the only actor of this tragedy! Since I must fall, I will press down some others with my ruins; since I must burn, my spiteful neighbours shall feel of my fire! Dost thou not perceive that my
25 diligent eyes have pierced through the cloudy mask of thy disguisement? Have I not told thee, O fool (if I were not much more fool), that I know thou wouldst abuse us with thy outward show? Wilt thou still attend the rage of love in a woman's heart? The girl, thy well chosen mistress, perchance shall defend thee when Basilius
30 shall know how thou hast sotted his mind with falsehood, and falsely sought the dishonour of his house. Believe it, believe it, unkind creature, I will end my miseries with a notable example of revenge; and that accursed cradle of mine shall feel the smart of my wound, thou of thy tyranny, and lastly, I confess, myself of my own
35 work!'

Cleophila (that had long before doubted herself to be discovered

1 savagest] savage Da, Je, Hm.   2 thine] thy Cl, Hm.   6 at] to As, Je.
8 into] to Ph, 93.   10 in too] into Hm, 93 (*corr.* 98).   11 continual] *om.* Bo,
Hm.   23 others] other Da, Ph, Je, Hm.   27 know] knew Ph, Je, Hm.
30 how] *om.* Ph, Je, Hm.   sotted] settled Da, Je (settled *corr. to* sotted Hm).
34 my] mine Cl, As, Ph, Je, Hm, 93.

by her, and now plainly finding it) was, as the proverb saith, like them that hold the wolf by the ears: bitten while they hold, and slain if they loose. If she held her off, in these wonted terms, she saw rage would make her love work the effects of hate; to grant unto her, her heart was so bound upon Philoclea, it had been worse than a thousand deaths. Yet found she it was necessary for her to come to a resolution; for Gynecia's sore could bide no leisure, and once discovered, besides the danger of Philoclea, her desires should be forever utterly stopped. She remembered withal the words of Basilius; how apt he was to leave this life, and return to his court (a great bar to her hopes). Lastly, she considered Dorus's enterprise might bring some strange alteration of this their well liked fellowship. So that, encompassed with these instant difficulties, she bent her spirits to think of a remedy which might at once both save her from them, and serve her to the accomplishment of her only pursuit. Lastly she determined thus: that there was no way but to yield to the violence of their desires, since striving did the more chafe them; and that following their own current, at length of itself it would bring her to the other side of her burning desires.

But methinks I hear the shepherd Dorus calling me to tell you something of his hopeful adventures. Whosoever hath found by experience how unspeakable a comfort a true friend is (where there is so sincere a participating of each other's fortune as a man is sure either to have help or comfort) may hold easily in his conjecture the present case of divided Dorus—divided betwixt love and friendship. But love carrying with it, besides all force of such arguments of which affectionated brains are never unprovided, the continual sting of insatiate desire, had (as you have heard) gotten the fort; though without prejudice of his loyal friendship, which doth never bar the mind from his free satisfaction. Yet still Dorus (a cruel judge over himself) thought he was some ways faulty, and applied his mind how to amend it with a speedy and behoveful return. But then was his first study how to get away, whereto already he had Pamela's consent, confirmed and concluded under the name of Mopsa in her

---

3 held] hold Cl, Da, Hm.   7 bide] bind Bo; ebyde Cl; abide Ph; *om*. Hm.
8 desires] desire Bo, Cl, Je, Hm.   9 utterly stopped] stopped utterly Cl, Je.
10 his] the Bo, Ph, Je.   12–13 fellowship] friendship Da, Ph, Hm.   14 spirits]
self Da; spirit Je.   20–9 But . . . friendship] Now in the meanwhile the divided
Dorus, long divided between love and friendship, and now for his love divided from his
friend, though indeed without prejudice of friendship's loyalty 93.   25 betwixt] be-
tween As, Da.   28 insatiate] insatiable As, Da; unsatiate Hm.   30 Dorus] *om*. 93.

own presence—Dorus taking this way, that whatsoever he would have of Pamela, he would ask her whether in such a case it were not best for Mopsa so to behave herself: thus was Mopsa's envy made an instrument of that she did envy, as already you have understood by the relation Dorus made thereof to Cleophila. Now that Dorus had passed over his first and most feared difficulty, he busied his spirits how to come to the harvest of his desires, whereof he had so fair a a show; and thereunto (having gotten leave for some days of his master Dametas, who began to account him as his son-in-law) he roamed round about the desert to find some unknown way, that might bring him to the next seaport, as much as might be out of all course of other passengers. Which all very well succeeding him, and he having hired a bark for his life's traffic, and provided horses to carry her thither, returned homeward, now come to the last point of his care: how to go beyond the loathsome watchfulness of these three uncomely companions. And therein did wisely consider how they were to be taken, with whom he had to deal, remembering that in the particularities of everybody's mind and fortune there are particular advantages by which they are to be held. The muddy mind of Dametas he found most easily stirred with covetousness; the cursed mischievous heart of Miso most apt to be tickled with jealousy, as whose rotten brain could think well of nobody; but young mistress Mopsa, who could open her eyes upon nothing that did not all to-bewonder her, he thought curiosity the fittest bait for her. And first for Dametas: Dorus, having employed a whole day's work about a ten mile off from the lodge (quite contrary way to that he meant to take with Pamela) in digging and opening the ground under an ancient oak that stood there, in such sort as might longest hold Dametas's greedy hopes in some show of comfort, he came to his master with a countenance mixed betwixt cheerfulness and haste; and taking him by the right hand as if he had a great matter of faithful secrecy to reveal unto him:

'Master', said he, 'I did never think that the gods had appointed my mind, freely brought up, to have so longing a desire to serve you, but that they minded thereby to bring some extraordinary fruit to one so beloved of them as your honesty makes me think you are.

3 thus . . . made] in that sort making Mopsa's envy 93.   4-5 as . . . had] so having 93.   6 feared OA, 93: fearful St.   9 began to account] now accounted 93.   12 succeeding] succeeded Ph, Hm, Je.   26 a ten mile] ten miles Cl; a ten miles As, Da, Ph, Je, Hm.   27 with] om. Ph, Je.   30 betwixt] between Cl, 05.   32 faithful] om. Cl, As, Da, Hm, 93.

This binds me even in conscience to disclose that which I persuade myself is allotted unto you, that your fortune may be of equal balance with your deserts.'

He said no further, because he would let Dametas play upon the bit awhile; who, not understanding what his words intended, yet well finding they carried no evil news, was so much the more desirous to know the matter as he had free scope to imagine what measure of good hap himself would. Therefore, putting off his cap to him (which he had never done before), and assuring him he should have Mopsa though she had been all made of cloth of gold, he besought Dorus not to hold him long in hope for that he found it a thing his heart was not able to bear.

'Master,' answered Dorus, 'you have so satisfied me with promising me the uttermost of my desired bliss that, if my duty bound me not, I were in it sufficiently rewarded. To you, therefore, shall my good hap be converted, and the fruit of all my labour dedicated.' Therewith he told him how under an ancient oak (the place he made him easily understand by sufficient marks he gave unto him) he had found, digging but a little depth, scatteringly lying a great number of rich medals; and that, piercing further into the ground, he had met with a great stone which, by the hollow sound it yielded, seemed to be the cover of some greater vault, and upon it a box of cypress with the name of the valiant Aristomenes graven upon it; and within the box he found certain verses which signified that some depth again under that all his treasures lay hidden, what time for the discord fell out in Arcadia he lived banished.

Therewith he gave Dametas certain medals of gold he had long kept about him, and asked him, because it was a thing much to be kept secret, and a matter one man in twenty hours might easily perform, whether he would have him go and seek the bottom of it— which he had refrained to do till he knew his mind—promising he would faithfully bring him what he found; or else that he himself would do it, and be the first beholder of that comfortable spectacle.

No man need doubt which part Dametas would choose, whose fancy had already devoured all this great riches, and even now began to grudge at a partner, before he saw his own share. Therefore,

1 in conscience] in my conscience Cl, Je; in very conscience Hm.   2 of] *om.*
Da, Je, Hm.   17 how] *om.* Ph, Hm.   22 greater] great Bo, Cl, Da, Ph.
23 and] and that 93.   within OA, 93: with St.   25 treasures] treasure Da, Ph, 13.
33 be Cl, As, Da, Ph, 93: by St, Bo, Je, Hm.   35 this] those Da; these Ph, Je;
his Hm.

taking straight a strong jade, laden with spades and mattocks (which he meant to bring back otherwise laden), he went in all speed thitherward, taking leave of nobody; only desiring Dorus he would look well to the princess Pamela, promising him mountains of his own labour,
5 which nevertheless he little meant to perform—like a fool, not considering that no man is to be moved with part that neglects the whole. Thus away went Dametas, having already made an image in his fancy what palaces he would build, how sumptuously he would fare, and among all other things imagined what money to employ
10 in making coffers to keep his money. His ten miles seemed twice so many leagues; and yet, contrary to the nature of it, though it seemed long, it was not wearisome. Many times he cursed his horse's want of consideration that in so important a matter would make no greater speed; many times he wished himself the back of an
15 ass to help to carry away the new-sought riches—an unfortunate wisher, for if he had as well wished the head, it had been granted him. At length, being come to the tree which he hoped should bear so golden acorns, down went all his instruments, and forthwith to the renting up of the hurtless earth; where by and by he was caught
20 with the lime of a few promised medals, which was so perfect a pawn unto him of his further expectation that he deemed a great number of hours well employed in groping further unto it (which with logs and great stones was made as cumbersome as might be), till at length with sweaty brows he came to the great stone—a stone, God
25 knows, full unlike to the cover of a monument, but yet there was the cypress box with Aristomenes graven upon it, and these verses written in it:

    A banished man, long barred from his desire
    By inward lets of them his state possessed,
30   Hid here his hopes, by which he might aspire
    To have his harms with wisdom's help redressed.

    Seek then, and see what man esteemeth best,
    All is but this, this is our labour's hire,
    Of this we live, in this we find our rest,
35   Who hold this fast no greater wealth require.

1 straight] *om.* 93.   laden Cl, Ph, Je, Hm: loaden St, Bo, As, Da, 93.   2 laden] loaden Da, Hm.   4 him] *om.* As, Je.   5 little] never Bo, Ph. 8 palaces] palace Bo, Je.   10 miles OA: mile St, 93.   13 important] importunate Cl, Da, Je, Hm.   15 the] his Bo, As, Ph, Je, Hm.   21 unto] into As, Da, Je, 93; in Hm.   28–p. 189, 2 *The poem is in* 93.   35 hold] holds Cl, Da, Je.

Look further then, so shalt thou find at least
A bait most fit for hungry-minded guest.

He opened the box, and to his great comfort read them, and with
fresh courage went about to lift up that stone.

But in the mean time I must tell you that Dametas was not half a 5
mile gone to the treasure-ward when Dorus came to Miso, whom he
found sitting in the chimney's end, babbling to herself, and showing
in all her gestures that she was loathsomely weary of the world, not
for any hope of a better life, but finding no-one good, neither in
mind nor body, whereout she might nourish a quiet thought, having 10
long since hated each thing else, began now to hate herself. Before
this sweet-humoured dame Dorus set himself, and framed towards
her such a smiling countenance as might seem **to** be mixed between
a tickled mirth and a forced pity. Miso (to whom cheerfulness in
others was ever a sauce of envy in herself) took quickly mark of his 15
behaviour, and with a look full of forworn spite:

'Now the devil', said she, 'take these villains that can never leave
grinning because I am not so fair as mistress Mopsa! To see how
the skipjack looks at me!'

Dorus, that had the occasion he desired, 'Truly mistress', 20
answered he, 'my smiling is not at you, but at them that are from
you; and indeed I must needs a little accord my countenance with
others' sport.' And therewithal took her in his arms, and rocking her
to and fro, 'In faith, mistress,' said he, 'it is high time for you to bid
good night forever, since others can possess your place in your own 25
time.'

Miso, that was never void of malice enough to suspect the utter-
most evil, to satisfy a further shrewdness took on a present mildness,
and gently desired him to tell her what he meant, 'for', said she, 'I
am like enough to be knavishly dealt with by that churl my husband.' 30

Dorus fell off from the matter again, as if he had meant no such
thing, till by much refusing her entreaty, and vehemently stirring
up her desire to know, he had strengthened a credit in her to that he
should say; and then with a formal countenance, as if the conscience
of the case had touched himself, 'Mistress,' said he, 'I am much 35

1 least] last Ph, Je, Hm.   2 bait] hart Ph, Hm.   5 I . . . that] ere 93.
not] *om.* 93.   6 when] *om.* 93.   8 in all] me all 93; by all 98.   19 the]
this 93.   22 needs] *om.* Ph, Je, Hm.   23 others'] other Da, Hm, 93 (*corr.*
98).   24 high] *om.* Ph, Je.   30 with] with all Cl, Ph, Je, Hm (all *deleted*
Bo).

perplexed in mine own determination, for my thoughts do ever will me to do honestly, but my judgement fails me what is honest, betwixt the general rule that entrusted secrecies are holily to be observed, and the particular exception that the dishonest secrecies
5 are to be revealed—especially there where by revealing they may either be prevented or at least amended. Yet in this balance your judgement weighs me down, because I have confidence in it, that you will use what you know moderately, and rather take such faults as an advantage to your own good desert than by your bitter using it
10 be content to be revenged on others with your own harms. So it is, mistress', said he, 'that yesterday driving my sheep up to the stately hill which lifts his head over the fair city of Mantinea I happened, upon the side of it in a little falling of the ground which was a rampire against the sun's rage, to perceive a young maid, truly of the
15 finest stamp of beauty; and that which made her beauty the more admirable, there was at all no art added to the helping of it. For her apparel was but such as shepherds' daughters are wont to wear; and as for her hair, it hong down at the free liberty of his goodly length, but that sometimes falling before the clear stars of her sight, she was
20 forced to put it behind her ears, and so open again the treasure of her perfections, which that for a while had in part hidden. In her lap there lay a shepherd, so wrapped up in that well liked place that I could discern no piece of his face; but as mine eyes were attent in that, her angelic voice strake mine ears with this song:

25   My true love hath my heart, and I have his,
          By just exchange, one for the other given.
          I hold his dear, and mine he cannot miss:
          There never was a better bargain driven.

          His heart in me, keeps me and him in one,
30   My heart in him, his thoughts and senses guides.
          He loves my heart, for once it was his own:
          I cherish his, because in me it bides.

1 mine] my Da, Ph, Je, Hm, 93 (*corr.* 98).   3 holily] wholly Cl, Ph.   8 faults]
fruits Bo, Ph.   9 own] *om.* Cl, As, Da.   desert] deserts Cl, Da.   10 content]
contented 93.   11 driving OA, 93: *om.* St.   13 was a] was Ph, Je, Hm.
18 hong] hanged Cl; hung Da; hangs Ph.   20 treasure] treasures As, Da.
21 perfections] perfection Ph, Je.   25-p. 191, 6 *The poem is in* Hy, Pu (*the
first eight lines only with the first line repeated after each quatrain), and* 93.   26 the
other OA, 93: thother St; another Hy, Pu.   27 his] it Da, Ph.   29 keeps
OA, Hy, Pu, 93: keep St.   me and him] him and me Je, Hy, Pu; me and I and he
Hm.

His heart his wound received from my sight:
My heart was wounded, with his wounded heart,
For as from me on him his hurt did light,
So still methought in me his hurt did smart:
    Both equal hurt, in this change sought our bliss: 5
    My true love hath my heart, and I have his.

But, as if the shepherd that lay before her had been organs which
were only to be blown by her breath, she had no sooner ended with
the joining her sweet lips together but that he recorded to her music
this rural poesy: 10

    O words which fall like summer dew on me,
    O breath more sweet than is the growing bean,
    O tongue in which all honeyed liquors be,
    O voice that doth the thrush in shrillness stain,
        Do you say still, this is her promise due,   15
        That she is mine, as I to her am true.

    Gay hair, more gay than straw when harvest lies,
    Lips red and plum, as cherry's ruddy side,
    Eyes fair and great, like fair great ox's eyes:
    O breast in which two white sheep swell in pride   20
        Join you with me, to seal this promise due,
        That she be mine, as I to her am true.

    But thou white skin, as white as cruds well pressed,
    So smooth as sleekstone-like it smooths each part,
    And thou dear flesh, as soft as wool new dressed,   25
    And yet as hard as brawn made hard by art;
        First four but say, next four their saying seal,
        But you must pay the gage of promised weal.

And with the conclusion of his song he embraced her about the
knees: 'O sweet Charita,' said he, 'when shall I enjoy the rest of 30
my toiling thoughts, and when shall your blissful promise (now due)
be verified with just performance?' With that I drew nearer to
them, and saw (for now he had lifted up his face to glass himself
in her fair eyes) that it was my master Dametas'—but here Miso

---

3 hurt] hart Ph, Hy.   11–28 *The poem is in* 93.   11–16 *om.* Da.
16 as] and Le, Je (and *corr. to* as As).   18 plum] plain Da, Ph.   23 cruds]
curds Bo, Cl, Le, Je.   24 sleek] slick Cl, Le, Da, Ph; sleight As; stick Je; silk Hm.
29 his] this Cl, As, Ph.   32 nearer] near Cl, As, Je.

interrupted his tale with railing at Dametas with all those exquisite terms which I was never good scold enough to imagine.

But Dorus (as if he had been much offended with her impatience) would proceed no further till she had vowed more stillness: 'For', said he, 'if the first drum thus chafe you, what will you be when it comes to the blows?' Then he told her how, after many familiar entertainments betwixt them, Dametas (laying before her his great credit with the duke, and withal giving her very fair presents, with promise of much more) had in the end concluded together to meet as that night at Mantinea in the Oudemian street at Charita's uncle's house about ten of the clock. After which bargain Dametas had spied Dorus, and calling him to him, had with great bravery told him all his good hap, willing him in any case to return to the old witch Miso ('for so indeed, mistress, of liveliness, and not of ill will, he termed you'), and to make some honest excuse of his absence; 'for', said he, kissing Charita, 'if thou didst know what a life I lead with that drivel, it would make thee even of pity receive me into thy only comfort.'

'Now mistress,' said he, 'exercise your discretion, which if I were well assured of, I would wish you to go yourself to Mantinea, and (lying secret in some one of your gossips' houses till the time appointed come) so may you find them together, and using mercy, reform my master from his evil ways.'

There had nothing more enraged Miso than the praises Dorus gave to Charita's beauty, which made her jealousy swell the more with the poison of envy; and that being increased with the presents she heard Dametas had given her (which all seemed torn out of her bowels), her hollow eyes yielded such wretched looks as one might well think Pluto at that time might have had her soul very good cheap. But when the fire of spite had fully caught hold of all her inward parts, then whosoever would have seen the picture of Alecto, or with what manner of countenance Medea killed her own children, needed but take Miso for the full satisfaction of that point of his knowledge. She, that could before scarce go but supported by crutches, now flew about the house, borne up with the wings of anger. There was no one sort of mortal revenge that had ever come to her ears but presented itself now to her gentle mind. At length,

6 how] *om.* Ph, Je, Hm.   7 his OA, 93: *om.* St.   9 had] and Bo, Je, Hm.
10 Oudemian Cl, As, 93: *om.* St, Da; Oudman Bo; Onken Ph; Enkin Je; Okin Hm.
11 spied] espied Da, Hm.   14 and] *om.* Ph, Je, Hm.   20 one] *om.* Cl, As, Ph.
26 which all OA, 93: withal St.   29 all] *om.* Da, Hm.   32 of that point] *om.*
As, Ph.

with few words (for her words were choked up with the rising of her revengeful heart), she ran down, and with her own hands saddled a mare of hers—a mare that seven year before had not been acquainted with a saddle—and so to Mantinea she went, casting with herself how she might couple shame with the punishment of her accursed 5 husband—but the person is not worthy in whose passion I should too long stand.

Therefore now must I tell you that mistress Mopsa (who was the last party Dorus was to practise his cunning withal) was, at the parting of her parents, attending upon the princess Pamela, whom 10 because she found to be placed in her father's house, she knew it was for suspicion the duke had of her. This made Mopsa, with a right base nature (which joys to see any hard hap happen to them they deem happy), grow proud over her, and use great ostentation of her own diligence in prying curiously into each thing that Pamela 15 did. Neither is there anything sooner overthrows a weak heart than opinion of authority (like too strong a liquor for so feeble a glass); which joined itself to the humour of envying Pamela's beauty so far that oft she would say to herself: 'if she had been born a duchess as well as Pamela, her perfections then should have been as well seen as 20 Pamela's.' With this manner of woman, and placed in these terms, had Dorus to play his last part, which he would quickly have dispatched, in tying her up in such a manner that she should little have hindered his enterprise, but that the virtuous Pamela (when she saw him so minded) by countenance absolutely forbade it, resolutely 25 determining she would not leave behind her any token of wrong, since the wrong done to herself was the best excuse of her escape. So that Dorus was compelled to take her in the manner he first thought of, and accordingly, Pamela sitting musing at the strange attempt she had condescended unto, and Mopsa hard by her (look- 30 ing in a glass with very partial eyes), Dorus put himself between them, and casting up his face to the top of the house, shrugging all over his body, and stamping sometimes upon the ground, gave Mopsa occasion (who was as busy as a bee to know anything) to ask her lover Dorus what ailed him that made him use so strange a 35 behaviour?

3 year] years Cl, As, Da, Ph, Je, Hm.   4 so] *om*. Ph, Je.   5 accursed] cursed Cl, Je.   6 too] so Ph, Hm (Je *omits* I . . . stand).   8 now must I Bo, Cl, As, Da, Ph, Hm, 93: must I St; must now I Je.   13 happen] *om*. Da, Ph, Je, Hm.   19 duchess] princess 98.   31 between] betwixt Da, Je.   35 him use] him to use Ph, Je.

He (as if his spirits had been ravished at some supernatural contemplation) stood still mute, sometimes rubbing his forehead, sometimes starting in himself; that he set Mopsa in such an itch of inquiry that she would have offered her maidenhead rather than be
5 long kept from it. Dorus not yet answering to the purpose, still keeping his amazement: 'O Hercules,' said he, 'resolve me in this doubt! A tree to grant one's wishes! Is this the cause of the duke's solitary life? Which part shall I take? Happy in either; unhappy because I cannot know which were my best hap!'

10   These doubtful self-speeches made Mopsa yet in a further longing of knowing the matter; so that the pretty pig, laying her sweet burden about his neck: 'My Dorus,' said she, 'tell me these wonders, or else I know not what will befall me. Honey Dorus, tell them me'.

Dorus, having stretched her mind upon a right last, 'Extremely
15 loved Mopsa,' said he, 'the matters be so great as my heart fails me in the telling them; but since you hold the greatest seat in it, it is reason your desire should add life unto it.' Therewith he told her a far-fet tale: how that many millions of years before Jupiter, fallen out with Apollo, had thrown him out of heaven, taking from him the
20 privilege of a god; so that poor Apollo was fain to lead a very miserable life, unacquainted to work, and never used to beg; that, in this order, having in time learned to be Admetus's herdman, he had (upon occasion of fetching a certain breed of goodly beasts out of Arcadia) come to that very desert, where, wearied with travel
25 and resting himself in the bough of a pleasant ash tree stood a little off from the lodge, he had with pitiful complaints gotten his father Jupiter's pardon, and so from that tree was received again to his golden sphere. But having that right nature of a god, never to be ungrateful, to Admetus he had granted a double life; and because
30 that tree was the chapel of his prosperous prayers, he had given it this quality: that whosoever, of such estate and in such manner as he then was, sat down in that tree, they should obtain whatsoever they wished. This Basilius having understood by the oracle was the only cause which had made him try whether, framing himself to the
35 state of a herdman, he might have the privilege of wishing only

5 long kept] kept long Cl, As, Hm.   7 duke's] king's 93 (*and throughout*).   8 either] neither As; other Hm.   12 wonders] words Da, Ph, Je, Hm, 93.   16 in the telling] in telling Bo, Ph, Hm.   23 goodly] *om.* Da, 93.   25 bough] boughs Cl, As, Je, 93.   tree stood] tree that stood Ph, Je.   a Cl, As, Ph: *om.* St, Bo, Da, Je, Hm, 93.   31 quality] property Je; equality 93 (*corr.* 98).   whosoever] whatsoever 93.   and in] was in Ph; or in Je, Hm.   35 a] an As, Ph.

granted to that degree. But that having often in vain attempted it,
because indeed he was not such, he had now opened the secret to
Dametas, making him swear he should wish according to his
direction. 'But because', said Dorus, 'Apollo was at that time with
extreme grief muffled round about his face with a scarlet cloak   5
Admetus had given him, and because they that must wish must be
muffled in like sort, and with like stuff, my master Dametas is gone
I know not whither to provide him a scarlet cloak, and tomorrow doth
appoint to return with it. My mistress, I cannot tell how, having
gotten some inkling of it, is trudged to Mantinea to get herself a 10
cloak before him, because she would have the first wish. My master
at his parting of great trust told me this secret, commanding me to
see nobody should climb that tree. But now, my Mopsa,' said he,
'I have here the like cloak of mine own, and am not so very a fool as,
though I keep his commandment in others, to bar myself. I rest only 15
extremely perplexed because, having nothing in the world I wish for,
but the enjoying you and your favour, I think it a much pleasanter
conquest to come to it by your own consent than to have it by such
a charming force as this is. Now therefore choose, since have you I
will, in what sort I shall have you.'   20
     But never child was so desirous of a gay puppet as Mopsa was to
be in the tree; and therefore without squeamishness promising all he
would, she conjured him by all her precious loves that she might
have the first possession of the wishing tree, assuring him that, for
the enjoying her, he should never need to climb far.   25
     Dorus, to whom time was precious, made no great ceremonies
with her; but helping her up to the top of the tree, from whence
likewise she could ill come down without help, he muffled her round
about the face so truly that she herself could not undo it. And so he
told her the manner was she should hold her mind in continual 30
devotion to Apollo, without making at all any noise, till at the
furthest within twelve hours' space she should hear a voice call her
by name three times; and that till the third time she must in no wise
answer: 'and then you shall not need to doubt your coming down,
for at that time', said he, 'be sure but to wish wisely, and in what 35
shape soever he come unto you, speak boldly unto him, and your

1 in vain attempted it] attempted it in vain Cl, Je.   6 that must wish] that wish
As, Da, Je.   7 like] that As, Je.   13 should] *om.* Cl, Je; to As.   14–15 as, though]
although Ph, Je.   15 keep] kept Cl, Je.   17 much pleasanter] much better *corr. to*
pleasanter Bo; pleasant As; more pleasanter Je.   25 enjoying her] enjoying of her
As, Da.   30 hold] have Da, Je.   35 but] *om.* Hm, 93.

wish shall have as certain effect as I have a desire to enjoy your sweet loves.' In this plight did he leave Mopsa, resolved in her heart to be the greatest lady of the world, and never after to feed on worse than furmenty.

5   Thus Dorus, having delivered his hands of his three tormentors, took speedily the benefit of his device, and mounting the gracious Pamela upon a fair horse he had provided for her, he thrust himself forthwith into the wildest part of the desert where he had left marks to guide him from place to place to the next seaport, disguising her
10 very fitly with scarves, although he rested assured he should meet that way with nobody till he came to his bark, into which he meant to enter by night. But Pamela who all this while transported with desire, and troubled with fear, had never free scope of judgement to look with perfect consideration into her own enterprise, but even by
15 the laws of love had bequeathed the care of herself upon him to whom she had given herself, now that the pang of desire with evident hope was quieted, and most part of the fear passed, reason began to renew his shining in her heart, and make her see herself in herself, and weigh with what wings she flew out of her native country, and
20 upon what ground she built so strange a determination. But love, fortified with her lover's presence, kept still his own in her heart, so that as they rid together, with her hand upon her faithful servant's shoulder, suddenly casting her bashful eyes to the ground, and yet bending herself towards him (like the client that commits the cause
25 of all his worth to a well trusted advocate) from a mild spirit said unto him these sweetly delivered words:

'Prince Musidorus (for so my assured hope is I may justly call you, since with no other my heart would ever have yielded to go; and if so I do not rightly term you, all other words are as bootless
30 as my deed miserable, and I as unfortunate as you wicked), my prince Musidorus, I say, now that the vehement shows of your faithful love towards me have brought my mind to answer it in so due a proportion that, contrary to all general rules of reason, I have laid in you my estate, my life, my honour, it is now your part to

1 as] a Da, Hm.   a desire] *om.* As, Da, Ph, Je, Hm.   sweet] *om.* Ph, Je, Hm.
3 of] in Bo, Cl, Ph, Je, Hm.   on] of Bo, Da, Ph, 93.   5 tormentors] torments
Da, Je.   8 wildest] midst As, Hm; wildish Da.   15 bequeathed] laid
Cl; *om.* As.   20 strange Bo, As, 93: strong St, Da, Ph, Je Hm (strong
corr. to strange Bo); *om.* Cl.   22 rid] rode As, Ph.   servant's] lover's As,
Hm.   23 to] down to Bo; unto Ph; upon Hm.   28 yielded OA, 93: yield St.
33 a] *om.* Cl, Hm.   34 now] *om.* 93.

double your former care, and make me see your virtue no less in
preserving than in obtaining, and your faith to be a faith as much in
freedom as bondage. Tender now your own workmanship, and so
govern your love towards me as I may still remain worthy to be
loved. Your promise you remember, which here by the eternal 5
givers of virtue I conjure you to observe. Let me be your own (as I
am), but by no unjust conquest. Let not our joys, which ought ever
to last, be stained in our own consciences. Let no shadow of repen-
tance steal into the sweet consideration of our mutual happiness.
I have yielded to be your wife; stay then till the time that I may 10
rightly be so. Let no other defiled name burden my heart. What
should I more say? If I have chosen well, all doubt is past, since
your action only must determine whether I have done virtuously
or shamefully in following you.'

Musidorus (that had more abundance of joy in his heart than 15
Ulysses had what time with his own industry he stale the fatal
Palladium, imagined to be the only relic of Troy's safety), taking
Pamela's hand, and many times kissing it, 'What I am,' said he, 'the
gods, I hope, will shortly make your own eyes judges; and of my
mind towards you, the mean time shall be my pledge unto you. Your 20
contentment is dearer to me than mine own, and therefore doubt not
of his mind whose thoughts are so thralled unto you as you are to
bend or slack them as it shall seem best unto you. You do wrong to
yourself to make any doubt that a base estate could ever undertake
so high an enterprise, or a spotted mind be able to behold your 25
virtues. Thus much only I must confess I can never do: to make the
world see you have chosen worthily; since all the world is not
worthy of you.'

In such delightful discourses kept they on their journey, main-
taining their hearts in that right harmony of affection which doth 30
interchangeably deliver each to other the secret workings of their
souls, till with the unused travel the princess being weary, they
lighted down in a fair thick wood which did entice them with the
pleasantness of it to take their rest there. It was all of pine trees,
whose broad heads meeting together yielded a perfect shade to the 35
ground, where their bodies gave a spacious and pleasant room to

3 as bondage] as in bondage Ph, Hm.   4 love Cl, As, Hm, 93: loves St, Bo,
Da, Ph, Je.   18 I am OA, 93: am I St.   21 to] unto As, Da, Hm.   mine]
my Bo, Da, Ph, Hm.   31 workings] working Cl, As, Da, Ph, Je, Hm.   34 rest]
rests Ph; ease Je, Hm.

walk in. They were set in so perfect an order that every way the eye being full, yet no way was stopped; and even in the midst of them were there many sweet springs which did loose themselves upon the face of the earth. Here Musidorus drew out such provision of fruits
5 and other cates as he had brought for that day's repast, and laid it down upon the fair carpet of the green grass. But Pamela had much more pleasure to walk under those trees, making in their barks pretty knots which tied together the names of Musidorus and Pamela, sometimes intermixedly changing them to Pamedorus and Musimela,
10 with twenty other flowers of her travailing fancies, which had bound themselves to a greater restraint than they could without much pain well endure. And to one tree, more beholding to her than the rest she entrusted the treasure of her thoughts in these verses:

> Do not disdain, O straight upraised pine,
15 > That wounding thee, my thoughts in thee I grave;
> Since that my thoughts, as straight as straightness thine,
> No smaller wound—alas! far deeper have.
>
> Deeper engraved, which salve nor time can save,
> Giv'n to my heart by my fore-wounded ey'n:
20 > Thus cruel to myself, how canst thou crave
> My inward hurt should spare thy outward rine?
>
> Yet still, fair tree, lift up thy stately line,
> Live long, and long witness my chosen smart,
> Which barred desires (barred by myself) impart.
>
25 > And in this growing bark grow verses mine.
> My heart my word, my word hath giv'n my heart.
> The giver giv'n from gift shall never part.

Upon a root of the tree that the earth had left something barer than the rest she wrate this couplet:

30 > Sweet root, say thou, the root of my desire
> Was virtue clad in constant love's attire.

1 every] Je *missing from here.*   7 those] these As, Ph; the Hm.   9 them]
there 93 (*corr.* 98).   14–27 *The poem is in* 93.   21 hurt] heart As,
Ph.   24 Which] With Cl, Le, Da, Hm.   28 the tree] a tree As, Hm.
29 wrate] writ Cl, Ph; wrote As.   30–1 *The couplet is in* Dd *and* 93.

Musidorus, seeing her fancies drawn up to such pleasant contempla-
tions, accompanied her in them, and made the trees as well bear the
badges of his passions, as this song engraved in them did testify:

You goodly pines, which still with brave ascent
In nature's pride your heads to heav'nward heave,   5
Though you besides such graces earth hath lent,
Of some late grace a greater grace receive,

By her who was (O blessed you) content,
With her fair hand, your tender barks to cleave,
And so by you (O blessed you) hath sent   10
Such piercing words as no thoughts else conceive:

Yet yield your grant, a baser hand may leave
His thoughts in you, where so sweet thoughts were spent,
For how would you the mistress' thoughts bereave
Of waiting thoughts all to her service meant?   15

Nay higher thoughts (though thralled thoughts) I call
My thoughts than hers, who first your rine did rent,
Than hers, to whom my thoughts alonely thrall
Rising from low, are to the highest bent;
Where hers, whom worth makes highest over all,   20
Coming from her, cannot but downward fall.

While Pamela, sitting her down under one of them, and making a
posy of the fair undergrowing flowers, filled Musidorus's ears with
the heavenly sound of her music, which before he had never heard,
so that it seemed unto him a new assault given to the castle of his   25
heart, already conquered; which to signify, and withal reply to her
sweet notes, he sang in a kind of still but ravishing tune a few
verses. Her song was this, and his reply follows:

Pamela. Like diverse flowers, whose diverse beauties serve
To deck the earth with his well-coloured weed,   30
Though each of them his private form preserve,
Yet joining forms one sight of beauty breed;
Right so my thoughts whereon my heart I feed;

2 as well] *om.* Da, 13.   4–21 *The poem is in* 93.   9 barks] bark Le,
Ph, Hm.   11 thoughts] thought Bo, As; thing Cl.   15 waiting] wailing
As; writing Le; wai[ ] Ph.   18 alonely] a lovely Cl, Le, Da, Hm; a lonely 93.
19 low] love Cl, Le, As, Da, Ph, Hm.   24 the] *om.* Ph; a Hm.   25 to] unto
As, Hm.   29–p. 200, 17 *The poem is in* 93.   30 his 93: this OA.

Right so my inward parts, and outward glass,
Though each possess a diverse working kind,
Yet all well knit to one fair end do pass:
That he to whom these sundry gifts I bind,
5   All what I am, still one, his own, do find.

Musidorus. All what you are still one, his own to find,
You that are born to be the world's eye,
What were it else, but to make each thing blind,
And to the sun with waxen wings to fly?

10   No, no, such force with my small force to try
Is not my skill, nor reach of mortal mind.
Call me but yours, my title is most high:
Hold me most yours, then my long suit is signed.

You none can claim but you yourself by right,
15   For you do pass yourself, in virtue's might.
So both are yours: I, bound with gaged heart;
You only yours, too far beyond desert.

In this virtuous wantonness suffering their minds to descend to each
tender enjoying their united thoughts, Pamela having tasted of the
20 fruits, and growing extreme sleepy, having been long kept from it
with the perplexity of her dangerous attempt, laying her head in his
lap, was invited by him to sleep with these softly uttered verses:

Lock up, fair lids, the treasures of my heart:
Preserve those beams, this age's only light:
25   To her sweet sense, sweet sleep, some ease impart—
Her sense too weak to bear her spirit's might.

And while, O sleep, thou closest up her sight
(Her sight where love did forge his fairest dart),
O harbour all her parts in easeful plight:
30   Let no strange dream make her fair body start.

---

4 these] this As, Hm; the Ph.   6 what] that Cl, Le.   11 nor] or 93.
14 none Cl, Hm, 93: now St, Bo, As, Da, Ph.   by right] be right Ph; aright 93.
20 extreme] extremely As, Da.   21 laying Cl, As, Ph, Hm, 93: lying St, Bo, Da.
23–p. 201, 6 *The poem is in* Dd, Hn, Hy, Ra, *and* 93.   23 Lock] Look Cl, As,
Da.   treasures] treasure Hm, Hy, Ra, 93.

But yet, O dream, if thou wilt not depart
In this rare subject from thy common right;
But wilt thyself in such a seat delight,

Then take my shape, and play a lover's part:
Kiss her from me, and say unto her sprite,   5
Till her eyes shine, I live in darkest night.

The sweet Pamela was brought into a sweet sleep with this song,
which gave Musidorus opportunity at leisure to behold her excellent
beauties. He thought her fair forehead was a field where all his
fancies fought, and every hair of her head seemed a strong chain that   10
tied him. Her fair lids (then hiding her fairer eyes) seemed unto him
sweet boxes of mother of pearl, rich in themselves, but containing
in them far richer jewels. Her cheeks, with their colour most deli-
cately mixed, would have entertained his eyes somewhile, but that
the roses of her lips (whose separating was wont to be accompanied   15
with most wise speeches) now by force drew his sight to mark how
prettily they lay one over the other, uniting their divided beauties,
and through them the eye of his fancy delivered to his memory the
lying (as in ambush) under her lips of those armed ranks, all armed
in most pure white, and keeping the most precise order of military   20
discipline. And lest this beauty might seem the picture of some
excellent artificer, forth there stale a soft breath, carrying good
testimony of her inward sweetness; and so stealingly it came out as
it seemed loath to leave his contentful mansion, but that it hoped to
be drawn in again to that well closed paradise, that did so tyrannize   25
over Musidorus's affects that he was compelled to put his face as
low to hers as he could, sucking the breath with such joy that he did
determine in himself there had been no life to a chameleon's, if he
might be suffered to enjoy that food. But each of these having a
mighty working in his heart, all joined together did so draw his will   30
into the nature of their confederacy that now his promise began to
have but a fainting force, and each thought that rase against those
desires was received but as a stranger to his counsel, well experienc-
ing in himself that no vow is so strong as the avoiding of occasions;

2 rare] fair Dd, Hn.   thy] the 93 (*corr.* 98).   6 night] light Cl, Le.   7 into
OA, 93: unto St.   11 fair] fairer 93.   19 of 93: *om.* OA.   23 stealingly
Cl, As, Da, 93: stealing St, Bo, Ph, Hm.   25 that did] which did 93.   29–p. 202, 8
But each . . . dozen] But long he was not suffered being within a while interrupted by
the coming of a company of 93.   31 their Bo, Cl, As, Da, Hm: his St; the Ph.
33 his OA: this St.
8118554   S

so that rising softly from her, overmastered with the fury of delight, having all his senses partial against himself and inclined to his well beloved adversary, he was bent to take the advantage of the weakness of the watch, and see whether at that season he could win the
5 bulwark before timely help might come. And now he began to make his approaches when (to the just punishment of his broken promise, and most infortunate bar of his long-pursued and almost-achieved desires) there came by a dozen clownish villains, armed with divers sorts of weapons, and for the rest, both in face and apparel, so
10 forwasted that they seemed to bear a great conformity with the savages; who (miserable in themselves, thought to increase their mischiefs in other bodies' harms) came with such cries as they awaked Pamela (whose sleep had been set upon with two dangers, the one of which had saved her from the other), and made Musidorus
15 turn unto them full of a most violent rage, with the look of a she-tiger when her whelps are stolen away.

But Cleophila (whom I left in the cave hardly bested, having both great wits and stirring passions to deal with) makes me lend her my pen awhile to see with what dexterity she could put by her dangers.
20 Cleophila (who had in one instant both to resist rage and go beyond wisdom, having to deal with a lady that had her wits awake in everything but in helping of her own hurt) saw now no other remedy in her case but to qualify her rage with hope, and to satisfy her wit with plainness. Yet (lest too abrupt a falling into it should
25 yield too great an advantage unto her) she thought good to come to it by degrees, with this kind of insinuation:

'Your wise but very dark speeches, most excellent lady, are woven up in so intricate a manner as I know not how to proportion mine answer unto them; so are your prayers mixed with threats, and so is
30 the show of your love hidden with the name of revenge, the natural effect of mortal hatred. You seem displeased with the opinion you have of my disguising; and yet if I be not disguised, you must needs be much more displeased, hope then (the only succour of perplexed minds) being quite cut off. You desire my affection, and yet you
35 yourself think my affection already bestowed. You pretend cruelty

1 overmastered OA: overmatched St.   7 infortunate] unfortuned Cl; unfortunate Da, Hm.   10 forwasted] far wasted Cl, Da, Ph, Hm.   11 thought Cl, As, Hm: taught St, Bo, Da, Ph, 93.   12 mischiefs] mischief Cl, Ph, Hm.   12–13 they awaked] they both awaked 93.   13–14 whose . . . other] om. 93.   20 Cleophila (who had] For having 93.   21 having] being 93.   22 of] om. 93.   saw] she saw 93.   24 a] om. 93.   27 woven] wound Cl, Da, Hm.   32 I] om. 93 (corr. 05).

before you have the subjection, and are jealous of the keeping that
which as yet you have not gotten. And that which is strangest in
your jealousy is both the unnatural unjustice of it (in being loath
that should come to your daughter which you deem good), and the
vainness, since you two are in so diverse respects that there is no 5
necessity one of you should fall to be a bar to the other. For neither
(if I be such as you fancy) can I marry you, which must needs be the
only end I can aspire to in her; neither need the marrying of her
keep me from a grateful consideration how much you honour me in
the love you vouchsafe to bear me.'   10

Gynecia (to whom the fearful agonies she still lived in made any
small reprieval sweet) did quickly find her words falling to a better
way of comfort; and therefore with a mind ready to show nothing
could make it rebellious against Cleophila but too extreme tyranny,
she thus said: 'Alas, too much beloved Cleophila, the thoughts are 15
but outflowings of the mind, and the tongue is but a servant of the
thoughts. Therefore, marvel not that my words suffer contrarieties,
since my mind doth hourly suffer in itself whole armies of mortal
adversaries. But, alas, if I had the use of mine own reason, then
should I not need, for want of it, to find myself in this desperate 20
mischief. But because my reason is vanished, so have I likewise no
power to correct my unreasonableness. Do you, therefore, accept the
protection of my mind (which hath no other resting place), and drive
it not, by being unguarded, to put itself into unknown extremities.
I desire but to have my affection answered, and to have a right 25
reflection of my love in you. That granted, assure yourself mine
own love will easily teach me to seek your contentment, and make me
think my daughter a very mean price to keep still in mine eyes the
food of my spirits. But take heed that contempt drive me not into
despair, the most violent cause of that miserable effect.'   30

Cleophila (that already saw some fruit of her last determined
fancy, so far as came to a mollifying of Gynecia's rage) seeing no
other way to satisfy suspicion (which was held open with the
continual pricks of love), resolved now with plainness to win trust—
which trust she might after deceive with a greater subtlety. There- 35
fore, looking upon her with a more relenting grace than ever she

---

1 of the keeping] of keeping 93.   3 unnatural] *om.* 93.   6 bar to] bar
unto Ph, Hm.   12 quickly] *om.* Cl, As.   16 servant of] servant to Cl; servant
of *corr. to* servant to As.   19 mine] my Da, Ph, Hm.   24 unguarded]
unregarded Cl, 93.   25 my] mine Cl, As.   26 mine] my Bo, Da, Ph.
32 a] *om.* As, Ph.   35 greater] great As, Ph.

had done before, pretending a great bashfulness before she could come to confess such a fault, she thus said unto her: 'Most worthy lady, I did never think till now that pity of another could make one betray himself, nor that the sound of words could overthrow any
5 wise body's determination; but your words, I think, have charmed me, and your grace bewitched me. Your compassion makes me open my heart to you, and leave unharboured mine own thoughts. For proof of it I will disclose my greatest secret, which well you might suspect, but never know, and so have your wandering hope in a more
10 painful wilderness, being neither way able to be lodged in any perfect resolution. I will, I say, unwrap my most hidden estate, and after make you judge of it—perchance director. The truth is I am a man. Nay, I will say further to you I am born a prince; and to make up your mind in a thorough understanding of me, since I came to
15 this place I may not deny I have had some sprinkling of I know not what good liking to my lady Philoclea. For how could I ever imagine the heavens would have rained down so much of your favour upon me? And of that side there was a show of possible hope, the most comfortable counsellor of love. The cause of this my changed attire
20 was a journey two years ago I made among the Amazons, where having sought to try my unfortunate valour, I met not one in all the country but was too hard for me; till, in the end, in the presence of their queen Senicia, I (hoping to prevail against her) challenged an old woman of fourscore years to fight on horseback to the uttermost
25 with me: who, having overthrown me, for saving of my life made me swear I should go like an unarmed Amazon till the coming of my beard did with the discharge of my oath deliver me of that bondage.'

Here Cleophila ended, not coming to a full conclusion, because she would see what this wrought in Gynecia's mind, having in her
30 speech sought to win a belief of her; and if it might be, by the disgrace of herself to diminish Gynecia's affection. For the first, it had much prevailed, but Gynecia whose end of loving her was not her fighting; neither could her love, too deeply grounded, receive diminishment; and besides she had seen herself sufficient proofs of
35 Cleophila's admirable prowess. Therefore (slightly passing over that

3 make one] make me Da, 93; om. Ph.   4 himself] myself corr. to himself Bo;
myself Da, 93; himself corr. to herself Ph.   5 words] worth Cl, As.   have]
hath Cl, As.   7 mine] my Bo, Da, Ph.   10 any] a 93.   11 most] om. 93.
13 to you] om. Bo; unto you Ph, Hm.   23 their] the Da, Ph, Hm.   Senicia]
Marpesia 93.   25 for saving] for the saving Bo, Da, 93.   29 this] om. Da; it 93.
35 sleightly] streightly corr. to sleightly Bo; straytly Cl, Ph.

point of her feigned dishonour, but taking good hold of the con-
fessing her manly sex), with the shamefast look of that suitor who,
having already obtained much, is yet forced by want to demand more,
put forth her sorrowful suit in these words:

'The gods', said she, 'reward thee for thy virtuous pity of my 5
overladen soul, who yet hath received some breath of comfort by
finding thy confession to maintain some possibility for my languish-
ing hope. But alas, as they who seek to enrich themselves by
mineral industry, their first labour is to find the mine, which to
their cheerful comfort being found, if after any unlooked-for stop 10
or casual impediment keep them from getting the desired ore, they
are so much the more grieved as the late-conceived hope adds
torment to their former want; so falls it out with me, happy or hap-
less woman as it pleaseth you to ordain, who am now either to
receive some guerdon of my long woeful labours, or to return into a 15
more wretched darkness, having had some glimmering of my bliss-
ful sun. O Cleophila, tread not upon a soul that lies under your feet!
Let not the abasing of myself make me more base in your eyes, but
judge of me according to that I am and have been, and let my errors
be made excusable by the immortal name of love!' 20

With that (under a feigned rage tearing her clothes) she dis-
covered some parts of her fair body, which, if Cleophila's heart had
not been so fully possessed as there was no place left for any new
guest, no doubt it would have yielded to that gallant assault. But
Cleophila so much the more arming her determination as she saw 25
such force threatened, yet still remembering she must wade betwixt
constancy and courtesy, embracing Gynecia and once or twice
kissing her: 'Dear lady', said she, 'he were a great enemy to himself
that would refuse such offered bliss, in the purchase of which a
man's life were blessedly bestowed. Nay, how can I ever yield due 30
recompense for so excessive a favour? But having no more to give
you but myself, take that—I must confess a small but a very free
present. What other affection soever I have had shall give place to
as great perfections, working besides upon the bond of gratefulness.

1 feigned] famed Bo; framed Ph.   7 for] of Cl, As, 93.   13 torment] torments
Cl, Ph.   15 long] most 93.   17 feet] foot Hm, 93.   22 parts] part As,
Da, Ph, Hm.   28 to himself] *om.* Cl, As.   29 offered bliss] an offer 93.
31 recompense] reverence Cl, As.   so] such Hm (such *corr. to* so Cl).   no more]
nothing 93.   33 present] gift 93.   34 perfections] perfection 93.   bond Cl,
As, 93: band St, Bo, Da, Ph; bound Hm.

The gods forbid I should either be so foolish as not to see, or so wicked as not to remember, how much my small deserts are over-balanced by your unspeakable goodness. Nay, happy may I well account my mishap among the Amazons, since that dishonour hath
5 been so true a path to my greatest honour, and the changing of my outward raiment hath clothed my mind in such inward contenta-tion. Take therefore, noble lady, as much comfort to your heart as the full commandment of me can yield you. Wipe your fair eyes, and keep them for nobler services. And now I will presume thus much
10 to say unto you: that you make of yourself for my sake that my joys of my new-obtained riches may be accomplished in you. But let us leave this place, lest you be too long missed; and henceforward quiet your mind from any further care, for I will now to my too much joy take the charge upon me within few days to work your
15 satisfaction and my felicity.'

Thus much she said, and withal led Gynecia out of the cave; for well she saw the boiling mind of Gynecia did easily apprehend the fitness of that lonely place. But indeed this direct promise of a short space, joined with the cumbersome familiar of womankind (I mean
20 modesty), stayed so Gynecia's mind that she took thus much at that present for good payment, remaining with a painful joy and a wearisome kind of comfort, not unlike to the condemned prisoner, whose mind still running upon the violent arrival of his cruel death, hears that his pardon is promised, but not yet signed. In this sort
25 they both issued out of that obscure mansion, Gynecia already half persuaded in herself (O weakness of human conceit!) that Cleophila's affection was turned towards her. For such, alas, are we all! In such a mould are we cast that, with the too much love we bear ourselves being first our own flatterers, we are easily hooked
30 with others' flattery, we are easily persuaded of others' love.

But Cleophila (who had now to play her prize), seeing no way things could long remain in that state, and now finding her promise had tied her trial to a small compass of time, began to throw her thoughts into each corner of her invention, how she might achieve
35 her life's enterprise. For well she knew deceit cannot otherwise be maintained but by deceit. And how to deceive such heedful eyes,

1 either] *om.* Cl, 93.   9–10 thus much to say] to say thus much Ph, Hm.
18 lonely] lovely Cl, Hm.   21–2 and a wearisome] and wearisome Cl, Hm.
27 are we] we are Da, 93.   30 with others'] with our own Da, 93 (*corr.* 13); with
other Ph.   34 invention] intention As; inventions Ph.

and how to satisfy, and yet not satisfy, such hopeful desires, it was
no small skill. But both their thoughts were called from themselves
with the sight of Basilius, who then lying down by his daughter
Philoclea upon the fair (though natural) bed of green grass, seeing
the sun what speed he made to leave our west to do his office in the 5
other hemisphere, his inward muses made him in his best music
sing this madrigal:

> Why dost thou haste away,
> O Titan fair, the giver of the day?
> Is it to carry news 10
> To western wights, what stars in east appear?
> Or dost thou think that here
> Is left a sun whose beams thy place may use?
> Yet stay, and well peruse
> What be her gifts that make her equal thee. 15
> Bend all thy light to see
> In earthly clothes enclosed a heav'nly spark.
> Thy running course cannot such beauties mark.
> No, no, thy motions be
> Hastened from us with bar of shadow dark, 20
> Because that thou, the author of our sight,
> Disdainst we see thee stained with other's light.

And having ended: 'Dear Philoclea', said he, 'sing something that may
divert my thoughts from the continual taste of their ruinous harbour.'
She (obedient to him, and not unwilling to disburden her secret 25
passion) made her sweet voice to be heard in these words:

> O stealing time, the subject of delay
> (Delay, the rack of unrefrained desire),
> What strange design hast thou my hopes to stay,
> My hopes which do but to mine own aspire? 30
>
> Mine own? O word on whose sweet sound doth prey
> My greedy soul, with gripe of inward fire.
> Thy title great, I justly challenge may,
> Since in such phrase his faith he did attire.

8-22 *The poem is in* 93.   8 Je *begins again here.*   11 appear] appears Le, Je, Hm.
15 make] makes Ph, Je, Hm.   20 shadow] shadows Ph, Je, Hm.   22 Disdainst
93: Disdains OA.   24 taste] task 93.   their] her Da; the Je, Hm.   26 voice
to be] voice be Cl, As, Da, Hm, 93.   27-p. 208, 6 *The poem is in* 93.   28 rack]
wrack Da, Je; lack Ph.   unrefrained] unrefram'd 93 (*corr.* 13).   29 design]
desire Cl, Ph; *blank left* Je.

O time, become the chariot of my joys;
As thou draw'st on, so let my bliss draw near.
Each moment lost, part of my hap destroys.

Thou art the father of occasion dear:
5   Join with thy son to ease my long annoys.
In speedy help thankworthy friends appear.

Philoclea brake off her song as soon as her mother with Cleophila
came near unto them, rising up with a kindly bashfulness, being not
ignorant of the spite her mother bare her, and stricken with the
10 sight of that person whose love made all those troubles seem fair
flowers of her dearest garland. Nay, rather, all those troubles made
the love increase. For as the arrival of enemies makes a town so
fortify itself as ever after it remains stronger, so that a man may say
enemies were no small cause to the town's strength; so to a mind
15 once fixed in a well pleasing determination, who hopes by annoyance
to overthrow it doth but teach it to knit together all his best grounds,
and so perchance of a changeable purpose make an unchangeable
resolution. But no more did Philoclea see the wonted signs of
Cleophila's affection towards her. She thought she saw another light
20 in her eyes, with a bold and careless look upon her (which was wont
to be dazzled with her beauty), and the framing of her courtesies
rather ceremonious than affectionate. And that which worse liked
her was that it proceeded with such quiet settledness as it rather
threatened a full purpose than any sudden passion. She found her
25 behaviour bent altogether to her mother, and presumed in herself
she discerned the well acquainted face of his fancies now turned to
another subject. She saw her mother's worthiness, and too well knew
her affection. These joining their diverse working powers together
in her mind (but yet a prentice in the painful mystery of passions)
30 brought Philoclea into a new traverse of her thoughts, and made her
keep her careful look the more attentive upon Cleophila's behaviour;
who indeed (though with much pain and condemning herself to
commit a sacrilege against the sweet saint that lived in her inmost
temple, yet strengthening herself in it, being the surest way to make
35 Gynecia bite of her other baits) did so quite overrule all wonted

10 fair OA, 93: fairer St.   12 so] to Cl, Je.   14 cause to] cause of Cl, Je, Hm.
15 pleasing] pleasant Da; pleased Ph, 93 (*corr.* 13).   17 changeable] chanceable
Bo, 93.   22 worse] worst Da, Je, 93.   28 affection] affections Da, Hm.
29 but] as 13.   prentice] princess Bo, As; apprentice Hm.   mystery] misery As, Da,
miseries Ph, Je; mysteries Hm.   35 quite OA, 93: quiet St.

shows of love to Philoclea, and convert them to Gynecia, that the part she played did work in both a full and lively persuasion: to Gynecia, such excessive comfort as the being preferred to a rival doth deliver to swelling desire. But to the delicate Philoclea (whose calm thoughts were unable to nourish any strong debate) it gave so 5 stinging a hurt that, fainting under the force of her inward torment, she withdrew herself to the lodge, and there (weary of supporting her own burden) cast herself upon her bed, suffering her sorrow to melt itself into abundance of tears. At length, closing her eyes, as if each thing she saw were a picture of her mishap, and turning upon 10 her heart side (which with vehement panting did summon her to consider her fortune), she thus bemoaned herself:

'Alas, Philoclea, is this the prize of all thy pains? Is this the reward of thy given-away liberty? Hath too much yielding bred cruelty, or can too great acquaintance make me held for a stranger? Hath the 15 choosing a companion made me left alone, or doth granting desire cause the desire to be neglected? Alas, despised Philoclea, why didst thou not hold thy thoughts in their simple course, and content thyself with the love of thy own virtue which would never have betrayed thee? Ah, silly fool, didst thou look for truth in him that 20 with his own mouth confessed his falsehood; for plain proceeding in him that still goes disguised? They say the falsest men will yet bear outward shows of a pure mind; but he that even outwardly bears the badge of treachery, what hells of wickedness must needs in the depth be contained? But, O wicked mouth of mine, how darest 25 thou thus blaspheme the ornament of the earth, the vessel of all virtue? O, wretch that I am, that will anger the gods in dispraising their most excellent work! O no, O no, there was no fault but in me, that could ever think so high eyes would look so low, or so great perfections would stain themselves with my unworthiness! Alas, 30 why could I not see I was too weak a band to tie so heavenly a heart? I was not fit to limit the infinite course of his wonderful destinies. Was it ever like that upon only Philoclea his thoughts should rest? Ah, silly soul that couldst please thyself with so impossible an imagination; an universal happiness is to flow from him! How was 35 I so inveigled to hope I might be the mark of such a mind? He did

4 But to the OA, 93: But the St. (corr. 98). side OA, 93: said St. 19 thy] thine Cl, Da, Je, 13. 32 infinite] om. Cl; insolent As. 10 were] was Da, 93. 11 heart] hurt 93 16 choosing a] choosing of a As, Da, Ph, 93. 28 O no, O no] O no, no Cl, Ph, Hm, 93. 34 Ah] a Da; Oh Hm. couldst 93: could OA.

thee no wrong, O Philoclea, he did thee no wrong! It was thy
weakness to fancy the beams of the sun should give light to no eyes
but thine! And yet, O prince Pyrocles (for whom I may well begin
to hate myself, but can never leave to love thee), what triumph
5 canst thou make of this conquest? What spoils wilt thou carry away
of this my undeserved overthrow? Could thy force find out no fitter
field than the feeble mind of a poor maid who at the first sight did
wish thee all happiness? Shall it be said the mirror of mankind hath
been employed to destroy a hurtless gentlewoman? O Pyrocles,
10 Pyrocles, let me yet call thee before the judgement of thine own
virtue! Let me be accepted for a plaintiff in a cause which concerns
my life! What need hadst thou to arm thy face with the enchanting
mask of thy painted passions? What need hadst thou to fortify thy
excellencies with so exquisite a cunning in making our own arts
15 betray us? What needest thou descend so far from thy incomparable
worthiness as to take on the habit of weak womankind? Was all this
to win the undefended castle of a friend; which being won, thou
wouldst after raze? Could so small a cause allure thee, or did not so
unjust a cause stop thee? O me, what say I more? This is my case:
20 my love hates me, virtue deals wickedly with me, and he does me
wrong whose doing I can never account wrong.'

   With that, the sweet lady turning herself upon her weary bed, she
haply saw a lute, upon the belly of which Gynecia had written this
song what time Basilius imputed her jealous motions to proceed of
25 the doubt she had of his untimely loves. Under which veil she
(contented to cover her never ceasing anguish) had made the lute a
monument of her mind; which Philoclea had never much marked till
now the fear of a competitor more stirred her than before the care
of a mother. The verses were these:

30   My lute within thyself thy tunes enclose,
       Thy mistress' song is now a sorrow's cry,
       Her hand benumbed with fortune's daily blows,
       Her mind amazed, can neither's help apply.
       Wear these my words as mourning weeds of woes,
35   Black ink becomes the state wherein I die.

1 O] *om.* Cl, As; Ah Je.   10 thine] thy Ph, Hm.   12 enchanting] enchanted
As, Ph (enchanted *corr. to* enchanting Bo).   20 does] doth Cl, As, Hm.   30–p. 211,
10 *The poem is in* 93.   30 within] which in 93 (*corr.* 98).   33 neither's]
neither Bo; never Je; not her Hm.   34 weeds Cl, Da, Ph, Je, Hm: weed St, Bo,
Le, As, 93 (*corr.* 05).   35 becomes] become Cl, Le, Da.

And though my moans be not in music bound,
Of written griefs, yet be the silent ground.

The world doth yield such ill consorted shows
(With circled course, which no wise stay can try)
That childish stuff which knows not friends from foes   5
(Better despised) bewonder gazing eye.
Thus noble gold down to the bottom goes,
When worthless cork aloft doth floating lie.
    Thus in thyself least strings are loudest found,
    And lowest stops do yield the highest sound.   10

Philoclea read them, and throwing down the lute: 'Is this the legacy
you have bequeathed me, O kind mother of mine', said she, 'did you
bestow the light upon me for this, or did you bear me to be the
author of my burial? A trim purchase you have made of your own
shame: robbed your daughter to ruin yourself! The birds unreason-   15
able, yet use so much reason as to make nests for their tender young
ones; my cruel mother turns me out of mine own harbour. Alas,
plaint boots not, for my case can receive no help; for who should give
me help? Shall I flee to my parents? They are my murderers. Shall
I go to him who (already being won and lost) must needs have killed   20
all pity? Alas, I can bring no new intercessions; he knows already
what I am is his! Shall I come home again to myself? O me,
contemned wretch, I have given away myself!'

With that the poor soul beat her breast as if that had been guilty
of her faults, neither thinking of revenge nor studying for remedy;   25
but, sweet creature, gave grief a free dominion, keeping her chamber
a few days after, not needing to feign herself sick, feeling even in her
soul the pangs of extreme pain. But little did Gynecia reck that,
neither when she saw her go away from them, neither when she
after found that sickness made her hide her fair face—so much had   30
fancy prevailed against nature. But, O you that have ever known how
tender to every motion love makes the lover's heart, how he measures
all his joys upon her contentment, and doth with respectful eye
hang all his behaviour upon her eyes, judge, I pray you, now of
Cleophila's troubled thoughts when she saw Philoclea with an   35

2 the] the *corr. to* they Cl; ihe As; they Ph, Hm.   5 That OA, 93: But St.
6 despised] despied Le; disguised Je.   bewonder] be wonder Cl, Le, Je; by wonder
Ph, Hm.   11 this the] this thy Ph; *om.* Je.   17 mine] my Bo, Da, Ph.
19 flee] fly Bo, As, Ph, Je, 93.   21 new] more Da, Je, Hm.   31 O] *om.* Cl, As, Da.

amazed kind of sorrow carry away her sweet presence, and easily found (so happy a conjecture unhappy affection hath) that her demeanour was guilty of that trespass. There was never foolish soft-hearted mother that, forced to beat her child, did weep first for
5 his pains, and doing that she was loath to do, did repent before she began, did find half that motion in her weak mind as Cleophila did, now that she was forced by reason to give an outward blow to her passions, and for the lending of a small time to seek the usury of all her desires. The unkindness she conceived Philoclea might conceive
10 did wound her soul; each tear she doubted she spent drowned all her comfort. Her sickness was a death unto her. Often would she speak to the image of Philoclea (which lived and ruled in the highest of her inward part), and use vehement oaths and protestations unto her that nothing should ever falsify the free-chosen vow she had
15 made. Often would she desire her that she would look well to Pyrocles' heart; for, as for her, she had no more interest in it to bestow it any way. 'Alas,' would she say, 'only Philoclea, hast thou not so much feeling of thine own force as to know no new conqueror can prevail against thy conquests? Was ever any dazzled with the
20 moon that had used his eyes to the beams of the sun? Is he carried away with a greedy desire of acorns that hath had his senses ravished with a garden of most delightful fruits? O Philoclea, Philoclea, be thou but as merciful a princess to my mind as thou art a sure possessor, and I shall have as much cause of gladness as
25 thou hast no cause of misdoubting! O no, no! when a man's own heart is the gage of his debt, when a man's own thoughts are willing witnesses to his promise, lastly, when a man is the gaoler over himself, there is little doubt of breaking credit, and less doubt of such an escape.'
30 In this combat of Cleophila's doubtful imaginations in the end reason (well backed with the vehement desire to bring her matters soon to the desired haven) did overrule the boiling of her inward kindness—though, as I say, with such a manifest strife that both Basilius's and Gynecia's well waiting eyes had marked her muses
35 had laboured in deeper subject than ordinary; which she likewise perceiving they had perceived, awaking herself out of those thoughts,

10 tear OA, 93: tree St.   13 part] parts As, Je.   14 free] fore As; true Je.
15 Often Cl, As, Ph, 93: Oft St, Bo, Da, Je, Hm.   19 conquests] conquest Da, Ph, Je, Hm.   21 a Bo, As, Ph, Je, Hm, 93: the St, Cl, Da.   24 sure] true Da, 93.
25 no cause] now cause Ph, Je, Hm.   27 the] om. Bo; a Ph.

and principally caring how to satisfy Gynecia (whose judgement and passion she stood most in regard of), bowing her head to her attentive ear, 'Madam,' said she, 'with practice of my thoughts I have found out a way by which your contentment shall draw on my happiness.'

Gynecia (delivering in her face as thankful a joyfulness as her 5 heart could hold) said it was then time to retire themselves to their rest; for what with the tumult the day before, and late sitting up for the eclogues, their bodies had dearly purchased that night's quiet. So went they home to their lodge, Cleophila framing of both sides bountiful measures of loving countenances, to either's joy and 10 neither's jealousy, but to the especial comfort of Basilius, whose weaker bowels were straight full with the least liquor of hope; so that (still holding her by the hand and sometimes tickling it) he went by her with the most gay conceits that ever had entered his brains, growing now so hearted in his resolution that he little respected 15 Gynecia's presence, but with a lustier note than wonted, clearing his voice and cheering his spirits, looking still upon Cleophila (whom now the moon did beautify with her shining almost at the full) as if her eyes had been his songbook, he did the message of his mind in singing these verses: 20

> When two suns do appear
> Some say it doth betoken wonders near,
> As prince's loss or change.
> Two gleaming suns of splendour like I see,
> And seeing feel in me 25
> Of prince's heart quite lost the ruin strange.

> But now each where doth range
> With ugly cloak the dark envious night;
> Who full of guilty spite,
> Such living beams should her black seat assail— 30
> Too weak for them our weaker sight doth veil.

> 'No', says fair moon, 'my light
> Shall bar that wrong, and though it not prevail
> Like to my brother's rays, yet those I send
> Hurt not the face, which nothing can amend.' 35

4 contentment OA, 93: commandment St.   7 tumult] riding abroad 93.   7–8 for the eclogues] for eclogues Je, Hm, 93.   10 joy OA, 93: joys St.   11 but] om. 93. 21–35 *The poem is in* 93.   29 spite OA, 93: spirit St.   34 rays] raise As, 93 (*corr.* 98).

And by that time being come to the lodge, and visited the sweet
Philoclea (with much less than natural care of the parents, and much
less than wonted kindness of Cleophila), each party, full fraught
with diversely working fancies, made their pillows weak props of
5 their overloaden heads. Yet of all other were Cleophila's brains most
turmoiled, troubled with love both active and passive, and lastly
and especially with care how to use her short limited time to the full
performance of her violent affection by some wise and happy
diverting her two lovers' unwelcome desires. But Cleophila, having
10 had the night her only counsellor in the busy enterprise she was to
undertake, and having all that time mused, and yet not fully
resolved how she might join obtaining with preventing, was offended
with the day's bold entry into her chamber, as if he had now by
custom grown an assured bringer of evil news; which she, taking a
15 cithern to her, did lay to Aurora's charge with these well sung verses:

> Aurora, now thou show'st thy blushing light
> (Which oft to hope lays out a guileful bait,
> That trusts in time to find the way aright
> To ease those pains which on desire do wait)

20
> Blush on for shame that still with thee do light
> On pensive souls (instead of restful bait)
> Care upon care (instead of doing right)
> To overpressed breasts, more grievous weight.

> As oh! myself, whose woes are never light,
25
> Tied to the stake of doubt, strange passions bait;
> While thy known course, observing nature's right,
> Stirs me to think what dangers lie in wait.
> For mischiefs great, day after day doth show;
> Make me still fear thy fair appearing show.

30   'Alas,' said she, 'am I not run into a strange gulf, that am fain
for love to hurt her I love; and because I detest the others, to
please them I detest? O, only Philoclea, whose beauty is matched
with nothing but with the unspeakable beauty of thy fairest mind, if

3 party] part Bo, Je.   4 of OA, 93: for St.   7–8 full . . . affection] best
purpose 93.   9 But] om. Cl, As, Da, Hm, 93.   12 obtaining] prevailing 93.
13 entry] entering Bo, Je, Hm.   16–29 The poem is in 93.   18 trusts] trust Bo,
Da, Je.   22 Care] Or Cl, Da; Are Le.   26 known] know Da; unknown Je.
28 doth] do Cl, Da, Je.   29 still fear] fear still Cl, Le, As.   30 I not] not I 93.

thou didst see upon what a rack my tormented soul is set, little would
you think I had free scope now to leap to any new change.'

With that with hasty hands she gat herself up, turning her sight to
everything, as if change of object might help her invention. So went
she again to the cave, where forthwith it came into her head that
should be the fittest place to perform her exploit—of which she had
now a kind of confused conceit, although she had not set down in her
fancy the meeting with each particularity that might fall out. But as
a painter doth at the first but show a rude proportion of the thing he
imitates, which after with more curious hand he draws to the
representing each lineament, so had her thoughts (beating about it
continually) received into them a ground plot of her device, although
she had not in each part shaped it according to a full determination.
But in this sort, having early visited the morning's beauty in those
pleasant deserts, she came to the duke and duchess, and told them
that, for the performance of certain her country devotions which
only were to be exercised in solitariness, she did desire their leave
she might for a few days lodge herself in the cave, the fresh sweetness
of which did greatly delight her in that hot country; and that for
that small space they would not otherwise trouble themselves in
visiting her, but at such times as she would come to wait upon them,
which should be every day at certain hours. Neither should it be
long she would desire this privileged absence of them. They (whose
minds had already taken out that lesson, perfectly to yield a willing
obedience to all her desires) with consenting countenance made her
soon see her pleasure was a law unto them, both indeed inwardly
glad of it: Basilius hoping that her dividing herself from them might
yet give him some freer occasion of coming in secret unto her, whose
favourable face had lately strengthened his fainting courage; but
Gynecia of all other most joyous, holding herself assured that this
was but a prologue to the play she had promised her. Thus both
flattering themselves with diversely grounded hopes, they rang a
bell which served to call certain poor women (which ever lay in
cabins not far off to do the household services of both lodges, and
never came to either but being called for), and commanded them to
carry forthwith Cleophila's bed and furniture of her chamber into

2 free] any 93.   3 gat] got Cl, 93.   9 a painter] the painter 93.   10 with OA, 93:
the St.   14 those OA, 93: these St.   15 duke and duchess] king and queen 93 (*and
throughout*).   23 this] that Je; his 93 (*corr.* 98).   25 with] which 93 (*corr.* 98).
28 freer] free Da, Ph, Hm; *om.* Je.   of OA, 93: in St; to As.   30 other] others Cl, Je.
34 services] service As, Je, Hm.   35–6 to carry forthwith OA, 93: forthwith to carry St.

the pleasant cave, and to deck it up as finely as it was possible for them, that their souls' rest might rest her body to her best pleasing manner. That was with all diligence performed of them, and Cleophila already in possession of her new chosen lodging where she (like one of Vesta's nuns) entertained herself for a few days in all show of straitness; yet once a day coming to do her duty to the duke and duchess, in whom the seldomness of the sight increased the more unquiet longing—though somewhat qualified, as her countenance was decked to either of them with more comfort than wonted, especially to Gynecia who (seeing her wholly neglect her daughter Philoclea) had now promised herself a full possession of Cleophila's heart, still expecting the fruit of the happy and hoped-for invention. But both she and Basilius kept such a continual watch about the precincts of the cave that either of them was a bar to the other from having any secret communing with Cleophila.

While in the mean time the sweet Philoclea (forgotten of her father, despised of her mother, and in appearance left of Cleophila) had yielded up her soul to be a prey to sorrow and unkindness, not with raging conceit of revenge (as had passed through the stout and wise heart of her mother), but with a kindly meekness taking upon herself the weight of her own woes, and suffering them to have so full a course in her as it did not a little weaken the state of her body. As well for which cause, as for that she could not see Cleophila without expressing (more than she would) how far now her love was imprisoned in extremity of sorrow, she bound herself to the limits of her own chamber. But Cleophila having now a full liberty to cast about every way how to bring her conceived attempt to a desired success, was oft so perplexed with the manifold difficulty of it that sometimes she would resolve by force to take her away, though it were with the death of her parents; sometimes to go away herself with Musidorus, and bring both their forces, so to win her. But lastly, even the same day that Musidorus, by feeding the humour of his three loathsome guardians, had stolen away the princess Pamela —whether it were that love meant to match them every way, or that

8 longing] lodging Ph, Je, Hm.   10 neglect] neglecting 93.   15 communing 05: commoning St, Cl, As, Hm, 93; communion Bo; conjoining Da; coloquence Ph; conning Je.   22 herself] her Da, 93.   23 in her] om. 93.   not a little] exceedingly 93.   26 herself to] herself first to 93.   27 chamber. But] chamber, and after (grief breeding sickness) of her bed. But 93.   32 so] om. Cl, Ph; set Da.   35 way,] 93 adds: or that her friend's example had holpen her invention,

indeed Cleophila forbare the practising her device till she found her
friend had passed through his—the same day, I say, thus she governed
her purpose: having curiously trimmed herself to the beautifying
her beauties (that being now at her last trial, she might come to it in
her best armour), having put on that kind of mild countenance 5
which doth encourage the looker-on to hope for a gentle answer,
according to her late-received manner, she left the pleasant darkness
of her melancholy cave to go take her dinner of the duke and duchess,
and give unto both them a pleasant food of seeing the owner of their
desires. But even as the Persians were anciently wont to leave no 10
rising sun unsaluted, but as his fair beams appeared clearer unto
them would they more heartily rejoice, laying upon them a great
foretoken of their following fortunes; so was there no time that
Cleophila encountered their eyes with her beloved presence but that
it bred a kind of burning devotion in them, yet so much the more 15
gladding their greedy souls as her countenance were cleared with
more favour unto them—which now being determinately framed to
the greatest descent of kindness, it took such hold of her unfortunate
lovers that, like children about a tender father from a long voyage
returned with lovely childishness hang about him, and yet with 20
simple fear measure by his countenance how far he accepts their
boldness, so were these two now thrown into so serviceable an
affection that the turning of Cleophila's eye was a strong stern
enough to all their motions, wending no way but as the enchanting
force of it guided them. But having made a light repast of the 25
pleasant fruits of that country, interlarding their food with such
manner of general discourses as lovers are wont to cover their

1 the practising] to practise 93.   2–3 thus . . . having] she resolved on a way to rid
out of the lodge her two cumbersome lovers, and in the night to carry away Philoclea—
whereunto she was assured her own love, no less than her sister's, would easily win her
consent; hoping that, although their abrupt parting had not suffered her to demand of
Musidorus which way he meant to direct his journey, yet either they should by some
good fortune find him, or if that course failed, yet they might well recover some town of
the Helots near the frontiers of Arcadia, who being newly again up in arms against the
nobility, she knew would be as glad of her presence as she of their protection. There-
fore, having taken order for all things requisite for their going, and first put on a slight
undersuit of man's apparel (which before for such purposes she had provided), she
93.   3–4 beautifying her] beautifying of her Bo, Ph, Hm, 93.   4 to] unto 93.
5 best] bravest 93.   having put] And so putting 93.   9 both them] them
both Ph, 93.   11 clearer] cleared Cl; clear Hm.   12 they] the Cl, Ph, Je.
16 were] was Bo, As, Je (were corr. to was Cl).   18 unfortunate] infortunatest
Bo; infortunate Cl, Da, Ph, Hm, 93.   19 a] om. Bo, Da.   20 lovely] loving
Cl, As.   22 two now As: now St, Bo, Da, Ph, Je, Hm, 93; two Cl.   an] om. Ph,
Hm.   24 wending] winding Cl; wandering Hm.   enchanting] enchanted Bo, Hm.

passions in when respect of a third person keeps them from plainer particulars, at the earnest entreaty of Basilius, Cleophila (first saluting the muses with a bass viol hung hard by her) sent this ambassade in versified music to both her ill-requited lovers:

5   Beauty hath force to catch the human sight.
       Sight doth bewitch the fancy ill awaked.
       Fancy, we feel, includes all passion's might.
       Passion rebelled, oft reason's strength hath shaked.

       No wonder then, though sight my sight did taint,
10   And though thereby my fancy was infected,
       Though (yoked so) my mind with sickness faint,
       Had reason's weight for passion's ease rejected.

       But now the fit is passed; and time hath given
       Leisure to weigh what due desert requireth.
15   All thoughts so sprung are from their dwelling driven,
       And wisdom to his wonted seat aspireth,
            Crying in me: 'Eye-hopes deceitful prove;
            Things rightly prized, love is the band of love.'

    And after her song, with an affected modesty, she threw down her
20 eye, as if the conscience of a secret grant her inward mind made had
suddenly cast a bashful veil over her; which Basilius finding, and
thinking now was the time to urge his painful petition, beseeching
his wife with more careful eye to accompany his sickly daughter
Philoclea, being rid for that time of her (who was content to grant
25 him any scope, that she might after have the like freedom), with a
gesture governed by the force of his passions, making his knees his
best supporters, he thus said unto her:
    'If either,' said he, 'O lady of my life, my deadly pangs could
bear delay, or that this were the first time the same were manifested
30 unto you, I would now but maintain still the remembrance of my
misfortune, without urging any further reward than time and pity
might procure for me. But alas, since my martyrdom is no less
painful than manifest, and that I no more feel the miserable danger
than you know the assured truth thereof, why should my tongue

1 plainer] plain As, Da, Hm, 93.   4 ambassade] embassade As; ambassage Da;
embassadge Ph, Hm; imbassage Je.   5–18 *The poem is in* 93.   7 includes]
eludes Cl, Da; include Je.   17 Eye-hopes] I hopes Cl; ay hopes Da; did hopes
Ph.   25 a OA, 93: *om.* St.

deny his service to my heart? Why should I fear the breath of my words who daily feel the flame of your works? Embrace in your sweet consideration, I beseech you, the misery of my case; acknowledge yourself to be the cause, and think it is reason for you to redress the effects! Alas, let not certain imaginative rules (whose 5 truth stands but upon opinion) keep so wise a mind from gratefulness and mercy, whose never failing laws nature hath planted in us. I plainly lay my death unto you, the death of him that loves you, the death of him whose life you may save. Say your absolute determination, for hope itself is a pain while it is overmastered with fear; and 10 if you do resolve to be cruel, yet is the speediest condemnation, as in evils, most welcome.'

Cleophila who had fully set to herself the train she would keep, yet knowing that who soonest means to yield doth well to make the bravest parley, keeping her countenance aloft: 'Noble prince,' said 15 she, 'your words are too well couched to come out of a restless mind, and thanked be the gods your face threatens no danger of death. These be but those swelling speeches which give the uttermost name to every trifle, which all were worth nothing if they were not enamelled with the goodly outside of love. Truly, love were very unlovely 20 if it were half so deadly as you lovers (still living) term it. I think well it may have a certain childish vehemency which for the time to one desire will engage all the soul, so long as it lasteth. But with what impatience, you yourself show, who confess the hope of it a pain, and think your own desire so unworthy as you would fain be 25 rid of it, and so with overmuch love sue hard for a hasty refusal.'

'A refusal,' cried out Basilius, amazed withal, but pierced with the last, 'now assure yourself whensoever you use that word definitively it will be the undoubted doom of my approaching death; and then shall your own experience know in me how soon the spirits dried up 30 with anguish leave the performance of their ministry, whereupon our life dependeth. But, alas, what a cruelty is this, not only to torment, but to think the torment slight! The terriblest tyrants would say by no man they killed, he died not; nor by no man they punished, that he escaped free. For of all other there is least hope of mercy where 35

1 Why should I fear] St *repeats these words on turning overleaf.*   2–3 in your sweet]
in sweet 93 (*corr.* 98).   12 evils] evil Da, Hm.   14 who] whoso Da, Ph.
means] mean Cl, As; *om.* Ph.   15 her] *om.* 93.   17 be] are 93.   21 you]
your 93 (*corr.* 13).   living] loving Ph, Je, Hm.   25 as you OA, 93: as if you St
(Hm *omits* as . . . rid of it).   31 the] their Ph, Je.   35 For of all OA, 93: For
all St.   least Bo, As, Da, Ph, Je, Hm, 93: less St; left Cl.

there is no acknowledging of the pain; and with like cruelty are my words, breathed out from a flamy heart, accounted as messengers of a quiet mind. If I speak nothing, I choke myself, and am in no way of relief; if simply, neglected; if confusedly, not understood; if by
5 the bending together all my inward powers they bring forth any lively expressing of that they truly feel, that is a token forsooth the thoughts are at too much leisure. Thus is silence desperate, folly punished, and wit suspected. But, indeed, it is vain to say any more, for words can bind no belief. Lady, I say, determine of me. I must
10 confess I cannot bear this battle in my mind, and therefore let me soon know what I may account of myself; for it is a hell of dolours when the mind, still in doubt for want of resolution, can make no resistance.'

'Indeed,' answered Cleophila, 'if I should grant to your request,
15 I should show an example in myself that I esteem the holy band of chastity to be but an imaginative rule (as you termed it), and not the truest observance of nature, the most noble commandment that mankind can have over themselves (as indeed both learning teacheth and inward feeling assureth). But first shall Cleophila's grave become
20 her marriage bed before my soul shall consent to his own shame, before I will leave a mark in myself of an unredeemable trespass. And yet must I confess that if ever my heart were stirred, it hath been with the manifest and manifold shows of the misery you live in for me. For in truth so it is, nature gives not to us her degenerate
25 children any more general precept than one to help the other, one to feel a true compassion of the other's mishap. But yet if I were never so contented to speak with you (for further never, O Basilius, look for at my hands), I know not how you can avoid your wife's jealous attendance, but that her suspicion shall bring my honour into
30 question.'

Basilius (whose small sails the least wind did fill) was forthwith as far gone into a large promising himself his desire as before he was stricken down with a threatened denial. And therefore, bending his brows as though he were not a man to take the matter as he had done:
35 'What,' said he, 'shall my wife become my mistress? Think you not that thus much time hath taught me to rule her? I will mew the

8 vain OA, 93: in vain St.   9 for] *om.* Da, Ph, Je, Hm.   16 an] and 93 (*corr.* 98).   termed OA, 93: term St.   24 to] *om.* Cl, As; unto Ph.   26–7 never . . . look] O Basilius never look Bo, Cl, Je.   28 hands OA, 93: hand St.   29 my] mine Cl, Je.   33 threatened] threatening Bo, Cl.   denial] devil 93 (*corr.* 98).

gentlewoman till she have cast all her feathers, if she rouse herself against me.' And with that he walked up and down, nodding his head as though they mistook him much that thought he was not his wife's master.

But Cleophila, now seeing it was time to conclude: 'Of your 5 wisdom and manhood,' said she, 'I doubt not, but that sufficeth not me; for both they can hardly tame a malicious tongue, and impossibly bar the freedom of thought—which be the things that must be my only witnesses of honour, or judges of dishonour. But that you may see I do not set light your affection, if tonight after your wife be 10 assuredly asleep (whereof by your love I conjure you to have a most precise care) you will steal handsomely to the cave unto me, there do I grant you as great proportion as you will take of free conference with me, ever remembering you seek no more, for so shall you but deceive yourself, and forever lose me.'   15

Basilius (that was old enough to know that women are not wont to appoint secret night meetings for the purchasing of land), holding himself already an undoubted possessor of his desires, kissing her hand, and lifting up his eyes to heaven, as if the greatness of the benefit did go beyond all measure of thanks, said no more, lest stir- 20 ring of more words might bring forth some perhaps contrary matter.

In which trance of joy Cleophila went from him, saying she would leave him to the remembrance of their appointment; and for her, she would go visit the lady Philoclea. Into whose chamber being come, keeping still her late-taken-on gravity, and asking her how she did 25 (rather in the way of dutiful honour than any special affection), with extreme inward anguish to them both she turned from her, and taking the duchess Gynecia, led her into a bay window of the same chamber, determining in herself not to utter to so excellent a wit as Gynecia had the uttermost point of her pretended device, but to 30 keep the clause of it for the last instant, when the shortness of the time should not give her spirits leisure to look into all those doubts that easily enter into an open invention. But with smiling eyes, and with a delivered-over grace (feigning as much love to her as she did counterfeit little love to Philoclea), she began with more credible than 35 eloquent speech to tell her that, with much consideration of a matter so nearly importing her own fancy and Gynecia's honour, she

had now concluded that the night following should be the fittest
time for the joining together their several desires, what time sleep
should perfectly do his office upon the duke her husband; and that the
one should come to the other into the cave (which place, as it was the
first receipt of their promised love, so it might have the first honour
of the due performance); that the cause why those few days past she
had not sought the like was lest the new change of her lodging might
make the duke more apt to mark any sudden event—which now the
use of it would take out of his mind. 'And therefore now, most
excellent lady,' said she, 'there resteth nothing but that quickly
after supper you train up the duke to visit his daughter Philoclea;
and then, feigning yourself not well at ease, by your going to bed
draw him not long to be after you. In the mean time I will be gone
home to my lodging, where I will attend you with no less devotion
(but, as I hope, with better fortune) than Thisbe did the too much
loving, and too much loved, Pyramus.'

The blood that quickly came into Gynecia's fair face was the only
answer she made, but that one might easily see contentment and
consent were both to the full in her—which she did testify with the
wringing Cleophila fast by the hand, closing her eyes, and letting
her head fall, as if she would give her to know she was not ignorant
of her fault, although she were transported with the violence of her
evil.

But in this triple agreement did the day seem tedious of all sides,
till his never erring course had given place to the night's succession.
And the supper, by each hand hasted, was with no less speed ended;
when Gynecia, presenting a heavy sleepiness in her countenance,
brought up both Basilius and Cleophila to see Philoclea, still
keeping her bed, and far more sick in mind than body, and more
grieved than comforted with any such visitation. Thence Cleophila
(wishing easeful rest to Philoclea) did seem to take that night's
leave of this princely crew; when Gynecia, likewise seeming some-
what diseased, desired Basilius to stay awhile with her daughter,
while she recommended her sickness to her bed's comfort, indeed
desirous to determine again of the manner of her stealing away—to
no less comfort of Basilius who, the sooner she was asleep, the sooner

2 joining] coming As; enjoying Da, Je, Hm.   3 perfectly Bo, Cl, Da, Ph, Je,
Hm, 93: partly St; perfect As.   4 into] to Cl; in Je.   8 duke] sic 93 (though
corr. as usual to king at 3 and 11); king 13.   12 feigning] framing Cl; finding As.
29 than body] than in body Cl, Ph.   30 Thence] Then Ph, Hm.   31 that night's]
the night's Da, Je.   32 this] her Bo; that Cl.   36 of] to Da, 93.

hoped to come by his long-pursued prey. Thus both were bent to deceive each other, and to take the advantage of either other's disadvantage.

But Gynecia having taken Cleophila into her bedchamber to speak a little with her of their sweet determination, Cleophila upon 5 a sudden (as though she had never thought of it before): 'Now the gods forbid', said she, 'so great a lady as you are should come to me, or that I should leave it to the hands of fortune if, by either the ill governing of your passion, or your husband's sudden waking, any danger might happen unto you! No! If there be any superiority in 10 the points of true love, it shall be yours; if there be any danger, since myself am the author of this device, it is reason it should be mine. Therefore do you but leave with me the keys of the gate, and upon yourself take my upper garment, that if any of Dametas's house see you they may think you to be myself; and I will presently lie down in 15 your place, so muffled for your supposed sickness as the duke shall nothing know me. And then, as soon as the duke is asleep, will I (as it much better becomes me) wait upon you; and if the uttermost of mischiefs should happen, I can assure you the duke's life shall sooner pay for it than your honour.' 20

And with the ending of her words she threw off her gown, not giving Gynecia any space to take the full image of this new change into her fancy; but seeing no ready objection against it in her heart, and knowing that there was no time then to stand long disputing, besides remembering the giver was to order the manner of his gift, 25 yielded quickly to this conceit—indeed, not among the smallest causes, tickled thereunto by a certain wanton desire that her husband's deceit might be the more notable. In this sort did Cleophila, nimbly disarming herself, possess Gynecia's place, hiding her head in such a close manner as grievous and overwatched sickness is wont 30 to invite to itself the solace of sleep.

And of the other side the duchess, putting on Cleophila's utmost apparel, went first into her closet, there quickly to beautify herself with the best and sweetest night deckings; but there casting a hasty eye over her precious things (which ever since Cleophila's coming 35

5 their] the Ph, Je; her Hm.   17 the duke] he 93.   18 and] But 93.
19 mischiefs] mischief Da, Je, Hm.   26 yielded OA, 93; yield St.   29 disarming]
disguising Ph; discern Je; disarraying 93.   32 utmost] uppermost Cl, As; outmost
Da, Je, 98; uttermost Ph; outermost Hm.   33 apparel] garment Cl, As.
35 over] on As, Ph.

her head, otherwise occupied, had left unseen), she happened to see
a bottle of gold, upon which down along were graved these verses:

> Let him drink this whom long in arms to fold
> Thou dost desire, and with free pow'r to hold.

5 She remembered the bottle, for it had been kept of long time by the
kings of Cyprus as a thing of rare virtue, and given to her by her
mother when she being very young married to her husband of much
greater age, her mother (persuaded it was of property to force love
with love's effects) had made a precious present of it to this her well
10 beloved child—though it had been received rather by tradition to
have such a quality than by any approved experiment. This Gynecia
(according to the common disposition, not only (though especially)
of wives, but of all other kinds of people, not to esteem much one's
own, but to think the labour lost employed about it) had never
15 cared to give it to her husband, but suffered his affection to run
according to his own scope. But now that love of her particular
choice had awaked her spirits, and perchance the very unlawfulness
of it had a little blown the coal, among her other ornaments with
glad mind she took most part of this liquor, putting it into a fair cup
20 all set with diamonds—for what dare not love undertake, armed with
the night and provoked with lust? And thus down she went to the
cave-ward, guided only by the moon's fair shining, suffering no
other thought to have any familiarity with her brains, but that which
did present unto her a picture of her approaching contentment.
25 She that had long disdained this solitary life her husband had
entered into now wished it much more solitary, so she might only
obtain the private presence of Cleophila. She that before would not
have gone alone so far (especially by night, and to so dark a place)
now took a pride in the same courage, and framed in her mind a
30 pleasure out of the pain itself. Thus with thick doubled paces she
went to the cave, receiving to herself for her first contentment the
only lying where Cleophila had done—whose pillow she kissed a
thousand times for having borne the print of that beloved head.

3-4 *This couplet is in* 93.   9 love's] love 93.   well] *om.* As, 93.   11 a] *om.*
As, Ph.   13 kinds] kind Cl, As, Ph, Hm.   14 the] that Cl, As.   lost OA, 93:
last St.   19 this] the Cl, As; his Hm.   it OA, 93: *om.* St; but As.   20 dare]
will Je; dares 93.   21 the night] night As, Ph.   thus down] this done, Bo, Cl;
this down As, Je.   26 she might OA, 93: that she might St.   28 alone so far]
so far As, Da, 93; so far alone Je; about so far Hm.   29 took a pride OA, 93: took
pride St.

And so keeping with panting heart her travailing fancies so attentive that the wind could stir nothing, but that she stirred herself as if it had been the pace of the longed-for Cleophila, she kept her side of the bed, defending only and cherishing the other side with her arm; till after a while waiting, counting with herself how many steps were 5 betwixt the lodge and the cave, and oft accusing Cleophila of more curious stay than needed, she was visited as you shall presently hear.

For Basilius, after his wife was departed to her feigned repose, as long as he remained with his daughter to give his wife time of unreadying herself, it was easily seen it was a very thorny abode he 10 made there, and the discourses with which he entertained his daughter not unlike to those of earnest players when, in the midst of their game, trifling questions be put unto them: his eyes still looking about, and himself still changing places; began to speak of a thing, and brake it off before it were half done; to any speech 15 Philoclea ministered unto him, with a sudden starting and casting up his head, made an answer far out of all grammar; a certain deep musing, and by and by out of it; uncertain motions, unstaid graces. Having borne out the limit of a reasonable time with as much pain as might be, he came darkling into his chamber, forcing himself to 20 tread as softly as he could. But the more curious he was, the more he thought everything creaked under him; and his mind being out of the way with another thought, and his eyes not serving his turn in that dark place, each coffer or cupboard he met, one saluted his shins, another his elbows; sometimes ready in revenge to strike 25 them again with his face. Till at length, fearing his wife were not fully asleep, he came lifting up the clothes as gently as I think poor Pan did when, instead of Iole's bed, he came into the rough embracings of Hercules, and laying himself down as tenderly as a new bride, rested awhile with a very open ear to mark each breath of his 30 supposed wife. And sometimes he himself would yield a long-fetched sigh, as though that had been a music to draw on another to

3 longed-for] longed As, Hm.   3-4 of the] of her As, Da.   7 as . . . hear]
with an unexpected guest 93.   presently] om. As, Je, Hm.   10 unreadying]
unridding Bo, Ph; unreading Je.   it was a] what a Cl, As.   14 began Cl, As,
Da, Je, Hm: begin St, Bo, 93; begun Ph.   15 brake] break As, 93.   17 made
Ph, Je, Hm: make St, As, Da, 93; made corr. to make Bo; would make Cl.
20 darkling OA, 93; darklong St.   22 creaked Bo, Cl, Je, Hm, 93: cracked St;
craked As; creked Da; crake Ph.   24 that] the Da, Hm.   28 into] in Da;
to Hm.   28-9 embracings] embracing As, Je.   30 rested] he rested Bo, Ph, Je, Hm.
32 that] he As; om. Da; it Je; there Hm.   been a music] been music As, Hm.
on] one As, Da, Ph, Je, Hm, 93 (corr. 13).

sleep. Till within a very little while, with the other party's well counterfeited sleep (who was as willing to be rid of him as he was to be gotten thence), assuring himself he left all safe there, in the same order stale out again; and putting on his nightgown, with much
5 groping and scrambling, he gat himself out of the little house. And then did the moonlight serve to guide his feet. Thus with a great deal of pain did Basilius go to her whom he fled, and with much cunning left the person for whom he had employed all his cunning. But when Basilius was once gotten (as he thought) into a clear coast,
10 what joy he then made; how each thing seemed vile in his sight, in comparison of his fortune; how far already he deemed himself in the chief tower of his desires, it were tedious to tell. But once his heart could not choose but yield this song as a fairing of his contentment:

15   Get hence foul grief, the canker of the mind;
       Farewell complaint, the miser's only pleasure;
       Away vain cares, by which few men do find
                Their sought-for treasure.

       Ye helpless sighs, blow out your breath to naught;
20   Tears, drown yourselves, for woe (your cause) is wasted;
       Thought, think to end, too long the fruit of thought
                My mind hath tasted.

       But thou, sure hope, tickle my leaping heart;
       Comfort, step thou in place of wonted sadness;
25   Forefelt desire, begin to savour part
                Of coming gladness.

       Let voice of sighs into clear music run;
       Eyes, let your tears with gazing now be mended;
       Instead of thought, true pleasure be begun
30   And never ended.

Thus imagining as then with himself, his joys so held him up that he never touched ground. Like a right old beaten soldier that knew well

2 counterfeited] counterfeit Je, 93.   was as] was As, Ph.   3 gotten] gone Da, Hm, 93.   5 scrambling] scambling Cl, Ph; stumbling As.   12 But] om. 93. 15-30 The poem is in 93.   19 sighs] sights As, Le.   24 step Bo, Ph, Je, Hm, 93: steep St, As; sleep Cl; slepp Da.   25 part] parts 93 (corr. 13). 26 coming] cunning Cl, Da, Ph.   32 Like] And like 93.   a right old] an old As, Da, Hm.

enough the greatest captains do never use long orations when it comes to the very point of execution, as soon as he was gotten into the cave, and (to the joyful, though silent, expectation of Gynecia) come close to the bed, never recking his promise to look for nothing but conference, he leapt into that side preserved for a more welcome 5 guest; and laying his lovingest hold upon Gynecia: 'O Cleophila,' said he, 'embrace in your favour this humble servant of yours! Hold within me my heart which pants to leave his master to come unto you.'

In what case poor Gynecia was when she knew the voice and felt 10 the body of her husband, fair ladies, it is better to know by imagination than experience; for straight was her mind assaulted, partly with the being deprived of her unquenched desire, but principally with the doubt that Cleophila had betrayed her to her husband—besides the renewed sting of jealousy what in the mean time might befall her 15 daughter. But of the other side her love, with a fixed persuasion she had had, taught her to seek all reason of hopes; and therein thought best, before discovering of herself, to mark the behaviour of her husband who, both in deeds and words still using her as taking her to be Cleophila, made Gynecia hope that this might be Basilius's 20 own enterprise which Cleophila had not stayed, lest she should discover the matter, which might be performed at another time. Which hope, accompanied with Basilius's manner of dealing (he being at that time fuller of livelier fancies than many years before he had been), besides the remembrance of her daughter's sickness, and 25 late strange countenance betwixt her and Cleophila, all coming together into her mind (which was loath to condemn itself of an utter overthrow) made her frame herself, not truly with a sugared joy, but with a determinate patience, to let her husband think he had found a very gentle and supple-minded Cleophila; which he, good 30 man, making full reckoning of, did melt in as much gladness as she was oppressed with divers ungrateful burdens.

But Pyrocles (who had at that present no more to play the part of Cleophila) having, as I told you, so naturally measured the manner

2 was] had Cl, As.   into] to Da, Ph.   3 though] thought As, Da.   4 come] came Cl, As, Ph, Je, Hm.   to look] of looking Cl, As.   5 that] the As, Hm. preserved] reserved 93.   6 lovingest] loving Cl; strongest As; longest Je, Hm. 7 embrace in] embracing Cl, Je, Hm.   11 ladies] lady As, Hm.   16 a fixed] affixed As, Je, Hm; om. Ph.   17 had had] had Ph, Je, Hm, 93.   18 discovering of herself] discovering herself Ph, Hm.   26 betwixt] between Bo, Cl. 27 into] in As, Je.   29 determinate] determined Cl, Da.   33 that] this Cl, As, Da.   present] instant Bo; time As, Ph, Je.   34 as I told you] om. 93.

of his breathing that Basilius made no doubt of his sound sleeping, having lain a pretty while with a quiet unquietness to satisfy his greedy desire, as soon as (by the debate betwixt Basilius's shins and the unregarding forms) he perceived that he had fully left the lodge, 5 after him went he with stealing steps, having his sword under his arm (still doubting lest some mischance might turn Basilius back again), down to the gate of the lodge, which not content to lock fast, he barred and fortified with as many devices as his wit and haste would suffer him, resolving to have full time to accomplish his 10 enterprise, and to have warning enough before they should come at him. For further ends of those ends, and what might ensue of this action, his love and courage well matched never looked after, holding for an assured ground that whosoever in great things will think to prevent all objections must lie still and do nothing. This 15 only generally he remembered: that so long as Gynecia bewrayed not the matter (which he thought she would not do, as well for her own honour and safety as for the hope she might still have of him— which is loath to die in a lover's heart), all the rest would turn but to a pretty merriment, and inflame his lover Basilius again to a new 20 casting about for the missed favour. This determination thus weighed, this first part thus performed, up to Philoclea's chamber door went Pyrocles, rapt from himself with the excessive forefeeling of his near coming contentment. Whatever pains he had taken, what dangers he had run into, and especially those saucy pangs of love, 25 doubts, griefs, languishing hopes, and threatening despairs, came all now to his mind in one rank to beautify this after-following blissfulness, and to serve for a most fit sauce, whose sourness might give a kind of life to the delightful cheer his imagination fed upon. All the great estate of his father seemed unto him but a trifling pomp, whose 30 good stands in other men's conceit, in comparison of the true com-

2 having] and 93.   lain] lyen Cl; laid Je.   2–3 to satisfy . . . desire] to perform his intended enterprise 93.   7 content OA, 93 : contented St.   9 would] could Cl, As.   9–11 resolving . . . at him] that so he might have full time, both for making ready Philoclea, and conveying her to her horse, before any might come in to find them missing 93.   11 further ends OA (Hm *omits* ends . . . and), 93 : further end St.   this Cl, As, Da, Ph, Hm, 93 : his St; that Bo; those Je.   14–20 This . . . favour] 93 *omits here*.   18 would turn but] would turn Ph; might turn 93.   19–20 a new casting] cast 93.   23 his near] his (as he assured himself) near 93.   pains] pain As, Je.   24 pangs As, Hm : pages St, Bo, Cl, Da, Ph, Je, 93.   26 this] his Ph, 93.   after-following] expected 93.   27 sourness] *blank left* As; sweetness Hm.   29 father seemed] father, all his own glory, seemed 93.   30 good] goods Bo, Ph, Je, Hm.

fort he found in the depth of his mind; and the knowledge of any misery that might ensue this joyous adventure was recked of but as a slight purchase of possessing the top of happiness. And yet well he found that extremity of joy is not without a certain joyful pain, by extending the heart beyond his wonted limits, and by so forcible a 5 holding all the senses to one object, that it confounds their mutual working, not without a charming kind of ravishing them from the free use of their own function. Thus grieved only with too much gladness, being come to the door which should be the entry to his happiness, he was met with the latter end of a song which Philoclea, 10 like a solitary nightingale, bewailing her guiltless punishment and helpless misfortune, had newly delivered over, meaning none should be judge of her passion but her own conscience. The song, having been accorded to a sweetly played-on lute, contained these verses which she had lately with some art curiously written to enwrap her 15 secret and resolute woes:

1   2   3   1   2   3
Virtue, beauty, and speech, did strike, wound, charm,

1   2   3   1   2   3
My heart, eyes, ears, with wonder, love, delight:

1   2   3   1   2   3
First, second, last, did bind, enforce, and arm,

1   2   3   1   2   3
His works, shows, suits, with wit, grace, and vow's might.   20

1   2   3   1   2   3
Thus honour, liking, trust, much, far, and deep,

1   2   3   1   2   3
Held, pierced, possessed, my judgement, sense, and will,

1   2   3   1   2   3
Till wrong, contempt, deceit, did grow, steal, creep,

1   2   3   1   2   3
Bands, favour, faith, to break, defile, and kill.

2 this] the As; his Da.   recked of] reckoned of Da; wrecked Je; racked Hm.
3-4 happiness . . . is not] happiness, for so far were his thoughts passed through
all perils that already he conceived himself safely arrived with his lady at the
stately palace of Pella, among the exceeding joys of his father, and infinite
congratulations of his friends, giving order for the royal entertaining of Philoclea,
and for sumptuous shows and triumphs against their marriage. In the thought
whereof, as he found extremity of joy, so well found he that extremity is not 93.
5 forcible a] forcibly Cl, As, Je.   7 working] workings Da; walking
Je; waking Hm.   17-p. 230, 6 The poem is in Hy and 93. Je and Hy do not
number the words.   20 suits] fruits Cl, Da, Hm.

    1   2   3   1   2   3
Then grief, unkindness, proof, took, kindled, taught,

  1   2   3   1   2   3
Well grounded, noble, due, spite, rage, disdain,

  1 2   3   1   2   3
But ah, alas! (in vain) my mind, sight, thought,

  1   2   3   1   2   3
Doth him, his face, his words, leave, shun, refrain,

      1   2   3   1   2   3
5   For no thing, time, nor place, can loose, quench, ease,

      1   2   3   1   2   3
Mine own, embraced, sought, knot, fire, disease.

The force of love, to those poor folk that feel it, is many ways very
strange, but no way stranger than that it doth so enchain the lover's
judgement upon her that holds the reins of his mind that whatsoever
10 she doth is ever in his eyes best. And that best, being by the con-
tinual motion of our changing life turned by her to any other thing,
that thing again becometh best; so that nature in each kind suffering
but one superlative, the lover only admits no positive. If she sit still,
that is best; for so is the conspiracy of her several graces held best
15 together to make one perfect figure of beauty. If she walk, no doubt
that is best; for besides the making happy the more places by her
steps, the very stirring adds a pleasing life to her native perfections.
If she be silent, that without comparison is best; since by that means
the untroubled eye most freely may devour the sweetness of his
20 object. But if she speak, he will take it upon his death that is best;
the quintessence of each word being distilled down into his affected
soul. Example of this was well to be seen in the given-over Pyrocles
who, with panting breath and sometimes sighs (not such as sorrow,
restraining the inward parts, doth make them glad to deliver, but
25 such as the impatience of desire, with the unsurety of never so sure
hope, is wont to breathe out), now being at the door, of the one side
hearing her voice (which, he thought, if the philosophers said true of
the heavenly seven-sphered harmony, was by her not only represented
but far surmounted), and of the other having his eyes overfilled
30 with her beauty—for the duke at his parting had left the chamber
open, and she at that time lay (as the heat of that country did well

8 than OA, 93: there St.   enchain] encharm Cl; enchange As.   12 kind] kinds
Da; thing Je.   16 that] it Da, Hm.   17 pleasing] pleasant Cl, Ph, Hm.
native] natural Cl; om. Je.   21 affected] afflicted Da; om. Je, Hm.   23 sighs]
sights As, Da.   25 desire] delay 93.   29 other having] other side having Ph, Je.

suffer) upon the top of her bed, having her beauties eclipsed with
nothing but with a fair smock (wrought all in flames of ash-colour
silk and gold), lying so upon her right side that the left thigh down
to the foot yielded his delightful proportion to the full view, which
was seen by the help of a rich lamp which, through the curtains a 5
little drawn, cast such a light upon her as the moon doth when it
shines into a thin wood—Pyrocles, I say, was stopped with the
violence of so many darts cast by Cupid altogether upon him that,
quite forgetting himself, and thinking therein already he was in the
best degree of felicity, I think he would have lost much of his time, and 10
with too much love omitted great fruit of his love, had not Philoclea's
pitiful accusing of him forced him to bring his spirits again to a
new bias. For she, laying her hand under her fair cheek, upon which
there did privily trickle the sweet drops of her delightful (though
sorrowful) tears, made these words wait upon her moanful song: 15

'And hath that cruel Pyrocles', said she, 'deserved thus much of
me, that I should for his sake lift up my voice in my best tunes, and
to him continually, with pouring out my plaint, make a disdained
oblation? Shall my soul still do this honour to his unmerciful
tyranny, by my lamenting his loss to show his worthiness and my 20
weakness? He hears thee not, simple Philoclea, he hears thee not;
and if he did, some hearts grow the harder, the more they find their
advantage. Alas, what a miserable constitution of mind have I!
I disdain my fortune, and yet reverence him that disdains me. I
accuse his ungratefulness, and have his virtue in admiration. O ye 25
deaf heavens, I would either his injury could blot out my affection,
or my affection could forget his injury!'

With that, giving a pitiful but sweet screech, she took again the
lute and began to sing this sonnet which might serve as an explaining
to the other: 30

> The love which is imprinted in my soul
> With beauty's seal, and virtue fair disguised,
> With inward cries puts up a bitter roll
> Of huge complaints that now it is despised.

2 colour] ash-coloured Da, Je, Hm.   6 such] forth Da, 93 (forth *corr.* to such Bo).
10 I think] *om.* 93.   11 great fruit of] the enterprise undertaken for 93.   13 under]
upon Cl, As (upon *corr. to* under Bo); over Je, Hm.   14 trickle] tickle 93.   18 dis-
dained] disdainful Cl, Da, Ph.   22 grow the harder OA, 93: grow harder St.
26 my] mine Da, 93.   28 but sweet] but a sweet Cl, Je; but [   ] As; *om.* Hm.
31–p. 232, 10 *The poem is in* 93; p. 232, 9–10 *only are in* Pu.   32 virtue] virtues
Ph, Je, Hm.   33 up] forth *corr. to* up Cl; out Je, Hm.

Thus, thus, the more I love, the wrong the more
Monstrous appears, long truth received late,
Wrong stirs remorsed grief, grief's deadly sore
Unkindness breeds, unkindness fost'reth hate.

5   But ah! the more I hate, the more I think
Whom I do hate, the more I think on him,
The more his matchless gifts do deeply sink
Into my breast, and loves renewed swim.
What medicine, then, can such disease remove
10   Where love draws hate, and hate engendreth love?

But Pyrocles (that had heard his name accused and condemned by
the mouth which of all the world, and more than all the world, he
most loved) had then cause enough to call his mind to his own home,
and with the most haste he could (for true love fears the accident of
15 an instant) to match the excusing of his fault with accomplishment
of his errand thither. And therefore (blown up and down with as
many contrary passions as Aeolus sent out winds upon the Trojan
relics guided upon the sea by the valiant Aeneas) he went into her
chamber; and with such a pace as reverent fear doth teach he came
20 to her bed side, where kneeling down, and having prepared a long
oration for her, his eyes were so filled with her sight that, as if they
would have robbed all their fellows of their services, both his heart
fainted and his tongue failed, in such sort that he could not bring
forth one word, but referred her understanding to his eyes' language.
25 But she in extremity amazed to see him there at so undue a season,
and ashamed that her beautiful body made so naked a prospect,
drawing in her delicate limbs into the weak guard of the bed, and
presenting in her face to him such a kind of pitiful anger as might
show this was only a fault, therefore, because she had a former
30 grudge unto him, turning away her face from him, she thus said
unto him:
'O Cleophila or Pyrocles (for whether name I use it much skills
not, since by the one I was first deceived, and by the other now
betrayed), what strange motion is the guide of thy cruel mind hither?
35 Dost thou not think the day torments thou hast given me sufficient,

4 hate] hath 93 (*corr.* 13).   13 own] *om.* Je, 93.   14 love] lovers Cl, As.
15 accomplishment] declaration 93.   19 and] *om.* 93.   19–20 he . . . side] *om.*
93.   21 oration] discourse 93.   27 the bed] her bed Ph, Je.   33 since] *om.*
93 (*added* 98).

but that thou dost envy me the night's quiet? Wilt thou give my sorrows no truce but, by making me see before mine eyes how much I have lost, offer me due cause of confirming my plaint? Or is thy heart so full of rancour that thou dost desire to feed thine eyes with the wretched spectacle of thine overthrown enemy, and so to satisfy 5 the full measure of thy undeserved rage with the receiving into thy sight the unrelievable ruins of my desolate life? O Pyrocles, Pyrocles, for thine own virtue's sake, let miseries be no music unto thee; and be content to take to thyself some colour of excuse, that thou didst not know to what extremity thy inconstancy, or rather false- 10 hood, hath brought me!'

Pyrocles, to whom every syllable she pronounced was a thunder-bolt to his heart, equally distracted betwixt amazement and sorrow, abashed to see such a stop of his desires, grieved with her pain, but tormented to find himself the author of it, with quaking lips and 15 pale cheer:

'Alas! divine lady,' said he, 'your displeasure is so contrary to my desert, and your words so far from all expectation, that I have least ability now I have most need to speak in the cause upon which my life dependeth. For my troth is so undoubtedly constant unto you, 20 my heart is so assured a witness to itself of his unspotted faith, that having no one thing in me whereout any such sacrilege might arise, I have likewise nothing in so direct a thing to say for myself but sincere and vehement protestations. For, in truth, there may most words be spent where there is some probability to breed of both 25 sides conjectural allegations; but in so perfect a thing as my love is of you, as it suffers no question so it seems to receive injury by any addition of words unto it. If my soul could have been polluted with treachery, it would likewise have provided for itself due furniture of colourable answers; but as it stood upon the naked confidence of his 30 untouched duty, so I must confess it is altogether unarmed against so unjust a violence as you lay upon me. Alas, let not the pains I

2 sorrows] sorrow Bo, As.   3 plaint] complaint Cl (complaint *corr. to* plaint Da); plaints Je, Hm.   4 thine] thy Bo, Ph.   5 thine Bo, Cl, Je, Hm, 93: thy St, As, Da, Ph.   6 with the receiving] with receiving Da, Je.   7 ruins OA, 93: raynes St.   8 thine Cl, As, Hm, 93: thy St, Bo, Da, Ph, Je.   13 dis-tracted] distraught 93.   14 stop] scope Ph; spot Je, Hm.   18 from] beyond 93. expectation] expectations As, 93.   22 whereout] whereunto Da; whence Je. 23 likewise nothing] nothing likewise Cl, Je.   25 of] on Cl, Ph, Je.   26 in] *om.* Cl, 93.   27 of] in Cl; to Je; towards Hm. any] *om.* As, 93.   28 words] any words 93.   30 stood] should 93 (*corr.* 13).   confidence] conscience Hm, 93.

have taken to serve you be now accounted injurious unto you! Let
not the dangerous cunning I have used to please you be deemed a
treason against you! Since I have deceived them whom you fear for
your sake, do not you destroy me for their sake. What can my words
5 further express? I have rid them both out of the house. There is
none here to be either hinderers or knowers of the perfecting the
mutual love which once my love wrought in you towards me, but
only the almighty powers, whom I invoke to be the triers of my
innocency. And if ever my thoughts did receive so much as a
10 fainting in their true affection; if they have not continually, with
more and more ardour, from time to time pursued the possession
of your sweetest favour; if ever in that profession they received
either spot or falsehood, then let their most horrible plagues fall
upon me; let mine eyes be deprived of the light, which did abuse the
15 heavenly beams that strake them; let my falsified tongue serve to no
use but to bemoan mine own wretchedness; let my heart empoisoned
with detestable treason be the seat of infernal sorrow; let my soul
with the endless anguish of his conscience become his own
tormentor!'

20 'O false mankind!' cried out the sweet Philoclea, 'how can an
impostumed heart but yield forth evil matter by his mouth? Are
oaths there to be believed where vows are broken? No, no! Who
doth wound the eternal justice of the gods cares little for the
abusing their name; and who, in doing wickedly, doth not fear due
25 recompensing plagues, doth little fear that invoking of plagues will
make them come ever a whit the sooner. But alas! What aileth this
new conversion? Have you yet another sleight to play; or do
you think to deceive me in Pyrocles' form, as you have done in
Cleophila's? Or rather, now you have betrayed me in both those, is
30 there some third sex left you into which you can transform yourself,

2 cunning] coming Cl; means Ph.   please] pleasure 93 (*corr.* 98).   4–9 my
words . . . innocency] I without you further do? Or to what more forwardness
can our counsel bring our desired happiness? I have provided whatsoever is needful
for our going. I have rid them both out of the lodge, so that there is none here to be
hinderers or knowers of our departure, but only the almighty powers, whom I invoke
as triers of mine innocency and witnesses of my well meaning 93.   10 true
affection] affections 93.   12 profession] possession 93.   13 falsehood 93:
fellowship OA; friendship Hm.   14 the light] their light Cl, Da, Ph.   abuse] abase
Cl, 93.   15 strake] strick Cl; strook Ph.   16 bemoan] be more 93 (*corr.* 98).   mine]
my Bo, Da, Hm (Ph *omits* mine own).   23 for the] for Je, 93/(doth . . . wickedly
om. Cl).   24 abusing their] abusing of their As, Hm.   name] names 93.
25 that] the Cl, As, Da, Ph, Je, Hm, 93.   27 conversion] conversation As, 93
(*corr.* 13).   29 those] these Je, Hm; *om.* 93.   30 there] *om.* 93.

to inveigle my simplicity? Enjoy, enjoy the conquests you have already won, and assure yourself you are come to the furthest point of your cunning! For my part, unkind Pyrocles, my only defence shall be belief of nothing; my comfort, my faithful innocency; and the punishment I desire of you shall be your own conscience.'   5

Philoclea's hard persevering in this unjust condemnation of him did so overthrow all the might of Pyrocles' mind (who saw that time would not serve to make proof by deeds, and that the better words he used, the more they were suspected of deceitful cunning) that, void of all counsel and deprived of all comfort, finding best deserts 10 punished and nearest hopes prevented, he did abandon the succour of himself, and suffered grief so to close his heart that his breath failing him, with a deathful shutting of his eyes, he fell down by her bedside, having had time to say no more but 'Oh, whom dost thou kill, Philoclea?'   15

She that little looked for such an extreme event of her doings, starting out of her bed like Venus rising from her mother the sea, not so much stricken down with amazement and grief of her fault as lifted up with the force of love and desire to help, she laid her fair body over his breast; and throwing no other water in his face but 20 the stream of her tears, nor giving him other blows but the kisses of her well formed mouth, her only cries were these lamentations:

'O unfortunate suspicions,' said she, 'the very mean to lose that we most suspect to lose! O unkind kindness of mine which returns an imagined wrong with an effectual injury! O folly to make 25 quarrels my supplications, or to use hate as the mediator of love! Childish Philoclea, hast thou thrown away the jewel wherein all thy pride consisted? Hast thou with too much haste overrun thyself?'

Then would she renew her kisses, and yet not finding the life return, redouble her plaints in this manner: 30

'O divine soul,' said she, 'whose virtue can possess no less than the highest place in heaven, if for my eternal plague thou hast utterly left this most sweet mansion, before I follow thee with

1 conquests] conquest Da, Je, Hm, 93.   7 so] *om*. As, Ph.   8 to make proof] to prove 93.   13 by] at 93.   16 little looked] looked As, Hm; looked little Ph.   17 starting] startling Ph; start 93.   21 him other] him no other Cl, Ph.   kissess] kissing Je, 93.   23 suspicions] suspicion Da, Je, Hm, 93.   24 most] must Bo; *om*. Ph.   mine] me Bo; mind As, Je.   returns] turns Cl, As.   25 O folly] fully Je; folly Hm; O fool 93.   26 quarrels . . . supplications] quarrel . . . supplication 93.   27 Childish] O childish Ph, Je, Hm.   hast] had 93 (*corr*. 98).   28 overrun] run over As; overthrown Je.   29 and yet not OA: and not St; O yet not 93 (*corr*. 98).   32 my] mine 93.

Thisbe's punishment of my rash unwariness, hear this true protesta-
tion of mine: that, as the wrong I have done thee proceeded of a
most sincere but unresistible affection, so led with this pitiful
example it shall end in the mortal hate of myself; and if it may be,
5 I will make my soul a tomb of thy memory!'
    But as she was rising, perchance to have begun some such

1 punishment of] punishment for 93.   true] *om.* 93.   2 proceeded] proceed As;
om. Je.   6 But as she . . . *to end of Book III*] 93 *substitutes*:
    At that word, with anguish of mind and weakness of body increased one by the other,
10 and both augmented by this fearful accident, she had fallen down in a swoon, but that
Pyrocles then first severing his eyelids, and quickly apprehending her danger (to him
more than death), beyond all powers striving to recover the commandment of all his
powers, stayed her from falling; and then, lifting the sweet burden of her body in his
arms, laid her again in her bed. So that she, but then the physician, was now become
15 the patient; and he, to whom her weakness had been serviceable, was now enforced
to do service to her weakness—which performed by him with that hearty care which
the most careful love on the best loved subject in greatest extremity could employ, pre-
vailed so far that ere long she was able (though in strength exceedingly dejected) to call
home her wandering senses to yield attention to that her beloved Pyrocles had to deliver.
20 But he, lying down on the bed by her, holding her hand in his, with so kind an accusing
her of unkindness as in accusing her he condemned himself, began from point to point
to discover unto her all that had passed between his loathed lovers and him: how he had
entertained, and by entertaining deceived, both Basilius and Gynecia; and that with
such a kind of deceit as either might see the cause in the other, but neither espy the
25 effect in themselves; that all his favours to them had tended only to make them strangers
to this his action, and all his strangeness to her to the final obtaining of her long pro-
mised, and now to be performed, favour—which device, seeing it had so well succeeded
to the removing all other hindrances, that only her resolution remained for the taking
their happy journey, he conjured her by all the love she had ever borne him she would
30 make no longer delay to partake with him whatsoever honours the noble kingdom of
Macedon, and all other Euarchus's dominions might yield him, especially since in this
enterprise he had now waded so far as he could not possibly retire himself back without
being overwhelmed with danger and dishonour. He needed not have used further argu-
ments of persuasion, for that only conjuration had so forcibly bound all her spirits that,
35 could her body have seconded her mind, or her mind have strengthened her body,
without respect of any worldly thing, but only fear to be again unkind to Pyrocles, she
condescended to go with him. But raising herself a little in her bed, and finding her own
unability in any sort to endure the air:
    'My Pyrocles,' said she (with tearful eyes and a pitiful countenance, such as well
40 witnessed she had no will to deny anything she had power to perform), 'if you can con-
vey me hence in such plight as you see me, I am most willing to make my extremest
danger a testimony that I esteem no danger in regard of your virtuous satisfaction.'
    But she fainted so fast that she was not able to utter the rest of her conceived speech—
which also turned Pyrocles' thoughts from expecting further answer to the necessary
45 care of reviving her in whose fainting himself was more than overthrown. And that
having effected with all the sweet means his wits could devise, though his highest hopes
were by this unexpected downfall sunk deeper than any degree of despair, yet, lest the
appearance of his inward grief might occasion her further discomfort, having racked

33–4 arguments of] *om.* 98.   43 But she 98: But if she 93.

enterprise, Pyrocles, severing his eyelids, and having for his first object her beloved beauty (which wrought in him not unlike to those who, lying abroad, are summoned by the morning sun to pay the tribute of their sight to his rising fairness), he was almost in as much danger of having his spirits again overpressed with this too excessive 5 joy; but that she, finding him alive, and forgetting natural bashfulness for the late fear of his loss, with her dear embracements added strength to his life. So that, coming again to the use of his feet, and lifting the sweet burden of Philoclea in his arms, he laid her on her

1 severing] serving As; fearing Da. 3 summoned] so moved Cl; soon moved As, Je (lying . . . tribute *om.* Ph). 9 on] in Je, Hm.

---

his face to a more comfortable semblance, he sought some show of reason to show she 10 had no reason, either for him, or for herself, so to be afflicted. Which in the sweet-minded Philoclea, whose consideration was limited by his words, and whose conceit pierced no deeper than his outward countenance, wrought within a while such quietness of mind, and that quietness again such repose of body, that sleep by his harbingers (weakness, weariness, and watchfulness) had quickly taken up his lodging in all her 15 senses. Then, indeed, had Pyrocles leisure to sit in judgement on himself, and to hear his reason accuse his rashness; who, without forecast of doubt, without knowledge of his friend, without acquainting Philoclea with his purpose or being made acquainted with her present estate, had fallen headlong into that attempt, the success whereof he had long since set down to himself as the measure of all his other fortunes. But calling 20 to mind how weakly they do that rather find fault with what cannot be amended than seek to amend wherein they have been faulty, he soon turned him from remembering what might have been done to considering what was now to be done; and when that consideration failed, what was now to be expected. Wherein having run over all the thoughts his reason, called to the strictest accounts, could bring before him, at length 25 he lighted on this: that as long as Gynecia bewrayed not the matter (which he thought she would not do, as well for her own honour and safety as for the hope she might still have of him, which is loath to die in a lover's heart), all the rest might turn to a pretty merriment, and inflame his lover Basilius again to cast about for the missed favour. And as naturally the heart stuffed up with woefulness is glad greedily to suck the thinnest 30 air of comfort, so did he, at the first, embrace this conceit as offering great hope, if not assurance, of well doing. Till looking more nearly into it, and not able to answer the doubts and difficulties he saw therein more and more arising, the night being also far spent, his thoughts even weary of their own burdens, fell to a straying kind of uncertainty; and his mind, standing only upon the nature of inward intelligences, left his 35 body to give a sleeping respite to his vital spirits, which he, according to the quality of sorrow, received with greater greediness than ever in his life before—according to the nature of sorrow, I say, which is past care's remedy. For care, stirring the brains and making thin the spirits, breaketh rest; but those griefs wherein one is determined there is no preventing do breed a dull heaviness which easily clothes itself in sleep. So as, 40 laid down so near the beauty of the world, Philoclea, that their necks were subject each to other's chaste embracements, it seemed love had come thither to lay a plot in that picture of death how gladly, if death came, their souls would go together.

---

31 at the first] at first 98.   34 their] his 98.

bed again, having so free scope of his serviceable sight that there
came into his mind a song the shepherd Philisides had in his
hearing sung of the beauties of his unkind mistress, which in
Pyrocles' judgement was fully accomplished in Philoclea. The song
5 was this:

What tongue can her perfections tell
In whose each part all pens may dwell?
Her hair fine threads of finest gold
In curled knots man's thought to hold;
10 But that her forehead says, 'in me
A whiter beauty you may see.'
Whiter indeed; more white than snow
Which on cold winter's face doth grow.
That doth present those even brows,
15 Whose equal lines their angles bows,
Like to the moon when after change
Her horned head abroad doth range;
And arches be to heav'nly lids,
Whose wink each bold attempt forbids.
20 For the black stars those spheres contain,
The matchless pair, e'en praise doth stain.
No lamp whose light by art is got,
No sun which shines, and seeth not,
Can liken them without all peer,
25 Save one as much as other clear;
Which only thus unhappy be
Because themselves they cannot see.
Her cheeks with kindly claret spread,
Aurora-like new out of bed,
30 Or like the fresh queen-apple's side,
Blushing at sight of Phoebus' pride.

6–p. 242, 28 *The poem is in* Dd; *it is transferred to Book II in* 90–93; *the first eight
lines are in* Cm, *and the last three in* Eg.   6 perfections] perfection As, Hm, 13.
8 threads of finest] laces made of Cl, Le, As, Da, Ph, Je, Hm; locks made of Cm.
9 thought] thoughts Bo, Le, Da, Je, Hm, Dd.   10 says] says *corr. to* said Bo;
sures Je; said Cm.   14 those] these Bo, Je, Hm.   even Dd, 90: eben *corr. to* even
St; eboene Bo; pretty Cl, Le, As, Da, Ph, Je, Hm.   15 lines] line Je, Hm, 90.
17 head abroad] face in heav'n Cl, Le, As, Da, Ph, Je, Hm.   18 heav'nly] those
fair Cl, Le, As, Da, Ph; these fair Je, Hm.   20 For the black] As for the Cl, Le,
As, Da, Ph, Je, Hm.   21 pair 90: praise OA, Dd.   29 *om.* Bo; Like crystal
underlaid with red Cl, Le, As, Da, Ph (*with new line added in margin*), Je, Hm.
30–1 *not in* Cl, Le, As, Da, Je, Hm; *in margin* Ph.

Her nose, her chin, pure ivory wears,
No purer than the pretty ears,
Save that therein appears some blood,
Like wine and milk that mingled stood.
In whose incirclets if you gaze   5
Your eyes may tread a lover's maze,
But with such turns the voice to stray,
No talk untaught can find the way.
The tip no jewel needs to wear;
The tip is jewel of the ear.   10
    But who those ruddy lips can miss,
Which blessed still themselves do kiss?
Rubies, cherries, and roses new,
In worth, in taste, in perfect hue,
Which never part but that they show   15
Of precious pearl the double row,
The second sweetly-fenced ward
Her heav'nly-dewed tongue to guard,
Whence never word in vain did flow.
    Fair under these doth stately grow   20
The handle of this pleasant work,
The neck, in which strange graces lurk.
Such be, I think, the sumptuous towers
Which skill doth make in princes' bowers.
    So good a say invites the eye   25
A little downward to espy
The lovely clusters of her breasts,
Of Venus' babe the wanton nests,
Like pommels round of marble clear,
Where azured veins well mixed appear,   30
With dearest tops of porphyry.
    Betwixt these two a way doth lie,

---

1 her chin, pure] and chin such Cl, Le, As, Da, Ph, Je, Hm.   2 No elephant so
perfect bears Cl, Le, As, Da, Ph, Je, Hm.   3-10 *not in* Cl, Le, As, Je, Hm;
added in margin Ph.   3 Save Bo: So St, Da, Dd, 90; but *corr. to* Save Bo; In Ph.
5 In Da, Ph, Dd, 90: On St, Bo.   you] ye Ph, 90.   7 stray] stay Da, Ph.
8 *om.* Dd.   9 needs] need Bo, Dd.   20 these] this Le, Dd.   21 pleasant]
precious 90.   24 skill] still Le, Hm, Dd.   princes'] princely Cl, Le.   25 So
good a say] So true a taste Cl, Le, As, Da, Ph, Je, Hm (true *corr. to* good Ph).   27 lovely]
lively 90.   28 babe] babb Cl; babes Da; baits Je; bait Hm.   31 dearest tops]
lickerous (lycoras Cl; lickerish As) stalks Cl, Le, As, Da, Ph (*corr. to* dearest tops),
Je, Hm.

A way more worthy beauty's fame
Than that which bears the milken name.
This leads unto the joyous field
Which only still doth lilies yield;
5   But lilies such whose native smell
The Indian odours doth excel.
Waist it is called, for it doth waste
Men's lives until it be embraced.
There may one see, and yet not see,
10   Her ribs in white well armed be,
More white than Neptune's foamy face
When struggling rocks he would embrace.
In these delights the wand'ring thought
Might of each side astray be brought,
15   But that her navel doth unite
In curious circle busy sight,
A dainty seal of virgin wax
Where nothing but impression lacks.
Her belly there glad sight doth fill,
20   Justly entitled Cupid's hill;
A hill most fit for such a master,
A spotless mine of alabaster,
Like alabaster fair and sleek,
But soft and supple, satin-like,
25   In that sweet seat the boy doth sport.
Loath, I must leave his chief resort;
For such an use the world hath gotten,
The best things still must be forgotten.
Yet never shall my song omit
30   Those thighs (for Ovid's song more fit)

2 milken] milker Je; milky 90.   3 This] These Cl, Le.   unto] into Hm, 90.
5 native] nature Le; natures As.   6 doth] do Cl, Le, Ph, Dd.   10 ribs in white]
tender ribs Cl, Le, As, Da, Ph, Je; tender tender ribs Hm.   well] all 90.   11-12 Cl,
Le, As, Da, Ph, Hm *read*:

    Like whitest stone in silver brook   stone] snow Cl.
    Fair through fair strikes of heedful look.   of] *om.* Le, As, Da, Ph.
Da, *also has St–Bo lines in its margin, prefixed by* alius. *The leaf containing these lines in* Je
is missing, but the catchword for line 11 is like.   13-28 *om.* As; Je *has these lines
in its margin.*   13–p. 241, 4 *om.* Hm.   13 these] those 90.   19–p. 241, 6 *om.,
apart from some initial word in the margin* Ph.   19 Her] The Bo, Cl, Je.   there]
then 90 (*corr.* 98).   25-6 *om.* Cl.   27 an] a 90.   29 Je *is missing from
here.*   30 Those thighs] Her thighs Ph (*margin*), 93; Thighs 90.

Which, flanked with two sugared flanks,
Lift up their stately swelling banks
That Albion cliffs in whiteness pass,
With haunches smooth as looking glass.
    But bow all knees, now of her knees   5
My tongue doth tell what fancy sees:
The knots of joy, the gems of love,
Whose motion makes all graces move;
Whose bought incaved doth yield such sight,
Like cunning painter shadowing white.   10
The gart'ring place with childlike sign
Shows easy print in metal fine.
    But there again the flesh doth rise
In her brave calves like crystal skies,
Whose Atlas is a smallest small,   15
More white than whitest bone of whale.
    There oft steals out that round clean foot,
This noble cedar's precious root;
In show and scent pale violets,
Whose step on earth all beauty sets.   20
    But back unto her back, my muse,
Where Leda's swan his feathers mews,
Along whose ridge such bones are met,
Like comfits round in marchpane set.
    Her shoulders be like two white doves,   25
Perching within square royal rooves,
Which leaded are with silver skin,
Passing the hate-spot ermelin.
    And thence those arms derived are;

---

7 gems] Gynnes Cl; iemes Le, Dd; Jinnes Ph; Ieames Hm.   9 incaved] en-
chained Cl; engraved As.   sight] light As, Hm.   10 painter] painters Cl, Le, Hm.
13 there] then 90.   14 crystal] morning Cl, Le, As, Da, Ph (*altered to* crystal),
Hm.   15 Whose Atlas is a] That limits have in Cl, Le, As, Da, Hm; That limits
have on Ph.   16 Whose even descent makes equal fall Cl, Le, As, Da, Ph (*with
St–Bo version also in margin*), Hm.   whale] all 90.   17 There oft] Thereof As,
Dd; Thereout 90.   22 Leda's] lo as Da; *blank left* Ph.   mews] muse Bo, Le,
As, Da; *om.* Cl, Ph.   26 within] upon Cl, Le, As, Da, Hm (upon *corr. to* within Ph).
27–8 Cl, Le, As, Da, Ph, Hm *read*:

Whose gentle rays such lustre find,
Like thinnest lawn with tinsel lined.   lawn] lawns Le.   tinsel] twysell As.

28 hate-spot Bo, Dd, 93: hate-sport St, 90.

The phoenix' wings be not so rare
For faultless length and stainless hue.
   Ah, woe is me, my woes renew!
Now course doth lead me to her hand,
5   Of my first love the fatal band,
Where whiteness doth for ever sit;
Nature herself enamelled it.
For there with strange compact doth lie
Warm snow, moist pearl, soft ivory.
10   There fall those sapphire-coloured brooks,
Which conduit-like, with curious crooks,
Sweet islands make in that sweet land.
As for the fingers of the hand,
The bloody shafts of Cupid's war,
15   With amethysts they headed are.
   Thus hath each part his beauty's part;
But how the Graces do impart
To all her limbs a special grace,
Becoming every time and place,
20   Which doth e'en beauty beautify,
And most bewitch the wretched eye!
How all this is but a fair inn
Of fairer guest which dwells within,
Of whose high praise, and praiseful bliss,
25   Goodness the pen, heav'n paper is;
The ink immortal fame doth lend.
As I began, so must I end:
   No tongue can her perfections tell,
   In whose each part all pens may dwell.

30   But do not think, fair ladies, his thoughts had such leisure as to
run over so long a ditty; the only general fancy of it came into his
mind, fixed upon the sense of that sweet subject. Where, using the
benefit of the time, and fortifying himself with the confessing her
late fault (to make her now the sooner yield to penance), turning the
35   passed griefs and unkindness to the excess of all kind joys (as

1 be] are As, Da, 90.   7 herself] itself Ph, Hm.   8 doth] do Le, Ph, Hm.
11 with] *om.* Bo, Dd.   12 make] makes Cl, Le, As.   13 the hand] that hand
As, Dd.   18 a special] especial Cl, Ph.   23 guest] guests Bo, Hm, 90.   dwells]
dwell Bo, Da, Ph, 90.   within] therein Cl, 13.   28 perfections] perfection As, Eg.
29 pens] tongues 90.   32 sense] senses As; sente Ph.   that] the Cl, As, Hm.
33 the time] her time Ph; his time Hm.

passion is apt to slide into his contrary), beginning now to envy
Argus's thousand eyes, and Briareus's hundred hands, fighting
against a weak resistance, which did strive to be overcome, he gives
me occasion to leave him in so happy a plight, lest my pen might
seem to grudge at the due bliss of these poor lovers whose loyalty 5
had but small respite of their fiery agonies. And now Lalus's pipe
doth come to my hearing, which invites me to his marriage that in
this season was celebrated between him and the handsome Kala
whom long he had loved; which, I hope your ears, fair ladies, be not
so full of great matters that you will disdain to hear.   10

The end of the third book.

1 his] all Cl; the As.   4 might] should Da, Hm.   7 my] *om.* Bo, Da, Ph,
Hm.   11 Here ends the third book or act Cl.

LALUS, not with many painted words, nor false-hearted promises, had won the consent of his beloved Kala, but with a true and simple making her know he loved her; not forcing himself beyond his reach
5 to buy her affection, but giving her such pretty presents as neither could weary him with the giving nor shame her for the taking. Thus the first strawberries he could find were ever in a clean washed dish sent to Kala. Thus posies of the spring flowers were wrapped up in a little green silk and dedicated to Kala's breasts. Thus sometimes
10 his sweetest cream, sometimes the best cake-bread his mother made, were reserved for Kala's taste. Neither would he stick to kill a lamb when she would be content to come over the way unto him. But then lo, how the house was swept, and rather no fire than any smoke left to trouble her. Then love songs were not dainty, when she would
15 hear them, and as much mannerly silence when she would not. In going to church, great worship to Kala, so that all the parish said never a maid they knew so well waited on; and when dancing was about the maypole, nobody taken out but she, and he after a leap or two to show her his own activity, would frame all the rest of his
20 dancing only to grace her. As for her father's sheep, he had no less care of them than his own; so that she might play her as she would, warranted with honest Lalus's carefulness. But if he spied Kala favoured any one of the flock more than his fellows, then that was cherished, shearing him so (when shorn he must be) as might
25 most become him; but while the wool was on, wrapping within it some verses (wherein Lalus had a special gift), and making the innocent beast his unwitting messenger. Thus constantly continuing, though he were none of the fairest, at length he wan Kala's heart, the honestest wench in all those quarters. And so, with consent
30 of both parents (without which neither Lalus would ask nor Kala grant), their marriage day was appointed; which, because it fell out in this time, I think it shall not be impertinent to remember a little our shepherds while the other greater persons are either sleeping or

---

1 om. Bo, Ph.　　2 Lalus] Thyrsis 93 (*and throughout*).　　false-hearted] falsified As, Da, 93.　　6 for] with Cl, Ph.　　14 left to] to Bo, Cl; should Hm. 19 show her his own As, Hm, 93: show his own St, Bo, Da, Ph; show her his Cl. 20 father's OA, 93: father St.　　23 favoured] favouring Cl; favour Hm. 25 within] in Ph, Hm.　　31 marriage] marring 93.

otherwise occupied. Lalus's marriage time once known, there needed
no inviting of the neighbours in that valley; for so well was Lalus
beloved that they were all ready to do him credit. Neither yet came
they like harpies to devour him, but one brought a fat pig, the other
a tender kid, a third a great goose; as for cheese, milk and butter 5
were the gossips' presents. Thither came of stranger shepherds only
the melancholy Philisides; for the virtuous Coredens had long since
left off all joyful solemnities, and as for Strephon and Klaius, they
had lost their mistress, which put them into such extreme sorrows
as they could scarcely abide the light of the day, much less the eyes 10
of men. But of the Arcadian-born shepherds, thither came good old
Geron, young Histor (though unwilling), and upright Dicus, merry
Pas, and jolly Nico; as for Dametas, they durst not presume, his
pride was such, to invite him; and Dorus they found might not be
spared. And there under a bower was made of boughs (for Lalus's 15
house was not able to receive them), they were entertained with
hearty welcome, and every one placed according to his age. The
women (for such was the manner of that country) kept together to
make good cheer among themselves, from which otherwise a certain
painful modesty restrains them. And there might the sadder matrons 20
give good counsel to Kala who, poor soul, wept for fear of that she
desired. But among the shepherds was all honest liberty; no fear of
dangerous telltales (who hunt greater preys), nor indeed minds in
them to give telltales any occasion, but one questioning with another
of the manuring his ground, and governing his flock. The highest 25
point they reached to was to talk of the holiness of marriage; to which
purpose, as soon as their sober dinner was ended, Dicus instead of
thanks sang this song with a clear voice and cheerful countenance:

> Let mother earth now deck herself in flowers,
> To see her offspring seek a good increase,   30
> Where justest love doth vanquish Cupid's powers
> And war of thoughts is swallowed up in peace
> Which never may decrease,

---

1 occupied] troubled 93.   time] *om.* Cl, Ph.   4 one brought] on bought 93 (*corr.*
98).   6 stranger] strangers Cl, As; strange Ph, Hm, 93.   7 Coredens]
Coridon 93.   8 all joyful] all his joyful As, Da, 93 (*corr.* 98).   16–17 they . . .
and] *om.* 93.   18 that] the As, 93; their Ph.   19 otherwise] otherwhiles Cl;
there was Hm.   25 manuring his] manuring of his Cl, As, Ph; manuring of their
Hm.   29–p. 248, 27 *The poem is in* 93.   29 in] with Bo, Le.   31 justest]
justice Le, As; instead Da; simple Ph.   32 war] wear Da; ware 93.

But like the turtles fair
Live one in two, a well united pair,
Which, that no chance may stain,
O Hymen long their coupled joys maintain.

5   O heav'n awake, show forth thy stately face;
Let not these slumb'ring clouds thy beauties hide,
But with thy cheerful presence help to grace
The honest bridegroom and the bashful bride,
       Whose loves may ever bide,
10   Like to the elm and vine,
With mutual embracements them to twine;
       In which delightful pain,
O Hymen long their coupled joys maintain.

Ye muses all which chaste affects allow,
15   And have to Lalus showed your secret skill,
To this chaste love your sacred favours bow,
And so to him and her your gifts distil,
       That they all vice may kill;
       And like to lilies pure
20   Do please all eyes, and spotless do endure;
       Where, that all bliss may reign,
O Hymen long their coupled joys maintain.

Ye nymphs in which the waters empire have,
Since Lalus' music oft doth yield you praise,
25   Grant to the thing which we for Lalus crave:
Let one time (but long first) close up their days,
       One grave their bodies seize,
       And like two rivers sweet
When they, though diverse, do together meet,
30   One stream both streams contain;
O Hymen long their coupled joys maintain.

Pan, father Pan, the god of silly sheep,
Whose care is cause that they in number grow,

19 to] as Cl; *om.* Ph.   20 Do . . . do] May . . . may 93.   23 empire] empires
Cl, As, Da; *om.* Ph.   27 Je *begins again.*   28 two] to Cl, Le. Ph, Je.
29 though] through Bo, Cl, Le; thought Da.

Have much more care of them that them do keep,
Since from these good the others' good doth flow,
   And make their issue show
   In number like the herd
   Of younglings which thyself with love hast reared,   5
   Or like the drops of rain;
   O Hymen long their coupled joys maintain.

Virtue, if not a god, yet God's chief part,
Be thou the knot of this their open vow:
That still he be her head, she be his heart,   10
He lean to her, she unto him do bow;
   Each other still allow,
   Like oak and mistletoe,
   Her strength from him, his praise from her do grow.
   In which most lovely train,   15
   O Hymen long their coupled joys maintain.

But thou foul Cupid, sire to lawless lust,
Be thou far hence with thy empoisoned dart
Which, though of glitt'ring gold, shall here take rust
Where simple love, which chasteness doth impart,   20
   Avoids thy hurtful art,
   Not needing charming skill
   Such minds with sweet affections for to fill,
   Which being pure and plain,
   O Hymen long their coupled joys maintain.   25

All churlish words, shrewd answers, crabbed looks,
All privateness, self-seeking, inward spite,
All waywardness which nothing kindly brooks,
All strife for toys, and claiming master's right,
   Be hence ay put to flight;   30
   All stirring husband's hate
   Gainst neighbours good for womanish debate
   Be fled as things most vain,
   O Hymen long their coupled joys maintain.

2 others'] other As, Ph, Je, Hm.   doth] do Bo, As, Je, Hm.   5 hast] hath
Bo, Je.   11 lean] cleave Cl, Le, Ph.   21 thy] the Cl, Le, As, Je, Hm; they
Da.

All peacock pride, and fruits of peacock's pride,
Longing to be with loss of substance gay
With recklessness what may thy house betide,
So that you may on higher slippers stay,
5   For ever hence away.
Yet let not sluttery,
The sink of filth, be counted housewifery;
But keeping wholesome mean,
O Hymen long their coupled joys maintain.

10   But above all, away vile jealousy,
The ill of ills, just cause to be unjust,
(How can he love, suspecting treachery?
How can she love where love cannot win trust?)
Go snake, hide thee in dust,
15   Ne dare once show thy face
Where open hearts do hold so constant place;
That they thy sting restrain,
O Hymen long their coupled joys maintain.

The earth is decked with flow'rs, the heav'ns displayed,
20   Muses grant gifts, nymphs long and joined life,
Pan store of babes, virtue their thoughts well stayed,
Cupid's lust gone, and gone is bitter strife,
Happy man, happy wife.
No pride shall them oppress,
25   Nor yet shall yield to loathsome sluttishness,
And jealousy is slain;
For Hymen will their coupled joys maintain.

'Truly Dicus,' said Nico, 'although thou didst not grant me the
prize the last day, when undoubtedly I wan it, yet must I needs say
30 thou for thy part hast sung well and thriftily.'

Pas straight desired all the company they would bear witness that
Nico had once in his life spoken wisely: 'For', said he, 'I will tell
it to his father, who will be a glad man when he hears such news.'

1 peacock] peacock's Cl, Da, Je, Hm.   3 recklessness] wretchlessness As; rack-
lessness Je, Hm; retchlessness 93.   thy] the Ph, Je, 13.   4 may Bo, Cl, Ph, Je,
93: main St, Hm; mean As; manie Da; om. Le.   higher] her sure Cl, Le.   16 do]
doth Da, Ph.   17 sting] string Bo; stings Le, Je.   21 thoughts] thought Le;
strength As.   33 hears] heareth Bo, Cl, Hm; hear Da.

'Very true,' said Nico, 'but, indeed, so would not thine in like case, for he would look thou shouldst live but one hour longer, that a discreet word wandered out of thy mouth.'

'And I pray thee,' said Pas, 'gentle Nico, tell me what mischance it was that brought thee to taste so fine a meat?'   5

'Marry, goodman blockhead,' said Nico, 'because he speaks against jealousy, the filthy traitor to true affection, and yet disguising itself in the raiment of love.'

'Sentences, sentences,' cried Pas, 'alas, how ripe-witted these young folks be nowadays! But well counselled shall that husband be   10 when this man comes to exhort him not to be jealous.'

'And so shall he,' answered Nico, 'for I have seen a fresh example, though it be not very fit to be known.'

'Come, come,' said Pas, 'be not so squeamish. I know thou longest more to tell it than we to hear it.'   15

But for all his words Nico would not bestow his voice till he was generally entreated of the rest; and then with a merry marriage look he sang this following discourse—for with a better grace he could sing than tell:

A neighbour mine not long ago there was   20
(But nameless he, for blameless he shall be)
That married had a trick and bonny lass
As in a summer day a man might see;
　　But he himself a foul unhandsome groom,
　　And far unfit to hold so good a room.   25

Now whether moved with self-unworthiness,
Or with her beauty, fit to make a prey,
Fell jealousy did so his brain oppress
That if he absent were but half a day,
　　He guessed the worst (you wot what is the worst)   30
　　And in himself new doubting causes nursed.

While thus he feared the silly innocent,
Who yet was good, because she knew none ill,

2 that] if Hm; than 13.   9–10 these . . . folks be] be these . . . folks
As, Da.   10 well] ill As; weak Je.   17 of the rest] of all the rest Je, Hm, 93.
20–p. 253, 14 *The poem is in* Ha *and* 93.   23 summer] summers Bo, Je, Hm, Ha.
27 with her] whether Cl, Le, Da; her fair Ph.   28 brain] brains Cl, Da, Ph, Je;
mind Ha.   30 wot] know Je, Ha.   31 doubting] doting As, Ha.   33 none]
no Bo, Da, Je, Hm, Ha (no *corr. to* none St); not Ph.

Unto his house a jolly shepherd went,
To whom our prince did bear a great goodwill,
  Because in wrestling and in pastoral
  He far did pass the rest of shepherds all.

5   And therefore he a courtier was benamed,
     And as a courtier was with cheer received
       (For they have tongues to make a poor man blamed
       If he to them his duty misconceived);
         And for this courtier should well like his table,
10   The goodman bad his wife be serviceable.

     And so she was, and all with good intent,
     But few days passed while she good manner used,
       But that her husband thought her service bent
       To such an end as he might be abused.
15   Yet, like a coward fearing stranger's pride,
         He made the simple wench his wrath abide.

     With chumpish looks, hard words, and secret nips,
     Grumbling at her when she his kindness sought,
       Asking her how she tasted courtier's lips,
20   He forced her think that which she never thought.
         In fine, it made her guess there was some sweet
         In that which he so feared that she should meet.

     When once this entered was in woman's heart,
     And that it had inflamed a new desire,
25   There rested then to play a woman's part,
         Fuel to seek and not to quench the fire;
           But (for his jealous eye she well did find)
           She studied cunning how the same to blind.

     And thus she did: one day to him she came
30   And (though against his will) on him she leaned,

---

5 was benamed] was by name Je; was he named Hm; he was named Ha.   9 well
like] like well Bo, Le.   his] this Da, Ph (this *corr. to* his Cl).   10 bad Bo, Cl,
Le, As, Da, Ph, Ha, 93: bid St; bed Je, Hm.   12 manner] manners Cl, Le, Da,
Ph, Je, Ha.   17 chumpish] clumpish Cl, Je; lumpish As; crumpish Ph, Ha.
21 it] he Je, Hm, Ha, 93.   23 entered] entry Je, Hm; kindled Ha.

And out gan cry, 'ah wellaway, for shame,
If you help not our wedlock will be stained!'
The goodman starting, asked what did her move?
She sighed, and said the bad guest sought her love.

He little looking that she should complain   5
Of that whereto he feared she was inclined,
Bussing her oft, and in his heart full fain,
He did demand what remedy to find;
    How they might get that guest from them to wend,
    And yet the prince (that loved him) not offend.   10

'Husband', quoth she, 'go to him by and by,
And tell him that you find I do him love,
And therefore pray him that of courtesy
He will absent himself, lest he should move
    A young girl's heart to that were shame for both,   15
    Whereto you know his honest heart were loath.

Thus shall you show that him you do not doubt,
And as for me, sweet husband, I must bear.'
Glad was the man when he had heard her out;
And did the same, although with mickle fear.   20
    For fear he did lest he the young man might
    In choler put, with whom he would not fight.

The courtly shepherd much aghast at this,
Not seeing erst such token in the wife,
Though full of scorn, would not his duty miss,   25
Knowing that ill becomes a household strife,
    Did go his way, but sojourned near thereby,
    That yet the ground hereof he might espy.

The wife thus having settled husband's brain
(Who would have sworn his spouse Diana was),   30
Watched when she a further point might gain;
Which little time did fitly bring to pass.
    For to the court her man was called by name,
    Whither he needs must go for fear of blame.

7 Bussing OA, Ha, 93: Busshing St.   12 that you] you do Ha, 93.   16 his]
this Cl; his *corr. to* an Ph; an Ha.   heart] mind Ph, Ha.   24 token] tokens As,
Ha.   28 hereof] thereof Bo, Cl, Je, Ha.

Three days before that he must sure depart,
She written had (but in a hand disguised)
A letter such which might from either part
Seem to proceed, so well it was devised.
    She sealed it first, then she the sealing brake,
    And to her jealous husband did it take.

With weeping eyes (her eyes she taught to weep)
She told him that the courtier had it sent:
'Alas', quoth she, 'thus women's shame doth creep.'
The goodman read on both sides the content;
    It title had: *Unto my only love.*
    Subscription was: *Yours most, if you will prove.*

The pistle self, such kind of words it had:
'My sweetest joy, the comfort of my sprite,
So may thy flocks increase, thy dear heart glad,
So may each thing e'en as thou wishest light,
    As thou wilt deign to read, and gently read,
    This mourning ink in which my heart doth bleed.

Long have I loved (alas, thou worthy art),
Long have I loved (alas, love craveth love),
Long have I loved thyself; alas, my heart
Doth break now tongue unto thy name doth move;
    And think not that thy answer answer is,
    But that it is my doom of bale or bliss.

The jealous wretch must now to court be gone;
Ne can he fail, for prince hath for him sent;
Now is the time we may be here alone,
And give a long desire a sweet content.
    Thus shall you both reward a lover true,
    And eke revenge his wrong suspecting you.'

And this was all, and this the husband read
With chafe enough, till she him pacified,
Desiring that no grief in him he bred
Now that he had her words so truly tried;

5
10
15
20
25
30

But that he would to him the letter show,
That with his fault he might her goodness know.

That straight was done, with many a boistrous threat
That to the duke he would his sin declare;
But now the courtier gan to smell the feat,   5
And with some words which showed little care,
 He stayed until the goodman was departed,
 Then gave he him the blow which never smarted.

Thus may you see the jealous wretch was made
The pander of the thing he most did fear.   10
Take heed, therefore, how you ensue that trade,
Lest that some marks of jealousy you bear;
 For sure no jealousy can that prevent
 Whereto two parties once be full content.

'Behold,' said Pas, 'a whole dicker of wit! He hath picked out such 15
a tale, with intention to keep a husband from jealousy, which were
enough to make a sanctified husband jealous, to see subtleties so
much in the feminine gender. But', said he, 'I will strike Nico dead
with the wise words shall flow out of my gorge'; and without further
entreaty thus sang: 20

Who doth desire that chaste his wife should be,
First be he true, for truth doth truth deserve.
Then such be he, as she his worth may see;
And one man still, credit with her preserve.

Not toying kind, nor causelessly unkind,   25
Not stirring thoughts, nor yet denying right,
Not spying faults, nor in plain errors blind;
Never hard hand, nor ever reins too light.

As far from want, as far from vain expense
(The one doth force, the latter doth entice);   30

1 he] she Cl, Da, Je.   2 fault] shame Ph, Ha.   4 duke] duke *corr. to* prince
Ph; king Ha, 93.   8 which] that Bo, Ha.   12 that some] that same As; you
like Ha; the same 93.   17 subtleties] subtleness As; subtlety Ph, Je.   19 shall]
that Cl, Ph, Hm.   20 thus sang] this song As; song this Je.   21–p. 254, 4
The poem is in Hn *and* 93.   25 causelessly] yet causeless As, Da.   28 ever]
never Cl, Le.   30 latter As, Ph, Je, Hm: later St, Cl, Le (latter *corr. to* later Da),
93 (*corr.* 98); tother Hn.

Allow good company, but keep from thence
All filthy mouths that glory in their vice.
This done, thou hast no more, but leave the rest
To virtue, fortune, time, and woman's breast.

5 'Well concluded', said Nico, 'when he hath done all, he leaves the
matter to his wife's discretion. Now whensoever thou marriest, let
her discretion deck thy head with Actaeon's ornament!'

Pas was so angry with his wish (being indeed towards marriage)
that they might perchance have fallen to buffets, but that Dicus
10 (who knew it more wisdom to let a fray than part a fray) desired
Philisides (who as a stranger sat among them, revolving in his mind
all the tempests of evil fortunes he had passed) that he would do so
much grace to the company as to sing one of his country songs.
Philisides knew it no good manners to be squeamish of his cunning,
15 having put himself in their company, and yet loath either in time
of marriage to sing his sorrows, more fit for funerals, or by any
outward matter to be drawn to such mirth as to betray (as it were)
that passion to which he had given over himself, he took a mean way
betwixt both and sang this song he had learned before he had ever
20 subjected his thoughts to acknowledge no master but a mistress:

As I my little flock on Ister bank
(A little flock, but well my pipe they couthe)
Did piping lead, the sun already sank
Beyond our world, and ere I gat my booth
25 Each thing with mantle black the night did soothe,
Saving the glow-worm, which would courteous be
Of that small light oft watching shepherds see.

3 This] Thus Cl, Da, Ph.   9 to] out into As; unto Da.   9–10 (who . . . fray)]
om. 93.   10 it more] it was more Cl, As, Da.   14 knew] knowing 93. cunning]
coming 93 (corr. 13).   15–19 and yet loath . . . and sang] 93 substitutes: without
further study began to utter that wherewith his thoughts were then (as always) most
busied; and to show what a stranger he was to himself spake of himself as of a third
person in this sort:
[Here follows 'The lad Philisides' (Ringler, OP 5)]
The whole company would gladly have taken this occasion of requesting Philisides in
plainer sort to discover unto them his estate. Which he willing to prevent (as knowing
the relation thereof more fit for funerals than the time of a marriage), began to sing
16–17 any outward matter OA: any other outward manner St; any inward matter Je.
18 a] om. Da, Je, Hm.   19 betwixt] between Cl, As, Da.   21–p. 259, 23 90
transferred the poem to the First Eclogues; 93 restored it to the Third Eclogues.
22 they] the Ph, 93 (corr. 13).   24 gat Bo, Cl, Le: got St, As, Da, Ph, Je, Hm,
90.   25 did OA: doth St. 90.   soothe OA: scothe St, 90.

The welkin had full niggardly enclosed
In coffer of dim clouds his silver groats,
Ycleped stars; each thing to rest disposed:
The caves were full, the mountains void of goats;
The birds' eyes closed, closed their chirping notes.   5
   As for the nightingale, wood-music's king,
   It August was, he deigned not then to sing.

Amid my sheep, though I saw naught to fear,
Yet (for I nothing saw) I feared sore;
Then found I which thing is a charge to bear,   10
For for my sheep I dreaded mickle more
Than ever for myself since I was bore.
   I sat me down, for see to go ne could,
   And sang unto my sheep lest stray they should.

The song I sang old Languet had me taught,   15
Languet, the shepherd best swift Ister knew,
For clerkly rede, and hating what is naught,
For faithful heart, clean hands, and mouth as true.
With his sweet skill my skill-less youth he drew
   To have a feeling taste of him that sits   20
   Beyond the heav'n, far more beyond our wits.

He said the music best thilke powers pleased
Was jump concord between our wit and will,
Where highest notes to godliness are raised,
And lowest sink not down to jot of ill.   25
With old true tales he wont mine ears to fill:
   How shepherds did of yore, how now, they thrive,
   Spoiling their flock, or while twixt them they strive.

   He liked me, but pitied lustful youth.
   His good strong staff my slipp'ry years upbore.   30

2 dim] dimmy Ph; divine Je, Hm.   3 Ycleped] Yeeldeped As; Eclipsed Je, Hm.
5 closed, closed] closed, closed up Cl; closed, did close As, Da; closed Ph, Je.
7 deigned] cared As; dared Ph.   10 found OA, 93: fond St, 90.   11 For] *om.*
Da; Far Ph; As 90.   dreaded Bo, Cl, As, Da, Ph, Je, Hm: dradded St, Le, 90 (feared
corr. to dreaded Cl).   see] so Cl, Le, Da.   15 *and* 16 Languet] Lanquet 90.
17 is] was As, Da.   21 our] your 90 (*corr.* 13).   26 mine] my Bo, Cl, Le.

He still hoped well, because I loved truth;
Till forced to part, with heart and eyes e'en sore,
To worthy Coredens he gave me o'er.
    But thus in oak's true shade recounted he
5   Which now in night's deep shade sheep heard of me.

Such manner time there was (what time I not)
When all this earth, this dam or mould of ours,
Was only woned with such as beasts begot;
Unknown as then were they that builden towers.
10 The cattle, wild or tame, in nature's bowers
    Might freely roam or rest, as seemed them;
    Man was not man their dwellings in to hem.

The beasts had sure some beastly policy;
For nothing can endure where order nis.
15 For once the lion by the lamb did lie;
The fearful hind the leopard did kiss;
Hurtless was tiger's paw and serpent's hiss.
    This think I well: the beasts with courage clad
    Like senators a harmless empire had.

20 At which, whether the others did repine
(For envy harb'reth most in feeblest hearts),
Or that they all to changing did incline
(As e'en in beasts their dams leave changing parts),
The multitude to Jove a suit imparts,
25   With neighing, bleaing, braying, and barking,
    Roaring, and howling, for to have a king.

A king in language theirs they said they would
(For then their language was a perfect speech).
The birds likewise with chirps and pewing could,
30 Cackling and chatt'ring, that of Jove beseech.
Only the owl still warned them not to seech
    So hastily that which they would repent;
    But saw they would, and he to deserts went.

1 I] *om.* Ph; he 90.   2 heart Cl, Le, As, Da, Je, Hm, 90: hearts St, Bo, Ph. 3 Coredens] Coridens Ph; Corydens Je, Hm; Coriden 90.   4 thus] this As, Da, Ph, Je, Hm.   he Bo, Cl, Le, As, Da, Je, 90: be St, Ph, Hm.   8 woned] woved Ph; wened Je, Hm.   9 as then were they] were they as then Bo, Le.   builden] builded Bo, Le, Ph, Je, Hm, 90.   11 roam] run Cl, As, Hm.   12 in to Bo, Cl, Le, Da, Je, 90: into St, Hm, 93; even to As; had not Ph.   14 nis] miss As, Da, Ph, Je, Hm.   29 pewing] pying Cl; pining Le, Ph.   31 still] *om.* Cl, Le, Ph.

Jove wisely said (for wisdom wisely says):
'O beasts, take heed what you of me desire.
Rulers will think all things made them to please,
And soon forget the swink due to their hire.
But since you will, part of my heav'nly fire   5
    I will you lend; the rest yourselves must give,
    That it both seen and felt may with you live.'

Full glad they were, and took the naked sprite,
Which straight the earth yclothed in his clay.
The lion, heart; the ounce gave active might;   10
The horse, good shape; the sparrow, lust to play;
Nightingale, voice, enticing songs to say.
    Elephant gave a perfect memory;
    And parrot, ready tongue, that to apply.

The fox gave craft; the dog gave flattery;   15
Ass, patience; the mole, a working thought;
Eagle, high look; wolf, secret cruelty;
Monkey, sweet breath; the cow, her fair eyes brought;
The ermine, whitest skin spotted with naught;
    The sheep, mild-seeming face; climbing, the bear;   20
    The stag did give the harm-eschewing fear.

The hare her sleights; the cat his melancholy;
Ant, industry; and cony, skill to build;
Cranes, order; storks, to be appearing holy;
Chameleon, ease to change; duck, ease to yield;   25
Crocodile, tears which might be falsely spilled.
    Ape great thing gave, though he did mowing stand:
    The instrument of instruments, the hand.

Each other beast likewise his present brings;
And (but they drad their prince they oft should want)   30
They all consented were to give him wings.
And ay more awe towards him for to plant,
To their own work this privilege they grant:
    That from thenceforth to all eternity
    No beast should freely speak, but only he.   35

2 you] ye As, Ph.   12 Nightingale] Nightingales As, Hm.   17 high] a As;
om. Da.   19 *om.* Le.   22 hare] bear Cl, Le; hart Je.   his] her Le, Je, Hm.
27 thing] things Da, Je, Hm.   mowing] moving Cl, Da, Je, Hm.   30 drad]
dread Bo, As, Ph, Je, Hm.   oft] *om.* Je; ought 90.

Thus man was made; thus man their lord became;
Who at the first, wanting or hiding pride,
He did to beasts' best use his cunning frame,
With water drink, herbs meat, and naked hide,
5   And fellow-like let his dominion slide,
    Not in his sayings saying 'I', but 'we';
    As if he meant his lordship common be.

But when his seat so rooted he had found
That they now skilled not how from him to wend,
10   Then gan in guiltless earth full many a wound,
Iron to seek, which gainst itself should bend
To tear the bowels that good corn should send.
    But yet the common dam none did bemoan,
    Because (though hurt) they never heard her groan.

15   Then gan he factions in the beasts to breed;
Where helping weaker sort, the nobler beasts
(As tigers, leopards, bears, and lions' seed)
Disdained with this, in deserts sought their rests;
Where famine ravin taught their hungry chests,
20   That craftily he forced them to do ill;
    Which being done, he afterwards would kill

For murder done, which never erst was seen,
By those great beasts. As for the weakers' good,
He chose themselves his guarders for to been
25   Gainst those of might of whom in fear they stood,
As horse and dog; not great, but gentle blood.
    Blithe were the commons, cattle of the field,
    Tho when they saw their foen of greatness killed.

But they, or spent or made of slender might,
30   Then quickly did the meaner cattle find,
The great beams gone, the house on shoulders light;
For by and by the horse fair bits did bind;
The dog was in a collar taught his kind.

---

1 their] *om*. Bo; the Da.   6 sayings] saying Cl, Le, As, Ph.   11 gainst]
against Cl, Da.   15 he] the 90.   20 That] Thus Le, As, Je, Hm.   21 after-
wards] after ward As, Da, Hm.   22 murder Bo, Cl, Le, As, Da, Ph, Je, Hm:
murders St, 90 (*corr.* 13).   23 weakers'] weaker Da, Je, Hm.   30 the] their
Cl, Da.   31 great] greaters Bo; greater Je, Hm.   33 collar Bo, Cl, Le, Da,
Ph, Hm, 90: choler St, As, Je.

As for the gentle birds, like case might rue
When falcon they, and goshawk, saw in mew.

Worst fell to smallest birds, and meanest herd,
Who now his own, full like his own he used.
Yet first but wool, or feathers, off he teared;   5
And when they were well used to be abused,
For hungry throat their flesh with teeth he bruised;
   At length for glutton taste he did them kill;
   At last for sport their silly lives did spill.

But yet, O man, rage not beyond thy need;   10
Deem it no gloire to swell in tyranny.
Thou art of blood; joy not to make things bleed.
Thou fearest death; think they are loath to die.
A plaint of guiltless hurt doth pierce the sky.
   And you, poor beasts, in patience bide your hell,   15
   Or know your strengths, and then you shall do well.

Thus did I sing and pipe eight sullen hours
To sheep whom love, not knowledge, made to hear;
Now fancy's fits, now fortune's baleful stours.
But then I homeward called my lambkins dear;   20
For to my dimmed eyes began t'appear
   The night grown old, her black head waxen grey,
   Sure shepherd's sign that morn would soon fetch day.

According to the nature of diverse ears, diverse judgements straight
followed: some praising his voice; others the words, fit to frame a   25
pastoral style; others the strangeness of the tale, and scanning what
he should mean by it. But old Geron (who had borne him a grudge
ever since, in one of their eclogues, he had taken him up over-
bitterly) took hold of this occasion to make his revenge and said he
never saw thing worse proportioned than to bring in a tale of he   30
knew not what beasts at such a banquet when rather some song of
love, or matter for joyful melody, was to be brought forth. 'But', said

4 Who] Whom 90.   7 throat] teeth 90.   9 At] And Le, As, Da, Ph, Je,
Hm.   their Cl, Le, As, Da, 90: the St, Bo, Ph, Hm.   11 gloire 90: glore St, Da;
glory Bo, Ph, Je, Hm, 93; praise Cl, Le, As.   12 make] see 90.   17 sullen]
solemn Cl, Le, Da, Ph.   20 homeward] homewards 90.   21 t'appear] to appear
Bo, Cl, As, Da, Ph, Hm.   23 would] should 90.

he, 'this is the right conceit of young men who think then they speak
wiseliest when they cannot understand themselves.' Then invited he
Histor to answer him in eclogue-wise; who, indeed, having been
long in love with the fair bride Kala, and now prevented, was grown
5   into a detestation of marriage. But thus it was:

Geron   Histor

Geron. In faith, good Histor, long is your delay
From holy marriage, sweet and surest mean
Our foolish lusts in honest rules to stay.
10   I pray thee do to Lalus' sample lean.
Thou seest how frisk and jolly now he is
That last day seemed he could not chaw a bean.
Believe me, man, there is no greater bliss
Than is the quiet joy of loving wife,
15   Which whoso wants, half of himself doth miss.
Friend without change, playfellow without strife,
Food without fullness, counsel without pride,
Is this sweet doubling of our single life.

Histor. No doubt to whom so good chance did betide
20   As for to find a pasture strowed with gold,
He were a fool if there he did not bide.
Who would not have a phoenix if he could?
The humming wasp, if it had not a sting,
Before all flies the wasp accept I would.
25   But this bad world few golden fields doth bring;
Phoenix but one, of crows we millions have;
The wasp seems gay, but is a cumbrous thing.
If many Kalas our Arcadia gave,
Lalus' example I would soon ensue;
30   And think I did myself from sorrow save.
But of such wives we find a slender crew;
Shrewdness so stirs, pride so puffs up their heart,
They seldom ponder what to them is due.

1 young men who think 90: a young man, think OA; a young man, who think Da.
2 wiseliest] wisely Da, Hm; wisest Ph.   3 in] *om.* Ph, Je.   4 bride] *om.* Bo,
90; bright Da.   6–p. 263, 24 90 *transferred this poem to the First Eclogues*; 93
restored it to the Third Eclogues.   9 lusts] lust 90.   12 chaw] chow Bo, Le;
chew Cl, As, Je, 90; shew Ph.   20 strowed] strewed Cl, Hm; araide Je; strawed
90.   24 flies Bo, Le, As, Da, Ph, Je, Hm, 90: flees St, Cl.   25 doth] do Da,
Ph, Je.   32 their] the 90.

With meagre looks, as if they still did smart,
  Puling and whimp'ring, or else scolding flat,
  Make home more pain than following of the cart.
Either dull silence, or eternal chat;
  Still contrary to what her husband says: 5
  If he do praise the dog, she likes the cat.
Austere she is, when he would honest plays;
  And gamesome then, when he thinks on his sheep;
  She bids him go, and yet from journey stays.
She war doth ever with his kinsfolk keep,   10
  And makes them fremd who friends by nature are,
  Envying shallow toys with malice deep.
And if, forsooth, there come some new-found ware,
  The little coin his sweating brows have got
  Must go for that, if for her lours he care;   15
Or else: 'Nay, faith, mine is the lucklest lot
  That ever fell to honest woman yet;
  No wife but I hath such a man, God wot.'
Such is their speech who be of sober wit;
  But who do let their tongues show well their rage,   20
  Lord, what by-words they speak, what spite they spit!
The house is made a very loathsome cage,
  Wherein the bird doth never sing, but cry
  With such a will that nothing can assuage.
Dearly the servants do their wages buy,   25
  Reviled for each small fault, sometimes for none;
  They better live that in a gaol do lie.
Let other fouler spots away be blown,
  For I seek not their shame; but still, methinks,
  A better life it is to lie alone.   30

Geron. Who for each fickle fear from virtue shrinks
  Shall in this life embrace no worthy thing;
  No mortal man the cup of surety drinks.
  The heav'ns do not good haps in handfuls bring,

4–6 *om.* Da, Ph, Je, Hm.   10 kinsfolk] kinsfolks Bo, As.   11 fremd]
fremd *corr. to* foes Cl; frend Da; freme Ph; frends Je.   14 have] hath Cl, Le, As,
Je.   15 lours] love Cl, Le, As; loves Da.   16 lucklest As, 90: looklest St;
luckliest Bo, Je; luckless Cl, Le, Da, Ph, Hm.   18 hath] have Bo, Cl, As, Je.   20 do]
doth Cl, Le, As, Da.   21 by-words] words Le; high words Ph.   24 that]
as 90.   30 lie] live Cl, Je, Hm.   32 this] his Le, 90.

But let us pick our good from out much bad;
That still our little world may know his king.
But certainly so long we may be glad
While that we do what nature doth require,
5   And for th'event we never ought be sad.
Man oft is plagued with air, is burnt with fire,
In water drowned, in earth his burial is;
And shall we not therefore their use desire?
Nature above all things requireth this:
10   That we our kind do labour to maintain;
Which drawn-out line doth hold all human bliss.
Thy father justly may of thee complain,
If thou do not repay his deeds for thee,
In granting unto him a grandsire's gain.
15   Thy commonwealth may rightly grieved be,
Which must by this immortal be preserved,
If thus thou murder thy posterity.
His very being he hath not deserved
Who for a self-conceit will that forbear
20   Whereby that being ay must be conserved.
And God forbid women such cattle were
As you paint them; but well in you I find,
No man doth speak aright who speaks in fear.
Who only sees the ill is worse than blind.
25   These fifty winters married I have been;
And yet find no such faults in womankind.
I have a wife worthy to be a queen,
So well she can command, and yet obey;
In ruling of a house so well she's seen.
30   And yet in all this time betwixt us tway,
We bear our double yoke with such consent,
There never passed foul word, I dare well say.
But these be your love-toys which still are spent
In lawless games, and love not as you should,
35   But with much study learn late to repent.

1 let Bo, Cl, Da, Ph, Je, Hm, 90: lets St, Le, As.   pick] *om.* Hm; pike 90.
our] or Bo; out Cl, As.   4 what] that Le, As.   12 justly may of thee] may
of thee justly Le, Je.   17 posterity] prosperity Da, Je.   23 who] that As,
Da; which Je, Hm.   25 winters] years Le, Je, Hm.   I have] have I Ph, 90.
29 she's 90: she is St, Bo, Cl, Le, As, Da, Hm; is Ph, Je.   30 tway] twain Da, Je,
Hm.   32 There] That 90.   33 be] are Cl, Le, As, 13.

How well last day before our prince you could
   Blind Cupid's works with wonder testify!
   Yet now the root of him abase you would.
Go to, go to, and Cupid now apply
   To that where thou thy Cupid mayst avow,   5
   And thou shalt find in women virtues lie.
Sweet supple minds which soon to wisdom bow,
   Where they by wisdom's rules directed are,
   And are not forced fond thraldom to allow.
As we to get are framed, so they to spare;   10
   We made for pains, our pains they made to cherish;
   We care abroad, and they of home have care.
O Histor, seek within thyself to flourish;
   Thy house by thee must live, or else be gone,
   And then who shall the name of Histor nourish?   15
Riches of children pass a prince's throne;
   Which touch the father's heart with secret joy
   When without shame he saith: 'these be mine own.'
Marry therefore; for marriage will destroy
   Those passions which to youthful head do climb,   20
   Mothers and nurses of all vain annoy.

Histor. Perchance I will, but now methinks it time
   We go unto the bride, and use this day
   To speak with her, while freely speak we may.

He spake these last words with such affection as a curious eye 25
might easily have perceived he liked Lalus's fortune better than he
loved his person. But then, indeed, did all arise, and went to the
women; where spending all the day and good part of the night in
dancing, carolling, and wassailing, lastly they left Lalus where he
long desired to be left, and with many unfeigned thanks returned 30
every man to his home. But some of them, having to cross the way

<hr />

1 our] your Cl, Je, Hm.   3 abase] abuse Ph, Hm.   5 thou] then Da, Hm.
thy] by Le; *om.* Da; to Ph.   8 rules] rule Le, 90.   9 are] yet Cl, Le, As.
11 for pains] our pains Le; for pain 90.   our pains they made] they made our pains
Cl, Le, As.   12 home] whom Da, Ph, Hm.   16 Riches Bo, Cl, Le, Da, Ph, Je,
Hm, 90: Richess St, As.   prince's Bo, Cl, As, Ph, Je, Hm, 90: princess St, Le;
princely Da.   18 mine] my Da, Hm.   22-4 *om.* 90 (*restored* 13).   22 me-
thinks] I think Bo, Da, Ph.   23 We] To 13.   25 these OA, 93: those St.
last] *om.* Hm, 93.   26 Lalus's] Thyrsis 93 (Lalus 13).   29 Lalus] Thyrsis 93
(Lalus 13).

of the two lodges, might see a lady making doleful lamentations over a body seemed dead unto them.

But methinks Dametas cries unto me, if I come not the sooner to comfort him, he will leave off his golden work hath already cost him so much labour and longing.

Here end the third eclogues.

1 lamentations] lamentation Cl, Je, Hm.   2 a body seemed] a body which seemed 93.   4 work hath] work which hath Je; work that hath 93.   6 Here ends the third eclogues Bo; Here end the third book and third eclogues Cl; Here endeth the third eclogues As, Ph, Je; Here ends the third eclogue Da, Hm; The end of the third book 93.

THE FOURTH BOOK OR ACT

THE everlasting justice (using ourselves to be the punishers of our faults, and making our own actions the beginning of our chastisement, that our shame may be the more manifest, and our repentance follow the sooner) took Dametas at this present (by whose folly the 5 others' wisdom might receive the greater overthrow) to be the instrument of revealing the secretest cunning—so evil a ground doth evil stand upon, and so manifest it is that nothing remains strongly but that which hath the good foundation of goodness. For so it fell out that Dametas, having spent the whole day in breaking up the 10 cumbersome work of the pastor Dorus, and feeling in all his labour no pain so much as that his hungry hopes received any stay, having with the price of much sweat and weariness gotten up the huge stone which he thought should have such a golden lining, the goodman in the great bed that stone had made found nothing but these two 15 verses written upon a piece of vellum:

Who hath his hire, hath well his labour placed;
Earth thou didst seek, and store of earth thou hast.

What an inward discountenance it was to master Dametas to find his hope of wealth turned to poor verses (for which he never cared 20 much) nothing can describe, but either the feeling in oneself the state of such a mind Dametas had, or at least the bethinking what was Midas's fancy when, after the great pride he conceived to be made judge between gods, he was rewarded with the ornament of an ass's ears. Yet the deep apprehension he had received of such 25

---

1 *om.* Ph; THE FOURTH BOOK OF THE COUNTESS OF PEMBROKE'S ARCADIA 93.   2–9 The everlasting . . . goodness] The almighty wisdom evermore delighting to show the world that by unlikeliest means greatest matters may come to conclusion; that human reason may be the more humbled, and more willingly give place to divine providence; as at the first it brought in Dametas to play a part in this royal pageant, so having continued him still an actor, now that all things were grown ripe for an end, made his folly the instrument of revealing that which far greater cunning had sought to conceal 93.   7–8 doth evil stand] doth stand Bo, As; doth evils stand Ph.   12 pain] pains Bo, Hm.   hopes] hope Cl, As.   14 lining] luning Bo; living Da; lying Hm.   17–18 Le *omits this poem; it is in* 93.   18 didst] dost Bo, Cl, As, Je.   19 discountenance] discontentation Da, Je; discontentment 13.   20 to] into Cl, Da.   22 mind Dametas] mind as Dametas Cl, Hm.   at] at the Da, Hm.   bethinking] thinking Cl, As, Ph.   24 between] betwixt Bo, Cl, As, Ph, Je, Hm.

8118554   Y

riches could not so suddenly lose the colour that had so thoroughly dyed his thick brain but that he turned and tossed the poor bowels of the innocent earth, till the far passing of the night, and the tediousness of his fruitless labour, made him content rather to
5 exercise his discontentation at home than there. Yet forced he was (his horse being otherwise burdened with digging instruments) to return, as he came, most part of the way on foot, with such grudging lamentations as a nobler mind would (but more nobly) make for the loss of his mistress. For so far had he fed his foolish soul with the
10 expectation of that which he reputed felicity that he no less accounted himself miserable than if he had fallen from such an estate his fancy had embraced. So then home again went Dametas, punished in conceit, as in conceit he had erred, till he found himself there from a fancied loss fallen to an essential misery. For entering
15 into his house three hours within night, instead of the lightsome countenance of Pamela (which gave such an inward decking to that lodge as proudest palaces might have cause to envy it), and of the grateful conversation of Dorus (whose witty behaviour made that loneliness to seem full of good company), instead of the loud
20 scolding of Miso, and the busy tumbling up and down of Mopsa (which, though they were so short as quite contrary to the others' praiseworthiness, yet were they far before them in filling of a house), he found nothing but a solitary darkness which, as naturally it breeds a kind of irksome ghastfulness, so it was to him a most present terror,
25 remembering the charge he had left behind, which he well knew imported no less than his life unto him. Therefore, lighting a candle, there was no place a mouse could have dwelled in but that he with quaking diligence sought into. But when he saw he could see nothing of that he most cared for, then became he the right pattern of a
30 wretch dejected with fear. For crying and howling, knocking his head to the wall, he began to make pitiful complaints where nobody could hear him; and with too much dread he should not recover her, leave all consideration how to recover her. But at length, looking like a she goat when she casts her kid, for very sorrow he took in his

---

1 so suddenly 93: suddenly OA.   3 far passing] surpassing Ph, Je; coming on 93.   5 Yet] But 93.   9 had he] he had Cl, As, Da, Ph.   13 he found] he had found Cl, Ph.   14 to an essential] to essential Bo, Da, Ph, Hm, 93; into an essential Cl; essential As.   15 within] before *corr. to* within Da; before 13.   19 loneliness] loveliness Cl, As, Hm; lowliness Da, Je; liveliness Ph.   20 tumbling] humming Ph; rumbling 93.   34 casts] hath cast Ph; cast Je; cares Hm.

own behalf, out of the lodge he went running as hard as he could, having now received the very form of hanging into his consideration. Thus running as a man that would gladly have run from himself, it was his foolish fortune to espy by the glimmering light the moon did then yield him one standing aloft among the boughs of a fair ash. He 5 (that would have asked counsel at that time of a dog) cast up his face as if his tooth had been drawing, and with much bending his sight he perceived it was mistress Mopsa, fitly seated there for her wit and dignity. There, I will not say with joy (for how could he taste of joy whose imagination was fallen from a palace to a gallows?), 10 but yet with some refreshing of comfort, in hope he should learn better tidings of her, he began to cry out: 'O Mopsa, my beloved chicken, here am I thine own father Dametas, never in such a towardness to hanging, if thou cannot help me!'

But never a word could his eloquence procure of Mopsa who, 15 indeed, was there attending for greater matters. This was yet a new burden to poor Dametas who thought all the world was conspired against him; and therefore, with a silly choler he began another tune: 'Thou vile Mopsa,' said he, 'now the vengeance of my fatherly curse light overthwart thee if thou do not straight answer me!' 20

But neither blessing nor cursing could prevail with Mopsa who was now great with child with the expectation of her may-game hopes, and did long to be delivered with the third time being named, which by and by followed; for Dametas, rubbing his elbow, stamping and whining, seeing neither of these take place, began to throw 25 stones at her, and withal to conjure her by the name of hellish Mopsa. But when he had named her the third time, no chime can more suddenly follow the striking of a clock than she, verily thinking it was the god that used her father's voice, throwing her arms abroad, and not considering she was muffled upon so high a tree, came 30 fluttering down like a hooded hawk, like enough to have broken her neck, but that the tree, full of boughs, tossed her from one bough to another, and lastly well bruised brought her to receive an unfriendly salutation of the earth. Dametas, as soon as she was down, came running to her, and finding her so close wrapped, pulled off 35

1 hard] fast Bo, Hm (fast *corr. to* hard Cl).   3 that] *om.* 93 (*added* 13).
would gladly] would Cl, Hm; gladly would Ph.   4 light the] light of the Hm, 93
(*corr.* 98).   8 for her wit] for wit 93 (*corr.* 13).   14 to] of Da, 93.   cannot]
canst not 93.   20 curse] course Ph, Je.   22 may-game] princely Ph; many
gay Hm.   28 a] the Bo, Ph, Je, Hm.   29 her arms] our arms 93 (*corr.* 98).
31 broken] broke Bo, Je; brake Hm.   33 another OA, 93: thother St.

the scarlet cloak—in good time for her; for, with the soreness of the fall, if she had not had breath given her, she had delivered a foolish soul to Pluto. But then Dametas began afresh to desire his daughter not to forget the pains he had taken for her in her childhood (which he 5 was sure she could not remember), and to tell him where Pamela was.

'O good Apollo,' said Mopsa, 'if ever thou didst bear love to Phaethon's mother, let me have a king to my husband.'

'Alas, what speakest thou of Phaethon?' said Dametas, 'if by thy circumspect means I find not out Pamela, thy father will be hanged 10 tomorrow.'

'It is no matter, though he be hanged,' answered Mopsa, 'do but thou make Dorus a king, and let him be my husband, good Apollo, for my courage doth much prick me towards him.'

'Ah, Mopsa,' cried out Dametas, 'where is thy wit? Dost thou 15 not know thy father? How hast thou forgotten thyself?'

'I do not ask wit of thee, mine own god,' said she, 'but I see thou wouldst have me remember my father, and indeed forget myself. No, no, a good husband!'

'Thou shalt have thy fill of husbands', said Dametas, 'and do but 20 answer me my question.'

'O, I thank thee,' said Mopsa, 'with all my heart, heartily; but let them be all kings.'

Dametas, seeing no other way prevail, fell down on his knees: 'Mopsa, Mopsa,' said he, 'do not thus cruelly torment me; I am al-25 ready wretched enough. Alas, either help me or tell me thou canst not.'

She (that would not be behind Apollo in courtesy) kneeled down on the other side: 'I will never leave tormenting thee', said Mopsa, 'until thou hast satisfied my longing; but I will proclaim thee a promise-breaker, that even Jupiter shall hear it.'

30 'Now, by the fostering thou hast received in this place, save my life', said Dametas.

'Now, by this fair ash', answered Mopsa, 'where thou didst receive so great a good turn, grant post-haste to my burning fancy.'

'O where is Pamela?' said Dametas.

35 'O a lusty husband!' said Mopsa.

Dametas (that now verily assured himself his daughter was mad) began utterly to despair of his life; and therefore amazedly catching her in his arms, to see whether he could bring her to herself, he might feel the weight of a great cudgel light upon his shoulders, and for the first greeting he knew his wife Miso's voice by the calling him 'ribald villain', and asking him whether she could not serve his turn as well as Charita. For Miso having, according to Dorus's 5 counsel, gone to Mantinea, and there harboured herself in an old acquaintance house of hers, as soon as ten of the clock was stricken (where she had remained closely all that while, I think with such an amiable cheer as when jealous Juno sat cross-legged to hinder the childbirth of her husband's love) with open mouth she went to 10 the magistrate appointed over such matters, and there, with the most scolding invective her rage rather than eloquence could bring forth, she required his aid to take Dametas, who had left his duty to the duke and his daughter to commit adultery in the house of Charita's uncle in the Oudemian street. But neither was the name of Charita 15 remembered, nor any such street known. Yet such was the general mislike all men had of Dametas's unworthy advancement that every man was glad to make himself a minister of that which might redound to his shame. Therefore, with pans, cries and laughters, there was no suspected place in all the city but was searched for, 20 under the title of, Dametas; Miso ever foremost encouraging them with all the shameful blazings of his demeanour, increasing the sport of hunting her husband with her diligent barking; till at length, having already done both him and herself as much infamous shame as such a tongue in such an action might perform, in the end (not 25 being able to find a thing that was not) to her mare again she went, having neither suspicion nor rage anything mitigated. But (leaving behind her a sufficient comedy of her tragical fancies) away homeward she came, imputing the not finding her husband to any chance rather than to his innocency; for her heart being apt to receive and 30 nourish a bitter thought, it had so swallowed up a determinate condemnation that in the very anatomy of her spirits one should have found nothing but devilish disdain and hateful jealousy. In this sort, grunting out her mischievous spite, she came by the tree even as Dametas was making that ill understood intercession to his foolish 35 Mopsa. As soon as she heard her husband's voice, she verily thought

7 of the clock OA, 93: of clock St.   14 and his daughter] and daughter Cl, As.
15 Oudemian] oaken (various spellings) Da, Ph, Hm; Eukian Je; Ondemian 93 (corr.
98).   17–18 every man] every one Bo, Je, Hm.   19 pans] Pannes St; Panns Bo;
Panns Cl; paynes As; pannes Da, Je; Pans Ph; Pane Hm; Panike 93.   21 foremost
encouraging OA, 93: foremost in encouraging St.   26 a] the As; any Ph.

she had her prey; and therefore stealing from her mare as softly as she could, she came creeping and halting behind him, even as he (thinking his daughter's little wits had quite left her great noll) began to take her in his arms, thinking perchance her feeling sense
5 might call her mind parts unto her. But Miso, who saw nothing but through the colour of revengeful anger, established upon the fore-judgement of his trespass, undoubtedly resolving that Mopsa was Charita, Dorus had told her of, mumping out her hoarse chafe, she gave him the wooden salutation you heard of. Dametas (that was
10 not so sensible in anything as in blows) turned up his blubbered face like a great lout new whipped: 'Alas, thou woman,' said he, 'what hath thy poor husband deserved to have his own ill luck loaden with thy displeasure? Pamela is lost! Pamela is lost!'

Miso, still holding on the course of her former fancy: 'What
15 tellest thou me, naughty varlet,' said she, 'of Pamela? Dost thou think that doth answer me for abusing the laws of marriage? Have I brought thee children; have I been a true wife unto thee, to be despised in mine old age?'

And ever among she would sauce her speeches with such bastin-
20 ados that poor Dametas began now to think that either a general madding was fallen, or else that all this was but a vision. But as for visions, the smart of the cudgel put out of his fancy; and therefore again turning to his wife, not knowing in the world what she meant: 'Miso,' said he, 'hereafter thou mayst examine me; do but now tell
25 me what is become of Pamela.'

'I will first examine this drab', said she; and withal let fall her staff as hard as she could upon Mopsa, still taking her for Charita.

But Mopsa (that was already angry, thinking she had hindered her from Apollo) leaped up and caught her by the throat, like to have
30 strangled her, but that Dametas from a condemned man was fain to become a judge and part this fray (such a picture of a rude discord where each was out with the other two), and then getting the opportunity of their falling out to hold himself in surety (who was indeed the veriest coward of the three), he renewed his earnest demand of
35 them. But it was a sport to see how the former conceits Dorus had printed in their imaginations kept still such a dominion in them

1 prey] play 93 (ex. 05).   3 wits] wit Ph, Je.   15 said she] om. Hm, 93.
18 mine] my Da, Ph.   23 again turning] turning again As, Ph, Je, Hm.
28 thinking she] thinking that she Da, 93.   31 of a rude] of rude Ph, Hm.
36 printed] painted Bo, Je; imprinted Cl.   such a dominion] such dominion Da,
Hm, 93.

that Miso, though now she found and felt it was her daughter Mopsa yet did Charita continually pass through her thoughts, which she uttered with such crabbed questions to Dametas that he, not possibly conceiving any part of her doubt, remained astonished; and the astonishment increased her doubt. And as for Mopsa, as first she 5 did assuredly take him to be Apollo, and thought her mother's coming did mar the bargain, so now much talking to and fro had delivered so much light into the misty mould of her capacity as to know him to be her father, yet remained there such footsteps of the foretaken opinion that she thought verily her father and mother 10 were hasted thither to get the first wish; and therefore to whatsoever they asked of her, she would never answer, but embracing the tree as if she feared it had been running away: 'Nay,' says she, 'I will have the first wish, for I was here first.'

Which they understood no more than Dametas did what Miso 15 meant by Charita; till at length with much urging them, being indeed better able to persuade both than to meet hand to hand with either, he prevailed so much with them as to bring them into the lodge to see what loss their negligence had suffered. Then, indeed, the near neighbourhood they bare to themselves made them leave 20 other toys, and look into what dangerous plight they were all fallen as soon as the duke should know his daughter's escape. And as for the women, they began afresh to enter into their brawling, whether were in the fault. But Dametas (who did fear that among his other evils the thunderbolt of that storm would fall upon his shoulders) 25 slipped away from them, but with so meagre a cheer as might much sooner engender laughter than pity: 'O true Arcadia,' would he say, tearing his hair and beard, and sometimes for too much woe making unwieldy somersaults, 'how darest thou bear upon thee such a felonious traitor as I am? And you, false-hearted trees, why would 30 you make no noise to make her ungracious departure known? Ah, Pamela, Pamela, how often when I brought thee in fine posies of all coloured flowers, wouldst thou clap me on the cheek, and say thou wouldst be one day even with me? Was this thy meaning: to bring me to an even pair of gallows? Ah, ill taught Dorus, that came hither to 35 learn good manners of me, did I ever teach thee to make thy master

3 possibly] possible Cl, Ph, Je, Hm.　　6 to be] for As, Ph.　　13 says] said Ph, Je; saith Hm.　　20–1 leave other] leave their Cl; leave off their Ph; leave off other Je.　　21 all] om. Bo, Cl, As, Hm.　　24 who] that Ph, Hm; om. Je.　　30 would Cl, As, Da, Je, Hm, 93; could St, Bo; should Ph.　　31 her OA, 93: om. St. 35 came] camest 93.

sweat out his heart for nothing, and in the mean time run away with
thy mistress? O my dun cow, I did think some evil was towards me
ever since the last day thou didst run away from me and hold up thy
tail, so pitifully. Did not I see an eagle kill a cuckoo, which was a plain
5 foretoken unto me Pamela should be my destruction? O wife Miso,
if I durst say it to thy face, why didst thou suspect thy husband that
loves a piece of cheese better than a woman? And thou little Mopsa,
that shalt inherit the shame of thy father's death, was it time for thee
to climb trees, which should so shortly be my best burial? O that I
10 could live without death, or die before I were aware! O heart, why
hast thou no hands at commandment to dispatch thee? O hands, why
want you a heart to kill this villain?'

   In this sort did he inveigh against everything, sometimes thinking
to run away while it was yet night; but he (that had included all the
15 world within his sheepcote) thought that worse than any death.
Sometimes for dread of hanging he meant to hang himself, finding
(as indeed it is) that fear is far more painful to cowardice than death
to a true courage. But his fingers were nothing nimble in that action,
and anything was let enough thereto, he being a true lover of him-
20 self without any rival. But lastly, guided by a far greater constellation
than his own, he remembered to search the other lodge, where it
might be Pamela that night had retired himself. So thither with
trembling hams he carried himself; but employing his double key
(which the duke for special credit had unworthily bestowed upon
25 him), he found all the gates so barred that his key could not prevail,
saving only one trap-door (which went down into a vault by the
cellar) which, as it was unknown of Pyrocles, so had he left it un-
guarded. But Dametas (that ever knew the buttery better than any
place) got in that way, and pacing softly to Philoclea's chamber
30 (where he thought most likely to find Pamela), the door being left
open, he entered in, and by the light of the lamp he might discern
one abed with her, which he, although he took to be Pamela, yet
thinking no surety enough in a matter touching his neck, he went

1 time run] time to run Hm, 93.   3 hold] held Da, 93.   7 loves Cl, Da,
Je, Hm: love St, Bo, As, Ph; loveth 93.   11 thee] me Cl, As.   12 villain]
villainy 93 (*corr.* 13).   13 inveigh] envy Ph, Je, Hm.   14 run] have 93 (*corr.*
98).   16 meant] went Cl, Ph.   17 cowardice] cowards Cl; cowardish men Ph.
25 could] would Cl, Ph, Hm (would *corr. to* could St).   26 trap-door] trapped door
93.   27–8 unguarded] unregarded 93.   28–9 any place] any other place Da, 93.
29 pacing] pasing Cl, Hm, 93; passing Ph, Je.   32 one abed with] on in bed
with Ph, 93; one on the bed by 98.   which he] which (he *crossed out*) Cl; which Ph.

hard to the bedside of these unfortunate lovers, who at that time, being not much before the break of day—whether it were they were so divinely surprised to bring their fault to open punishment; or that the too high degree of their joys had overthrown the wakeful use of their senses; or that their souls, lifted up with extremity of 5 love after mutual satisfaction, had left their bodies dearly joined to unite themselves together so much more freely as they were freer of that earthly prison; or whatsoever other cause may be imagined of it—but so it was that they were as then possessed with a mutual sleep, yet not forgetting with viny embracements to give any eye a 10 perfect model of affection. But Dametas, looking with the lamp in his hand, but neither with such a face nor mind, upon these excellent creatures, as Psyche did upon her unknown lover, and giving every way freedom to his fearful eyes, did not only perceive it was Cleophila (and therefore much different from the lady he sought), 15 but that this same Cleophila did more differ from the Cleophila he and others had ever taken her for. Satisfied with that, and not thinking it good to awake the sleeping lion, he went down again, taking with him Pyrocles' sword (wherewith upon his shirt Pyrocles came only apparelled thither), being sure to leave no weapon in the cham- 20 ber. And so, making the door as fast as he could on the outside, hoping with the revealing of this fault to make his own the less, or at least that this injury would so fill the duke's head that he should not have leisure to chastise his negligence (like a fool not considering that the more rage breeds the crueller punishment), he went first 25 into the duke's chamber, and not finding him there, he ran down crying with open mouth, the duke was betrayed, and that Cleophila did abuse his daughter. The noise he made, being a man of no few words, joined to the yelping sound of Miso and his unpleasant inheritrix, brought together some number of the shepherds, to whom 30 he, without any regard of first reserving it for the duke's knowledge, spattered out the bottom of his stomach, swearing by him he never knew that Cleophila, whom they had taken all that while to be a

1 hard] heard 93 (*corr.* 05).   these] those Cl, As, Je.   2 of day] of the day As, Da, Ph, Hm.   3 divinely] by fore appointment Cl; before appointment As. 3-4 their . . . joys] this whole matter to be destinied (*corr. to* the destined 98) conclusion, or that the unresistible force of their sorrows 93.   4 degree] degrees Ph, Je, Hm. 5-9 or that . . . that they] *om.* 93.   8 may] light Cl, Ph.   10 viny] *blank left* As; veʳnny Ph; very nye Je; *om.* Hm.   12 nor] or Da, Je.   13 Psyche] *blank left* As; he Ph.   17 for] 93 *adds* wherein the change of her apparel chiefly confirmed his opinion.   19 shirt] slight undersuit 93.   22 this fault] this (as he thought) greater fault 93.   29 to] with Cl, As.   31 first] *om.* 93.

woman, was as arrant a man as himself was, whereof he had seen sufficient signs and tokens; and that he was as close as a butterfly with the lady Philoclea. The poor men, jealous of their prince's honour, were ready with weapons to have entered the lodge, standing
5 yet in some pause, whether it were not better first to hear some news of the duke himself, when by the sudden coming of other shepherds, which with astonished looks ran from one cry to the other, their griefs were surcharged with the evil tidings of the duke's death. Turning therefore all their minds and eyes that way, they ran to the
10 cave where they said he lay dead, the sun beginning now to send some promise of his coming light, making haste, I think, to be spectator of the following tragedies.

But of Basilius, thus it had fallen out: the duke, having passed over the night, more happy in contemplation than action, having
15 had his spirits sublimed with the sweet imagination of embracing the much desired Cleophila, doubting lest the cave's darkness might deceive him in the day's approach, thought it now season to return to his wedlock bed, remembering the promise he had made Cleophila to observe due orders towards Gynecia. There-
20 fore departing, but not departing without bequeathing by a will of words, sealed with many kisses, a full gift of all his love and life to his misconceived bedfellow, he went to the mouth of the cave, there to apparel himself; in which doing, the motion of his joy could not be bridled from uttering suchlike words: 'Blessed be thou, O night,'
25 said he, 'that hast with thy sweet wings shrouded me in the vale of bliss! It is thou that art the first gotten child of time. The day hath been but an usurper upon thy delightful inheritance. Thou invitest all living things to comfortable rest. Thou art the stop of strife, and the necessary truce of approaching battles.' And therewith, he sang
30 these verses to confirm his former praises:

> O night, the ease of care, the pledge of pleasure,
> Desire's best mean, harvest of hearts affected,
> The seat of peace, the throne which is erected
> Of human life to be the quiet measure.

1 a] om. Ph, Hm.   3 jealous OA, 93: zealous St.   their OA, 93: the St.
5 yet] then Da, Je.   better] best As, 93.   first] om. As, Ph.   6 of the] from the
93.   11 his] om. 93.   13 But . . . duke] For Basilius 93.   16 much] most
Cl, As, Da, 93.   18 wedlock Bo, Cl, As, Ph, Je, Hm, 93: wedlocks St, Da.
19 due] true Cl, Da, Ph.   orders] order Cl, As.   31–p. 275, 10 The poem is in
93.   32 harvest] harnest 93 (corr. 13).

Be victor still of Phoebus' golden treasure,
Who hath our sight with too much sight infected,
Whose light is cause we have our lives neglected,
Turning all nature's course to self-displeasure.

These stately stars in their now shining faces, 5
With sinless sleep, and silence, wisdom's mother,
Witness his wrong which by thy help is eased.

Thou art therefore of these our desert places
The sure refuge, by thee and by no other
My soul is blest, sense joyed, and fortune raised. 10

And yet further would his joy needs break forth: 'O Basilius,'
said he, 'the rest of thy time hath been but a dream unto thee. It is
now only thou beginnest to live; now only thou hast entered into
the way of blissfulness. Should fancy of marriage keep me from this
paradise? Or opinion of I know not what promise bind me from 15
paying the right duties to nature and affection? O who would have
thought there could have been such difference betwixt women? Be
not jealous no more, good Gynecia, but yield to the pre-eminence of
more excellent gifts; support thyself upon such marble pillars as she
doth; deck thy breast with those alabaster bowls that Cleophila doth; 20
then accompanied with such a title, perhaps thou mayst recover the
possession of my otherwise-inclined love. But alas, Gynecia, thou
canst not show such evidence; therefore thy plea is vain.'

Gynecia heard all this he said, who had cast about her Cleophila's
garment wherein she came thither, and had followed Basilius even 25
to the cave's entry, full of inward vexation betwixt the deadly accu-
sation of her own guiltiness and the spiteful doubt she had Cleophila
had abused her. But because of the one side, finding the duke did
think her to be Cleophila, she had liberty to imagine it might rather
be the duke's own unbridled enterprise which had barred Cleophila 30
than Cleophila's cunning deceiving of her; and that of the other
part, if she should headily seek a violent revenge, her own honour
might be as much interested as Cleophila endangered; she fell to
this determination: first, with fine handling of the duke to settle in

5 now] new Ph, Je.   6 sinless] slily Cl; sweetest Da; senseless Ph, 05 (only); simple Je.
11 joy] joys 93.   needs] still As; om. Je.   13 beginnest Da, Ph, Hm, 93: begins
St, Bo, Cl, As, Je.   18 not] om. 93.   good] O 93.   19 upon] with Bo, 93.
21 title] little Cl; ability Ph; tittle 93 (corr. 98).   25 even] om. 93.   28 of]
on Da, Je.   31 cunning] coming Cl, Ph.   32 part] side Cl; om. 93.
33 Cleophila] Cleophila's As, Je, Hm.   34 settle] set As, Ph, Je, Hm.

him a perfect good opinion of her; and then, as she should learn how things had passed, so take into herself new devised counsels. But this being her first action: having given unlooked-for attendance to the duke, she heard with what partiality he did prefer her to herself;
5 she saw in him how much fancy doth not only darken reason but beguile sense; she found opinion mistress of the lover's judgement. Which serving as a good lesson to her wise conceit, she went out to Basilius, setting herself in a grave behaviour and stately silence before him, until he (who at the first thinking her by so much
10 shadow as he could see to be Cleophila, was beginning his loving ceremonies) did now (being helped by the peeping light wherewith the morning did overcome the night's darkness) know her face and his error. Which acknowledging in himself with starting back from her, she thus with a modest bitterness spake unto him:
15 'Alas, my lord, well did your words decipher your mind; and well be those words confirmed with this gesture. Very loathsome must that woman be from whom a man hath cause to go back; and little better liked is that wife before whom the husband prefers them he never knew. Alas, hath my faithful observing my part of duty made
20 you think yourself ever a whit the more exempted? Hath that which should claim gratefulness been a cause of contempt? Is the being the mother of Pamela become an odious name unto you? If my life hitherto led have not avoided suspicion; if my violated truth to you be deserving of any punishment; I refuse not to be chastised with
25 the most cruel torment of your displeasure; I refuse not misery purchased by mine own merit. Hard I must needs say (although till now I never thought I should have had cause to say) is the destiny of womankind, the trial of whose virtue must stand upon the loving them that employ all their industry not to be beloved. If
30 Cleophila's young years had not had as much gravity hidden under a youthful face as your grey hairs have been but the visor of a far unfitting youthfulness, your vicious mind had brought some fruits of late repentance; and Gynecia might then have been with much more right so basely despised.'
35 Basilius (that was more ashamed to see himself so overtaken than Vulcan was when with much cunning he proved himself a cuckold)

2 so take] so to take Cl; to take 93.   counsels] counsellors Da; counsel 93.   3 to OA, 93: unto St.   6 beguile] beguiled Cl, Je.   7 wise] good 93.   24 any] my As; om. Hm.   25 torment] torments Da, Je.   26 mine] my Cl, Ph, Hm. 29 loving them] loving of them 93.   30 as] so Da, Hm, 93.   31 the] a As, Da. a far] om. 93.   33 late] om. 93.   35 so] om. Hm, 13.

began to make certain extravagant excuses. But the matter in itself
hardly brooking any purgation, with the suddenness of the time,
which barred any good conjoined invention, made him sometimes
allege one thing, to which by and by he would bring in a contrary:
one time with flat denial, another time with mitigating the fault; 5
now brave, then humble, use such a stammering defensive that
Gynecia (the violence of whose sore, indeed, ran another way) was
content thus to fasten up the last stitch of her anger:

'Well, well, my lord,' said she, 'it shall well become you so to
govern yourself as you may be fit rather to direct me than to be 10
judged of me, and rather be a wise master of me than an unskilful
pleader before me. Remember the wrong you do me is not only to
me, but to your children, whom you had of me; to your country,
when they shall find they are commanded by him that cannot
command his own undecent appetites; lastly to yourself, since with 15
these pains you do but build up a house of shame to dwell in. If
from those movable goods of nature (wherewith in my first youth
my royal parents bestowed me upon you) bearing you children and
increase of years have withdrawn me, consider, I pray you, that as
you are the cause of the one, so in the other, time hath not left to 20
work his never failing effects in you. Truly, truly, sir, very untimely
are these fires in you. It is high season for us both to let reason enjoy
his due sovereignty. Let us not plant anew those weeds which by
nature's course are content to fade.'

Basilius that would rather than his life this matter had been ended, 25
the best rhetoric he had was flat demanding pardon of her, swearing
it was the very force of Apollo's destiny which had carried him thus
from his own bias; but that now, like far travellers were taught to
love their own country, he had such a lesson without book of affec-
tion unto her as he would repay the debt of this error with the 30
interest of a great deal more true honour than ever before he had
borne her.

'Neither am I to give pardon to you, my lord,' said she, 'nor you to
bear honour to me. I have taken this boldness for the unfeigned love I
owe you, to deliver my sorrow unto you, much more for the care I 35

11 rather be] rather to be Ph, Hm, 93.   12 do me] have done Da, 93.   14 by]
of Bo, As.   17 those] these Bo, Cl, As, Je, Hm.   20 the cause] cause Da,
Hm, 93 (ex. 05).   22 high season] time 93.   23 us not] not us Bo; us Je, Hm.
25 this] the Cl, As, Da, 93.   28 like] like as 93.   30 this] his Bo, Da, Ph, Hm.
32 borne] done Da, 93.   34 to me] unto me Bo, Je.   35 owe you] owe unto
you, Da, Je, 93.

have of your well doing than for any other self-fancy. For well I know that by your good estate my life is maintained; neither, if I would, can I separate myself from your fortune. For my part, therefore, I claim nothing but that which may be safest for yourself; my life, will, honour, and whatsoever else, shall be but a shadow of that body.'

How much Basilius's own shame had found him culpable, and had already even in soul read his own condemnation, so much did this unexpected mildness of Gynecia captive his heart unto her, which otherwise perchance would have grown to a desperate carelessness. Therefore, embracing her and confessing that her virtue shined in his vice, he did even with a true resolved mind vow unto her that, so long as he unworthy of her did live, she should be the furthest and only limit of his affection. He thanked the destinies that had wrought her honour out of his shame; and that had made his own striving to go amiss to be the best mean ever after to hold him in the right path.

Thus reconciled to Basilius's great contentation, who began something to mark himself in his own doings, his hard hap guided his eye to the cup of gold wherein Gynecia had put the liquor meant for Cleophila, and having failed of that guest, was now carrying it home again. But he (whom perchance sorrow, perchance some long disaccustomed pains, had made extremely thirsty, took it out of her hands, although she directly told him both of whom she had it, what the effect of it was, and the little proof she had seen thereof, hiding nothing from him, but that she meant to minister it to another patient. But the duke, whose belly had no ears, and much drought kept from the desiring a taster, finding it not unpleasant to his palate, drank it almost off, leaving very little to cover the cup's bottom. But within a while that from his stomach the drink had delivered to his principal veins his noisome vapours, first with a painful stretching and forced yawning, then with a dark yellowness dyeing his skin and a cold deadly sweat principally about his temples, his body by natural course longing to deliver his heavy burden to his earthly dam, wanting force in his knees (which utterly abandoned him), with heavy fall gave soon proof whither the operation of that unknown potion tended. For, with pang-like groans and ghastly

9–10 carelessness Bo, Cl, Da, Ph, Je, Hm, 93: carefulness St, As.   12 so] as 93.
13 limit 93: limits OA.   15 striving 93: finding OA.   17–18 something] somewhat
Ph; sometimes Je, Hm.   24 thereof] of it Ph, Je.   25 from him Cl, As, Da, Ph, Je,
Hm, 93: from St; him Bo.   26 the duke] Basilius Cl, As; the king 13.
35 gave soon] soon gave Cl; gave some As, Je, Hm, 93.   36 pang-like] pangly As, Da.

turning of his eyes, immediately all his limbs stiffened and his eyes fixed, he having had time to declare his case only in these words: 'O Gynecia, I die! Have care—.' Of what, or how much further he would have spoken, no man can tell. For Gynecia, having well perceived the changing of his colour and those other evil signs, yet had not looked for such a sudden overthrow, but rather had bethought herself what was best for him, when she suddenly saw the matter come to that period, coming to him, and neither with any cries getting a word of him, nor with any other possible means able to bring any living action from him, the height of all ugly sorrows did so horribly appear before her amazed mind that at the first it did not only distract all power of speech from her but almost wit to consider, remaining as it were quick buried in a grave of miseries. Her painful memory had straight filled her with the true shapes of all the forepassed mischiefs. Her reason began to cry out against the filthy rebellion of sinful sense, and to tear itself with anguish for having made so weak a resistance; her conscience (a terrible witness of the inward wickedness) still nourishing this debateful fire; her complaint now not having an end directed to it, something to disburden sorrow; but as a necessary downfall of inward wretchedness, she saw the rigour of the laws was like to lay a shameful death upon her—which being for that action undeserved, made it the more insupportable; and yet in depth of her soul most deserved, made it more miserable. At length, letting her tongue go as her dolorous thoughts guided it, she thus, with lamentable demeanour, spake:

'O bottomless pit of sorrow in which I cannot contain myself, having the firebrands of all furies within me, still falling and yet by the infiniteness of it never fallen! Neither can I rid myself, being fettered with the everlasting consideration of it. For whither should I recommend the protection of my dishonoured fall? To the earth? It hath no life, and waits to be increased by the relics of my shamed carcass. To men, who are always cruel in their neighbours' faults, and make others' overthrow become the badge of their ill-masked virtue? To the heavens? O unspeakable torment of conscience which dare not look unto them; no sin can enter there! O, there is

2 fixed, Cl, Da, Ph, Je, Hm, 93: closed St, Bo; *om*. As.   16 filthy] *om*. Cl, As.
18 this] his Da, Je, Hm; the Ph.   19 her] the As; *om*. Da.   directed to it]
directed unto it Cl, Da, Ph; to be directed unto 93.   20 as] *om*. 93.   23-4
insupportable . . . more] *om*. As, Je, Hm.   30 the everlasting] everlasting Da; the
infinite Je.

no receipt for polluted minds! Whither, then, wilt thou lead this
captive of thine, O snaky despair? Alas, alas, was this the free-
holding power that accursed poison hath granted unto me: that, to
be held the surer, it should deprive life? Was this the folding in
5 mine arms promised: that I should fold nothing but a dead body?
O mother of mine, what a deathful suck have you given me! O
Philoclea, Philoclea, well hath my mother revenged upon me my
unmotherly hating of thee! O Cleophila, to whom yet, lest any
misery should fail me, remain some sparks of my detestable love,
10 if thou hast (as now, alas, my mind assures me thou hast) deceived
me, there is a fair scene prepared for thee: to see the tragical end of
thy hated lover.'

With that word, there flowed out two rivers of tears out of her
fair eyes, which before were dry, the remembrance of her other
15 mischiefs being dried up in a furious fire of self-detestation, love
only (according to the temper of it) melting itself into those briny
tokens of passion. Then, turning her eyes again upon the body, she
remembered a dream she had had some days before, wherein,
thinking herself called by Cleophila, passing a troublesome passage,
20 she found a dead body which told her there should be her only rest.
This no sooner caught hold of her remembrance than that she
(determining with herself it was a direct vision of her fore-appointed
end) took a certain resolution to embrace death as soon as it should
be offered unto her, and no way to seek the prolonging of her
25 annoyed life. And therefore, kissing the cold face of Basilius:

'And even so will I rest', said she, 'and join this faulty soul of
mine to thee, if so much the angry gods will grant me.'

As she was in this plight (the sun now climbing over our horizon),
the first shepherds came by; who, seeing the duke in that case, and
30 hearing the noise Dametas made of the lady Philoclea, ran with the
doleful tidings of Basilius's death unto him; who presently with all
his company came to the cave's entry where the duke's body lay—
Dametas, for his part, more glad for the hope he had of his private
escape than sorry for the public loss his country received of a prince

2 snaky Cl, As, Da, Ph, Je, Hm, 93: foul fiend St, Bo.   3 hath] had 93.
8 unmotherly] unworthily Ph; unworthy Je, Hm.   10 now, alas my] now, alas,
now my Bo, As, Ph, Hm, 93.   11 fair Bo, As, Ph, Je, Hm, 93: fairer St, Da.
scene] stage 93.   12 thy] a Ph; om. Je.   lover] love Bo, Da, Hm; loves 93 (corr. 98).
16 briny] brinish Bo; brine Cl.   18 had had some] had some As, Da, Ph, Hm.
days] nights Da, 93.   28 climbing] glymng Cl; shining As.   29 shepherds]
shepherd Ph, Je, Hm.   34 of] for Da, 93.

not to be misliked. But in Gynecia nature prevailed above
judgement, and the shame she conceived to be taken in that order
overcame for that instant the former resolution; so that, as soon as
she saw the foremost of the pastoral troop, the wretched princess ran
to have hid her face in the next woods, but with such a mind that   5
she knew not almost herself what she could wish to be the ground of
her safety. Dametas (that saw her run away in Cleophila's upper
raiment, and judging her to be so) thought certainly all the spirits in
hell were come to play a tragedy in those woods, such strange change
he saw every way: the duke dead at the cave's mouth; the duchess   10
(as he thought) absent; Pamela fled away with Dorus; his wife and
Mopsa in diverse frenzies. But of all other things Cleophila con-
quered his capacity, suddenly from a woman grown a man, and
from a locked chamber gotten before him into the fields, which he
gave the rest quickly to understand. For, instead of doing anything   15
as the exigent required, he began to make circles and all those
fantastical defences that he had ever heard were fortifications against
devils. But the other shepherds (who had both better wits and more
faith) forthwith divided themselves; some of them running after
Gynecia, taking her to be Cleophila and esteeming her running   20
away a great condemnation of her own guiltiness; others going to
their prince to see what service was left for them, either in recovery
of his life, or honouring his death. They that went after the duchess
had soon overtaken her, in whom now the first fears were stayed,
and the resolution to die had repossessed his place in her mind. But 25
when they saw it was the duchess, to whom, besides the obedient
duty they owed to her state, they had always carried a singular love
for her courteous liberalities and other wise and virtuous parts
which had filled all that people with affection and admiration, they
were all suddenly stopped, beginning to ask pardon for their follow- 30
ing her in that sort, and desiring her to be their good lady as she had
ever been. But the duchess (who now thirsted to be rid of herself
whom she hated above all things), with such an assured countenance
as they have who already have dispensed with shame and digested
the sorrows of death, she thus said unto them: 35

5 to have hid] to hide As, Hm; to have hide Ph.   8 raiment] garment Da, Ph,
Hm.   9 those] these Ph, Je, 93.   13 grown a man] grown to be a man Je;
grown to a man Hm, 93.   17 fantastical] imaginative Da, Ph, Je, Hm.
20 taking . . . Cleophila] om. Da, 93.   22 their] the As, Hm.   left] best Cl, Ph.
25 repossessed Bo, As, Da, Ph, 93: possessed St, Cl, 05 (only); reposed Je, Hm.
28 other wise and virtuous] otherwise virtuous Da, Je.

'Continue, continue, my friends! Your doing is better than your excusing; the one argues assured faith, the other want of assurance. If you loved your prince when he was able and willing to do you much good, which you could not then requite to him, do you now
5 publish your gratefulness when it shall be seen to the world there are no hopes left to lead you unto it. Remember, remember, you have lost Basilius: a prince to defend you, a father to care for you, a companion in your joys, a friend in your wants. And if you loved him, show you hate the author of his loss. It is I, faithful Arcadians,
10 that have spoiled this country of their protector. I, none but I, was the minister of his unnatural end. Carry, therefore, my blood in your hands to testify your own innocency. Neither spare for my title's sake, but consider it was he that so entitled me. And if you think of any benefits received by my means, think with it that I was but the in-
15 strument, and he the spring. What, stay ye, shepherds, whose great shepherd is gone? You need not fear a woman, reverence your lord's murderer, nor have pity of her who hath not pity of herself.'

With this she presented her fair neck; some by name, others by signs, desiring them to do justice to the world, duty to their good
20 duke, honour to themselves, and favour to her. The poor men looked one upon the other, unused to be arbiters in princes' matters, and being now fallen into a great perplexity betwixt a prince dead and a princess alive. But once for them she might have gone whither she would, thinking it a sacrilege to touch her person, when she, finding
25 she was not a sufficient orator to persuade her own death by their hands:

'Well,' said she, 'it is but so much more time of misery; for my part, I will not give my life so much pleasure from henceforward as to yield to his desire of his own choice of death. Since all the rest is
30 taken from me, yet let me excel in misery. Lead me, therefore, whither you will, only happy because I cannot be more wretched.'

But neither so much would the honest shepherds do, but rather with many tears bemoaned this increase of their former loss, till she was fain to lead them, with a very strange spectacle: either that a
35 princess should be in the hands of shepherds, or a prisoner should direct her guardians, lastly before either witness or accuser a lady

10 this] the Je, 93.   12 title's] title As, Ph, Je.   14 received] *om.* 93.
16 reverence your] nor reverence your Cl, Da; reverence not your Ph, Je.
17 have] take Cl, As.   not] no Da, Ph.   19 desiring] desired 93 (*corr.* 13).
21 the other] an other Bo, Cl, As, Da, Je, Hm.   22 betwixt] between Cl,
Da, Je.   23 But once] But as Da; *om.* Je.   30 from me] of me Cl; away 93.

condemn herself to death. But in such moanful march they went towards the other shepherds, who in the mean time had left nothing unassayed to revive the duke. But all was bootless, and their sorrows increased the more they had suffered any hopes vainly to arise. Among other trials they made to know at least the cause of his end, having espied the unhappy cup, they gave the little liquor that was left in it to a dog of Dametas, in which within short space it wrought the same effect; although Dametas did so much to recover him that for very love of his life he dashed out his brains. Now all together, and having Gynecia among them (who, to make herself the more odious, did continually record to their minds the excess of their loss), they yielded themselves over to all those forms of lamentation that doleful images do imprint in the honest but over-tender hearts, especially when they think the rebound of the evil falls to their own smart. Therefore, after the ancient Greek manner, some of them remembering the nobility of his birth, continued by being like his ancestors; others his shape which, though not excellent, yet favour and pity drew all things now to the highest point; others his peaceable government, the thing which most pleaseth men resolved to live of their own; others his liberality which, though it cannot light upon all men, yet all men naturally hoping it may be they, makes it a most amiable virtue; some calling in question the greatness of his power, which increased the compassion to see the present change (having a doleful memory how he had tempered it with such familiar courtesy among them, that they did more feel the fruits than see the pomps of his greatness). All with one consent giving him the sacred titles of good, just, merciful, the father of the people, the life of his country, they ran about his body tearing their beards and garments; some sending their cries to heaven; others inventing particular howling musics; many vowing to kill themselves at the day of his funerals; generally giving a true testimony that men are loving creatures when injuries put them not from their natural course, and how easy a thing it is for a prince by succession deeply

5 least OA, 93: last St.   7 in it] *om.* Da, 93.   within short] within a short 93. space] time Da, Je, 93.   8 same] like Da, Ph, Je, 93.   9 Now] But now 93. all together 93: altoger St; altogether OA.   12 over to all] over to Ph; all over to Hm.   lamentation] lamentations Da, Ph, Hm.   13 hearts OA, 93: heart St. 14 evil] evils Cl, As, Je, Hm.   16–17 continued . . . ancestors] *om.* Cl, As.   21 yet all men] yet men 93 (*corr.* 98).   21–2 they, makes], they make As, Da, Je, Hm, 93.   23 increased] increaseth As, Je.   29 sending] sounding Da, Je. 30 musics] music Da, Je, 93.   33 easy] easily 93 (*corr.* 05).

to sink into the souls of his subjects—a more lively monument than Mausolus's tomb. Lastly, having one after the other cryingly sung the duke's praise and his own lamentation, they did all desire Agelastus, one notably noted among them as well for his skill in poetry as for an austerely maintained sorrowfulness (the cause of which, as it were too long to tell, so yet the effect of an Athenian senator to become an Arcadian shepherd), to make an universal complaint for them in this universal mischief; who did it in this sestine:

Since wailing is a bud of causeful sorrow,
Since sorrow is the follower of ill fortune,
Since no ill fortune equals public damage,
Now prince's loss hath made our damage public,
Sorrow pay we unto the rights of nature,
And inward grief seal up with outward wailing.

Why should we spare our voice from endless wailing,
Who justly make our hearts the seats of sorrow,
In such a case where it appears that nature
Doth add her force unto the sting of fortune,
Choosing alas, this our theatre public,
Where they would leave trophies of cruel damage?

Then since such pow'rs conspire unto our damage
(Which may be known, but never helped with wailing)
Yet let us leave a monument in public,
Of willing tears, torn hair, and cries of sorrow.
For lost, lost is by blow of cruel fortune
Arcadia's gem, the noblest child of nature.

O nature doting old, O blinded nature,
How hast thou torn thyself, sought thine own damage,

2–p. 285, 20 Lastly . . . wailing] 93 *transferred the prose introduction and the sestina to the Fourth Eclogues.*   2–4 Lastly . . . one] Nevertheless, of that number one Agelastus 93.   2 the other] another Bo, Da, Hm.   4–5 in poetry] in their poetry Cl, As, Da, Hm.   5–7 (the cause . . . shepherd)] wherewith he seemed to despise the works of nature Cl, As, Da, Ph, Je, Hm, 93.   7 to make] framing 93.   8 for them] *om.* 93.   this] that 93.   who did] uttered 93.   9 sestine] fashion Ph; sort Je.   13 prince's Bo, As, Da, Je, Hm, 93: princess St, Cl, Le, Ph.   14 unto the] to thee the 93.   17 make] makes Le, Ph.   seats] seat Je, 93.   22 conspire] conspired Da, Ph, Je, Hm, 93.   25 hair] hairs As, Da, 93; cheer Je; hearts Hm.   29 thine Cl, Le, As, Da, 93: thy St, Bo, Ph, Je, Hm.

In granting such a scope to filthy fortune,
By thy imp's loss to fill the world with wailing!
Cast thy stepmother eyes upon our sorrow,
Public our loss, so see thy shame is public.

O that we had, to make our woes more public,   5
Seas in our eyes, and brazen tongues by nature,
A yelling voice, and hearts composed of sorrow,
Breath made of flames, wits knowing naught but
    damage,
Our sports murdering ourselves, our musics wailing,   10
Our studies fixed upon the falls of fortune.

No, no, our mischief grows in this vile fortune,
That private pangs cannot breathe out in public
The furious inward griefs with hellish wailing;
But forced are to burden feeble nature   15
With secret sense of our eternal damage,
And sorrow feed, feeding our souls with sorrow.

Since sorrow then concludeth all our fortune,
With all our deaths show we this damage public.
His nature fears to die who lives still wailing.   20

They did with such hearty lamentation disperse among those
woods their resounding shrieks that, the sun (the perfectest mark of
time) having now gotten up two hours' journey in his daily-changing
circle, their voice, helped with the only answering echo, came to the
ears of the faithful and worthy gentleman Philanax; who at that 25
time was coming, accompanied with divers of the principal Arcadian
lords, to visit the duke upon this occasion. Fame (the charge of many
ears and governor of many tongues) had delivered to the attentive
ear of Philanax the late drunken commotion of the Phagonians, with
so large an increase that he (who well knew that too much provision 30
might well lose some charge, but too little might lose all) had speedily

4 so] to Cl, Da, Ph.   7 yelling] yielding As, Hm.   8 wits] with Cl, Hm.
10 musics] music Da, Ph, Je, Hm.   13 pangs] pains 93.   21 They did ... dis-
perse] But as with such hearty lamentation they dispersed 93.   those] these Bo, Je.
22 that] *om.* 93.   23 now] *om.* Cl, As, Hm.   26-p. 286, 13 accompanied ... done]
to visit the king, accompanied with divers of the worthy Arcadian lords, who with him
had visited the places adjoining for the more assurance of Basilius's solitariness, a thing
after the late mutiny he had usually done, and since the princesses' return more diligently
continued; which having now likewise performed, 93.   29 ear] ears Cl; care Da, Hm.

assembled in the frontiers where he lay five hundred horse, and came with all diligence, giving order more should be in readiness if more needed. But being come to the very town itself of Phagona (as it was not out of his way), he there understood how far the virtue of 5 Cleophila had made Basilius fortunate, and that those dangers feared were utterly passed; yet to avoid any such other disturbance to his master's quiet (whom he loved with incomparable loyalty), suffering those that were pardoned to enjoy the fruits of a prince's word, he placed garrisons in all the towns and villages anything near the 10 lodges, over whom he appointed captains of such wisdom and virtue as might not only with the force of their soldiers keep the inhabitants from outrage, but might unpartially look to the discipline both of the men of war and people. That done, thinking it as well his duty to see the duke as of good purpose, being so near, to receive his 15 further direction, accompanied as abovesaid, he was this morning coming unto him, when these unpleasant voices gave his mind an uncertain presage of his near approaching sorrow. For by and by he saw the body of his dearly esteemed prince, and heard Gynecia's waymenting, not such as the turtle-like love is wont to make for the 20 ever over-soon loss of her only loved make, but with cursings of her life, detesting her own wickedness, seeming only therefore not to desire death because she would not show a love of anything. The shepherds, especially Dametas, knowing him to be the second person in authority, gave forthwith relation unto him what they knew and 25 had proved of this dolorous spectacle, besides the other accidents of his children. But he (principally touched with his master's loss), lighting from his horse, with a heavy cheer came and kneeled down by him; where finding he could do no more than the shepherds had for his recovery, the constancy of his mind surprised before he might 30 call together his best rules, could not refrain suchlike words:

'Ah, dear master', said he, 'what change it hath pleased the almighty justice to work in this place! How soon (not to your loss, who have lived long to nature, and now live longer by your well deserved glory, but longest of all in the eternal mansion you now

3 town] village Da, Ph, Je, Hm.   6 such other] other such Cl; such Da.
8 word] words As, Hm.   9 anything] something As; om. Ph.   16 these]
those Cl, As.   18 esteemed] beloved Cl, As, Ph, Hm.   19 waymenting]
lamenting Ph, 93.   20 ever] om. Ph, Hm.   only] om. As; well Ph.   make] mate Ph,
Je, Hm.   cursings] cursing As, Da, Je.   21 only therefore] therefore only Cl, Hm.
27 came and] om. Cl, As.   29 might] could As, Je.   33 have] having 93.
now live] to time 93.

possess), but how soon, I say, to our ruin have you left the frail bark of your estate! O that the words my most faithful duty delivered unto you when you first entered this solitary course might have wrought as much persuasion in you as they sprang from truth in me! Perchance your servant Philanax should not now have had cause in your loss to bewail his own overthrow.' And therewith taking himself: 'And, indeed, ill fitteth it me,' said he, 'to let go my heart to womanish complaints, since my prince being undoubtedly well, it rather shows love of myself, which makes me bewail mine own loss. No, the true love must be proved in the honour of your memory; and that must be showed with seeking just revenge upon your unjust and unnatural enemies. And far more honourable it will be for your tomb to have the blood of your murderers sprinkled upon it than the tears of your friends. And if your soul look down upon this miserable earth, I doubt not it had much rather your death were accompanied with well deserved punishment of the causers of it than with the heaping on it more sorrows with the end of them to whom you vouchsafed your affection. Let them lament that have woven this web of lamentation! Let their own deaths make them cry out for your death that were the authors of it!'

Therewith, carrying manful sorrow and vindicative resolution in his face, he rose up, so looking upon the poor guiltless princess, transported with an unjust justice, that his eyes were sufficient heralds for him to denounce a mortal hatred. She (whom furies of love, firebrands of her conscience, shame of the world, with the miserable loss of her husband, towards whom now the disdain of herself bred more love, with the remembrance of her vision wherewith she resolved assuredly the gods had appointed that shameful end to be her resting place, had set her mind in no other way but to death) used suchlike speeches to Philanax as she had done before to the shepherds, willing him not to look upon her as a woman but a monster; not as a princess but a traitor to his prince; not as Basilius's wife but as Basilius's murderer. She told him how the world required at his hands the just demonstration of his friendship. If he now forgot his prince he should show he had never loved but his fortune,

2 my most] in most 93; I in most 98.   7 it] *om.* Da, Hm.   said he] saith he Cl, Ph; *om.* Hm.   9 mine] my Cl, Da, Ph, Hm.   14 And if OA, 93: if St. 18 this] the Da, Hm, 93.   19 for] of Cl, Hm.   22 rose] rase Bo, Cl, As. so looking 93: looking OA.   upon] on Da, 93.   25 with the] with As, Da. 29 in] to 93.   30 done] *om.* 93.   32 but a traitor] but as a traitor Cl, Da. 35 had] *om.* Bo, Cl, As, Hm.   fortune, 93: fortune, but OA.

like those vermin which suck of the living blood and leave the body as soon as it is dead—poor princess, needlessly seeking to kindle him who did most deadly detest her; which he uttered in this bitter answer:

5 'Madam,' said he, 'you do well to hate yourself, for you cannot hate a worse creature; and though we feel enough your hellish disposition, yet we need not doubt you are a counsel to yourself of much worse than we know. But now fear not, you shall not long be cumbered with being guided by so evil a soul. Therefore prepare 10 yourself, that if it be possible you may deliver up your spirit so much purer as you more wash your wickedness with repentance.'

Then, having presently given order for the bringing from Mantinea a great number of tents for the receipt of the principal Arcadians, the manner of that country being that where the prince died 15 there should be order taken for the country's government, and in the place any murder was committed the judgement should be given there before the body was buried, both concurring in this matter and already great part of the nobility being arrived, he delivered the duchess to a gentleman of great trust. And as for Dametas, taking 20 from him the keys of both the lodges, calling him the moth of his prince's estate, and only spot of his judgement, he caused him with his wife and daughter to be fettered up in as many chains and clogs as they could bear, and every third hour to be cruelly whipped, till the determinate judgement should be given of all these matters. 25 That done, having sent already at his first coming to all the quarters of the country to seek Pamela, although with small hope of overtaking them, he himself went well accompanied to the lodge where the two unfortunate lovers were attending a cruel conclusion of their long-painful, late-pleasant, affection.

30 Dametas's clownish eyes having been the only discoverers of Pyrocles' stratagem, he had no sooner taken a full view of them (which in some sights would rather have bred anything than an accusing mind) and locked the door upon these two young folks (now made prisoners for love as before they had been prisoners to

1 those] the Cl; these As.   which] that 93.   2 as soon] so soon Cl, Hm.   7 a counsel] of counsel 93.   9 by] with Bo, Cl, Ph (with *corr. to* by St).   11 more] *om.* Cl, As.   15 order] orders 93 (*ex.* 05).   17 was] were Cl, Ph, Je. in] is 93 (*corr.* 98).   19 duchess] princess Ph, 93.   20 moth] mouth Da, Hm (mouth *corr. to* moth St).   24 these] those Bo, Cl.   25 first] *om.* 93. 29 long-painful, late-pleasant] long painful and late most painful 93.   31 he] *om.* 93.   33 these] those Cl, Ph; them As.

love) but that, immediately upon his going down (whether with noise
Dametas made, or with the creeping in of the light, or rather, as I think,
that as he had but little slept that night so the sweet embracement
he enjoyed gave his senses a very early salve to come to themselves),
but so it was that Pyrocles awaked, grudging in himself that sleep 5
(though very short) had robbed him of any part of those his highest
contentments, especially considering that he was then to prepare
himself to return to the duke's bed, and at his coming to set such a
comical face of the matter as he should find by the speeches of
Basilius and Gynecia should be most convenient. But being now 10
fully awaked, he might hear a great noise under the lodge which (as
affection is full of sudden doubts) made him leap out of his bed,
having first with earnest kissing the peerless Philoclea (who then
soundly sleeping was the natural image of exact beauty) received
into his sense a full proportion of the greatest delight he could 15
imagine under the moon. But being up, the first ill handsel he had
of the ill case wherein he was was the seeing himself deprived of his
sword, from which he had never separated himself in any occasion,
and even that night, first by the duke's bed, and then there, had laid
it as he thought safe, putting great part of the trust of his well doing 20
in his own courage, so armed. For, indeed, the confidence in oneself
is the chief nurse of true magnanimity; which confidence notwith-
standing doth not leave the care of necessary furnitures for it, and
therefore of all the Grecians Homer doth ever make Achilles the
best armed. But that, as I say, was his first ill token. But by and by 25
he perceived he was a prisoner before any arrest; for the door, which
he had left open, was made so fast of the outside that, for all the
force he could employ unto it, he could not undo Dametas's doing.
Then went he to the window to see if that way there were any escape
for him and his dear lady. But as vain he found all his employment 30
there, not having might to break out, but only one bar, wherein
notwithstanding he strained his sinews to the uttermost; and that
he rather took out to use for other services than for any possibility

1 but that OA, 93: but St.   with noise] with the noise Da, Je.   2 as I
think] *om*. 93.   3 that as he] that he Cl, Da.   slept] sleep Ph, Hm.
embracement] embracements Da, Ph, Je.   3–4 he had . . . gave] extreme grief
had procured his sleep so extreme care had measured his sleep, giving 93.   4 early]
easy Cl; earthly Da.   salve] saluë 93.   5 but . . . was that] *om*. 93.
5–16 grudging . . . moon] *om*. 93.   12 sudden] *om*. Bo, Cl.   16 But] And 93.
being] looking Cl, As.   22 true] *om*. Da, Ph, Je, Hm, 93.   23 furnitures] furni-
ture As, Da.   25 as] *om*. Cl, As.   his] the Ph, 93.   27 of] on Bo, Da, Je, Hm.
29 window] windows Hm, 93.   33 services] service 93.

he found of escape. For even then it was that Dametas, having gathered together the first-coming shepherds, did blabber out what he had found in the lady Philoclea's chamber. Pyrocles markingly hearkened to all that Dametas said (whose voice and mind acquain-
5 tance had taught him sufficiently to know). But when he assuredly perceived all his action with the lady Philoclea was fully discovered, remembering withal the cruelty of the Arcadian laws which, without exception, did condemn all to death who were found in act of marriage without solemnity of marriage, assuring himself, besides the
10 law, that the duke and duchess would use so much more hate against their daughter as they had found themselves sotted by him in the pursuit of their love; lastly, seeing they were not only in the way of death but fitly encaged for death, looking with a hearty grief upon the honour of love, the fellowless Philoclea (whose innocent soul
15 now enjoying his own goodness did little know the danger of his ever fair, then sleeping, harbour), his excellent wit, strengthened with virtue but guided by love, had soon described to himself a perfect vision of their present condition. Wherein having presently cast a resolute reckoning of his own part of the misery, not only the
20 chief but sole burden of his anguish consisted in the unworthy case which was like to fall upon the best deserving Philoclea. He saw the misfortune, not the mismeaning, of his work was like to bring that creature to end in whom the world, as he thought, did begin to receive honour. He saw the weak judgement of man would condemn
25 that as a death-deserving vice in her which had in truth never broken the bands of a true living virtue. And how often his eye turned to his attractive adamant so often did an unspeakable horror strike his noble heart, to consider so unripe years, so faultless a beauty, the mansion of so pure goodness, should have her youth so untimely cut
30 off, her natural perfections unnaturally consumed, her virtue rewarded with shame. Sometimes he would accuse himself of negligence, that had not more curiously looked to all the house entries; and yet could he not imagine the way Dametas was gotten in. And

1 found of] had to 93.   that] when Bo, Hm.   6 all] as As; that 93.   action] being 93.   6–7 discovered, remembering] discovered, and by the folly or malice, or rather malicious folly, of Dametas her honour therein touched in the highest degree, remembering 93.   8 in act] (as Dametas reported of them) in act 93.   10 that] *om.* Da, Je, 93.   the duke and duchess] the king and the queen 93.   so] *om.* As, Je. 14 fellowless] silly Ph; fellowes 93 (*corr.* 98).   16 ever] *om.* Ph; over Hm. 22 that] the Da, Hm.   25 a] *om.* 93.   vice] voice 93 (*corr.* 98).   26 bands] bonds 93.   30 unnaturally] so unnaturally Ph, Hm.   32 that had] that he had Da, Hm.

to call back what might have been to a man of wisdom and courage carries but a vain shadow of discourse. Sometimes he could not choose but, with a dissolution of his inward might, lamentably consider with what face he might look upon his (till then) joy, Philoclea, when the next light waking should deliver unto her should perchance 5 be the last of her hurtless life; and that the first time she should bend her excellent eyes upon him she should see the accursed author of her dreadful end. And even this consideration, more than any other, did so settle itself in his well disposed mind that, dispersing his thoughts to all the ways that might be of her safety, finding a very 10 small discourse in so narrow limits of time and place, at length in many difficulties he saw none bear any likelihood for her life, but his death. For then he thought it would fall out that when they found his body dead, having no accuser but Dametas (as by his speech he found there was not), it might justly appear that either Philoclea in 15 defending her honour, or else he himself in despair of achieving, had left his carcass proof of his fact but witness of her clearness. Having a small while stayed upon the greatness of his resolution, and looked to the furthest of it:

'Be it so,' said the valiant Pyrocles, 'never life for better cause, 20 nor to better end, was bestowed; for if death be to follow this fact (which no death of mine shall ever make me repent), who is to die so justly as myself? And if I must die, who can be so fit executioners as mine own hands which, as they were accessaries to the fact, so in killing me they shall suffer their own punishment?'   25

But then arose there a new impediment; for Dametas having carried away anything which he thought might hurt as tender a man as himself, he could find no fit instrument which might give him a final dispatch. At length, making the more haste lest his lady should awake, taking the iron bar (which being sharper something at the 30 one end than the other, he hoped, joined to his willing strength, might break off the slender thread of mortality):

'Truly,' said he, 'fortune, thou hast well persevered mine enemy, that wilt grant me no fortune to be unfortunate, nor let me have an easy passage, now I am to trouble thee no more. But,' said he, 'O bar, 35 blessed in that thou hast done service to the chamber of the paragon

2 discourse OA, 93: disdain St.   9 settle] set 93.   17 fact] intent 93.
21 fact] doing 93.   22 shall . . . repent] could make me leave undone 93.   24 fact]
doing 93.   31 than the] than at the Bo, Cl, Da, Ph, Je, Hm.   33 persevered
Cl, As, 93: preserved St, Bo, Da, Ph, Je, Hm (preserved *corr. to* persevered Cl).
34 wilt] will Cl, As, Da, Ph, Je, Hm.

of life, since thou couldst not help me to make a perfecter escape,
yet serve my turn, I pray thee, that I may escape from myself.'

Therewithal, yet once looking to fetch the last repast of his eyes,
and new again transported with the pitiful case he left her in,
5 kneeling down he thus prayed unto Jupiter:

'O great maker and great ruler of this world,' said he, 'to thee do
I sacrifice this blood of mine; and suffer, O Jove, the errors of my
youth to pass away therein. And let not the soul by thee made, and
ever bending unto thee, be now rejected of thee. Neither be offended
10 that I do abandon this body, to the government of which thou hadst
placed me, without thy leave, since how can I know but that thy
unsearchable mind is I should so do, since thou hast taken from me
all means longer to abide in it? And since the difference stands but
in a short time of dying, thou that hast framed my heart inclined
15 to do good, how can I in this small space of mine benefit so much all
the human kind as in preserving thy perfectest workmanship, their
chiefest honour? O justice itself, howsoever thou determinest of me,
let this excellent innocency not be oppressed. Let my life pay her
loss. O Jove, give me some sign that I may die with this comfort.'
20 And pausing a little, as if he had hoped for some token: 'And when-
soever, to the eternal darkness of the earth, she doth follow me, let
our spirits possess one place, and let them be more happy in that
uniting.'

With that word, striking the bar upon his heart side with all the
25 force he had, and falling withal upon, to give it the througher
passage, the bar in truth was too blunt to do the effect; although it
pierced his skin and bruised his ribs very sore, so that his breath
was almost past him. But the noise of his fall drave away sleep from
the quiet senses of the dear Philoclea, whose sweet soul had an early
30 salutation of a deadly spectacle unto her; with so much more astonish-
ment as the falling asleep but a little before she had left herself
in the uttermost point of contentment, and saw now before her eyes
the most cruel enterprise that human nature can undertake, without

1 perfecter] perfect Cl, Ph; profitter Je.   3 yet] *om.* Da, Hm.   5 unto
Jupiter] *om.* 93.   7 O Jove] Lord 93.   errors] error Ph; cares Hm (since . . . in
it *om.* Ph).   10 hadst Bo, Cl, As, Da, Ph, 93: hast St, Je, Hm.   13 means]
mean Cl, As.   14 heart] soul Da, Ph, Je, Hm, 93.   16 their] thy Cl, As;
the Je.   19 Jove] Lord 93.   20 as if he had hoped] as though he had looked
Da, Ph.   24 word] *om.* Cl, As.   25 througher] thorow As, Da, Hm; thorower 93.
31 she had] had Cl, As; *om.* Da, Ph, Je, Hm.   31–2 left herself in] retired herself
from 93.   32 contentment] woefulness 93.   now before] now again before 93.

discerning any cause thereof. But the lively print of her affection had soon taught her not to stay long upon deliberation in so urgent a necessity. Therefore getting with speed her well accorded limbs out of her sweetened bed (as when jewels are hastily pulled out of some rich coffer), she spared not the nakedness of her tender feet, 5 but I think borne as fast with desire as fear carried Daphne, she came running to Pyrocles; and finding his spirits something troubled with the fall, she put by the bar that lay close to him, and straining him in her most beloved embracement:

'My comfort, my joy, my life,' said she, 'what haste have you to 10 kill your Philoclea with the most cruel torment that ever lady suffered? Do you not yet persuade yourself that any hurt of yours is a death unto me, and that your death should be my hell? Alas, if any sudden mislike of me (for other cause I see none) have caused you to loathe yourself; if any fault or defect of mine hath bred this 15 terriblest rage in you, rather let me suffer the bitterness of it, for so shall the deserver be punished, mankind preserved from such a ruin, and I, for my part, shall have that comfort that I die by the noblest hand that ever drew sword.'

Pyrocles, grieved with his fortune that he had not in one instant 20 cut off all such deliberation, thinking his life only reserved to be bound to be the unhappy news-teller: 'Alas,' said he, 'my only star, why do you this wrong to God, yourself, and me, to speak of faults in you? No, no, most faultless, most perfect lady, it is your excellency that makes me hasten my desired end. It is the right I owe to 25 the general nature that (though against private nature) makes me seek the preservation of all that she hath done in this age. Let me, let me die! There is no way to save your life, most worthy to be conserved, than that my death be your clearing.'

Then did he, with far more pain and backward loathness than 30 the so near killing himself was (but yet driven with necessity to make her yield to that he thought was her safety), make her a short but pithy discourse what he had heard by Dametas's speeches, confirming the rest with a plain demonstration of their imprisonment. And then sought he new means of stopping his breath, but that by 35 Philoclea's labour above her force he was stayed to hear her, in whom

3 her well] her weak though well 93.   8 that] which Da, Je.   9 beloved] loving
Cl, As, Da.   13 a] om. Cl, Da, Ph.   15 fault or defect] desert or default As;
fault or desert Cl; default or defect Ph.   hath Cl, As, Da, Ph, Je, Hm, 93: had St;
have Bo.   16 terriblest] terrible As, Da, Je, 05 (only).   21 such] om. Bo, Da.
25 hasten] haste Da, Je.   27 hath] had Cl, As.   32 make] made Da, Je.

a man might perceive what small difference in the working there is betwixt a simple voidness of evil and a judicial habit of virtue. For she, not with an unshaked magnanimity, wherewith Pyrocles weighed and despised death, but with an innocent guiltlessness, not knowing
5 why she should fear to deliver her unstained soul to God, helped with the true loving of Pyrocles, which made her think no life without him, did almost bring her mind to as quiet attending all accidents as the unmastered virtue of Pyrocles. Yet, having with a pretty paleness (which did leave milken lines upon her rosy cheeks) paid
10 a little duty to human fear, taking the prince by the hand, and kissing the wound he had given himself:

'O the only life of my life and, if it fall out so, the comfort of my death,' said she, 'far, far from you be the doing me such wrong as to think I will receive my life as a purchase of your death. But well
15 may you make my death so much more miserable as it shall anything be delayed after my only felicity. Do you think I can account of the moment of death like the unspeakable afflictions my soul should suffer so oft as I call Pyrocles to my mind, which should be as oft as I breathed? Should these eyes guide my steps, that had seen your
20 murder? Should these hands feed me, that had not hindered such a mischief? Should this heart remain within me, at every pant to count the continual clock of my miseries? O no, if die we must, let us thank death he hath not divided so true an union. And truly, my Pyrocles, I have heard my father and other wise men say that the
25 killing oneself is but a false colour of true courage, proceeding rather of fear of a further evil, either of torment or shame. For if it were a not respecting the harm, that would likewise make him not respect what might be done unto him; and hope being of all other the most contrary thing to fear, this being an utter banishment of hope, it
30 seems to receive his ground in fear. Whatsoever (would they say) comes out of despair cannot bear the title of valour, which should be lifted up to such a height that, holding all things under itself, it should be able to maintain his greatness even in the midst of miseries. Lastly, they would say God had appointed us captains of
35 these our bodily forts, which without treason to that majesty were never to be delivered over till they were redemanded.'

4 guiltlessness] guiltiness As, Je, Hm.   7 did OA, 93: and did St.   13 far, far] far Ph, Hm.   doing me] doing of me Cl, As.   16 my] mine Cl, As.   16 can account] cannot count As, Ph.   23 divided] denied Cl, Ph.   25 killing oneself] killing of oneself Bo, Ph.   34 they would Bo, Cl, As, Da, Ph, 93: the would St; would they Je; they will Hm.

Pyrocles (who had that for a law unto him not to leave Philoclea in anything unsatisfied), although he still remained in his former purpose, and knew the time would grow short for it, yet hearing no noise (the shepherds being as then run to Basilius), with settled and humbled countenance, as a man that should have spoken of a thing that did not concern himself, bearing even in his eyes sufficient shows that it was nothing but Philoclea's danger which did anything burden his heart, far stronger than fortune, having with vehement embracings of her got yet some fruit of his delayed end, he thus answered the wise innocency of Philoclea:

'Lady most worthy not only of life but to be the very life of all things, the more notable demonstrations you make of the love so far beyond my desert with which it pleaseth you to overcome fortune in making me happy, the more am I even in course of humanity (to leave that love's force which I neither can nor will leave) bound to seek requital's witness that I am not ungrateful; to do which, the infiniteness of your goodness being such as it cannot reach unto it, yet doing all I can and paying my life, which is all I have, though it be far (without measure) short of your desert, yet shall I not die in debt to mine own duty. And truly, the more excellent arguments you made to keep me from this passage (imagined far more terrible than it is), the more plainly it makes me see what reason I have to prevent the loss, not only Arcadia but all the face of the earth, should receive if such a tree (which even in his first spring doth not only bear most beautiful blossoms but most rare fruits) should be so untimely cut off. Therefore, O most truly beloved lady, to whom I desire for both our goods that these may be my last words, give me your consent even out of that wisdom which must needs see that (besides your unmatched betterness, which perchance you will not see) it is fitter one die than both. And since you have sufficiently showed you love me, let me claim by that love you will be content rather to let me die contentedly than wretchedly; rather with a clear and joyful conscience than with desperate condemnation in myself that I, accursed villain, should be the mean of banishing from the sight of men the true example of virtue. And because there is nothing left me to be imagined which I so much desire as that the

3 the time] that time Hm, 93.   4 run] come As, Hm.   9 embracings] embracing Cl, Da; embracement As; embracements Hm.   got yet some OA, 93: got some St. 11 very] *om.* Ph, Je.   17 it cannot] I cannot As, Ph; cannot Da.   23 only Arcadia] only of Arcadia Hm, 93.   29 betterness] bitterness Ph; betters Hm. 35 men OA, 93: man St.

memory of Pyrocles may ever have an allowed place in your wise judgement, I am content to draw so much breath longer as, by answering the sweet objections you alleged, may bequeath (as I think) a right conceit unto you that this my doing is out of judgement, 5 and not sprung of passion. Your father, you say, was wont to say that this like action doth more proceed of fear of further evil or shame than of a true courage. Truly first, they put a very guessing case, speaking of them who can never after come to tell with what mind they did it. And as for my part, I call the immortal truth to 10 witness that no fear of torment can appal me, who know it is but diverse manners of apparelling death, and have long learned to set bodily pain in the second form of my being. And as for shame, how can I be ashamed of that for which my well meaning conscience will answer for me to God, and your unresistible beauty to the world? But 15 to take that argument in his own force, and grant it done for avoiding of further pain or dishonour (for as for the name of fear, it is but an odious title of a passion given to that which true judgement performeth), grant I say it is to shun a worse case; and truly I do not see but that true fortitude, looking into all human things with a persisting resolu- 20 tion, carried away neither with wonder of pleasing things nor astonishment of unpleasant, doth not yet deprive itself of the discerning the difference of evils, but rather is the only virtue with which an assured tranquillity shuns the greater by valiant entering into the less. Thus for his country's safety he will spend his life; for the saving of a limb he 25 will not niggardly spare his goods; for the saving of all his body he will not spare the cutting off a limb—where indeed the weak-hearted man will rather die than see the face of a surgeon, who might with as good reason say that the constant man abides the painful surgery for fear of a further evil, but he is content to wait for death itself. But neither is 30 true, for neither hath the one any fear, but a well choosing judgement; nor the other hath any contentment, but only fear, not having a heart actively to perform a matter of pain, is forced passively to abide a greater damage. For to do requires a whole heart, to suffer falls easiliest

1 wise] *om.* Cl, Ph.   3 the] *om.* As; your Ph.   6 more] rather Cl; *om.* Da; now Ph.   8 never] ever 93 (*corr.* 13).   after come] come after Cl; come Da. 9 the] them 93 (*corr.* 98).   10 know] knows Cl, As, Je (who . . . death *blank left* Ph).   12 pain in] pain but in Cl, 93.   15 done] *om.* Bo; due Hm.   15–16 of further] of a further Bo, Cl, As, Da, Ph; a further Je, Hm.   21 of unpleasant] of the unpleasant Bo, As, Je, Hm, 93; of unpleasing things Cl.   22 evils] evil 93. 23 shuns] shames Ph; shows Hm.   by valiant] by the valiant 93.   31 fear, not] fear, and not 93.   33 falls Bo, Ph: false *corr. to* faults St (false *on cancelled folio*); falleth Cl, As, Je, Hm, 93; faults *corr. to* falleth Da.   easiliest] easily Da, Hm.

in the broken minds; and if in bodily torments thus, much more in
shame wherein, since valour is a virtue, and virtue is ever limited, we
must not run so infinitely as to think the valiant man is willingly to
suffer any thing, since the very suffering of some things is a certain
proof of want of courage; and if anything unwillingly, among the   5
chiefest may shame go. For if honour be to be held dear, his contrary
is to be abhorred; and that not for fear, but of a true election. Which is
the less inconvenient, either the loss of some years more or less (for
once we know our lives be not immortal), or the submitting ourselves
to each unworthy misery which the foolish world may lay upon us? As   10
for their reason that fear is contrary to hope, neither do I defend fear,
nor much yield unto the authority of hope; to either of which, great
inclining shows but a feeble reason, which must be guided by his
servants; and who builds not upon hope shall fear no earthquake of
despair. Their last alleging of the heavenly powers, as it bears the   15
greatest name so it is the only thing that at all bred any combat in
my mind. And yet I do not see but that, if God have made us masters
of anything, it is of our own lives, out of which without doing wrong
to anybody we are to issue at our own pleasure; and the same argu-
ment would as much prevail to say we should for no necessity lay   20
away from us any of our joints, since they being made of him,
without his warrant we shall not depart from them; or if that may
be for a greater cause, we may pass to a greater degree. And if we
be lieutenants of God in this little castle, do you not think we must
take warning of him to give over our charge when he leaves us   25
unprovided of good means to tarry in it?'

'No, certainly do I not,' answered the sorrowful Philoclea, 'since
it is not for us to appoint that mighty majesty what time he will help
us. The uttermost instant is scope enough for him to revoke every-
thing to one's own desire. And therefore, to prejudicate his deter-   30
mination is but a doubt of goodness in him who is nothing but
goodness. But when, indeed, he doth either by sickness or outward
force lay death upon us, then are we to take knowledge that such is
his pleasure, and to know that all is well that he doth. That we should
be masters of ourselves we can show at all no title, nor claim; since   35

1 torments] torment As, 93.   3 willingly] willing Ph, Je, Hm.   5 unwillingly] *om*. Cl;
unwilling Hm.   7 Which] For which 93.   8 inconvenient] inconvenience Cl, Ph, Hm.
9 submitting ourselves] submitting of ourselves As, Hm.   12 unto] to Cl, Da, Ph, Je, 93.
14 fear] feel Cl, Da.   16 bred] breeds As, Da, Ph, Je, Hm.   17 that] *om*. As, Ph.
have] had Da; hath Je, Hm, 93.   20 no] our As, Ph.   22 shall] should Bo, Da, Je,
Hm, 93; may Ph.   27 answered] answereth As; answers Da.

neither we made ourselves, nor bought ourselves, we can stand upon no other right but his gift, which he must limit as it pleaseth him. Neither is there any proportion betwixt the loss of any other limb and that, since the one bends to the preserving all, the other to the

5 destruction of all; the one takes not away the mind from the actions for which it is placed in the world, the other cuts off all possibility of his working. And truly, my most dear Pyrocles, I must needs protest unto you that I cannot think your defence even in rules of virtue sufficient. Sufficient and excellent it were, if the question

10 were of two outward things wherein a man might by nature's freedom determine whether he would prefer shame to pain, present smaller torment to greater following, or no. But to this (besides the comparison of the matters' values) there is added of the one part a direct evil doing, which maketh the balance of that side too much unequal,

15 since a virtuous man, without any respect whether the grief be less or more, is never to do that which he cannot assure himself is allowable before the everliving rightfulness, but rather is to think honours or shames (which stand in other men's true or false judgements), pains or not pains (which yet never approach our souls) to be nothing in regard

20 of an unspotted conscience. And these reasons do I remember I have heard good men bring in: that since it hath not his ground in an assured virtue, it proceeds rather of some other disguised passion.'

Pyrocles was not so much persuaded as delighted by her well conceived and sweetly pronounced speeches. But when she had

25 closed her pitiful discourse and, as it were, sealed up her delightful lips with the moistness of her tears (which followed still one another like a precious rope of pearl), now thinking it high time: 'Be it as you say,' said he, 'most virtuous beauty, in all the rest; but never can God himself persuade me that Pyrocles' life is not well lost for

30 to preserve the most admirable Philoclea. Let that be, if it be possible, written on my tomb, and I will not envy Codrus's honour.'

With that, he would again have used the bar, meaning if that failed to leave his brains upon the wall, when Philoclea, now brought to that she most feared, kneeled down unto him, and embracing so

35 his legs that without hurting her (which for nothing he would have

2 he] we Cl, As.   10 were of] were not of Cl, As.   12–13 comparison] comparisons Cl, Da, Je.   13 values] valures Da, 98; value Ph.   14 of] on Da, Je, Hm (of . . . unequal Ph *substitutes* nothing).   16 more] no Da, Je.   which] *om.* As, Da.   17 rather is] rather Cl, As; is rather Je.   18 judgements] judgement Da, Je.   20 these OA, 93: those St; this Da.   31 on] in Cl, As.   33 failed] fail Ph, Je.   Philoclea, now] now Philoclea Ph, Je.

done) he could not rid himself from her, she did, with all the conjuring words which the authority of love may lay, beseech him he would not now so cruelly abandon her; he would not leave her comfortless in that misery to which he had brought her; that then indeed she would even in her soul accuse him to have most foully betrayed her; 5 that then she should have cause to curse the time that ever the name of Pyrocles came to her ears, which otherwise no death could make her do. 'Will you leave me', said she, 'not only dishonoured as unchaste with you, but as a murderer of you? Will you give mine eyes such a picture of hell before my near approaching death as to see the 10 murdered body of him I love more than all the lives that nature can give?' With that, she sware by the highest cause of all devotions that, if he did persevere in that cruel resolution, she would not only confess to her father that with her consent this act had been committed but, if that would not serve, after she had pulled out her own 15 eyes (made accursed by such a sight), she would give herself so terrible a death as she might think the pain of it would countervail the never dying pain of her mind: 'Now therefore kill yourself, to crown our virtuous action with infamy; kill yourself, to make me (whom you say you love), as long as I after-live you, change my 20 loving admiration of you to a detestable abhorring your name. And so, indeed, you shall have the end you shoot at; for instead of one death you shall give me a thousand, and yet in the mean time deprive me of the help God may send me.'

Pyrocles, even overweighed with her so wisely uttered affection, 25 finding her determination so fixed that his end should but deprive them both of a present contentment, and not avoid a coming evil (as a man that ran not unto it by a sudden qualm of passion, but by a true use of reason, preferring her life to his own), now that wisdom did manifest unto him that way would not prevail, he retired himself 30 with as much tranquillity from it as before he had gone unto it, like a man that had set the keeping or leaving of the body as a thing without himself, and so had thereof a freed and untroubled consideration. Therefore throwing away the bar from him, and taking

8–9 as unchaste] as supposed unchaste 93.   9 mine] nty Cl, Da.   13 would not] would (though untruly) not 93.   19 our] your Ph; this 93 (to . . . yourself om. Cl).   20 after-live you] live after you Ph; after live 93.   21 abhorring your] abhorring of your Cl, Hm.   28 ran] came Ph, Hm.   not OA, 93: om. St. unto] into Cl, As (he . . . unto it om. Bo).   of passion] om. Cl, As.   31 unto] into Cl; to Je.   32 of] om. Ph, Hm.   the body] that body As; a body Hm. 33 had thereof] had therefore Bo; thereof had Cl, Da.   freed] free Ph, Hm.

her up from the place where he thought the consummating of all
beauties very unworthily lay, suffering all his senses to devour up
their chiefest food, which he assured himself they should shortly
after forever be deprived of: 'Well', said he, 'most dear lady, whose
5 contentment I prefer before mine own, and judgement esteem more
than mine own, I yield unto your pleasure. The gods send you have
not won your own loss! For my part, they are my witnesses that I
think I do more at your commandment in delaying my death than
another would in bestowing his life. But now', said he, 'as thus far I
10 have yielded unto you, so grant me in recompense thus much again,
that I may find your love in granting as you have found your
authority in obtaining: my humble suit is you will say I came in by
force into your chamber, for so I am resolved now to affirm, and
that will be the best for us both. But in no case name my name,
15 that whatsoever come of me my house be not dishonoured.'

Philoclea, fearing lest refusal would turn him back again to his
violent refuge, gave him a certain countenance that might show she
did yield to his request, the latter part whereof indeed she meant for
his sake to perform. Neither could they spend more words together,
20 for Philanax, with twenty of the noblest personages of Arcadia after
him were come into the lodge. Philanax, making the rest stay below
for the reverence he bare to womanhood, as stilly as he could came
to the door, and opening it, drew the eyes of these two doleful lovers
unto him; Philoclea closing again for modesty's sake within her bed
25 the richess of her beauties, but Pyrocles took hold of his bar,
minding at least to die before the excellent Philoclea should receive
any outrage. But Philanax rested awhile upon himself, stricken with
admiration at the goodly shape of Pyrocles, whom before he had
never seen, and withal remembering the notable act he had done
30 (when with his courage and eloquence he had saved Basilius, per-
chance the whole state, from utter ruin), he felt a kind of relenting
mind towards him. But when that same thought came waited on
with the remembrance of his master's death, which he by all

4 forever be deprived of] be deprived of Da, Ph; be deprived of forever Je.
5 mine] my Da, Ph, Hm.   10 you OA, 93: om. St.   11 love in] loving Bo, As.
12 humble OA, 93: humblest St.   in] om. Da, Hm.   13 I am] am I Bo, Da, Je, 93.
resolved now] resolved Cl; now resolved Hm.   14 will OA, 93: shall St.   20 the
noblest] the most noblest Da, Je.   23 these] those Cl, As, Je Hm.   24 unto]
upon Cl, As, Da, Je, 93; to Ph; towards Hm.   within her bed] within the bed Bo;
om. Cl, Je.   25 richess] riches Cl, As, Da, Ph, Je, Hm.   29 remembering the]
remembering besides others the 93.   32 that] the Cl, Da, Ph, Hm (the corr. to
that St).   33 with the remembrance] with remembrance As, Je.

probabilities thought he had been of counsel unto with the duchess, compassion turned to hateful passion, and left in Philanax a strange medley betwixt pity and revenge, betwixt liking and abhorring.

'O lord,' said he to himself, 'what wonders doth nature in our time to set wickedness so beautifully garnished; and that which is 5 strangest, out of one spring to make wonderful effects both of virtue and vice to issue!'

Pyrocles seeing him in such a muse, neither knowing the man nor the cause of his coming, but assuring himself it was not for his good, yet thought best to begin with him in this sort: 'Gentleman,' 10 said he, 'what is the cause of your coming to my lady Philoclea's chamber? Is it to defend her from such violence as I might go about to offer unto her? If it be so, truly your coming is vain, for her own virtue hath been a sufficient resistance. There needs no strength to be added to so inviolate chastity. The excellency of her mind makes 15 her body impregnable, which for mine own part I had soon yielded to confess with going out of this place (where I found but little comfort, being so disdainfully received) had I not been, I know not by whom, presently upon my coming hither so locked into this chamber that I could never escape hence, where I was fettered in 20 the most guilty shame that ever man was, seeing what a paradise of unspotted goodness my filthy thoughts sought to defile. If for that therefore you come, already I assure you your errand is performed. But if it be to bring me to any punishment whatsoever for having undertaken so unexcusable presumption, truly I bear such an accuser 25 about me of mine own conscience that I willingly submit myself unto it. Only thus much let me demand of you, that you will be a witness unto the duke what you hear me say, and oppose yourself, that neither his sudden fury nor any other occasion may offer any hurt to this lady, in whom you see nature hath accomplished so 30 much that I am fain to lay mine own faultiness as a foil of her purest excellency. I can say no more, but look upon her beauty; remember her blood; consider her years; and judge rightly of her virtues, and I doubt not a gentleman's mind will then be a sufficient instructor unto you in this, I may term it, miserable chance, happened unto 35 her by my unbridled audacity.'

2 and left] had left Da, Je.   strange] strong Bo, Hm.   9–10 was not for his good] was not for no good Da, Je; was for no good 93.   13 is vain] is in vain Cl, Da, Hm.   16 mine] my Cl, Da.   17 with] by Cl, As, Je.   26 mine] my Da Hm.   27 thus] this 93 (corr. 05).   31 mine] my Bo, Hm.   34 then] there Ph; om. Hm.

Philanax was content to hear him out, not for any favour he owed him, but to see whether he would reveal anything of the original cause and purpose of the duke's death. But finding it so far from that that he named Basilius unto him as supposing him alive, think-ing it rather cunning than ignorance: 'Young man,' said he, 'whom I have cause to hate before I have mean to know, you use but a point of skill by confessing the manifest smaller fault, to be believed here-after in the denial of the greater. But for that matter, all passeth to one end, and hereafter we shall have leisure to seek by torments the truth—if the love of truth itself will not bring you unto it. As for my lady Philoclea, if it so fall out as you say, it shall be the more fit for her years, and comely for the great house she is come of, that an ill-governed beauty have not cancelled the rules of virtue. But howso-ever that be, it is not for you to teach an Arcadian what reverent duty we owe to any of that progeny. But', said he, 'come you with me without resistance, for the one cannot avail, and the other may procure pity.'

'Pity,' said Pyrocles with a bitter smiling, disdained with so cur-rish an answer, 'no, no, Arcadian, I can quickly have pity of myself, and I would think my life most miserable which should be a gift of thine. Only I demand this innocent lady's security, which until thou hast confirmed unto me by an oath assure thyself the first that lays hands upon her shall leave his life for a testimony of his sacrilege.'

Philanax with an inward scorn, thinking it most manifest they were both, he at least, of counsel with the duke's death: 'Well', said he, 'you speak much to me of the duke. I do here swear unto you by the love I have ever borne him she shall have no worse (howsoever it fall out) than her own parents.'

'And upon that word of yours I yield', said the poor Pyrocles, deceived by him that meant not to deceive him.

Then did Philanax send for apparel for him, and having arrayed him, delivered him into the hands of a nobleman in the company, everyone desirous to have him in his charge, so much did his goodly presence (in whom true valour shined) breed a delightful admiration

---

3 finding it so OA, 93: finding so St.   8 in the denial] in denial As, Ph.
9 to seek by torments] by torments to seek 93.   11 be the more OA, 93: be more
St.   12 is come] came Cl, Hm.   13 have] hath Cl, Ph, Je, 93.   14 that
be] it be Cl, Ph, Je, Hm, 93.   15 you] *om.* Bo, Hm, 13.   20 would]
will Da, Je.   24 scorn] storm 93 (*corr.* 98).   25 at least] at the least Ph, Je.
of] *om.* Cl; a Hm.   31-2 send . . . arrayed him] *om.* 93.   32 delivered]
deliver 93.   34 breed] bred Cl, As, Hm.

in all the beholders. Philanax himself stayed with Philoclea, to see whether of her he might learn some disclosing of this former confusion. But she, sweet lady, whom first a kindly shamefastness had separated from Pyrocles (they being both left in a more open view than her modesty would well bear), then the attending her father's 5 coming and studying how to behave herself towards him for both their safeties had called her spirits all within her, now that upon a sudden Pyrocles was delivered out of the chamber from her, at the first she was so surprised with the extreme stroke of the woeful sight that, like those that in their dream are taken with some ugly vision 10 they would fain cry for help but have no force, so remained she awhile quite deprived, not only of speech, but almost of any other lively action. But when indeed Pyrocles was quite drawn from her eyes, and that her vital strength began to return unto her, now not knowing what they did to Pyrocles, but according to the nature of 15 love fearing the worst, wringing her hands and letting abundance of tears be the first part of her eloquence, bending her amber-crowned head over her bedside, to the hard-hearted Philanax: 'O Philanax, Philanax,' said she, 'I know how much authority you have with my father; there is no man whose wisdom he so much esteems, nor whose 20 faith he so much reposeth upon. Remember how oft you have promised your service unto me; how oft you have given me occasion to believe that there was no lady in whose favour you more desired to remain. Now my chance is turned, let not your troth turn. I present myself unto you, the most humble and miserable suppliant 25 living; neither shall my desire be great. I seek for no more life than I shall be thought worthy of. If my blood may wash away the dishonour of Arcadia, spare it not; although through me it hath never been willingly dishonoured. My only suit is you will be a mean for me that, while I am suffered to enjoy this life, I may not be separated 30 from him to whom the gods have joined me; and that you determine

2 this] his Da, Ph, Hm.   2–3 confusion] conclusion Je, 93.   3 she] the 93.
4 they being] having been 93.   both] *om.* Hm. 93.   5 the attending] they attend-
ing Ph, Hm.   10 dream] dreams 93.   15 did to] did unto Cl, As.   21 he
so much reposeth upon Cl, Je, Hm: so much reposeth upon St, Bo, As, Ph; more
reposeth upon Da; so much he reposeth upon 93.   22 me; how oft] me; how
often Cl, As.   23 you more desired] you desired more Cl, Hm; more you desired
Ph.   24 remain] 93 *adds*: and if the remembrance be not unpleasant to your
mind, or the rehearsal unfitting for my fortune, remember there was a time when I could
deserve it.   26 seek for no] seek no As, Hm.   27 thought] found 93.
28–9 hath never been willingly] never hath been willingly Je; hath indeed never
been 93.

nothing more cruelly of him than you do of me. But if you rightly judge of our virtuous marriage, whereto our innocencies were the solemnities, and the gods themselves the witnesses, then procure we may live together. But if my father will not so conceive of us, as the
5 fault (if any were) was united, so let the punishment be united also.'
   There was no man that ever loved either his prince or anything pertaining unto him with a truer zeal than Philanax did. This made him even to the depth of his heart receive a most vehement grief to see his master made, as it were, more miserable after death. And for
10 himself, there was nothing could have kept him from falling to all tender pity but the perfect persuasion he had that all this was joined to the pack of his master's death, which the speech of marriage made him the more believe. Therefore, first muttering to himself suchlike words: 'the violence the gentleman spake of is now turned to
15 marriage. He alleged Mars, but she speaks of Venus. O unfortunate master, this hath been that fair devil Gynecia, sent away one of her daughters, prostituted the other, empoisoned thee to overthrow the diadem of Arcadia.' But at length thus unto herself he said: 'If your father, madam, were now to speak unto, truly there should nobody
20 be found a more ready advocate for you than myself; for I would suffer this fault, though very great, to be blotted out of my mind by your former led life, and being daughter to such a father. But since among yourselves you have taken him away in whom was the only power to have mercy, you must now be clothed in your own working,
25 and look for no other than that which dead pitiless laws may allot unto you. For my part, I loved you for your virtue; but now where is that? I loved you for your father; unhappy folks, you have robbed the world of him.'
   These words of her father were so little understood of the only
30 well understanding Philoclea that she desired him to tell her what he meant to speak in such dark sort unto her of her lord and father,

1 more cruelly of him] of him more cruelly 93. But] And Cl, As; *om.* 93. 2-3 our . . . witnesses] what hath passed, wherein the gods (that should have been of our marriage) are witnesses of our innocencies 93. 6 either] *om.* Cl, Je, Hm. 7 unto] to Da, Hm, 93. 9 death OA, 93: his death St. 10 himself,] 93 *adds*: calling to mind in what sort his life had been preserved by Philoclea what time, taken by Amphialus, he was like to suffer a cruel death. 12 speech] misconceived speech 93. 13 first] *om.* Cl, Ph. 15 speaks] spake Cl, Ph; speaketh Hm. 18 unto] to Da, Je, Hm. herself] her As, Je. 19 unto] unto you As, Da (you *cancelled* St). 22 life,] 93 *adds*: your benefit towards myself, 25 no] none 93. 27 that?] 93 *adds*: I loved you in respect of a private benefit; what is that in comparison of the public loss? 29 of] by 93. only] *om.* Ph, Je.

whose displeasure was more dreadful unto her than her punishment; that she was free in her own conscience she had never deserved evil of him but in this last fact, wherein notwithstanding if it pleased him to proceed with patience he should find her choice had not been unfortunate.

He that saw her words written in the plain table of her fair face thought it impossible there should therein be contained deceit; and therefore so much the more abashed: 'Why,' said he, 'madam, would you have me think that you are not of conspiracy with the princess Pamela's flight and your father's death?'

With that word the sweet lady gave a pitiful cry, having straight in her face and breast abundance of witnesses that her heart was far from any such abominable consent. 'Ah, of all sides utterly ruined Philoclea,' said she, 'now indeed I may well suffer all conceit of hope to die in me. Dear father, where was I that might not do you my last service before soon after miserably following you?'

Philanax perceived the demonstration so lively and true in her that he easily acquitted her in his heart of that fact; and the more was moved to join with her in most hearty lamentation. But remembering him that the burden of the state and punishment of his master's murderers lay all upon him: 'Well,' said he, 'madam, I can do nothing without all the states of Arcadia. What they will determine of you, I know not; for my part your speeches would much prevail with me, but that I find not how to excuse your giving over your body to him that for the last proof of his treason lent his garments to disguise your miserable mother in the most vile fact she hath committed. Hard surely it will be to separate your causes, with whom you have so nearly joined yourself.'

'Neither do I desire it,' said the sweetly weeping Philoclea, 'whatsoever you determine of him, do that likewise to me; for I know from the fountain of virtue nothing but virtue could ever proceed.'

Philanax, feeling his heart more and more mollifying to her, renewed the image of his dead master in his fancy, and using that for the spurs of his revengeful choler, went suddenly without any more speech from the desolate lady; to whom now fortune seemed

1 unto OA, 93: to St. 3 but] no not 93. notwithstanding] *om.* 93.
7 should therein be contained] should be therein contained Cl, As; should be contained therein Ph; should be contained Hm. 9 the] *om.* Cl, Hm. 13 any] *om.* Ph, Hm. 14 well] *om.* Cl, As, Ph, Hm. 27 surely] sure Je, 93.
31 proceed] 93 *adds*: only as you find him faultless, let him find you favourable, and build not my dishonour upon surmises. 32 to her] unto her As, Ph, 93.

to threaten unripe death and undeserved shame among her least
evils. But Philanax, leaving good guard upon the lodge, went him-
self to see the order of his other prisoners, whom even then as he
issued he found increased with unhoped means—the order of which
5 shall be from the beginning thereof declared.

Long methinks it is since anything hath been spoken of the noble
prince Musidorus, especially having been left in so impatient a case
as he should hardly brook a tedious respite. But so sovereign a
possession the charming Philoclea had stolen into that her eldest
10 sister was almost forgotten; who, having delivered over the burden
of her fearful cares to the natural ease of a well refreshing sleep,
reposing both body and mind upon the trusted support of her
princely shepherd, was with the braying cries of a rascal company
robbed of her quiet, at what time she was in a shrewd likelihood to
15 have had great part of her trust in Musidorus deceived, and found
herself robbed of that she had laid in store as her dearest jewel—so
did her own beauties enforce a force against herself. But a greater
peril preserved her from the less, and the coming of enemies defended
her from the violence of a friend; so that both she at one instant
20 opened her eyes (which in so double a danger had great need to look
to themselves) and the every way enraged Musidorus rase from her—
enraged betwixt a repentant shame of his promise-breaking attempt
and the tyrannical fire of lust (which, having already caught hold of
so sweet and fit a fuel, was past the calling back of reason's counsel),
25 and now betwixt the doubt he had what these men would go about
and the spite he conceived against their cumbersome presence. But
the clowns, having with their hideous noise brought them both to
their feet, had soon knowledge what guests they had found. For
indeed these were the scummy remnant of those Phagonian rebels
30 whose naughty minds could not trust so much to the goodness of
their prince as to lay their hang-worthy necks upon the constancy

1 among] amongst Da, Je, Hm.   4 with] by this 93.   4–10 the order . . .
forgotten] *om*. 93.   9 possession] *om*. Ph; passion Hm.   10 who] The noble
Pamela 93.   12 body] her body Cl, As, Da, Hm.   13 was] when 93.
13–14 company robbed] company she was robbed 93.   14–19 at what . . . friend]
om. 93.   14 in a shrewd] in shrewd Bo, Da, Ph.   17 greater] great Cl, Ph.
18 and the coming OA: and coming St.   19 both] *om*. Cl, As, 93.   she at one
instant] at one instant she 93.   20–1 (which . . . themselves)] *om*. 93.   21 the every
way Bo, Cl, As, Da, Ph, Je: they every way St; the very way Hm; the 93.   rase]
rose Da, Ph, 93.   22–5 betwixt . . . and now] *om*. 93.   22 a] the Cl; *om*. Ph,
Hm.   23 the tyrannical OA: tyrannical St.   26 cumbersome] ill-pleasing 93.
29 Phagonian] *om*. 93.

of his promised pardon. Therefore, when the rest (who as sheep had
but followed their fellows) so sheepishly had submitted themselves,
these only committed their safety to the thickest part of those desert
woods; who, as they were in the constitution of their minds little
better than beasts, so were they apt to degenerate to a beastly kind 5
of life, having these few days already framed their gluttonish
stomachs to have for food the wild benefits of nature, the uttermost
end they had being but to draw out as much as they could the line of a
tedious life. In this sort vagabonding in those untrodden places, they
were guided by the everlasting justice to be chastisers of Musidorus's 10
broken vow; whom, as soon as they saw turned towards them,
they full well remembered it was he that, accompanied with some
other honest shepherds, had come to the succour of Cleophila,
and had left among some of them bloody tokens of his valour. As for
Pamela, they had many times seen her. Thus, first stirred up with a 15
rustical revenge against him, and then desire of spoil to help their
miserable wants, but chiefly thinking it was the way to confirm their
own pardon to bring the princess back unto her father, whom (they
were sure) he would never have sent so far so slightly accompanied,
they did, without any other denouncing of war, set all together upon 20
the worthy Musidorus; who, being beforehand as much inflamed
against them for the interrupting his vehement pursuit, gave them
so brave a welcome that the smart of some made the rest stand
further off, crying and prating against him, but like bad curs rather
barking than closing; he, in the mean time, placing his trembling 25
lady to one of the fair pine trees, and so setting himself before her
as might show the cause of his courage grew in himself, but the
effect was only employed in her defence. The villains (that now had
a second proof how ill wards they had for such a sword) turned all
the course of their violence into throwing darts and stones—indeed, 30
the only way to overmaster the valour of Musidorus who, finding
them some already touch, some fall so near his chiefest life
Pamela, that in the end some one or other might hap to do an

6 these few days already] now 93.   gluttonish] gluttonous Ph, Je.   9 those OA,
93: these St.   10–11 to be . . . vow] using themselves to be punishers of their faults,
and making their own actions the beginning of their chastisements (unhappily both for
him and themselves) to light on Musidorus 93.   10 be chastisers] be the chastisers
Ph, Hm.   11 they] he Ph, Je.   12–13 some other honest shepherds] some
honest shepherds Bo, Hm; Basilius 93.   20 they did] om. 93.   22 for . . .
pursuit] om. 93.   26 fair] om. Hm, 93.   29 wards] words As, Ph, 93 (corr.
98).   30 throwing darts OA, 93: throwing of darts St.   32 them] that Da;
om. Hm.   33 some . . . other] some other Cl; some one other Da.

unsuccourable mischief, setting all his hope in despair, ran out from
his lady among them; who straight (like so many swine when a hardy
mastiff sets upon them) dispersed themselves. But the first he over-
took as he ran away, carrying his head as far before him as those
5 manner of runnings are wont to do, with one blow strake it so clean off
that, it falling betwixt the hands, and the body falling upon it, it made
a show as though the fellow had had great haste to gather up his head
again. Another, the speed he made to run for the best game bare him
full butt against a tree, so that tumbling back with a bruised face
10 and a dreadful expectation, Musidorus was straight upon him, and
parting with his sword one of his legs from him, left him to make a
roaring lamentation that his mortar-treading was marred for ever.
A third, finding his feet too slow as well as his hands too weak, sud-
denly turned back, beginning to open his lips for mercy, but before
15 he had well entered a rudely compiled oration, Musidorus's blade
was come betwixt his jaws into his throat; and so the poor man rested
there for ever with a very ill mouthful of an answer. Musidorus
in this furious chafe would have followed some other of these hate-
ful wretches but that he heard his lady cry for help, whom three
20 of that villainous crew had (whilst Musidorus followed their fellows),
compassing about some trees, suddenly come upon and surprised,
threatening to kill her if she cried, and meaning to convey her out of
sight while the prince was making his bloodthirsty chase. But she
that was resolved no worse thing could fall unto her than the being
25 deprived of him on whom she had established all her comfort, with
a pitiful cry fetched his eyes unto her; who then, thinking so many
weapons thrust into his eyes as with his eyes he saw bent against her,
made all hearty speed to her succour. But one of them, wiser than
his companions, set his dagger to her alabaster throat, swearing
30 if he threw not away his sword he would presently kill her. There
was never poor scholar that, having instead of his book some playing
toy about him, did more suddenly cast it from him at the child-
feared presence of a cruel schoolmaster than the valorous Musidorus
discharged himself of his only defence, when he saw it stood upon
35 the instant point of his lady's life; and holding up his noble hands to
so unworthy audience:

4 away] *om.* Cl, As.   16 betwixt] between Je, 93.   18 these] those Cl, Hm.
20 that] this 93.   whilst] whiles 93.   21 come] came Bo; ran Je, Hm.   32 at
Bo, As, Da, Je, 93: as St. Cl, Hm; and Ph.   33 valorous] valiant Da,
Je, 93.

'O Arcadians, it is I, it is I, that have done you the wrong! She is your princess,' said he, 'she never had will to hurt you; and you see she hath no power. Use your choler upon me that have better deserved it. Do not yourselves the wrong to do her any hurt, which in no time nor place will ever be forgiven you.'   5

They, that yet trusted not to his courtesy, bad him stand further off from his sword, which he obediently did—so far was love above all other thoughts in him. Then did they call together the rest of their fellows who, though they were few, yet according to their number possessed many places. And then began those savage 10 senators to make a consultation what they should do; some wishing to spoil them of their jewels and let them go on their journey (for that, if they carried them back, they were sure they should have least part of the prey); others, preferring their old homes to anything, desiring to bring them to Basilius as pledges of their surety; 15 and there wanted not which cried the safest way was to kill them both—to such an unworthy thraldom were these great and excellent personages brought. But the most part resisted to the killing of the princess, foreseeing their lives would never be safe after such a fact committed, and began to wish rather the spoil than death of 20 Musidorus; when the villain that had his leg cut off came scrawling towards them, and being helped to them by one of the company, began with a groaning voice and a disfigured face to demand the revenge of his blood which, since he had spent with them in their defence, it were no reason he should be suffered by them to die discontented. 25 The only contentment he required was that by their help with his own hands he might put his murderer to some cruel death. He would fain have cried more against Musidorus, but that the much loss of blood, helped on with this vehemency, choked up the spirits of his life, leaving him to make betwixt his body and soul an ill-favoured 30 partition. But they, seeing their fellow in that sort die before their faces, did swell in new mortal rages, all resolved to kill him, but now only considering what manner of terrible death they should invent for him. Thus was a while the agreement of his slaying broken by the disagreement of the manner of it; and extremity of cruelty grew 35 for a time to be the stop of cruelty. At length they were resolved

everyone to have a piece of him, and to become all as well hangmen
as judges; when Pamela, tearing her hair and falling down among
them, sometimes with all the sort of humble prayers, mixed with
promises of great good turns (which they knew her estate was able to
5 perform), sometimes threatening them that, if they killed him and
not her, she would not only revenge it upon them but upon all their
wives and children, bidding them consider that, though they might
think she was come away in her father's displeasure, yet they might
be sure he would ever show himself a father; that the gods would
10 never if she lived put her in so base estate but that she should have
ability to plague such as they were; returning afresh to prayers and
promises, and mixing the same again with threatenings, brought
them (who were now grown colder in their fellow's cause, who was
past aggravating the matter with his cries) to determine with them-
15 selves there was no way but either to kill them both or save them
both. As for the killing, already they having answered themselves
that that was a way to make them citizens of the woods for ever,
they did in fine conclude they would return them back again to the
duke, which they did not doubt would be cause of a great reward,
20 besides their safety from their fore-deserved punishment. Thus
having, either by fortune, or the force of these two lovers' inward
working virtue, settled their cruel hearts to this gentler course, they
took the two horses, and having set upon them their princely pris-
oners, they returned towards the lodge. The villains, having decked
25 all their heads with laurel branches, as thinking they had done a
notable act, singing and shouting, ran by them in hope to have
brought them the same day again to the duke. But the time was so
far spent that they were forced to take up that night's lodging in the
midst of the woods where, while the clowns continued their watch
30 about them, now that the night, according to his dark nature, did
add a kind of desolation to the pensive hearts of these two afflicted
lovers, it is said that Musidorus, taking the tender hand of Pamela
and bedewing it with his tears, in this sort gave an issue to the
swelling of his heart's grief:
35   'Most excellent lady,' said he, 'in what case think you am I
with myself? How unmerciful judgements do I lay upon my soul

13 were now] now were Ph, Hm.   16 already they having] they having Ph; they
having already Je.   21 these] those 93 (corr. 05).   22 gentler] gentle Da, Hm.
23 their] these As; the two Hm.   27 again to the duke] to the duke Cl; to the
duke again Ph.   31 these] the Cl, As; those Hm.   32 it is said that] om. 93.
35 am I] I am Cl, As, Hm.

now that I know not what god hath so reversed my well meaning
enterprise as, instead of doing you that honour which I hoped (and
not without reason hoped) Thessalia should have yielded unto you,
am now like to become a wretched instrument of your discomfort?
Alas, how contrary an end have all the inclinations of my mind taken! 5
My faith falls out a treason unto you, and the true honour I bear you
is the field wherein your dishonour is like to be sown. But I invoke
that universal and only wisdom (which examining the depth of
hearts, hath not his judgement fixed upon the event) to bear testi-
mony with me that my desire, though in extremest vehemency, yet 10
did not so overgo my remembrance but that, as far as man's wit
might be extended, I sought to prevent all things that might fall to
your hurt. But now that all the ill fortunes of ill fortune have crossed
my best framed intent, I am most miserable in that I cannot only
not give you help but, which is worst of all, am barred from giving 15
you counsel. For how should I open my mouth to counsel you in
that wherein, by my counsel, you are most undeservedly fallen?'
    The fair and wise Pamela, although full of cares of the unhappy
turning of this matter, yet seeing the grief of Musidorus only stirred
for her, did so tread down all other motions with the true force of 20
virtue that she thus answered him, having first kissed him (which
before she had never done), either love so commanding her (which
doubted how long they should enjoy one another) or of a lively spark
of nobleness to descend in most favour to one when he is lowest in
affliction: 'My dear and ever dear Musidorus,' said she, 'a great 25
wrong you do to yourself that will torment you thus with grief for
the fault of fortune. Since a man is bound no further to himself than
to do wisely, the chance is only to trouble them that stand upon
chance. But greater is the wrong (at least, if anything comes from you
may bear the name of wrong) you do unto me to think me either so 30
childish as not to perceive your faithful faultlessness; or perceiving
it, so basely disposed as to let my heart be overthrown, standing upon
itself in so unspotted a pureness. Hold for certain, most worthy
Musidorus, it is yourself I love, which can no more be diminished

---

2 as OA, 93: and St.　　　7 wherein OA, 93: whereon St.　　　11 overgo] over-
charge Da, Je, 93.　　as far] so far Da, Je.　　　13 have] hath As, Da, Ph, Je, Hm.
17 undeservedly] unworthily Cl; unworthy As.　　　19 this matter] his matter Cl;
these matters Da.　　　25 great] greater 93.　　　26 you do] do you As, Da, Je, Hm,
93.　　　28 the chance] chance 93.　　　29 anything comes] anything that comes 93.
31 faithful faultlessness] faultlessness Da; faultiness Je; faithful faithfulness Hm
(faithfulness *corr. to* faultiness St).　　　34 yourself] you yourself As, Hm.

by these showers of ill hap than flowers are marred with the timely rains of April. For how can I want comfort that have the true and living comfort of my unblemished virtue; and how can I want honour as long as Musidorus (in whom indeed honour is) doth honour me?
5 Nothing bred from myself can discomfort me, and fools' opinions I will not reckon as dishonour.'

Musidorus, looking up to the stars, 'O mind of minds,' said he, 'the living power of all things which dost with all these eyes behold our ever varying actions, accept into thy favourable ears this prayer
10 of mine. If I may any longer hold out this dwelling on the earth which is called a life, grant me ability to deserve at this lady's hands the grace she hath showed unto me; grant me wisdom to know her wisdom, and goodness so to increase my love of her goodness that all mine own chosen desires be to myself but second to her deter-
15 minations. Whatsoever I be, let it be to her service. Let me herein be satisfied that for such infinite favours of virtue I have some way wrought her satisfaction. But if my last time approacheth, and that I am no longer to be among mortal creatures, make yet my death serve her to some purpose, that hereafter she may not have cause to repent
20 herself that she bestowed so excellent a mind upon Musidorus.'

Pamela could not choose but accord the conceit of their fortune to these passionate prayers, insomuch that her constant eyes yielded some tears, which wiping from her fair face with Musidorus's hand, speaking softly unto him, as if she had feared more that anybody
25 should be witness of her weakness than of anything else she had said:

'You see,' said she, 'my prince and only lord, what you work in me by your too much grieving for me. I pray you think I have no joy but in you, and if you fill that with sorrow, what do you leave for me? What is prepared for us we know not, but that with sorrow we cannot
30 prevent it, we know. Now let us turn from these things, and think how you will have me behave myself towards you in this matter.'

Musidorus, finding the authority of her speech confirmed with direct necessity, the first care came into his mind was of his dear friend and cousin, the prince Pyrocles, with whom at his parting he had

1 showers] flowers Cl; savours Je.   5 Nothing As, Da, Je, Hm, 93: No things St, Bo, Cl, Ph.   opinions OA, 93: opinion St.   8 living Bo, Cl, As, Da, Je, Hm, 93: liking St; being Ph.   these] those Cl, Da, Hm.   11 this OA, 93: these St. 14 mine] my Da, Je.   14–15 determinations] determination Cl, As.   18 am] be As (be corr. to am Bo).   among] amongst 93.   24 that] om. Da, Ph, Je, Hm, 93. 27 too] om. 93 (added 98).   33 care came into] care that came into As, Ph; care came to 93.   34 the prince] om. Je, Hm, 93.   at his parting] long before 93.

concluded what names they should bear if upon any occasion they were forced to give themselves out for great men, and yet not make themselves fully known. Now fearing lest, if the princess name him for Musidorus, the fame of their two being together would discover Pyrocles, holding her hand betwixt his hands a good while together: 5

'I did not think, most excellent princess,' said he, 'to have made any further request unto you; for having been already to you so unfortunate a suitor, I know not what modesty can bear any further demand. But the estate of one young man whom (next to you, far before myself) I owe more than all the world, one both worthy of all well 10 being for the notable constitution of his mind, and most unworthy to receive hurt by me, whom he doth in all faith and constancy love, the pity of him only goes beyond all resolution to the contrary.'

Then did he, to the princess's great admiration, tell her the whole story so far as he knew of it; and that when they made the grievous 15 disjunction of their long company, they had concluded Musidorus should entitle himself Palladius, prince of Caria, and Pyrocles should be Timopyrus of Lycia.

'Now,' said Musidorus, 'he keeping a woman's habit is to use no other name than Cleophila, but I that find it best of the one side for 20 your honour it be known you went away with a prince, and not with a shepherd; of the other side accounting any death less evil than the betraying that sweet friend of mine, will take this mean betwixt both, and using the name of Palladius (if the respect of a prince will stop your father's fury, that will serve as well as Musidorus) until 25 Pyrocles' fortune being some way established, I may freely give good proofs that the noble country of Thessalia is mine. And if that will not mitigate your father's opinion to me-wards, nature, I hope, working in your excellencies will make him deal well by you. For my part, the image of death is nothing fearful unto me, and this good I 30 shall have reaped by it, that I leave my most esteemed friend in no danger to be disclosed by me. And besides (since I must confess I am not without a remorse of her case) my virtuous mother shall not

5 hand] hands As, Da, Hm.   9 whom] *om.* Ph, Hm.   9–10 before] above 93.
11 notable] noble Cl, As.   his] the 93 (*corr.* 98).   15 knew of it] knew it Bo, Cl.
16 company] combination 13.   17 Caria] Iberia 93.   18 Timopyrus] Daiphantus
93 (*and throughout*).   20 of the one] on the one Da; of the on 93.   21 it be
known] *om.* 93.   22 any] my 93.   23 betraying that] betraying of that 93.
betwixt OA, 93: between St.   26 being] be Da, Hm.   some way] somewhat Bo,
As, Je, Hm; some ways Da.   27 proofs] proof 93.   28 to me-wards] towards
me Da, Hm.   29 by] with As, Je, 05 (*only*).   31 leave] shall leave 93.
33 her case] his case Je, 93 (*corr.* 98).

know her son's violent death hid under the fame will go of Palladius. But as long as her years (now of good number) be counted among the living, she may joy herself with some possibility of my return.'

Pamela, promising him upon no occasion ever to name him, fell
5 into extremity of weeping, as if her eyes had been content to spend all their seeing moistness, now that there was speech of the loss of that which they held as their chiefest light. So that Musidorus was forced to repay her good counsels with sweet consolations, which continued betwixt them until it was about midnight that their
10 thoughts, even weary of their own burdens, fell to a strange kind of uncertainty; and the minds standing only upon the nature of their inward intelligences, left their bodies to give a sleeping respite to their vital spirits, which they (according to the quality of sorrow) received with greater greediness than ever in their lives before—
15 according to the nature of sorrow, I say, that which is past care's remedy. For care, stirring the brain and making thin the spirits, breaketh rest; but those griefs wherein one is determined there is no preventing, do breed a dull heaviness which easily clothes itself in sleep. As it fell out in these personages who, delicately wound up
20 one in another's arms, laid a plot in that picture of death how gladly, if death came, their souls would go together. But as soon as that morning appeared to play her part (which, as you have heard, was laden with so many well occasioned lamentations), their lobbish guard (who all night had kept themselves awake with prating how
25 valiant deeds they had done, when they ran away; and how fair a death their fellow died, who at his last gasp sued to be a hangman) awaked them and set them upon their horses; to whom the very shining force of excellent virtue (though in a very harsh subject) had wrought a kind of reverence in them. Musidorus, as he rid among
30 them (of whom they had no other hold but the hold of Pamela), thinking it want of a well squared judgement to leave any mean unassayed of saving their lives, to this purpose spake to his unseemly guardians, using a plain kind of phrase to make his speech the more credible:

8 repay] repair 93.   9 until] till As, Da.   9–23 their . . . laden] sleep, having stolen into their heavy senses and now absolutely commanding in their vital powers, left them delicately wound one in another's arms quietly to wait for the coming of the morning; which, as soon as she appeared to play her part, laden (as you have heard) 93.
11 minds] mind Cl, Da.   12 respite] respect As; rest Da.   16 thin OA: them St.   17 those] these As, Hm.   21 that] the As, Da, Je.   24 how] what Da, Je.   26 died] had died Da, Je.   30 but the hold of] but of Da, Je, Hm, 93.

'My masters,' said he, 'there is no man that is wise but hath in whatsoever he doth some purpose whereto he directs his doing, which so long he follows till he see that either that purpose is not worth the pains or that another doing carries with it a better purpose. That you are wise in what you take in hand, I have to my cost learned; 5 that makes me desire you to tell me what is your end in carrying the princess and me back again unto her father.'

'Pardon', said one. 'Reward', cried another.

'Well,' said he, 'take both; although I know you are so wise to remember that hardly they both will go together, being of so contrary 10 a making. For the ground of pardon is an evil. Neither any man pardons, but remembers an evil done. The cause of reward is the opinion of some good act; and whoso rewardeth that, holds the chief place of his fancy. Now one man of one company to have the same consideration both of good and evil, but that the conceit of pardon- 15 ing, if it be pardoned, will take away the mind of rewarding, is very hard, if not impossible. For either even in justice will he punish the fault, as well as reward the desert, or else in mercy balance the one by the other; so that the not chastising shall be a sufficient satis- fying. Thus then you may see that in your own purpose rests great 20 uncertainty; but I will grant that by this your deed you shall obtain your double purpose. Yet consider, I pray you, whether by another mean that may not better be obtained, and then I doubt not your wisdoms will teach you to take hold of the better. I am sure you know anybody were better have no need of a pardon than enjoy a 25 pardon; for as it carries with it the surety of a preserved life so bears it a continual note of a deserved death. This, therefore (besides the danger you may run into, my lady Pamela being the undoubted inheritrix of this state, if she shall hereafter seek to revenge your wrong done her), shall be continually cast in your teeth, as men dead 30 by the law. The honester sort will disdain your company and your children shall be the more basely reputed of, and you yourselves in every slight fault hereafter, as men once condemned, aptest to be overthrown. Now if you will, as I doubt not you will (for you are wise), turn your course and guard my lady Pamela thitherward 35 whither she was going first, you need not doubt to adventure your fortunes where she goes], and there shall you be assured in a country as good and rich as this, of the same manners and language, to be so far from the conceit of a pardon as we both shall be forced to acknowledge we have received by your means whatsoever we hold dear in this life; and so for reward, judge you whether it be not more likely you shall there receive it where you have done no evil, but singular and undeserved goodness, or here where this service of yours shall be diminished by your duty and blemished by your former fault. Yes: I protest and swear unto you by the fair eyes of that lady there shall no gentleman in all that country be preferred. You shall have riches, ease, pleasure, and that which is best to such worthy minds, you shall not be forced to cry mercy for a good fact. You only, of all the Arcadians, shall have the praise in continuing in your late valiant attempt, and not basely be brought under a halter for seeking the liberty of Arcadia.'

These words in their minds (who did nothing for any love of goodness but only as their senses presented greater shows of profit) began to make them waver, and some to clap their hands, and scratch their heads and swear it was the best way; others (that would seem wiser than the rest) to capitulate what tenements they should have, what subsidies they should pay; others to talk of their wives (in doubt whether it were best to send for them or take new where they went); most like fools, not readily thinking what was next to be done, but imagining what cheer they would make when they came there; one or two only of the least discoursers beginning to turn their faces towards the woods which they had left, and come within the plain near to the lodges, when unhappily they espied a troop of horsemen. But then their false hearts had quickly, for the present fear, forsaken their last hopes. And therefore keeping on the way towards the lodge with songs and cries of joy, these horsemen (who were some of them Philanax had sent out to the search of Pamela) came galloping unto them, marvelling who they were that in such a general mourning durst sing joyful tunes, and in so public a ruin

5 for reward] forward As; rewarding Da, Je.   judge] *om.* Da, Je.   7 this service of yours] your service Da; the service of yours Je.   10 gentleman] gentlemen 93 (*ex.* 05).   13 continuing OA, 93: continuance St.   14–15 and . . . Arcadia] *om.* Cl, As.   14 a halter] an halter Bo, Je.   22 or take] or to take Bo, As, Da, Je, 93.   23 readily thinking] thinking readily Cl; thinking Hm.   25 only] *om.* Je, Hm, 93.   discoursers] discourses 93.   26 and come] and coming Cl; But being come 93.   27 when] *om.* 93.   espied] spied Da, Ph.   29 the way] their way Cl, Da, Je.   29 and cries of joy] and cries for joy Je; of cries and joy 93.   these] the Je, Hm, 93.   33 so public a] such a public As, Ph.

wear the laurel tokens of victory. And that which seemed strangest, they might see two among them, unarmed like prisoners, but riding like captains. But when they came nearer, they perceived the one was a lady, and the lady Pamela. Then glad they had by hap found that which they so little hoped to meet withal, taking these clowns 5 (who first resisted them for the desire they had to be the deliverers of the two excellent prisoners), learning that they were of those Phagonians which had made the dangerous uproar, as well under colour to punish that as this their last withstanding them, but indeed their principal cause being because they themselves would have the 10 only praise of their own quest, they suffered not one of them to live. Marry, three of the stubbornest of them they left their bodies hanging upon the trees, because their doing might carry the likelier form of judgement—such an unlooked-for end did the life of justice work for the mighty-minded wretches, by subjects to be executed that 15 would have executed princes, and to suffer that without law which by law they had deserved. And thus these young folks, twice prisoners before any due arrest, delivered of their gaolers but not of their gaol, had rather change than respite of misery. These soldiers (that took them with very few words of entertainment), hasting to carry 20 them to their lord Philanax, to whom they came even as he (going out of the lady Philoclea's chamber) had overtaken Pyrocles whom before he had delivered to the custody of a nobleman of that country.

When Pyrocles (led towards his prison) saw his friend Musidorus with the noble lady Pamela in that inexpected sort returned, his grief 25 (if any grief were in a mind which had placed everything according to his natural worth) was very much augmented; for, besides some small hope he had, if Musidorus had once been clear of Arcadia, by his dealing and authority to have brought his only gladsome desires to a good issue. The hard estate of his friend did no less, nay rather 30 more, vex him than his own; for so, indeed, it is ever found where valour and friendship are perfectly coupled in one heart—the reason being that the resolute man having once digested in his judgement the worst extremity of his own case, and either having quite repelled or at least expelled all passion which ordinarily follows an over- 35 thrown fortune, not knowing his friend's mind so well as his own,

8 Phagonians] rebels 93.   10 their] the Ph, Hm.   11 quest] conquest As; gift Ph, Hm.   15 for the] for these Da; for those Je.   18 gaolers] captors Da; gallows Ph.   19 These] The Da, Je, Hm.   21 came] ran Ph, Hm.   25 with the noble OA, 93: with noble St.   27 worth] worthiness Bo, Ph.   34–5 repelled . . . expelled] expelled . . . repelled 93.

nor with what patience he brooks his case (which is, as it were, the material cause of making a man happy or unhappy), doubts whether his friend account not himself more miserable, and so, indeed, be more lamentable. But as soon as Musidorus was brought by the
5 soldiers near unto Philanax, Pyrocles not knowing whether ever after he should be suffered to see his friend, and determining there could be no advantage by dissembling a not-knowing of him, leapt suddenly from their hands that held him, and passing with a strength strengthened with a true affection through them that encompassed
10 Musidorus, he embraced him as fast as he could in his arms, and kissing his cheek:

'O my Palladius,' said he, 'let not our virtue now abandon us. Let us prove our minds are no slaves to fortune, but in adversity can triumph over adversity.'

15 'Dear Timopyrus', answered Musidorus (seeing by his apparel his being a man was revealed), 'I thank you for this best care of my best part. But fear not, I have kept too long company with you to want now a thorough determination of these things. I well know there is nothing evil but within us; the rest is either natural or acci-
20 dental.'

Philanax (finding them of so near acquaintance) began presently to examine them apart; but such resolution he met within them that by no such means he could learn further than it pleased them to deliver; so that he thought best to put them both in one place with
25 espial of their words and behaviour, that way to sift out the more of these forepassed mischiefs, and for that purpose gave them both unto the nobleman who before had the custody of Pyrocles, by name Sympathus, leaving a trusty servant of his own to give diligent watch to what might pass betwixt them.

30 No man that hath ever passed through the school of affection needs doubt what a tormenting grief it was to the noble Pamela to have the company of him taken from her to whose virtuous company she had bound her life. But weighing with herself it was fit for her honour, till her doing was clearly manifested, that they should remain sepa-
35 rate, kept down the rising tokens of grief, showing passion in nothing but her eyes which accompanied Musidorus even unto the

3 account] accounts Bo, Cl, As, Da, Ph, 93.   indeed, be] *om.* Da, Ph, Je, Hm.
5 unto] to Ph, Je.   7 a not-knowing] and not knowing As, Da, Je, Hm.   9 with
a] *om.* As; with Je.   11 cheek] cheeks 93.   18 now] *om.* Da, Ph.   27 unto]
to Ph, Hm.   28–9 watch to what OA, 93: watch what St.   29 betwixt]
between Bo, As.   34–5 separate] separated Ph, Hm.   36 unto] to Ph, Hm.

tent whither he and Pyrocles were led. Then with a countenance more princely than she was wont, according to the wont of highest hearts (like the palm tree striving most upward when he is most burdened), she commanded Philanax to bring her to her father and mother, that she might render them account of her doings. Philanax, 5 showing a sullen kind of reverence unto her, as a man that honoured her as his master's heir but much misliked her for her (in his conceit) dishonourable proceedings, told her what was passed, rather to answer her than that he thought she was ignorant of it. But her good spirit did presently suffer a true compassionate affliction of those 10 hard adventures; which, crossing her arms, looking a great while on the ground with those eyes which let fall many tears, she well declared. But in the end remembering how necessary it was for her not to lose herself in such an extremity, she strengthened her well created heart, and stoutly demanded Philanax what authority then 15 they had to lay hands of her person, who being the undoubted heir was then the lawful princess of that dukedom.

Philanax answered: 'Her grace knew the ancient laws of Arcadia bare she was to have no sway of government till she came to one and twenty years of age, or were married.'   20

'And married I am,' replied the wise princess, 'therefore I demand your due allegiance.'

'The gods forbid', said Philanax, 'Arcadia should be a dowry of such marriages.' Besides, he told her, all the estates of her country were ill satisfied touching her father's death, which likewise according 25 to the statutes of Arcadia was even that day to be judged of, before the body were removed to receive his princely funerals. After that passed, she should have such obedience as by the laws was due unto her, desiring God she would show herself better in public government than she had done in private.   30

She would have spoken to the gentlemen and people gathered about her, but Philanax, fearing lest thereby some commotion might arise, or at least a hindrance of executing his master's murderers, which he longed after more than anything, hasted her up to the lodge where her sister was, and there with a chosen company of 35 soldiers to guard the place, left her with Philoclea, Pamela protesting they laid violent hands of her, and that they entered into rebellious attempts against her.

But high time it was for Philanax so to do, for already was all the whole multitude fallen into confused and dangerous divisions. There was a notable example how great dissipations monarchal governments are subject unto; for now their prince and guide had left them, they had not experience to rule, and had not whom to obey. Public matters had ever been privately governed, so that they had no lively taste what was good for themselves, but everything was either vehemently desireful or extremely terrible. Neighbours' invasions, civil dissension, cruelty of the coming prince, and whatsoever in common sense carries a dreadful show, was in all men's heads, but in few how to prevent: hearkening on every rumour, suspecting everything, condemning them whom before they had honoured, making strange and impossible tales of the duke's death; while they thought themselves in danger, wishing nothing but safety; as soon as persuasion of safety took them, desiring further benefits as amendment of forepassed faults (which faults notwithstanding none could tell either the grounds or effects of); all agreeing in the universal names of liking or misliking, but of what in especial points infinitely disagreeing; altogether like a falling steeple, the parts whereof (as windows, stones, and pinnacles) were well, but the whole mass ruinous. And this was the general case of all, wherein notwithstanding was an extreme medley of diversified thoughts: the great men looking to make themselves strong by factions; the gentlemen, some bending to them, some standing upon themselves, some desirous to overthrow those few which they thought were over them; the soldiers desirous of trouble as the nurse of spoil; and not much unlike to them (though in another way) were all the needy sort; the rich, fearful; the wise, careful. This composition of conceits brought forth a dangerous tumult, which yet would have been more dangerous but that it had so many parts that nobody well knew against whom chiefly to oppose themselves. For some there were that cried to have the state altered and governed no more by a prince; marry, in the alteration many would have the Lacedemonian government of few chosen senators; others the Athenian, where the people's

1 of] upon Cl; on Da, Ph, Je.   3 all] *om.* Cl, As.   5 dissipations OA, 93: disputations St.   5-6 governments are] government is Da, Je, 93.   14 had] *om.* As, Ph.   19 grounds] ground Cl, Hm.   effects] the effects As, Hm.   23 case] rate Bo; care As; *om.* Da, Je; cause Hm.   24 diversified] diverse Cl, As; diverse fed Ph.   26 desirous] *om.* Bo, Je.   33 chiefly] *om.* Cl, Ph, Hm.   36 of few] of a few Ph, Je.

voice held the chief authority. But these were rather the discoursing sort of men than the active, being a matter more in imagination than practice. But they that went nearest to the present case (as in a country that knew no government without a prince) were they that strave whom they should make; whereof a great number there were 5 that would have the princess Pamela presently to enjoy it; some, disdaining that she had as it were abandoned her own country, inclining more to Philoclea; and there wanted not of them which wished Gynecia were delivered and made regent till Pamela were worthily married. But great multitudes there were which, having been ac- 10 quainted with the just government of Philanax, meant to establish him as lieutenant of the state, and these were the most popular sort who judged by the commodities they felt. But the principal men in honour and might, who had long before envied his greatness with Basilius, did much more spurn against any such preferment of him. 15 For yet before their envy had some kind of breathing out his rancour by laying his greatness as a fault to the prince's judgement, who showed in Dametas he might easily be deceived in men's value. But now, if the prince's choice by so many mouths should be confirmed, what could they object to so rightly esteemed an excellency? They 20 therefore were disposed sooner to yield to anything than to his raising, and were content (for to cross Philanax) to stop those actions which otherwise they could not but think good. Philanax himself, as much hindered by those that did immoderately honour him (which brought both more envy and suspicion upon him) as by them that 25 did manifestly resist him, but (standing only upon a constant desire of justice and a clear conscience) went forward stoutly in the action of his master's revenge, which he thought himself particularly bound to. For the rest, as the ordering of the government, he accounted himself but as one, wherein notwithstanding he would employ all 30 his loyal endeavour.

But among the noblemen, he that most openly set himself against him was named Timautus, a man of middle age but of extreme ambition, as one that had placed his uttermost good in greatness, thinking small difference by what means he came by it; of commendable 35 wit, if he had not made it a servant to unbridled desires; cunning to

1 discoursing OA, 93: discovering St.   2–3 than practice] than in practice Bo, Je.
3 nearest] near Cl, As.   8 of them] *om.* Cl, As; some Da.   22 for] *om.* Cl, Ph,
Je.   32 openly] notably Bo; *om.* Cl.   33 named] *om.* Bo, As, Hm.   Timautus]
Timantus Cl, 93 (*corr.* 98), *so spelt throughout in* Cl *and* 93.

creep into men's favours, which he prized only as they were service-
able unto him. He had been brought up in some soldiery, which he
knew how to set out with more than deserved ostentation; servile
(though envious) to his betters, and no less tyrannically minded to
them he had advantage of; counted revengeful, but indeed measur-
ing both revenge and reward as the party might either help or hurt
him; rather shameless than bold, and yet more bold in practices
than in personal adventures; in sum, a man that could be as evil as he
listed, and listed as much as any advancement might thereby be
gotten. As for virtue, he counted it but a school name. He even at
the first assembling together, finding the great stroke Philanax
carried among the people, thought it his readiest way of ambition to
join with him; which, though his pride did hardly brook, yet the
other vice, carrying with it a more apparent object, prevailed over
the weaker, so that (with those liberal protestations of friendship
which men that care not for their word are wont to bestow) he
offered unto him the choice in marriage of either the sisters, so he
would likewise help him to the other, and make such a partition of
the Arcadian state, wishing him that, since he loved his master
because he was his master (which showed the love began in himself),
he should rather, now occasion was presented, seek his own good
substantially than affect the smoke of a glory by showing an untimely
fidelity to him that could not reward it, and have all the fruit he
should get in men's opinions; which would be as diverse, as many,
few agreeing to yield him due praise of his true heart.

But Philanax, who had limited his thoughts in that he esteemed
good (to which he was neither carried by the vain tickling of un-
certain fame nor from which he would be transported by enjoying
anything whereto the ignorant world gives the excellent name of
goods), with great mislike of his offer he made him so peremptory
an answer (not without threatening if he found him foster any such
fancy) that Timautus went with an inward spite from him whom
before he had never loved; and measuring all men's marches by his
own pace, rather thought it some further fetch of Philanax (as that
he would have all to himself alone) than was any way taken with the
lovely beauty of his virtue, whose image he had so quite defaced in

---

4 tyrannically OA, 93: tyrannical St.   6 help or hurt OA, 93: hurt or help St.
17 either the] either of the As, Ph, Je, Hm.   22 showing an untimely] showing
untimely Cl, As, Hm.   23 to him] unto him Ph, Hm.   30 goods] good Cl,
As, Ph, Hm; goodness Je.

his own soul that he had left himself no eyes to behold it. But stayed
waiting fit opportunity to execute his desires, both for himself and
against Philanax, when by the bringing back of Pamela the people
being divided in many motions (which both with murmuring
noises and putting themselves into several troops they well showed),   5
he thought apt time was laid before him (the waters being, as the
proverb saith, troubled, and so the better for his fishing). Therefore
going among the chiefest lords whom he knew principally to repine
at Philanax, and making a kind of convocation of them, he inveighed
against his proceedings, drawing everything to the most malicious   10
interpretation that malice itself could instruct him to do. He said it
was season for them to look to such a weed that else would overgrow
them all. It was not now time to consult of the dead but of the living,
since such a sly wolf was entered among them that could make
justice the cloak of tyranny and love of his late master the destruction   15
of his now being children. 'Do you not see', said he, 'how far his
corruption hath stretched that he hath such a number of rascals'
voices to declare him lieutenant, ready to make him prince, but that
he instructs them matters are not yet ripe for it. As for us, because
we are too rich to be bought, he thinks us the fitter to be killed. Hath   20
Arcadia bred no man but Philanax? Is she become a stepmother to
all the rest, and hath given all her blessings to Philanax? Or if there
be men among us, let us show we disdain to be servants to a servant.
Let us make him know we are far worthier not to be slaves than he
to be a master. Think you he hath made such haste in these matters   25
to give them over to another man's hand? Think you he durst be-
come the gaoler of his princess but either meaning to be her master
or her murderer? And all this for the dear goodwill, forsooth, he
bears to the duke's memory, whose authority as he abused in his life
so he would now persevere to abuse his name after his death! O   30
notable affection, for the love of the father to kill the wife and disin-
herit the children! O single-minded modesty, to aspire to no less
than to the princely diadem! No, no, he hath veered all this while
but to come the sooner to his affected end. But let us remember
what we be: in quality, his equals; in number, far before him. Let us   35
deliver the duchess and our natural princesses, and leave them no

2 opportunity] opportunities As, Je.   3 when] which Da, 93.   11 itself]
himself Cl, Hm.   17 rascals'] rascal Ph, Je.   21–2 Is she . . . Philanax?]
om. Bo, Je.   22 blessings] blessing As, Hm.   26 hand] hands As, Ph.
28 forsooth] om. Cl, Ph.   31–2 disinherit] disherit As, Da.   33 to the princely]
the princely Bo, Je.   veered] viewed Cl; *blank left* As, Je; desired Da; tarried Hm.

longer under his authority, whose proceedings would rather show
that he himself had been the murderer of the duke than a fit guardian
of his posterity.'

These words pierced much into the minds already inclined that
5 way; insomuch that most part of the nobility confirmed Timautus's
speech and were ready to execute it, when Philanax came among
them and with a constant but reverent behaviour desired them they
would not exercise private grudges in so common a necessity. He
acknowledged himself a man, and a faulty man; to the clearing or
10 satisfying of which he would at all times submit himself. Since his
end was to bring all things to an upright judgement, it should ill fit
him to fly the judgement. 'But,' said he, 'my lords, let not Timautus's
railing speech (who whatsoever he finds evil in his own soul can with
ease lay it upon another) make me lose your good favour. Consider
15 that all well doing stands so in the middle betwixt his two contrary
evils that it is a ready matter to cast a slanderous shade upon the
most approved virtues. Who hath an evil tongue can call severity
cruelty, and faithful diligence diligent ambition. But my end is not
to excuse myself, nor to accuse him; for both those, hereafter will
20 be time enough. There is neither of us whose purging or punishing
may so much import to Arcadia. Now I request you for your own
honours' sake, and require you by the duty you owe to this state
that you do presently (according to the laws) take in hand the chas-
tisement of our master's murderers, and laying order for the govern-
25 ment; by whomsoever it be done, so it be done, and justly done, I am
satisfied. My labour hath been to frame things so as you might
determine; now it is in you to determine. For my part, I call the
heavens to witness the care of my heart stands to repay that wherein
both I and most of you were tied to that prince, with whom all my
30 love of worldly action is dead.'

As Philanax was speaking his last words there came one running
to him with open mouth and fearful eyes, telling him that there were
a great number of the people which were bent to take the young men
out of Sympathus's hands, and as it should seem by their acclama-
35 tions, were like enough to proclaim them princes.

'Nay,' said Philanax, speaking aloud and looking with a just anger
upon the other noblemen, 'it is now season to hear Timautus's idle
slanders, while strangers become our lords and Basilius's murderers

sit in his throne. But whosoever is a true Arcadian, let him follow me.'

With that, he went towards the place he heard of, followed by those that had ever loved him and some of the noblemen; some other remaining with Timautus, who in the mean time was conspiring by strong hand to deliver Gynecia, of whom the weakest guard was had. But Philanax where he went found them all in an uproar, which thus was fallen out: the greatest multitude of people that were come to the death of Basilius were the Mantineans, as being the nearest city to the lodges. Among these the chief man, both in authority and love, was Kerxenus, he that not long before had been host to the two princes whom, though he knew not so much as by name, yet their noble behaviour had bred such love in his heart towards them as both with tears he parted from them when they left him (under promise to return) and did keep their jewels and apparel as the relics of two demigods. Among others he had entered the prison and seen them, which forthwith so invested his soul both with sorrow and desire to help them (whom he tendered as his children) that, calling his neighbours the Mantineans unto him, he told them all the praises of those two young men, swearing he thought the gods had provided for them better than they themselves could have imagined. He willed them to consider that, when all was done, Basilius's children must enjoy the state, who since they had chosen, and chosen so as all the world could not mend their choice, why should they resist God's doing and their princesses' pleasure? This was the only way to purchase quietness without blood, where otherwise they should at one instant crown Pamela with a crown of gold and a dishonoured title, which whether ever she would forget, he thought it fit for them to weigh. 'Such', said he, 'heroical greatness shines in their eyes, such an extraordinary majesty in all their actions, as surely either fortune by parentage or nature in creation hath made them princes. And yet a state already we have. We need but a man; who, since he is presented unto you by the heavenly providence, embraced by your undoubted princess, worthy for their youth of compassion, for their beauty of admiration, for their excellent virtue to be monarchs of

7 an uproar OA, 93: one uproar St.   10 these OA, 93: those St.   11 Kerxenus]
Kalander 93 (*and throughout*).   12 yet their] yet besides the obligation he stood
bound to them in, for preserving the lives of his son or (and 98) nephew, their 93.
13 such love] much love Cl, As.   15 did keep] kept Cl, As, Da, Ph, Hm.
20 those] the Cl, As; these Da, Hm.   23 and chosen] *om.* Cl, As, Ph.   24 mend
Bo, Cl, Da, Ph, Je, Hm, 93: amend St, As.   30 either] *om.* Cl, Hm.

the world, shall we not be content with our own bliss? Shall we put out our eyes because another man cannot see; or rather, like some men when too much good happens unto them, they think themselves in a dream and have not spirits to taste their own good? No, no, my
5 friends, believe me, I am so unpartial that I know not their names, but so overcome with their virtue that I shall then think the destinies have ordained a perpetual flourishing to Arcadia when they shall allot such a governor unto it.'

This, spoken by a man both grave in years and known honest,
10 prevailed so with all the Mantineans that with one voice they ran to deliver the two princes. But Philanax came in time to withstand them, both sides yet standing in arms, and rather wanting a beginning than minds to enter into a bloody conflict; which Philanax foreseeing, thought best to remove the prisoners secretly, and (if need were)
15 rather without form of justice to kill them than against justice (as he thought) to have them usurp the state. But there again arose a new trouble; for Sympathus, the nobleman that kept them, was so stricken in compassion with their excellent presence that, as he would not falsify his promise to Philanax to give them liberty, so
20 yet would he not yield them to himself, fearing he would do them violence. Thus tumult upon tumult arising, the sun, I think, a-weary to see their discords, had already gone down to his western lodging. But yet to know what the poor shepherds did (who were the first descriers of these matters) will not to some ears perchance be a
25 tedious digression.

Here ends the fourth book or act.

1 content] contented Cl, As.   4 good] goods Da, Je, 93.   8 governor] government Cl, As; governance Da; governess Ph, Hm; governours Je.   9 both] om. Da, 93.   years and] years, great in authority, near allied to the prince, and 93. 10 so] still Cl; much Ph.   16 arose] arase Cl; rose Da.   26 Here ends] The end of Cl; Here endeth Bo, Da, Je, Hm.   or act] om. Cl, Da.

THE FOURTH ECLOGUES

THE shepherds, finding no place for them in these garboils, to which
their quiet hearts (whose highest ambition was in keeping themselves
up in goodness) had at all no aptness, retired themselves from among
the clamorous multitude, and (as sorrow refuseth not sorrowful 5
company) went up together to the western side of a hill whose pros-
pect extended it so far as they might well discern many of Arcadia's
beauties. And there, looking upon the sun's as then declining race,
the poor men sat pensive of their present miseries, as if they found
a wearisomeness of their woeful words; till at last good old Geron 10
(who as he had longest tasted the benefits of Basilius's government
so seemed to have a special feeling of the present loss), wiping his
eyes and long white beard bedewed with great drops of tears, began
in this sort to complain:

'Alas, poor sheep', said he, 'which hitherto have enjoyed your 15
fruitful pasture in such quietness as your wool, among other things,
hath made this country famous, your best days are now passed. Now
must you become the victual of an army, and perchance an army of
foreign enemies. You are now not only to fear home wolves but alien
lions; now, I say, now that Basilius, our right Basilius is deceased. 20
Alas, sweet pastures, shall soldiers that know not how to use you
possess you? Shall they that cannot speak Arcadian language be
lords over your shepherds? For, alas, with good cause may we look
for any evil, since Basilius our only strength is taken from us.'

To that all the other shepherds present uttered pitiful voices, 25
especially the very born Arcadians. For, as for the other, though
humanity moved them to pity human cases, especially of a prince
under whom they had found a refuge of their miseries and justice
equally administered, yet they could not so naturally feel the lively
touch of sorrow, but rather used this occasion to record their own 30

1 THE FOURTH ECLOGUES] HERE BEGIN THE FOURTH ECLOGUES
Cl.   5–6 refuseth . . . company] desires company Cl, As, Da, Ph, Je, Hm, 93.
7 extended it so] extended so Cl, Ph; extends it so As; attended so Da; extended itself so
Hm.   10 wearisomeness] weariness 93.   at last] at the last Ph, Hm.   16 among]
amongst Cl, 93.   17 hath] have As, Je.   18 must you] you must 93.   20 now
that Basilius, our right Basilius] now that our right Basilius 93.   27 of] for Ph; in 93.
29 they could] could they 93.   30–p. 344, 16 but rather . . . my delight] 93 *sub-
stitutes* pp. 284, 2–285, 30 n. Nevertheless, of that number one Agelastus . . . still wailing.

private sorrows which they thought would not have agreed with a joy-
ful time. Among them the principals were Strephon, Klaius, and
Philisides. Strephon and Klaius would require a whole book to re-
count their sorrows and the strange causes of their sorrows—another
5 place perchance will serve for the declaring of them. But in short two
gentlemen they were both in love with one maid of that country
named Urania, thought a shepherd's daughter, but indeed of far
greater birth. For her sake they had both taken this trade of life,
each knowing other's love, but yet of so high a quality their friend-
10 ship was that they never so much as brake company one from the
other, but continued their pursuit, like two true runners both
employing their best speed, but one not hindering the other. But
after many marvellous adventures, Urania never yielding better than
hate for their love, upon a strange occasion had left the country,
15 giving withal strait commandment to these two by writing that they
should tarry in Arcadia until they heard from her. And now some
months were passed that they had no news of her; but yet rather
meaning to break their hearts than break her commandment, they
bare it out as well as such evil might be until now that the general
20 complaints of all men called in like question their particular griefs,
which eclogue-wise they specified in this double sestine:

Strephon   Klaius

Strephon. Ye goat-herd gods, that love the grassy mountains,
Ye nymphs, which haunt the springs in pleasant valleys,
25   Ye satyrs, joyed with free and quiet forests,
Vouchsafe your silent ears to plaining music
Which to my woes gives still an early morning,
And draws the dolour on till weary evening.

Klaius. O Mercury, foregoer to the evening,
30   O heav'nly huntress of the savage mountains,
O lovely star, entitled of the morning,
While that my voice doth fill these woeful valleys,

1–2 a joyful] a more joyful Cl, As.   5 the declaring] the better declaring Cl, As.
6 maid of that] made in that Cl, Hm.   10 that] as As, Je.   18 than break
her Bo, Cl, As, Da, Ph: than break their St; than her Je, Hm.   20 griefs] groans As;
grief Da.   22–p. 330, 33 *The poem is in* Ra; 90 *transferred it to the First Eclogues;*
93 *to the Second Eclogues.*   23 Ye] You Ra, 90 (*only*).   24 Ye] You Ra, 90
(*only*).   which] that Da, Ra, 90 (*only*).   haunt OA, Ra, 90: hunt St.   25 Ye;
You Ra, 90 (*only*).   forests OA, Ra, 90: frosts St.   26 plaining] playing Cl, Da,
Ph.   27 gives] give Ra, 93.

Vouchsafe your silent ears to plaining music,
Which oft hath Echo tired in secret forests.

Strephon. I that was once free burgess of the forests,
　Where shade from sun, and sport I sought in evening,
　I that was once esteemed for pleasant music,   5
　Am banished now among the monstrous mountains
　Of huge despair, and foul affliction's valleys,
　Am grown a screech-owl to myself each morning.

Klaius. I that was once delighted every morning,
　Hunting the wild inhabiters of forests,   10
　I that was once the music of these valleys,
　So darkened am that all my day is evening,
　Heart-broken so, that molehills seem high mountains,
　And fill the vales with cries instead of music.

Strephon. Long since, alas, my deadly swannish music   15
　Hath made itself a crier of the morning,
　And hath with wailing strength climbed highest mountains.
　Long since my thoughts more desert be than forests.
　Long since I see my joys come to their evening,
　And state thrown down to over-trodden valleys.   20

Klaius. Long since the happy dwellers of these valleys
　Have prayed me leave my strange exclaiming music,
　Which troubles their day's work, and joys of evening.
　Long since I hate the night, more hate the morning.
　Long since my thoughts chase me like beasts in forests,   25
　And make me wish myself laid under mountains.

Strephon. Meseems I see the high and stately mountains
　Transform themselves to low dejected valleys.
　Meseems I hear in these ill-changed forests
　The nightingales do learn of owls their music.
　Meseems I feel the comfort of the morning   30
　Turned to the mortal serene of an evening.

1 plaining] playing Cl, Da, Ph; pleasant Hm, Ra.   2 tired Bo, Cl, Le, As, Da,
Ph, 90: tried St. Je, Hm; cried Ra.   4 sport OA, Ra: sports St, 90.   in] at 90.
6 Am] And Cl, Le.   among] amongst Cl, Le, Je, Hm, Ra.   10 of forests] of
the forests Cl, As, Hm, Ra.   11 these] the Cl; those As, Da.   14 vales] valleys
Cl, As, Ph, Hm, Ra.   16 the OA, Ra, 90: this St.   25 beasts Cl, As, Da, Ph,
Hm, Ra, 90: beast St, Bo, Je.   32 Turned] Turn Cl, Hm, Ra.   serene] siren Cl,
Da, Hm, Ra; sereme Le; serien As; *blank left* Ph; sering *corr. to* syryen Je.

Klaius. Meseems I see a filthy cloudy evening
  As soon as sun begins to climb the mountains.
  Meseems I feel a noisome scent the morning
  When I do smell the flowers of these valleys.
5 Meseems I hear (when I do hear sweet music)
  The dreadful cries of murdered men in forests.

Strephon. I wish to fire the trees of all these forests;
  I give the sun a last farewell each evening;
  I curse the fiddling finders-out of music;
10 With envy I do hate the lofty mountains,
  And with despite despise the humble valleys;
  I do detest night, evening, day, and morning.

Klaius. Curse to myself my prayer is, the morning;
  My fire is more than can be made with forests;
15 My state more base than are the basest valleys;
  I wish no evenings more to see, each evening;
  Shamed, I hate myself in sight of mountains,
  And stop mine ears lest I grow mad with music.

Strephon. For she, whose parts maintained a perfect music,
20 Whose beauties shined more than the blushing morning,
  Who much did pass in state the stately mountains,
  In straightness passed the cedars of the forests,
  Hath cast me, wretch, into eternal evening,
  By taking her two suns from these dark valleys.

25 *Klaius.* For she, with whom compared the Alps are valleys,
  She, whose least word brings from the spheres their music,
  At whose approach the sun rase in the evening,
  Who, where she went, bare in her forehead morning,
  Is gone, is gone from these our spoiled forests,
30 Turning to deserts our best pastured mountains.

Strephon. These mountains witness shall, so shall these valleys,

Klaius. These forests eke, made wretched by our music,
  Our morning hymn this is, and song at evening.

4 these] the Cl; those Ra.   7 wish OA, Ra, 90: which St.   8 last] late Hm, Ra.   11 despise] do spite Cl, Da.   12 day, and morning] and morning Hm; and the morning Ra.   15 are] is Cl, Da. Ph, Hm, Ra.   16 evenings] evening Cl, Le, Da, Ph, Hm, Ra.   17 hate] have 90 (*only*).   20 beauties] beauty Ra, 90.   25 with] that Hm; to Ra, 90.   26 word] words As, Hm, Ra.   27 rase] rose Hm Ra, 90.   33 this is] is this 90.

But, as though all this had been but the taking of a taste to their wailings, Strephon again began this dizain, which was answered unto him in that kind of verse which is called the crown:

Strephon. I joy in grief, and do detest all joys;
    Despise delight, am tired with thought of ease.   5
    I turn my mind to all forms of annoys,
    And with the change of them my fancy please.
    I study that which most may me displease,
    And in despite of that displeasure's might
    Embrace that most that most my soul destroys;   10
    Blinded with beams, fell darkness is my sight;
    Dwell in my ruins, feed with sucking smart,
    I think from me, not from my woes, to part.

Klaius. I think from me, not from my woes to part,
    And loathe this time called life, nay think that life   15
    Nature to me for torment did impart;
    Think my hard haps have blunted death's sharp knife,
    Not sparing me in whom his works be rife;
    And thinking this, think nature, life, and death
    Place sorrow's triumph on my conquered heart.   20
    Whereto I yield, and seek no other breath
    But from the scent of some infectious grave;
    Nor of my fortune aught but mischief crave.

Strephon. Nor of my fortune aught but mischief crave,
    And seek to nourish that which now contains   25
    All what I am. If I myself will save,
    Then must I save what in me chiefly reigns,
    Which is the hateful web of sorrow's pains.
    Sorrow then cherish me, for I am sorrow;
    No being now but sorrow I can have;   30
    Then deck me as thine own; thy help I borrow,
    Since thou my riches art, and that thou hast
    Enough to make a fertile mind lie waste.

4– p.334, 6 90–93 *transferred this poem to the Second Eclogues.*   5 am] and Cl, Ph, 90 (*only*).   tired Bo, Le, As, Da, Ph, Je, Hm, Ra, 90: tried St; tyer Cl. thought] thoughts Cl, Da.   8 most may me] may me most 90.   12. Dwell in my ruins, feed] Dwell in my ruins, fed Cl, Ph: Dwell in my ruins fled Da; Dull in my ruins, feed Hm; Dole on my ruin feeds 90 (*only*).   15 nay] may Cl, Da. 20 heart] breast 90 (*only*).   21 no OA: none St, 90.   32 riches] richess Bo; reckless Cl, Le.

Klaius. Enough to make a fertile mind lie waste
 Is that huge storm which pours itself on me.
 Hailstones of tears, of sighs a monstrous blast,
 Thunders of cries; lightnings my wild looks be,
5 The darkened heav'n my soul which naught can see;
 The flying sprites which trees by roots up tear
 Be those despairs which have my hopes quite waste.
 The difference is: all folks those storms forbear,
 But I cannot; who then myself should fly,
10 So close unto myself my wracks do lie.

Strephon. So close unto myself my wracks do lie;
 Both cause, effect, beginning, and the end
 Are all in me: what help then can I try?
 My ship, myself, whose course to love doth bend,
15 Sore beaten doth her mast of comfort spend;
 Her cable, reason, breaks from anchor, hope;
 Fancy, her tackling, torn away doth fly;
 Ruin, the wind, hath blown her from her scope;
 Bruised with waves of care, but broken is
20 On rock, despair, the burial of my bliss.

Klaius. On rock, despair, the burial of my bliss,
 I long do plough with plough of deep desire;
 The seed fast-meaning is, no truth to miss;
 I harrow it with thoughts, which all conspire
25 Favour to make my chief and only hire.
 But, woe is me, the year is gone about,
 And now I fain would reap, I reap but this,
 Hate fully grown, absence new sprongen out.
 So that I see, although my sight impair,
30 Vain is their pain who labour in despair.

Strephon. Vain is their pain who labour in despair.
 For so did I when with my angle, will,
 I sought to catch the fish torpedo fair.
 E'en then despair did hope already kill;

6 tear] tears Cl, Ph. 7 waste] raste Cl, Le, As. 8 those] these Da, Je.
18 her] me Cl; *om.* Le. 19 care] cares 90. 22 do] to Da, Hm.
28 new] now Le, Da, Hm. sprongen] spring Bo; sprong Cl, Le, As, Ph, 98.
32 my] mine Cl, As.

Yet fancy would perforce employ his skill,
And this hath got: the catcher now is caught,
Lamed with the angle which itself did bear,
And unto death, quite drowned in dolours, brought
To death, as then disguised in her fair face.   5
Thus, thus alas, I had my loss in chase.

Klaius. Thus, thus alas, I had my loss in chase
When first that crowned basilisk I knew,
Whose footsteps I with kisses oft did trace,
Till by such hap as I must ever rue   10
Mine eyes did light upon her shining hue,
And hers on me, astonished with that sight.
Since then my heart did lose his wonted place,
Infected so with her sweet poison's might
That, leaving me for dead, to her it went.   15
But ah, her flight hath my dead relics spent.

Strephon. But ah, her flight hath my dead relics spent,
Her flight from me, from me, though dead to me,
Yet living still in her, while her beams lent
Such vital spark that her mine eyes might see.   20
But now those living lights absented be,
Full dead before, I now to dust should fall,
But that eternal pains my soul have hent,
And keep it still within this body thrall;
That thus I must, while in this death I dwell,   25
In earthly fetters feel a lasting hell.

Klaius. In earthly fetters feel a lasting hell
Alas I do; from which to find release,
I would the earth, I would the heavens sell.
But vain it is to think those pains should cease,   30
Where life is death, and death cannot breed peace.
O fair, O only fair, from thee, alas,
These foul, most foul, disasters to me fell;
Since thou from me (O me) O sun didst pass.

6 alas, I had] I had, alas 90 (*only*).   7 alas, I had] I had, alas 90 (*only*).   13 lose]
loose Le, As, 90.   14 with her OA, 90: whither St.   poison's] poison Ph;
poisonous Le, Da.   21 those] these Cl, Je.   22 should] shall 93 (*corr.* 98).
23 have] hath Je, Hm; should 90 (*only*).   25 That] Thus Da, Je, Hm.   29 sell]
fell Da, Ph, Hm, 90.   30 those] these Ph, Je, Hm, 90.   32 only fair, from OA, 90:
only from St.   33 disasters] distresses Ph, 90 (*only*).   fell] fall Cl, Ph; sell Hm.

Therefore esteeming all good blessings toys,
I joy in grief, and do detest all joys.

Strephon. I joy in grief, and do detest all joys.
But now an end, O Klaius, now an end,
5 For e'en the herbs our hateful music stroys,
And from our burning breath the trees do bend.

When they had ended, with earnest entreaty they obtained of
Philisides that he would impart some part of the sorrow his coun-
tenance so well witnessed unto them. And he (who by no entreaty
10 of the duke would be brought unto it) in this doleful time was content
thus to manifest himself:

'The name of Samothea is so famous that, telling you I am of that,
I shall not need to extend myself further in telling you what that
country is. But there I was born, of such parentage as neither left
15 me so great that I was a mark for envy nor so base that I was subject
to contempt, brought up from my cradle age with such care as
parents are wont to bestow upon their children whom they mean to
make the maintainers of their name. And as soon as my memory grew
strong enough to receive what might be delivered unto it by my
20 senses, they offered learning unto me, especially that kind that
teacheth what in truth and not in opinion is to be embraced, and
what to be eschewed. Neither was I barred from seeking the natural
knowledge of things so far as the narrow sight of man hath pierced
into it. And because the mind's commandment is vain without the
25 body be enabled to obey it, my strength was exercised with horse-
manship, weapons, and suchlike other qualities as, besides the
practice, carried in themselves some serviceable use; wherein I so
profited that, as I was not excellent, so I was accompanable. After
that by my years, or perchance by a sooner privilege than years
30 commonly grant, I was thought able to be mine own master, I was
suffered to spend some time in travel, that by the comparison of
many things I might ripen my judgement; since greatness, power,
riches, and suchlike standing in relation to another, who doth
know none but his own, doth not know his own. Then being home
35 returned, and thought of good hope (for the world rarely bestows

4 But] And 90.   5 hateful] mournful 90 (*only*).   26 suchlike] such
Cl, As.   27 I so] so I Cl, Da, Ph, Je, Hm.   28 so I was] so was I Cl, As; so I
was not Ph, Hm.   30 mine] my Da, Ph.

a better title upon youth), I continued to use the benefits of a quiet mind; in truth (I call him to witness that knoweth hearts) even in the secret of my soul bent to honesty—thus far you see, as no pompous spectacle, so an untroubled tenor of a well guided life. But alas, what should I make pathetical exclamations to a most true event? 5 So it happened that love (which what it is, your own feeling can best tell you) diverted this course of tranquillity; which, though I did with so much covering hide that I was thought void of it as any man, yet my wound which smarted to myself brought me in fine to this change, much in state but more in mind. But how love first took me 10 I did once, using the liberty of versifying, set down in a song, in a dream indeed it was; and thus did I poetically describe my dream:

Now was our heav'nly vault deprived of the light
With sun's depart; and now the darkness of the night
Did light those beamy stars which greater light did dark. 15
Now each thing which enjoyed that fiery quickning spark
Which life is called were moved their spirits to repose,
And wanting use of eyes, their eyes began to close.
A silence sweet each where with one concent embraced
(A music sweet to one in careful musing placed); 20
And mother earth, now clad in mourning weeds, did breathe
A dull desire to kiss the image of our death;
When I, disgraced wretch, not wretched then, did give
My senses such release as they which quiet live,
Whose brains boil not in woes, nor breasts with beatings ache, 25
With nature's praise are wont in safest home to take.
Far from my thoughts was aught whereto their minds aspire
Who under courtly pomps do hatch a base desire.
Free all my powers were from those captiving snares
Which heav'nly purest gifts defile in muddy cares. 30
Ne could my soul itself accuse of such a fault
As tender conscience might with furious pangs assault.
But like the feeble flow'r (whose stalk cannot sustain
His weighty top) his top doth downward drooping lean;

8 so] too Bo, Da, Je.   11 did] had Da, Je.   13–p. 340, 28 90–93 *transferred the poem to Book III of* NA.   16 which] that Je, 90.   19 A] And Cl, As, Hm. 20 musing] music Cl, Ph, Hm.   24 release] relief 90.   25 boil] boils Le, Hm; broil 90.   beatings] heating Da; bitings Ph; heatings Je.   26 safest] safety Cl, Le; saftest Je.   34 doth downward] downward doth 93.   drooping] dropping Bo, Cl, Da, Ph.

Or as the silly bird in well acquainted nest
Doth hide his head with cares but only how to rest,
So I in simple course, and unentangled mind,
Did suffer drowsy lids mine eyes then clear to blind;
5   And laying down my head, did nature's rule observe,
Which senses up doth shut the senses to preserve.
They first their use forgot, then fancies lost their force,
Till deadly sleep at length possessed my living corse.
A living corse I lay; but ah, my wakeful mind
10   (Which made of heav'nly stuff no mortal change doth bind)
Flew up with freer wings of fleshly bondage free;
And having placed my thoughts, my thoughts thus placed
       me:
Methought, nay sure I was, I was in fairest wood
15   Of Samothea land; a land which whilom stood
An honour to the world, while honour was their end,
And while their line of years they did in virtue spend.
But there I was, and there my calmy thoughts I fed
On nature's sweet repast, as healthful senses led.
20   Her gifts my study was, her beauties were my sport;
My work her works to know, her dwelling my resort.
Those lamps of heav'nly fire to fixed motion bound,
The ever turning spheres, the never moving ground;
What essence dest'ny hath; if fortune be or no;
25   Whence our immortal souls to mortal earth do flow;
What life it is, and how that all these lives do gather,
With outward maker's force, or like an inward father.
Such thoughts, methought, I thought, and strained my single
       mind
30   Then void of nearer cares, the depth of things to find.
When lo, with hugest noise (such noise a tower makes
When it blown up with mine a fall of ruin takes;
Or such a noise it was as highest thunders send,
Or cannons thunder-like, all shot together, lend),

3 unentangled] unitangled Cl; uninfangled As; in untangled Da.   4 mine] my
Bo, As, Da.   9 lay] say As, Ph, Hm.   10 bind Bo, Cl, Le, As, Ph, Je, Hm:
blind St, Da, 90.   25 Whence] When Da, Hm.   26 do gather Cl, Le, Da, Ph,
Je, 90: doth gather St, Bo, Hm; together As.   30 depth] depths Cl, Da.
31 When] Who Cl, Ph, Hm.   a] as Cl, Le; no Da, Ph, Je, Hm.   32 up with
mine] down with wind 90.   33 Or] But Da, Ph, Je, Hm.

The moon asunder rent (O gods, O pardon me,
That forced with grief reveals what grieved eyes did see),
The moon asunder rent; whereat with sudden fall
(More swift than falcon's stoop to feeding falconer's call)
There came a chariot fair by doves and sparrows guided,   5
Whose storm-like course stayed not till hard by me it bided.
I, wretch, astonished was, and thought the deathful doom
Of heav'n, of earth, of hell, of time and place was come.
But straight there issued forth two ladies (ladies sure
They seemed to me) on whom did wait a virgin pure;   10
Strange were the ladies' weeds, yet more unfit than strange.
The first with clothes tucked up, as nymphs in woods do range,
Tucked up e'en with the knees, with bow and arrows prest;
Her right arm naked was, discovered was her breast.
But heavy was her pace, and such a meagre cheer   15
As little hunting mind (God knows) did there appear.
The other had with art (more than our women know,
As stuff meant for the sale set out to glaring show)
A wanton woman's face, and with curled knots had twined
Her hair which, by the help of painter's cunning, shined.   20
When I such guests did see come out of such a house,
The mountains great with child I thought brought forth a
    mouse.
But walking forth, the first thus to the second said:
'Venus, come on.' Said she: 'Diane, you are obeyed.'   25
Those names abashed me much, when those great names I
    heard;
Although their fame (meseemed) from truth had greatly jarred.
As I thus musing stood, Diana called to her
Her waiting nymph, a nymph that did excel as far   30
All things that erst I saw, as orient pearls exceed
That which their mother hight, or else their silly seed;
Indeed a perfect hue, indeed a sweet concent
Of all those graces' gifts the heav'ns have ever lent.
And so she was attired, as one that did not prize   35
Too much her peerless parts, nor yet could them despise.

1-3 (O gods . . . rent] *om.* 90.   2 with OA, 90: much St.   3 whereat] whereout 90.
10 seemed] seem Da, Je.   13 e'en with] e'en to Cl, Le.   16 did there]
there did Da, Hm.   25 Diane] Diana Cl, Le, Da, Ph, Hm.   30 Her OA: The
St, 90.   32 their OA, 90: her St.   36 Too] So St, Cl, Le, Da.

But called, she came apace; a pace wherein did move
The band of beauties all, the little world of love.
And bending humbled eyes (O eyes, the sun of sight)
She waited mistress' will, who thus disclosed her sprite:
5 'Sweet Mira mine', quoth she, 'the pleasure of my mind,
In whom of all my rules the perfect proof I find,
To only thee thou seest we grant this special grace
Us to attend, in this most private time and place.
Be silent therefore now, and so be silent still
10 Of what thou seest; close up in secret knot thy will.'
She answered was with look, and well performed behest.
And Mira I admired; her shape sank in my breast.
But thus with ireful eyes, and face that shook with spite,
Diana did begin: 'What moved me to invite
15 Your presence, sister dear, first to my moony sphere,
And hither now, vouchsafe to take with willing ear.
I know full well you know what discord long hath reigned
Betwixt us two; how much that discord foul hath stained
Both our estates, while each the other did deprave,
20 Proof speaks too much to us that feeling trial have.
Our names are quite forgot, our temples are defaced;
Our off'rings spoiled, our priests from priesthood are displaced.
Is this thy fruit, O strife? those thousand churches high,
Those thousand altars fair now in the dust to lie?
25 In mortal minds our minds but planets' names preserve;
No knee once bowed, forsooth, for them they say we serve.
Are we their servants grown? no doubt a noble stay;
Celestial pow'rs to worms, Jove's children serve to clay.
But such they say we be; this praise our discord bred,
30 While we for mutual spite a striving passion fed.
But let us wiser be; and what foul discord brake,
So much more strong again let fastest concord make.
Our years do it require; you see we both do feel
The weak'ning work of time's for ever whirling wheel.

3 sun Cl, Da, Ph, Hm, 90: sum St, Bo, Le, As, Je.   sight] light Cl, Da, Ph.
10 what] that 90.   12 sank] cank Bo; sonke 90.   13 face that shook] face
trembling Ph, Je; trembling face Hm.   15 moony] moovy Cl; moonish As; mani
Da; mony Ph.   22 off'rings] offsprings As, Je (offsprings *corr. to* offrings St, Da).
priests] priest 90 (*only*).   23 thy] the Da, Ph, Je, 90.   O] of Cl, Je, 90;
or As.   26 knee OA: knees St, 90.   32 fastest] safest Cl; fattest Da.
33 it] yet Cl, Le, Da, Ph, Hm.

Although we be divine, our grandsire Saturn is
With age's force decayed, yet once the heav'n was his.
And now before we seek by wise Apollo's skill
Our young years to renew (for so he saith he will)
Let us a perfect peace betwixt us two resolve;   5
Which, lest the ruinous want of government dissolve,
Let one the princess be, to her the other yield;
For vain equality is but contention's field.
And let her have the gifts that should in both remain;
In her let beauty both and chasteness fully reign;   10
So as, if I prevail, you give your gifts to me;
If you, on you I lay what in my office be.
Now resteth only this: which of us two is she
To whom precedence shall of both accorded be.
For that (so that you like) hereby doth lie a youth   15
(She beckoned unto me), as yet of spotless truth,
Who may this doubt discern; for better wit than lot
Becometh us; in us fortune determines not.
This crown of amber fair (an amber crown she held)
To worthiest let him give when both he hath beheld;   20
And be it as he saith.' Venus was glad to hear
Such proffer made, which she well showed with smiling
    cheer;
As though she were the same as when by Paris' doom
She had chief goddesses in beauty overcome.   25
And smirkly thus gan say: 'I never sought debate,
Diana dear, my mind to love and not to hate
Was ever apt; but you my pastimes did despise.
I never spited you, but thought you over wise.
Now kindness proffered is, none kinder is than I;   30
And so most ready am this mean of peace to try.
And let him be our judge; the lad doth please me well.'
Thus both did come to me, and both began to tell
(For both together spake, each loath to be behind)
That they by solemn oath their deities would bind   35
To stand unto my will; their will they made me know.
I that was first aghast, when first I saw their show,

4 he saith] saith he Le, Ph.   5 betwixt] between 90.   8 contention's]
a contentious Ph, Hm.   13–14 *om.* Je.   14 precedence Bo, Da, Ph, 90:
precedents St, Cl, Le, Hm; president As.   29 over wise] ever wise Da, Hm.

Now bolder waxed, waxed proud that I such sway might bear;
For near acquaintance doth diminish reverent fear.
And having bound them fast by Styx they should obey
To all what I decreed, did thus my verdict say:
'How ill both you can rule, well hath your discord taught;
Ne yet, for what I see, your beauties merit aught.
To yonder nymph therefore (to Mira I did point)
The crown above you both for ever I appoint.'
I would have spoken out, but out they both did cry:
'Fie, fie, what have we done? ungodly rebel, fie!
But now we must needs yield to what our oaths require.'
'Yet thou shalt not go free,' quoth Venus, 'such a fire
Her beauty kindle shall within thy foolish mind
That thou full oft shalt wish thy judging eyes were blind.'
'Nay then,' Diana, said, 'the chasteness I will give
In ashes of despair, though burnt, shall make thee live.'
'Nay thou', said both, 'shalt see such beams shine in her face
That thou shalt never dare seek help of wretched case.'
And with that cursed curse away to heav'n they fled,
First having all their gifts upon fair Mira spread.
The rest I cannot tell, for therewithal I waked
And found with deadly fear that all my sinews shaked.
Was it a dream? O dream, how hast thou wrought in me
That I things erst unseen should first in dreaming see?
And thou, O traitor sleep, made for to be our rest,
How hast thou framed the pain wherewith I am oppressed?
O coward Cupid, thus dost thou thy honour keep,
Unarmed, alas unwarned, to take a man asleep?

In such, or suchlike, sort in a dream was offered unto me the
sight of her in whose respect all things afterwards seemed but blind
darkness unto me. For so it fell out that her I saw, I say that sweet
and incomparable Mira (so like her which in that rather vision than
dream of mine I had seen), that I began to persuade myself in my
nativity I was allotted unto her; to her, I say, whom even Coredens

---

1 might] should Ph; must 90.   4 what] that Le, Je, Hm, 13 (that *corr. to* what
St).   6 what] aught Cl, 90; *om.* Le.   7–p. 342, 12 Je *omits, leaving a blank
leaf.*   11 must needs] needs must 90.   what OA: that St, 90.   14 shalt] shall
Bo, Hm.   15 the] thee Cl, Le, Ph.   19 heav'n] heav'ns Cl, Le, As.
22 sinews] senses Le, Hm.   25 thou] then Bo, Cl, Da, Ph.   28 unwarned]
unarmed Cl, As, Da, Ph, Hm; unwares 90 (*only*).   32 incomparable Cl, As:
uncomparable St, Bo, Da, Ph, Hm.

made the upshot of all his despairing desires, and so, alas, from all
other exercises of my mind bent myself only to the pursuit of her
favour. But having spent some part of my youth in following of her,
sometimes with some measure of favour, sometimes with unkind
interpretations of my most kind thoughts, in the end having   5
attempted all means to establish my blissful estate, and having
been not only refused all comfort but new quarrels picked against
me, I did resolve by perpetual absence to choke mine own ill
fortunes. Yet before I departed these following elegiacs I sent unto
her: 10

$$- \cup \cup - - - - - - - - \cup \cup - -$$

$$- - - \cup \cup - - \cup \cup - \cup \cup -$$

Unto the caitiff wretch whom long affliction holdeth,
    and now fully believes help to be quite perished,
Grant yet, grant yet a look, to the last monument of his   15
    anguish,
    O you (alas so I find) cause of his only ruin.
Dread not a whit (O goodly cruel) that pity may enter
    Into thy heart by the sight of this epistle I send;
And so refuse to behold of these strange wounds the recital,   20
    Lest it might thee allure home to thyself to return
(Unto thyself I do mean, those graces dwell so within thee,
    gratefulness, sweetness, holy love, hearty regard).
Such thing cannot I seek (despair hath giv'n me my answer,
    despair most tragical clause to a deadly request);   25
Such thing cannot he hope that knows thy determinate
    hardness;
    hard like a rich marble; hard, but a fair diamond.
Can those eyes, that of eyes drowned in most hearty
    flowing tears   30
    (tears, and tears of a man) had no return to remorse;
Can those eyes now yield to the kind conceit of a
    sorrow,
    which ink only relates, but ne laments, ne replies?

7 refused all] refused of all Cl, Hm.   8 mine] my Cl, Da, Ph.   11 -p. 344, 16
The poem is in Hn; *90–93 transferred to Book III of* NA; Cm *has the first 16 lines only.*
11–12 *Scansions in* St, Bo, Cl, As, Hm *only*; St, Bo, *show extra final syllable.*   13 the
OA: the *changed by a later hand to* a St; a Cm, 90.   15 monument] moment As,
Ph, Hm.   21 thee] the Bo, As, Cm; the' Hn; th' 90.   25 clause]cause As, Hm.
29 those] these Da, Hm.

Ah, that, that do I not conceive, though that to me lief were
    more than Nestor's years, more than a king's diadem.
Ah, that, that do I not conceive; to the heaven when a
    mouse climbs
5   then may I hope t'achieve grace of a heavenly tiger.
But, but alas, like a man condemned doth crave to be heard
    speak,
    not that he hopes for amends of the disaster he feels,
But finding th'approach of death with an inly relenting,
10   gives an adieu to the world, as to his only delight;
Right so my boiling heart, inflamed with fire of a fair eye,
    bubbling out doth breathe signs of his hugy dolours,
Now that he finds to what end his life and love be reserved,
    and that he thence must part where to live only I lived.
15   O fair, O fairest, are such the triumphs to thy fairness?
    can death beauty become? must I be such a monument?
Must I be only the mark shall prove that virtue is angry?
    shall prove that fierceness can with a white dove abide?
Shall to the world appear that faith and love be rewarded
20   with mortal disdain, bent to unendly revenge?
Unto revenge? O sweet, on a wretch wilt thou be revenged?
    shall such high planets tend to the loss of a worm?
And to revenge who do bend would in that kind be re-
    venged,
25   as th'offence was done, and go beyond if he can.
All my 'offence was love; with love then must I be chastened,
    and with more by the laws that to revenge do belong.
If that love be a fault, more fault in you to be lovely;
    love never had me oppressed, but that I saw to be
30   loved.
You be the cause that I love; what reason blameth a shadow
    that with a body't goes, since by a body it is?

1–2 *om*. Da.   1 that do I] that I do I Bo, 90 (*corr.* 13); I do Cl.   1–3 though
. ˙. conceive] *om.* As.   me lief] me life Bo, Le; me sure Ph; my bliss 90.   3 that
do I] I do Cl, Da; that I do Hn, 90, 98, 05.   9 inly] ugly 90 (*only*).   11 so] to
Bo, Ph.   12 breathe] breath Bo, As, Hn, 90.   13 Je *begins again here.*
14 thence] hence Cl, 90 (*only*).   live only I lived] live only he loved 90; live only
he lived 93.   15 the] to the Bo; *om.* As; thy Da, 93.   16 I be such a] I be
such Bo, Cl, Je, Hm, Hn, 93; be such a 90.   18 that] the Ph (the *corr. to* that Cl).
20 to unendly] to the unendly Da, Je.   22–3 *om.* Cl.   22 tend] tread Da; end
90 (*only*).   25 was] is Cl, Ph; were Da.   26 must I be] must be Ph, Hm.
27 do] *om.* Bo; doth Hn.   31 love] loved 90.

If the love hate you did, you should your beauty have
　　hidden;
you should those fair eyes have with a veil covered.
But fool, fool that I am, those eyes would shine from a
　　dark cave;   5
what veils then do prevail, but to a more miracle?
Or those golden locks (those locks which lock me to bond-
　　age)
torn you should disperse unto the blasts of a wind.
But fool, fool that I am, though I had but a hair of her head   10
　　found,
ee'n as I am, so I should unto that hair be a thrall.
Or with a fair hand's nails (O hand which nails me to this
　　death)
you should have your face (since love is ill) blemished.   15
O wretch, what do I say? should that fair face be defaced?
should my too much sight cause so true a sun to be lost?
First let Cimmerian darkness be my onl'habitation,
first be mine eyes pulled out, first be my brain perished,
Ere that I should consent to do such excessive a damage   20
unto the earth by the hurt of this her heavenly jewel.
O not but such love you say you could have afforded,
as might learn temp'rance void of a rage's events.
O sweet simplicity, from whence should love be so learned?
unto Cupid that boy shall a pedant be found?   25
Well, but faulty I was; reason to my passion yielded,
passion unto my rage, rage to a hasty revenge.
But what's this for a fault, for which such faith be
　　abolished,
such faith, so stainless, inviolate, violent?   30
Shall I not? O may I not thus yet refresh the remembrance
what sweet joys I had once, and what a place I did hold?

1 the] that Ph, Hn, 90.　　hate you did] you hate Ph; you did hate 90.　　　7 lock]
locks Le, Ph; looked Da; locked Je.　　　12 I should] should I Da, Hm.　　　13 with
a fair Bo, Cl, Le, As, Ph, Hm, Hn: with fair St, Da, Je, 90.　　　this] *om*. Cl, Le, As,
Da.　　　16 do] did Bo, Cl, Le, As, Da, Ph, Je, Hm, Hn.　　　19 mine] my As, Je.
20 such] so 93.　　a] *om*. Le, Hm.　　　21 jewel] Ivill Bo; evil Cl.　　　22 not] no 90
(*only*).　　　23 a rage's] outrageous Cl; rages Le, Ph, Je.　　　events] event Le, As, Ph,
Hn.　　　24 be so] so be 90 (*only*).　　　25 shall] should Cl, Le, As.　　a pedant As,
Da, 90: a padante St; a pechante Bo; a pendaunt Cl, Le; a picture Ph; apelante Je;
a pendantes Hm; a pedantee Hn.　　　28 faith be] faith is Le; fault is 90
(*only*).

Shall I not once object that you, you granted a favour
    unto the man whom now such miseries you award?
Bend your thoughts to the dear sweet words which then
    to me giv'n were;
5   think what a world is now, think who hath altered her heart.
What? was I then worthy such good, now worthy so much
    evil?
    now fled, then cherished? then so nigh, now so remote?
Did not a rosed breath, from lips more rosy proceeding,
10   say that I well should find in what a care I was had?
With much more: now what do I find but care to abhor me,
    care that I sink in grief, care that I live banished?
And banished do I live, nor now will seek a recov'ry,
    since so she will, whose will is to me more than a law.
15 If then a man in most ill case may give you a farewell;
    farewell, long farewell, all my woe, all my delight.

Philisides would have gone on in telling the rest of his unhappy
adventures, and by what desperate works of fortune he was become
a shepherd; but the shepherd Dicus desired him he would for that
20 time leave particular passions, and join in bewailing this general
loss of that country which had been a nurse to strangers as well as a
mother to Arcadians. And so, having purchased silence, Agelastus
rather cried out than sang this following lamentation:

    Since that to death is gone the shepherd high
25   Who most the silly shepherd's pipe did prize,
        Your doleful tunes sweet muses now apply.

1 you, you] yon you Bo; you me Ph; you have Je; you now Hm.   5 think OA,
Hn, 90: I think St.   6 such Bo, Le, Da, Ph, Je, Hm, 90: of such St, Cl, As, Hn. so
much] too much Ph; such Le, 90.   9 a rosed] arosed Bo; a rosy Le, Hn.
10 well should] will should As; should well 90 (corr. 98).   11 With] What As;
Which Ph.   17–23 Philisides . . . lamentation] It seemed that this complaint of
Agelastus had awaked the spirits of the Arcadians, astonished before with exceedingness
of sorrow; for he had scarcely ended when divers of them offered to follow his example in
bewailing the general loss of that country which had been as well a nurse to strangers as
a mother to Arcadians. Among the rest one accounted good in that kind, and made the
better by the true feeling of sorrow, roared out a song of lamentation which (as well as
might be) was gathered up in this form 93.   18 works] work Cl, As.
20 passions] passion Cl, As.   22 Agelastus] he Cl, As, Da, Ph, Je, Hm.
24–p. 348, 90 transferred this poem to Book III of NA, where Cm leaves a blank space for
it; 93 replaced it in the Fourth Eclogues.   25 Who] Whom 90 (only)   prize OA,
90: praise St.

And you, O trees (if any life there lies
   In trees) now through your porous barks receive
   The strange resound of these my causeful cries;
And let my breath upon your branches cleave,
   My breath distinguished into words of woe,   5
   That so I may signs of my sorrows leave.
But if among yourselves some one tree grow
   That aptest is to figure misery,
   Let it ambassade bear your griefs to show.
The weeping myrrh I think will not deny   10
   Her help to this, this justest cause of plaint.
   Your doleful tunes sweet muses now apply.

And thou, poor earth, whom fortune doth attaint
   In nature's name to suffer such a harm
   As for to lose thy gem, our earthly saint,   15
Upon thy face let coaly ravens swarm;
   Let all the sea thy tears accounted be;
   Thy bowels with all killing metals arm.
Let gold now rust, let diamonds waste in thee;
   Let pearls be wan with woe their dam doth bear;   20
   Thyself henceforth the light do never see.
And you, O flow'rs, which sometimes princes were,
   Till these strange alt'rings you did hap to try,
   Of prince's loss yourselves for tokens rear.
Lily in mourning black thy whiteness dye.   25
   O hyacinth let ai be on thee still.
   Your doleful tunes sweet muses now apply.

O echo, all these woods with roaring fill,
   And do not only mark the accents last
   But all, for all reach not my wailful will;   30
One echo to another echo cast
   Sound of my griefs, and let it never end
   Till that it hath all woods and waters passed.

---

3 these OA, 90: this St.   4 cleave] leave 90 (*only*).   6 sorrows] sorrow Le,
90.   9 ambassade Bo, As: embasshade St; (embraced) Cl; imbassage Le;
ambassage Da, Je; imbusshed Ph; embashed Hm; embassage 90.   15 lose] loose
Cl, Le, Ph, Je, Hm, 90.   our earthly] or earthly Cl, Le; thy earthly Je; and such a 90.
25 in mourning] in morning Cl, Le; O mourn in Da, Hm; O morn in Ph, Je.   thy
whiteness dye] and whiteness fly Da, Ph, Je, Hm.   28 roaring Cl, Le, As, Da,
Hm, 90: roarings St, Bo, Je; scritching Ph.   29-31 *om.* As.   30 not] out 90.

Nay, to the heav'ns your just complainings send,
 And stay the stars' inconstant constant race
 Till that they do unto our dolours bend;
And ask the reason of that special grace
5 That they, which have no lives, should live so long,
 And virtuous souls so soon should lose their place?
Ask if in great men good men so do throng
 That he for want of elbow-room must die?
 Or if that they be scant, if this be wrong?
10 Did wisdom this our wretched time espy
 In one true chest to rob all virtue's treasure?
 Your doleful tunes sweet muses now apply.

And if that any counsel you to measure
 Your doleful tunes, to them still plaining say
15 To well felt grief, plaint is the only pleasure.
O light of sun, which is entitled day,
 O well thou dost that thou no longer bidest;
 For mourning night her black weeds may display.
O Phoebus with good cause thy face thou hidest
20 Rather than have thy all-beholding eye
 Fouled with this sight while thou thy chariot guidest.
And well (methinks) becomes this vaulty sky
 A stately tomb to cover him deceased.
 Your doleful tunes sweet muses now apply.

25 O Philomela with thy breast oppressed
 By shame and grief, help, help me to lament
 Such cursed harms as cannot be redressed.
Or if thy mourning notes be fully spent,
 Then give a quiet ear unto my plaining;
30 For I to teach the world complaint am bent.
Ye dimmy clouds, which well employ your staining
 This cheerful air with your obscured cheer,
 Witness your woeful tears with daily raining.

1 complainings] complaining Da, Ph, Hm, 90. 2 inconstant] unconstant Cl,
Le; inconst As; in constant Da, Ph. 3 our] your As, Ph. 6 lose] loose Bo,
Ph, Je, Hm; leave Cl. 7 so do] do so Da, Ph, 90. 14 plaining] playing Bo,
Cl, Da. 18 night] light 90 (*corr.* 13). 21 Fouled Cl, Le, As, Hm, 90: Iould
St, Bo, Da, Je; Would Ph. thy] the Cl, Ph. 31 Ye] You 90.

And if, O sun, thou ever didst appear
   In shape which by man's eye might be perceived,
   Virtue is dead, now set thy triumph here.
Now set thy triumph in this world, bereaved
   Of what was good, where now no good doth lie;   5
   And by thy pomp our loss will be conceived.
O notes of mine, yourselves together tie;
   With too much grief methinks you are dissolved.
   Your doleful tunes sweet muses now apply.

Time ever old and young is still revolved   10
   Within itself, and never taketh end;
   But mankind is for ay to naught resolved.
The filthy snake her aged coat can mend,
   And getting youth again, in youth doth flourish;
   But unto man, age ever death doth send.   15
The very trees with grafting we can cherish,
   So that we can long time produce their time;
   But man which helpeth them, helpless must perish.
Thus, thus, the minds which over all do climb,
   When they by years' experience get best graces,   20
   Must finish then by death's detested crime.
We last short while, and build long-lasting places.
   Ah, let us all against foul nature cry;
   We nature's works do help, she us defaces.
For how can nature unto this reply: 25
   That she her child, I say, her best child killeth?
   Your doleful tunes sweet muses now apply.

Alas, methinks my weakened voice but spilleth
   The vehement course of this just lamentation;
   Methinks my sound no place with sorrow filleth.   30
I know not I, but once in detestation
   I have myself, and all what life containeth,
   Since death on virtue's fort hath made invasion.
One word of woe another after traineth;
   Ne do I care how rude be my invention,   35
   So it be seen what sorrow in me reigneth.

1 sun] sin 93 (*corr.* 98).   6 thy] the Cl, Da, Ph, 93 (*corr.* 98)   11 taketh
OA: takest St; tasteth 90.   12 resolved] dissolved Le, As, Da, Ph, Je, Hm.
14 again, in youth] in youth again Cl, Le.   24 We OA, 90: When St.
25 reply] apply Cl, Le.

O elements, by whose (they say) contention
  Our bodies be in living pow'r maintained,
  Was this man's death the fruit of your dissension?
O physic's power, which (some say) hath refrained
5   Approach of death, alas thou helpest meagrely
  When once one is for Atropos distrained.
Great be physicians' brags, but aid is beggarly;
  When rooted moisture fails, or groweth dry,
  They leave off all, and say death comes too eagerly.
10   They are but words therefore which men do buy
  Of any since god Aesculapius ceased.
  Your doleful tunes sweet muses now apply.

Justice, justice is now, alas, oppressed;
  Bountifulness hath made his last conclusion;
15   Goodness for best attire in dust is dressed.
Shepherds bewail your uttermost confusion;
  And see by this picture to you presented,
  Death is our home, life is but a delusion.
For see, alas, who is from you absented.
20   Absented? nay, I say for ever banished
  From such as were to die for him contented.
Out of our sight in turn of hand is vanished
  Shepherd of shepherds, whose well settled order
  Private with wealth, public with quiet, garnished.
25 While he did live, far, far was all disorder;
  Example more prevailing than direction,
  Far was home-strife, and far was foe from border.
His life a law, his look a full correction;
  As in his health we healthful were preserved,
30   So in his sickness grew our sure infection;
His death our death. But ah, my muse hath swarved
  From such deep plaint as should such woes descry,
  Which he of us for ever hath deserved.
The style of heavy heart can never fly
35   So high as should make such a pain notorious.
  Cease muse, therefore; thy dart, O death, apply;
And farewell prince, whom goodness hath made glorious.

1 they] men 90.   2 pow'r] pow'rs Le, Hm.   4 refrained] restrained Cl, 90.
10 which] that 90.   11 god] good Bo, Ph, Je, Hm; *om.* Cl.   17 by] with Da, Je.
32 plaint] plaints Le, Hm.

Agelastus, when he had ended his song, thus maintained the
lamentation in this rhyming sestine, having the doleful tune of the
other shepherds' pipes joined unto him:

Farewell O sun, Arcadia's clearest light;
Farewell O pearl, the poor man's plenteous treasure;   5
Farewell O golden staff, the weak man's might;
Farewell O joy, the woeful's only pleasure.
Wisdom farewell, the skill-less man's direction;
Farewell with thee, farewell all our affection.

For what place now is left for our affection,   10
Now that of purest lamp is queint the light
Which to our darkened minds was best direction;
Now that the mine is lost of all our treasure,
Now death hath swallowed up our worldly pleasure,
We orphans left, void of all public might?   15

Orphans indeed, deprived of father's might;
For he our father was in all affection,
In our well doing placing all his pleasure,
Still studying how to us to be a light.
As well he was in peace a safest treasure;   20
In war his wit and word was our direction.

Whence, whence alas, shall we seek our direction
When that we fear our hateful neighbours' might,
Who long have gaped to get Arcadians' treasure?
Shall we now find a guide of such affection,   25
Who for our sakes will think all travail light,
And make his pain to keep us safe his pleasure?

No, no, for ever gone is all our pleasure;
For ever wand'ring from all good direction;
For ever blinded of our clearest light;   30
For ever lamed of our surest might;

1-3 Agelastus . . . unto him] Many were ready to have followed this course, but the
day was so wasted that only this rhyming sestine, delivered by one of great account
among them, could obtain favour to be heard 93.   1 he] Dicus Cl, As, Da,
Ph, Je, Hm.   4-p. 350, 11 *The poem is in* 93.   4 clearest] chiefest Bo, Je;
cearest Ph.   7 woeful's] joyful's 93.   8 skill-less] skill of Da; skillest Ph, Je.
10 now is OA 93: is now St.   11 queint] quynt Le; quienc As; quench'd Ph, 93;
quenchest Je; queccht Hm.   15 left] *om.* Ph; made 93.   24 Arcadians']
Arcadian Cl, Le, Ph; Arcadias Hm.   31 surest] fairest Ph; sured 93.

For ever banished from well placed affection;
For ever robbed of our royal treasure.

Let tears for him therefore be all our treasure,
And in our wailful naming him our pleasure.
5   Let hating of ourselves be our affection,
And unto death bend still our thoughts' direction.
Let us against ourselves employ our might,
And putting out our eyes seek we our light.

Farewell our light, farewell our spoiled treasure;
10   Farewell our might, farewell our daunted pleasure;
Farewell direction, farewell all affection.

The night began to cast her dark canopy over them; and they,
even wearied with their woes, bended homewards, hoping by a
sleep, forgetting themselves, to ease their present dolours, when
15 they were met with a troop of twenty horsemen. The chief of which
asking them for the duke, and understanding the hard news, did
thereupon stay among them, and send away with speed to Philanax.
But since the night is an ease of all things, it shall at this present ease
my memory, tired with these troublesome matters.

20   Here end the fourth eclogues.

2 of our] of all our 93.   3 for him therefore] therefore for him Le, Da.
8 our eyes] of eyes Cl, Le.   10 daunted] dainted Bo, Cl; dampned Hm.
13 wearied] weary 93.   13–14 by a sleep] by sleep 93.   15 horsemen] horse Je, 93.
16 the hard OA, 93: they herd St.   16–17 did thereupon stay] thereupon stayed 93.
17 and send away OA: and sent away St; expecting the return of a messenger whom 93.
18–19 But . . . matters] om. 93.   18 of] to As, Hm.   20 Here end the fourth
eclogues Bo, Da: om. St; Here end the fourth eclogues and the fourth book or act Cl;
The end of the fourth eclogues As; Here endeth the fourth eclogues Je; Here ends the
fourth eclogues Hm; The end of the fourth book 93.

THE LAST BOOK OR ACT

THE dangerous division of men's minds, the ruinous renting of all estates, had now brought Arcadia to feel the pangs of uttermost peril (such convulsions never coming but that the life of that government draws near his necessary period), when to the honest 5 and wise Philanax, equally distracted betwixt desire of his master's revenge and care of the state's establishment, there came (unlooked-for) a Macedonian gentleman who in short but pithy manner delivered unto him that the renowned Euarchus, king of Macedon, having made a long and tedious journey to visit his old friend and 10 confederate the duke Basilius, was now come within half a mile of the lodges, where having understood by certain shepherds the sudden death of their prince, had sent unto him (of whose authority and faith he had good knowledge) desiring him to advertise him in what security he might rest there for that night; where willingly he 15 would (if safely he might) help to celebrate the funerals of his ancient companion and ally; adding he need not doubt, since he had brought but twenty in his company, he would be so unwise as to enter into any forcible attempt with so small force.

Philanax (having entertained the gentleman as well as in the midst 20 of so many tumults he could), pausing a while with himself, considering how it should not only be unjust and against the law of nations not well to receive a prince whom goodwill had brought among them, but in respect of the greatness of his might very dangerous to give him any cause of due offence, remembering withal 25 the excellent trials of his equity which made him more famous than his victories, he thought he might be the fittest instrument to redress the ruins they were in, since his goodness put him without suspicion and his greatness beyond envy. Yet weighing how hard many heads were to be bridled, and that in this monstrous confusion 30 such mischief might be attempted of which late repentance should after be but a simple remedy, he judged best first to know how the people's minds would sway to this determination. Therefore,

1 THE FIFTH AND LAST BOOK OR ACT Cl; THE FIFTH BOOK: OR LAST ACT Je; THE FIFTH BOOK OF THE COUNTESS OF PEMBROKE'S ARCADIA 93. 6 his master's] *om.* Cl, As. 10 having made . . . to visit] purposing to have visited 93. 12 by] be 93 (*corr.* 98). 29 beyond] without Ph, Hm. weighing how] weighing with himself how 93.

desiring the gentleman to return to the king his master and to
beseech him (though with his pains) to stay for an hour or two
where he was till he had set things in better order to receive him,
he himself went first to the noblemen, then to Kerxenus and the
5 principal Mantineans who were most opposite unto him, desiring
them that, as the night had most blessedly stayed them from entering
into civil blood, so they would be content in the night to assemble
the people together to hear some news which he was to deliver unto
them. There is nothing more desirous of novelties than a man that
10 fears his present fortune. Therefore they, whom mutual diffidence
made doubtful of their utter destruction, were quickly persuaded to
hear of any new matter which might alter at least, if not help, the
nature of their fear; namely the chiefest men who, as they had most
to lose so were most jealous of their own case, and were already
15 grown as weary to be followers of Timautus's ambition as before
they were enviers of Philanax's worthiness. As for Kerxenus and
Sympathus, as in the one a virtuous friendship had made him
seek to advance, in the other a natural commiseration had made him
willing to protect, the two excellent (though unfortunate) prisoners, so
20 were they not against this convocation; for having nothing but just
desires in them, they did not mistrust the justifying of them. Only
Timautus laboured to have withdrawn them from this assembly,
saying it was time to stop their ears from the ambitious charms of
Philanax:

25 'Let them first deliver Gynecia and her daughters,' said he,
'which were fit persons to hear, and then they might begin to speak;
that this was but Philanax's cunning, to link broil upon broil,
because he might avoid the answering of his trespasses which, as he
had long intended so had he prepared coloured speeches to disguise
30 them.'

But as his words expressed rather a violence of rancour than any
just ground of accusation so pierced they no further than to some
partial ears; the multitude yielding good attention to what Philanax
would propose unto them, who (like a man whose best building was
35 a well framed conscience), neither with plausible words nor fawning

---

1 and to] and Cl, As.   4 Kerxenus] Kalander 93 (and throughout).
8 unto] om. Cl, Hm.   10 fears] feareth Bo, Ph.   14 case] care Bo, Hm.
17 in the one OA, 93: in one St.   19 willing] om. Da, Ph, Je, Hm.   two] om.
As, 93.   25 said he] om. Da, Ph, Je, Hm, 93.   27 cunning] coming 93 (corr.
13).   28 trespasses] trespass Da, Je.   33 what] that Cl, As, Je.
35 fawning] faining As; frowning Hm.

countenance, but even with the grave behaviour of a wise father whom nothing but love makes to chide, he thus said unto them:

'I have', said he, 'a great matter to deliver unto you, and thereout am I to make a greater demand of you. But truly, such hath this late proceeding been of yours that I know not what is not to be 5 demanded of you. Methinks I may have reason to require of you, as men are wont among pirates, that the life at least of him that never hurt you may be safe. Methinks I am not without appearance of cause, as if you were cyclops or cannibals, to desire that our prince's body (which hath thirty years maintained us in a flourishing 10 peace) be not torn in pieces or devoured among you, but may be suffered to yield itself (which never was defiled with any of your bloods) to the natural rest of the earth. Methinks not as to Arcadians, renowned for your faith to prince and love of country, but as to sworn enemies of this sweet soil, I am to desire you that at least, if 15 you will have strangers to your princes, yet you will not deliver the seigniory of this goodly dukedom to your noble duke's murderers. Lastly I have reason, as if I had to speak to madmen, to desire you to be good to yourselves; for, before God, what either barbarous violence or unnatural folly hath not this day had his seat in your 20 minds, and left his footsteps in your actions? But in truth I love you too well to stand long displaying your faults; I would you yourselves did forget them, so you did not fall again into them. For my part I had much rather be an orator of your praises. But now, if you will suffer attentive judgement and not fore-judging passion to be the 25 weigher of my words, I will deliver unto you what a blessed mean the heavens have sent unto you, if you list to embrace it. I think there is none among you so young either in years or understanding but hath heard the true fame of that just prince, Euarchus, king of Macedon—a prince with whom our late master did ever hold most 30 perfect alliance. He, even he, is this day come, having but twenty horse with him, within two miles of this place, hoping to have found the virtuous Basilius alive, but now willing to do honour to his death. Surely, surely, the heavenly powers have in so full a time

2 he thus] thus Ph, 93.   3 thereout] thereunto Da; therewith Hm.   4 make] demand Cl, As.   greater] great Cl, As, Hm.   7 at least] *om.* Cl, As, 93.   9 or] and As, Ph.   11 but OA, 93: *om.* St.   13 bloods] blood Cl, As.   13–14 to Arcadians] Arcadians Bo, Ph.   14–15 to sworn] sworn Cl, Je.   24 much] *om.* Cl, Da.   26 a] *om.* Da, Ph.   mean] means Ph, Je.   27 heavens] gods 93.   28 you so young either] you either so young Cl, Da.   29 that] the Da, Je, Hm.

bestowed him on us to unite our disunions. For my part, therefore, I wish that, since among ourselves we cannot agree in so manifold partialities, we do put the ordering of all these things into his hands, as well touching the obsequies of the duke, the punishment of his 5 death, as the marriage and crowning of our princess. He is, both by experience and wisdom, taught how to direct his greatness such as no man can disdain to obey him, his equity such as no man need to fear him; lastly, as he hath all these qualities to help so hath he (though he would) no force to hurt. If, therefore, you so think good, 10 since our laws bear that our prince's murder be chastised before his murdered body be buried, we may invite him to sit tomorrow in the judgement seat; after which done, you may proceed to the burial.'

When Philanax first named Euarchus's landing there was a muttering murmur among the people, as though in that ill-ordered 15 weakness of theirs he had come to conquer their country. But when they understood he had so small a retinue, whispering one with another and looking who should begin to confirm Philanax's proposition, at length Sympathus was the first that allowed it, then the rest of the noblemen; neither did Kerxenus strive, hoping so 20 excellent a prince could not but deal graciously with two such young men; whose authority, joined to Philanax, all the popular sort followed. Timautus, still blinded with his own ambitious haste, not remembering factions are no longer to be trusted than the factious may be persuaded it is for their own good, would needs strive 25 against the stream, exclaiming against Philanax that now he showed who it was that would betray his country to strangers. But well he found that who is too busy in the foundation of a house may pull the building about his ears; for the people, already tired with their own divisions (of which his clampering had been a principal nurse), and 30 beginning now to espy a haven of rest, hated anything that should hinder them from it. And so asked one another whether this were not he whose evil tongue no man could escape; whether it were not Timautus that made the first mutinous oration to strengthen the troubles; whether Timautus, without their consent, had not gone 35 about to deliver Gynecia. And thus inflaming one another against him, they threw him out of the assembly, and after pursued him

1 on] upon Cl, Da, Je.   disunions] divisions 93.   2 manifold] many As, Ph, Hm.
11 to sit tomorrow] tomorrow to sit Bo, Hm.   12 after which done, you may]
which done, you may after 93.   20 two such] such two Cl, Je.   27 too]
om. Da, Je.   a house] an house Je, 93.   31 And so asked] asked Cl, As, Da,
Ph, Je, Hm, 93; asking 13.   33-4 the troubles] their troubles Ph, Hm.

with stones and staves; so that, with loss of one of his eyes, sore wounded and beaten, he was fain to fly to Philanax's feet for the succour of his life—giving a true lesson that vice itself is forced to seek the sanctuary of virtue. For Philanax, who hated his evil but not his person, and knew that a just punishment might by the manner be unjustly done, remembering withal that, although herein the people's rage might have hit right enough, yet if it were nourished in this, no man knew to what extremities it might extend itself, with earnest dealing and employing the uttermost of his authority, he did protect the trembling Timautus. And then having taken a general oath that they should, in the nonage of the princess, or till these things were settled, yield full obedience to Euarchus, so far as were not prejudicial to the laws, customs, and liberties of Arcadia; and having taken a particular oath of Sympathus that the prisoners should be kept close, without conference to any man, he himself, honourably accompanied with a great number of torches, went to the king Euarchus, whom he found taking his rest under a tree with

2 fly Bo, As, Da, Je, Hm, 93: flee St, Cl.   2–3 for the succour] for succour 93.
7 hit] it As, Ph; in it Da.   right enough] rightly 93.   12 so far] *om.* Ph; as far
Hm.   14 taken a OA, 93: taken St. oath] bond 93.   Sympathus that] Sympathus
(under whom he had a servant of his own) that 93.   15 to any] with any 93.
17–p. 359, 21 whom he found . . . as soon] 93 *reads*: whose coming in this sort into
Arcadia had thus fallen out:

The woeful prince Plangus, receiving of Basilius no other succours but only certain to conduct him to Euarchus, made all possible speed towards Byzantium, where he understood the king, having concluded all his wars with the winning of that town, had now for some good space made his abode. But being far gone on his way, he received certain intelligence that Euarchus was not only some days before returned into Macedon but since was gone with some haste to visit that coast of his country that lay towards Italy: the occasion given by the Latins who, having already gotten into their hands, partly by conquest and partly by confederacy, the greatest part of Italy, and long gaped to devour Greece also (observing the present opportunity of Euarchus's absence and Basilius's solitariness, which two princes they knew to be in effect the whole strength of Greece), were even ready to lay an unjust gripe upon it, which after they might beautify with the noble name of conquest. Which purpose, though they made not known by any solemn denouncing of war, but contrariwise gave many tokens of continuing still their former amity, yet the staying of his subjects' ships trafficking as merchants into those parts, together with the daily preparation of shipping and other warlike provisions in ports most convenient for the transporting of soldiers, occasioned Euarchus (not unacquainted with such practices) first to suspect, then to discern, lastly to seek to prevent, the intended mischief. Yet, thinking war never to be accepted until it be offered by the hand of necessity, he determined so long openly to hold them his friends as open hostility bewrayed them not his enemies; not ceasing in the mean time by letters and messages to move the states of Greece, by uniting their strength, to make timely provision against this peril; by many reasons making them see that, though in respect of place some of them might seem further removed from the first violence of the storm, yet being embarked in the same ship the final wrack must needs be common to them all. And knowing the mighty force of example, with the weak effect of fair discourses not waited on with agreeable actions, what he persuaded them himself performed, leaving in his own realm nothing either undone or unprovided which might be thought necessary for withstanding an invasion. His first care was to put his people in a readiness for war, and by his experienced soldiers to train the unskilful to martial exercises. For the better effecting whereof, as also for meeting with other inconveniences in such doubtful times incident to the most settled states, making of the divers regions of his whole kingdom so many divisions as he thought convenient, he appointed the charge of them to the greatest, and of greatest trust, he had about him, arming them with sufficient authority to levy forces within their several governments, both for resisting the invading enemy, and punishing the disordered subject. Having thus prepared the body and assured the heart of his country against any mischief that might attaint it, he then took into his careful consideration the external parts, giving order both for the repairing and increasing his navy and for the fortifying of such places, especially on the sea coast, as either commodity of landing, weakness of the country, or any other respect of advantage was likeliest to draw the enemy unto. But being none of them who think all things done for which they have once given direction, he followed everywhere his commandment with his presence; which witness of every man's slackness or diligence, chastising the one and encouraging the other, suffered not the fruit of any profitable counsel, for want of timely taking, to be lost. And thus making one place succeed another in the progress of wisdom and virtue, he was now come to Aulon, a principal port of his realm, when the poor Plangus, extremely wearied with his long journey (desire of succouring Erona no more relieving than fear of not succouring her in time aggravating his travail), by a lamentable narration of his children's death, called home his cares from encountering foreign enemies to suppress the insurrection of inward passions. The matter so heinous, the manner so villainous, the loss of such persons in so unripe years, in a time so dangerous to the whole state of Greece, how vehemently it moved to grief and compassion others, only not blind to the light of virtue nor deaf to the voice of their country, might perchance by a more cunning workman in lively colours be delivered. But the face of Euarchus's sorrow, to the one in nature, to both in affection, a father, and judging the world so much the more unworthily deprived of those excellencies as himself was better judge of so excellent worthiness, can no otherwise be shadowed out by the skilfullest pencil than by covering it over with the veil of silence. And indeed that way himself took, with so patient a quietness receiving this pitiful relation that, all words of weakness suppressed, magnanimity seemed to triumph over misery, only receiving of Plangus perfect instruction of all things concerning Plexirtus and Artaxia, with promise not only to aid him in delivering Erona but also, with vehement protestation never to return into Macedon till he had pursued the murderers to death, he dispatched with speed a ship for Byzantium, commanding the governor to provide all necessaries for the war against his own coming, which he purposed should be very shortly. In this ship Plangus would needs go, impatient of stay for that in many days before he had understood nothing of his lady's estate. Soon after whose departure news was brought to Euarchus that all the ships detained in Italy were returned; for the Latins, finding by Euarchus's proceedings their intent to be frustrate (as before by his sudden return they doubted it was discovered), deeming it no wisdom to show the will, not having the ability, to hurt, had not only in free and friendly manner dismissed them but for the time wholly omitted their enterprise, attending the opportunity of fitter occasion. By means whereof Euarchus, rid from the cumber of that war (likewise otherwise to have stayed him longer), with so great a fleet as haste would suffer him to assemble, forthwith embarked for Byzantium. And now, followed with fresh winds, he had in short time run a long course, when on a night encountered with an extreme tempest, his ships were so scattered that scarcely any two were left together. As for the king's own ship, deprived of all company, sore bruised and weatherbeaten,

no more affected pomps than as a man that knew, howsoever he was
exalted, the beginning and end of his body was earth.

But first it were fit to be known what cause moved this puissant
prince to come in this sort to Arcadia. Euarchus did not further
exceed his meanest subject with the greatness of his fortune than he 5
did surmount the greatness of his fortune with the greatness of his
mind; in so much that those things which oftentimes the best sort
think rewards of virtue, he held them not at so high price, but
esteemed them servants to well doing, the reward of virtue being in
itself; on which his inward love was so fixed that it never was 10
dissolved into other desires, but keeping his thoughts true to
themselves, was neither beguiled with the painted gloss of pleasure
nor dazzled with the false light of ambition. This made the line of

8 high price] high a price Cl, Da, Hm.   9 to] of Ph, Hm.   12 neither] never
As, Da, Je.

---

able no longer to brook the sea's churlish entertainment, a little before day it recovered
the shore. The first light made them see it was the unhappy coast of Laconia; for no
other country could have shown the like evidence of unnatural war. Which having long
endured between the nobility and the Helots, and once compounded by Pyrocles under
the name of Daiphantus, immediately upon his departure had broken out more violently
than ever before. For the king, taking the opportunity of their captain's absence, refused
to perform the conditions of peace, as extorted from him by rebellious violence. Where-
upon they were again deeply entered into war, with so notable an hatred towards the
very name of a king that Euarchus (though a stranger unto them) thought it not safe
there to leave his person where neither his own force could be a defence nor the sacred
name of majesty a protection. Therefore calling to him an Arcadian (one that coming
with Plangus had remained with Euarchus, desirous to see the wars), he demanded of
him for the next place of surety where he might make his stay until he might hear some-
what of his fleet, or cause his ship to be repaired. The gentleman, glad to have this
occasion of doing service to Euarchus and honour to Basilius (to whom he knew he
should bring a most welcome guest), told him that, if it pleased him to commit himself
to Arcadia (a part whereof lay open to their view), he would undertake ere the next
night were far spent to guide him safely to his master Basilius. The present necessity
much prevailed with Euarchus, yet more a certain virtuous desire to try whether by
his authority he might withdraw Basilius from burying himself alive, and to employ
the rest of his old years in doing good, the only happy action of man's life. For, besides
the universal case of Greece deprived by this means of a principal pillar, he weighed
and pitied the pitiful state of the Arcadian people, who were in worse case than if death
had taken away their prince. For so yet their necessity would have placed someone
to the helm; now a prince being, and not doing like a prince, keeping and not exercising
the place, they were in so much more evil case as they could not provide for their evil.
These rightly wise and virtuous considerations especially moved Euarchus to take his
journey towards the desert, where arriving within night, and understanding to his great
grief the news of the prince's death, he waited for his safe conduct from Philanax; in
the mean time taking his rest under a tree with no more affected pomps than as a man
that knew, howsoever he was exalted, the beginning and end of his body was earth.
But Philanax, as soon

his actions straight and always like itself, no worldly thing being able to shake the constancy of it; which, among many other times, yielded some proof of itself when Basilius, the mightiest prince of Greece next to Euarchus, did so suddenly without the advice or
5 allowance of his subjects, without either good show of reasonable cause, or good provision for likely accidents, in the sight of the world put himself from the world, as a man that not only unarmed himself but would make his nakedness manifest. This measured by the minds of most princes, even those whom great acts have entitled
10 with the holy name of virtue, would have been thought a sufficient cause (where such opportunity did offer so great a prey into their hands) to have sought the enlarging of their dominions, wherein they falsely put the more or less felicity of an estate. But Euarchus, that had conceived what is evil in itself no respect can make good, and
15 never forgat his office was to maintain the Macedonians in the exercise of goodness and happy enjoying their natural lives, never used war (which is maintained with the cost and blood of the subject) but when it was to defend their right whereon their well being depended. For this reckoning he made: how far soever he extended
20 himself, neighbours he must have; and therefore, as he kept in peace time a continual discipline of war, and at no time would suffer injury, so he did rather stand upon a just moderation of keeping his own in good and happy case than, multiplying desire upon desire, seeking one enemy after another, put both his honour and people's
25 safety in the continual dice of fortune. So that, having this advantage of Basilius's country laid open unto him, instead of laying an unjust gripe upon it (which yet might have been beautified with the noble name of conquest), he straight considered the universal case of Greece deprived by this means of a principal pillar. He weighed and
30 pitied the pitiful case of the Arcadian people, who were in worse case than if death had taken away their prince. For so yet their necessity would have placed someone to the helm; now a prince being, and not doing like a prince, keeping and not exercising the place, they were in so much more evil case as they could not provide
35 for their evil. He saw the Asiatics of the one side, the Latins of the other, gaping for any occasion to devour Greece, which was no way

to be prevented but by their united strength, and strength most to
be maintained by maintaining their principal instruments. These
rightly wise and temperate considerations moved Euarchus to take
this laboursome journey, to see whether by his authority he might
withdraw Basilius from this burying himself alive, and to return 5
again to employ his old years in doing good, the only happy action
of man's life. Neither was he without a consideration in himself to
provide the marriage of Basilius's two daughters for his son and
nephew against their return, the tedious expectation of which,
joined with the fear of their miscarrying (having been long without 10
hearing any news from them), made him the willinger to ease that
part of melancholy with changing the objects of his wearied senses
and visiting his old and well approved acquaintance. So, having left
his country for the short time of his absence in very perfect state,
and having thoroughly settled his late conquests, taking with him a 15
good number of galleys to waft him in safety to the Arcadian shore,
he sailed with a prosperous wind to a port not far from Mantinea;
where landing no more with him but the small company you have
heard of, and going towards the desert, he understood to his great
grief the news of the prince's death, and waited in that sort for his 20
safe conduct, till Philanax came; who, as soon as he was in sight of
him, lighting from his horse, presented himself unto him in all
those humble behaviours which not only the great reverence of the
party but the conceit of one's own misery is wont to frame. Euarchus
rase up unto him with so gracious a countenance as the goodness of 25
his mind had long exercised him unto, careful so much more to
descend in all courtesies as he saw him bear a low representation of
his afflicted state. But to Philanax, as soon as by near looking on him
he might perfectly behold him, the gravity of his countenance and
years not much unlike to his late deceased but ever beloved master, 30
brought his form so lively into his memory, and revived so all the
thoughts of his wonted joys with him, that instead of speaking to
Euarchus, he stood a while like a man gone a far journey from him-
self, calling as it were with his mind an account of his losses, imagin-
ing that his pain needed not if nature had not been violently stopped 35
of her own course, and casting more loving than wise conceits what a

1 and strength] *om.* Da, Je.   4 this] his Cl, Hm.   5 withdraw] draw Cl, As,
Ph.   this] *om.* Da; the Je.   13–14 So . . . absence] *om.* Cl, As.   16 in safety]
safely Ph; *om.* Hm.   18 the] a Bo, Hm.   25 unto] to Ph, Hm.   31 into]
unto 93.   32 with] within As, Da, Ph, 93.   35 his] this Bo, Cl, Ph, Je, 93.
36 her] his Ph, Je.

world this would have been if this sudden accident had not inter-
rupted it. And so far strayed he into this raving melancholy that his
eyes, nimbler than his tongue, let fall a flood of tears, his voice
being stopped with extremity of sobbing—so much had his friend-
5 ship carried him to Basilius that he thought no age was timely for his
death. But at length, taking the occasion of his own weeping, he thus
did speak to Euarchus:

'Let not my tears, most worthily renowned prince, make my
presence unpleasant or my speech unmarked of you; for the justness
10 of the cause takes away any blame of weakness in me, and the
affinity that the same beareth to your greatness seems even lawfully
to claim pity in you: a prince, of a prince's fall; a lover of justice, of
a most unjust violence. And give me leave, excellent Euarchus, to
say it: I am but the representer of all the late flourishing Arcadia,
15 which now with my eyes doth weep, with my tongue doth complain,
with my knees doth lay itself at your feet which never have been
unready to carry you to the virtuous protecting of innocents.
Imagine, vouchsafe to imagine, most wise and good king, that here
is before your eyes the pitiful spectacle of a most dolorously ending
20 tragedy, wherein I do but play the part of all this now miserable
province which, being spoiled of her guide, doth lie like a ship
without a pilot, tumbling up and down in the uncertain waves, till it
either run itself upon the rock of self-division or be overthrown by
the stormy wind of foreign force. Arcadia, finding herself in these
25 desolate terms, doth speak, and I speak for her, to thee not vainly,
puissant prince, that since now she is not only robbed of the natural
support of her lord but so suddenly robbed that she hath not
breathing time to stand for her safety; so unfortunately that it doth
appal their minds, though they had leisure; and so mischievously
30 that it doth exceed both the suddenness and infortunateness of it.
Thou wilt lend thine arms unto her, and as a man take compassion of
mankind, as a virtuous man chastise most abominable vice, and as a
prince protect a people which all have with one voice called for thy
goodness, thinking that, as thou art only able, so thou art fully able,

8 worthily] worthy Cl, Da, Je, Hm.   10 any blame of weakness] the blame of any
weakness 93.   11 beareth] bears Ph, Je.   13–14 to say it] to say 93.   14 all]
om. Da, Ph.   15 my] mine Cl, Da, Je, 93.   doth weep] do weep Cl, As.
19 dolorously OA, 93: dolorous St.   20 this] the Da, Ph, 93.   now] new 93.
21 her] their Da, Je, 93.   22 tumbling] turning Da, Je; trembling Hm.
23 rock] rocks Hm, 93.   30 both] om, As, Je.   infortunateness] unfortunateness
Bo, Cl, As, Ph, Je, Hm.   31 arms] arm Cl, As, Ph, Je, 93; ears Hm.

to redress their imminent ruins. They do, therefore, with as much
confidence as necessity, fly unto you for succour. They lay themselves
open to you—to you, I mean yourself, such as you have ever been;
that is to say, one that hath always had his determinations bounded
with equity. They only reserve the right to Basilius's blood, the 5
manner to the ancient prescribing of their laws; for the rest, without
exception, they yield over unto you as to the elected protector of this
dukedom, which name and office they beseech you, till you have laid
a sufficient foundation of tranquillity, to take upon you. The parti-
cularities, both of their statutes and demands, you shall presently 10
after understand. Now only I am to say unto you that this country
falls to be a fair field to prove whether the goodly tree of your virtue
will live in all soils. Here, I say, will be seen whether either fear can
make you short or the lickerousness of dominion make you beyond
justice. And I can for conclusion say no more but this: you must 15
think, upon my words and your answer depend not only the quiet
but the lives of so many thousand, which for their ancient confederacy
in this their extreme necessity desire neither the expense of your
treasure nor hazard of your subjects but only the benefit of your
wisdom, whose both glory and increase stands in the exercising of it.' 20

The sum of this request was utterly unlooked-for of Euarchus,
which made him the more diligent in marking his speech, and after
his speech take the greater pause for a perfect resolution. For, as of
the one side he thought nature required nothing more of him than
that he should be a help to them of like creation, and had his heart 25
no whit commanded with fear, thinking his life well passed, having
satisfied the tyranny of time with the course of many years, the
expectation of the world with more than expected honour, lastly
the tribute due to his own mind with the daily offering of most
virtuous actions, so of the other he weighed the just reproach that 30
followed those who easily enter into other folk's business with the
opinion might be conceived love of seigniory rather than of justice
had made him embark himself thus into a matter nothing appertain-
ing unto him. But in the end, wisdom being an essential and not an

2 fly Bo, As, Da, Ph, Je, Hm, 93: flee St, Cl.   3 open to you] open unto you As,
Je.   4 determinations] determination Ph, Hm.   9–10 particularities] particu-
larity 93.   17 thousand] thousands Cl, Je, Hm, 93.   26 whit] way Cl, As;
what Ph.   27 with] which 93 (corr. 98).   33–4 appertaining] pertaining Da,
Ph, Je, Hm, 93.   34 unto] to Da, Je, Hm, 93.   him. But] him, especially in
a time when earnest occasion of his own business so greatly required his presence.
But 93.

opinionate thing, made him rather bend to what was in itself good than what by evil minds might be judged not good. And therein did see that, though that people did not belong unto him, yet doing good (which is enclosed within no terms of people or place) did belong
5   unto him. To this, the secret assurance of his own worthiness (which, although it be never so well clothed in modesty, yet always lives in the worthiest minds) did much push him forward, saying unto himself: the treasure of those inward gifts he had were bestowed by the gods upon him to be beneficial and not idle. On which determina-
10 tion resting, and yet willing before he waded any further to examine well the depth of the other's proffer, he thus, with that well appeased gesture unpassionate nature bestoweth upon mankind, made answer to Philanax's most urgent petition:

'Although long experience hath made me know all men (and so
15 princes, which be but men) to be subject to infinite casualties, the very constitution of our lives remaining in continual change, yet the affairs of this country, or at least my meeting so jumply with them, makes me even abashed with the strangeness of it. With much pain I am come hither to see my long-approved friend, and now I find if I
20 will see him, I must see him dead; after for mine own security I seek to be warranted mine own life. And here am I suddenly appointed to be a judge of other men's lives. Though a friend to him, yet am I a stranger to the country; and now of a stranger you would suddenly make a director. I might object to your desire my weakness, which
25 age perhaps hath wrought both in mind and body, and justly I may pretend the necessity of mine own country, to which, as I am by all true rules more nearly tied so can it not long bear the delay of my absence. But though I would and could dispense with these difficulties, what assurance can I have of the people's will, which having so

1 opinionate] opinious Cl; *blank left* Hm.   rather bend] rather to bend 93.
4 is . . . no] is not enclosed within any 93.   or place] *om.* 93.   5 him. To] him; and if necessity forced him for some time to abide in Arcadia, the necessity of Arcadia might justly demand some fruit of abiding. To 93.   this, the secret] this secret 93.
9 gods] heavens Da, Ph, Je, Hm, 93.   11 of the other's OA, 93: of other's St.
proffer] profit Ph; offer Hm.   appeased] apposed Hm; poised 13.   12 bestoweth] bestowed Da, Ph.   18 me even abashed] me abashed Ph, 93.   20 mine] my Da, Hm.   21 mine] my As, Da, Ph, Hm.   And . . . appointed] And here am I appointed suddenly Cl; And her I am suddenly appointed As, Ph; And there suddenly am I appointed 93.   22 be a judge] be judge Ph, Je.   23 suddenly] *om.* As, Hm.   24 make a] make me a Cl, Je, Hm.   25 both] *om.* 93.   26 mine own] my own Bo, Da, Ph; my As, Hm.   country] affairs 93.   to which] which 93 (*corr.* 13).   27 more] *om.* Cl; most Je, 93.   it] they 93.   28 I would and could OA, 93: I would I could St.   29 will OA, 93: wills St.

many circles of imaginations can hardly be enclosed in one point? Who knows a people that knows not a sudden opinion makes them hope, which hope, if it be not answered, they fall to hate, choosing and refusing, erecting and overthrowing, according as the presentness of any fancy carries them? Even this their hasty drawing to me makes me think they may be as hastily withdrawn from me; for it is but one ground of inconstancy soon to take or soon to leave. It may be they have heard of Euarchus more than cause; their own eyes will be perhaps more curious judges. Out of hearsay they may have builded many conceits which I cannot, perchance will not, perform. Then will undeserved repentance be a greater shame and injury unto me than their undeserved proffer is honour. And to conclude, I must be fully informed how the patient is minded before I can promise to undertake the cure.'

Philanax was not of the modern minds who make suitors magistrates, but did ever think the unwilling worthy man was fitter than the undeserving desirer. Therefore the more Euarchus drew back, the more he found in him that the cunningest pilot doth most dread the rocks, the more earnestly he pursued his public request unto him. He desired him not to make any weak excuses of his weakness, since so many examples had well proved his mind was strong to overpass the greatest troubles, and his body strong enough to obey his mind; and that, so long as they were joined together, he knew Euarchus would think it no wearisome exercise to make them vessels of virtuous actions. The duty to his country he acknowledged, which as he had so settled as it was not to fear any sudden alteration so, since it did want him, as well it might endure a fruitful as an idle absence. As for the doubt he conceived of the people's constancy in this their election, he said it was such a doubt as all human actions are subject unto; yet as much as in politic matters (which receive not geometrical certainties) a man may assure himself, there was evident likelihood to be conceived of the continuance both in their unanimity and his worthiness, whereof the one was apt to be held and the other to hold, joined to the present necessity, the firmest band of mortal minds. In sum, he alleged so many reasons to

2 not a sudden] not sudden 93.   3 to] in 93.   5 fancy] fancies Cl, As.
6 may] will Da, Je, 93.   from] form 93 (*corr.* 98).   10 many conceits] many
imaginative conceits Da, Ph, Je, Hm.   15 make] makes As, Ph, Hm.
16 was fitter] more fit Cl, As; *om.* Ph.   17 undeserving] undeserved Ph;
unwilling Hm.   desirer] desire As, Ph; desirous Je; deserver Hm.   18–19 the
rocks] a rock Cl, As.   request] requests Cl, As.   30 politic OA, 93: public St.

Euarchus's mind (already inclined to enter into any virtuous action) that he yielded to take upon himself the judgement of the present cause, so as he might find indeed that such was the people's desire out of judgement and not faction. Therefore, mounting on their
5 horses, they hasted to the lodges, where they found, though late in the night, the people wakefully watching for the issue of Philanax's ambassade, no man thinking the matter would be well done without he had his voice in it, and each deeming his own eyes the best guardians of his throat in that unaccustomed tumult. But when they
10 saw Philanax return, having on his right hand the king Euarchus, on whom now they had placed the greatest burden of their fears, with joyful shouts and applauding acclamations, they made him and the world quickly know that one man's sufficiency is more available than ten thousand's multitude—so ill balanced be the extremities of
15 popular minds, and so much natural imperiousness there rests in a well formed spirit. For, as if Euarchus had been born of the princely blood of Arcadia, or that long and well acquainted proof had engrafted him in their community, so flocked they about this stranger, most of them already from dejected fears rising to ambitious
20 considerations who should catch the first hold of his favour; and then from those crying welcomes to babbling one with another, some praising Philanax for his well succeeding pains, others liking Euarchus's aspect, and as they judged his age by his face, so judging his wisdom by his age. Euarchus passed through them like a man that
25 did neither disdain a people nor yet was anything tickled with their flatteries, but always holding his own, a man might read a constant determination in his eyes. And in that sort dismounting among them, he forthwith demanded the convocation to be made, which accordingly was done with as much order and silence as it might appear
30 Neptune had not more force to appease the rebellious wind than the admiration of an extraordinary virtue hath to temper a disordered multitude. He, being raised up upon a place more high than the rest where he might be best understood, in this sort spake unto them:
'I understand,' said he, 'faithful Arcadians, by my lord Philanax
35 that you have with one consent chosen me to be the judge of the

4 faction] factions Cl, As.   7 ambassade] ambassage Ph; embassage Hm, 93.
11 now they had] they had now Da, 93.   12 acclamations] exclamations Da, Je,
Hm.   14 thousand's multitude] thousand multitudes Da, Ph, Je, Hm.   18 community] country 93.   21 another] the other As, Da, Ph, 93.   22 well] *om.* 93.
pains] pain 93.   30 wind] winds Cl, Hm.   32 up upon OA, 93: up on St.
34 said he] saith he Cl; *om.* Hm.

late evils happened, orderer of the present disorders, and finally protector of this country till therein it be seen what the customs of Arcadia require.'

He could say no further, being stopped with a general cry that so it was, giving him all the honourable titles and happy wishes they could imagine. He beckoned unto them for silence, and then thus again proceeded:

'Well,' said he, 'how good choice you have made, the attending must be in you, the proof in me. But because it many times falls out we are much deceived in others, we being the first to deceive ourselves, I am to require you not to have an overshooting expectation of me—the most cruel adversary of all honourable doings—nor promise yourselves wonders out of a sudden liking. But remember I am a man; that is to say, a creature whose reason is often darkened with error. Secondly, that you will lay your hearts void of foretaken opinions, else whatsoever I do or say will be measured by a wrong rule, like them that have the yellow jaundice, everything seeming yellow unto them. Thirdly, whatsoever debates have risen among you may be utterly extinguished, knowing that even among the best men are diversities of opinions, which are no more in true reason to breed hatred than one that loves black should be angry with him that is clothed in white; for thoughts and conceits are the very apparel of the mind. Lastly, that you do not easily judge of your judge; but since you will have me to command, think it is your part to obey. And in reward of this, I will promise and protest unto you that to the uttermost of my skill, both in the general laws of nature, especially of Greece, and particularly of Arcadia (wherein I must confess I am not unacquainted), I will not only see the past evils duly punished, and your weal hereafter established, but for your defence in it, if need shall require, I will employ the forces and treasures of mine own country. In the mean time, this shall be the first order I will take: that no man, under pain of grievous punishment name me by any other name but protector of Arcadia; for I will not leave any possible colour to any of my natural successors to make claim to this, which by free election you have bestowed upon me. And so I vow unto you to depose myself of it as soon as the judgement is passed,

6 then] *om.* Cl, Hm.   11 an] any Cl, As, 05 (*only*)   26 both] but 93 (*corr.* 98). especially As, Ph, Je, Hm, 93: special St, Bo, Cl, Da.   26–7 of Greece OA, 93: Greece St.   27 particularly Je, Hm: particular St, Bo, Cl, As, Da, Ph, 93 (*ex.* 05). 30 mine] my Bo, Da, Ph, Hm.

the duke buried, and his lawful successor appointed. For the first
whereof (I mean the trying which be guilty of the duke's death and
these other heinous trespasses), because your customs require such
haste, I will no longer delay it than till tomorrow, as soon as the sun
5 shall give us fit opportunity. You may, therefore, retire yourselves to
your rest, that you may be the readier to be present at these so great
important matters.'

With many allowing tokens was Euarchus's speech heard; who
now by Philanax (that took the principal care of doing all due
10 services unto him) was offered a lodging made ready for him (the
rest of the people, as well as the small commodity of that place
would suffer, yielding their weary heads to sleep), when, lo, the
night, thoroughly spent in these mixed matters, was for that time
banished the face of the earth. And Euarchus, seeing the day begin
15 to disclose his comfortable beauties, desiring nothing more than to
join speed with justice, willed Philanax presently to make the
judgement-place be put in order; and as soon as the people (who
yet were not fully dispersed) might be brought together, to bring
forth the prisoners and the duke's body, which the manner was
20 should in such cases be held in sight, though covered with black
velvet, until they that were accused to be the murderers were
quitted or condemned—whether the reason of the law were to show
the more grateful love to their prince, or by that spectacle the more
to remember the judge of his duty. Philanax (who now thought in
25 himself he approached to the just revenge he so much desired) went
with all care and diligence to perform his charge.

But first it shall be well to know how the poor and princely
prisoners passed this tedious night. There was never tyrant exercised
his rage with more grievous torments upon any he most hated than
30 the afflicted Gynecia did crucify her own soul, after the guiltiness of
her heart was surcharged with the suddenness of her husband's
death; for although that effect came not from her mind, yet her mind
being evil, and the effect evil, she thought the justice of God had for
the beginning of her pains coupled them together. This incessantly
35 boiled in her breast, but most of all when, Philanax having closely

1 successor] successors Ph, Hm.   6 the readier] ready Da; readier Je, 93.   these]
the As; those Ph.   7 important] apportunate Ph; importunate Hm.   8 With]
Which 93 (corr. 98).   17–18 who yet] who as yet Cl, As, Je.   20 held] om. Ph;
had Hm.   22 quitted] acquitted Da, Je.   25 approached to] approached by
93 (corr. 13).   32 that effect Bo, Cl, Da, Ph, Je, Hm, 93: that the effect St; the
effect As.

imprisoned her, she was left more freely to suffer the firebrands of her own thoughts; especially when it grew dark and had nothing left by her but a little lamp, whose small light to a perplexed mind might rather yield fearful shadows than any assured sight. Then began the heaps of her miseries to weigh down the platform of her 5 judgement; then began despair to lay his ugly claws upon her. She began to fear the heavenly powers she was wont to reverence, not like a child but like an enemy. Neither kept she herself from blasphemous repining against her creation. 'O gods,' would she cry out, 'why did you make me to destruction? If you love goodness, why 10 did you not give me a good mind? Or if I cannot have it without your gift, why do you plague me? Is it in me to resist the mightiness of your power?' Then would she imagine she saw strange sights, and that she heard the cries of hellish ghosts. Then would she screech out for succour; but no man coming unto her, she would fain have killed 15 herself, but knew not how. At some times again the very heaviness of her imaginations would close up her senses to a little sleep; but then did her dreams become her tormentors. One time it would seem unto her Philanax was haling her by the hair of the head, and having put out her eyes, was ready to throw her into a burning 20 furnace. Another time she would think she saw her husband making the complaint of his death to Pluto, and the magistrates of that infernal region contending in great debate to what eternal punishment they should allot her. But long her dreaming would not hold but that it would fall upon Cleophila, to whom she would think she 25 was crying for mercy, and that he did pass away by her in silence without any show of pitying her mischief. Then waking out of a broken sleep, and yet wishing she might ever have slept, new forms (but of the same miseries) would seize her mind. She feared death, and yet desired death. She had passed the uttermost of shame, and 30 yet shame was one of her cruellest assaulters. She hated Pyrocles as the original of her mortal overthrow, and yet the love she had conceived to him had still a high authority in her passions. 'O Cleophila,' would she say (not knowing how near he himself was to

4 sight] light Cl, As.   5 weigh] ware As; make Ph.   14 would she screech OA, 93: would screech St.   18 tormentors] torments Ph, Hm.   19 the head] her head Ph, Je.   23 to] *om.* Cl, As.   24 allot her] allot unto her Cl, As.   dreaming] dream Da, Je.   26 he did] she did Da, 93.   29 but of] but Cl; but that As.   miseries OA, 93: mysteries St.   31 assaulters] assaults Cl, As, Ph, Hm, 13.   33 still a] still an As, Je.   in] of Da, Je, 93.   O] *om.* Da, Je.

as great a danger), 'now shalt thou glut thy eyes with the dishonoured death of thy enemy—enemy (alas, enemy), since so thou hast well showed thou wilt have me account thee. Couldst thou not as well have given me a determinate denial, as to disguise thy first
5 disguising with a double dissembling? Perchance if I had been utterly hopeless, the virtue was once in me might have called together his forces, and not have been led captive to this monstrous thraldom of punished wickedness.' Then would her own knowing of good inflame anew the rage of despair, which becoming an unresisted
10 lord in her breast, she had no other comfort but in death, which yet she had in horror when she thought of. But the wearisome detesting of herself made her long for the day's approach, at which time she determined to continue her former course in acknowledging anything which might hasten her end; wherein, although she did not
15 hope for the end of her torments (feeling already the beginning of hell-agonies), yet (according to the nature of pain, the present being most intolerable) she desired to change that, and put to adventure the ensuing. And thus rested the restless Gynecia.

No less sorrowful, though less rageful, were the minds of the
20 princess Pamela and the lady Philoclea, whose only advantages were that they had not consented to so much evil, and so were at greater peace with themselves; and that they were not left alone, but might mutually bear part of each other's woes. For when Philanax, not regarding Pamela's princely protestations, had by force left her
25 under guard with her sister, and that the two sisters were matched as well in the disgraces of fortune as they had been in the best beauties of nature, those things that till then bashfulness and mistrust had made them hold reserved one from the other, now fear (the underminer of all determinations) and necessity (the victorious
30 rebel of all laws) forced them interchangeably to lay open; their passions, then so swelling in them as they would have made auditors of stones rather than have swallowed up in silence the choking adventures were fallen unto them. Truly, the hardest hearts which have at any time thought woman's tears to be a matter of slight
35 compassion (imagining that fair weather will quickly after follow), would now have been mollified, and been compelled to confess that,

---

1 thy eyes] thine eyes Cl, As, Hm.   2 thy enemy] thine enemy Cl, As, Ph, Je.
6 hopeless Bo, Cl, Da, Ph, Hm, 93: helpless St; hapless As, Je.   7 this] his Da, Je.
16 hell-agonies] her agonies As; hellish agonies Je.   34 woman's] women's Cl, Da, Ph, Hm.   35 fair OA, 93: fairer St.

the fairer a diamond is, the more pity it is it should receive a blemish; although no doubt their faces did rather beautify sorrow than sorrow could darken that which even in darkness did shine. But after they had, so long as their other afflictions would suffer them, with doleful ceremonies bemoaned their father's death, they 5 sat down together, apparelled as their misadventures had found them—Pamela in her journeying weeds, now converted to another use; Philoclea only in her nightgown, which she thought should be the raiment both of her marriage and funerals. But when the excellent creatures had, after much panting with their inward 10 travail, gotten so much breathing power as to make a pitiful discourse one to the other what had befallen them, and that, by the plain comparing the case they were in, they thoroughly found that their griefs were not more like in regard of themselves than like in respect of the subject (the two princes, as Pamela had learned of 15 Musidorus, being so minded as they would ever make both their fortunes one), it did more unite, and so strengthen, their lamentation, seeing the one could not any way be helped by the other, but rather the one could not be miserable but that it must necessarily make the other miserable also. That, therefore, was the first matter 20 their sweet mouths delivered, the declaring the passionate beginning, troublesome proceeding, and dangerous ending, their never ending loves had passed; and when at any time they entered into the praises of the young princes, too long it would have exercised their tongues but that their memory forthwith warned them the 25 more praiseworthy they were, the more at that time they were worthy of lamentation. Then again to crying and wringing of hands, and then anew as unquiet grief sought each corner to new discourses; from discourses to wishes; from wishes to prayers— especially the tender Philoclea who, as she was in years younger and 30 had never lifted up her mind to any opinion of sovereignty, so was she apter to yield to her misfortune, having no stronger debates in her mind than a man may say a most witty childhood is wont to nourish, as to imagine with herself why Philanax and the other noblemen should deal so cruelly by her that had never deserved 35 evil of any of them; and how they could find in their hearts to imprison such a personage as she did figure Pyrocles, whom she

1 fairer a] fairer that a As, Da.   9 the . . . both] both . . . raiment Hm; the raiment 93.   marriage and] om. 93.   18–19 could . . . one] om. Je, 93.   26 that] any Da, Je. 32 apter] apt Ph, Hm; the apter Je, 93.   35 by] with As, Ph, Je (with corr. to by Bo).

thought all the world was bound to love as well as she did. But
Pamela, although endued with a virtuous mildness, yet the know-
ledge of herself, and what was due unto her, made her heart full of
a stronger disdain against her adversity; so that she joined the
5 vexation for her friend with the spite to see herself, as she thought,
rebelliously detained, and mixed desirous thoughts to help with
revengeful thoughts if she could not help. And as in pangs of death
the stronger heart feels the greater torment, because it doth the
more resist to his oppressor, so her mind, the nobler it was set (and
10 had already embraced the higher thoughts), so much more it did
repine; and the more it repined, the more helpless wounds it gave
unto itself. But when great part of the night was passed over the
doleful music of these sweet ladies' complaints, and that leisure
(though with some strife) had brought Pamela to know that an
15 eagle when she is in a cage must not think to do like an eagle,
remembering with themselves that it was likely the next day the
lords would proceed against those they had imprisoned, they
employed the rest of the night in writing unto them, with such
earnestness as the matter required, but in such styles as the state
20 of their thoughts was apt to fashion.

In the mean time Pyrocles and Musidorus were recommended to
so strong a guard as they might well see it was meant they should
pay no less price than their lives for the getting out of that place,
which they like men indeed (fortifying courage with the true
25 rampire of patience) did so endure as they did rather appear gover-
nors of necessity than servants to fortune; the whole sum of their
thoughts resting upon the safety of their ladies and their care one for
the other, wherein (if at all) their hearts did seem to receive some
softness. For sometimes Musidorus would feel such a motion to his
30 friend and his unworthy case that he would fall into such kind
speeches: 'My Pyrocles,' would he say, 'how unhappy may I think
Thessalia that hath been as it were the middle way to this evil
state of yours. For if you had not been there brought up, the sea
should not have had this power thus to sever you from your dear
35 father. I have therefore (if complaints do at any time become a
man's heart) most cause to complain, since my country, which
received the honour of Pyrocles' education, should be a step to his

4 a stronger] stronger Cl; strong As, Hm.   adversity] adversary Ph, Je.   5 as
she thought] om. Da, Je.   6 desirous] desires, Da, Ph.   13 these] the Cl, As.
16 likely] like Cl, As.   22 see] know Da; think Je.   31 speeches] of speech
Cl, As (of deleted Bo).   34 thus to . . . you] to . . . you thus Cl; to . . . you Hm.

overthrow—if human chances can be counted an overthrow to him that stands upon virtue.'

'O excellent Musidorus,' answered Pyrocles, 'how do you teach me rather to fall out with myself and my fortune, since by you I have received all good, you only by me this affliction. To you and 5 your virtuous mother I in my tenderest years, and father's greatest troubles, was sent for succour. There did I learn the sweet mysteries of philosophy. There had I your lively example to confirm that which I learned. There, lastly, had I your friendship which no unhappiness can ever make me say but that hath made me happy. Now see 10 how my destiny (the gods know, not my will) hath rewarded you. My father sends for you away out of your land, whence, but for me, you had not come. What after followed, you know; it was my love, not yours, which first stayed you here. And therefore, if the heavens ever held a just proportion, it were I, and not you, that should feel the smart.' 15

'O blame not the heavens, sweet Pyrocles,' said Musidorus, 'as their course never alters, so is there nothing done by the unreachable ruler of them, but hath an everlasting reason for it. And to say the truth of those things, we should deal ungratefully with nature if we should be forgetful receivers of her good gifts, and so diligent 20 auditors of the chances we like not. We have lived, and have lived to be good to ourselves and others. Our souls (which are put into the stirring earth of our bodies) have achieved the causes of their hither coming. They have known, and honoured with knowledge, the cause of their creation. And to many men (for in this time, place, and 25 fortune, it is lawful for us to speak gloriously) it hath been behoveful that we should live. Since, then, eternity is not to be had in this conjunction, what is to be lost by the separation but time? Which, since it hath his end, when that is once come, all what is past is nothing; and by the protracting, nothing gotten but labour and 30 care. Do not me, therefore, that wrong (who something in years, but much in all other deserts, am fitter to die than you) as to say you have brought me to any evil, since the love of you doth overbalance all bodily mischiefs; and those mischiefs be but mischiefs to the baser minds too much delighted with the kennel of this life. Neither 35 will I any more yield to my passion of lamenting you, which howsoever it might agree to my exceeding friendship, surely it would nothing to your exceeding virtue.'

'Add this to your noble speech, my dear cousin', said Pyrocles,
5 'that if we complain of this our fortune, or seem to ourselves faulty in having one hurt the other, we show a repentance of the love we bear to those matchless creatures, or at least a doubt it should be over dearly bought, which for my part (and so dare I answer for you) I call all the gods to witness, I am so far from that
10 no shame, no torment, no death, would make me forgo the least part of the inward honour, essential pleasure, and living life I have enjoyed in the presence of the faultless Philoclea.'

'Take the pre-eminence in all things but in true loving', answered Musidorus, 'for the confession of that no death shall get of me.'
15 'Of that,' answered Pyrocles, soberly smiling, 'I perceive we shall have a debate in the other world—if, at least, there remain anything of remembrance in that place.'

'I do not think the contrary,' said Musidorus, 'although you know it is greatly held that with the death of body and senses (which are
20 not only the beginning but dwelling and nourishing of passions, thoughts, and imaginations), they failing, memory likewise fails (which riseth only out of them), and then is there left nothing but the intellectual part or intelligence which, void of all moral virtues (which stand in the mean of perturbations) doth only live in the
25 contemplative virtue and power of the omnipotent God (the soul of souls and universal life of this great work); and therefore is utterly void from the possibility of drawing to itself these sensible considerations.'

'Certainly,' answered Pyrocles, 'I easily yield that we shall not
30 know one another, and much less these past things, with a sensible or passionate knowledge; for the cause being taken away, the effect follows. Neither do I think we shall have such a memory as now we have, which is but a relic of the senses, or rather a print the senses have left of things past in our thoughts; but it shall be a vital power
35 of that very intelligence which, as while it was here it held the chief seat of our life, and was as it were the last resort to which of all our knowledges the highest appeal came, and so by that means was never

6 hurt] helped Da; hart Ph, Hm; help Je.   7 those] these Cl, As, Da, Ph, 93.
16 at least OA, 93: at the least St.   25 God] good Cl, Da, 93.   33 of the senses]
cf senses As, Hm,

ignorant of our actions (though many times rebelliously resisted, always with this prison darkened), so much more being free of that prison, and returning to the life of all things, where all infinite knowledge is, it cannot but be a right intelligence, which is both his name and being, of things both present and past, though void of 5 imagining to itself anything, but even grown like to his creator, hath all things with a spiritual knowledge before it. The difference of which is as hard for us to conceive as it had been for us when we were in our mothers' wombs to comprehend (if anybody could have told us) what kind of light we now in this life see, what kind of 10 knowledge we now have. Yet now we do not only feel our present being but we conceive what we were before we were born; though remembrance make us not do it, but knowledge. And though we are utterly without any remorse of any misery we might then suffer, even such and much more odds shall there be at that second 15 delivery of ours when, void of sensible memory or memorative passion, we shall not see the colours but lives of all things that have been or can be; and shall, as I hope, know our friendship, though exempt from the earthly cares of friendship, having both united it and ourselves in that high and heavenly love of the unquenchable 20 light.'

As he had ended his speech, Musidorus, looking with a heavenly joy upon him, sang this song unto him he had made before love turned his muse to another subject.

> Since nature's works be good, and death doth serve 25
> As nature's work, why should we fear to die?
> Since fear is vain but when it may preserve,
> Why should we fear that which we cannot fly?
>
> Fear is more pain than is the pain it fears,
> Disarming human minds of native might; 30
> While each conceit an ugly figure bears,
> Which were not ill, well viewed in reason's light.
>
> Our owly eyes, which dimmed with passions be,
> And scarce discern the dawn of coming day,

4 but be] be but Da, Ph. 8 had been] hath been Cl; had 93; was 13. 9 could] would Hm, 93. 10 light] life Da, Je. 13 make us not do] makes us not to do Da, Je, Hm. 19 cares] care Cl, Je (though . . . friendship *om.* As). 25–p. 374, 4 *The poem is in* 93. 26 work] works Cl, Le. 32 well viewed] well weighed Cl, Le; *blank left* Ph. 33 owly] only As, Ph, 13.

Let them be cleared, and now begin to see
Our life is but a step in dusty way.
Then let us hold the bliss of peaceful mind,
Since this we feel, great loss we cannot find.

5 Thus did they, like quiet swans, sing their own obsequies, and
virtuously enable their minds against all extremities which they did
think would fall upon them, especially resolving that the first care
they would have should be, by taking the fault upon themselves, to
clear the two ladies, of whose case (as of nothing else that had
10 happened) they had not any knowledge; although their friendly host,
the honest gentleman Kerxenus, seeking all means how to help them,
had endeavoured to speak with them and to make them know who
should be their judge. But the curious servant of Philanax forbad
him the entry upon pain of death; for so it was agreed upon that no
15 man should have any conference with them for fear of new tumults,
in so much that Kerxenus was constrained to retire himself, having
yet obtained thus much: that he would deliver unto the two princes
their apparel and jewels, which being left with him at Mantinea
(wisely considering that their disguised weeds, which were all as
20 then they had, saving a certain mean raiment Philanax had cast upon
Pyrocles, would make them more odious in the sight of the judges),
he had that night sent for, and now brought unto them. They
accepted their own with great thankfulness, knowing from whence it
came, and attired themselves in it against the next day; which being
25 indeed rich and princely, they accordingly determined to maintain
the names of Palladius and Timopyrus (as before it is mentioned).
Then gave they themselves to consider in what sort they might defend
their causes (for they thought it no less vain to wish death than
cowardly to fear it), till something before morning, a small slumber
30 taking them, they were by and by after called up to come to the
answer of no less than their lives imported.

But in this sort was the judgement ordered: as soon as the morn-
ing had taken a full possession of the element, Euarchus called
unto him Philanax, and willed him to draw out into the midst of the
35 green (before the chief lodge) the throne of judgement seat in which
Basilius was wont to sit, and according to their customs was ever

3-4 om. Ph.   4 this] that Da, Je.   13 curious] heedful Cl, As.   15 any]
om. As, Je.   20-1 saving . . . Pyrocles] om. 93.   26 is] was Bo, Cl, As.
30 up to come] up again Cl; up again to come As.   30-1 the answer] answer
Cl; their answer Ph, Hm.

carried with the prince. For Euarchus did wisely consider the people
to be naturally taken with exterior shows far more than with inward
consideration of the material points; and therefore in this new entry
into so entangled a matter he would leave nothing which might be
either an armour or ornament unto him; and in these pompous 5
ceremonies he well knew a secret of government much to consist.
That was performed by the diligent Philanax; and therein Euarchus
did sit himself, all clothed in black, with the principal men who
could in that suddenness provide themselves of such mourning
raiments, the whole people commanded to keep an orderly silence of 10
each side, which was duly observed of them, partly for the desire
they had to see a good conclusion of these matters, and partly
stricken with admiration as well at the grave and princely presence
of Euarchus as at the greatness of the cause which was then to come
in question. As for Philanax, Euarchus would have done him the 15
honour to sit by him, but he excused himself, desiring to be the
accuser of the prisoners in his master's behalf; and therefore, since
he made himself a party, it was not convenient for him to sit in the
judicial place.

Then was it a while deliberated whether the two young ladies 20
should be brought forth in open presence. But that was stopped by
Philanax, whose love and faith did descend from his master to his
children, and only desired the smart should light upon the others
whom he thought guilty of his death and dishonour, alleging for this
that neither wisdom would they should be brought in presence of the 25
people, which might thereupon grow to new uproars, nor justice
required they should be drawn to any shame, till somebody accused
them. And as for Pamela, he protested the laws of Arcadia would
not allow any judgement of her, although she herself were to deter-
mine nothing till age or marriage enabled her. 30

Then, the duke's body being laid upon a table just before
Euarchus, and all covered over with black, the prisoners (namely
the duchess and two young princes) were sent for to appear in
the protector's name (which name was the cause they came not to
knowledge how near a kinsman was to judge of them, but thought 35
him to be some nobleman chosen by the country in this extremity—

1 the prince] their prince Cl, Ph.   6 government] judgement Ph, Hm.   8 sit]
set Bo, Da, Je, Hm, 93.   principal] noble Cl, As.   10 raiments] raiment Ph, Hm.
12 these] the Cl, As; those Hm.   16 to sit] to have him sit Cl, Ph.   19 place]
seat Da, Hm.   26 thereupon] hereupon Da, Je, 93.   new] more Da, Je.   justice]
justly Da, Ph.

so extraordinary a course had the order of the heavens produced at this time that both nephew and son were not only prisoners but unknown to their uncle and father, who of many years had not seen them, and Pyrocles was to plead for his life before that throne, in
5 which throne lately before he had saved the duke's life).

But first was Gynecia led forth in the same weeds that the day and night before she had worn, saving that, instead of Cleophila's garment, in which she was found, she had cast on a long cloak which reached to the ground, of russet coarse cloth, with a poor felt hat
10 which almost covered all her face, most part of her goodly hair (on which her hands had laid many a spiteful hold), so lying upon her shoulders as a man might well see had no artificial carelessness; her eyes down on the ground of purpose not to look on Pyrocles' face, which she did not so much shun for the unkindness she conceived of
15 her own overthrow as for the fear those motions at this short time of her life should be revived which she had with the passage of infinite sorrows mortified. Great was the compassion the people felt to see their princess's estate and beauty so deformed by fortune and her own desert, whom they had ever found a lady most worthy of all
20 honour. But by and by the sight of the other two prisoners drew most of the eyes to that spectacle.

Pyrocles came out, led by Sympathus, clothed after the Greek manner in a long coat of white velvet reaching to the small of his leg, with great buttons of diamonds all along upon it. His neck, without
25 any collar, not so much as hidden with a ruff, did pass the whiteness of his garments, which was not much in fashion unlike to the crimson raiment our knights of the order first put on. On his feet he had nothing but slippers which, after the ancient manner, were tied up by certain laces which were fastened under his knee, having
30 wrapped about (with many pretty knots) his naked leg. His fair auburn hair (which he ware in great length, and gave at that time a delightful show with being stirred up and down with the breath of a gentle wind) had nothing upon it but a white ribbon, in those days used for a diadem, which rolled once or twice about the uppermost
35 part of his forehead, fell down upon his back, closed up at each end with the richest pearl were to be seen in the world. After him

---

1 a] *om.* 93.   of the heavens OA, 93: of heavens St.   7 that] *om.* Cl, As.
10 all] *om.* Ph, Hm.   16 passage] passions Cl; passing Hm.   27 our] of Cl;
the Hm.   29 by] with Da, Ph, Je, Hm, 93 (with *corr. to* by Bo).   30 leg]
legs 93.   His] *om.* Da, Je.   33 ribbon] riband Cl, As, Je.

followed another nobleman, guiding the noble Musidorus who had upon him a long cloak after the fashion of that which we call the apostle's mantle, made of purple satin—not that purple which we now have, and is but a counterfeit of the Gaetulian purple (which yet was far the meaner in price and estimation), but of the right 5 Tyrian purple (which was nearest to a colour betwixt our murrey and scarlet). On his head (which was black and curled) he ware a Persian tiara all set down with rows of so rich rubies as they were enough to speak for him that they had to judge of no mean personage. In this sort, with erected countenances, did these unfortunate 10 princes suffer themselves to be led, showing aright by the comparison of them and Gynecia how to diverse persons compassion is diversely to be stirred. For as to Gynecia, a lady known of great estate and greatly esteemed, the more miserable representation was made of her sudden ruin, the more men's hearts were forced to bewail such 15 an evident witness of weak humanity; so to these men, not regarded because unknown, but rather (besides the detestation of their fact) hated as strangers, the more they should have fallen down in an abject semblance, the more, instead of compassion, they should have gotten contempt; but therefore were to use (as I may term it) the 20 more violence of magnanimity, and so to conquer the expectation of the lookers with an extraordinary virtue. And such effect, indeed, it wrought in the whole assembly, their eyes yet standing as it were in balance to whether of them they should most direct their sight. Musidorus was in stature so much higher than Pyrocles as commonly 25 is gotten by one year's growth; his face, now beginning to have some tokens of a beard, was composed to a kind of manlike beauty; his colour was of a well pleasing brownness; and the features of it such as they carried both delight and majesty; his countenance severe, and promising a mind much given to thinking; Pyrocles of a pure 30 complexion, and of such a cheerful favour as might seem either a woman's face on a boy or an excellent boy's face in a woman; his look gentle and bashful, which bred the more admiration having showed such notable proofs of courage. Lastly, though both had both, if there were any odds, Musidorus was the more goodly and 35 Pyrocles the more lovely. But as soon as Musidorus saw himself so

4 of the] of that Cl; of Ph.   5 of the right OA, 93: of right St.   8 so] *om.* Ph, Je; such Hm.   10 countenances] countenance Ph, Hm.   18–19 fallen . . . have] *om.* Da, Je.   19 abject] object Cl, As, Ph.   compassion] passion Cl; pity Ph, Hm.   32 on a boy] in a boy As, 13; *om.* Ph.

far forth led among the people that he knew to a great number of them his voice should be heard, misdoubting their intention to the princess Pamela (of which he was more careful than of his own life), even as he went (though his leader sought to interrupt him), he thus
5 with a loud voice spake unto them:

'And is it possible, O Arcadians,' said he, 'that you can forget the natural duty you owe to your princess Pamela? Hath this soil been so little beholding to her noble ancestors? Hath so long a time rooted no surer love in your hearts to that line? Where is that faith to your
10 prince's blood, which hath not only preserved you from all dangers heretofore but hath spread your fame to all the nations in the world? Where is that justice the Arcadians were wont to flourish in, whose nature is to render to everyone his own? Will you now keep the right from your prince who is the only giver of judgement, the key
15 of justice, and life of your laws? Do you hope in a few years to set up such another race, which nothing but length of time can establish? Will you reward Basilius's children with ungratefulness, the very poison of manhood? Will you betray your long-settled reputation with the foul name of traitors? Is this your mourning for your
20 duke's death: to increase his loss with his daughters' misery? Imagine your prince do look out of the heavens unto you; what do you think he could wish more at your hands than that you do well by his children? And what more honour, I pray you, can you do to his obsequies than to satisfy his soul with a loving memory, as you
25 do his body with an unfelt solemnity? What have you done with the princess Pamela? Pamela, the just inheritrix of this country; Pamela, whom this earth may be happy that it shall be hereafter said she was born in Arcadia; Pamela, in herself your ornament, in her education your foster child, and every way your only princess; what account
30 can you render to yourselves of her? Truly, I do not think that you all know what is become of her, so soon may a diamond be lost, so soon may the fairest light in the world be put out. But look, look unto it! O Arcadians, be not wilfully robbed of your greatest treasure! Make not yourselves ministers to private ambitions, who
35 do but use yourselves to put on your own yokes! Whatsoever you determine of us (who I must confess are but strangers), yet let not

8 beholding] beholden Bo, Da.   9 no surer] no Cl; so sure Ph, Hm.   to that line] that live Cl; to that love Ph.   13 render] tender Ph, Je, Hm.   16 such] *om.* Cl, As.   21-2 do you think OA, 93: do think St.   22 could] would Ph, Hm.   wish more] wish for more Cl, As.   27 shall] should Cl, As.   35 your own yokes OA, 93: your yokes St.   35-6 you determine] you do determine As, Hm.

Basilius's daughters be strangers unto you. Lastly, howsoever you bar her from her public sovereignty (which if you do, little may we hope for equity where rebellion reigns), yet deny not that child's right unto her, that she may come and do the last duties to her father's body. Deny not that happiness (if in such a case there be 5 any happiness) to your late duke, that his body may have his last touch of his dearest child.'

With suchlike broken manner of questions and speeches was Musidorus desirous, as much as in passing by them he could, to move the people to tender Pamela's fortune. But at length, by that 10 they came to the judgement place, both Sympathus and his guider had greatly satisfied him, with the assurance they gave him, that this assembly of people had neither meaning nor power to do any hurt to the princess, whom they all acknowledged as their sovereign lady; but that the custom of Arcadia was such, till she had more 15 years, the state of the country to be guided by a protector, under whom he and his fellow were to receive their judgement. That eased Musidorus's heart of his most vehement care, when he found his beloved lady to be out of danger. But Pyrocles, as soon as the duchess of the one side, he and Musidorus of the other, were stayed 20 before the face of their judge (having only for their bar the table on which the duke's body lay), being nothing less vexed with the doubt of Philoclea than Musidorus was for Pamela, in this sort with a lowly behaviour, and only then like a suppliant, he spake to the protector: 25

'Pardon me, most honoured judge,' said he, 'that uncommanded I begin my speech unto you, since both to you and me these words of mine shall be most necessary. To you, having the sacred exercise of justice in your hand, nothing appertains more properly than truth nakedly and freely set down. To me, being environed round about 30 with many dangerous calamities, what can be more convenient than at least to be at peace with myself in having discharged my conscience in a most behoveful verity. Understand therefore, and truly understand, that the lady Philoclea (to whose unstained virtue it hath been my unspeakable misery that my name should become a blot), if she 35

---

3 for] of Je, 93.   12 that] *om*. Da, Je, 93.   17 their] *om*. Ph, Hm.   20 of the one] on the one Da, Ph, Je.   of the other] on the other Bo, As, Da, Hm.   21 the face of] *om*. Ph, Je.   their] the Bo, Ph, Hm.   22 on which] whereon Bo, Ph. 24 to OA, 93: unto St.   29 hand] hands Da Ph, Je, Hm.   30 round] *om*. Cl, Je, Hm.   31 many] *om*. Cl, As.

be accused, is most unjustly accused, of any dishonourable fact which by my means she may be thought to have yielded unto. Whatsoever hath been done hath been my violence, which notwithstanding could not prevail against her chastity. But whatsoever hath
5 been informed, was my force; and I attest the heavens, to blaspheme which I am not now in fit time, that so much as my coming into her chamber was wholly unwitting unto her. This your wisdom may withal consider: if I would lie, I would lie for mine own behoof. I am not so old as to be weary of myself, but the very sting of my
10 inward knowledge, joined with the consideration I must needs have what an infinite loss it should be to all those who love goodness in good folks if so pure a child of virtue should wrongfully be destroyed, compels me to use my tongue against myself, and receive the burden of what evil was upon my own doing. Look therefore with
15 pitiful eyes upon so fair beams, and that misfortune which by me hath fallen unto her. Help to repair it with your public judgement; since whosoever deals cruelly with such a creature shows himself a hater of mankind and an envier of the world's bliss. And this petition I make even in the name of justice: that before you proceed
20 further against us, I may know how you conceive of her noble, though unfortunate, action; and what judgement you will make of it.'

He had not spoken his last word when all the whole people, both of great and low estate, confirmed with an united murmur Pyrocles' demand, longing, for the love generally was borne Philoclea, to know
25 what they might hope of her. Euarchus, though neither regarding a prisoner's passionate prayer nor bearing over-plausible ears to a many-headed motion, yet well enough content to win their liking with things in themselves indifferent, he was content first to seek as much as might be of Philoclea's behaviour in this matter; which
30 being cleared by Pyrocles and but weakly gainsaid by Philanax (who had framed both his own and Dametas's evidence most for her favour), yet finding by his wisdom that she was not altogether faultless, he pronounced she should all her life long be kept prisoner

3 violence] only attempt 93.   4 could not prevail] was never intended 93.
5 force] fault 93.   6 time] tune 93.   8 mine] my Bo, Da, Ph.   9 myself]
myself corr. to my life Cl; my life Ph.   11 who] that Da, Ph, Je, Hm.   14 my]
mine Cl, As, Da, 98.   16 unto] upon Da, Hm, 93.   17 himself a] himself an As,
Je.   20 further] om. Cl, As.   22 whole] om. Cl, As, Ph, Je, Hm.   24 borne
Philoclea] borne to Philoclea Ph, Je.   25 neither] never Ph; nothing Je.
32 favour), yet] favour), and in truth could have gone no further than conjecture. Yet
93.   33 pronounced she] pronounced that she Cl, As.

among certain women of religion like the vestal nuns, so to repay the
touched honour of her house with well observing a strict profession
of chastity. Although this were a great prejudicating of Pyrocles'
case, yet was he exceedingly joyous of it, being assured of his lady's
life, and in the depth of his mind not sorry that, what end soever he 5
had, none should obtain the after-enjoying that jewel whereon he
had set his life's happiness.

After it was by public sentence delivered what should be done
with the sweet Philoclea (the laws of Arcadia bearing that what was
appointed by the magistrates in the nonage of the prince could not 10
afterwards be repealed), Euarchus (still using to himself no other
name but protector of Arcadia) commanded those that had to say
against the duchess Gynecia to proceed, because both her estate
required she should be first heard and also for that she was taken to
be the principal in the greatest matter they were to judge of. 15
Philanax incontinently stepped forth, and showing in his greedy
eyes that he did thirst for her blood, began a well thought-on
discourse of her (in his judgement) execrable wickedness. But
Gynecia, standing up before the judge, casting abroad her arms, with
her eyes hidden under the breadth of her unseemly hat, laying open 20
in all her gestures the despairful affliction to which all the might of
her reason was converted, with suchlike words stopped Philanax
as he was entering into his invective oration:

'Stay, stay, Philanax,' said she, 'do not defile thy honest mouth
with those dishonourable speeches thou art about to utter against a 25
woman, now most wretched, lately thy mistress! Let either the
remembrance how great she was move thy heart to some reverence,
or the seeing how low she is stir in thee some pity. It may be truth
doth make thee deal untruly, and love of justice frames unjustice in
thee. Do not therefore (neither shalt thou need) tread upon my 30
desolate ruins. Thou shalt have that thou seekest, and yet shalt not
be the oppressor of her who cannot choose but love thee for thy
singular faith to thy master. I do not speak this to procure mercy, or
to prolong my life. No, no, I say unto you, I will not live; but I am

1 repay the] repay their 93 (corr. 98).   4 exceedingly] exceeding Bo, Da,
Hm.   6 that OA, 93: the St.   10 by the magistrates] by magistrates Cl, As.
15 be the principal] be principal Bo, Da.   16 greedy Je, 93: grieved St, Bo, Cl, As,
Da, Ph (Hm omits incontinently . . . that he).   20 breadth] brimes Ph; breath Hm.
25 those] these Cl, Ph.   31 yet shalt Cl, As, Ph, Hm, 93: yet shall St, Bo, Da,
Je.   32 be the oppressor] be oppressor Cl, As, Da, Je, 93.   33 faith] love
Cl, As; truth Hm

only loath my death should be engrieved with any wrong thou shouldst do unto me. I have been too painful a judge over myself to desire pardon in others' judgement. I have been too cruel an executioner of mine own soul to desire that execution of justice should be stayed for me. Alas, they that know how sorrow can rent the spirits, they that know what fiery hells are contained in a self-condemning mind, need not fear that fear can keep such a one from desiring to be separated from that which nothing but death can separate! I therefore say to thee, O just judge, that I, and only I, was the worker of Basilius's death. They were these hands that gave unto him that poisonous potion that hath brought death to him and loss to Arcadia. It was I, and none but I, that hastened his aged years to an unnatural end, and that have made all this people orphans of their royal father. I am the subject that have killed my prince. I am the wife that have murdered my husband. I am a degenerate woman, an undoer of this country, a shame of my children. What couldst thou have said more, O Philanax? And all this I grant. There resteth, then, nothing else to say, but that I desire you you will appoint quickly some to rid me of my life, rather than these hands which else are destinied unto it; and that indeed it may be done with such speed as I may not long die in this life which I have in so great horror.'

With that, she crossed her arms and sat down upon the ground, attending the judge's answer. But a great while it was before anybody could be heard speak, the whole people concurring in a lamentable cry; so much had Gynecia's words and behaviour stirred their hearts to a doleful compassion. Neither, in truth, could most of them in their judgements tell whether they should be more sorry for her fault or her misery, for the loss of her estate or loss of her virtue. But most were most moved with that which was under their eyes, the sense most subject to pity. But at length the reverent awe they stood in of Euarchus brought them to a silent waiting his determination; who having well considered the abomination of the fact, attending more the manifest proof of so horrible a trespass, confessed by herself, and proved by others, than anything relenting to those tragical phrases of hers (apter to stir a vulgar pity than his mind which

1 only] *om.* Da, Je, Hm.   4 mine] my Da, Je, Hm.   6–7 self-condemning]
self-condemned Ph, Hm.   11 to] unto Cl, As, Ph.   13 this] his Ph, 93.
16 couldst] wouldst Da, Je, 93.   19 my] *om.* Bo, Ph.   28 her fault] the fault
Da, Ph.   29 or loss] or the loss Da, Ph, Hm.

hated evil in what colours soever he found it), having conferred a while with the principal men of the country and demanded their allowance, he definitively gave this sentence:

'That whereas, both in private and public respects, this woman had most heinously offended (in private, because marriage being the 5 most holy conjunction that falls to mankind, out of which all families, and so consequently all societies, do proceed, which not only by community of goods but community of children is to knit the minds in a most perfect union which whoso breaks dissolves all humanity, no man living free from the danger of so near a neighbour, 10 she had not only broken it but broken it with death, and the most pretended death that might be; in public respect, the prince's person being in all monarchal governments the very knot of the people's welfare and light of all their doings, to which they are not only in conscience but in necessity bound to be loyal, she had 15 traitorously empoisoned him, neither regarding her country's profit, her own duty, nor the rigour of the laws); that therefore, as well for the due satisfaction to eternal justice and accomplishment of the Arcadian statutes as for the everlasting example to all wives and subjects, she should presently be conveyed to close prison, and 20 there be kept with such food as might serve to sustain her alive until the day of her husband's burial; at which time she should be buried quick in the same tomb with him, that so his murder might be a murder to herself, and she forced to keep company with the body from which she had made so detestable a severance; and lastly 25 death might redress their disjoined conjunction of marriage.'

His judgement was received of the whole assembly as not with disliking so with great astonishment, the greatness of the matter and person as it were overpressing the might of their conceits. But when they did set it to the beam with the monstrousness of her ugly 30 misdeed, they could not but yield in their hearts there was no overbalancing. As for Gynecia, who had already settled her thoughts not only to look but long for this event, having in this time of her vexation found a sweetness in the rest she hoped by death, with a

1 colours] colour Bo, Cl, As, Da, Ph, Je, Hm.   conferred] considered Da, 93.
7 so] *om.* Cl, Ph, Je.   8 community of goods . . . of children] community goods but community children 93 (*corr.* 98).   10 so near] such Ph, Hm.
13 person] persons 93.   16 empoisoned] poisoned Bo, Ph.   18–19 of the Arcadian OA, 93: of Arcadian St.   23 so] *om.* Da, Je.   24 to herself] unto herself Bo, Da.   29 and person] *om.* Da, Je.   overpressing] overgrowing Bo; dazzling Ph.   34 hoped by] hoped for by Da, Hm.

countenance witnessing she had beforehand so passed through all
the degrees of sorrow that she had no new look to figure forth any
more, rose up and offered forth her fair hands to be bound or led as
they would, being indeed troubled with no part of this judgement
5 but that her death was, as she thought, long delayed. They that were
appointed for it conveyed her to the place she was in before, where
the guard was relieved and the number increased to keep her more
sure for the time of her execution. None of them all that led her,
though most of them were such whose hearts had been long hardened
10 with the often-exercising such offices, being able to bar tears from
their eyes and other manifest tokens of compassionate sorrow—so
goodly a virtue is a resolute constancy that even in ill-deservers it
seems that party might have been notably well deserving. Thus the
excellent lady Gynecia, having passed five and thirty years of her
15 age even to admiration of her beautiful mind and body, and having
not in her own knowledge ever spotted her soul with any wilful vice
but her inordinate love of Cleophila, was brought, first by the
violence of that ill-answered passion, and then by the despairing
conceit she took of the judgement of God in her husband's death and
20 her own fortune, purposely to overthrow herself, and confirm by a
wrong confession that abominable shame which, with her wisdom,
joined to the truth, perhaps she might have refelled.

Then did Euarchus ask Philanax whether it were he that would
charge the two young prisoners, or that some other should do it, and
25 he sit according to his estate as an assistant in the judgement.
Philanax told him, as before he had done, that he thought no man
could lay manifest the naughtiness of those two young men with so
much either truth or zeal as himself, and therefore he desired he
might do this last service to his faithfully beloved master as to
30 prosecute the traitorous causers of his death and dishonour; which
being done, for his part, he meant to give up all dealing in public
affairs, since that man was gone who had made him love them.

Philanax thus being ready to speak, the two princes were commanded
to tell their names; who answered, according to their agreement,

1 beforehand] before Cl, As, Hm.   so passed through 93: passed so through St, Bo,
Ph, Hm; passed through Cl, As, Da, Je.   2 sorrow] sorrows Cl, As.   3 rose]
rase Cl, Hm, 93.   11 other] others 93 (*corr.* 98).   14 her] *om.* Ph, Hm.
17 inordinate] moderate Da; immoderate Ph, Je, 93.   19 of] by Bo; in As.
20 confirm] confirmed Bo, Da, Hm.   by] with Cl, As.   23 would] could Da, Je.
25 sit] set Ph, Je.   27 those] these Bo, Ph, Je.   29 this] this his Ph; his Je.
faithfully] *om.* Da; well Ph; faithful Je, Hm.   31 for his part] *om.* Cl, As.
dealing in] dealings in Cl, Hm; *om.* As.   34 agreement] agreements 93.

that they were Timopyrus, despota of Lycia, and Palladius, prince of Caria. Which when they had said, they demanded to know by what authority they could judge of them, since they were not only foreigners, and so not born under their laws, but absolute princes, and therefore not to be touched by laws. But answer was presently 5 made them that Arcadia laws were to have their force upon any were found in Arcadia, since strangers have scope to know the customs of a country before they put themselves in it, and when they once are entered, they must know that what by many was made must not for one be broken, and so much less for a stranger, as he is 10 to look for no privilege in that place to which in time of need his service is not to be expected. As for their being princes, whether they were so or no, the belief stood but in their own words, which they had so diversely falsified as they did not deserve belief. But whatsoever they were, Arcadia was to acknowledge them but as 15 private men, since they were neither by magistracy nor alliance to the princely blood to claim anything in that region. Therefore, if they had offended (which now by the plaintiff and their defence was to be judged) against the laws of nations, by the laws of nations they were to be chastised; if against the peculiar ordinances of 20 the province, those peculiar ordinances were to lay hold of them.

The princes stood a while upon that, demanding leisure to give perfect knowledge of their greatness. But when they were answered that in the case of a prince's death the law of that country had ever been that immediate trial should be had, they were forced to yield, 25 resolved that in those names they would as much as they could cover the shame of their royal parentage, and keep as long as might be (if evil were determined against them) the evil news from their careful kinsfolk. Wherein the chief man they considered was Euarchus, whom the strange and secret working of justice had 30 brought to be the judge over them—in such a shadow or rather pit of darkness the wormish mankind lives that neither they know how to

1 Timopyrus, despota of Lycia] Timopyrus, despata of Lycia Cl; Timopyrus ⟨   ⟩ of Lycia As; Daiphantus of Lycia 93.   2 Caria] Iberia 93. to know] *om.* Ph, Je.   5 and therefore] *om.* Da, Je (Hm *omits* but absolute . . . laws). 6 any] anyone As; any that Je, Hm.   8 in it] into it Bo, Hm.   13 but] *om.* Da, Je, 93.   15 was to . . . but as] was but to . . . but as As; was but to . . . as Ph; was to . . . as Hm.   19 by the laws of nations] *om.* Cl, Da.   21 those] these As, Ph.   24 in the case] in that case Ph; in a case 93.   25 immediate] immediately As, Ph, Je.   27 as might OA, 93: as they might St.   29 kinsfolk] kinsfolks Da, Je.   31 the] *om.* Cl, As, Da, Ph, Hm.   such a shadow] such shadow Cl, As.

foresee nor what to fear, and are but like tennis balls tossed by the racket of the higher powers. Thus, both sides ready, it was determined, because their causes were separate, first Philanax should be heard against Pyrocles (whom they termed Timopyrus), and that
5 heard, the other's cause should follow, and so receive together such judgement as they should be found to have deserved.

But Philanax, that was even short-breathed at the first with the extreme vehemency he had to speak against them, stroking once or twice his forehead, and wiping his eyes (which either wept, or he
10 would at that time have them seem to weep), looking first upon Pyrocles as if he had proclaimed all hatefulness against him, humbly turning to Euarchus (who with quiet gravity showed great attention), he thus began his oration:

'That which all men who take upon them to accuse another are
15 wont to desire, most worthy protector, to have: many proofs of many faults in them they seek to have condemned; that is to me in this present action my greatest cumber and annoyance. For the number is so great, and the quality so monstrous, of the enormities this wretched young man hath committed that neither I in myself
20 can tell where to begin (my thoughts being confused with the horrible multitude of them), neither do I think your virtuous ears will be able to endure the report of them, but will rather imagine you hear some tragedy invented of the extremity of wickedness than a just recital of a wickedness indeed committed. For such is the
25 disposition of the most sincere judgements that, as they can believe mean faults and such as man's nature may slide into so, when they pass to a certain degree—nay, when they pass all degrees of unspeakable naughtiness—then find they in themselves a hardness to give credit that human creatures can so from all humanity be
30 transformed. But in myself, the strength of my faith to my dead master will help the weakness of my memory; in you, your excellent love of justice will force you to vouchsafe attention. And as for the matter, it is so manifest, so pitiful evidences lie before your eyes of it, that I shall need to be but a brief recounter, and no rhetorical
35 enlarger, of this most harmful mischief. I will, therefore, in as few words as so huge a trespass can be contained, deliver unto you the

2 of the higher] of higher Da, Ph.   3 causes] cases Bo, Cl, As, Ph, Je, Hm, 93.
separate] separated 93.   5 other's] other Cl, Hm.   16 many] my 93 (om. 98).
22 of them] om. 93.   24 of a] of Da, Je.   28 hardness] hardiness Ph, Hm.
30 faith] love Cl, As.   31 my memory] my dead memory Da, Je.   35 in as]
in so Da, Ph, Je.

sum of this miserable fact, leaving out a great number particular
tokens of his naughtiness, and only touching the essential points of
this doleful case.

This man, whom to begin withal I know not how to name, since
being come into this country unaccompanied like a lost pilgrim, 5
from a man grew a woman, from a woman a ravisher of women,
thence a prisoner, and now a prince; but this Timopyrus, this
Cleophila, this what you will (for any shape or title he can take
upon him that hath no restraint of shame), having understood the
solitary life my late master lived, and considering how open he had 10
laid himself to any traitorous attempt, for the first mask of his
falsehood disguised himself like a woman (which, being the more
simple and hurtless sex, might easier hide his subtle harmfulness),
and presenting himself to my master (the most courteous prince
that lived), was received of him with so great graciousness as might 15
have bound not only any grateful mind, but might have mollified
any enemy's rancour. But this venomous serpent, admitted thus into
his bosom, as contagion will easily find a fit body for it, so had he
quickly fallen into so near acquaintance with this naughty woman,
whom even now you have most justly condemned, that this was her 20
right hand; she saw with no eyes but his, nor seemed to have any
life but in him, so glad she was to find one more cunning than
herself in covering wickedness with a modest veil. What is to be
thought passed betwixt two such virtuous creatures, whereof the
one hath confessed murder and the other rape, I leave to your wise 25
consideration. For my heart hastens to the miserable point of
Basilius's murder, for the executing of which with more facility
this young nymph of Diana's bringing up feigned certain rites she
had to perform—so furious an impiety had carried him from all
remembrance of goodness that he did not only not fear the gods, as 30
the beholders and punishers of so ungodly a villainy, but did
blasphemously use their sacred holy name as a minister unto it.
And forsooth a cave hereby was chosen for the temple of his devo-
tions, a cave of such darkness as did prognosticate he meant to

---

1 number particular] number of his particular Da; number of particular Je, 93.
5 unaccompanied] uncompanied Da; unacquainted Hm.   6 woman a] woman
to a Da, Je, Hm.   7–8 Timopyrus, this Cleophila, this what] Timopyrus, this
what Da, Je, Hm; Timopyrus, what Ph; Zelmane, this Daiphantus, this what 93.
10 late] om. As, Hm.   11 mask] om. As; mark Hm.   12 disguised] disguising
As, Ph.   16 any] a Cl, As; my Ph.   28 feigned] feigning Da, Je.   30 only
not fear] only fear Da, Hm.

please the infernal powers; for there this accursed caitiff upon the altar of falsehood sacrificed the life of the virtuous Basilius. By what means he trained him thither, alas, I know not; for if I might have known it, either my life had accompanied my master, or this
5   fellow's death had preserved him. But this may suffice: that in the mouth of the cave where this traitor had his lodging and chapel, when already master shepherd, his companion, had conveyed away the undoubted inheritrix of this country, was Gynecia found by the dead corpse of her husband newly empoisoned, apparelled in the
10   garments of the young lady, and ready, no question, to have fled to some place according to their consort, but that she was by certain honest shepherds arrested. While in the mean time, because there should be left no revenger of this bloody mischief, this noble Amazon was violently gotten into the chamber of the lady Philoclea
15   where, by the mingling of her shame with his misdeed, he might enforce her to be the accessary to her father's death; and under the countenance of her and her sister (against whom they knew we would not rebel), seize as it were with one gripe into their treacherous hands the regiment of this mighty province. But the almighty eye
20   prevented him of the end of his mischief by using a villain, Dametas's hand, to enclose him in there, where with as much fortification as in a house could be made he thought himself in most security. Thus see you, most just judge, a short and simple story of the infamous misery fallen to this country—indeed infamous, since by
25   an effeminate man we should suffer a greater overthrow than our mightiest enemies have been ever able to lay upon us. And that all this which I have said is most manifest, as well of the murdering of Basilius as the ravishing of Philoclea (for those two parts I establish of my accusation), who is of so incredulous a mind, or rather who
30   will so stop his eyes from seeing a thing clearer than the light, as not to hold for assured so palpable a matter? For (to begin with his most cruel misdeed) is it to be imagined that Gynecia (a woman, though wicked, yet witty) would have attempted and achieved an enterprise no less hazardous than horrible without having some counsellor in
35   the beginning and some comforter in the performing? Had she, who

---

6 the cave] this cave Je, 93.   10 the young] this young As, Da.   11 consort]
comfort Cl; cunforth Ph; consent Je.   13 revenger] revenge Ph, Hm.
15 mingling of] mingling (as much as in him lay) of 93.   16 be the accessary]
be accessary Cl, As, Da, Ph, Je.   18 treacherous] *om.* Ph, Hm.   19 this]
the 93.   24 to] upon 93.   26 been ever] ever been Cl, Ph.   32 misdeed]
deed Ph, Hm.   is it] it is Cl (it is *corr. to* is it St); is Je.

showed her thoughts were so overruled with some strange desire as, in despite of God, nature, and womanhood, to execute that in deeds which in words we cannot hear without trembling? Had she, I say, no practice to lead her unto it? Or had she a practice without conspiracy? Or could she conspire without somebody to conspire 5 with? And if one were, who so likely as this, to whom she communicated, I am sure, her mind; the world thinks, her body? Neither let her words, taking the whole fault upon herself, be herein anything available. For to those persons who have vomitted out of their souls all remnants of goodness there rests a certain pride in evil, and 10 having else no shadow of glory left them, they glory to be constant in iniquity; and that, God knows, must be held out to the last gasp without revealing their accomplices, as thinking great courage is declared in being neither afeard of the gods nor ashamed of the world. But let Gynecia's action die with herself. What can all the 15 earth answer for his coming hither? Why alone, if he be a prince? How so richly jewelled, if he be not a prince? Why then a woman, if now a man? Why now Timopyrus, if then Cleophila? Was all this play for nothing? Or if it had an end, what end but the end of my dear master? Shall we doubt so many secret conferences with 20 Gynecia, such feigned favour to the over-soon beguiled Basilius, a cave made a lodging, and the same lodging made a temple of his religion, lastly such changes and traverses as a quiet poet could scarce fill a poem withal, were directed to any less scope than to this monstrous murder? O snaky ambition which can wind thyself in 25 so many figures to slide thither thou desirest to come! O corrupted reason of mankind that can yield to deform thyself with so filthy desires! And O hopeless be those minds whom so unnatural desires do not with their own ugliness sufficiently terrify! But yet even of favour let us grant him thus much more as to fancy that in these 30 foretold things fortune might be a great actor perchance to an evil end, yet to a less evil end all these entangled devices were intended. But I beseech your ladyship, my lady Timopyrus, tell me what excuse can you find for the changing your lodging with the duchess that very instant she was to finish her execrable practice? How can 35

6–7 communicated] committed Ph, Hm.   13–14 courage is declared] courages declared Da, Je.   14 afeard] afraid Cl, Ph.   gods] heavens Da, Ph, Je, Hm, 93. 16 alone Bo, Cl, As, Ph, Je, Hm, 93: allow St; above Da.   22 same lodging made] same made Cl, As.   24 a poem] a pen Cl, Da; *blank left* Ph.   25 in] into Cl, As.   28 O hopeless] full graceless Cl, As.   34 can you] you can Cl, As, Ph.   lodging] garments Cl, As.

you cloak the lending of your cloak unto her? Was all that by chance too? Had the stars sent such an influence unto you as you should be just weary of your lodging and garments when our prince was destinied to the slaughter? What say you to this, O shameful and
5 shameless creature, fit indeed to be the dishonour of both sexes? But alas, I spend too many words in so manifest and so miserable a matter. They must be four wild horses (which according to our laws are the executioners of men which murder our prince) which must decide this question with you.

10   Yet see, so far had my zeal to my beloved prince transported me that I had almost forgotten my second part and his second abomination, I mean his violence offered (I hope but offered) to the lady Philoclea, wherewith (as if it had well become his womanhood) he came braving to the judgement seat; indeed, our laws appoint not so
15 cruel a death (although death too) for this fact as for the other. But whosoever well weighs it shall find it sprung out of the same fountain of mischievous naughtiness: the killing of the father, dishonouring the mother, and ravishing the child. Alas, could not so many benefits received of my prince, the justice of nature, the
20 right of hospitality, be a bridle to thy lust, if not to thy cruelty? Or if thou hadst (as surely thou hast) a heart recompensing goodness with hatred, could not his death (which is the last of revenges) satisfy thy malice, but thou must heap upon it the shame of his daughter? Were thy eyes so stony, thy breast so tigerish, as the sweet and
25 beautiful shows of Philoclea's virtue did not astonish thee? O woeful Arcadia, to whom the name of this mankind courtesan shall ever be remembered as a procurer of thy greatest loss! But too far I find my passion, yet honest passion, hath guided me. The case is every way too too much unanswerable. It resteth in you, O excellent protector,
30 to pronounce judgement; which, if there be hope that such a young man may prove profitable to the world, who in the first exercise of his own determinations far passed the arrantest strumpet in luxuriousness, the cunningest forger in falsehood; a player in disguising, a tiger in cruelty, a dragon in ungratefulness, let him be preserved

1 that by chance] that but by chance Cl, As.   6 and so] and Da, Ph, Je, Hm.
8 our] their Da; your Ph.   11 his] the Cl, As.   12 I hope but offered] *om.*
Da, Ph, Je, Hm, 93.   20 bridle to] bridle unto Bo; bridle for Cl.   24 breast]
breasts Bo, Cl.   26 courtesan] *blank left* As; Christian Ph.   28 case] cause
Hm, 13.   29 too too much] too much Cl, Ph.   32 determinations] determination Ph, Hm. 93.   34 tiger] pirate Da, Ph, Je, Hm.   ungratefulness]
ingratefulness 93.

like a jewel to do greater mischief. If his youth be not more defiled with treachery than the eldest man's age, let, I say, his youth be some cause of compassion. If he have not every way sought the overthrow of human society, if he have done anything like a prince, let his naming himself a prince breed a reverence to his base wickedness. If he have not broken all laws of hospitality, and broken them in the most detestable degree that can be, let his being a guest be a sacred protection of his more than savage doings. Or if his whorish beauty have not been as the highway of his wickedness, let the picture drawn upon so poisonous a wood be reserved to show how greatly colours can please us. But if it is as it is, what should I say more—a very spirit of hellish naughtiness? If his act be to be punished, and his defiled person not to be pitied, then restore unto us our prince by duly punishing his murderers; for then we shall think him and his name to live when we shall see his killers to die. Restore to the excellent Philoclea her honour by taking out of the world her dishonour; and think that at this day in this matter are the eyes of the world upon you, whether anything can sway your mind from a true administration of justice. Alas, though I have much more to say, I can say no more; for my tears and sighs interrupt my speech and force me to give myself over to my private sorrow.'

Thus, when Philanax had uttered the uttermost of his malice, he made sorrow the cause of his conclusion. But while Philanax was in the course of his speech, and did with such bitter reproaches defame the princely Pyrocles, it was well to be seen his heart was unused to bear such injuries, and his thoughts such as could arm themselves better against anything than shame. For sometimes blushing, his blood with diverse motions coming and going, sometimes closing his eyes and laying his hand over them, sometimes again giving such a look to Philanax as might show he assured himself he durst not so have spoken if they had been in indifferent place, with some impatience he bare the length of his oration; which being ended, with as much modest humbleness to the judge as despiteful scorn to the accuser, with words to this purpose he defended his honour:

'My accuser's tale may well bear witness with me, most rightful judge, in how hard a case, and environed with how many troubles, I may esteem myself. For if he (who shows his tongue is not unacquainted with railing) was in an agony in the beginning of his

speech with the multitude of matters he had to lay unto me (wherein notwithstanding the most evil could fall unto him was that he should not do so much evil as he would), how cumbered do you think may I acknowledge myself who, in things no less importing than my life,
5 must be mine own advocate, without leisure to answer or foreknowledge what should be objected? In things, I say, promoted with so cunning a confusion as, having mingled truths with falsehoods, surmises with certainties, causes of no moment with matters capital, scolding with complaining, I can absolutely neither grant
10 nor deny. Neither can I tell whether I come hither to be judged, or before judgement to be punished, being compelled to bear such unworthy words, far more grievous than any death unto me. But since the form of this government allows such tongue-liberty unto him, I will pick as well as I can out of his invective those few points
15 which may seem of some purpose in the touching of me, hoping that, as by your easy hearing of me you will show that though you hate evil yet you wish men may prove themselves not evil, so in that he hath said you will not weigh so much what he hath said as what he hath proved, remembering that truth is simple and naked, and that
20 if he had guided himself under that banner, he needed not out of the way have sought so vile and false disgracings of me, enough to make the untruest accusation believed. I will, therefore, using truth as my best eloquence, repeat unto you as much as I know in this matter; and then, by the only clearness of the discourse, your wisdom, I
25 know, will find the difference betwixt cavilling supposition and direct declaration.

This prince Palladius and I being inflamed with love (a passion far more easily reprehended than refrained) to the two peerless daughters of Basilius, and understanding how he had secluded
30 himself from the world, that like princes there was no access unto him, we disguised ourselves in such forms as might soonest bring us to the revealing of our affections. The prince Palladius had such event of his doings that, with Pamela's consent, he was to convey her out of the thraldom she lived in, to receive the subjection of a

9 absolutely] absolute 93.   12 words far] words of this coward creature, far Da, Ph, Je, Hm.   13 this OA, 93: his St.   13–14 unto him] to handless and heartless people Da, Ph, Je, Hm.   16 as] *om.* 93.   though] although Cl, As. 21 way have] way to have Da, Je, Hm.   disgracings] disgracing As, Da, Ph, Je. make] have made Cl, Ph.   24 the discourse] this discourse Cl, Ph.   28 easily reprehended] easily to be reprehended Bo, Je.   two peerless] two poor peerless Da, Je.

greater people than her own, until her father's consent might be obtained. My fortune was more hard, for I bare no more love to the chaste Philoclea than Basilius, deceived in my sex, showed to me, insomuch that by his importunacy I could have no time to assail the constant rock of the pure Philoclea's mind, till this policy I found: 5 taking (under colour of some devotions) my lodging to draw Basilius thither with hope to enjoy me, which likewise I revealed to the duchess, that she might keep my place, and so make her husband see his error, while I in the mean time being delivered of them both, and having locked so the doors as I hoped the immaculate Philoclea 10 should be succourless, my attempt was such as even now I confessed, and I made prisoner there, I know not by what means, when being repelled by her divine virtue, I would fainest have escaped. Here have you the thread to guide you in the labyrinth this man of his tongue had made so monstrous. Here see you the true discourse 15 which he (mountebank fashion) doth make so wide a mouth over. Here may you conceive the reason why the duchess had my garment, because in her going to the cave in the moonshine night she might be taken for me, which he useth as the knot of all his wise assertions; so that, as this double-minded fellow's accusation was double, 20 double likewise my answer must perforce be to the murder of Basilius and violence offered to the inviolate Philoclea. For the first, O heavenly gods, who would have thought any mouth could have been found so immodest as to have opened so slight proofs of so horrible matters? His first argument is a question: who would 25 imagine that Gynecia would accomplish such an act without some accessaries; and if any, who but I? Truly, I am so far from imagining anything that, till I saw these mourning tokens, and heard Gynecia's confession, I never imagined the duke was dead. And for my part, so vehemently and more like the manner of passionate than 30 guilty folks, I see the duchess prosecute herself, that I think condemnation may go too hastily over her, considering the unlikelihood, if not impossibility, her wisdom and virtue so long nourished should

4–5 assail . . . mind] obtain the like favour of the pure Philoclea 93.   10–12 hoped . . . made] hoped if the immaculate Philoclea would condescend to go with me, there should be none to hinder our going. I was made 93.   15 discourse] discourses Da, Ph, Je, Hm.   16 mountebank] ⟨ ⟩ bank As; in mountebank Da, Je; ⟨ ⟩ in bank Ph; meant in bank Hm.   18 in] by Cl; om. As.   23 mouth OA, 93: match St. 24 immodest] mercenary Da, Ph, Je, Hm, 93.   slight OA, 93: light St.   27 am] and 93 (corr. 98).   28 these OA, 93: this St.   31 prosecute Bo: psecute St, As, Da, Ph, Je, Hm; persecute Cl, 93.

in one moment throw down itself to the uttermost end of wickedness. But whatsoever she hath done (which, as I say, I never believed), yet how unjustly should that aggravate my fault? She found abroad, I within doors (for, as for the wearing my garment, I have told you 5 the cause); she seeking, as you say, to escape, I locking myself in a house; without perchance the conspiracy of one poor stranger might greatly enable her attempt, or the fortification of the lodge (as the trim man alleged) might make me hope to resist all Arcadia. And see how injuriously he seeks to draw from me my chiefest clearing by 10 preventing the credit of her words wherewith she hath wholly taken the fault upon herself. An honest and unpartial examiner!—her words may condemn her, but may not absolve me. Thus, void of all probable allegation, the craven crows upon my affliction, not leaving out any evil that ever he hath felt in his own soul to charge my youth 15 withal. But who can look for a sweeter breath out of such a stomach, or for honey from so filthy a spider? What should I say more? If in so inhuman a matter (which he himself confesseth sincerest judgements are loathest to believe), and in the severest law, proofs clearer than the sun are required, his reasons are only the scum of a 20 base malice, my answers most manifest, shining in their own truth. If there remain any doubt of it (because it stands betwixt his affirming and my denial), I offer, nay I desire, and humbly desire, I may be granted the trial by combat—by combat; wherein, let him be armed, and me in my shirt. I doubt not justice will be my shield, 25 and his heart will show itself as faint as it is false.

Now come I to the second part of my offence, towards the young lady, which I confess, and for her sake heartily lament. But in fine I offered force to her; love offered more force to me. Let her beauty be compared to my years, and such effects will be found no miracles. 30 But since it is thus, as it is, and that justice teacheth us not to love punishment, but to fly to it for necessity, the salve of her honour (I mean as the world will take it, for else in truth it is most untouched)

---

1 throw down] participate Da, Ph, Je, Hm.   4 wearing my] wearing of my Cl, As.   9 injuriously] treacherously Da, Ph, Je, Hm, 93.   10 hath] had Da, Je, 93. 11 An Cl, As, Da, Ph, Je, Hm, 98: A St, Bo, 93.   14 ever he hath] he hath ever Ph, Hm.   16–17 If in so inhuman] If in human As; of so inhuman Da; If so inhuman Ph; If so in ^un^human Je; If in so human Hm, (If ^in^ so inhuman St.)   18 severest] sweetest Da, Je.   law] laws Cl, As, 93.   19 scum] some Ph; showing Hm.   21 If Bo, Cl: *om.* St, As, Da, Ph, Je, Hm, 93. 23 —by combat] *om.* 93.   24 me] I As, Ph.   27 which I] which, howsoever you term it, so far forth as I have told ou, I 93.   in fine] if herein 93.   31 fly to it] flee yt Cl; fly y^t As.

must be my marriage and not my death, since the one stops all mouths, the other becomes a doubtful fable. This matter requires no more words, and your experience, I hope, in these cases shall need no more. For myself, methinks I have showed already too much love of my life to bestow so many. But certainly it hath been love of 5 truth which could not bear so unworthy falsehood, and love of justice that would brook no wrong to myself nor other, and makes me now even in that respect to desire you to be moved rather with pity at a just cause of tears than with the bloody tears this crocodile spends, who weeps to procure death and not to lament death. It will 10 be no honour to Basilius's tomb to have guiltless blood sprinkled upon it, and much more may a judge overweigh himself in cruelty than in clemency. It is hard, but it is excellent where it is found: a right knowledge when correction is necessary, when grace doth more avail. For my own respect, if I thought in wisdom I had deserved 15 death, I would not desire life; for I know nature will condemn me to die, though you do not, and longer I would not wish to draw this breath than I may keep myself unspotted of any horrible crime. Only I cannot, nor ever will, deny the love of Philoclea, whose violence wrought violent effects in me.'   20

With that he finished his speech, casting up his eyes to the judge, and crossing his hands, which he held on their length before him, declaring a resolute patience in whatsoever should be done with him.

Philanax, like a watchful adversary, curiously marked all that he said, saving that in the beginning he was interrupted by two letters 25 were brought him from the princess Pamela and the lady Philoclea, who having all that night considered and bewailed their estate, careful for their mother likewise, of whom they could never think so much evil. But considering with themselves that she assuredly should have so due trial by the laws as either she should not need 30 their help or should be past their help, they looked to that which nearliest touched them, and each wrate in this sort for him in whom their lives' joy consisted:

The humble-hearted Philoclea wrate much after this manner:

'My lords, what you will determine of me is to me uncertain, but 35

15 my] mine Cl, As, Je, 98.   19 nor ever Bo, Cl, Da, Ph, Je, Hm, 93: nor never St; or ever As.   21 he finished] he had finished As, Hm.   22 on] in Da, Ph, Je, Hm, 93.   23 in] with Ph, _om._ Hm.   24-5 he said] he had said As, Ph, Hm. 27 that] the Cl; _om._ Je.   28 for their] of their Cl, Ph; _om._ As.   32 nearliest] nearestly Cl; near best Da; nearest Ph, Hm.   34-p. 398, 6 Bo, Ph, Hm _reverse the order of the two sister's letters._

what I have determined of myself I am most certain of; which is no longer to enjoy my life than I may enjoy him for husband whom the gods for my highest glory have bestowed upon me. Those that judge him, let them execute me. Let my throat satisfy their hunger of 5 murder; for, alas, what hath he done that had not his original in me? Look upon him, I beseech you, with indifference, and see whether in those eyes all virtue shines not; see whether that face could hide a murderer. Take leisure to know him, and then yourselves will say it hath been too great an inhumanity to suspect such excellency. 10 Are the gods, think you, deceived in their workmanship? Artificers will not use marble but to noble uses. Should those powers be so overshot as to frame so precious an image of their own, but to honourable purposes? O speak with him, O hear him, O know him, and become not the putters-out of the world's light! Hope you to 15 joy my father's soul with hurting him he loved above all the world? Shall a wrong suspicion make you forget the certain knowledge of those benefits this house hath received by him? Alas, alas, let not Arcadia for his loss be accursed of the whole earth and of all posterity! He is a great prince. I speak unto you that which I know, for 20 I have seen most evident testimonies. Why should you hinder my advancement? Who, if I have passed my childhood hurtless to any of you, if I have refused nobody to do what good I could, if have often mitigated my father's anger, ever sought to maintain his favour towards you, nay if I have held you all as fathers and brothers 25 unto me, rob me not of more than my life comes unto, tear not that which is inseparably joined to my soul. But if he rest misliked of you (which, O God, how can it be?), yet give him to me. Let me have him; you know I pretend no right to your state. Therefore it is but a private petition I make unto you. Or if you be hard-heartedly bent 30 to appoint otherwise (which, O sooner let me die than know), then, to end as I began, let me by you be ordered to the same end, without for more cruelty you mean to force Philoclea to use her own hands to kill one of your duke's children.'

Pamela's letter (which she meant to send with her sister's to the

---

1 certain of; which] certain which Cl, Ph, Hm, 93.   2 for husband] for my husband Cl, As, Da, Ph, Je, Hm, 93.   3 gods] heavens Da, Ph, Je, Hm, 93.   4 their] the Cl, As.   7 could] would Bo, Ph.   8 murderer] murder Cl, As, Da, Ph, Je, Hm, 93.   11 those] these As, Je.   24 all] *om.* As, Hm. 26 inseparably] unseparable Cl, Ph, Je.   28 it is] is it 93.   29 hard-heartedly] hardly hearted Cl; hard, hardly As.   34 with her sister's] *om.* Cl, As, Da, Ph, Je, Hm, 93.

general assembly of the Arcadian nobility—for so closely they were kept as they were utterly ignorant of the new-taken orders) was thus framed:

'In such a state, my lords, you have placed me as I can neither write nor be silent. For how can I be silent, since you have left me nothing but my solitary words to testify my misery? And how should I write (for as for speech I have none but my gaoler that can hear me), who neither can resolve what to write nor to whom to write? What to write is as hard for me to say as what I may not write, so little hope have I of any success, and so much hath no injury been left undone to me-wards. To whom to write, where may I learn, since yet I wot not how to entitle you? Shall I call you my sovereigns? Set down your laws that I may do you homage. Shall I fall lower, and name you my fellows? Show me, I beseech you, the lord and master over us. But shall Basilius's heir name herself your princess? Alas, I am your prisoner. But whatsoever I be, or whatsoever you be, O all you beholders of these doleful lines, this do I signify unto you, and signify it with a heart that shall ever remain in that opinion: the good or evil you do to the excellent prince was taken with me, and after by force from me, I will ever impute it as either way done to my own person. He is a prince and worthy to be my husband, and so is he my husband by me worthily chosen. Believe it, believe it; either you shall be traitors for murdering of me or, if you let me live, the murderers of him shall smart as traitors. For what do you think I can think? Am I so childish as not to see wherein you touch him you condemn me? Can his shame be without my reproach? No, nor shall be, since nothing he hath done that I will not avow. Is this the comfort you bring me in my father's death, to make me fuller of shame than sorrow? Would you do this if it were not with full intention to prevent my power with slaughter? And so do, I pray you. It is high time for me to be weary of my life too long led, since you are weary of me before you have me. I say again, I say it infinitely unto you, I will not live without him, if it be not to revenge him. Either do justly in saving both, or wisely in killing both. If I be your princess, I command his preservation. If but a private person, then are we both to suffer. I take all truth to witness

4 a state] estate As, Je.   12 wot not how OA, 93: wot how St.   17 you be-holders] ye beholders Ph, Je.   18 ever] om. Cl, As.   19 the excellent] that excellent Bo, As.   21 my] mine As, Je, Hm, 93.   32 I say again] I say it again Bo, Ph, Hm; om. Da, Je.   35 princess] prince Cl, Ph, Hm.

he hath done no fault but in going with me. Therefore, to conclude; in judging him, you judge me. Neither conceive with yourselves the matter you treat is the life of a stranger (though even in that name he deserved pity), nor of a shepherd (to which estate love of me made 5 such a prince descend); but determine most assuredly the life that is in question is of Pamela, Basilius's daughter.'

Many blots had the tears of these sweet ladies made in their letters, which many times they had altered, many times torn, and written anew, ever thinking something either wanted or were too 10 much, or would offend, or (which was worst) would breed denial. But at last the day warned them to dispatch; which they accordingly did, and calling one of their guard (for nobody else was suffered to come near them), with great entreaty they requested him that he would present them to the principal noblemen and gentlemen 15 together, for they had more confidence in the numbers' favour than in any one, upon whom they would not lay the lives they held so precious. But the fellow, trusty to Philanax (who had placed him there), delivered them both to him (what time Pyrocles began to speak); which he suddenly opened, and seeing to what they tended 20 by the first words, was so far from publishing them (whereby he feared, in Euarchus's just mind, either the princesses might be endangered or the prisoners preserved, of which choice he knew not which to think the worst) that he would not himself read them over, doubting his own heart might be mollified, so bent upon revenge. 25 Therefore utterly suppressing them, he lent a spiteful ear to Pyrocles, and as soon as he had ended, with a very willing heart desired Euarchus he might accept the combat, although it would have framed but ill with him, Pyrocles having never found any match near him besides Musidorus.

30 But Euarchus made answer: since bodily strength is but a servant to the mind, it were very barbarous and preposterous that force should be made judge over reason.

Then would he also have replied in words unto him, but Euarchus (who knew what they could say was already said), taking their 35 arguments into his mind, commanded him to proceed against the other prisoner, and that then he would sentence them both together.

Philanax, nothing the milder for Pyrocles' purging himself, but

---

7 these] those As; the Da, Je, 93 (*corr.* 13).   16 the lives] their lives Da, Je (*blank left for* lives Cl).   23 worst] worse Da, Hm.   28 having never found] never having found Cl, Da, Hm.

rather (according to the nature of arguing, especially when it is bitter) so much the more vehement, entered thus into his speech against Musidorus, being so overgone with rage that he forgat in this oration his precise method of oratory:

'Behold, most noble protector, to what a state Arcadia is come, 5 since such manner of men may challenge in combat the faithfullest of the nobility, and having merited the shamefullest of all deaths, dare name in marriage the princesses of this country. Certainly, my masters, I must say you were much out of taste if you had not rather enjoy such ladies than be hanged. But the one you have as 10 much deserved as you have dishonoured the other. But now my speech must be directed to you, good master Dorus, who with Pallas' help, pardie, are lately grown Palladius. Too much, too much, this sacred seat of justice grants unto such a fugitive bondslave who, instead of these examinations, should be made confess with a whip 15 that which a halter should punish. Are not you he, sir, whose sheep-hook was prepared to be our sceptre, in whom lay the knot of all this tragedy? Or else, perchance, they that should gain little by it were dealers in the murder; you only (that had provided the fruits for yourself) knew nothing of it, knew nothing. Hath thy companion 20 here infected thee with such impudency as even in the face of the world to deny that which all the world perceiveth? The other pleads ignorance, and you, I doubt not, will allege absence. But he was ignorant when he was hard by, and you had framed your absence just against the time the act should be committed—so fit a lieutenant 25 he knew he had left of his wickedness that for himself his safest mean was to convey away the lady of us all, who once out of the country, he knew we would come with olive branches of intercession unto her, and fall at his feet to beseech him to leave keeping of sheep and vouchsafe the tyrannizing over us. For to think they are princes, as 30 they say (although in our laws it behoves them nothing), I see at all no reason. These jewels certainly with their disguising sleights they have pilfered in their vagabonding race. And think you such princes should be so long without some followers after them? Truly, if they be princes, it manifestly shows their virtues such as all their subjects 35 are glad to be rid of them. But be they as they are, for we are to

4 this] his Cl, As, Je.   precise OA, 93: privy St (being . . . oratory *om.* Ph).   5 a state] estate Cl, Je, Hm.   10 the one you Cl, Da, Ph, Je, Hm, 93: the one of you St, As.   13 Too much, too much] Too much Da, Ph, 93.   17 knot] plot Da, Je.   20 knew nothing.] knew nothing of it. As, Ph, Hm.   30 think they] think that they Cl, As.

consider the matter and not the men. Basilius's murder hath been the cause of their coming. Basilius's murder they have most treacherously brought to pass. Yet that, I doubt not, you will deny as well as your fellow. But how will you deny the stealing away of the
5 princess of this province, which is no less than treason? So notably hath the justice of the gods provided for the punishing of these malefactors as, if it were possible, men would not believe the certain evidences of their principal mischief; yet have they discovered themselves sufficiently for their most just overthrow. I say,
10 therefore (to omit my chief matter of the duke's death), this wolvish shepherd, this counterfeit prince, hath traitorously, contrary to his allegiance (having made himself a servant and subject) attempted the depriving this country of our natural princess; and therefore by all right must receive the punishment of traitors. This matter is so
15 assured as he himself will not deny it, being taken and brought back in the fact. This matter is so odious in nature, so shameful to the world, so contrary to all laws, so hurtful to us, so false in him, as if I should stand further in declaring or defacing it, I should either show great doubts in your wisdom or in your justice. Therefore I will
20 transfer my care upon you, and attend, to my learning and comfort, the eternal example you will leave to all mankind of disguisers, falsifiers, adulterers, ravishers, murderers, and traitors.'

Musidorus, while Philanax was speaking against his cousin and him, had looked round about him, to see whether by any means he might
25 come to have caught him in his arms, and have killed him—so much had his disgracing words filled his breast with rage. But perceiving himself so guarded as he should rather show a passionate act than perform his revenge, his hand trembling with desire to strike, and all the veins in his face swelling, casting his eyes over the judgement seat:
30 'O gods,' said he, 'and have you spared my life to bear these injuries of such a drivel? Is this the justice of this place, to have such men as we are submitted not only to apparent falsehood but most shameful reviling? But mark, I pray you, the ungratefulness of the wretch; how utterly he hath forgotten the benefits both he and all
35 this country hath received of us. For if ever men may remember their own noble deeds, it is then when their just defence and others' unjust unkindness doth require it. Were not we the men that killed

the wild beasts which otherwise had killed the princesses if we had not succoured them? Consider, if it please you, where had been Timopyrus's rape, or my treason, if the sweet beauties of the earth had then been devoured? Either think them now dead, or remember they live by us. And yet full often this telltale can acknowledge the 5 loss they should have by their taking away, while maliciously he overpasseth who were their preservers. Neither let this be spoken of me as if I meant to balance this evil with that good, for I must confess that saving of such creatures was rewarded in the act itself, but only to manifest the partial jangling of this vile pickthank. But if 10 we be traitors, where was your fidelity, O only tongue-valiant gentleman, when not only the young princesses but the duke himself was defended from uttermost peril, partly by me, but principally by this excellent young man's both wisdom and valour? Were we that made ourselves against hundreds of armed men openly 15 the shields of his life like secretly to be his empoisoners? Did we then show his life to be dearer to us than our own because we might after rob him of his life, to die shamefully? Truly, truly, master orator, whosoever hath hired you to be so busy in their matters who keep honester servants than yourself, he should have bid you in so 20 many railings bring some excuse for yourself why in the greatest need of your prince, to whom you pretend a miraculous goodwill, you were not then as forward to do like a man yourself, or at least to accuse them that were slack in that service. But commonly they use their feet for their defence, whose tongue is their weapon. Certainly, 25 a very simple subtlety it had been in us to repose our lives in the daughters when we had killed the father. But as this gentleman thinks to win the reputation of a copious talker by leaving nothing unsaid which a filthy mind can imagine, so think I (or else all words are vain) that to wisemen's judgement our clearness in the duke's 30 death is sufficiently notorious. But at length, when the merchant hath set out his gilded baggage, lastly he comes to some stuff of importance, and saith I conveyed away the princess of this country.

than his daughters' lives and his state's preservation. Were 93.   2–3 had been
... treason OA: had Timopyrus's rape, or my treason, been St; had been Daiphantus's
rape, or my treason 93.   7 of] by Cl, Da.   8 as if I OA, 93: as I St.
9 that saving] that the saving Bo, Cl; the saving Ph; saving Je.   11 be traitors] be
the traitors Cl, As, Je, Hm, 93.   your] our As, Hm.   12 princesses] princes Ph,
Hm; princess 93.   22 a] om. Cl, As, Da.   24 in that] in this As; in their Ph,
Je.   they] the 93 (corr. 98).   26 been in us] been for us Cl, Hm.   28 copious
talker] gallant speaker Cl, As; compendious talker Hm.   30 judgement] judge-
ments Ph, Je.   33 saith] said Ph, Je.

And is she indeed your princess? I pray you, then, whom should I
wait of else but her that was my mistress by my professed vow, and
princess over me while I lived in this soil? Ask her why she went;
ask not me why I served her. Since accounting me as a prince you
5 have not to do with me, taking me as her servant, then take withal
that I must obey her. But you will say I persuaded her to fly away.
Certainly I will for no death deny it, knowing to what honour I
should bring her from the thraldom, by such fellows' counsel as
you, she was kept in. Shall persuasion to a prince grow treason
10 against a prince? It might be error in me, but falsehood it could not
be, since I made myself partaker of whatsoever I wished her unto.
Who will ever counsel his king if his counsel be judged by the event,
and if he be not found wise shall therefore be thought wicked?
But if I be a traitor, I hope you will grant me a correlative to whom I
15 shall be the traitor; for the princess (against whom treasons are
considered), I am sure, will avow my faithfulness, without you will
say that I am a traitor to her because I left the country, and a traitor
to the country because I went with her. Here do I leave out my just
excuses of love's force; which, as thy narrow heart hath never had
20 noble room enough in it to receive, so yet those manlike courages
that by experience know how subject the virtuous minds are to love
a most virtuous creature (witnessed to be such by the most excellent
gifts of nature) will deem it a venial trespass to seek the satisfaction
of honourable desires—honourable even in the curiousest points of
25 honour, whereout there can no disgrace nor disparagement come
unto her. Therefore, O judge, who I hope dost know what it is to be
a judge, that your end is to preserve and not to destroy mankind,
that laws are not made like lime twigs or nets to catch everything that
toucheth them, but rather like sea marks to avoid the shipwrack of
30 ignorant passengers, since that our doing in the extremest interpreta-
tion is but a human error, and that of it you may make a profitable
event (we being of such estate as their parents would not have
misliked the affinity), you will not, I trust, at the persuasion of this
brabbler burn your house to make it clean, but like a wise father

10 against] to Da, Je, 93.   13 he] it Cl, Da, Je, 93.   therefore] it Cl;
om. As.   15 whom treasons] whom the treasons Cl, Da, Je, Hm, 93;
whom the treason Ph.   17 that] *om.* Cl, As, Da, Hm.   19 thy] the
Cl, Ph, Hm.   20 yet those 1627: yet to those St, Bo, Cl, As, Ph,
Je, 93; yet to these Da, Hm.   25 whereout] whereat Bo; whereunto Hm.
there] there they Da; *om.* Je.   29 shipwrack] shipwracks Cl, Hm.   31 a human]
an human Da, Je.   33 misliked the] misliked their Cl, Hm; misliked our As.

turn even the fault of your children to any good that may come of it, since that is the fruit of wisdom and end of all judgements.'

While this matter was thus handling, a silent and, as it were, astonished attention possessed all the people; a kindly compassion moved the noble gentleman Sympathus; but as for Kerxenus, 5 everything was spoken either by or of his dear guests moved an effect in him: sometimes tears, sometimes hopeful looks, sometimes whispering persuasions in their ears that stood by him, to seek the saving the two young princes. But the general multitude waited the judgement of Euarchus who, showing in his face no motions either 10 at the one's or other's speech, letting pass the flowers of rhetoric and only marking whither their reasons tended, having made the question to be asked of Gynecia (who continued to take the whole fault upon herself), and having caused Dametas with Miso and Mopsa (who by Philanax's order had been held in most cruel prison) to make a full 15 declaration how much they knew of these past matters, and then gathering as assured satisfaction to his own mind as in that case he could, not needing to take leisure for that whereof a long practice had bred a well grounded habit in him, with a voice and gesture directed to the universal assembly, in this form pronounced sentence: 20

'This weighty matter, whereof presently we are to determine, doth at the first consideration yield two important doubts: the first, whether these men be to be judged; the second, how they are to be judged. The first doubt ariseth because they give themselves out for princes absolute, a sacred name and to which any violence seems to 25 be an impiety; for how can any laws (which are the bonds of all human society) be observed if the lawgivers and law rulers be not held in an untouched admiration? But hereto although already they have been sufficiently answered, yet thus much again I may repeat unto you: that whatsoever they be or be not, here they be no princes, 30 since betwixt prince and subject there is as necessary a relation as between father and son, and as there is no man a father but to his child, so is not a prince a prince but to his own subjects. Therefore is not this place to acknowledge in them any principality, without it should at the same time by a secret consent confess subjection. Yet 35

6 of] for As, Da, Je, 93.   his dear guests] his guests Da, Je; his own dear guests 93.
7 effect] affect 93 (*ex.* 05).   9 saving the] saving of the Cl, As, Ph, Hm.
10 showing] showed 93.   11 or other's] or at the other's Da; or the other's Hm; or other 93 (*corr.* 98).   speech] speeches Da, Je.   19 voice and] voice of 93 (*corr.* 98).   25-6 to be] *om.* Cl, As, Hm.   26 bonds] bands Bo, Da.   29 may repeat] will repeat Cl, As, Da, 93; will report Je; mean to report Hm.

hereto may be objected that the universal civility, the law of nations (all mankind being as it were coinhabiters or world citizens together), hath ever required public persons should be of all parties especially regarded, since not only in peace but in war, not only princes but
5 heralds and trumpets are with great reason exempted from injuries. This point is true, but yet so true as they that will receive the benefit of a custom must not be the first to break it, for then can they not complain if they be not helped by that which they themselves hurt. If a prince do acts of hostility without denouncing war, if he break
10 his oath of amity, or innumerable such other things contrary to the law of arms, he must take heed how he fall into their hands whom he so wrongeth, for then is courtesy the best custom he can claim; much more these men who have not only left to do like princes but to be like princes, not only entered into Arcadia, and so into the
15 Arcadian orders, but into domestical services, and so by making themselves private deprived themselves of respect due to their public calling. For no proportion it were of justice that a man might make himself no prince when he would do evil, and might anew create himself a prince when he would not suffer evil. Thus, there-
20 fore, by all laws of nature and nations, and especially by their own putting themselves out of the sanctuary of them, these young men cannot in justice avoid the judgement, but like private men must have their doings either cleared, excused, or condemned.

There resteth, then, the second point: how to judge well. And
25 that must undoubtedly be done, not by a free discourse of reason and skill of philosophy, but must be tied to the laws of Greece and municipal statutes of this dukedom. For although out of them these came, and to them must indeed refer their offspring, yet because philosophical discourses stand in the general consideration of
30 things, they leave to every man a scope of his own interpretation; where the laws, applying themselves to the necessary use, fold us within assured bounds, which once broken, man's nature infinitely rangeth. Judged therefore they must be, and by your laws judged. Now the action offereth itself to due balance betwixt the accuser's
35 twofold accusation and their answer accordingly applied, the questions being, the one of a fact simply, the other of the quality of a fact. To the first they use direct denial, to the second qualification

---

2 world] worldly Ph, Hm.   5 trumpets] trumpeters Da, Ph.   14 the] *om*˙
Ph, Hm.   27 dukedom] kingdom Cl, 93.   32 bounds] bonds Bo'
Da, Hm.

and excuse. They deny the murder of the duke, and against mighty presumptions bring forth some probable answers, which they do principally fortify with the duchess's acknowledging herself only culpable. Certainly, as in equality of conjectures we are not to take hold of the worst, but rather to be glad we may find any hope that mankind is not grown monstrous (being undoubtedly less evil a guilty man should escape than a guiltless perish), so if in the rest they be spotless, then is this no further to be remembered. But if they have aggravated these suspicions with new evils, then are those suspicions so far to show themselves as to cause the other points to be thoroughly examined and with less favour weighed; since this no man can deny: they have been accidental, if not principal, causes of the duke's death.

Now, then, we are to determine of the other matters which are laid to them, wherein they do not deny the fact but deny, or at least diminish, the fault. But first I may remember (though it were not first alleged by them) the services they had before done, truly honourable and worthy of great reward, but not worthy to countervail with a following wickedness. Reward is proper to well doing, punishment to evil doing, which must not be confounded no more than good and evil are to be mingled. Therefore it hath been determined in all wisdoms that no man, because he hath done well before, should have his present evils spared, but rather so much the more punished, as having showed he knew how to be good, would against his knowledge be naught. The fact, then, is nakedly without passion or partiality to be viewed. Wherein, he that terms himself Timopyrus denies not he offered violence to the lady Philoclea, an act punished by all the Grecian laws with being thrown down from a high tower to the earth—a death which doth no way exceed the proportion of the trespass; for nothing can be imagined more

---

1 against mighty] mighty against 93 (*corr.* 13).   5 worst] worse As, Da, 93.
6 undoubtedly] Je *missing from here to the end*.   8 this] it Cl, As; *om.* Da, 93.
21 it] *om.* 93.   24 be] do Cl, As, Hm.   26–p. 406, 11 Wherein . . . by the loss] 93 *substitutes*:
    Wherein without all question they are equally culpable. For though he that terms himself Daiphantus were sooner disappointed of his purpose of conveying away the lady Philoclea than he that persuaded the princess Pamela to fly her country and accompanied her in it, yet seeing in causes of this nature the will by the rules of justice standeth for the deed, they are both alike to be found guilty, and guilty of heinous ravishment. For though they ravished them not from themselves, yet they ravished them from him that owed them, which was their father—an act punished by all the Grecian laws by the loss
28–9 a high] an high Bo, Da, Hm.

unnatural than by force to take that which, being holily used, is the
root of humanity, the beginning and maintaining of living creatures,
whereof the confusion must needs be a general ruin. And since the
wickedness of lust is by our decrees punished by death, though both
5 consent, much more is he whose wickedness so overflows as he will
compel another to be wicked.

The other young man confesseth he persuaded the princess
Pamela to fly her country, and accompanied her in it—without all
question a ravishment no less than the other; for, although he
10 ravished her not from herself, yet he ravished her from him that
owed her, which was her father. This kind is chastised by the loss of
the head, as a most execrable theft; for if they must die who steal
from us our goods, how much more they who steal from us that for
which we gather our goods. And if our laws have it so in the private
15 persons, much more forcible are they to be in princes' children,
where one steals as it were the whole state and well being of that
people, tied by the secret of a long use to be governed by none but
the next of that blood. Neither let any man marvel our ances-
tors have been so severe in these cases, since the example of the
20 Phoenician Europa, but especially of the Grecian Helen, hath
taught them what destroying fires have grown of such sparkles.
And although Helen was a wife and this but a child, that booteth
not, since the principal cause of marrying wives is that we may
have children of our own.

25 But now let us see how these young men (truly for their persons
worthy of pity, if they had rightly pitied themselves) do go about to
mitigate the vehemency of their errors. Some of their excuses are
common to both, some peculiar only to him that was the shepherd;
both remember the force of love, and as it were the mending up of
30 the matter by their marriage. If that unbridled desire which is
entitled love might purge such a sickness as this, surely we should
have many loving excuses of hateful mischiefs. Nay rather, no
mischief should be committed that should not be veiled under the
name of love. For as well he that steals might allege the love of
35 money, he that murders the love of revenge, he that rebels the love
of greatness, as the adulterer the love of a woman; since they do in

15 persons] person Da, Ph.   forcible] *om* Da, Ph.   16 that] the Bo, Ph, Hm.
17 tied] being tied 93.   18 that blood] the blood Cl, Hm; blood As.
19 cases] causes As, Ph, Hm.   21 sparkles] sparks Ph, Hm.   26 had 13:
have OA, 93.   28 peculiar OA, 93: particular St.   32 mischiefs] mischief 93.

all speech affirm they love that which an ill-governed passion maketh them to follow. But love may have no such privilege. That sweet and heavenly uniting of the minds, which properly is called love, hath no other knot but virtue; and therefore if it be a right love, it can never slide into any action that is not virtuous. The other, and 5 indeed more effectual, reason is that they may be married unto them, and so honourably redress the dishonour of them whom this matter seemeth most to touch. Surely, if the question were what were convenient for the parties, and not what is just in the never-changing justice, there might be much said in it. But herein we must 10 consider that the laws look how to prevent by due examples that such things be not done, and not how to salve such things when they are done. For if the governors of justice shall take such a scope as to measure the foot of the law by a show of conveniency, and measure that conveniency not by the public society but by that which is 15 fittest for them which offend, young men, strong men, and rich men shall ever find private conveniences how to palliate such committed disorders as to the public shall not only be inconvenient but pestilent. The marriage perchance might be fit for them, but very unfit were it to the state to allow a pattern of such procurations of 20 marriage. And thus much do they both allege. Further goes he that went with the princess Pamela, and requireth the benefit of a counsellor, who hath place of free persuasion, and the reasonable excuse of a servant, that did but wait of his mistress. Without all question, as counsellors have great cause to take heed how they 25 advise anything directly opposite to the form of that present government, especially when they do it simply without public allowance, so yet is this case much more apparent; since neither she was an effectual princess, her father being then alive, and though he had been dead, she not come to the years of authority, 30 nor he her servant in such manner to obey her, but by his own preferment first belonging to Dametas, and then to the duke, and therefore, if not by Arcadia laws, yet by household orders, bound to have done nothing without his agreement. Thus, therefore, since the deeds accomplished by these two are both abominable and 35

1 speech] speeches Ph, 93. 2 them to follow] them follow As, Da.
10 be much] much be As, Da, 93 (*corr.* 13). 15 the] *om.* Da, Ph. 16 which]
to Cl; that Da. 20 to the] for the Cl, Ph, Hm. 21 marriage] marriages Bo,
As. 24 wait of] wait on As, Da. 27 simply] singly 93. 28 this] the Da,
93. 33 not by . . . yet by OA, 93: not by the . . . yet by the St (if . . . thus *om.*
Ph). Arcadia] Arcadian Cl, Hm.

inexcusable, I do in the behalf of justice, and by the force of
Arcadia laws pronounce that Timopyrus shall be thrown out of a
high tower to receive his death by his fall; Palladius shall be
beheaded: the time, before sunset; the place, in Mantinea; the
5 executioner, Dametas. Which office he shall execute all the days of
his life, for his beastly forgetting the careful duty he owed to his
charge.'

This said, he turned himself to Philanax and two of the other
noblemen, commanding them to see the judgement presently
10 performed. Philanax, more greedy than any hunter of his prey, went
straight to lay hold of the excellent prisoners who, casting a farewell
look one upon the other, represented in their faces as much unappalled
constancy as the most excellent courage can deliver in outward
graces. Yet if at all there were any show of change in them, it was
15 that Pyrocles was something nearer to bashfulness, and Musidorus
to anger, both overruled by reason and resolution. But as with great
number of armed men Philanax was descending unto them, and
that Musidorus was beginning to say something in Pyrocles' behalf,
behold Kerxenus that with arms cast abroad and open mouth came
20 crying to Euarchus, holding a stranger in his hand that cried much
more than he, desiring they might be heard speak before the pris-
oners were removed. Even the noble gentleman Sympathus aided
them in it, and taking such as he could command, stopped Philanax
betwixt entreaty and force from carrying away the princes until it
25 were heard what new matters these men did bring. So again mount-
ing to the tribunal, they hearkened to the stranger's vehement
speech, or rather appassionate exclaiming.

But first you will be content to know what he was, and what
cause and mean brought him thither. It is not, I hope, forgotten how
30 in the first beginning of Musidorus's love, when in despite of his
best-grounded determinations he became a slave to affection, how
leaving the place of his eye-infection, he met with the shepherd
Menalcas, by the help of whose raiment he advanced himself to that
estate which he accounted most high because it might be serviceable

2 Arcadia] Arcadian Cl, Hm; Arcadia's As.   4 before sunset] before the sunset
Cl, As, Da, Hm.   6 his beastly] the beastly Ph, Hm.   11 of] on As, Ph.
22 noble gentleman] nobleman Bo, Hm; now gentleman As.   27 appassionate]
a passionate Cl, Da, Ph, Hm; passionate As.   28-30 But first . . . Musidorus's
love] It was indeed Kalodoulus, the faithful servant of Musidorus, to whom his master
93.   30 first] *om.* Cl, Hm.   31-3 how . . . Menalcas] had sent the shepherd
Menalcas to be arrested 93.   33 raiment he] raiment in the mean time he 93.

to that fancy which he had placed most high in his mind; and how, lest by his presence his purpose might be revealed, he hired him to go into Thessalia, writing by him to a trusty servant of his that he should arrest him until he knew his further pleasure. Menalcas faithfully performed his errand, and was as faithfully imprisoned by 5 Kalodoulus, for such was the gentleman's name to whom Musidorus directed him. But as Kalodoulus performed the first part of his duty in doing the commandment of his prince, so was he with abundance of sincere loyalty extremely perplexed when he understood of Menalcas the strange disguising of his beloved master. For as the 10 acts he and his cousin Pyrocles had done in Asia and Egypt had filled all the ears of the Thessalians and Macedonians with no less joy than admiration, so was the fear of their loss no less grievous unto them when by the noise of report they understood of their lonely committing themselves to the sea, the issue of which they 15 had yet no way learned. But now that by Menalcas he perceived where he was, guessing the like of Pyrocles, comparing the unusedness of this act with the unripeness of their age, seeing in general conjecture they could do it for nothing that might not fall out dangerous, he was somewhile troubled with himself what to do, 20 betwixt doubt of their hurt and doubt of their displeasure. Lastly he resolved his safest and honestest way was to reveal it to the king Euarchus, that both his authority might prevent any damage, and under his wings he himself might remain safe. Thitherward, therefore, he went. But being come to the city of Pella, where he had 25 heard the king lay, he found him not long before departed towards Arcadia. This made him, with all the speed he could, follow Euarchus, as well to advertise him, if need were, as to do his prince service in his uncle's thither coming. And so it happened that,

1-4 and how . . . pleasure] om. 93.   4-5 Menalcas faithfully] For Menalcas having faithfully 93.   6-7 for such . . . directed him] om. 93.   7 directed him] wrote As, Da, Ph; had wrote Hm.   11 and Egypt] om. 93.   13 the fear Bo, Cl, Ph, Hm, 93: their fear St (joy . . . no less om. As, Da).   15 lonely] lovely Bo, Cl, As, Da, Ph, Hm, 13.   16 yet no way] no way Cl, As, Da, 93; not yet Ph, Hm.   learned] understood As, Da, Ph, Hm.   17-18 unusedness] blank left As; unadvisedness Ph. 21-2 Lastly he resolved his] Often he was minded (as his 93.   22 honestest] honest As, Da. was] om. 93.   23 damage] damage to them 93.   24-9 Thitherward . . . coming.] But considering a journey to Byzantium (where as yet he supposed Euarchus lay) would require more time than he was willing to remain doubtful of his prince's estate, he resolved at length to write the matter to Euarchus, and himself the while to go into Arcadia, uncertain what to do when he came thither, but determined to do his best service to his dear master, if by any good fortune he might find him. 93.

being even this day come to Mantinea, and as warily as he could inquiring after Euarchus, he straight received a strange rumour of these things, but so uncertainly as popular reports carry so rare accidents. But this by all men he was willed: to seek out Kerxenus,
5 a great gentleman of that country, who would soonest satisfy him of all those occurrents. Thus instructed, he came even about the midst of Euarchus's judgement to the desert, where seeing great multitudes, and hearing unknown names of Palladius and Timopyrus, and not able to press to the place where Euarchus sat, he inquired for
10 Kerxenus, and was soon brought unto him, partly because he was generally known unto all men, and partly because he had withdrawn himself from the press when he perceived by Euarchus's words whither they tended, not being able to endure his guests' condemnation. He inquired forthwith of Kerxenus the cause of the assembly,
15 and whether he had heard of Euarchus. Who with many tears made a doleful recital unto him, both of the amazon and shepherd, setting forth their natural graces, and lamenting their pitiful undoing. But his description made Kalodoulus immediately know the shepherd was his duke, and so judging the other to be Pyrocles,
20 and speedily communicating it to Kerxenus, who he saw did favour their case, they brake the press with astonishing every man with their cries. And being come to Euarchus, Kalodoulus fell at his feet, telling him those he had judged were his own son and nephew, the one the comfort of Macedon, the other the only stay of Thessalia,
25 with many suchlike words, but as from a man that assured himself in that matter he should need small speech; while Kerxenus made it known to all men what the prisoners were. To whom he cried they should salute their father, and joy in the good hap the gods had sent them; who were no less glad than all the people amazed at the strange
30 event of these matters. Even Philanax's own revengeful heart was mollified when he saw how from diverse parts in the world so near kinsmen should meet in such a necessity; and withal the fame of Pyrocles and Musidorus greatly drew him to a compassionate conceit, and had already unclothed his face of all show of malice.
35   But Euarchus stayed a good while upon himself, like a valiant man

1 warily] warily and attentively 93.   2 inquiring after Euarchus] giving ear to all reports, in hope to hear something of them he sought 93.   5 who] he Da, Hm.
6 those] these Cl, 93 (om. 13).   15 he had heard] the fame were true 93.
Euarchus] Euarchus's presence 93.   21 case] causes As; cause Da.   30 these OA, 93: those St.   31 how] om. 93.   in the world] of the world Cl, Ph, 93.

that should receive a notable encounter, being vehemently stricken with the fatherly love of so excellent children, and studying with his best reason what his office required. At length, with such a kind of gravity as was near to sorrow, he thus uttered his mind:

'I take witness of the immortal gods', said he, 'O Arcadians, that 5 what this day I have said hath been out of my assured persuasion what justice itself and your just laws require. Though strangers then to me, I had no desire to hurt them; but leaving aside all considerations of the persons, I weighed the matter which you committed into my hands with my most unpartial and furthest reach of reason, 10 and thereout have condemned them to lose their lives, contaminated with so many foul breaches of hospitality, civility, and virtue. Now, contrary to all expectation, I find them to be mine only son and nephew; such upon whom you see what gifts nature hath bestowed; such who have so to the wonder of the world heretofore behaved 15 themselves as might give just cause to the greatest hopes that in an excellent youth may be conceived; lastly, in few words, such in whom I placed all my mortal joys, and thought myself now near my grave to recover a new life. But, alas, shall justice halt, or shall she wink in one's cause which had lynx's eyes in another's? Or rather, shall 20 all private respects give place to that holy name? Be it so, be it so. Let my grey hairs be laid in the dust with sorrow. Let the small remnant of my life be to me an inward and outward desolation, and to the world a gazing stock of wretched misery. But never, never, let sacred rightfulness fall. It is immortal, and immortally ought to 25 be preserved. If rightly I have judged, then rightly have I judged mine own children, unless the name of a child should have force to change the never-changing justice. No, no, Pyrocles and Musidorus, I prefer you much before my life, but I prefer justice as far before you. While you did like yourselves, my body should willingly have 30 been your shield; but I cannot keep you from the effects of your own doing. Nay, I cannot in this case acknowledge you for mine; for never had I shepherd to my nephew, nor never had woman to my

7 strangers OA, 93: stranger St.　　　10 into] unto Ph; to Hm.　　with my most] with most As, 93 (corr. 98).　　13 expectation] expectations 93.　　mine] my Cl, Da, Ph, Hm, 93.　　14 what gifts nature hath bestowed Bo, Cl, As, Da, Ph, 93: what gifts of nature hath bestowed St; nature hath bestowed her gifts Hm.　　19 recover OA, 93: receive St.　　or OA, 93: as St.　　20 lynx's] Lynceus As; princes Ph; links Hm.　　25 immortally] immortal Cl, As; imortall yt Da; Immortallytye Ph.　　26 rightly have I] I have rightly Bo, Cl, Hm, 93.　　27 mine] my Da, Ph.　　32 doing] doings As, Ph.　　33 nor never had] nor ever had Bo, Hm, 93; nor As, Da, Ph.

son. Your vices have degraded you from being princes, and have disannulled your birthright. Therefore, if there be anything left in you of princely virtue, show it in constant suffering that your unprincely dealing hath purchased unto you. For my part, I must
5 tell you, you have forced a father to rob himself of his children. Do you, therefore, O Philanax, and you my other lords of this country, see the judgement be rightly performed in time, place, and manner as before appointed.'

With that, though he would have refrained them, a man might
10 perceive the tears drop down his long white beard, which moved not only Kalodoulus and Kerxenus to roaring lamentations, but all the assembly dolefully to record that pitiful spectacle. Philanax himself could not abstain from great shows of pitying sorrow, and manifest withdrawing from performing the king's commandment. But
15 Musidorus, having the hope of his safety and recovering of the princess Pamela (which made him most desire to live) so suddenly dashed, but especially moved for his dear Pyrocles, for whom he was ever resolved his last speech should be, and stirred up with rage of unkindness, he thus spake:
20 'Enjoy thy bloody conquest, tyrannical Euarchus,' said he, 'for neither is convenient the title of a king to a murderer, nor the remembrance of kindred to a destroyer of his kindred. Go home and glory that it hath been in thy power shamefully to kill Musidorus. Let thy flattering orators dedicate crowns of laurel unto thee, that
25 the first of thy race thou hast overthrown a prince of Thessalia. But for me, I hope the Thessalians are not so degenerate from their ancestors but that they will revenge my injury and their loss upon thee. I hope my death is no more unjust to me than it shall be bitter to thee. Howsoever it be, my death shall triumph over thy cruelty.
30 Neither as now would I live to make my life beholding unto thee. But if thy cruelty hath not so blinded thy eyes that thou canst not see thine own hurt, if thy heart be not so devilish as thou hast no power but to torment thyself, then look upon this young Pyrocles with a manlike eye, if not with a pitiful. Give not occasion to the
35 whole earth to say "see how the gods have made the tyrant tear his own bowels". Examine the eyes and voices of all this people, and

11 Kerxenus] Kalander 98.   15 recovering of the] recovering the Cl, Hm.
16 desire] desirous 93.   18-19 with rage] with the rage Cl, 98 (corr. 13).
21 murderer OA, 93: murder St.   31 thy eyes] thine eyes Bo, Cl, As, Da, 93.
32 thine] thy Bo, Ph, Hm.   hurt] heart 93 (corr. 98).

what all men see, be not blind in thine own case. Look, I say, look upon him in whom the most curious searcher is able to find no fault but that he is thy son. Believe it, thy own subjects will detest thee for robbing them of such a prince, in whom they have right as well as thyself.' 5

Some more words to that purpose he would have spoken, but Pyrocles (who oft had called to him) did now fully interrupt him, desiring him not to do him the wrong to give his father ill words before him, willing him to consider it was their own fault and not his unjustice; and withal to remember their resolution of well suffering 10 all accidents, which this impatience did seem to vary from. And then kneeling down with all humbleness, he took the speech in this order to Euarchus:

'If my daily prayers to the almighty gods had so far prevailed as to have granted me the end whereto I have directed my actions, I 15 should rather have been now a comfort to your mind than an example of your justice, rather a preserver of your memory by my life than a monument of your judgement by my death. But since it hath pleased their unsearchable wisdoms to overthrow all the desires I had to serve you, and make me become a shame unto you, since the 20 last obedience I can show you is to die, vouchsafe yet, O father (if my fault have not made me altogether unworthy so to term you), vouchsafe, I say, to let the few and last words your son shall ever speak not to be tedious unto you. And if the remembrance of my virtuous mother (who once was dear unto you) may bear any sway 25 with you, if the name of Pyrocles have at any time been pleasant, let one request of mine (which shall not be for my own life) be graciously accepted of you. What you owe to justice is performed in my death. A father to have executed his only son will leave a sufficient example for a greater crime than this. My blood will satisfy the highest point 30 of equity. My blood will satisfy the hardest hearted of this country. O save the life of this prince; that is the only all I will with my last breath demand of you. With what face will you look upon your sister when, in reward of nourishing me in your greatest need, you take away, and in such sort take away, that which is more dear to her 35 than all the world, and is the only comfort wherewith she nourisheth

7 oft had] had oft Cl; often had As, Da, 93.   10 unjustice] injustice Da, Ph.
11 impatience] impatiency 93.   16–17 example of] example to Da, Hm.
19 their] your Da; the Hm.   24 not to be] not be Cl, As, Hm, 93 (*corr.* 13).
27 my own] mine own Cl, As, 93.   28 in OA, 93: by St.   31 hearted of]
hearts of Cl; hearted in As, Da, Ph, 93.

her old age? O give not such an occasion to the noble Thessalians for ever to curse the match that their prince did make with the Macedonian blood. By my loss there follows no public loss, for you are to hold the seat, and to provide yourself perchance of a worthier
5 successor. But how can you, or all the earth, recompense the damage that poor Thessalia shall sustain, who sending out (whom otherwise they would no more have spared than their own eyes) their prince to you, and you requesting to have him, by you he should thus dishonourably be extinguished? Set before you, I beseech you, the face
10 of that miserable people when no sooner shall the news come that you have met your nephew but withal they shall hear that you have beheaded him. How many tears they shall spend, how many complaints they shall make, so many just execrations will light upon you. And take heed, O father (for since my death answers my fault
15 while I live I may call upon that dear name), lest seeking too precise a course of justice, you be not thought most unjust in weakening your neighbour's mighty estate by taking away their only pillar. In me, in me, this matter began; in me, let it receive his ending. Assure yourself, no man will doubt your severe observing the laws
20 when it shall be known Euarchus hath killed Pyrocles. But the time of my ever farewell approacheth. If you do think my death sufficient for my fault, and do not desire to make my death more miserable than death, let these dying words of him that was once your son pierce your ears. Let Musidorus live, and Pyrocles shall live in him,
25 and you shall not want a child.'

'A child', cried out Musidorus, 'to him that kills Pyrocles!'

With that again he fell to entreat for Pyrocles, and Pyrocles as fast for Musidorus, each employing his wit how to show himself most worthy to die, to such an admiration of all the beholders that
30 most of them, examining the matter by their own passions, thought Euarchus (as often extraordinary excellencies, not being rightly conceived, do rather offend than please) an obstinate-hearted man, and such a one, who being pitiless, his dominion must needs be insupportable. But Euarchus, that felt his own misery more than they,
35 and yet loved goodness more than himself, with such a sad assured behaviour as Cato killed himself withal, when he had heard the uttermost of that their speech tended unto, he commanded again they should be carried away, rising up from the seat (which he would much

rather have wished should have been his grave), and looking who
would take the charge, whereto everyone was exceeding backward.

But as this pitiful matter was entering into, those that were next
the duke's body might hear from under the velvet wherewith he was
covered a great voice of groaning; whereat every man astonished, 5
and their spirits, appalled with these former miseries, apt to take
any strange conceit. When they might perfectly perceive the body
stir, then some began to fear spirits, some to look for a miracle, most
to imagine they knew not what. But Philanax and Kerxenus, whose
eyes honest love (though to diverse parties) held most attentive, 10
leapt to the table, and putting off the velvet cover, might plainly
discern, with as much wonder as gladness, that the duke lived.
Which how it fell out in few words shall be declared.

So it was that the drink he had received was neither (as Gynecia
first imagined) a love potion nor (as it was after thought) a deadly 15
poison, but a drink made by notable art, and as it was thought not
without natural magic, to procure for thirty hours such a deadly
sleep as should oppress all show of life. The cause of the making of
this drink had first been that a princess of Cyprus, grandmother to
Gynecia, being notably learned (and yet not able with all her learn- 20
ing to answer the objections of Cupid), did furiously love a young
nobleman of her father's court, who fearing the king's rage, and not
once daring either to attempt or accept so high a place, she made that
sleeping drink, and found means by a trusty servant of hers (who of
purpose invited him to his chamber) to procure him, that suspected 25
no such thing, to receive it. Which done, he no way able to resist,
was secretly carried by him into a pleasant chamber in the midst of
a garden she had of purpose provided for this enterprise, where that
space of time pleasing herself with seeing and cherishing of him,
when the time came of the drink's end of working (and he more 30
astonished than if he had fallen from the clouds), she bade him
choose either then to marry her, and to promise to fly away with her
in a bark she had made ready, or else she would presently cry out,
and show in what place he was, with oath he was come thither to
ravish her. The nobleman in these straits, her beauty prevailed; he 35
married her and escaped the realm with her, and after many
strange adventures were reconciled to the king, her father, after

9 Kerxenus] Kalander 98.   13 Which . . . declared] *om*. 93.   14 So] For so
93.   20 and yet not OA, 93: and not St.   23 either] neither Ph; *om*. Hm.
32 either then] either As, Ph; then either Hm.

whose death they reigned. But she, gratefully remembering the
service that drink had done her, preserved in a bottle (made by
singular art long to keep it without perishing) great quantity of it,
with the foretold inscription. Which wrong interpreted by her
5 daughter-in-law, the queen of Cyprus, was given by her to Gynecia
at the time of her marriage; and the drink, finding an old body of
Basilius, had kept him some hours longer in the trance than it would
have done a younger.

But a good while it was before good Basilius could come again to
10 himself. In which time Euarchus (more glad than of the whole
world's monarchy to be rid of his miserable magistracy, which even
in justice he was now to surrender to the lawful prince of that
country) came from the throne unto him, and there with much ado
made him understand how these intricate matters had fallen out.
15 Many garboils passed through his fancy before he could be persuaded
Cleophila was other than a woman. At length, remembering the
oracle, which now indeed was accomplished (not as before he had
imagined), considering all had fallen out by the highest providence,
and withal weighing in all these matters his own fault had been the
20 greatest, the first thing he did was with all honourable pomp to send
for Gynecia (who, poor lady, thought she was leading forth to her
living burial), and (when she came) to recount before all the people
the excellent virtue was in her, which she had not only maintained
all her life most unspotted but now was content so miserably to die
25 to follow her husband. He told them how she had warned him to
take heed of that drink. And so, with all the exaltings of her that
might be, he publicly desired her pardon for those errors he had
committed. And so kissing her, left her to receive the most honour-
able fame of any princess throughout the world, all men thinking
30 (saving only Pyrocles and Philoclea who never bewrayed her) that
she was the perfect mirror of all wifely love. Which though in that
point undeserved, she did in the remnant of her life duly purchase
with observing all duty and faith, to the example and glory of
Greece—so uncertain are mortal judgements, the same person most
35 infamous and most famous, and neither justly.

Then with princely entertainment to Euarchus, and many kind
words to Pyrocles (whom still he dearly loved, though in a more

16 Cleophila] Zelmane 98.   24 content] contented Da, 93.   32 duly] daily
As, Hm, 93 (corr. 13).   34 are mortal OA, 93: are the mortal St.   · 37 in a
more OA, 93: in more St.

virtuous kind), the marriage was concluded, to the inestimable joy
of Euarchus (towards whom now Musidorus acknowledged his
fault), betwixt these peerless princes and princesses; Philanax for
his singular faith ever held dear of Basilius while he lived, and no less
of Musidorus who was to inherit that dukedom, and therein con- 5
firmed to him and his the second place of that province, with great
increase of his living to maintain it; which like proportion he used to
Kalodoulus in Thessalia. Sympathus, Euarchus took with him into
Macedon, and there highly advanced him. But as for Kerxenus,
Pyrocles (to whom his father in his own time gave the whole kingdom 10
of Thrace) held him always about him, giving him in pure gift the
great city of Abdera.

But the solemnities of these marriages, with the Arcadian
pastorals full of many comical adventures happening to those rural
lovers, the strange story of the fair queens Artaxia of Persia and 15
Erona of Lydia, with the prince Plangus's wonderful chances, whom
the latter had sent to Pyrocles, and the extreme affection Amasis,
king of Egypt, bare unto the former, the shepherdish loves of
Menalcas with Kalodoulus's daughter, and the poor hopes of the
poor Philisides in the pursuit of his affections, the strange continu- 20
ance of Klaius's and Strephon's desire, lastly the son of Pyrocles
named Pyrophilus, and Melidora the fair daughter of Pamela by
Musidorus, who even at their birth entered into admirable fortunes,
may awake some other spirit to exercise his pen in that wherewith
mine is already dulled. 25

The last book or act.

3 these] those Cl, As, Da.   5 dukedom] kingdom 98.   8–9 Sympathus . . .
him] Highly honouring Kalander while he lived; and after his death continuing in the
same measure to love and advance his (98: this 93) son Clitophon 93.   9 Ker-
xenus] Sympathus 93.   15–18 story . . . former] stories of Artaxia and Plexirtus,
Erona and Plangus, Helen and Amphialus, with the wonderful chances that befell them
93.   15 queens] queen Cl, As, Da, Hm.   16 whom OA: *om.* St.   19 and]
om. 93.   20–1 continuance] countenance Cl, Hm.   21 desire] desires Bo, Hm.
22 named] *om.* Cl, As.   26 The last book or act] Here endeth the fifth and last
book or act of the Countess of Pembroke's Arcadia Cl; *om.* As, Da; FINIS 93; The end
of the fifth and last book of Arcadia 98.

COMMENTARY

DEDICATION

THIS was printed on sigs. A3ʳ–A4ʳ of the 1590 edition of the *New Arcadia*, and reprinted in the 1593 and all the later folios. Although it is not in any of the *Old Arcadia* manuscripts, it must have been composed for the earlier completed work. It was evidently sent by Sidney to his sister, from whom the editors of 90 must have obtained it, with her manuscript copy of the *Old Arcadia* (P), and no copy was placed with his own OA transcript (T).

PAGE **3**, 3. *most dear . . . lady.* This is the first phrase copied in Folger Shakespeare Library, MS. V. b. 83 (formerly 413. 3); ff. 1–15 contain extracts taken from 93 or a later folio edition of the *Arcadia*. Cf. Marston, *The Malcontent*, iv. 1, 'and so ye shall ever remain most dear, and worthy to be most dear ladies'; and Harington, Dedication to Queen Elizabeth.

4 and 15. See Ringler, 383, for comment on this negligent pose of the Renaissance gentleman, maintained even in the family circle, and Introduction, p. xvi; and cf. AS **18**. 9, 'My youth doth waste, my knowledge brings forth toys'.

6–9. *as the cruel . . . father.* Goldman, 146, compares Castiglione, *The Courtier*, trans. Hoby, ed. Raleigh, p. 367, '[his book] deserved not to have any more store made of him, but (like an untimely birth) to be left in the highway for the benefit of nature'.

16–17. *being done . . . presence.* A good deal of the *Old Arcadia* was almost certainly written while Sidney was staying with his sister at Wilton; see Introduction, pp. xv ff.

THE FIRST BOOK OR ACT

PAGE **4**, 3–14. *Arcadia . . . done so.* Brie, 71, suggests that this description of the well-tempered minds of the Arcadians was based on Aristotle, *Politics*, iv. 15 and iii. 4; but, as the next sentence indicates (see note to p. 6, 26–7), Sidney could scarcely write of Arcadian shepherds without having Virgil's *Eclogues* in mind. Cf. *Defence of Poesy* (*Works*, iii. 22), where Sidney claims that pastorals 'sometimes show that contentions for trifles can get but a trifling victory, where perchance a man may see that even Alexander and Darius, when they strave who should be cock of this world's dunghill, the benefit they got was that the after-livers may say, *Haec memini et victum frustra contendere Thirsim. Ex illo Coridon, Coridon est tempore nobis.*' [Virgil, *Eclogues*, vii. 69–70.]

31–2. *nature is no stepmother.* Cf. p. 285, 3, AS **vii**. 1 and Sir Thomas Chaloner, trans. Erasmus, *The Praise of Folly*, ed. C. H. Miller, p. 29, 'nature . . . rather a stepdame than a mother'.

PAGE **5**, 5–6. *perpetual . . . life.* Cf. p. 150, 29, AS **39**. 2, and Sidney's metrical version of Psalm **39**. 40. Parallels from Cicero and Seneca for this contrast between the earth or the body and the heavens or the soul as a *hospitium* rather than a *domus* are cited in *N. & Q.* xxxvii (1868), 516 and xxxviii (1869), 541.

7–8. *wherein . . . uncertainty.* There are no pre-nineteenth-century citations for this 'sentence' in *O.D.E.P.*, but cf. Guevara, *A Dispraise of the Life of a Courtier* (1548), C1^r, 'there is nothing in this world so certain as that all things is uncertain'; and Tilley, N276, 'I know nothing except that I know not' (1542), and N316, 'Nothing is so certain as death' (for which the earliest citation in *O.D.E.P.* is dated *c.* 1300).

15–21. Ringler, OA 1 and p. 383. See Introduction, pp. xxxiv–xxxv, for Sidney's use of the oracle, and p. lxii, for comment on the additional lines in NA.

PAGE 6, 26–7. *sports . . . excel.* The Arcadians were famous for their skill in music; cf. Virgil, *Eclogues*, x. 32, 'Soli cantare periti Arcades'.

36–PAGE 8, 32. *Most . . . imagined.* Lanham, 241–4, compares the rhetorical structure of Philanax's address to Basilius with that of Sidney's *Discourse to the Queen's Majesty*; see also Goldman, 206, and again in *J.E.G.P.* liv (1955), 526–48.

PAGE 7, 3–9. *wisdom . . . virtue.* Brie, 118, compares Aristotle, *Ethics*, iv. 13; and Dent, 215, compares *The Duchess of Malfi*, II. ii. 311–14.

8. *oppress it.* 'oppress virtue'.

16–17. *But since . . . done.* Fraunce, 43, quotes as an example of epistrophe, 'conversion or turning to the same sound in the end, is when the like sound is iterated in the endings'.

29–31. *no destiny . . . goodness.* Brie, 118, compares Aristotle, *Politics*, iv. 1.

PAGE 8, 22–4. *O no . . . unassayed.* Fraunce, 43, quotes as an example of epistrophe, and again on 111, with the rest of the sentence, to illustrate utterance; he misread *unassayed* in St as *unassayld*.

Abelard, *Dialectics*, maintained that all knowledge is good, even that which relates to evil, because a righteous man must have it. Since he must guard against evil, it is necessary that he should know it beforehand, otherwise he could not shun it (cited in Taylor, *The Medieval Mind* (1914), ii. 379). *that* (line 24), 'the test'.

26. The blank left for *seemed* in Bo and the unsatisfactory alteration in Ph indicate that T was confused, and I have adopted 90's tidying up of the text.

PAGE 9, 26. *towardness. fowndnes* was probably a misreading. When he saw that there was no hope of furthering his argument, Philanax descended to capping Basilius's pliant reeds with firm rocks; see Introduction, pp. xxix f.

30. *the beauty of the world.* Ringler, 553, notes that Sir John Harington headed his transcript of AS x 'To the beauty of the world'. Harington knew that Stella represented Penelope Rich in AS; but even if he took the phrase (probably a common one; cf. p. 237, 41 and *Hamlet*, II. ii. 310) from his OA MS., it does not necessarily follow that he thought Philoclea was also intended to represent her.

PAGE 10, 9 and 34 f. Ringler, 376, shows that the geography in OA is vague and meagre compared with the precise indications in NA. Nevertheless, Sidney may have glanced at a map of Greece when he named the three countries that attacked Euarchus simultaneously on three fronts. Epirus lay to the west of Macedon and Thessalia; Pannonia was a large country to the north of Dalmatia;

and Thrace stretched away to the east. Like Philip of Macedon (who also con-
quered Pannonia), Euarchus reduced Thrace to subjection. When the princes
took ship from Thessalia for Byzantium they could have been driven to the coast
of Lydia (p. 11, 2); but Ringler is rightly sceptical of their one year's adventures
extending over Asia Minor, Syria, and Egypt.

20–30. *Pyrocles . . . well doing.* Davis, *Map*, 157, compares the *paideia* out-
lined in Plato's *Republic.* Zandvoort, 143, compares the birth and education of
Rogel de Grèce and his cousin Agesilan in *Amadis de Gaule*, XI. iii.

PAGE 11, 5–6. *it is work . . . mine.* Some of the adventures are related in the OA
eclogues; but Sidney's remark could be taken as evidence that when he under-
took the expansion of them in NA he was embarking on a higher form of art.

14–15. *wherein . . . dazzled.* 'rulers have most difficulty in seeing the true
nature of their own countries'.

22–31. *picture . . . suspected.* For Sidney's interest in the technique of the
artist see Ringler's note on AS **7.** 3–4 and Buxton, 151.

38—PAGE 12, 3. *it received . . . love.* In the *Amadis* both Agesilan and Amadis
fall in love through seeing pictures of their ladies; see Introduction, p. xxii.
There is a further parallel in *Primaléon de Grèce*, i. 50, 'Comme don Douard,
fils aîné du Roi d'Angleterre, s'enamoura de la belle Gridonie, voyant son
portrait contre un mur'.

PAGE 12, 25–6. *would . . . it.* 'was sometimes willing to consign away his whole
estate for the sake of the grass on which Philoclea might tread'.

PAGE 13, 1–3. *For . . . laws.* Unlike Pyrocles, Musidorus has been pursuing the
proper educative purposes of foreign travel for a young prince. Cf. Sidney's
letter to his brother Robert (*Works*, iii. 124–7).

PAGE 14, 23–PAGE 17, 9. *And yet . . . lovers.* 'Whether the contemplative or the
active life do excel' is one of the examples of the subjects that philosophers
wrangle about in the *Defence of Poesy* (*Works*, iii. 20). Petrarch's *De Vita Soli-
taria*, I. v, chapter 2, develops the theme that 'woods, fields, and streams are of
great advantage to the solitary'; cf. 'O sweet woods, the delight of solitariness'
(p. 166). *The Praise of Solitariness, set down in the form of a dialogue wherein is
contained a discourse philosophical, of the life active and contemplative* (1577) was
dedicated by the translator, Roger Baynes, 'To my approved friend, the right
worshipful Mr. Edward Dyer', who may have brought it to Sidney's notice.
See also note to p. 85, 19–21 and Castiglione, *The Courtier*, IV. xxiv–xxvi. Fogel,
197, compares Sidney's letter to Languet of 1 March 1578 (*Works*, iii. 119–
21); Rudenstine, 16–22, cites Languet's letters of 22 October 1578 and 24
October 1580 reproaching Sidney for retiring into a life of solitude. The rhetoric
of this debate is studied by P. A. Duhamel in *S.P.* xlv (1948), 134–50; and, with
emphasis on the comic intention, by Lanham, 244–56.

27–8. *the mind . . . broken.* Cf. Tilley, B561, and Sidney's letter to Languet of
11 February 1574 (Pears, 36), 'in your letters I fancy I see a picture of the age in
which we live: an age that resembles a bow too long bent, it must be unstrung
or it will break'.

PAGE 15, 2–3. *Eagles . . . together.* Cited by Tilley, E7, from this passage, which appears in Ling's *Politeuphuia*, 167b, in the section headed 'Proverbs', with the reading 'flock together'—as in *The Duchess of Malfi*, v. ii. 31–2 (Dent, 247).

14–27. *Do you . . . perfection.* Cf. *Diana*, ed. Kennedy, 292:

For who would not wonder at the lively green of this wood? and not be amazed at the beauty of this goodly meadow? For, to behold the diversity of coloured flowers, and the pleasant melody of chirping birds, is a thing so full of content and delight, that the glorious pomp and wealth of the bravest and most famous court is not comparable to it.

Marenco in *English Miscellany*, xvii (1966), 13, compares Lucretius v. 785, 'florida fulserunt viridanti prata colore'. Rudenstine, 21, draws attention to similar praise of nature by the old shepherd Dorcas in LM (*Works*, ii. 335 f.).

PAGE 16, 16–19. *the gods . . . employ them.* This is quoted in both *Palladis Tamia* and *Politeuphuia*. Dent, 291, compares *The Devil's Law-Case*, I. i. 70–2.

PAGE 17, 4–9. *or else . . . lovers.* Cf. Shakespeare, *A Midsummer Night's Dream*, v. i. 2–22.

11. *tarantula.* O.E.D. cites this passage for the use of the name of the spider for the disease, *tarantism*, which its bite was thought to cause. In NA it is made clear that the person suffering from this hysterical disease danced (*Works*, i. 58 f.). The reference was apparently introduced to England by Hoby's translation of *The Courtier* (1561); but cf. *Amadis de Gaule*, XI. lvi, where Lardenie and Diane, trying to revive Daraïde from a swoon, recall that music can even cure wounds, as it does 'en une contrée ceux qui sont piquez des serpens nommez Tarantes'.

PAGE 18, 3–4. *even . . . laurel.* Apollo chased Daphne in the valley of Tempe, which Musidorus has just mentioned. The story is told in Ovid, *Met.* i. 452 ff., and was a favourite subject of Renaissance poets and painters. K. Duncan-Jones, 18–19, refers to the illustration in the *Metamorphoses*, ed. Virgil Solis (Frankfort, 1563), I. xiv; and to the decorated capital D used in Pasqual Caracciolo, *La Gloria del Cavallo* (Venice, 1566), p. 246. Sidney recommended this book to his brother (*Works*, iii. 133). See also Kalstone, 49 and 115.

8–12. *I am . . . husband.* See Introduction, pp. xxi f., for the parallels in *Amadis*.

21. *Cleophila.* Agesilan's friend Garaye falls in love with Cléophile in *Amadis*, xi. Sidney may have worked back to 'Philoclea' from this name, or formed his heroine's name on the analogy of Heliodorus's Chariclea.

PAGE 19, 4–8. *born . . . home.* Rudenstine, 19 and 214, compares Languet's reproaches to Sidney (Pears, 2 and 185), and AS 21. 6–11.

10–11. *drown . . . haven.* Cf. Tilley, H219.

14–PAGE 23, 5. *the reasonable . . . possesseth me.* The whole debate on earthly and heavenly love, love and beauty, love and virtue, echoes passages in the *Symposium* and *Phaedrus*, with some resemblances to Serranus's introductions to these works in Stephanus's edition of Plato, which was sent to Sidney in 1579. A summary version of the debate is to be found in AS 14. 6–13 (Ringler, 466); and Musidorus's plea to Pyrocles to respect his birth and education is echoed in AS 21. 5–7:

> That Plato I read for naught, but if he tame
> Such coltish gyres, that to my birth I owe
> Nobler desires . . .

See also Davis, *Map*, 69–72.

14–16. *the reasonable . . . rebellion.* Ringler, 461, compares AS **5.** 1–4:

> It is most true that eyes are formed to serve
> The inward light: and that the heavenly part
> Ought to be king, from whose rules who do swerve,
> Rebels to nature, strive for their own smart.

17–21. *wherein . . . womanish.* Ringler, 475, compares AS **47.** 9–11.

18–21. *Nay, . . . womanish.* Fraunce, 43, quotes as his third example of epistrophe, reading 'I will not, *is* womanish'; Hoskyns also quotes, from NA (*Works*, i. 77), as a kind of division.

28–30. *there . . . viciousness.* Cf. Languet to Sidney, 28 November 1577 (Pears, 126):

> You are in error if you suppose that men naturally grow better as they grow older: the case is very rare. They do indeed become more cautious, and learn to conceal their moral faults and their evil affections; but if you know an old man in whom you think there are some remains of honesty, be sure he was a good man in his youth.

PAGE **20,** 21. *distaff-spinner.* In NA (*Works*, i. 75–6), when he was disguised as a woman, Pyrocles adopted the device of Hercules spinning wool for Omphale. Cf. *Defence of Poesy* (*Works*, iii. 40).

PAGE **21,** 17–18. *are framed . . . as we are*; and 33. *virtue in a fair lodging.* Cf. *England's Parnassus*, no. 1754:

> . . . Women be
> Framed with the same parts of the mind as we,
> Nay nature triumphed in their beauties' birth,
> And women made the glory of the earth:
> The life of beauty, in whose supple breasts,
> And in her fairest lodging virtue rests,
> Whose towering thoughts, attended with remorse,
> Do make their fairness be of greater force.

26. *since . . . hawk.* Cf. Tilley, K114.

PAGE **22,** 5–22. *And poor . . . loves.* Rudenstine, 47–8, compares *Defence of Poesy* (*Works*, iii. 30):

> Alas Love, I would thou couldst as well defend thyself as thou canst offend others. I would those on whom thou dost attend could either put thee away or yield good reason why they keep thee. But grant love of beauty to be a beastly fault, although it be very hard, since only man and no beast hath that gift to discern beauty; grant that lovely name of love to deserve all hateful reproaches (although even some of my masters the philosophers spent a good deal of their lamp oil in setting forth the excellency of it); grant, I say, what they will have granted, that not only love, but lust, but vanity, but if they list scurrility, possess many leaves of the poets' books; yet think I, when this is granted, they will find their sentence may with good manners put the last words foremost; and not say that poetry abuseth man's wit, but that man's wit abuseth poetry.

20–1. *virtue . . . book.* Cf. p. 91, 31–2 and p. 322, 10 and note.

PAGE **23,** 3. *disputations . . . schools.* An admission that Sidney has just given us another of the popular debating topics in places where they teach; see note to p. 14, 23–p. 17, 9.

PAGE **24,** 17–18. *insomuch . . . deal with me.* Fraunce, 123, quotes as an example of the shaking of the head to denote grief; like Je, he reads *grief* for *griefs*.

20–2. *If you seek . . . imperfections.* Fraunce, 103, quotes as an example of sufferance, 'when we mockingly give leave to do somewhat'. With Pyrocles' expostulation to Musidorus compare AS 14, 'Alas, have I not pain enough my friend'; and AS 21.

23. *swan . . . blackness.* Sidney's version of Tilley, C851, 'The crow thinks her own birds whitest'.

36. *crossing his arms.* A common sign of melancholy; cf. AS **viii.** 19.

PAGE **26,** 24–5. *careless . . . art.* Cf. *Defence of Poesy* (Works, iii. 43), and Shepherd, 231.

26. *paragon.* See Introduction, p. lxv, for comment on the variants. *Paragon* is used for 'a model for comparison' in NA (*Works,* i. 104); and as a verb (*Works,* i. 110—the earliest citation in *O.E.D.*); see also *Diana,* ed. Kennedy, **126.** 37 and **397.** 21.

31–3. *Upon . . . in it.* J. A. van Dorsten in *English Studies,* xlviii (1967), 1–7, notes that Sidney's arms have the same colours as Pyrocles' blue and gold doublet.

PAGE **27,** 6. *a certain mantle.* This is the reading of all the texts, except for the omission of *certain* in Je, and is no vaguer than 'a kind of doublet' (p. 26, 31); and the title-page of 93 shows Pyrocles in a medium-length cloak. Nevertheless, Sidney may have intended a contrast with the long apostle's mantle worn by Pyrocles at the trial scene (p. 373, 2 and note), and wrote *curtal* or *curted*—a curtal friar was one who wore a short cloak.

9–12. *rich . . . eagle.* Sidney's interest in devices (see Buxton, 148–50) finds expression in the knights' imprese in NA: there are only two more, both jewels, in OA (see p. 37 and p. 108). The eagle (Pyrocles) has been overcome by the dove (Philoclea).

13–14. *such a look . . . grieved him.* The paradox of contrary emotions in one face was much affected by Achilles Tatius; for example *Clitophon and Leucippe,* VI. vii, 'with tears and laughter'. Cf. NA (*Works,* i. 6), 'sorrow seemed to smile'.

28. *mettle.* The spellings in the manuscripts and *O.E.D.* citations indicate that the word was scarcely distinguished from *metal* at this date.

PAGE **28,** 16–21. *Yet . . . with him.* Cf. Tilley, S927, 'It is hard/folly to strive against the stream'; and p. 354, 24–5.

30–PAGE **29,** 8. Ringler, OA 2 and p. 384, where the improvements effected by the revisions preserved in 90 are analysed. The poem is copied in C.U.L. MS. Dd.5.75(2), f. 38, probably from another manuscript miscellany, deriving in turn from an OA MS., with no indication of authorship. There is also a copy in B.M. MS. Addit. 34064, f. 28, taken from 93, with no indication of authorship (Ringler, 554–5).

PAGE **29,** 32. *pantable.* This was the commonest corruption 1580–1650, and the readings of the manuscripts suggest that Dametas used it rather than *pantofle.*

PAGE **30,** 23–PAGE **31,** 4. Ringler, OA 3 and p. 384, where earlier examples of English mock blazons are given. C. W. Lemmi in *M.L.N.* xlii (1927), 78–9, and Scott, 16–17, cite Berni's Sonnet II, 'Sopra le bellezze della sua innamorata' (imitated by Du Bellay, *Regrets*, 91, and by M. de Saint-Gelais). Berni does not invoke the characteristics of the gods, and borrowing seems to be confined to two or three 'precious things' in Sidney's sestet; but see A. Guidi in *Paideia*, xv (1960), 3–8. T. N. Marsh in *English Miscellany*, xiii (1962), 25–9, compares Tasso, *Rime* xxxvii, 'Sopra la bellezza', and suggests that Donne's 2nd elegy was influenced by Sidney's poem; see also *The Elegies . . . of John Donne*, ed. H. Gardner, p. 138.

The poem is copied in C.U.L. MS. Dd.5.75(2), f. 37ᵛ, with no indication of authorship; in B.M. MS. Harl. 6910, f. 145ᵛ, subscribed 'P.S.'; and in Harl. 7392(2), f. 75, attributed to Sidney—all substantive texts (Ringler, 554, 556, and 557). Another copy, from one of the printed editions, is in the Bodleian MS. Rawl. Poet. 142, f. 26ᵛ (Ringler, 558). It is no. 2058 in *England's Parnassus*, where it is printed from 98 (Ringler, 565). It was imitated in 'An old ditty of Sir Philip Sidney's omitted in the printed Arcadia' printed in 1655 and later editions of *Arcadia*, and also attributed to Sidney in four late seventeenth-century MSS.; it was probably composed by Sir John Mennes or James Smith (Ringler, 351). There is another imitation in a seventeenth-century miscellany (Bodleian, MS. Eng. Poet. f. 27, pp. 99–101) entitled 'An Imitation of Sir Philip Sidney's Encomium of Mopsa'.

23. *What length of verse.* Sidney uses the lumbering poulter's measure (for the first and last time) to underline his burlesque intention.

29. Saturn is ugly, Venus wanton.

30. Pan is rough and shaggy, Juno wrathful. Ringler emends *Iris* to *Isis* who was *faced* like a cow, on the grounds that Iris is 'fast' and it is not ironical to call her so. 'Faste' (the spelling of several of the texts) is a normal spelling for 'faced', and gives a satisfactory rhyme for 'chaste'. But *Iris* is the reading of all the texts, and *fast* as well as 'swift' also means 'steadfast'. The rainbow that 'comes and goes' is the opposite of steadfast.

31. Cupid is blind, Vulcan lame.

32. Momus is censorious.

33. Jacinth is blue or yellow, opal many-coloured.

34. *twinkling . . . pearl.* Cf. Berni, 'occhi di perle vaghi'.

PAGE **31**, 1. *crapal.* Chelonitis, the stone in the head of a toad described in the bestiaries, generally as tortoiseshell in colouring, occasionally green. Cotgrave gives the word as 'crapaudine' and the common English form would appear to have been 'crapaud'—Sidney's derives from med. L. *crapollus*.

mouth . . . wide. Cf. Berni, 'bocca ampia celeste'.

2. *Her skin . . . gold.* Cf. Berni, 'un bel viso d'oro'.

untried. unsmelted silver ore is black.

3–4. W. Blount quotes Ovid's account of Apollo gazing upon Daphne 'si qua latent meliora putat' (*Met.* i. 502); cf. Golding's version (lines 606–7) with Sidney's couplet.

4. Ringler, 48, compares AS **77**. 14, 'Yet ah, my Maiden Muse doth blush to tell the best!'

will. This seems marginally the better reading; and I have therefore stuck to my copy-text rather than adopting, as Ringler does with some reservation, the reading of the earlier manuscripts and of 90, *well.*

5–22. *The beginning . . . herdman.* Danby and Muir in *N. & Q.* cxcv (1950), 51, suggest that Shakespeare may have had in mind Sidney's distinction between 'rudeness' and 'plainness' in *King Lear*, I. i. 131 and 150, and more particularly when, later in the play, to Kent's declaration that it is his 'occupation to be plain', Cornwall retorts that Kent calls his 'saucy roughness' plainness (II. ii. 98–110).

19–20. *fancied . . . wisdom.* Basilius thought that Dametas would become wise through conversing with him. In NA the sentence is altered to 'fancied that his weakness with his presence would much be mended' (*Works*, i. 22).

31–2. *Hercules . . . head.* Raging Hercules became a stock character like Herod and Termagant. For Sidney's contrast between actor and character, cf. *A Midsummer Night's Dream*, I. ii. 25, where Bottom declares that he could 'play Ercles rarely', and *Love's Labour Lost*, V. ii. 584, where the diminutive Moth plays Hercules.

PAGE **32**, 29–30. *Maid Marian.* In may-games and morris dances the part of Maid Marian was often taken by a man dressed as a woman—Dametas is evidently suspicious.

38. *Latona.* When she knelt down to quench her thirst at a fountain in Delos, she was insulted by some Lycian clowns, who were then turned into frogs (Ovid, *Met.* vi. 160).

PAGE **34**, 35–6. *was . . . approaches.* Ph substitutes 'he ran back again to the lodge, as if he had told the duke he would take his part in anything but blows'. This has no authority; Dametas does withdraw a little, but remains within earshot (p. 37, 1).

PAGE **36**, 21–3. *Senicia . . . Pyrrhus.* W. Blount refers to Virgil, *Aeneid*, i. 491 ff., but in his Commentary Servius says that Penthesilea was killed by Achilles; the deed is attributed to his son Pyrrhus by Dares, by Lydgate in *Troy Book*, iv. 4321–36, and by other writers, and this is the tradition followed by Spenser, *The Faerie Queene*, II. iii. 31. 'Senicia' would seem to be a coinage analogous to 'Gynecia'.

33–4. *well acquainted passengers.* 'well known travellers'; the rapacity of the innkeeper is brought out in NA by substituting 'well paying' (*Works*, i. 89).

PAGE **37**, 14. *mountainets.* The correction in 90, and the unfamiliarity of the word (the first citation in *O.E.D.* is from this passage in NA, the next being from the Countess of Pembroke's metrical version of Psalm **68**. 41) support this reading.

18 (var.). The change from *impresa* (the earliest citation in *O.E.D.* is from Greene's *Menaphon*, 1589) to *picture* (line 15) shows that the aside was intentionally omitted from St and Bo. The reflection is inappropriate as Pamela had decided not to have a motto; in NA the jewel has a different emblem and a motto. Cf. Ruscelli's statement, echoed by numerous writers, that the *parole* is the *anima* of an impresa. See note to p. 27, 9–12.

25–6. *net . . . disposition.* Cf. AS **12**. 2.

PAGE **38**, 17. *these great princes.* The reading of St is 'thies great Princesse'. I think that Pyrocles wished to include Basilius, to whom he has just explained (p. 36, 20) that it is against the custom of his country to make obeisance.

PAGE **39**, 34–PAGE **40**, 15. *she might . . . thee.* Fraunce, 88, quotes as an example of a perfect prosopopoeia.

34–5. *apparel of a shepherd.* See Introduction, p. xxii, for the parallel in *Amadis.*

PAGE **40**, 3–12. Ringler, OA 4 and p. 385, where *guest* in line 5 is explained as Musidorus's body in shepherd's clothes. The poem was printed in *England's Helicon* from 98 (Ringler, 564); and the second stanza was set to music for five voices by Francis Pilkington, *The Second Set of Madrigals and Pastorals* (1624), no. 14; the words were taken from one of the printed editions. Words and music were edited by E. H. Fellowes, *The English Madrigal School*, xxvi (1923) (Ringler, 567); and the words are reprinted in Fellowes, 3rd edn., p. 197.

PAGE **41**, 27. *servant of his.* His name is given as Kalodoulus on p. 409.

PAGE **42**, 7–8. *I . . . express it.* Sidney invented the speech in NA (*Works*, i. 113).

PAGE **44**, 2. *pastorals . . . termed.* O.E.D. cites this passage to illustrate *pastorals* B †2, 'pastoral games and pastimes'. Sidney's explanation indicates the novelty of the term.

32. *so as.* 'provided that'.

PAGE **45**, 33. *but after.* 'except in'.

PAGE **46**, 6. *pebble stones.* The commonest spelling in the manuscripts is *pible*; St's nasalized form is found in Frampton, *Joyful News* (1577), 'pure pimple stones of a brook or river'.

PAGE **47**, 21–6. *strake . . . force.* The changes made in this combat reduce the gravity of Cleophila's wound, but increase to two the blows that she gives the lion.

29. *Arethusa . . . Alpheus.* The story is told in Ovid, *Met.* v. 572 ff.; but, as A. B. Taylor notes in *N. & Q.* xci (1969), 455, Arethusa was naked, and Sidney's ensuing description is closer to that of Daphne fleeing from Apollo in lines 530–3, and in *Met.* i (cf. in particular Golding's translation, lines 606–7 and 641–5). Sidney refers to the story of Daphne on pp. 18, 143, and 293.

32. *twice-wounded.* Once by his love for Philoclea, and once by the lion.

PAGE **48**, 31–3. *unnatural . . . blood.* The idea goes back to Pliny; cf. 1 *Henry IV*, II. iv. 268–9, 'the lion will not touch the true prince'.

PAGE **49**, 15 ff. See Introduction, p. xxii, for Sidney's indebtedness to the *Amadis* for his story.

PAGE **50**, 6–9. *For both . . . beauty.* Gynecia's skill in surgery has many precedents, starting with the royal Agamede who knew all herbs and their virtues (*Iliad* xi. 740). Cf. Harington, 147, marginal note to xix. 16 on surgery: 'This art, as Sir P. Sidney noteth in his Arcadia, was in great estimation in time past.'

32–4. *with mind . . . Pamela.* There seems no reason why this passage should have been cancelled; indeed NA's '(thinking of her friend Dorus)' (*Works*, i. 121) would seem to derive from it. I have therefore concluded that the omission in St and Bo was accidental.

PAGE **51,** 9–20. Ringler, OA 5 and p. 385, where Cm, 90, and 93 variants are dismissed as errors in G. Dametas appropriately gives thanks to Pan, the god of shepherds.

9–14. These lines, taken from one of the printed folios 93–05, were set as a round for six voices by Thomas Ravenscroft, *Pammelia. Music's Miscellany* (1609), no. 95. The words and music were edited by P. Warlock (1928); and the words are printed in Fellowes, 3rd edn., p. 218. Ravenscroft's music and version of Sidney's words were transcribed as no. 68 in 'Ane buik of roundells . . . collected and notted by david Melvill 1612'; this manuscript (now in the Library of Congress) was edited by G. Bantock and H. O. Anderton for the Roxburghe Club, 1916. J. P. Cutts prints Ravenscroft's music and Melvill's copy in *Renaissance News*, xi (1958), 183–8 (Ringler, 567).

13–14. Fraunce, 25, quotes these lines as an example of synedoche of the general, 'when by the general we intend the special, so the plural for the singular'. They are inaccurately quoted by Sir John Harington in a note to *The Metamorphosis of Ajax* (1594), ed. Donno, p. 203, and there attributed to 'Dametas in *Arcadia*'.

PAGE **52,** 16–17. *But long . . . for.* Ph substitutes 'And much further he would have used that present action is hard to be guessed of'.

28. *of reward.* Ph adds 'though not the reward he aspired unto'.

33–PAGE **53,** 1. *For . . . death.* The usual action of a coward, according to Ariosto; cf. *The Faerie Queene*, II. iii. 21, where Braggadochio 'crept under a bush'.

PAGE **53,** 16. *Pallas . . . Gorgon.* Perseus gave the head of Medusa, one of the three Gorgons, to Minerva (Pallas Athena), who had helped to arm him.

17–18. *killing . . . lion.* The first labour of Hercules.

THE FIRST ECLOGUES

PAGE **56.** The first set of eclogues is concerned, like the preceding book, with the theme of unrequited love. For the description of the musical and poetical Arcadians, which was used and expanded at the beginning of NA (*Works*, i. 14 ff.), see p. 6, 26–7 and note.

PAGE **57,** 6. *speaking in looks.* Ph substitutes 'both with foot and hand'.

8. *ambassade.* Sidney liked this word, and *heraldry, herald*, were probably scribal substitutions.

11. *corrosive.* Cl's *corosy* was an attempt to reproduce the more correct form rather than the corrupt *corsie*.

15. *a combat.* The copyist of St seems to have accepted *accombat* as a word; see p. 48, 6.

35–PAGE **58,** 14. Ringler, OA 6 and p. 385. This poem is not in Le. It is no. 64 in *England's Helicon*, headed 'The Shepherds' brawl, one half answering the other'; the text is taken from 98 (Ringler, 564).

35 and PAGE 58, 2. These lines may have inspired the opening of Weelkes, *Balletts and Madrigals* (1598), no. 18, 1–2:

> I love and have my love regarded,
> And sport with sport as well rewarded.

See Fellowes, 3rd edn., p. 289.

E. Seaton compares P. Fletcher, *Venus and Anchises* (ed. 1926, p. 103):

> He no play regarded
> And fit love to reward, and with love to be rewarded.

PAGE 58, 4 and 6. 'Affection's snare is sweet; but care, full of despair, is sour'.
8. 'Who can despair if he is borne up by hope?'

17–22. *which . . . Dorus.* Neither Cl's insertion for *For* before *which*, nor 90's omission of *he* before *began* (20), really tidies up the construction, which requires some verb after *Lalus*—e.g. 'which Lalus . . . *proceeded to do*'. Lalus (renamed Thyrsis in 93) is the name of an old shepherd in LM.

23–PAGE 64, 4. Ringler, OA 7 and pp. 385–7. The poem was revised in T after St and Bo were copied; these revisions appear in 90, but 93 reverted to the OA text in P for some readings. The earliest English example of a singing-match appears to be the contest between Therion and Espilus in LM, which is a simpler affair than this poem or the one in Spenser's 'August'. Spenser concentrates on the song, Sidney on the match as a contest of skill. Dorus has to reply to each of Lalus's stanzas in the same metre, using the same kind of rhyme; the roles are reversed, and Lalus is finally defeated. The progressive stages of the competition are analysed by Ringler, 385–6. Sidney outdoes his probable models, Sannazaro's 2nd Eclogue in *Arcadia*, and Gil Polo's Third Song in Book VI of the *Diana* (ed. Kennedy, 224).

23–8 and PAGE 59, 1–6. Sir John Harington, Preface to *Orlando Furioso* (G. G. Smith, *Elizabethan Critical Essays*, ii. 221), quotes from these two stanzas in his defence of two- and three-syllable rhymes:

> But in a word to answer this, and to make them for ever hold their peaces of this point, Sir Philip Sidney not only useth them, but affecteth them—*signify*, *dignify*, *shamed is*, *named is*, *blamed is*, *hide away*, *bide away*. Though if my many blotted papers that I have made in this kind might afford me authority to give a rule of it, I would say that to part them with a one syllable metre between them would give it best grace.

In the *Defence of Poesy* (*Works*, iii. 44–5), Sidney argues that English was superior to French or Italian for poetry, because it was rich in masculine, feminine, and three-syllable rhymes.

27–8. Ph substitutes:

> He gathers up each word a true heart scattereth,
> For in a yielding praise his triumph framed is.

29. Cf. p. 142, 9–10 and p. 329, 30 and note.
30. Cf. Tilley, W742, 'Wood half-burnt is easily kindled'.
31. Cf. Tilley, W930 (first citation from Lyly's *Euphues*), 'The wound that bleedeth inwardly is most dangerous'.
32. Ringler, 362, compares LM 2. 14, 'As shallow brooks do yield the greatest sound'. This is the earliest example in *O.D.E.P.*; cf. Tilley, W130 and W123.

PAGE 59, 11. *historify.* The earliest citation in *O.E.D.* is from the Countess of

Pembroke's metrical version of Psalm **76**. 10, which begins like this poem by rhyming on *signify/dignify*.

15–16. *help . . . spilled is*. Ph substitutes:

> best her nobleness notify
> A golden fire where sugar still distilled is.

16. *though . . . bee*. Rubel, 158, cites as an example of antanaclasis.

PAGE **60**, 12. *keep*. Ringler emends to *sheep*; but *keep*, the reading of all the texts, gives good sense: 'Shall I accustom myself to taking care of sheep?' See *O.E.D.*, s.v. keep, ii. 2.

13–14. *love of her . . . heart*. Ph substitutes: 'my senses harnished/In complete love'.

23. *and if . . . pleasure*. Ringler, 386, explains 'and if the failing of hope should end the pleasure of life'.

PAGE **61**, 1–12. Ringler, 386, calls attention to Dorus's reference to Pamela's swoon when she saw the bear (p. 52).

10. *open rays*. Pamela's eyes; *open* seems the correct reading, but *opened* has been determinedly squashed into St.

31–PAGE **62**, 1. Rubel, 158, cites as an example of a song made up of hybrid anadiplosis and internal rhyme that gives the effect of antistrophe.

33. W. Blount quotes Virgil, *Eclogues*, ii. 19–21 (Ringler, 387). Ringler, 363, compares LM **2**. 19, where Espilus wooes with the remark, 'Two thousand sheep I have as white as milk'.

34. *which . . . burn*. Ringler, 468, compares AS **22**. 14, 'The sun which others burned, did her but kiss'.

PAGE **62**, 20. *spirit's wars*. Ringler prints *spirits'*; but I think that the flowers represent the wars of Dorus's spirit, to correspond with 'despair my field'.

34–PAGE **63**, 4. These lines are copied in Bodleian MS. Rawl. Poet. 85, f. 65ᵛ, without ascription (Ringler, 557).

PAGE **63**, 12. Ringler prints *others'*; but I fancy that Dorus has his only being in Pamela's head.

14 (var.). Nashe quotes from 90 in *Summer's Last Will and Testament* (*Works*, ed. McKerrow, iii. 238):

> True is it that divinest Sidney sung,
> *O he is marred, that is for others made.*

23. This line is quoted by Davison, *A Poetical Rhapsody*, 'To the Reader' (ed. Rollins, i. 4 and note).

PAGE **64**, 1–4. A covert appeal by Musidorus to Pamela to pierce his disguise, which was heard 'without attention'.

18–28. *But . . . there*. Ringler notes that this picture and the verses that follow form an emblem.

34–PAGE **65**, 1. *indeed . . . title*. See Ovid, *Met.* i. 588 ff., for the story of Jove and Io; as Ringler notes, that Argus begot Cupid on Io is Sidney's invention. It is referred to as such in Florio's *Second Fruits* (1591), Y4:

> *Silvestro*. You run wide Sir, Love is the grandchild of nature, and first born of beauty, by her husband pleasure.

Pandolpho. There lay a straw, for you to shoot wide, hold your hand a while, his grandam was idleness (as Seneca says), his mother beggary, as Plato tells us, his father Erebus, as Lucian reporteth, or Argus, as Sir Philip Sidney declareth in drawing of his pedigree.

PAGE **65,** 5–6. The story of Pan and Syrinx is told by Ovid, *Met.* i. 689 ff. Cf. Sannazaro, *Arcadia*, 10th Prose; and p. 143, 19–20.

9–PAGE **66,** 22. Ringler, OA 8 and pp. 387–8. The poem was revised in T after St and Bo had been copied; 93 returns to P.

18. 'Cupid caused Phoebus to fall in love with Daphne (Ovid, *Met.* i. 452 ff.). That Love was the youngest and oldest of the gods had been a commonplace since the time of Plato (*Symposium*, 178 B and 197 A)' (Ringler).

19–20. 'The arrow of gold kindles love, that of lead causes disdain (*Met.* i. 470–1); the third arrow with the head of horn (for cuckoldry) is Sidney's invention' (Ringler, 387).

21–6. See note to p. 64, 34–p. 65, 1.

33–PAGE **66,** 4. Davis, *Map*, 123, commenting on NA (*Works*, i. 239–40), where the poem is transferred to Miso's prayer book, considers that part of the joke is that a description of Pan is taken for one of Eros. Dicus may have taken the cloven foot and horned head from Pan to show his opinion of love; Ringler remarks on the inconsistency of giving the song to Dicus who later praises married love (p. 245); but he does not do so in the Second Eclogue (p. 137).

PAGE **66,** 21. *hangman.* Cf. *Much Ado*, III. ii. 9–11, 'He hath twice or thrice cut Cupid's bow-string, and the little hangman dare not shoot at him'.

PAGE **67,** 27. *Otanes.* Sidney probably took the name from a Persian nobleman of the time of Darius, mentioned by Herodotus. In NA he becomes Tiridates, king of Armenia; but there is an Otanes (spelt Otaues in 90), brother of Barzanes. Some OA MSS. spell Octaves or Otaues.

PAGE **68,** 27–8. *Plangus . . . Iberia.* At p. 67, 2–3 Plangus is merely 'an Iberian nobleman'; in NA he is the king's only son.

PAGE **71,** 31. *Philisides.* Sidney's name for his poetic persona, formed by adding a Greek termination to the first elements of his names; the derivation φιλ-sidus, 'star-lover', was probably an afterthought, later replaced by the etymologically sounder *Astrophil*. He is discovered in the customary pose of the poet introduced into his own pastoral poem (e.g. Sannazaro as Sincero in his *Arcadia*), established by the opening of Virgil's 1st Eclogue, 'Tityre, tu patulae recubans sub tegmine fagi'.

PAGE **72,** 3–PAGE **76,** 4. Ringler OA 9 and pp. 388–9, where the indebtedness to Sannazaro's 8th Eclogue is recorded, but Sidney's more intricate metrical structure and more dramatic debate, are pointed out. Rudenstine, 35–9, suggests that Geron's moral advice is closer to that of the wise old shepherds in Mantuan's 2nd and 3rd Eclogues (he cites the versions of George Turberville and Barnabe Googe). Cf. also Cuddie and Thenot in Spenser's 'February'.

3–7. Fraunce, 54, quotes with the note, 'Sir Philip Sidney, i, hath a rhyme wherein the last word of the first doth jump in sound with the middle of the second'.

11. This is the earliest citation in *O.D.E.P.*; cf. Tilley, O28.

34. Rubel, 158, cites as an example of antanaclasis, combined with epizeuxis and zeugma.

PAGE **73,** 7–12. Fogel, 236, suggests that this is Geron's criticism of CS 3, 'The fire to see my wrongs for anger burneth'. Cf. line 9 with CS **3.** 20, 'Fire, air, sea, earth, fame, time, place, show your power'. As Ringler, 420, remarks, 'the four elements as ground of invention for a poem was a favourite device'; cf. p. 262, 6–7 and note.

12–14. Cf. p. 19, 14–16, where Musidorus urges the need to overthrow so unnatural a rebellion as that of the senses against reason.

16–30. Ringler, 388, notes that the attack on women is similar to that in Mantuan's 4th Eclogue, but that lines 22–4 translate Sannazaro's *Arcadia*, 8th Eclogue, 10–12:

> Nel'onde solca e nel'arene semena;
> E'l vago vento spera in rete accogliere
> Chi sue speranze fonda in cor de femina.

The idea in Sidney's line 22 is as old as the *Greek Anthology*, is found in Virgil and Ovid, and was given currency by Erasmus (see Tilley, S87, S89, and S184). Wyatt's version is close to Sidney:

> For he that believeth bearing in hand
> Ploweth in water and soweth in sand.
>
> *(Poems*, ed. Muir and Thomson, no. xiv)

Ringler, 428, compares the similar idea (Tilley, W114) in CS 13, 'Out of Catullus'; and CS **28.** 38–40, which is translated from the *Diana*, and Montemayor's next song (ed. Kennedy, 16) repeats the conceit. Cf. also p. 118, 29. The earliest English citation in Tilley, W416, for the idea in line 23 is from Wyatt:

> Since in a net I seek to hold the wind.
>
> *(Poems*, ed. Muir and Thomson, no. vii)

Sidney's lines were borrowed in *Two Italian Gentlemen* (Malone Society Reprint, 683–6), and in *Alcilia* (1595), Part II, Sonnet 26.

28–30. Ringler compares p. 161, 32–3, and Dyer, 'A Fancy':

> O frail unconstant kind, and safe in trust to no man,
> No women angels be, and lo, my mistress is a woman.

31–4. These two couplets of Histor's are an interpolation in the terza rima. Ringler, 388, suggests that Sidney added them to T after P was transcribed to cover the unwonted borrowing from Sannazaro in lines 22–4; but Fogel is probably right in thinking that they refer to the immediately preceding lines, so strikingly similar to Dyer's two. Histor's second couplet is much more appropriate to Dyer's 'He that his mirth hath lost' than to Sannazaro's Eclogue.

PAGE **74,** 1–2 and 12–13. Rudenstine, 112, compares Rixus's speech to the old shepherd Dorcas in LM (*Works*, ii. 334).

16–18. Ringler, 388, refers to Antipater's remark that the old orator Demades was like an animal that had been eaten at a sacrificial feast; there were left only the belly and the tongue.

18. Rubel, 157, cites as an example of synoeciosis.

34–6. Fogel compares Languet's letter to Sidney of 2 May 1578 (Pears, 147):
And yet, let them [men] be never so strong, in this respect they are inferior to many of the brutes. Make use then of that particle of the Divine Mind. . . .

PAGE 75, 22–31. Ringler, 388, notes that Geron's prescriptions are similar to those of Sannazaro's Eugenio (8th Eclogue, 121 ff.), but are even closer to Ovid's *Remedia Amoris*, 315–16 and 178–210.

PAGE 76, 12–13. *Melampus* and *Laelaps*. The names of two of Actaeon's dogs in Ovid, *Met.* iii. 206 and 211; in vii. 771 the dog given by Diana to Procris is called Lelaps. One of Montano's dogs in Sannazaro's 2nd Eclogue is called Melampus. See also Harington, *The Metamorphosis of Ajax*, ed. Donno, p. 110.

18–PAGE 79, 12. Ringler, OA 10 and p. 389. See Introduction, pp. xix–xx and xxxiii for Sidney's use of an 'old rustic language'; *mickle*, *sicker*, *sneb* are glossed by E. K. in *The Shepherds' Calendar*; *red* and *sickerly* are glossed by Speght in his edition of Chaucer.

19. With this line and p. 79, 12 compare Sannazaro's 2nd Eclogue, in which Montano urges his dogs against the wolves, 'Ite miei cani, ite Melampo, ed Adro'.

27. *jarl*. *O.E.D.* cites this passage and Sidney's letter to his brother Robert of 18 October 1580 (*Works*, iii. 132), 'The odd 30l. shall come with the hundred or else my father and I will jarle'. Wright records the word for Oxon., Wilts., and Worcs.

PAGE 77, 20. 'You who are fond of your dogs acknowledge your gratitude to them.'

33. Three children's games. In *blow point* small pieces of wood were puffed through a tube; see Brewer. However, W. Milgate, *The Satires, Epigrams . . . of John Donne*, p. 106, follows Grosart in equating *blow point* with *dust point*. In *hot cockles* one blindfolded player knelt down and had to guess the names of those who struck him; *keels* is a variant spelling of *kayles*, ninepins, mentioned in OP 4. 47.

PAGE 78, 12. *mickle warse*. I have followed the texts giving the form *warse* as being likely to represent Sidney's intentions.

23–PAGE 79, 1. Ringler comments that the fable, similar to Ovid's story of why the raven is black (*Met.* ii. 534 ff.), is probably Sidney's invention, and compares the previous invention concerning Cupid's parentage (p. 64, 34–6). Sidney ignores the popular belief that the swan sings only at death (but see p. 81, 33 and p. 329, 15), and concentrates on accounting for its silence during life. His explanation rests on the characteristic attributed to it in the bestiaries: jealousy (see J. A. W. Bennett, *The Parlement of Foules. An Interpretation*, p. 150).

27. *pie's pilled flattery*. Chaucer, *Parl.* 345, has the 'jangling pie'. For the probable pun in *pilled*, see Glossary.

28. *Cormorant's glut*. Cf. Chaucer, *Parl.* 362, 'The hote cormerant of glutonye'.

29. *falcon's fierceness*. Chaucer, *Parl.* 336, has the conventional 'gentle' (i.e. noble). *sparrow's lechery*. Chaucer, *Parl.* 351, calls him Venus' son. Cf. p. 257, 11.

30. Cf. Chaucer, *Parl.* 358, 'The waker goos; the cukkow ever unkinde'.

31. Hitherto the jealous swan has been accusing birds of their accepted faults; he now slanders the 'turtle true' (Chaucer, *Parl.* 557).

32–6. The ending of the fable with the calling of a parliament and the passing of a statute is surely intended to recall Chaucer's *The Parlement of Foules*.

PAGE 79, 22–PAGE 80, 12. Ringler, OA 11 and pp. 389–94. Dorus repeats the laments he and Pyrocles had uttered (pp. 42 ff.); he also attempts to advance his suit. The scansion model does not indicate the permissible variations.

24. M. Poirier in *Études Anglaises*, xi (1958), 152, compares Petrarch, Sonnet 99 'Amor, Fortuna e la mia mente, schiva'; and Sonnet 151, 'Amor, natura e la bella alma umile'; and Desportes, *Diane*, ii. vii, 'Madame, Amour, Fortune et tous les éléments'.

PAGE 80, 1. *choler adusted.* Ringler, 393, compares CS **17.** 51–2:

for physic true doth find
Choler adust is joyed in womankind.

and explains that when choler (one of the four humours of the body) loses its moisture through heat, melancholy results.

4. *Heraclitus.* Cf. *Defence of Poesy (Works,* iii. 22), where Sidney says that Heraclitus bewailed 'the weakness of mankind, and the wretchedness of the world'.

6. *a beauty divine.* Pamela.

13–PAGE **81,** 6. *Nota.* This note was evidently written on a loose sheet of paper, and not placed with T until fairly late. The scribe of St wrote it in the margins of 'Fortune, Nature, Love' and of the subsequent prose link. The scribe of As has a note on f. 39b, immediately after 'Fortune, Nature, Love', 'Write these rules', and f. 40a is left blank. The Note was first printed by Ringler in *Ph.Q.* xxix (1950), 70–4, and it is reprinted in Ringler, 391; I have gratefully followed his paragraphing and punctuation. He identifies the rules with those which Spenser reported to Harvey in October 1579 that Sidney and Dyer had prescribed for English measured verse; in April 1580 these rules are further stated to be 'the very same which M. Drant devised, but enlarged with M. Sidney's own judgement'. Ringler suggests that Sidney's rules may have had their starting-point in the copy of Gualtherus's *De Syllabarum et Carminum ratione* he owned at Shrewsbury; and that his interest in applying the principles to English verse may have been stimulated by such continental works as C. Tolomei's *Versi e regole della nuova poesia toscana* (1539), as well as by the experiments of the earlier English humanists. As Ringler notes, Sidney follows the Latin rule of position, but this conflicts with his adoption of English pronunciation as a guide to quantity. D. Attridge, 'The Elizabethan Experiments in English Quantitative Verse' (unpublished D.Phil. Diss., University of Cambridge, 1971), pp. 194–215, considers Sidney's rules and experiments.

33. *denizened.* Cf. AS **15.** 8.

PAGE **81,** 11. *fair . . . shamefastness.* Ph substitutes 'sweet deal of blushing blood'.

16–PAGE **82,** 14. Ringler, OA 12 and p. 394. The scansion model in St should also indicate alternative short final syllables in lines 2 and 4. CS 5 is written in rhyming sapphics, and OA 59 (p. 226) is 'an imitation in accentual iambics of a sapphic stanza' (Ringler, 409). Greville, *Caelica,* vi, also rhymes, and starts with eyes as messengers, 'Eyes, why did you bring unto me these graces'. Fraunce, 30, quotes the first three stanzas as an example of sapphics; at p. 81, 30 he attempts to emend St by reading 'become our losses'. Gil, *Logonomia Anglica*, ed. Jiriczek, p. 149, quotes the first stanza from 90.

28. Ph reads 'Yet dying our death be to her an honour'.

33. See p. 78, 23–p. 79, 1 and note.

PAGE **82,** 1. *the mute.* Whereas Da, Ph, and 90 added *the,* the metre is saved in St by spelling *muett* as a dissyllable; cf. p. 137, 27 and note.

23–PAGE **88,** 15. Ringler, OA 13 and pp. 394–5, where there is a discussion of the metre and the use of elisions not indicated graphically. The variants in 93 (see also Ringler, 374) are explained as original readings from P, later altered by Sidney. Certainly the manuscript readings at p. 83, 6 and 27 and p. 85, 10 make rather better sense and not much worse sound. Rubel, 123–4, illustrates several rhetorical figures from this poem. P. 86, 17–p. 87, 33; p. 87, 15–18 and 20–8 are copied, without attribution, in Bodleian MS. Rawl. Poet. 85, f. 22^{r-v} (Ringler, 557).

27–8. Fraunce, 8, quotes as an example of metonymia of the subject. In line 27 he alters to 'Here ye do find in truth'; and emends St's *ride* to *rides* in line 28.

29. Cf. Dyer, no. xii in Sargent, 'And love is love, in beggars and in kings'; and Tilley, L519, 'Love lives in cottages as well as in courts', cited from Lodge's *Rosalynde* (1590).

30. C. W. Lemmi in *M.L.N.* xlii (1927), 78, compares Dante, *Vita Nuova,* xi, where Love reproaches him for diverting his attention from Beatrice to another lady, 'Ego tanquam centrum circuli, cui simili modo se habent circumferentiae partes; tu autem non sic'.

PAGE **83,** 2. *sacred muse.* Philoclea, to whom Pyrocles hopes, in vain, to reveal his love in this poem.

6 (var.). *sweet Cyparissus.* Possibly the reference is to the youth (Ovid, *Met.* x. 106–42), but 'sweet cyparis', a bog plant, may have been confused with the 'stately cypress tree'; at p. 86, 24 it is the juniper that is sweet.

7. *unfortunate Echo.* Narcissus did not return her love (Ovid, *Met.* iii. 358).

9. *Idea.* Pamela.

10 and 13–14. Pyrocles is trying to indicate that whereas Musidorus is disguised as a shepherd, he is disguised as a woman.

PAGE **84,** 2. *Which.* Who.

22. *richess.* I take this to be the correct reading; cf. p. 85, 15.

29–32. W. Blount quotes Virgil, *Eclogues,* i. 59–63.

31. Fraunce, 31, quotes as an example of a hexameter. Cf. NA (*Works,* i. 415–16), 'A greyhound, which overrunning his fellow, and taking the hare, yet hurts it not when it takes it'.

PAGE **85,** 4–5. *by my judgement.* 'in my view'.

12. *worth of a walnut.* Cf. Tilley, N366, 'not worth a nutshell'.

14. *rich.* Line 12 confirms that this is the correct reading.

19–21. M. Poirier in *Études Anglaises,* xi (1958), 154, suggests that this was borrowed from Gosson's *The School of Abuse* (ed. Arber, p. 58): 'It is not a soft shoe that healeth the gout; nor a golden ring that driveth away the cramp; nor a crown of pearl that cureth the megrim'. The essay in Plutarch's *Moralia* which Sir Thomas Wyatt translated from Budé's Latin version as *The Quiet of Mind* contains the sentence, 'Sore toes are not eased with gorgeous shows, nor the whitlow with a ring, nor the headache with a crown' (*Poems*, ed. Muir and Thomson, p. 442). This was one of the four essays in the *Moralia* to which Sidney drew the attention of Edward Denny (*T.L.S.* 24 March 1972); see also Introduction, p. xxvii. Cf. Tilley, C863, 'What cares wait upon a crown'; and 2 *Henry IV*, III. i. 4–31.

27. J. Buxton, *Elizabethan Taste* (1963), p. 251, notes that Lady Anne Clifford, Countess of Dorset, Montgomery, and Pembroke, remembered this line when she wrote in her diary, 'the marble pillars of Knole in Kent and Wilton in Wiltshire were to me oftentimes but the gay arbours of anguish'. *harbour/arbour* had much the same meaning, and I have kept *harbour* as it is the form in all the texts.

32. *adherent.* See *O.E.D.*, adj. 2 *fig.*, with the earliest citation from Fraunce, *The Lawyer's Logic* (1588).

PAGE **86,** 7. *sorrow's.* Ringler prints *sorrows*; *sorrows'* is also possible.

20–PAGE **87,** 6. Ringler, 395, remarks that tree lists with their traditional attributes have been popular ever since Ovid, who in *Met.* x. 90 ff. named eleven of Sidney's sixteen trees; Sannazaro has a list at the beginning of his *Arcadia*, and there is one in *The Parlement of Foules*, 176–82 (see notes to p. 78, 23–p. 79, 1 and p. 79, 32–6). Musidorus develops the *topos* by using the trees' properties as part of his love argument.

23. *Cypress.* In NA (*Works*, i. 445) the furniture of the knight of the tomb was appropriately composed of cypress branches.

24. *Sweet juniper.* K. Duncan-Jones, 89, compares the knight Nestor in NA (*Works*, i. 105–6) whose 'impresa in his shield was a fire made of juniper with this word, *More easy, and more sweet*', and quotes *Batman upon Bartholomew* (1582), xvii. lxxxiv:

If it take fire, it keepeth and holdeth it long time . . . Fire is called *Pir* in Greek, therefore this tree is called juniper as it were breeding fire.

25. *boy.* Cupid.

27. *barren.* This refers to the tree; Plutarch, *Quaest. Conv.* II. vi, observes that though firs grow great, some bear no fruit at all (Ringler, 395).

30. *his shadow is hurtful.* The only tree characteristic that Sidney appears to have invented. 'The fig was usually referred to as having a sweet fruit and a bitter root (Plutarch, *Quaest. Conv.* v. ix)' (Ringler, 395).

PAGE **87,** 11. Palms never bore fruit unless planted one beside the other, and were therefore used as emblems of a happy marriage. For this reason Argalus's shield bore the device of 'two palm trees, near one another' in NA (*Works*, i. 423).

PAGE **88,** 5. *dear diamond.* Cf. 'nature's diamond' (p. 165, 30).

26. *Death.* Sleep as the elder brother of Death was proverbial from the time of Homer (whom W. Blount quotes); see Tilley, S526.

PAGE **89**–PAGE **90.** This passage, in Je and Hm (whence it was copied in Qu) only, has several times been reprinted and discussed—notably by Ringler, 389–93, and earlier in *Ph.Q*.xxix (1950), 70–4. My text is based on Je with some emendations from Hm. The excision of the passage in T was evidently done rather roughly, so that the ending of the Eclogues in Da and Ph appears in a mangled form; the text was somewhat tidied up before Cl was copied, and again emended before As, Bo, and St were copied. Ringler, 389, suggests that Sidney may have removed the passage because the debate on the respective merits of quantitative and rhyming verses is summarized in the *Defence of Poesy* (*Works*, iii. 44). If Sidney did not hear of de Baïf's Académie de Poésie et de Musique when he was in Paris in 1572, Daniel Rogers—who recalled hearing Ronsard sing de Baïf's poems (Dorsten, *Poets*, 100)—may have told him about it. Dicus certainly seems to be relying on the arguments of the French humanists for 'la musique mesurée à l'antique'. See also Shepherd, 233–5.

8. *the country muses*. I have accepted Ringler's emendation of *that* to *the*; but possibly *that country's muses* was intended.

19 and 37 *time . . . time . . . time*. Because Sidney uses *time* to signify the recurring pattern of the scansion reflected in the musical pattern, and *measure* for the quantitative value of a word or syllable, I have kept the reading of the manuscripts at line 37. Cf. *The Phoenix Nest* (1593), ed. Rollins, p. 98: 'When love on time and measure makes his ground.' The same minim confusion occurs in the similar passage in the *Defence of Poesy*, where Olney reads *tune* and Ponsonby and the Penshurst MS. read *time*: 'the ancient (no doubt) more fit for music, both words and time observing quantity.'

33. Cf. Tilley, O97: 'You bring owls to Athens.'

PAGE 90, 3. *implied*. I have kept Je's word as it has the same meaning here as *applied* (cf. p. 89, 39), 'accommodated to', and Sidney might well have wished to vary his terms.

6. *popular philosopher*. Cf. *Defence of Poesy* (*Works*, iii. 16): 'the poet is indeed the right popular philosopher.'

14–15. *Tuscan and Arcadian shepherds*. Tuscan would seem to be an anachronistic glance at Italian rhyming verse; Ringler, 393, points out that the shepherds in the OA do not recite quantitative poems, which are the province of the young princes and Philisides. Despite the defence of measured verse as more fit for music, Sidney's poems in quantitative metres did not attract the attention of the musicians.

THE SECOND BOOK OR ACT

PAGE 91, 3. *cup of poison*. Ringler, 467, compares AS **16**. 14 and OP **4**. 165.

6–9. *yet . . . Gynecia*. Having stayed up late, Gynecia rose again at break of dawn. NA tidies up the temporal sequence.

20–3. *Insomuch . . . said she*. Fraunce, 124, quotes as an example of the use of the eyes in an oration.

31–2. *O virtue . . . thing*. See note to p. 322, 10.

PAGE 92, 4–10. *But wretch . . . womankind*. Fraunce, 65, quotes as an example of exclamation.

11–23. *Yet if . . . shame*. Fraunce, 94–5, quotes as an example of addubitation.

He transcribes *given thee* (line 20) and *bereave thee of* (line 21), confirming my text of St. The pronoun *thee* is often spelt *the*, and the manuscripts vary in both instances. The direct address to Philoclea is the better reading, supported by the bulk of the texts.

28. *near away.* 'not far away'; Da omits the words.

PAGE 93, 3–16. Ringler, OA 14. The poem is copied from 93 in B.M. MS. Addit. 34064, f. 29 without any indication of authorship (Ringler, 555).

PAGE 95, 15–28. Ringler, OA 15. The first eight and last two lines are copied from some manuscript source, without attribution, in B.M. MS. Harl. 6910, f. 154^v (Ringler, 556). The whole poem is copied in B.M. MS. Addit. 34064, f. 28, probably from 93 (Ringler, 555); and in Bodleian MS. Rawl. Poet. 172, f. 6 from 90 (Ringler, 558). There is a fifteen-line poem based on the text of this one in 90 in what was Rosenbach MS. 197, p. 81 (Ringler, 560). Cf. the song of the foolish old courtier Mauruccio in Ford's *Love's Sacrifice*, II. i.

15–18. Scott, 16, suggests that this is a reminiscence of Ronsard:

> Soit qu'un sage amoureux, ou soit qu'un sot me lise,
> Il ne doit s'esbahir, voyant mon chef grison,
> Si je chante d'Amour: tousjours un vieil tison
> Cache un germe de feu dessous la cendre grise.
> Le bois verd à grand peine en le soufflant s'attise,
> Le sec sans le souffler brusle en toute saison.

Cf. Tilley, W140, 'Old wood is best to burn'.

23–8. Rubel, 156, cites as an example of anaphora, with ploce in the concluding couplet, the couplet itself being an example of epiphenomena.

PAGE 97, 8 ff. For Pyrocles' plight, compare the similar situation of Agesilan in *Amadis*; see Introduction, p. xxii.

PAGE 98, 18. *When* . . . The clause is never followed by the expected *then*, Sidney having lost his way in the parenthesis about Dametas.

28–9. *restrained . . . servitude.* 'restricted to being unworthily served'.

29–PAGE 99, 20. *Dorus . . . song.* This is the only prose passage included in Le.

34–5. *nothing . . . forward.* Cf. Tilley, N319 and N320, 'Nothing venture, nothing have/win'.

PAGE 99, 21–30. Ringler, OA 16 and p. 395, where it is explained that the song is constructed on two schemes: the anaphora of 'since', and the anadiplosis of 'sight'. It is copied from 93 in B.M. MS. Addit. 34064, f. 28, without attribution (Ringler, 555).

PAGE 101, 7. *patronage.* The scribal variations indicate that various forms of the word were current; *patrociny* occurs in Yong's translation of the *Diana* (ed. Kennedy, 243).

19. *to think.* Evidently missing in T and G, and conjecturally supplied by Cl and 90, with an independent emendation in Da.

32–PAGE 102, 1. *throwing sheep's eyes on.* 'looking amorously at'.

PAGE 102, 15–16. *I find . . . love.* Cf. AS 61. 14, 'That I love not, without I leave to love'.

21. *quab. O.E.D.* cites as Dorset dialect (1663). It is a variant of *quap*, 'quiver like a jelly'; evidently Sidney decided that the word was too obscure.

34. *so is . . . persons.* 'the same act varies in merit according to the quality of the doer.'

PAGE **103,** 1–3. *There is . . . reneweth.* Cf. Languet to Sidney, 14 June 1577 (ed. Pears, 108):

I felt incredible satisfaction from our intercourse during so many days, but I have experienced what a man does who drinks largely and eagerly of cold water when he is hot, and by this means brings on a fever;

and in a later letter of 2 May 1578 (ed. Pears, 149):

. . . and I fear they will meet with the fate of a man who drinks cold water in a fever, who feels a slight refreshment for a very short time, and then his fever rages far more fiercely than if he had not drunk at all.

For *heat/rage* in line 3, see Introduction, p. lxv.

28–34. *In the country . . . sound.* Fraunce, 79, quotes as an example of epanorthosis, 'the calling back of a man's self followeth when anything is revoked, and it is as it were a cooling of that heat of exclamation whereof we lately spake'.

PAGE **104,** 19. *widowed. O.E.D.* cites this passage for the attributive use of *widowhead.* I have followed St as it is impossible to tell which form Sidney favoured.

PAGE **105,** 16. *we find.* The scribe of St wrote *we*, but omitted *find*; then a later hand deleted *we*.

29–30. *But alas . . . persuade.* Fraunce, 50, quotes as an example of paronomasia; Hoskyns, 130, cites from 90, commenting that the figure can become tedious.

PAGE **106,** 3. *that veil. that* draws attention to the particular disgrace of shepherd's weeds; *y^t* and *y^e* are easily confused.

13. *pattern.* As all the other texts read *pattern* here, and St does so elsewhere, I have not kept the older form *patron.*

22. *his meanness.* Musidorus's humble status as a shepherd.

PAGE **107,** 4–11. Ringler, OA 17 and p. 395. There is a copy in Marsh's Library, Dublin, MS. Z.3.5.21, f. 19ᵛ, descending from T through some intermediary source (Ringler, 559–60); and another, signed with the initials 'T.L.', deriving from a similar original, in the Folger Shakespeare Library, MS. V.a.339 (formerly 2071.7), f. 187 (Ringler, 561). There is also a copy, preceded by a prose extract, in B.M. MS. Sloane 1925, f. 13, taken from one of the printed editions (Ringler, 557). The poem is no. 65 in *England's Helicon*, the text being taken from 98.

4. Cf. T. Lodge, *Rosalynde* (*Works*, i. 18), 'My sheep are turned to thoughts'.

19. *salamander.* A mythical lizard-like creature, supposed to be able to live in the fire, which purifies. Dorus's answer turns the allusion to Prometheus who stole fire from heaven; cf. AS **14.** 1–4.

PAGE **108,** 2. *quaint.* Cf. *quaint phrase* (p. 58, 28); here Mopsa may be using it in the bad sense of 'cunning, crafty' (*O.E.D.* 1b). Rubel, 164, notes that the word is glossed by Speght, and by E. K. in 'October', 114.

11–15. *It was . . . vobis.* For Sidney's use of devices see note to p. 27, 9–12. In Ovid, *Met.* vi. 109, and most other accounts, but not in Cartari, it was Pollux who was born a god, and whose brother Castor was made an immortal at his request. *Sic vos non vobis* was a popular motto, deriving from pseudo-Virgil. K. Duncan-Jones, 83, suggests that the immediate source may have been Ruscelli who applies the motto to a hive of bees, and gives an account of its origin. *Sic nos non nobis* was the motto borne by Sidney's attendants when he performed as one of the *Four Foster Children of Desire*, the tilt which he devised for the entertainment of the French Ambassadors on 15 May 1581. See also K. Duncan-Jones in *Journal of the Warburg and Courtauld Institutes*, xxiii (1970), 323–4. Both device and motto are changed in NA.

PAGE **109**, 30–PAGE **110**, 12. Ringler, OA 18 and p. 396, where W. Blount's reference to a similar situation, Dido's oath in *Aeneid*, iv. 24–7, is cited.

PAGE **110**, 18. *But neither . . . and.* We should expect *nor* after *neither*, but the sentence survives unchanged in NA.

29–PAGE **111**, 6. Ringler, OA 19 and p. 396.

PAGE **111**, 32. *Caeneus.* A Thessalian woman, called Caenis, being ravished by Neptune, was given power to change her sex, and her name to Caeneus (Ovid, *Met.* xii. 172 and 479).

PAGE **113**, 1. *disastered.* 'ill-starred'; the scribal variants indicate the unfamiliarity of the word, which is cited from this passage in *O.E.D.*

2. *thy.* i.e. her bed's.

16. *with a little.* 'with little', i.e. none at all.

27. *unhap.* The scribes were puzzled by this obsolete word; this is the last instance given in *O.E.D.*, and the previous one is for 1523.

PAGE **114**, 6–19. Ringler, OA 20 and p. 396, where the song is described as 'a heaping of contraries, a device which Sidney ridiculed in AS 6'. R. Jakobson discusses the grammatical structure in *Studies . . . in Honour of Margaret Schlauch* (Warsaw, 1966). The poem, preceded by prose extracts, is copied in B.M. MS. Sloane 1925, f. 13, from one of the printed editions (Ringler, 557).

6–9. Rubel, 157, cites as an example of epanalepsis, combined with epizeuxis, traductio, and antistrophe.

15. Cf. p. 65, 14 for the blind Cupid.

23–4. *holding . . . shower.* Jove fell in love with Danae and came down from heaven disguised as a shower of gold (Ovid, *Met.* iv. 611). K. Duncan-Jones, 19–21, shows that the inspiration of the old governess who lifts up a dish with both hands or her apron (cf. *Timon of Athens*, IV. iii. 134–5, 'Hold up, you sluts/Your aprons mountant') was pictorial and not literary. Her first appearance seems to be in Titian's later versions of the subject, painted in 1554–5; one (now in the Prado) was dispatched to Philip II in 1554, and could not have been seen by Sidney; the other two are workshop copies, now in Vienna and Leningrad. The governess motif was taken over by Tintoretto, some of those pictures Sidney almost certainly saw, and her gesture became a recognized sign of female avarice. Without knowing one of these pictures, it might not be realized that the governess and Basilius threw up their hands in a gesture of misdirected eagerness, and not in amazement or supplication.

PAGE **116**, 13. *high thoughts*. See Introduction, p. lxv.

PAGE **117**, 23. *mettle*. See note to p. 27, 28, where *mettle* is clearly required. Here *metal* is possible; cf. p. 137, 20.

32-3. *much . . . suffer*. This qualifying phrase seems rather telling; but it is possible that Sidney felt it to be tasteless, and therefore it was cancelled in T before As, Bo, and St were transcribed. The passage is rewritten in NA.

PAGE **118**, 15-32. Ringler, OA 21 and p. 396. The poem is copied in Bodleian MS. Rawl. Poet. 85, f. 23ᵛ, from some MS. source, and attributed to Sidney (Ringler, 557). There are further MS. copies in B.M. MS. Addit. 34064, f. 28, from 93 (Ringler, 555); in B.M. MS. Harl. 3511, ff. 74ᵛ-75, from one of the printed editions (Ringler, 556); in Bodleian MS. Rawl. Poet. 148, ff. 99-100, from 98 (Ringler, 558). It is no. 11 in Robert Jones, *The Second Book of Songs and Airs* (1601)—the words being taken from one of the prints 90-99, and arranged with a three-part setting; words and music were edited by E. H. Fellowes, *The English School of Lutenist Song Writers*, v (1926); the words are printed in Fellowes, 3rd edn., 566-7 (Ringler, 567). Ringler, lvii, notes the elaborate figures used by Cleophila to invoke the four elements. Fraunce, 36, quotes lines 15-18 as examples of anadiplosis.

19. *watered eyes*. Ringler, 396, accepts *watery eyes* as an emendation in Bo, Cl, and 90 of a d/e graphical error in T, and compares p. 170, 26 where, however, some MSS. again read *watered eyes*.

29. See note to p. 73, 16-30.

PAGE **119**, 13. *straitly*. 'closely'; *straightly*, 'immediately', the spelling of St and some other MSS., is possible. The word is omitted in NA.

PAGE **120**, 16. This wing of the sentence was cancelled in T (note the addition of *and* before *my end*); perhaps Sidney felt that Pyrocles should not express a hope of deserving Philoclea's favour, since he goes on to hope only for her pity.

PAGE **121**, 4. *candle . . . presence*. Cf. Tilley, S988.

23. *decayed*. See Introduction, pp. xxx-xxxi n.

PAGE **122**, 1. *never hath*. 'never hath declined'.

11. *marriage*. Ph adds 'what further might have happened it is not my skill to know'.

17. *quickly*. The manuscript tradition indicates that *quietly* is a misreading in 90, possibly influenced by the assumption that a contrast with the *unquiet heart* of Gynecia (line 18) was intended.

33. *Trojan women*. Cf. *Aeneid*, v. 604 ff.

PAGE **123**, 3-16. Ringler, OA 22 and p. 396, where attention is drawn to the fact that this is not a sonnet, but two stanzas of rhyme royal. The poem is copied, without attribution, from a manuscript source, in Bodleian MS. Rawl. Poet. 85, f. 23 (Ringler, 557).

19-21. *same disdainful . . . weaving*. Arachne challenged Minerva, goddess of art, to a contest in weaving; although her piece was perfect, she was defeated and hanged herself in despair. Minerva changed her into a spider (Ovid, *Met*. vi. 1 ff.).

PAGE 124, 17. *one eagle . . . kites*. This sounds proverbial. In NA (*Works*, i. 311) it is altered to 'the odds between an eagle and a kite'); cf. p. 21, 26 and note.

31–PAGE 125, 11. Ringler, OA 23 and p. 396, where the continuation of the imagery of Musidorus's previous song (p. 107) is noted; as also that this and the following answer poem (p. 125) are not sonnets, but are made up of twelve lines of terza rima, with a concluding couplet. The poems were omitted from NA because the role of Philisides had been changed.

32. *sun's approach*. the favour of Pamela.

PAGE 125, 16–29. Ringler, OA 24 and pp. 396–7, where other examples of answer poems which parallel the structure but reverse the sentiment of another poem are given; and attention is drawn to Gil Polo's two sonnets with identical rhyme words in Book III of the *Diana Enamorada*.

17. *My sun is gone*. Mira has withdrawn her favour.

28. *Leave leaving not*. Ringler regards this as an error in T, and substitutes the opening phrase of the stanzas 'Leave off my sheep', to give an exact repetition as in the previous poem, 'Feed on my sheep'. But 'Cease not ceasing to maintain my mourning' gives good sense, and is the sort of subtle variation that Sidney liked.

PAGE 126, 19. *face of wood*. the closed wooden gates.

26–9. *Bacchus . . . allarum*. Fraunce, 4, quotes as an example of metonymia of the cause 'as when the author and inventor is put for the things by him invented and found'. W. Blount has a note on Bacchus's rebirth from Jupiter, god of thunder; the story is told in Ovid, *Met.* iii. 3.

35. *Phagona*. Sidney invented this town from φαγών, 'glutton'; presumably he changed it from a village to a town when he made the rebellion so formidable.

PAGE 128, 7–19. *Thus . . . mischief*. Wolff, 360, compares Heliodorus, 1. i. 9–10: . . . the tables were furnished with delicate dishes, some whereof lay in the hands of those that were slain, being instead of weapons. . . . Besides the cups were overthrown, and fell out of the hands, either of them that drank, or those who had instead of stones used them. For that sudden mischief wrought new devices, and taught them instead of weapons to use pots . . . brewing blood with wine, joining battle with banqueting.

14. *Some . . . other*. *Some* took swords and bills, in contrast with *other(s)* who took pitchforks. But some MSS. (and this is the arrangement in the revised passage in NA) punctuate 'some swords and bills there were; other took pitchforks'.

PAGE 129, 24–34. *An unused . . . people*. This passage is cited by Fraunce, 101, with the heading 'Cleophila to the inconstant multitude' as an example of preoccupation

. . . when we prevent and meet with that which might be objected, and do also make answer to the same; of the first part, it is called preoccupation, or the laying down of the objection; of the second, subjection, or answering thereunto. So that commonly it hath a kind of prosopopoeia adjoined unto it. This preventing therefore is either indirect, most fit for beginnings, and more used of orators than of poets.

At line 30 Fraunce, like 90, reads *manlike*. Cleophila's oratory is discussed by Challis in *S.P.* lxii (1965), 567, and by Lanham, 267–9.

PAGE **130**, 7. *stranger . . . succour.* Pyrocles has not previously claimed, nor does he later make the point, that (as the Amazon Cleophila) he has fled to Arcadia for succour. We are intended to admire the powerful oratory with which he sways the crowd rather than to scrutinize his arguments.

PAGE **131**, 14. *to inflame . . . knots.* Cf. Tilley, F251 and K167.

32. *sheep's draught.* bitter medicine.

PAGE **132**, 24–35. Ringler, OA 25 and p. 397. This corresponds to the triumphant song of the cowardly Dametas at the end of Book I.

27. As Ringler remarks, *bobbed* must be the right reading because it continues the anaphora of the previous three lines. For this reason I question his gloss 'let the man who wishes to receive blows *be mocked*' instead of '*be hit*' (see *O.E.D.* s.v. bob v²). *bobbed* is the reading of Cm and 93; the correction of *bould* to *bobde* in St is in another hand.

31. *make brave lame shows.* 'make a boastful exhibition of how lamed they have been by their wounds'; cf. Donne, 'Satire III', *brave scorn*, 'fine show of scorn'.

34. 'Keeping his eyes averted from swords and his ears remote from the cries of battle.'

PAGE **133**, 14. *daughters.* Page 134, 4 shows that this is the correct reading.

22–3. *yet . . . remained.* 'yet his care for Pamela had not disappeared, since the basis for it remained in his heart.'

27. *it which.* I have kept the reading of all the manuscripts, as this is a possible construction; though Sidney may have written y^t, 'that'.

34. *selfness.* The earliest citation in *O.E.D.* is from AS **61**. 7, followed by two from Fulke Greville.

PAGE **134**, 7–22. Ringler OA 26 and pp. 397–8, where it is noted that, in spite of the mythological details, the spirit of the song is entirely Christian, albeit completely at variance with Basilius's intentions. The notes on this poem are based on Ringler's.

7. So Phaethon addressed his father:

> O lux immensi publica mundi,
> Phoebe pater
> (Ovid, *Met.* ii. 35–6)

8. *little world.* The microcosm, the mind of man. *dost.* Apollo is the subject here, and the antecedent of 'Which' in the following line.

11–12. After the flood which overwhelmed the world had receded, the huge serpent Python was born from the mud of the Nile and was killed by the young archer-god Apollo (Ovid, *Met.* i. 434–44).

13–14. Latona (Leto) was prevented by the anger of Juno from remaining anywhere at rest, and finally bore the twins Apollo and Diana on the floating island of Delos (Ovid, *Met.* vi. 332–8).

14. 'Shows how difficult it is to learn what is good.'

27. In As the following couplet is written on the right-hand side at the foot of the page:

> Could the stars that bred such wit
> In force no longer fixed sit?

THE SECOND ECLOGUES

PAGE **135,** 9. *appassionate.* The earliest citation in *O.E.D.* is from the *Arcadia*; the MSS. variants here, and at p. 155, 35 and p. 408, 37, indicate its unfamiliarity. It was used by Yong in his translation of the *Diana* (ed. Kennedy, **11.** 22; **178.** 22; **244.** 4; **263.** 14), and he then went on to coin *unappassionate* (**81.** 33) and *unappassionately* (**223.** 6).

13–PAGE **136,** 30. Ringler, OA 27 and p. 398, where it is noted that this song announces the theme of the eclogues to follow, just as the dance of the Arcadian shepherds announces the theme of the First Eclogues (p. 56). This poem is copied in B.M. MS. Addit. 34064, f. 27, probably from 93, without indication of authorship (Ringler, 555).

19. *rule the roast.* Cf. Tilley, R144.

PAGE **137,** 2. *convoy.* See Introduction, p. lv n.

4. Dicus has already shown that he despises love; see note to p. 65, 33–p. 66, 4.

10–PAGE **141,** 15. Ringler, OA 28 and p. 398, where it is noted that the metrical pattern is similar to that of the second poem in the First Eclogues (the verse contest between Dorus and Lalus, pp. 58 ff.). Mrs. Kennedy in her edition of *Diana*, 425, notes that Sidney is much more successful in his original tercetos esdrujolos than either Wilson or Yong (**26.** 2) is in imitating Montemayor's.

20. *metal.* This spelling is adopted for the sake of the metaphor; see notes to p. 27, 28 and p. 117, 23.

27. *muett.* I have kept the spelling of the MSS., giving a dissyllable, for the sake of the scansion; see note to p. 82, 1.

PAGE **138,** 22. *warefulness.* This and the previous citation from Thomas, *Italian Dictionary* (1548), '*sagacita*, wisdom or warefulness', are the only examples given in *O.E.D.*

24. 'Love's hands are bountifulness and could never have skill in frugality' (Ringler).

PAGE **139,** 15. 'And Venus appears to have exhausted her resources in order to complete Pamela.'

5–6. The changes in 90 do not seem necessary, and are not, I think, authorial.

PAGE **140,** 1–5. 'The authorial changes made in T provide a better ordering of images and improve the rhymes' (Ringler). In the variant reading, the sense demands *leeches*, but the rhyme required *loaches*.

5. *shepherd.* The texts divide; Ringler reads *shepherds'*, which rather over-emphasizes the subordination of Dorus and Dicus.

22. *seal.* Most scribes and compositors seem to have had difficulty in accepting this word—we should say 'stamp'.

PAGE **141,** 25–PAGE **146,** 12. Ringler, OA 29 and pp. 399–400, where this rustic flyting is shown to be a comic interlude similar to 'Poor painters oft' in the First Eclogues (pp. 65–6), deriving much of its humour from its parody of Virgil's 3rd Eclogue, and containing the conventional four parts: the preliminary banter, the wager, the singing match, and the judgement. An analysis of the verse forms used follows. The mention of Dorcas (p. 141, 33), who, like Lalus, was a character in LM confused the scribes.

25–PAGE **142**, 20. Ringler quotes the opening dialogue between Menalcas and Damoetas in Abraham Fleming's 'awkwardly literal' translation of Virgil's 3rd Eclogue, published in 1575.

PAGE **142**, 1. *rayed*. Ringler regards this as an error in T and emends to *raged*; but I think *raid*, *rayed*, 'berayed'; 'diseased'; 'disfigured', was intended. Cf. *The Taming of the Shrew*, II. ii. 55; IV. i. 5.
2. *Cosma*. She is called Hyppa in the earlier manuscripts.
6. *crouch to bless*. 'crutch to wound'; Grosart was probably right in suggesting a pun on 'cross to bless'. Cf. the pun on *mate* in line 14.
9–10. Cf. p. 58, 29 and p. 329, 30 and note.

PAGE **143**, 7. *eft*. Ringler glosses 'moreover'; 'e' and 'o' are easily confused, and 'oft' may be the correct reading.
13–24. Fraunce, 11, cites these lines as an example of 'a continued Ironia between Pas and Nico'.
19–20. Syrinx fleeing from Pan was turned into a reed on which he blew, so inventing the shepherd's pipe (Ovid, *Met*. i. 689). Cf. p. 65, 5–6.
22–3. See p. 18, 3–4 and note.
32. *barleybreak*. The most elaborate description of this country game is in OP **4**. 208–416; see Ringler's note, pp. 495–6.

PAGE **144**, 13–14. 'This is Skelton's "sparrow white as milk" (*Philip Sparrow*, 213); cf. AS 83 and OP **4**. 83–104' (Ringler).
22–4. Ringler compares Spenser's 'April', 73–81.
32. Ringler compares OP **5**. 112:

> She is the herdess fair that shines in dark.

PAGE **145**, 2–3. Ringler follows Grosart in taking *fell* to mean 'skin'; but I would construe 'she made the water cleaner and finer with the beauties that fell from her'. This is supported by his comparison with Greville, *Caelica*, xxii. 26, 'Washing the water with her beauties, white'.
8. *spy her baby*. 'look at her reflection.' Ringler compares AS **11**. 10, 'thou straight lookst babies in her eyes'. This is a common phrase in Elizabethan poetry for a lover's looking at his reflection in his mistress's eyes.
10–12. Cf. CS **29**. 1–9, translated from Montemayor (Ringler).

PAGE **146**, 4–12. Ringler quotes the conclusion to Virgil's 3rd Eclogue, which also contains two riddles and the award of the prize. 'Virgil's riddles contain learned literary allusions, Sidney's are of the simple nursery variety. The answer to Sidney's first may be a man on crutches wearing spectacles; I give up the second' (Ringler). Cf. the riddle poems in *Diana*, ed. Kennedy, 391–6.
14 (var.). Although eyeskip from 'But' to 'But' is a possibility, I conjecture that Sidney cancelled this sentence in T before St and Bo were copied because it accords ill with Dicus's 'Enough, enough'; it is not included in 90 (*Works*, i. 348), where the editors were working from T⁵.

26–PAGE **152**, 18. Ringler, OA 30 and pp. 401–2. The poem is transferred to Book II in NA (*Works*, i. 227 ff.), where Basilius takes the part of Boulon.

30. *refrain*. Boulon 'restrains' the violence of Plangus's laments with essentially biblical arguments (Ringler).

PAGE **147,** 5–6. Cf. John Wilbye, *The First Set of English Madrigals* (1598), no. 26, 9 (Fellowes, 3rd edn., p. 309):

My throat is sore, my voice is hoarse, with skriking.

14. *Balls to the stars*. W. Blount quotes Plautus, *Captivi*, Prol. 22, 'Enim vero di nos quasi pilas homines habent', for this commonplace. Cf. p. 385, 32–p. 386, 2 and note.

17. Ringler quotes Sidney's disapproval of naughty play-makers in the *Defence of Poesy* (*Works*, iii. 23).

20–2. Ringler cites Wisdom 7: 3; cf. Eccles. 1: 18. Dent, 223, compares *The Duchess of Malfi*, III. v. 81–4, 93–5.

23. *shop of shame*. Poirier in *Études Anglaises*, xi (1958), 153, compares Spenser's 'September', 36.

26–8. 'The four elements warring for mastery are the bases of the four bodily humours; only in a perfect man would they be in perfect equipoise' (Ringler).

30. Ringler compares Virgil, *Aeneid*, vii. 383, 'Dant animos plagae'. Cf. Greville (ed. Bullough, i. 136), 'Life is a top which whipping sorrow driveth'.

PAGE **148,** 1–4. John Ward, *The First Set of English Madrigals* (1613), no. 12, fashioned these lines into a five-line song with a setting for four voices. The text was taken from one of the folios 98–13. The words and music were edited by E. H. Fellowes, *The English Madrigal School*, xix (1922) (Ringler, 401 and 567). The words are reprinted in Fellowes, 3rd edn., p. 268.

31–3. W. Blount cites Zeus's speech in the *Odyssey*, i. 32–4.

34–PAGE **149,** 5. 'The usual proof texts for the sweet uses of adversity (cited, for example, by St. Augustine, *De Patientia*, I. xiv) are Proverbs 3: 11–12 and Wisdom 3: 4–6' (Ringler).

PAGE **149,** 35. *Phaethon's dam*. Clymene, the mother of Phaethon by Phoebus Apollo, the sun god (Ovid, *Met*. i. 756) (Ringler). Cf. p. 268, 6.

36–PAGE **150,** 5. Vulcan the smith, husband of Venus, was made a cuckold by her amour with Mars (Ovid, *Met*. iv. 169 ff.) (Ringler). Cf. *An Apology for Poetry*, ed. Shepherd, p. 131 and note.

PAGE **150,** 19. Ringler, 460, compares AS **2.** 14, 'While with a feeling skill I paint my hell'.

23. *most prone*. 'most inclined to'. Ringler prefers the reading of the majority of the manuscripts, *must prove* (though *prone* rather than *proue* may be the word in some of them), and glosses 'must experience', making 'to feel' redundant.

29. *baiting place*. See note to p. 5, 5–6.

PAGE **151,** 6. *she*. Erona.

14. Ringler draws attention to the same anachronism when Shakespeare's Cleopatra asks Charmian to cut her lace.

PAGE **153,** 28. *horse-load of a mast*. *Horse-load* is used here to indicate a great weight. The reading of St, like that of the other manuscripts, may be *mase*, but *mast* was clearly intended—giants were customarily armed with tree trunks.

PAGE **155**, 30. *king of Egypt*. The fabulous deeds of Sesostris, king of Egypt, are recounted by Herodotus, ii. 102 ff. and by Strabo, xvi.

31. *policied*. The scribal variants indicate unfamiliarity with this word.

35. *appassionate*. See note to p. 135, 9.

PAGE **156**, 26. *Amasis*. In Herodotus he is a common soldier who became king of Egypt and is not the son of Sesostris.

31. *ordinary . . . hate*. Possibly Phaedra, the archetype for this situation, was in Sidney's mind, but see Introduction, p. xxiii, for other analogues.

PAGE **158**, 31. *Artaxia hated them*. She hated the two princes because they had killed her brother (see pp. 67 ff.).

PAGE **159**, 26–8. *Lalus . . . more*. Lalus sang the praises of Kala in his song with Dorus (see pp. 58 ff.).

PAGE **160**, 4–PAGE **162**, 28. Ringler, OA 31 and pp. 402–3, where earlier and later examples of continental and English echo poems are noted. Sidney's poem was imitated by Sir William Alexander in 'An Echo' (*Aurora* (1604), K4); see also 2 *Return to Parnassus*, II. ii. 583–620. Ringler, 557–8, draws attention to a note on f. 85 of Bodleian MS. Rawl. Poet. 85, indicating that the MS. originally contained this poem 'on a leaf near the beginning which is now missing'. The poem was printed from one of the later folios in the 1638 edition of Dousa's *Lusus Imaginis Iocosae sive Echus*, pp. 93–6. Ringler considers that the imperfections in the metre indicate that this is one of Sidney's earliest experiments in measured verse. He regards 90's emendations as editorial and often erroneous, and takes his text from 93, which was based on P.

5. Cf. Golding's trans. of Ovid, *Met.* iii. 474.

6–9. These lines are quoted from 90 in Gil, *Logonomia Anglica*, ed. Jiriczek (1903), p. 149.

16–19 and 29–PAGE **161**, 2. Fraunce, 55, quotes these lines as examples of strange rhymes.

PAGE **161**, 10. The corrections in St are written in the same hand as the text, but would seem to be without authority as they appear neither in the other OA MSS., nor in 90 (from T), nor in 93 (from P).

22–3. Cf. p. 73, 28–30 and note.

PAGE **162**, 15. *th'hast narrowly*. Ringler explains agreement between 90 and 93 as conjectural emendation of scribal error in T by 90, and correct reading from P in 93.

PAGE **163**, 7–PAGE **164**, 31. Ringler, OA 3 2and p. 403, where it is stated that Sidney's metre is found in several of the '*Anacreontea*, the Greek text of which was first printed with a Latin translation by Sidney's friend H. Stephanus in 1554. Sidney was, with Spenser and Watson, among the first Englishmen to make use of motifs from this collection.'

7. The scansion model fails to indicate that the last syllable may be short or long.

8–15. Fraunce, 33, quotes these lines to illustrate Anacreontics, but gives a faulty scansion model.

30–PAGE **164**, 2. Brie, 199, cites Ovid, *Met.* xii. 210 ff.; ii. 833 ff.; x. 519 ff.; iv. 169 ff. Page 164, 2 refers to the story of Endymion.

PAGE **164**, 15. *she.* Pyrocles' muse.
    21. *she.* Philoclea.

PAGE **165**, 3–PAGE **166**, 3. Ringler, OA 33 and pp. 403–4. *Phaleuciacs* is apparently Sidney's coinage for Phaleucian hendecasyllables, a favourite metre of Catullus. Fraunce, 29–30, quotes this poem as an example of a 'Phaleucium'. There are four examples of poems in this metre in Davison's *A Poetical Rhapsody.* The poem is copied, without attribution, in Bodleian MS. Rawl. Poet. 85, f. 24 (Ringler, 557). Ringler contrasts the greater skill with which the siege image is used in AS 2.
    30. *nature's diamond.* Ringler compares 'dear diamond' (p. 88, 5).

8–PAGE **167**, 16. Ringler, OA 34 and p. 404, where it is suggested that the imperfections of Sidney's asclepiads indicate, like the similar defects in 'Fair Rocks' (see note to p. 160, 4–p. 162, 28), an early experiment. In spite of the seemingly deliberate contrast between this polysyllabic poem by Musidorus and the monosyllables of Pyrocles' 'My muse' (p. 163, 7 ff.), Ringler considers that it is inappropriately placed so soon after the Phagonian insurrection. A more appropriate placing would be after Pyrocles' praise of solitariness in Book I (see p. 14, 23–p. 17, 9 and note).
    9–10. These first two lines are used as the opening of each of the four stanzas of no. 10 in John Dowland's *The Second Book of Songs or Airs* (1600). The words of Dowland's first stanza were copied in Bodleian MS. Douce 280, f. 69; and the words of all four stanzas are printed in Fellowes, 3rd edn., pp. 470–1. Another musical setting of Dowland's stanzas, by Henry Lawes, is in the Beconsfield MS. (B.M. MS. Loan 35, f. 9ᵛ) (Ringler, 404 and 566).
    9. Wilson, 314, compares the beginning of della Casa's sonnet, 'O dolce selva solitaria, amica'.
    9–17. Rudenstine, 48–9, compares *Defence of Poesy* (*Works*, iii. 8):

Only the poet, disdaining to be tied to any such subjection, lifted up with the vigour of his own invention, doth grow in effect into another nature . . . not enclosed within the narrow warrant of her gifts, but freely ranging within the zodiac of his own wit.

    23–30. Fraunce, 28, quotes these lines for the metre.

PAGE **167**, 18. *quietly.* This is the reading of all the texts, but *quickly* may have been intended.

THE THIRD BOOK OR ACT

At the point where 90 breaks off in the middle of a sentence, 93 prints the following note to introduce the *Old Arcadia*, Books III–V:

How this combat ended, how the ladies by the coming of the discovered forces were delivered, and restored to Basilius, and how Dorus again returned to his old master Dametas, is altogether unknown. What afterwards chanced, out of the author's own writings and conceits hath been supplied as followeth.

Although this bridge passage appears in 13 on sig. Ff3ʳ, it was clearly meant to be replaced by the last paragraph of the following extended note on an unpaged inserted leaf Ee5:

Thus far the worthy author had revised or enlarged that first written Arcadia of his, which only passed from hand to hand, and was never printed; having a purpose likewise to have new ordered, augmented, and concluded the rest, had he not been prevented by untimely death. So that all which followeth here of this work remained as it was done and sent away in several loose sheets (being never after reviewed, nor so much as seen all together by himself), without any certain disposition or perfect order. Yet, for that it was his, howsoever deprived of the just grace it should have had, was held too good to be lost; and therefore with much labour were the best coherencies that could be gathered out of those scattered papers made, and afterwards printed as now it is, only by her noble care to whose dear hand they were first committed, and for whose delight and entertainment only undertaken.

What conclusion it should have had, or how far the work have been extended (had it had his last hand thereunto) was only known to his own spirit, where only those admirable images were (and nowhere else) to be cast.

And here we are likewise utterly deprived of the relation how this combat ended, and how the ladies by discovery of the approaching forces were delivered and restored to Basilius; how Dorus returned to his old master Dametas. All which unfortunate maim we must be content to suffer with the rest.

The first two paragraphs are a conflation of Sidney's Dedication (p. 3 above) and Hugh Sanford's Preface to 93 (see Introduction, pp. xlix–l; 13 is the only edition to omit this Preface). Some copies of 13 contain 'A supplement of the said defect by Sir W. A.'. The edition of 1621 omitted the link passages in 93 and 13, and followed Sir William Alexander's Supplement with the statement, 'From hence the history is again continued out of the author's own writings and conceits as followeth'.

The principal changes made by the editors of 93 in the *Old Arcadia*, Books III–V, are discussed on pp. lx–lxii.

PAGE **168**, 16–24. *for, indeed . . . gladness*. Ringler, 498, compares OP **6**. 6, 'Make but one mind in bodies three', and OA 45, 'My true love hath my heart, and I have his' (p. 190, 25–p. 191, 6).

24–PAGE **172**, 25. *Then would . . . so to do*. Sidney may himself have indicated the excision of this passage, for traces of some of the sentences are to be found in NA (*Works*, i. 57, 94, 153, 177, 180); and the glove as a love token had been used in NA (*Works*, i. 222–5) where Amphialus's dog takes one of Philoclea's gloves. The prose introduction to the songs refers back too obviously to the state of affairs in Book II of OA to follow the long captivity episode of Book III of NA convincingly; and as Ringler, 404, remarks, the poems had to be omitted from 93 'because at this point in the revised narrative Dorus had not received any indication of love from Pamela'.

29. *have been*. The insertion of *have* seems to be required by the other *haves* in this speech, and in the next; its omission by the copyist of T would have been an easy error to make.

PAGE **169**, 6. *stanzas*. This is apparently the earliest use of the word in English. Puttenham cites it as an Italian word: 'Staff in our vulgar poesy. . . . The Italians called it *stanza*.' Both St and Bo spellings were current at the end of the sixteenth century: Harington has *stanse*; Florio defines *stanze* as 'a stance or staff of verses or songs'; and Shakespeare introduces the word as part of the pedantry of Holofernes, 'Let me hear a staff, a stanze, a verse' (*Love's Labour's Lost*, IV. ii. 107).

7–22. Ringler, OA 35 and p. 404. The poem is copied, without attribution, in C.U.L. MS. Dd.5.75(2), f. 36ᵛ (Ringler, 554).

15–22. Fraunce, 39, quotes this verse as an example of 'climax, gradation', which 'is a reduplication continued by divers degrees and steps, as it were, of the same word or sound, for these two be of one kind'. Rubel, 160, finds climax combined with ploce and traductio; see also Ringler, lvii.

15. Poirier in *Études Anglaises*, xi (1958), 151, compares Petrarch, Sonnet 166, 9–11:

> Candido, leggiadretto e caro guanto,
> Che copria netto avorio e fresche rose,
> Chi vide al mondo mai si dolci spoglie?

PAGE **170**, 19–36. Ringler, OA 36.

19–20. Ringler follows St in putting a comma after *wait* (Cl puts it after *them*); I have omitted it altogether as I take *them* to mean *those whom*.

26. *watered*. See note to p. 118, 19.

PAGE **171**, 13–30. Ringler, OA 37 and p. 405, where it is noted that Cleophila uses the same stanza and words as Dorus in the previous poem; see note to p. 125, 16–29.

21–4. 'But at no change does he take such extreme care as when harvest sends pleasing displays of corn; for at the great sight of the hoped-for bliss, reason will make its loss great, so great is the fear to fail to obtain it.'

28. *flow'r of fruit*. 'flower that produces fruit'.

PAGE **172**, 25–9 (var.). *kindest . . . unkindness*. Cf. p. 174, 6–7.

PAGE **173**, 3. *folly*. The other readings in OA MSS. may simply be scribal carelessness; but they could reflect dissatisfaction with Dorus's exasperated attribution of folly to the well-grounded suspicions of Dametas, Miso, and Mopsa.

10–11. *The eternal . . . me*. 93 and some OA MSS. punctuate so as to make this qualify the preceding sentence; but I think that Pyrocles wants to emphasize that the parting with his friend is worse than death.

PAGE **174**, 1–2. *so much . . . friendship*. Fraunce, 76, quotes as an example of epiphonema, 'a kind of exclamation when after the discourse ended, we add some short acclamation, as a conclusion or shutting up all in wondering wise'.

PAGE **175**, 4–5, and PAGE **176**, 10–11. *the guide . . . fortune*; *make . . . virtues*. Brie, 118–19, compares Aristotle, *Ethics*, I. ii. Cf. p. 318, 12–14 and *Defence of Poesy* (*Works*, iii. 18):

. . . for indeed poetry ever sets virtue so out in her best colours, making fortune her well-waiting handmaid, that one must needs be enamoured of her. Well may you see Ulysses in a storm and in other hard plights, but they are but exercises of patience and magnanimity, to make them shine the more in the near following prosperity.

This supports the reading of St, Bo, Cl, and 93, 'make fortune to wait on'; see Introduction, p. lxvi.

23–4. *That . . . damage.* 'That friendship which puts a man's own vulnerability before the injury of a friend produces hatred.'

PAGE **176**, 8. *our. your* in 93 takes *departure* in the modern sense; but it is clear from line 15 that it is the separation of the two friends that is sorrowful.

21. *took. take* Da, Ph, and Je, is possible, gaining some support from *keep* in the variant reading of 93.

26–9. *Basilius . . . unto her.* This sentence was presumably deleted in 93 because of the similar inquiry Basilius made to Philoclea in NA (*Works*, i. 329).

PAGE **177**, 6. *know.* The scribe of T probably wrote *knew*, and Bo and Hm emended conjecturally.

15–31. Ringler OA 38 and p. 405. The poem is copied, and attributed to Sidney, in Bodleian MS. Rawl. Poet. 85, f. 5ᵛ (Ringler 557). See Ringler, 461, where he compares the play with love and idolatry in AS **4.** 13; **5.** 5–8; **40.** 12–14.

15. Cf. Arundel Harington MS., no. 188, 'Blush, Phoebus, blush, thy glory is forlorn' (see *R.E.S.* xiii (1962), 405). See note to p. 213, 2.

16. This line is the object of *forget* in line 3.

26, 28–9. The rhymes are clearer in the original spelling: *defaste, raste, taste.*

PAGE **178**, 23–4. *age cooleth the blood.* Cf. Tilley, A63 and A64, for which the earliest citation in *O.D.E.P.* is from Greene's *Menaphon* (1589).

25–6. *daintiness . . . granting.* Cf. Marston, *The Malcontent*, v. ii:

. . . a squeamish affected niceness is natural to women, and that the excuse of their yielding is only (forsooth) the difficult obtaining.

PAGE **179**, 18. *farewell.* Ph adds:

And as folks do in an ague take cold water which breeds the greater heat, she would fill her eyes with his sight, which should after make her feel the greater emptiness.

The simile may have been suggested by p. 103, 1–3.

19–28. *she saw . . . mansion.* Descriptions of caves abound in pastoral literature; cf. Sannazaro's 10th Prose.

22–3. *yielding . . . bed.* The Tagus was celebrated for its golden sands in antiquity. Thomas Cooper, *Thesaurus* (1565) notes under *Tagus*, 'Wherein hath been found gravel of gold'; cf. Wyatt, 'Tagus, farewell' (*Poems*, ed. Muir and Thomson, no. xcix).

33–PAGE **180**, 12. Ringler, OA 39 and p. 405, where attention is drawn to AS 89, Petrarch's Sonnet 18, 1–8, and Bembo's 'E cosa natural fuggir da morte', in which all the lines end with either 'morte' or 'vita'.

33–PAGE **180**, 2. Rudenstine, 266, compares AS **104.** 5–8:

Ah, is it not enough, that I am thence,
Thence, so far thence, that scarcely any spark
Of comfort dare come to this dungeon dark,
Where rigour's exile locks up all my sense?

PAGE **180**, 5. *windows . . . light.* 'my five senses' (Ringler).

26–PAGE **181**, 6. Ringler, OA 40.

PAGE **181**, 9–16. Ringler OA 41. This octave is copied, without attribution, in C.U.L. MS. Dd.5.75(2), f. 26ᵛ and Bodleian MS. Rawl. Poet. 85, f. 21ᵛ (Ringler, 554 and 557).

12. *his.* 'my mind's'.

13. *Joys.* Ringler prints *Joie's*; but I take the meaning to be 'Joys seem to be strangers'.

16. Cf. Shakespeare's Sonnet 147, 1–2:

> My love is as a fever longing still
> For that which longer nurseth the disease.

30–PAGE **182**, 10. Ringler, OA 42 and p. 405.

30–PAGE **182**, 4. These lines are copied in C.U.L. MS. Dd.5.75(2), f. 26ᵛ, without attribution (Ringler, 554).

30. *sun.* Pyrocles.

30–1. A. Davenport, *The Poems of John Marston* (1961), compares 'The Scourge of Villainy', iv. 125, 'Who says the sun is cause of ugly night?', and NA (*Works*, i. 408), 'that eternal causes should bring forth chanceable effects is as sensible as that the sun should be author of darkness'; and *As You Like It*, III. ii. 27–8, 'a great cause of the night is lack of the sun'.

32–PAGE **182**, 4. Ringler compares AS 10.

PAGE **182**, 8. *Tire on.* Ringler compares AS **14**. 2; see also note to p. 207, 32.

12–19. Ringler, OA 43 and p. 406, where there is a note on correlative or reporting verse, and a list of Sidney's other poems in this popular form, including the even more elaborate OA 60.

PAGE **183**, 6. *footsteps . . . virtue.* Ringler, 460, compares AS **2**. 9, 'footstep of lost liberty', where he glosses *footstep*, 'trace'.

PAGE **184**, 1–2. *The savagest . . . mollified.* Quasi-proverbial phrases on the pattern of Tilley, D618.

1–3. *The savagest . . . worthy.* Fraunce, 125, quotes as a speech for which an arm gesture would be appropriate.

19–35. *'O', said . . . work.* Fraunce, 110, quotes Gynecia's speech in full as one requiring 'a bitter, angry, choleric, and furious voice'.

21. *hard-hearted tiger.* Cf. 3 *Henry VI*, I. iv. 137, 'O tiger's heart in a woman's hide'.

27–8. *Wilt . . . attend.* 'Will you delay for ever in paying attention to.'

PAGE **185**, 1–3. *as the proverb . . . loose.* Cf. Tilley, W603 and Plutarch's *The Quiet of Mind*, trans. Wyatt (*Poems*, ed. Muir and Thomson, p. 460):

. . . and as though he held the wolf by the ears, as the proverb saith, could neither hold the tree for weariness and discommodity of the chance, nor let it go for fear of the dreadful peril.

8. *danger of Philoclea.* 'danger to her'.

17. *their desires.* Gynecia's desire for Cleophila, and Cleophila's desire for Philoclea.

17–19. *since . . . desires.* Cf. Tilley, S927 and S930.

27. *affectionated.* O.E.D. †3 cites Florio (1578), Hooker (1586), and NA (*Works*, i. 35), 'lamentable and truly affectionated speeches'.

PAGE **186**, 8. *all to-bewonder her.* The earliest citation for *bewonder* in O.E.D. is from p. 211, 6; *all to-* are intensives (see O.E.D. s.v. *to prefix*² 3).

PAGE **187**, 20 and 27. *medals*. This is the earliest citation in *O.E.D.*; the manuscript spellings suggest that Sidney may have imported the word in the form *medaille* or *medailla*.

23. *Aristomenes*. Ringler, 406, refutes the suggestion of Brie, 206, that Sidney took the name from the famous Messenian general whose deeds are described by Pausanias, IV. xiii–xxiv. He suggests that Sidney is more likely to have found the name in Alciati's emblem 'Signa fortium', where the verses praise Aristomenes as a great and brave man without any indication of nationality. Characters called Aristomenes and Charite (see pp. 191–2) occur in Apuleius, *The Golden Ass*.

PAGE **188**, 1–2. *laden*. I have adopted the less archaic form as the St scribe is indifferent (cf. p. 182, 31); the agreement of St and 93 in reading *loaden* . . . *laden* probably indicates nothing more than coincidental indifference.

5–7. *like* . . . *whole*. Dametas ought to have reflected that if Musidorus had wanted the gold he would have helped himself to the lot.

18. *instruments*. Ph adds 'with as much eagerness as the belly of Sinon's wooden horse was opened in the last night of unfortunate Troy'.

28–PAGE **189**, 2. Ringler, OA 44 and p. 406.

29. 'By the privy hindrances of those who possessed his estate.'

PAGE **189**, 2. Ringler notes the pun on *bait*, a place for rest and refreshment on a journey, and food put out to entrap animals.

15. *sauce*. The word is spelt *sawse* in most manuscripts; it adds spice to Miso's envy rather than produces it (*source*).

PAGE **190**, 25–PAGE **191**, 6. Ringler, OA 45 and pp. 406–7. The poem is copied in B.M. MS. Harl. 7392(2), f. 68 (Ringler, 557). There is a musical setting in B.M. MS. Addit. 15117, f. 18ᵛ in which the final couplet is used as a refrain after each quatrain; the text is taken from one of the folios 1593–1613 (Ringler, 566). There is a three-part setting in John Ward, *The First Set of English Madrigals* (1613), nos. 1 and 2 (words and music are printed in E. H. Fellowes, *The English Madrigal School*, xix (1922)); the text is taken from one of the folios 1598–1613 (Ringler, 567). The words are printed in Fellowes, 3rd edn., p. 266. Ringler informs me that there are many more nineteenth- and twentieth-century settings listed in the New York Public Library Music Index than items 314–24 in S. A. Tannenbaum, *Sidney: a Concise Bibliography* (1941). The first two quatrains, with the first line repeated as a refrain (indicating that the source was a musical setting made before 1589), are quoted by Puttenham, 225, with this introduction:

> Epimone, or the love-burden . . . or the long repeat, in one respect because that one verse alone beareth the whole burden of the song according to the original: in another respect, for that it comes by large distances to be often repeated, as in this ditty made by the noble knight Sir Philip Sidney.

Ringler notes that, like OA 72 and AS 24, these are *serpentina carmina*.

11–28. Ringler, OA 46 and p. 407, where it is noted that 'Sidney deliberately contrasts the complex rhetorical structure and the simple rural images of this song'. He then analyses the framework of this correlative verse. The whole poem, omitting the refrain, is no. 2059 in *England's Parnassus*.

30. *Charita*. See note to p. 187, 3.

PAGE **192**, 10. *Oudemian Street.* This name evidently puzzled the copyists. The scribe of T may have written *unkenned*, 'unknown', and then corrected it to *Oudemian*. With 'nor any such place known' (p. 269, 16), this would suggest that Sidney derived his street name from οὐδαμοῦ, 'nowhere'; though his form is closer to δήμιον, and the suggestion of Ringler, xli, that Sidney intended 'street without inhabitants' may be correct.

30. *picture of Alecto.* She was one of the Furies, pictured with flaming torches, her head covered with serpents, and breathing vengeance, war, and pestilence. She appeared to Turnus in *Aeneid*, vii. 417. Cf. NA (*Works*, i. 256).

31. *Medea.* K. Duncan-Jones, 21, notes that 'there are nine epigrams on paintings and statues of Medea killing her children in the *Greek Anthology*, which Sidney may have known in the edition printed by Stephanus (*Florilegium diversorum epigrammatum veterum* (Paris, 1566))'; and that there is a picture on the subject by Veronese, now in the Accademia, Venice.

PAGE **193**, 34. *as busy as a bee.* Cf. Tilley, B262, with the first citation from Lyly (1580), and the third from NA (*Works*, i. 94). *O.D.E.P.* cites from Chaucer.

PAGE **194**, 3. *that.* 'so that'.

11–12. *so that . . . wonders.* Fraunce, 11, quotes as an example of ironia.

12. *wonders.* Presumably this was indistinctly written in the OA foul papers; Sidney may have made the correction in T himself before Cl and As were copied.

14. *having . . . last.* The metaphor is from the cobbler's trade.

18–29. *how that . . . life.* No doubt Dorus hopes that Mopsa will be the more inclined to fall for his ridiculous tale if he starts with the well-known story of Apollo's banishment and tending of Admetus's flock for nine years. The episode is referred to in Sannazaro's 3rd Prose.

29. *double life.* Apollo persuaded the Fates to grant Admetus deliverance from death if his father, mother, or wife would die for him. His wife Alcestis died in his stead, but was brought back from the underworld by Hercules.

PAGE **196**, 12. *But Pamela.* 'But as for Pamela.'

PAGE **197**, 16–17. *Ulysses . . . safety.* His theft, with Diomedes, of the statue of Pallas Athena from Troy is narrated in the *Iliad*, x; cf. Ovid, *Met.* xiii. 1 ff.

PAGE **198**, 10. *travailing.* With *restraint, travelling* might be the meaning intended.

14–27. Ringler, OA 47. This is one of eight poems copied from 93, without indication of authorship, in B.M. MS. Addit. 34064, ff. 27–31 (Ringler, 555).

21. *rine.* This older form of *rind* is used as here for the sake of the rhyme in Spenser's 'February', 111. I have kept it medially in Musidorus's accompanying poem at p. 199, 17.

26–7. Fraunce, 27, quotes as an example of rhyme, reading *hand* instead of *word*.

30–1. Ringler, OA 48. The poem is copied, without indication of authorship, in C.U.L. MS. Dd.5.75(2), f. 26ᵛ (Ringler, 554).

PAGE **199**, 4–21. Ringler, OA 49.

4. W. Blount cites Propertius:

> Vos exitis testes si quos habet arbor amores
> Fagas et Arcadia pinus amata deo.

17. *rine.* See note to p. 198, 21.

29–PAGE **200**, 17. Ringler, OA 50 and p. 407. Although Ringler prints Pamela's song and Musidorus's reply as one poem, the introductory prose and the different stanza forms suggest that these are two separate poems.

PAGE **200**, 1. *outward glass.* 'external appearance, which reflects her mind' (Ringler).

9. 'Referring to the myth of Icarus (Ovid, *Met.* viii. 183 ff.), usually interpreted as exemplifying the golden mean and the disaster that overtakes those who aspire too high' (Ringler).

23–PAGE **201**, 6. Ringler, OA 51 and pp. 407–8. The poem is copied, without indication of authorship, in C.U.L. MS. Dd.5.75(2), f. 26, and in the Arundel Harington MS., no. 191; attributed to 'Syd' in B.M. MS. Harleian 7392(2), f. 38ᵛ; and to 'S.P.S.' in Bodleian MS. Rawl. Poet. 85, f. 9 (Ringler, 554, 553, and 557). The first eight and the last six lines are set for five voices as nos. 8 and 9 in Thomas Vautor, *The First Set: Being Songs of divers Airs and Natures* (1619–20); the words were taken from one of the folios 93–13. Words and music were edited by E. H. Fellowes, *The English Madrigal School*, xxxiv (1924), and the words are printed in Fellowes, 3rd edn., p. 263. There is a setting of the whole poem for four voices in Martin Peerson, *Private Music, or the First Book of Airs and Dialogues* (1620), no. 13; the words were probably taken from one of the folios 93–13 (Ringler, 567). The words are printed in Fellowes, 3rd edn., p. 180.

23–6. Fraunce, 116, quotes these lines as an illustration of 'the application of the voice' to various emotions.

PAGE **201**, 18–19. *and through . . . lips.* Ph substitutes 'saving that there was so much space left that he might espy part of'.

28. *no life to.* 'no life compared to'. Cf. Tilley, M226, 'A man cannot live on air like a chameleon'. Shakespeare's earliest use of this proverb also associates the lover with the chameleon (*Two Gentlemen of Verona*, II. i. 178).

29–PAGE **202**, 8. See Introduction, pp. lxi–lxii, for the omission of this passage in 93.

PAGE **202**, 6. *approaches.* Ph adds: '(how much he would have proceeded, whom may I desire you to imagine)'.

PAGE **203**, 15–17. *the thoughts . . . thoughts.* Fraunce, 45, quotes this as an example of epanalepsis, 'when the same sound is iterated in the beginning and ending'; he mistranscribed 'out-' as 'ouer-'.

24. *unguarded.* This seems to follow from *protection*; but *unregarded* would fit the love-lorn Gynecia almost as well.

PAGE **204**, 23. *Senicia.* Pyrocles told Basilius that he was queen Senicia's niece (p. 36), and the statement is kept in 90. He had no reason to change the name in his tale to Gynecia; the editors of 93 may have read *Senicia* as *Gynecia*, an error for the name intended, failed to check in Book I, and substituted the celebrated Amazonian queen, Marpesia.

24. *fight on horseback.* Ph substitutes 'run at tilt'.

32. *Gynecia whose.* 'Gynecia's.'

35. *sleightly*. The MSS. spellings vary, and *slightly*, as well as *straitly*, or *straightly*, are possible; but I fancy it suited Gynecia to overlook Pyrocles' story of his dishonourable defeat.

PAGE 206, 31. *play her prize*. 'engage in her contest for victory'.

PAGE 207, 7. *madrigal*. Ringler, 408, notes that this appears to be the first appearance in England of the word and the type of poem (a single stanza of long and short lines, with varying rhyme scheme), which had become popular in Italy in the early sixteenth century.

8–22. Ringler, OA 52 and p. 408.

13. *a sun*. Pyrocles.

21–2. Poirier in *Études Anglaises*, xi (1958), 152, compares Petrarch's Sonnet 183, 12–14, and Sonnet 92, 12–14.

22. Ringler compares p. 144, 22–4.

24. *taste*. The metaphor is confused, but 93's *task* is scarcely an improvement.

27–PAGE 208, 6. Ringler, OA 53 and p. 408.

27. *subject*. in the political sense (Ringler).

27–30. Fraunce, 37, quotes as an example of anadiplosis.

32. *gripe*. Ringler, 466, compares this line with AS **86.** 4 and **14.** 2, 'Upon whose breast a fiercer gripe doth tire'; and notes that the reference to the vulture that rends the vitals of Prometheus was 'a commonplace for describing the effects of love'. Cf. p. 182, 8.

33. *Thy title*. 'Time's right of possession' (Ringler).

PAGE 208, 4. *occasion dear*. Ringler notes that Opportunity is 'usually personified as a young woman (see Alciati's emblem "In occasionem"), but described as a man in *Phaedrus*, v. viii'.

PAGE 209, 34–5. *Ah . . . imagination*. Fraunce, 113 (emending St.'s *could* to *couldest*), quotes as a passage requiring the use of a sobbing flexible voice in lamentation.

PAGE 210, 30–PAGE 211, 10. Ringler, OA 54 and p. 408. There is a musical setting in B.M. MS. Loan 35, f. 1ᵛ, probably taken from 05 or a later folio (Ringler, 566). J. Hollander, *The Untuning of the Sky* (1961), 139–40, analyses Sidney's use of musical terms relating to the technique of lute-playing in this poem.

33. *neither's help*. 'help of neither hand nor mind'.

PAGE 211, 2. *ground*. 'surface, also musical accompaniment' (Ringler).

9–10. W. Milgate, *The Satires, Epigrams . . . of John Donne*, p. 124, compares Satire I. 77–8:

> And as fiddlers stop low'st, at highest sound,
> So to the most brave, stoops he nigh'st ground.

10. *stops*. 'frets', in both musical and non-musical senses.

12–15. *O kind . . . ruin yourself*. Fraunce, 11–12, quotes as an example of ironia.

PAGE 212, 6. *motion . . . mind*. Ph substitutes 'same rising of blood, about the heart'.

19–22. *Was ever . . . fruits.* Cf. Tilley, M1120, 'The moon is not seen where the sun shines'; and A21, 'Acorns were good till bread was found', for which the earliest citation in *O.D.E.P.* is from this passage; cf. *O.D.E.P.*, 'To esteem acorns better than corn', for which the earliest citation is dated 1581.

PAGE **213,** 7. *tumult.* The change in 93 takes account of the adventures in Book III of 90; but the editors failed to remove the reference to *recent* eclogues.

21–35. Ringler, OA 55 and p. 408, where it is noted that Basilius's song 'duplicates the metrical form of his earlier madrigal (OA 52) and continues its praise of Cleophila as a second sun'.

21. Cf. Spenser, *F.Q.* v. iii. 19, 'As when two sunnes appeare in the azure skye'; and Tilley, S992, 'Two suns cannot shine in one sphere'. See note to p. 177, 15–31.

23–6. The reader may be meant to catch the irony of Basilius's impending doom.

PAGE **214,** 12. *obtaining.* The alliteration of 93's *prevailing* with *preventing* is attractive; but the editors of 93 were alert to any suggestion that Pyrocles might intend to ravish Philoclea (see the alteration at lines 7–8).

16–29. Ringler, OA 56 and pp. 408–9, where the use of *bait* for 'trap' (line 17), a 'stopping place for refreshment' (line 21), and for Pyrocles 'teased' by passions like a bear tied to a stake and baited by dogs (line 25) is noted; cf. p. 189, 2. Cf. no. 188 in the Arundel Harington MS., and see note to p. 177, 15–31.

26. *nature's right.* The spelling *rite* (in St alone) is possible.

PAGE **215,** 9–11. *a painter . . . lineament.* See note to p. 11, 22–31.

PAGE **216,** 2. *their souls' rest.* The place where Basilius's and Gynecia's souls rested: Cleophila.

10. *neglect.* The reading of 93 is possible, but the -*ing* may have been repeated by the compositor from *seeing.*

35 (var.) and PAGE **217,** 1 (var.). For the alterations in 93 see Introduction, pp. lx ff.

PAGE **218,** 4. *ambassade.* See note to p. 57, 8.

5–18. Ringler, OA 57 and p. 409, where it is noted that the first stanza is built on the figure anadiplosis.

8. *Passion rebelled.* 'Passion having rebelled against reason.'

17. *Eye-hopes.* 'hopes induced by appearances'.

PAGE **220,** 33–PAGE **221,** 4. *And therefore . . . master.* Fraunce, 114, quotes as an example of the voice 'in anger, shrill, sharp, quick, short'.

36–PAGE **221,** 1. *mew . . . rouse.* Basilius is using a hawking image.

33. *open invention.* 'acute intelligence'.

PAGE **222,** 15–16. *Thisbe . . . Pyramus.* Cf. Ovid, *Met.* iv. 55–166.

29. *disarming.* Pyrocles certainly had his sword with him (see p. 228, 5–6); but 93's *disarraying* could be the correct reading.

PAGE **224,** 1–11. *a bottle . . . experiment.* Goldman, 204–5, compares the little flacket of gold given by Isoud's mother to her daughter's gentlewoman to give to king Mark, but its contents were drunk by Tristram. See Introduction, p. xxiii, for a closer parallel in Apuleius, *The Golden Ass.*

3–4. Ringler, OA 58.

21. *thus down*. The As and Je reading confirms that Bo and Cl *this done* was an intelligent emendation following a misreading of T's *thus* as *this*.

PAGE **225**, 11. *unreadying*. This is the earliest citation in *O.E.D.*; the variants indicate the unfamiliarity of the word.

14–17. *began . . . brake . . . made*. The confusion of tenses in the MSS. evidently goes back to Sidney; the disjointed sentences are intended to reflect Basilius's mental state, 'out of all grammar'.

24–6. *coffer . . . face*. Fraunce, 16, cites as an example of metaphor. Cf. Heliodorus, v. iii where Cnemon

hurried away, stumbling as he went, now getting his feet tripped up, now suddenly running into the walls: here it was against a lintel, there against some utensil hanging by chance from the roof, that he knocked his head.

27–8. *Pan . . . Hercules*. Ringler, 363, compares LM **3**. 7–12:

> When wanton Pan, deceived with lion's skin,
> Came to the bed where wound for kiss he got,
> To woe and shame the wretch did enter in,
> Till this he took for comfort of his lot:
> 'Poor Pan', he said, 'although thou beaten be,
> It is no shame, since Hercules was he'.

Ringler notes that 'Ovid, *Fasti*, ii. 303–58, tells how Faunus (whom he equates with Pan), seeking Omphale's bed, gets into that of Hercules'. K. Duncan-Jones, 28, notes that Omphale is not actually mentioned by name in Ovid's account; hence perhaps the confusion with Iole on the part of Sidney and others, including Gower, Tasso, and Spenser. In NA (*Works*, i. 75–6) Sidney has Hercules spinning for Omphale.

29. *bride*. Ph adds: 'doth, that will not seem to know what metal a man is made'.

PAGE **226**, 4. *nightgown*. Ph adds:

the same order was encountered with his professed enemies, the turks and stools, so that much he feared he had new awaked his wife, yet rather adventuring anything than now to retire.

Cf. p. 225, 24–6. Presumably *turks* are *ottomans*, for which the earliest citation in *O.E.D.* is for 1806.

6–8. *Thus . . . cunning*. See Introduction, pp. xxii–xxiii, for parallels with Pyrocles' stratagem to unite Basilius and Gynecia in the *Amadis* and Heliodorus.

15–30. Ringler, OA 59 and p. 409, where it is noted that this 'song is an imitation, in accentual iambics, of a sapphic stanza (cf. OA 12)' [p. 81, 16–p. 82, 14].

PAGE **227**, 23. *dealing*. Ph adds: 'within a warm bed they say is not without some force of persuasion'.

32. *burdens*. Ph adds: 'as well of mind as otherwise'.

PAGE **228**, 2. *unquietness*. Ph adds: 'as the fox doth when he lurks'.

2–3. *to satisfy . . . desire*. *Greedy* was often used where we might prefer *eager*; cf. p. 212, 21 and p. 217, 16, and Castiglione's *The Courtier*, trans. Hoby (Everyman edn., p. 27), 'clean quenched the fire of his greedy desire'.

14-20. *This . . . favour.* 93 transfers this sentence to the end of this Book or Act.

24. *pangs.* There is no trace of a bookish metaphor, and the reading of St, etc., and 93 must have arisen from a misreading of *pāges.*

PAGE **229**, 10–11. *Philoclea . . . guiltless punishment.* The epithet has been transferred from Philoclea to punishment—if indeed it does not belong to the nightingale; for Sidney has in mind the tale of Philomela (Ovid, *Met.* vi. 565). See p. 346, 25–7 and note.

17–PAGE **230**, 6. Ringler, OA 60 and p. 409, where it is noted that this is Sidney's most elaborate example of correlative verse (see note to p. 182, 12–19). Rubel, 158, notes that the poem is built entirely on the figure of brachylogia. Fraunce, 56, quotes the poem in full. It is copied without attribution in B.M. MS. Harl. 7392(2), f. 66 (Ringler, 557). It is included in *England's Helicon* (1600), taken from 98, headed 'An excellent sonnet of a nymph'.

PAGE **230**, 7–22. *The force . . . soul.* Florizel's description of his feelings for Perdita in *The Winter's Tale*, IV. iv. 136–46, is strongly reminiscent of this passage; see C. B. Mount in *N. & Q*. iii (1893), 305.

PAGE **231**, 2–3. *ash-colour silk and gold.* Philoclea wears ash-colour in token of submission to her fate, while the gold represents her steadfast love.

31–PAGE **232**, 10. Ringler OA 61 and p. 409.

PAGE **232**, 9–10. These lines are cited from a manuscript source in Puttenham, 217, reading *breeds* for *draws*, as an example of acclamatio, 'the surclose or consenting close', with the remark that 'Sir Philip Sidney very prettily closed up a ditty in this sort'.

PAGE **234**, 5–19. *There . . . tormentor.* Fraunce, 74, cites as an example of exclamation (cursing).

9–10. *And . . . affection.* W. Blount cites Puttenham, 213, adapting him as follows: 'Petrarch wrote in the like sort translated by Sir Thom. Wiat', and quoting from him the first fourteen lines of 'Perdie I said it not'.

14. *which.* Pyrocles' eyes.

PAGE **236**, 1. *Thisbe's punishment.* Pyrocles had used the same comparison to Gynecia; see p. 222, 15–16 and note.

9–PAGE **237**, 43. See Introduction, p. lxi, for comment on the passage substituted in 93.

PAGE **237**, 41. *The beauty . . . Philoclea.* See p. 9, 30 and note.

PAGE **238**, 2. *Philisides.* The song was presumably written in praise of Mira. Some of the phrases in it are quoted in AS v as examples of the praise that the poet has already lavished on the mistress to whom this song is addressed. Ringler, 484, argues from this that AS v was originally addressed to Mira. In NA the song is transferred from Philisides to Zelmane (Pyrocles), who is said to have composed it when he saw Philoclea bathing in the river Ladon (*Works*, i. 218).

6–PAGE **242**, 29. Ringler OA 62 and pp. 409–11, where Sidney's many revisions to the poem are discussed. As it was transferred to Book II in 90, 93 takes its text (with the latest revisions made in T) from 90 and not from P. Cm contains lines 1–8 only (for comment on their readings see Ringler, 371). The poem is copied from a miscellany in which the text was taken from a MS. similar to St, without attribution, in C.U.L. MS. Dd.5.75(2), f. 26 (the first two lines), and ff. 36ᵛ–37 (complete) (Ringler, 554). The last three lines occur upside down (previous leaves torn out), taken from a MS. similar to As, in B.M. MS. Egerton 2421, f. 46ᵛ (Ringler, 555). The first four lines, probably copied from one of the folios, are in B.M. MS. Add. 27406, f. 117, and the whole poem is copied from 93 in B.M. MS. Add. 34064, ff. 30–1 (Ringler, 555). B.M. MS. Sloane 1925, ff. 13–14 contains the NA introductory prose and the following lines in this order: p. 239, 9–10; p. 241, 7–8; p. 242, 8–9 and 6–7; p. 240, 15–18 and 7–8; p. 239, 11–12; p. 238, 26–7, taken from one of the printed editions (Ringler, 557). The poem is copied in Corpus Christi College, Oxford MS. 328, ff. 85–6ᵛ, from 93 or a later print, headed 'In commendation of a beautiful lady' (Ringler, 559). The poem is copied from 1621 or a later print in the Folger Shakespeare Library MS. V. a. 162 [formerly 452. 4], ff. 93–6ᵛ (Ringler, 560). It is no. 2012 in *England's Parnassus*. Puttenham, 244, refers to this poem under '*Icon.* or Resemblance by Imagery':

> Sir Philip Sidney in the description of his mistress excellently well handled this figure of resemblance by imagery, as ye may see in his book of *Arcadia*.

Ringler, 411, traces the development of these anatomical catalogues from the thirteenth century onwards, and refers to some of the many imitations of Sidney's poem. The description of a fair shepherdess in Sannazaro's 4th Prose, and several other parallels, are quoted by W. Blount. The various texts differ in the arrangement of the paragraphs; I have begun a new one for each part of the body.

8–9; PAGE **239**, 11–16; PAGE **240**, 3–4. Cf. AS **v.** 38–9:

> Nor blushing lilies, nor pearls' ruby-hidden row,
> Nor of that golden sea, whose waves in curls are broken:

14. *That.* her forehead.

    even. I have kept Ringler's reading, though with some doubts. It is not easy to tell whether *even* or *eben* was the final choice in St; but Bo's *eboene* might be the result of *ebon* corrected to *even* in the copy (T). Mira had golden hair, with which black eyebrows, though not impossible, would be unusual. The somewhat similar description of Belphoebe, who also had golden hair (*F.Q.* II. iii. 25), has 'Vnder the shadow of her euen browes'; though *shadow* suggests that *eben* might have been intended. For *ebony brows* evidently became a commonplace; cf. *Greene's Mourning Garment* (*c.* 1590), 'When fro' th'arches eben black flew looks as a lightning' (ed. Collins, ii. 274); and P. Fletcher, *Piscatory Eclogues*, VII. xvii, 'Her eyebrow black, like to an ebon bow'. W. Blount notes (he is quoting from Puttenham, 244), as though he had *ebon* and not *even* before him, 'One writeth thus, describing a lady: "Her brows two bows of ebony".' Finally, *even brows* simply repeats Sidney's *equal lines* of line 15.

20; PAGE **240**, 2; PAGE **242**, 14. Ringler compares AS **v.** 10–11:

> I said thine eyes were stars, thy breasts the milk'n way,
> Thy fingers Cupid's shafts, thy voice the angels' lay.

21. *pair.* 'An emendation by 90, or a late correction by Sidney himself of

T's scribal error "praise". The line as corrected means "They are so perfect that even praise will blemish them"' (Ringler).

26–7. Cf. OP **4**. 451, 'Those eyes which nothing like themselves can see'.

30. *queen-apple's side*. Cf. Spenser, 'June', 43. Grosart quotes Parkinson, *Paradisus Terrestris* (1629), 'The queen-apple is of two sorts, both of them great, fair red apples, and well relished, but the greater is the best'.

PAGE **239**, 3. *Save that*. Ringler prints *So that*, and does not record Bo's emendation, which the sense requires.

11–16. See note to p. 238, 8–9.

25. *a say*. Sidney may have written *assay*, but the aphetic form was not unusual.

29. *pommels*. Sidney may have been influenced by Sannazaro's 'duo ritondi pomi', but not have wished to repeat the comparison with apples already used for the lady's cheeks (p. 238, 30).

PAGE **240**, 1–4. See note to p. 238, 8–9 and to p. 238, 20.

2. *milken name*. The Milky Way. G. Bullough, edn. of Greville's *Works*, i. 257, compares Greville's Sonnet VI.

11–12. Fraunce, 5, quotes as an example of metonymia. Cl's *snow* (given currency by Feuillerat) is an error for *stone*.

19. *Her*. Ringler reads *The*; but he evidently thought *Her*, the reading of St, was an error peculiar to 90. It is *her navel* at line 15.

26–7. E. Seaton, editing P. Fletcher, *Venus and Anchises*, p. 106, compares stanza 29, 'For now the shameless world of best things is ashamed', written in a similar context.

30. *Ovid's song*. Cf. Elegy I. v (Marlowe's translation):

> What arms and shoulders did I touch and see!
> How apt her breasts were to be press'd by me!
> How smooth a belly under her waist saw I,
> How large a leg, and what a lusty thigh!

PAGE **241**, 3. *Albion cliffs*. After 'Ovid's song', this naturalizes the convention in England, though it is no less inappropriate in Arcadia; however, Philisides, the author of the poem, is a 'stranger shepherd'.

7. *gems of love*. *gins* is a possible reading with *knots*.

10. K. Duncan-Jones, 65, suggests that Sidney may be recalling his conversation with Hilliard (see Buxton, 151); and notes that Edward Norgate, *Miniatura* (ed. M. Hardie (1919), p. 22) advised the limner 'ever to remember that in all or most of the shadows white is ever a daily guest, and seldom absent but in the deepest shadows'.

15. *Atlas*. 'the muscle of her calf supporting the heavens of her body' (Ringler).

16. *whale*. This is spelt *whall* for the sake of the eye-rhyme in most of the manuscripts.

28. *hate-spot ermelin*. The misreading of *spott* as *sport* in St and 90 displays ignorance of the ermine's proverbial purity; cf. p. 257, 19, NA (*Works*, i. 108), and AS **86**. 5.

PAGE **242**, 9. Ringler compares Petrarch's 'calde neve' and AS **v**. 37, 'Think now

no more to hear of warm, fine, odoured snow'. Davenport in *N. & Q.* cxciv
(1949), 555, compares *A Midsummer Night's Dream*, v. i. 59, 'That is hot ice and
wondrous strange snow'.

   10. *sapphire-coloured.* blue.

   14. See note to p. 238, 20.

   14–15. Ringler compares OP **4.** 147–8:

> Her hands, which pierced the soul's sev'n-double shield,
> Were now his darts leaving his wonted fight.

   15. *amethysts.* Purple or violet stones. The texts use the alternative spelling
amatists.

   26–9. See headnote to the poem.

PAGE **243,** 2. *Argus . . . Briareus.* Actually Argus had one hundred eyes (Ovid,
Met. i. 13–14). Evidently the Hm scribe could not read *Briareus*, the owner of
one hundred hands and fifty heads, and so substituted *Cerberus*, Pluto's dog,
who had fifty heads, and added 'and heads'.

THE THIRD ECLOGUES

PAGE **244,** 2 (var.). *Thyrsis.* 93 changed Lalus to Thyrsis in the First and
also in the Second Eclogues (p. 159), but left the reference to Lalus in the
Second Eclogues in the duologue between Nico and Pas (p. 142, 6 and 9). 90
left Lalus in the First Eclogues, did not use the passage in the Second Eclogues
at p. 159, and kept the reference to Lalus in the duologue. The editors of 93 may
have felt that the name was too like Lelius in NA; if so, they overlooked the
reference to the fine shepherd Lalus whom once Basilius 'had afore him in
pastoral sports, and had greatly delighted in his wit, full of pretty simplicity'
(*Works*, i. 107)—though this occurs in Book I, and Basilius evidently refers to
pastoral sports that took place before the story begins.

   9. *green silk.* The colour for lovers.

   29–30. *And so . . . appointed.* This seems to point the contrast between the
honest loves of Lalus and Kala, leading to marriage with parental approval, and
the clandestine embraces of Pyrocles and Philoclea in the preceding book.

PAGE **245, 7.** *Coredens.* This is the usual spelling in the OA MSS.; 93 has *Coridon*.
Ringler, 413–14, suggests that Sidney made up the compound 'co-red[i]ens',
meaning 'returning with', perhaps to refer to Edward Wotton with whom
Sidney returned to England in the spring of 1575. At p. 256, 3 Languet, who
frequently sent greetings to 'noster Wottonus', hands Philisides over to Coredens.
Another possible candidate would be Lodowick Bryskett, who went with Sidney
to Italy when he left Languet in Vienna. On p. 340 Coredens is, like Phili-
sides, in love with Mira. The close friend of Sidney known to have addressed
poems to a Mira was Fulke Greville. His posthumously published *Works* (1633)
were said to have been 'written in his youth and familiar exercise with Sir
Philip Sidney', and Sidney and Greville are referred to as Philisides and
Mirafilus in one of the funeral elegies in *Exequiae* (1587). But Greville was not
in Vienna with Sidney, and was exactly the same age. Edward Dyer was not in
Vienna with Sidney either, and Languet did not meet him until he came to

England in 1579; but he was appropriately nine years older than Sidney. The protagonist of his poems 'Alas my heart' and 'Amaryllis' is called Corydon; but Sargent's anagram 'Cos^n Dier' from 'Coridens' is somewhat unconvincing— 'cor Sidne' is just as likely, and would serve for any one of his friends. In sum, Coredens combines features pointing to both Greville and Dyer; but the 'Ister Bank' poem (pp. 254 ff.) points to someone who was not only older than Sidney (like Dyer), but also, like Wotton or Bryskett, was with him in Vienna and left the town with him.

27. *Dicus*. This shepherd has hitherto been represented as one who detested love (pp. 64 ff. and pp. 137 ff.). Either Sidney has forgotten this, or he felt that it enhanced the celebration of Lalus and Kala that such a character should be moved to sing their marriage song, or he thought one misogynist shepherd was enough now that Histor, disappointed in his love for Kala, has fallen into 'a detestation of marriage' (see p. 260).

29–PAGE **248**, 27. Ringler, OA 63 and pp. 411–12, where he notes that this is the first English epithalamium, and that 'Sidney derived his stanza form from the "Versos Franceses" sung by Arsileo at the marriage of Syreno and Diana in Book IV of Gil Polo's *Diana Enamorada*'. He finds the only similarities in content are in the opening line, 'De flores matizadas se vista 'l verde prado' and in two lines of the last stanza:

> Concorde paz os tenga contentos muchos años,
> sin ser de la raviosa sospecha atormentados.

which Sidney expands in his eighth and tenth stanzas (see *Diana*, ed. Kennedy, 378, for Yong's translation of Gil Polo's poem). Ringler analyses the structural pattern of this correlative verse.

PAGE **249**, 20–PAGE **253**, 14. Ringler, OA 64 and p. 412. There is a very free version of this poem in B.M. MS. Harl. 6910, ff. 173^v–175, subscribed 'P.S.', and dated 1601. Ringler considers this a substantive source, not deriving from any of the prints; but he does not record the variants as they are clearly sophistications, and I have likewise ignored them. Nico's fabliau is similar to 'The unwittingly complaisant confessor', Boccaccio, *Decameron*, 3rd Day, Novella 3.

21. Cf. Harington, 232, Note to Book XXVIII, 'As I have heard of one of honest calling (But nameless he, for blameless he must be)'.

PAGE **250**, 5. *benamed*. Rubel, 153, compares Spenser's 'November', and notes that Sidney's passage is cited in *O.E.D.* as the first of three examples of the word used with complement. There are one or two other examples of dialect or archaic terms in this poem.

17. *chumpish*. The variants indicate the unfamiliarity of the word.

21. *it*. Ringler reads *he*, as in Je, Hm and 93.

26. Cf. p. 72, 11 and note for another glance at the proverbs, 'Oil on the fire is not the way to quench', and 'No quenching fire with tow'.

PAGE **251**, 7. *Bussing*. Sidney may have been aware of some older tradition summed up in Herrick's 'We buss our wantons, but our wives we kiss' (*Poems*, ed. L. C. Martin, p. 189).

PAGE **252**, 13. *pistle*. Sidney may have written 'Th'epistle' as in Je, rather than the aphetic form.

PAGE **253,** 4. *duke.* Ph's *prince* brings the nomenclature into line with p. 251, 10 and p. 252, 26; the slip was either Nico's or Sidney's, and as such I have left it.

8. Cf. Harington, 232, Note to Book XXVIII, 'Moral. In Jocundo and Astolfo both, may be noted the vanity of beauty in men, and how weak a protection it is, against the blow that never smarteth, as some have termed it.'

12. *marks of jealousy.* Horns, as W. Blount is quick to point out, with an anecdote.

13–14. Cf. Harington, 97, Note to Book XIII. 9:

> When love hath knit two hearts in perfect unity,
> They seldom fail to find their opportunity.

Sentence. Ovid. Non caret effectu quod volvere duo. Sir Philip Sid. made it thus. For why no jealousy can that prevent, to which two parties once give full consent.

The line from Ovid (*Amores,* II. iii. 16) is quoted by W. Blount, and also appears partly erased in the Folger Shakespeare Library copy of the 1598 edition of the *Arcadia.* Cf. Alexander Nicholas, *Discourse of Marriage and Wiving,* 1615 (*Harl. Misc.* ii. 158):

> No policy, they say, can that prevent,
> Whereto two parties give their full consent.

15. *dicker.* Half a score was the customary unit of exchange, especially for hides or skins; *O.E.D.* cites this passage for the *transf.* use.

21–PAGE **254,** 4. Ringler, OA 65 and p. 412. Harington, 87, Note to Book XI on the 'Moral', quotes this poem in full with this introduction:

> And therefore that excellent verse of Sir Philip Sidney in his first *Arcadia* (which I know not by what mishap is left out in the printed book) is in mine opinion worthy to be praised and followed to make a good and virtuous wife.

And at the end of the poem he remarks, 'In which you see his opinion of the two extremities of want and vain expense'. Harington's 'printed book' was 90, and he might have been expected to have observed that the text ends before the Third Eclogues. The poem is no. 141 in *England's Parnassus*; the text is taken from Harington (Ringler, 565).

24. *one man still.* 'always remaining the same, maintaining the same course' (Ringler).

PAGE **254,** 7. *Actaeon's ornament.* Ovid, *Met.* iii. 138 ff.; 'the horns (of a cuckold)'.

15–19 (var.). I have not printed 'The lad Philisides'; it is readily available as OP 5 in Ringler; it has an English setting, and is not appropriate to the theme of marriage in the Third Eclogues.

21–PAGE **259,** 23. Ringler, OA 66 and pp. 412–15. In transferring this poem to the First Eclogues the editors of 90 gave it to 'a young shepherd'; the editors of 93 restored it to Philisides in the Third Eclogues. This is Sidney's tribute to Hubert Languet who, in the words of Daniel Rogers (14 January 1579) addressed to Sidney, 'guided you through the histories and origins of states; he was the tutor who determined your judgement' (Dorsten, *Poets,* 65). They were together in Vienna in August 1573 and August 1574, and we are to suppose that the fable was told Philisides by Languet in one of these months before 'they were forced to part'. There are many tributes to masters in Renaissance pastoral poetry (see Goldman, 81 and 176); here Sidney is closest to the fable in Spenser's 'February' related by the shepherd Thenot, which he learnt from his master Tityrus (Chaucer). Like Spenser, he uses an old rustic language, and both fables may have a contemporary application (see the inquiry on p. 259, 26–7); both have been interpreted as attacks on the French marriage, opposed by Sidney in his *Discourse to the Queen's Majesty*. The general moral is clear: a powerful aristocracy is the best safeguard of the common people against tyranny. This is in accordance with the Tudor theory of mixed government by a threefold system of monarch, aristocracy, and commons. Cf. L. Stone, *The Crisis of the Aristocracy* 1558–1641 (1965), pp. 14–15:

> The early Tudors had striven, not without success, to undermine the strength of the nobility, which they regarded as a menace to quasi-absolute monarchy. In the reign of Elizabeth it was thought that the balance of society was just about right, with the aristocracy filling a useful role as 'brave half paces between a throne and a people', to use Fulke Greville's famous phrase.

See p. 320, 3–p. 321, 31 for a discussion of monarchical government.

21. *Ister*. The setting on the Danube is natural in that it was at Vienna that Sidney was under Languet's tutelage. Ringler notes that pastorals are usually sung by day, and the night setting underlines Sidney's apprehensions that the sheep, the common people, might be led astray in the darkness of their ignorance.

22. *couthe*. Rubel, 154–5, notes that this is glossed in Spenser's 'January', and that 'September' has 'coulde' and 'December' 'kidst'.

25. *did soothe*. Ringler reads *doth soothe*, and does not record *did*, the reading of the MSS. that supplied him with *soothe*. Sidney might, however, have been trying to produce a pseudo-archaic word *scothe*, meaning to 'scarf' or 'cover'. Ringler, 413, draws attention to the confusion Sidney's archaisms caused to the copyists.

PAGE 255, 15. *Languet*. See headnote to the poem.

18 and 30. Rudenstine, 294, compares Languet's letter of 22 October 1578:

> I confess that in the splendour of a court, there are so many temptations to vice that it is very hard for a man to hold himself unspotted by them, and keep his feet on so slippery ground. But you must stand firm on your principle and strength of mind against these difficulties, knowing the harder the conflict, the greater the glory of a triumph (Pears, 155).

On p. 308 he draws attention to some further passages in the Languet–Sidney correspondence (Pears, 2–5, 29–30, and 46–9) that 'relate closely to the tone and spirit' of this poem.

21. *our wits*. Ringler reads *your wits* with 90–93, and does not record the reading of OA and 13.

PAGE 256, 3. *Coredens*. See note to p. 245, 7.

6–17. Sidney combines the Golden Age described by Ovid (*Met.* i. 89–112) and the millennial kingdom prophesied by Isaiah 11: 6–8, when the wolf will dwell with the lamb, and the leopard lie down with the kid. Cf. Greville, *A Treatise of Monarchy*, st. 122 (*Remains*, ed. G. A. Wilkes, p. 64).

8. *woned*. Rubel, 155, notes that Sidney's use is peculiar, and that E. K. erroneously glosses *haunt* in 'February' and 'September'. Speght glosses *wone*.

11. *as seemed them*. 'as seemed best to them'.

18. *beasts with courage clad*. the aristocrats.

20 ff. Sidney combines the late classical myth of Prometheus, who when he created man from earth gave him the characteristics of each living creature, with Aesop's fable of the frogs who asked Jupiter for a king (Ringler).

PAGE 257, 10–21. Cf. George Herbert, 'Humility' (*Poems*, ed. F. E. Hutchinson, p. 70).

11. *sparrow*. Cf. p. 78, 29.

13. *elephant . . . memory*. Cf. Pliny, *Natural History*, viii. 5.

14. *parrot*. Cf. p. 78, 17–22.

19. *ermine*. See note to p. 241, 28.

28. Cf. the Dedication by the publisher, T. Thorpe, to John Florio of *Epictetus his Manual*, trans. J. Healey (1618), 'This Manual of Epictetus . . . hath been held by some the hand to philosophy, the instrument of instruments'.

PAGE 258, 4. *water drink, herbs meat*. At first man drank only water and was a vegetarian.

23. *weakers'*. *themselves* (line 24) demands the plural.

28. *foen of greatness*. Ringler glosses 'their foes the nobler beasts'; they were killed on account of their greatness.

29. *they*. The nobler beasts, i.e. the aristocracy.

31. 'The structure of government, unsupported by a strong aristocracy, crushes the common people' (Ringler).

PAGE 259, 11. *gloire*. See Introduction, p. lxv.

12–13. Fraunce, 52, quotes these lines as an example of polyptoton, 'often falling or declining, of one word, is when as words of one offspring have diverse fallings or terminations'.

16. *Or know your strengths*. 'Be aware that the aristocrats are the protectors of the commons against tyranny.'

19. *stour*. The earliest citation in *O.E.D.* for this extension of the original meaning of 'armed conflict' is from Spenser's 'January', 27, where E. K. glosses it 'a fit'.

24–PAGE 260, 5. *According . . . it was*. 90 uses this prose link in the First Eclogues.

25–6. *words . . . style*. This statement contrasts with Sidney's later reservation about the 'old rustic language' of *The Shepherds' Calendar* in the *Defence of Poesy* (*Works*, iii. 37).

26–7. *strangeness . . . mean by it*. Cf. p. 56, 8–9 where it is said that the Arcadian shepherds 'under hidden forms utter such matters as otherwise were not fit for their delivery' (altered in NA (*Works*, i. 28) to the less equivocal 'as otherwise they durst not deal with').

27. For Geron's grudge against Philisides see pp. 74 ff.

31. *banquet*. Kala's wedding feast. 93 follows 90, which had altered to *sport-meeting* as more appropriate to the context in the First Eclogues.

PAGE 260, 6–PAGE 263, 24. Ringler, OA 67 and p. 415. 90 transferred this poem to the First Eclogues, but 93 restored it to its original position. Fogel, 239–40, compares with Geron's defence of marriage Languet's letter to Sidney of 8 January 1578 (Pears, 133).

12. *chaw*. Ringler prefers *chew*; but I think that Geron would have used the vulgar form.

PAGE **261**, 4. *chat*. Rubel, 154, compares Turberville, *Eclogues*, p. 13, 'Tush Amyntas, let us chat'. E. K. glosses 'to holden chat' in Spenser's 'July'.

4–6. These lines were evidently omitted by the transcriber of T, but later restored, probably by Sidney himself.

11. *fremd*. Rubel, 153, notes that Speght glosses *frened*, *frend*, 'stranger', and *fremed*, 'wild, strange'; and compares Spenser's 'April', 28, 'So now his frend is changed for a frenne'.

PAGE **262**, 1–2. 'Our "little world" is the microcosm, the individual man, which knows (acknowledges) its king (reason) by rationally choosing the good' (Ringler).

6–7. W. Milgate, *The Satires, Epigrams . . . of John Donne*, p. 197, compares Donne's epigram on 'Hero and Leander':

> Both robbed of air, we both lie in one ground,
> Both whom one fire had burnt, one water drowned.

6–8. Ringler compares *Defence of Poesy* (*Works*, iii. 31), 'With a sword thou maist kill thy father, and with a sword thou maist defend thy prince and country'.

11. *drawn-out line*. 'line of descendants'.

25. *I have*. Ringler prints *have I*, the reading of Ph and 90–93, and does not record the reading of the other OA MSS.

PAGE **263**, 1–2. This refers to Histor's prose account of the miseries inflicted on Erona for despising love in the First Eclogues; see pp. 67, 13 ff.

11. *for pains*. Ringler prints *for pain* from 90–93, and does not record the OA reading.

21–3. 'Omitted in 90 because the poem had been transferred to the First Eclogues where there was no mention of a bride. 93, though it replaced the poem in the Third Eclogues, took its text from 90 and also omitted these lines; 13 restored them from an *Old Arcadia* manuscript' (Ringler).

THE FOURTH BOOK OR ACT

PAGE **265**, 2–9 (var.). As the princes were no longer guilty, 93 transferred the passage about 'everlasting justice' to apply to the rebellious peasants, p. 307, 10–11 (var.).

17–18. Ringler, OA 68. These lines are copied in Bodleian, MS. Rawl. Poet. 148, f. 5ᵛ from 98 (Ringler, 558).

23–5. *Midas's . . . ears*. Midas judged that Pan was superior in singing and playing on the flute to Apollo, who thereupon turned his ears into those of an ass to show his stupidity and ignorance (Ovid, *Met*. xi. 5 ff.). The illustration, appropriate in itself, may have occurred to Sidney here because of Midas's golden touch.

PAGE **266**, 1. *so suddenly*. I have adopted 93's *so*, which may, however, be editorial rather than derived from P, as the rest of the sentence with *but that* requires it.

3. *far passing*. This is apparently what Sidney wrote; but as Dametas got

home 'three hours within night' (line 15), 93's *coming on* is a reasonable emendation, accepted by 13, which thought the time-sequence further improved by having Dametas return 'three hours *before* night'.

PAGE **267**, 12. *chicken.* Ph adds: 'the bedstaff of my age, the spectacle of my eyes, the plum porridge to my mouth'.

13. *me.* Ph adds: 'my honey egg'.

15. *attending for.* Je has *attending far*, which is tempting, but 'waiting for' is perfectly good sense.

18. *said he.* Ph adds: 'the drone of my hive, the cobweb of my house, the pole-cat of my chamber'.

23. *third time named.* See p. 195, 32–4.

25. *seeing . . . place.* 'as neither blessing nor cursing had any effect'.

PAGE **268**, 7. *Phaethon's mother.* Cf. p. 149, 35 and note.

19–22. *Thou . . . kings.* Harington, 404, quotes this exchange between Dametas and Mopsa; see Introduction, p. xxxix.

PAGE **269**, 6–7. *an old . . . hers.* 'a house of an old acquaintance of hers', or 'a house she used to frequent'. The sequence of the narrative would be greatly improved by transferring *as . . . stricken* to follow *husband's love.*

9–10. *Juno . . . love.* The story is told in Ovid, *Met.* ix. 273 ff.

17. *Dametas's unworthy advancement.* This is hyperbaton: 'the advancement of which Dametas was unworthy'.

19. *pans, cries and laughters.* There is something uncomfortable about pans and cries so flatly juxtaposed. Nevertheless, taken with Miso's 'increasing the sport of hunting her husband with her diligent barking', I think that the *pans* were metal vessels beaten in order to flush out the game (Dametas). The spirit is that of a skimmington (the earliest citation in *O.E.D.* is for 1607, but no doubt the custom was much older amongst country people), or of the pursuit of the fox in Chaucer, 'Nonnes Preestes Tale', 560–80. Cf. the Phagonian rebels who seized their pots as weapons (p. 128, 7–19 and note). The readings of the manuscripts point to 'Pannes' or 'pannes' in T; the spelling and punctuation of St are 'Pannes, cryes and Laughters', whereas the god is invariably spelt 'Pan'. '*Panike*' in 93 could derive from P, but it is more likely to be the learned and pedantic Hugh Sanford's misreading as 'Pan's cries', which he interpreted as a reference either to Pan as a hunter or to the causeless fear that Pan was supposed to inspire in crowds. 93's usage is not recorded in *O.E.D.*, where the earliest citations for *panic* are both from Holland's translation of Plutarch's *Moralia* (1603).

PAGE **270**, 4. *feeling sense.* 'sense of touch'.

6. *colour.* Cl spells *choller*, and this may indicate a play on words; cf. *Defence of Poesy* (*Works*, iii. 42):

And we having noted the grace of those words, hale them in sometimes to a familiar epistle, when it were too much choler to be choleric.

17. *children.* Mopsa is the only offspring we hear about.

PAGE **272**, 9. *trees. . . . burial.* Dametas refers to his coffin, with a shudder at the gallows.

20. *greater constellation*. The stars governing the fortunes of Pyrocles and Musidorus.

24. *unworthily*. See note to p. 269, 17.

29. *pacing*. The alternative spelling *pasing* gave rise to *passing* in some manuscripts.

32. *which he*. The omission of *he* in Cl and Ph brings the sentence structure closer to modern usage; but there are several other examples of the repetition of pronominal subjects in long sentences.

PAGE 273, 5–8. *or that . . . prison*. Sidney appears to be drawing on neo-Platonic descriptions of ecstasy; see *The Elegies . . . of John Donne*, ed. H. Gardner, Appendix D, and J. Carey in *R.E.S.* xvi (1965), 50–3.

10. *viny*. The word, which puzzled the copyists (Je's *very nigh* is ingenious) is first recorded for 1570 in *O.E.D.*, and the earliest citation for the figurative meaning is from this passage.

13. *Psyche . . . lover*. Deceived by her sisters into thinking her unknown lover lover was a monster, Psyche broke her promise to Cupid and one night when he was asleep drew near him with a lamp and beheld the most handsome of the gods. The story is told in Apuleius, *The Golden Ass*, xxii.

17–18. *not thinking . . . lion*. This is the earliest citation in Tilley, L317; but cf. W7, for which the earliest citation in *O.D.E.P.* ('Let sleeping dogs lie') is from Chaucer.

29–30. *Miso . . . inheritrix*. Evidently Miso and Mopsa, attracted by the noise, have followed Dametas.

32–3. *him he never knew*. Presumably Dametas swears by Apollo.

PAGE 274, 2. *close as a butterfly*. Cf. 'butterfly kiss'.

3. *jealous*. St's *zealous* is possible; the words have the same root.

18. *wedlock*. *wedlock's*, as indicated by the reading of St and Da, is possible; I have accepted the majority reading.

20–1. *will of words*. 'verbal testament'.

26. *first . . . time*. There may be an intended irony as truth was the daughter of time.

31–PAGE 275, 10. Ringler, OA 69 and p. 415. Ringler, lix, notes the Petrarchan rhyme scheme and hendecasyllabic lines. Cf. AS 39.

PAGE 275, 6. *sinless sleep*. Ringler glosses *Witness his wrong* in the next line as 'testify to his suffering'; if this is taken to mean suffering caused by others' wrongdoing, then sleep is *sinless* because it is without such wrongs. I confess to sharing the uneasiness of some of the copyists. The conjecture of Ph and 05, *senseless*, is the most intelligent; but given the contrast between night and day in the whole poem—in the previous lines the presence of Phoebus is blamed for Basilius's displeasure during the day—*sunless* may have been intended. The u/i confusion is a common one, and *sunless* would emphasize the contrast in Phoebus's absence.

silence wisdom's mother. Several proverbs deal with the merits of silence; cf. Tilley, W519, 'No wisdom like silence', for which the earliest citation is dated 1620. Cf. Plutarch, *De Liberis educ.*, 14. 10 E, 'There is wisdom in timely silence which is better than speech'.

8. *our desert places*. The lonely country round the lodges and the cave.

14. *fancy of marriage.* 'fanciful conception of the holiness of marriage'.

24. *heard . . . said.* Modern usage requires the transference of the main sentence to the end of the clause after *abused her* (line 28).

PAGE **276,** 4. *her to herself.* Pyrocles to Gynecia.

30–4. *Cleophila's . . . despised.* Gynecia hints that Pyrocles' good sense accounts for her presence in his place in the cave.

36. *Vulcan . . . cuckold.* Vulcan, husband of Venus, caught her and Mars in a net, and exposed the guilty pair to the laughter of the assembled gods (Ovid, *Met.* iv. 169 ff.).

PAGE **277,** 17. *movable goods of nature.* 'transitory natural advantages', such as good looks.

20. *the one . . . the other.* 'the bearing of children . . . the getting older'.

26. *the best rhetoric.* Basilius's rhetoric is not so 'flat' as to lack a metaphor from bowls, a simile with a proverbial ring (cf. Tilley, A10, 'Absence sharpens love'), and another simile, this time commercial.

29. *lesson without book.* 'lesson learnt by rote'; cf. AS **56.** 2.

PAGE **278,** 4. *will.* This could be a copying error for *wele*; but the only support is from Ph, *weale.*

9–10. *carelessness.* In desperation Basilius might have had no solicitude for either Gynecia or his public reputation; *carefulness* (St and As) would mean 'state of being full of anxiety'.

13 and 15. *limit; striving.* The readings of 93 have been adopted on the assumption that the inferior MSS. readings derive from an error in T.

19. *cup of gold.* See note to p. 224, 1–11.

25. *from him.* St and Bo suggest that there was an attempt to delete these words in T.

26. *whose . . . ears.* Cf. Tilley, B284.

35. *gave soon.* Cl's *soon gave* suggests that *soon* was the reading in T; *sone* and *some* are easily confused.

36. *unknown potion.* 'potion whose properties were unknown'.

PAGE **279,** 2. *fixed.* See Introduction, p. lv n. 3.

19–21. *directed . . . she saw.* The text is rather confused here, perhaps to mirror Gynecia's perplexity. The editors of 93 endeavoured to tidy it up, but mistakenly put a full stop after 'inward wretchedness'.

34–5. *ill-masked virtue.* 'sin poorly or wickedly disguised as virtue'; Gynecia means hypocrisy.

PAGE **280,** 2. *snaky.* *O.E.D.*, s.v. snaky 3, cites p. 389, 25 as the first example of the word with the meaning 'deceitful'; see Glossary, under *snakish*; and Introduction, p. lv.

10. *now . . . my mind.* The repetition of *now* in 93 and in several manuscripts may be correct.

11. *fair.* St and Da may be correct, and the scene is *fairer* (ironically) than the one Cleophila had engineered.

16. *briny.* Bo and Cl variants indicate the unfamiliarity of the word, and *O.E.D.* citations suggest that this may have been Sidney's coinage. Lyly and

Shakespeare, also applying the word to tears, preferred the form 'brinish', which is found in Bo.

30. *made of.* 'made about'.

PAGE **282**, 18. *some by name.* This is governed by *desiring* and not by *presented*, as the Cl copyist supposed in writing *to some*.

23. *But once for them.* 'But as for them' (the reading of Da).

34. *fain to lead.* 'obliged to lead the way', as the shepherds refused to lead her as requested at line 30.

PAGE **283**, 20. *of their own.* 'with their own possessions intact'.

21–2. *they, makes.* 'who benefit' is to be understood after *they*. The meaning is clearer in this reading, though it can be extracted from the reading of As, Da, Je, Hm, and 93.

PAGE **284**, 2. *Mausolus's tomb.* This splendid monument was built by his disconsolate widow, Artemisia.

4–7. *Agelastus . . . shepherd.* The St-Bo text seems to show an intention to build up the character of Agelastus. Both manuscripts give 'Since that to death is gone the shepherd high' (see p. 344, 24) to him instead of to Dicus.

10–PAGE **285**, 20. Ringler, OA 70 and pp. 415–16, where there is a note on the sestina and its adoption by Sidney. See p. 328, 22–p. 330, 33 for his double sestina, and p. 349, 4–p. 350, 11 for a rhyming one. Sidney was the first English poet to use the form (Spenser's in 'August' was probably inspired by his example), and is credited with the introduction of the word (in the form *sestine*) into English in the *O.E.D.* The editors of 93 transferred the poem to the Fourth Eclogues, perhaps because two of the poems had been removed for insertion in the NA narrative.

PAGE **285**, 3. *stepmother eyes.* For nature as a stepmother cf. p. 4, 31–2.

PAGE **286**, 3. *Phagona.* See note to p. 126, 35.

4–6. *he there . . . passed.* This refers to Pyrocles' handling of the rebels at the end of Book II.

33. *have . . . now live.* The readings of 93, with *to time* balancing *to nature*, are perhaps smoother; possibly Sidney wrote 'and now live longer to time'.

PAGE **287**, 6. *taking himself.* 'taking himself up'.

22. *so looking.* 93's *so* is to be taken with *that* (line 23), and could easily have been overlooked by T's copyist.

27. *vision.* Gynecia's 'vision of her fore-appointed end' is described on p. 280, 17–20.

PAGE **290**, 7–9. *cruelty . . . marriage.* Cf. 'L'aspra legge di Scozia, empia e severa' which imposed the death penalty on Ginevra in *Orlando Furioso*, iv. 59, and the case of Ricciardetto in xxv. 22–70. Amadis and Oriane were threatened by a similar harsh law in the *Amadis de Gaule*.

PAGE **291**, 5. *when . . . unto her.* 'when the next light of day that waking should bring her'.

PAGE **292**, 6–PAGE **300**, 9. *O great . . . life.* Brie, 134–5, regards the whole debate on suicide as a paraphrase of Aristotle, *Ethics* iii. 9–11. Sidney probably knew

Socrates' arguments, as well as Seneca's; he was also conversant with Duplessis-Mornay, who comes perilously near to justifying suicide. We are meant to consider that Pyrocles contemplates suicide from the highest motives in order to protect Philoclea, but that there is no doubt that her arguments, based as she tells us on the views of 'wise men' (p. 294, 24), are the correct ones.

26. *to do the effect.* 'to bring about the result wanted'. Cl's *the fact*, 'the deed', is a possibility; the other manuscripts read the palaeographically similar *theffect*.

31. The omission of *she* or *she had* in some manuscripts improves the sentence structure.

PAGE **293**, 6. *Daphne.* See note to p. 18, 3–4.

15. *fault or defect.* The manuscript variants show attempts to complete the rhetorical figure, with palaeographical confusion of *defect* with *defert*, contributed to by *deferver* in line 17.

PAGE **294**, 23–36. *And truly . . . redemanded.* Cf. St. Augustine, *City of God*, trans. G. E. McCracken (1957), i. 97:

Those who have laid violent hands upon themselves are perhaps to be admired for the greatness of their souls, but not to be praised for the soundness of their wisdom. If, however, you take reason more carefully into account, you will not really call it greatness of soul which brings anyone to suicide because he or she lacks strength to bear whatever hardships or sins of others may occur.

F. Marenco, *Arcadia Puritana* (Bari, 1968), 145 n., cites La Primaudaye, *Academie Françoise* (Paris, 1577), f. 86. Philoclea states the accepted Christian position.

PAGE **295**, 11–20. *Lady . . . duty.* This long sentence is variously punctuated in the MSS.; the general meaning is 'the more love Philoclea shows for him, the more Pyrocles feels bound to requite it'.

22–PAGE **297**, 9. *the more plainly . . . immortal.* The copyist of St inadvertently recopied this passage, which he had begun on f. 159, on f. 160 recto and verso, and then crossed it out.

24–5. *such a tree . . . fruits.* K. Duncan-Jones, 144, suggests that Sidney intends the orange tree, a symbol of eternal fruitfulness because it blossoms and fruits simultaneously, and compares the description of orange trees in NA (*Works*, i. 462).

PAGE **297**, 1–15. *since valour . . . despair.* Brie, 116, compares Aristotle, *Ethics*, ii. 7 and iii. 9, 11, where bravery is differentiated on the one side from foolhardiness, and on the other from cowardice.

PAGE **298**, 20. *these reasons.* This may be intended to refer back to the previous arguments, but grammatically it refers to the single reason which follows; this seems to have struck the copyist of Da only.

31. *Codrus's honour.* When the Dorians attacked Athens, an oracle declared that the victory would go to the country whose king was killed in battle. Codrus disguised himself and got killed; the victorious Athenians honoured his name by resolving that he should have no successor, and thereafter Athens was ruled by archons.

PAGE **299**, 20. *after-live.* Neither 93 nor Ph cared for this verb, and Sidney may simply have put his adverb in front of the verb. It is not recorded in *O.E.D.*, but *after-liver n.* is given as compounded by Sidney (see Shepherd, 186); and see also p. 110, 4.

25. *even . . . affection.* Ph substitutes: 'cast his eye upon her as a mother doth upon a most [*corr. from* her well] beloved child that refuseth to take the only potion which may save him from present death yet'.

PAGE **300**, 25. *richess.* See note to p. 84, 22.

PAGE **301**, 3. *medley.* The word means both 'combat' and 'mixture'.

PAGE **303**, 24 (var.), PAGE **304,** 10 (var.), 22 (var.), and 27 (var.). In NA Philoclea obtained Philanax's release after he had been taken prisoner by Amphialus (*Works*, i. 400).

PAGE **307**, 6. *gluttonish.* The earliest citation in *O.E.D.* is from this passage; its unfamiliarity is suggested by *gluttonous* in Ph and Je.

10–11 (var.). As Musidorus is no longer guilty of intending to rape Pamela, in 93 the outlaws have become the recipients instead of the instruments of divine justice. 93's words are taken from the reflection on everlasting justice and the two princes which 93 cut from the beginning of Book IV; see p. 265, 2–9 (var.) and note.

PAGE **312**, 2–4. *For how . . . honour me.* 93 let these words on Musidorus's honour stand, though the irony is lost as he has not contemplated dishonourable action in this version.

34. *at his parting.* 93's *long before* takes account of the use of the names Daiphantus and Palladius right at the beginning of NA.

PAGE **313**, 17 (var.). *Iberia.* In OA Plangus was the second son of the king of Iberia; see p. 67 and p. 68.

PAGE **314**, 1. *hid . . . Palladius.* This is the word order in all the sources.

9–23 (var.). The description of Musidorus and Pamela falling asleep is cut here by 93 because it had been transferred to Pyrocles and Philoclea; see p. 237, 34–9. Rowe in *M.P.* xxxvii (1939), 176 n., compares Heliodorus, 55:

. . . but their manifold miseries passed the greatness of their calamities present, and the uncertainty of that which was to come did hinder and darken the reasonable part of the mind. . . . At length . . . Theagenes sat down on a stone and Chariclea leaned on him, and strived a great while to overcome sleep, for desire to consider somewhat of their present affairs. But they with sorrow and labour much abated, although against their wills, were constrained to obey nature, and out of their heaviness they fell into a pleasant sleep. Thus was the reasonable part of the mind of force constrained to agree with the affection of the body.

PAGE **316**, 25. *and come.* 93's *But being come*, with the omission of *when*, is smoother, but probably editorial.

PAGE **317**, 8. *Phagonians* (*rebels* 93). Cf. p. 306, 29.

PAGE **318**, 12–14. *let not . . . adversity.* Cf. p. 175, 4–5 and p. 176, 10–11 and the *Defence of Poesy* (*Works*, iii. 32):

Only Alexander's example may serve, who by Plutarch is accounted of such virtue that fortune was not his guide, but his footstool.

PAGE **319,** 4–6. *like the palm . . . burdened.* Cf. Tilley, P37, and *O.D.E.P.*, 'the straighter grows the palm . . .', where the earliest citation is dated 1540.

11. *which, crossing.* The original MS. may have had wth w^{ch}, as in Cl.

PAGE **320,** 3–PAGE **321,** 10. *But . . . married.* Cf. p. 258, 21–p. 259, 23 and note.

PAGE **321,** 33. *Timautus.* Davis, *Map*, 155, considers that this character is based on Plato's timocratic man, and compares *Republic*, trans. F. M. Cornford, p. 422 and pp. 546–8.

PAGE **322,** 10. *As for . . . name.* Cf. p. 22, 20–1, and p. 91, 31–2, and *Defence of Poesy* (*Works*, iii. 20), 'For even those hard-hearted evil men who think virtue a school name'.

PAGE **323,** 6–7. *the waters . . . fishing.* Cf. Tilley, F334, cited from Harington; *O.D.E.P.* gives earlier citations, including this example.

33. *veered.* Sidney's spelling was *vired* (cf. French *viré*); the MSS. variants, and the later date of the citations in *O.E.D.* under *veer* vb.²4, indicate the unfamiliarity of the figurative use.

PAGE **324,** 11. *fit.* Long s and f are hard to distinguish in the MSS., and *sit* would be equally appropriate here.

PAGE **325,** 12 (var.). *son or nephew.* The editors of 93 probably meant to check which it should be; 98 changed *or* to *and*. In NA (*Works*, i. 38 ff.) Kalander and his *son* Clitophon are rescued by Pyrocles and Musidorus.

PAGE **326,** 9 (var.). The addition indicates the closer relationship of Kalander to the royal family in NA than that of Kerxenus in OA.

THE FOURTH ECLOGUES

PAGE **327,** 22. *Arcadian language.* It is not clear what enemies Geron has in mind. Musidorus (p. 316, 2) told the Phagonian rebels that in Thessalia the people spoke the same language as themselves.

30–PAGE **344,** 16. *but rather . . . my delight.* 93 substitutes the prose link and sestina of Agelastus from p. 284, 2–p. 285, 30. The double sestina of Strephon and Klaius (p. 328, 22 ff.) was transferred to the Second Eclogues by 93 (90 had already used it in the First Eclogues). Their second poem (p. 331, 4 ff.) was transferred by both 90 and 93 to the Second Eclogues, where in 90 it was repeated by Lamon, and in 93 by Histor and Damon. 93 omits Philisides' autobiographical prose passage, and follows 90 in transferring the poem describing his dream of Mira (p. 335, 13 ff.) to Amphialus (*Works*, i. 394 ff.). The elegiacs which Philisides says he sent to Mira (p. 341, 11 ff.) are transferred by 90, followed by 93, to Musidorus in a verse letter to Pamela (*Works*, i. 357 ff.).

PAGE **328,** 2–21. *Among . . . sestine.* Like Philisides and Coredens, Strephon and Klaius are non-Arcadian shepherds (in NA they are Arcadians), and may be intended to represent Sidney's friends; Greville and Dyer (for the older Klaius) are obvious candidates. Their first falling in love with Urania is described in OP 4 (which 93 inserted at the end of the First Eclogues). Ringler, 495, notes that Urania was Spenser's name for the Countess of Pembroke in *Colin Clout's*

Come Home Again, but he also points out that in *The Tears of the Muses* Urania is the Heavenly Muse, as in Du Bartas. At p. 328, 3–5 the reappearance of her lovers Strephon and Klaius at the beginning of NA is forecast, and their mysterious quality is suggested in the image of *two true runners* (p. 328, 11). See K. Duncan-Jones in *R.E.S.* xvii (1966), 123–32, where attention is drawn to Plato's καλὸν γὰρ τὸ ἆθλον, καὶ ἡ ἐλπὶς μεγάλη (*Phaedo* 114 c (Loeb edn., p. 390)), and to 'Let us run with patience the race that is set before us' (Heb. 12: 1; cf. 1 Cor. 9: 24–7).

22–PAGE **330**, 33. Ringler, OA 71 and pp. 416–17, where the arrangement of this sestina is discussed. See also Kalstone, 32–5, 73–82 and in *Comp. Lit.* xv (1963), 234–49. There are earlier analyses in W. Empson, *Seven Types of Ambiguity* (1930), pp. 45–50, and J. C. Ransom, *The New Criticism* (1941), pp. 108–14. The poem is copied in Bodleian MS. Rawl. Poet. 85, ff. 20–1ᵛ (Ringler, 557).

23. *goat-herd gods.* Wilson, 309, cites 'dieux chièvres-pieds' as one of the compounds used by French sixteenth-century poets, without giving any precise references. *O.E.D.* cites this passage as an example of a quasi-adjective.

PAGE **329**, 9–10. Poirier in *Études Anglaises*, xi (1958), 151, compares Ovid, *Met.* vii. 804–5:

> Sole fere radiis feriente cacumina primis
> Venatum in silvas juveniliter ire solebam.

13. *Molehills . . . mountains.* Cf. Tilley, M1035.

15. Cf. p. 78, 23–p. 79, 1, p. 81, 33, and p. 374, 5.

25. Ringler suggests that Sidney 'may have had in mind the myth of Actaeon who was torn to pieces by his own dogs, which was often applied by renaissance poets to the lover tormented by his own thoughts'.

30. Cf. Tilley, N181, 'The nightingale and the cuckoo sing both in one month', for which the earliest citation in *O.D.E.P.* is from Nicholas Breton's *Soothing of Proverbs* (?1617). Cf. *O.D.E.P.*, 'When the owl sings, the nightingale will hold her peace', for which the earliest citation, again from Breton, is dated 1603. Cf. p. 58, 29 and p. 142, 9–10.

32. *serene.* The earliest citation in *O.E.D.* is from Florio, *First Fruits* (1578); the MSS. variants suggest its unfamiliarity.

PAGE **330**, 19. *she.* Urania.

24. *her two suns.* Urania's eyes.

PAGE **331**, 1 and 2. *dizain*; *crown.* The earliest citation in *O.E.D.* for *crown* is from this passage, and for *dizain* Gascoigne (1575) is cited, and then this passage. See L. Martz, *Poetry of Meditation* (1954), p. 107.

4–PAGE **334**, 6. Ringler, OA 72 and p. 417, where the dependence of 93 on 90, apart from errors in seven lines corrected from P, is noted.

PAGE **332**, 7. *waste.* Ringler notes the apocopation of *wasted* for the sake of the rhyme. As *waste* is the rhyme-word of the first line of the stanza, *raste* (*razed*) in Cl-Le-As may be the correct reading; but see note to p. 333, 29.

32–PAGE **333**, 6. Ringler refers to the habits of the torpedo (the electric ray or cramp fish), which, when caught, paralyses the angler (Pliny, *Natural History*, ix. 65 and xxxii. 2), and notes the 'numerous references from classical and renaissance sources' in E. M. Denkinger in *S.P.* xxviii (1931), 162–83. There is a close parallel in Du Bartas's 'Fifth Day, First Week' (tr. Sylvester (1608), 246–77). This is the emblem chosen by Amphialus in NA (*Works*, i. 415) to indicate that he has been overcome by his intended victim, Philoclea. Sidney's 'the catcher now is caught' is close to Tilley, B429, 'the biter bit', cited for 1693; but cf. D179, 'He that deceives another is oft deceived himself' (1484), and D182, 'To deceive the deceiver is no deceit' (*c.* 1550).

PAGE 333, 8. *crowned basilisk.* The basilisk was so named from the crown on its head. Pliny, *Natural History*, viii. 33, is the source for the belief that its glance was lethal.

29. *sell.* Ringler takes this to be the correct reading as *fell* is the rhyme word to line 33; but he accepted the use of *waste* twice (see note to p. 332, 7), and this was a permitted licence provided that the word was used in a different sense, or was a different part of speech. Long s and f are difficult to distinguish (Feuillerat misread Cl's *sell* as *fell*); and I am not absolutely convinced that Klaius would express a wish to sell rather than to destroy the earth and sky.

PAGE 334, 9–10. (*who . . . unto it*). Philisides asked to be excused when Basilius requested him to relate his own fortunes during the Second Eclogues; see p. 159.

12–PAGE 335, 12. *The name . . . dream.* Sidney continues his fictionalized self-portrait; his friendship with Languet is celebrated in the Ister Bank poem (p. 254, 21 ff.). Ringler, 365 n., notes the parallel between p. 334, 31–4, *in travel . . . know his own,* and Sidney's letter to his brother Robert of February 1579 (*Works*, iii. 125):

. . . for hard sure it is to know England without you know it by comparing it with others . . . as greatness of itself is a quantity, so yet the judgement of it, of might, riches &c. stands in the predicament of relation. . . .

Ringler, 418, also compares Virgil as Tityrus in his *Eclogues*, Spenser as Colin Clout in *The Shepherds' Calendar*, and Sannazaro who as Sincero recites his autobiography in the 7th Prose of the *Arcadia.* He thinks that as Mira ('Wonderful') is first seen in a dream she may be imaginary; at this date she could scarcely have been Penelope Devereux, but might be intended to represent one of the other attendants on Queen Elizabeth ('Diana'). Mira disappears from NA, and Philisides has become an Iberian knight in love with the 'Star' (*Works*, i. 285). Ringler also rejects the suggestion of Sargent, 68–9, that Mira (an anagram of Mari) represents the Countess of Pembroke, whom Thomas Moffet (her son's tutor) referred to as Mira in his *Silkworms and their Flies* (1599), F8ᵛ. Mira's identity hinges on that of Coredens, who is also in love with her (p. 340, 34 f.); see note to p. 245, 7.

PAGE 335, 13—PAGE 340, 28. Ringler, OA 73 and pp. 417–19, where it is noted that Philisides' dream is an adaptation of the story of the judgement of Paris, similar to the epigram on the actress Ariadne in the *Greek Anthology* (v. 222). Cf. also Montemayor's *Diana*, ed. Kennedy, 81, and Peele's *The Arraignment of Paris*, where the apple is awarded to Queen Elizabeth.

28. *hatch.* The first citation in *O.E.D.*, vb.³, 'to close as with a hatch', is from AS 38. 2:

This night while sleep begins with heavy wings
To hatch mine eyes.

PAGE **336**, 12–14 Fraunce, 37, quotes as an example of anadiplosis.

23. *ground*. 'The earth, which in the Ptolemaic system does not move' (Ringler).

PAGE **337**, 22–3. Cf. Tilley, M1215.

31–2. The reference is to mother-of-pearl and tiny seed pearls.

PAGE **338**, 5. *Mira*. See note to p. 334, 12–p. 335, 12.

15. *moony*. The earliest citation in *O.E.D.* is from this passage; the manuscript variants indicate the unfamiliarity of the word.

PAGE **339**, 29. *over wise*. Venus's flattery makes the reading of Da and Hm, *ever wise*, attractive.

PAGE **340**, 2. Cf. Tilley, F47, and *O.D.E.P.*, 'familiarity breeds contempt'.

3. *Styx*. Ringler notes that this was the usual oath of the Olympian gods and compares CS **17**. 6 and AS **74**. 7.

9–10. Fraunce, 68, quotes these lines as an example of an exclamation expressing indignation.

12–20. Ringler, 498, compares OP **5**. 112, 'She is the herdess fair that shines in dark'.

34. *Coredens*. See notes to p. 334, 12–p. 335, 12 and p. 245, 7.

PAGE **341**, 11–PAGE **344**, 16. Ringler, OA 74 and p. 419. The poem is no. 229 in the Arundel Harington MS.; Harington comments on the transfer of the poem in NA to Musidorus, who leaves it in the 'standish' of Pamela (*Works*, i. 356). Fraunce, 31, quotes p. 343, 26–7 as an example of elegiac verse and as a hexameter joined to a pentameter. For the scansion see note to p. 80, 13–p. 81, 6. I have followed Ringler in accepting the 90 contractions required by the metre, but not in the rather spasmodic use of capitals for semi-personified abstract qualities. Rubel, 125, discusses some of the rhetorical figures used in this poem.

15. *monument*. this verse epistle.

PAGE **342**, 15 and 20 and PAGE **343**, 27. Ringler, 484–5, suggests that AS v was probably part of the 'hasty revenge' that Philisides said he took when Mira first disdained him. He compares AS **v.** 7–8:

> I said thou wert most fair, and so indeed thou art;
> I said thou wert most sweet, sweet poison to my heart.

Cf. also AS **8.** 12 and **21.** 14.

16. *monument*. Ringler points out that the metre requires this to be made disyllabic by syncopation.

PAGE **343**, 18. *Cimmerian darkness*. From *Odyssey*, xi. 14 ff. this became a commonplace for utter darkness. The earliest citation in *O.E.D.* is from Marston (1598), but in addition to Sidney's usage here, Spenser, 'Virgil's Gnat', 370, has 'Cymerian shades'. Cf. Marlowe's 2 *Tamburlaine*, v. ii. 170, and Shakespeare's *Titus Andronicus*, II. iii. 72.

25. *pedant*. Ringler notes the Italian pronunciation and compares 'pedanteria' in the *Defence of Poesy* (*Works*, iii. 3). The unfamiliarity of the word for 'schoolmaster' is indicated by the MS. variants; the earliest citation in *O.E.D.* is from *Love's Labour's Lost*, and it occurs again in *The Taming of the Shrew* and in

Twelfth Night. Marlowe also used it in his translation of Ovid, *Amores*, I. xiii. 17–18.

PAGE **344**, 17–23 (var.). The link passage in 93 follows immediately after the sestina of Agelastus (see note to p. 327, 30–p. 344, 16). The words *Among the rest . . . form* are taken from 90.

22. *Agelastus's.* Bo–St reading indicates that Sidney had decided to transfer this lament from Dicus to Agelastus; see note to p. 284, 4–7.

24–PAGE **348**, 37. Ringler, OA 75 and pp. 419–21. In NA (*Works*, i. 498) this song becomes the lament for the death of Amphialus in Book III. Ringler notes that this poem and Spenser's lament for Dido in 'November' are the earliest examples of formal pastoral elegy in English. He notes that Sidney's immediate model was the 11th Eclogue of Sannazaro's *Arcadia*, but that in the latter part of his poem Sidney departs from Sannazaro because he is writing a lament by a pagan shepherd for a pagan ruler who did not have the consolation of Christian immortality. He quotes the lines in Sannazaro's eclogue that Sidney imitates most closely: p. 344, 24–6 are compared with Sannazaro's opening lines; p. 345, 1–11 and 28–p. 346, 3 are elaborated from the hint in Sannazaro, 7–9 and 13–15; p. 345, 12–27 are an expansion of Sannazaro, 16–18 and 25–33; p. 346, 25–30 are compared with Sannazaro, 46–54; p. 347, 7–27 are compared with Sannazaro, 55–63.

PAGE **345**, 9. *ambassade.* See note to p. 57, 8.

10. *myrrh.* Ringler notes that the tree exudes sap from its trunk and so appears to weep, and compares p. 86, 20 and Ovid, *Met.* x. 310.

18. *all killing. all-killing* may be intended; cf. p. 346, 20.

20. *dam.* Their mother, the earth.

26. Like Moschus, *Elegy on Bion*, v. 5 ff. and Ovid, *Met.* x. 215, Sidney uses the detail of the Greek cry of lament αἴ which appeared on the leaves when Hyacinth was changed into a flower.

PAGE **346**, 20. *all-beholding eye.* Cf. 'tou' voyans yeux' in Du Bellay, 'L'honeste amour', Sonnet 9.

25–7. Sannazaro's eleventh eclogue was the immediate source, but the story of Philomela (cf. Ovid, *Met.* vi. 565 ff.) is referred to elsewhere by Sidney; cf. p. 229, 10–11. Ringler, 426–7, compares CS 4, particularly lines 6–7:

Her throat in tunes expresseth
What grief her breast oppresseth

and OP **4.** 474:

The nightingales for woe their songs refrain

and NA (*Works*, i. 13):

The nightingales (striving one with the other which could in most dainty variety recount their wrong-caused sorrow) made them put off their sleep, . . .

PAGE **348**, 6 and 14. *distrained*; *conclusion.* Sidney is here using legal terms in the midst of the medical discourse.

8. 'When the vital spirits decay.'

PAGE **349**, 1. *Agelastus.* See note to p. 344, 22. 93 does not name the shepherd who sings the next song.

4–Page 350, 11. Ringler, OA 76 and p. 421, where he notes that the form is the same as that of Agelastus's first sestina (p. 284, 10 ff.), with the added complication that the end words rhyme ababcc in the first strophe.

11. *queint*. The variants indicate the unfamiliarity of the form; cf. Spenser, *F.Q.* II. v. 11.

THE LAST BOOK OR ACT

Page 352, 2. *though with his pains*. 'though with Philanax's regrets and apologies'.

Page 353, 9. *cyclops or cannibals*. Sidney is using the plural of the older form *cyclop*; cf. *Defence of Poesy* (*Works*, iii. 8). Homer described them as a gigantic and lawless race of shepherds in Sicily who devoured human beings and cared nothing for Zeus. Although the earliest citation for *cannibal* in *O.E.D.* dates back to 1553, Shakespeare felt it necessary to gloss the word from old-world terminology in *Othello*, I. iii. 142, 'the cannibals that each other eat, the anthropophagi'.

Page 354, 1. *disunions*. *divisions* in 93 may be the correct reading.

24–5. *strive . . . stream*. Cf. Tilley, S927 and p. 28, 16–21.

31. *And so asked*. The readings in St, Bo, and 13 show dissatisfaction with the sentence construction.

Page 355, 4–5. *hated . . . person*. Cf. Tilley, P238, 'Hate not the person but the vice'. This, and the related proverb K64, 'A king hates the treason but loves the traitor', are to be found in Shakespeare; cf. *Measure for Measure*, II. ii. 37, 'condemn the fault and not the actor of it'.

17–Page 357 (var.). *whom he found . . . as soon*. See Introduction, p. lxi, for the revised journey of Euarchus in 93.

Page 357, 4–7. *Euarchus . . . mind*. The curtailment of the character sketch of Euarchus in 93 is accounted for by the description of him in NA (*Works*, i. 186), where this sentence is rephrased. Sidney may have had Philip of Macedon in mind. For comparisons with Plato's *Republic* and Erasmus's *The Education of a Christian Prince*, see Davis, *Map*, 148–9.

Page 358, 3–35. *when Basilius . . . evil*. F. Marenco, *Arcadia Puritana*, pp. 32–41, discusses Basilius's abdication from his role as shepherd of his people and cites, among other works, R. Taverner's translation of Erasmus's *Proverbs or Adages* (1569), p. 42, and Greville, *Life*, 11.

Page 360, 13–33. *And give . . . people*. Fraunce, 91–2, quotes as an example of prosopopoeia.

14. *say it*. The omission of *it* in 93 makes the sentence run more smoothly; possibly y^t ('that') was misread as *yt*.

Page 364, 7. *ambassade*. See note to p. 57, 8.

14–16. *so ill . . . spirit*. Fraunce, 76, quotes as an example of epiphonema.

Page 365, 17. *yellow jaundice*. Cf. Tilley, A160, and *O.D.E.P.*, 'To the jaundiced eye all things look yellow', citing this passage, preceded by an analogue from

Chaucer, and followed by a citation from Webster, *The White Devil*, I. ii. 12—
to which Dent, 81, adds a citation from Montaigne. The black jaundice is
referred to on p. 33, 22, where, as here, most manuscripts spell 'janders' or
'jaunders'.

PAGE 366, 8. *With . . . tokens.* This is expanded in Ph to 'With great clapping of
hands and many other allowing tokens'.

PAGE 368, 6. *hopeless.* This reading gives the correct sense: Gynecia is blaming
Pyrocles for giving her grounds for hoping that he returned her passion.

29–30. *necessity . . . laws.* Cf. Tilley, N76, 'Need (Necessity) knows no laws'.

35. *fair . . . follow.* Cf. Tilley, C442, R8, and S908.

PAGE 370, 15. *an eagle . . . eagle.* Cf. Tilley, B361, 'Better to be a bird of the wood
than of the cage', cited from 1566–8.

25–6. *governors . . . fortune.* Pyrocles and Musidorus are making 'a virtue of
necessity'; cf. Tilley, V73 and *O.D.E.P.*, where some of the English examples
antedate Tilley's, and the proverb is traced back to Quintilian, who based his
maxim on Aristotle's magnanimous man opposing his Virtue to Fortune.

31. *such kind speeches. of speech* in As-Cl has been rejected as the emphasis is
on the emotion of *kindness*, and the copyist of Bo wrote *of* and then deleted it.

PAGE 371, 17. *unreachable.* The earliest citation in *O.E.D.* is from this passage.
The weight of the MS. evidence and the alliteration suggest that it is the correct
reading; but *unsearchable* in St is the common periphrasis for the almighty; cf.
p. 292, 12, 'thy [Jove's] unsearchable mind', and p. 413, 19, 'their [the gods']
unsearchable wisdoms'.

23–4. *Our souls . . . bodies.* See note to p. 372, 16–p. 373, 21, and cf. *Defence of
Poesy* (*Works*, iii. 11):

. . . to lead and draw us to as high a perfection as our degenerate souls, made worse by
their clayey lodgings, can be capable of . . . to know, and by knowledge lift up the mind
from the dungeon of the body to the enjoying his own divine essence.

28. *then.* This must have been written *thē* in T.

PAGE 372, 16–PAGE 373, 21. *a debate . . . light.* In Cl Musidorus's speech (p. 372,
18–28) is underlined and the word *Memory* has been written in the margin in
dark ink. Superficially, Musidorus appears to be reporting Aristotle's theory of
memory based on his theory of knowledge expounded in the *De Anima*; the
'moral' (miscopied as *mortal* in Cl only) virtues of line 23, standing 'in the mean
of perturbations', make it clear that Sidney is writing of Aristotle's *virtus moralis*
as distinct from *virtus intellectualis* (Sidney's 'contemplative virtue'). However,
Pyrocles' reply (p. 372, 29–p. 373, 21) departs from Aristotle and follows Plato
in its assumption that there is a true knowledge not derived from sense impres-
sions, but derived from the memory of pre-existence. The two theories are
discussed by F. A. Yates, *The Art of Memory* (1966), chapter ii, 'The Art of
Memory in Greece: Memory and the Soul'. Sidney may have read the Com-
mentary on the *Phaedo* by J. Serranus (see Introduction, p. xxvii n.); and he
may have recollected, if only to reject, the suggestion that the soul may not be
utterly devoid of 'sense' after death in Xenophon's *Cyropaedia*, viii. 7 (ed.
Watson and Dale, p. 279). D. P. Walker in *Bibliothèque d'Humanisme et Renais-*

sance, xvii (1955), 252–77, comments that this discussion on the after-life suggests that Pyrocles and Musidorus are good heathens who are 'saved', and remarks that Calvinists were inclined to damn all heathens—albeit sometimes regretfully—unless like Duplessis-Mornay they considered that the *prisca theologia* of Orpheus, etc., derived from Jewish pre-Christian knowledge. Davis, *Map*, 63 n., regards chapter xiv, 'That the soul of man is immortal, or dieth not', of Duplessis-Mornay's *A Work concerning the trueness of the Christian religion* as the immediate source of the whole prison scene, and quotes A. Golding's translation (1587), p. 246:

> And therefore we ought surely to say that this mind or reason ought not to be ever in prison; that one day it shall see clearly, and not by these dim and cloudy spectacles; that it shall come in place where it shall have the true object of understanding; and that he shall have his life free from these fetters and from all the affections of the body. To be short, that as man is prepared in his mother's womb to be brought forth into the world, so is he also after a sort prepared in this body and in this world to live in another world.

See also N. R. Lindheim in *English Literary Renaissance*, ii (Winter 1972), 142–6.

PAGE 373, 25–PAGE 374, 4. Ringler, OA 77 and p. 422. The poem is copied from 93 or a later print in B.M. MS. Egerton 2877, f. 105, headed 'Verses against fear of death; made by Sir ph: sidney' (Ringler, 556).

29. Fraunce, 45, quotes this line as an example of epanalepsis. Cf. *O.D.E.P.*, 'Fear of death is worse than death itself', with the earliest citation dated 1594.

PAGE 374, 5. *swans . . . obsequies*. See note to p. 329, 15.
26. *as before . . . mentioned*. See p. 313, 16 f.

PAGE 376, 4–5. *in which . . . before*. The omission of *throne* in Je conforms with modern usage. 93 might have been expected to omit *lately* in view of the events which have occurred in NA since Pyrocles' speech to the rebels from the judgement seat in Book II (see p. 129, 11 ff.).

9. *russet . . . hat*. K. Duncan-Jones, 170, comments that russet here represents real humility, not the ample hope of Pamela in Book I (p. 37, 8). For the unseemly hat as an indication of melancholy she refers to Roy Strong in *Apollo*, lxxix (1964), 264–9. See also the account of Donne's portrait in Appendix E of *The Elegies . . . of John Donne*, ed. H. Gardner, p. 268. J. C. Maxwell in the New Cambridge Shakespeare edition of the *Poems*, p. 224, accepts as plausible the suggestion of S. Walker that 'A Lover's Complaint', 29–35, owe something to this description of Gynecia.

27. *knights of the order*. Elias Ashmole, *Laws & Ceremonies of the most noble Order of the Garter* (1672), p. 213, declares that:

> by the Sovereign's Warrants entered in the great Wardrobe, towards the end of the reign of king Henry the eighth, and since, it is manifest the surcoats of the sovereign and all the knights-companions were of crimson velvet.

In the time of Elizabeth the garter mantle seems to have been purple, but see p. 377, 3–7 and note for the various tints in the scarlet/purple range.

PAGE 377, 3. *apostle's mantle*. Sidney refers to the long cloaks in which the

apostles were portrayed in pictures and tapestries. *O.E.D.*, mantle 1†e, cites
this passage, and refers to *Dives and Pauper* (1496):

The apostles commonly . . . [were] painted with mantles . . . and a mantle is a loose
clothing not fast to the body but loose.

3–7. *not that purple . . . scarlet.* This distinction is made by Pliny, *Natural
History*, ix. 60 (Loeb trans.):

The best Asiatic purple is at Tyre, the best African is at Meninx and on the Gaetulian
coast of the Ocean, the best European in the district of Sparta. The official rods and
axes of Rome clear it a path, and it also marks the honourable estate of boyhood; it
distinguishes the senate from the knighthood, it is called in to secure the favour of the
gods; and it adds radiance to every garment, while in a triumphal robe it is blended with
gold.

In 62, Pliny goes into the different colours in the purple/scarlet range, and says
of Tyrian purple that

its highest glory consists in the colour of congealed blood, blackish at first glance but
gleaming when held up to the light; this is the origin of Homer's phrase, 'blood of purple
hue'.

In 63, Pliny gives the prices of violet purple dye as 100 denarii per pound, and of
double-dyed Tyrian purple as 1,000 denarii. Cf. also the description of Calli-
gone's bridal dress in Achilles Tatius, *Clitophon and Leucippe*, II. xi:

the purple with which it was dyed was no casual tint, but that kind which (according to
the story the Tyrians tell) was discovered by the shepherd's dog, with which they dye
Aphrodite's robe to this day.

The dog crushed a murex shell in its mouth, which then appeared to be bleeding.

26. *one year's growth.* The editors of 93 failed to correct in accordance with
the revised ages and age differential of the princes in NA (*Works*, i. 190), where
Musidorus is said to be three or four years older than Pyrocles.

PAGE **378,** 25. *unfelt solemnity.* Musidorus contrasts the possibility that Basilius's
soul might be cognizant of his subjects' *loving memory* in the heavens with the
fact that his body could not feel the pomp accorded to his corpse. He seems
conscious, in his parenthesis, of the contradiction at p. 379, 5–7; but his mind
has gone back to the debate with Pyrocles on the immortality of the soul.

33–PAGE **380,** 21. *Understand . . . of it.* Pyrocles' equivocation over what
happened in Philoclea's chamber is justified by his desire to protect her honour
and safety. As he did not sleep with her in the 93 version the reader does not
have to condone his lack of candour, and his self-accusation at p. 380, 3–4 could
be removed.

PAGE **380,** 16. *judgement.* Ph adds: 'do not like bats see worst in the sunshine'.

PAGE **381,** 16. *greedy.* The reading of Je (Hm omits the whole clause) and 93
seems more likely to be right with *thirst*; but Sidney could have altered the
word in T to remind us that Philanax's thirst for vengeance was caused by
grief at the death of his old master.

20. *unseemly hat.* See note to p. 376, 9.

PAGE **382,** 9–17. *I therefore . . . grant.* Fraunce, 77, quotes as an example of
licence and liberty of speech in exclamation.

PAGE 383, 32–PAGE 384, 3. *As for . . . rose up. so* was probably inserted indeterminately in T, and I have adopted the placing of it in 93; but the construction of the sentence has got lost in the parenthesis, and *she* is wanted before *rose up*.

PAGE 385, 1–2. *that . . . Caria.* Cf. p. 312, 34 and note.

1. *despota.* The variants indicate the unfamiliarity of the word, which Sidney has picked up in the vocative case. The earliest citation under *despot* in *O.E.D.* is dated 1562, but the author, J. Shute, is translating and keeps the Italian form *dispotto*; the next citation, using the now-established English form, is dated 1585.

9. *by many.* 'with respect to/affecting a large number of people'.

32–PAGE 386, 2. *in such . . . powers.* Sidney intervenes to point the irony of the situation. Dent, 259 and 265, compares *The Duchess of Malfi*, V. V. 104–5:

> In what a shadow, or deep pit of darkness,
> Doth (womanish and fearful) mankind live!

and v. iv. 63–4:

> We are merely the stars' tennis balls, struck and banded
> Which way please them.

For the ball metaphor see p. 147, 14 and note, and cf. NA (*Works*, i. 508), 'balls to injurious fortune'.

PAGE 386, 3. *causes.* I have preferred the reading of St and Da as all manuscripts have *cause* at line 5.

14–PAGE 391, 21. *That . . . sorrow.* Wolff, 317, compares the opening of Thersander's invective in Achilles Tatius, *Clitophon and Leucippe*, VIII. vii. Sidney shows a certain hostility towards Philanax and his practised oratory; and L. Challis in *S.P.* lxii (1965), 569–71, notes the emotional and loaded phrases of Philanax, led astray by strong affection for Basilius. She contrasts Euarchus's judgement, based on reason, and remarks Aristotle's principle that forensic oratory should not attempt to arouse the feelings of the public. Myrick, however, notes (2nd edn., 63) that Cicero did not hesitate to appeal to the feelings, and though Quintilian accepted Aristotle's principle, he added that 'when the cause is of greater moment, it will be proper to speak of heinous crimes in a tone of invective, and of mournful occurrences in one of pity' (*Institutes*, i. 298). See also Lanham, 294–300.

PAGE 388, 11. *consort.* The manuscript variants indicate the unfamiliarity of the word in the sense of 'agreement' or 'partnership'; the earliest citation in *O.E.D.* is from Scot, *Discovery of Witchcraft* (1584).

15 (var.). (*as much as in him lay*). I am treating this parenthesis in 93 as an editorial addition, but it could derive from P and have been carelessly omitted in T (99 omitted it inadvertently); for it is in line with Philanax's statements at p. 375, 21–8 and p. 302, 10–13. See p. 390, 12 where (*I hope but offered*) is omitted from 93 and the earlier OA MSS.

PAGE 389, 29–PAGE 390, 2. *But yet . . . chance too.* Fraunce, 104, quotes as an example of granting 'when we jestingly admit of any speech or argument', and remarks:

This figure delighteth very much when we grant that which hurteth him to whom it is granted, as it many times falleth out in contentious disputations.

PAGE 390, 11. *my second part.* B. Vickers, *Francis Bacon and Renaissance Prose* (1968), pp. 42 and 273, draws attention to Sidney's use of the figure of partition in Philanax's speech and Pyrocles' reply. Throughout his forensic oratory Philanax is conscious of his 'method'.

20. *right of hospitality. right* is the spelling in all the texts, but modern *rite* may have been intended.

34 (var.). *pirate.* This was presumably Sidney's first thought, to alliterate with *player,* but then an animal to match the ensuing *dragon* seemed preferable.

PAGE 391, 8–10. *his whorish . . . please us.* Cf. p. 121, 23 and OP 4. 124, 'But gold can gild a rotten piece of wood'.

PAGE 392, 12 (var.). *of this coward creature.* Sidney may have cancelled these words as being too close to *the craven crows* at p. 394, 13.

13–14 (var.). *to handless and heartless people.* Again, the removal of this phrase would seem to be authorial pruning of the rhetoric.

14. *out of his invective.* Ph alters to 'of the dunghill of his invective'.

PAGE 393, 4–5 (var.) and 10–12 (var.). These revisions in 93 accord with the other changes made, but lines 12–13, *when . . . escaped,* have not been altered, nor has the climax of Pyrocles' speech (p. 394, 26 f.).

16. *mountebank.* The various manuscript readings indicate the unfamiliarity of the word; the earliest citation in *O.E.D.* is for 1577, and the second is from Sidney's *Defence of Poesy* (*Works,* iii. 36), 'Poets are almost in as good reputation as the mountebanks of Venice.'

16. *make . . . over;* and 24–5. *immodest . . . matters.* These phrases seem to glance at the proverb 'to open one's mouth wide' (= to ask too high a price), for which the earliest citation in *O.D.E.P.* is for 1891; but cf. Tilley, M1263, 'to make up one's mouth' (Heywood, 1546), and S10, 'A short sack has a wide mouth' (1583). *Mercenary* seems perfectly satisfactory in the context of over-pricing goods, but perhaps Sidney did not want to labour the proverbial reference. The substitute, *immodest,* is recorded in *O.E.D.* †1, with the earliest citation for 1570.

31. *prosecute.* This seems closer to the effect of Gynecia's confession than *persecute*—the abbreviation ꝑ is used in the manuscripts for *par, per, pro,* and *pre.*

PAGE 394, 1. *throw down. participate* is awkward as a reflexive, and I suspect (see previous note) that it is an error for the true reading *precipitate* (the earliest citation in *O.E.D.* is for 1575). The meaning, but not the word, was subsequently restored in T.

13. *the craven crows.* Pyrocles is taking a metaphor from cock fighting to introduce his challenge to single combat. The adjective *craven* was common in ME.; for the noun *O.E.D.,* B. 1A gives 1. 'A confessed coward', with the earliest citation for 1581 and the next from Shakespeare, *Henry V,* IV. vii. 139, 'He is a craven, and a villain else'; and 2. 'A cock that is not game', with the earliest citation from *The Taming of the Shrew,* II. i. 228, 'No cock of mine, you crow too like a craven'. Cf. Tilley, C486, 'Every cock is bold on his own dunghill'.

16. *honey . . . spider.* Cf. Tilley, B208.

21. *If.* This is probably an intelligent scribal insertion made independently by the copyists of Bo and Cl.

PAGE **395**, 9–10. *bloody . . . death.* Cf. Tilley, C831, and *O.D.E.P.*, where the proverb is traced back to Erasmus, and the earliest English citation is from Cooper (1548), who comments 'A proverb applied unto them which, hating another man whom they would destroy, or have destroyed, they will seem to be sorry for him'.

19–20. *whose violence.* the violence of his love for Philoclea.

PAGE **397**, 4–PAGE **398**, 6. *In such . . . daughter.* Pamela's letter, as befits her status as heir to the dukedom and her character, is more imperious and ironic in tone than that of the humble-hearted Philoclea.

PAGE **399**, 10–11. *But the one . . . other.* 'But you have deserved hanging as much as you have dishonoured the ladies.'

11–13. *But now . . . Palladius.* Fraunce, 81, quotes as an example of apostrophe. Presumably Philanax chose Pallas not only for the alliteration but also as protectress of agriculture.

PAGE **400**, 38–PAGE **401**, 2. *killed . . . them.* Musidorus refers to the killing of the lion and the bear at the end of Book I.

PAGE **401**, 15–18. *Were we . . . shamefully.* He now refers to the rescue of Basilius from the drunken mob at the end of Book II.

PAGE **402**, 6–PAGE **403**, 2. *But you will say . . . judgements.* Fraunce, 102, refers to this passage as a 'full and perfect example' of preoccupation, which he defines (p. 100) as

> when we prevent and meet with that which might be objected, and do also make answer to the same. . . . This preventing therefore is either indirect, most fit for beginnings, and more used of orators than of poets.

20. *yet those.* I have adopted the emendation in the edition of 1627; when Sidney wrote *yet to those*, he probably intended to use a different construction.

28. *lime twigs and nets.* Twigs smeared with bird-lime and nets were both used for snaring birds.

34. *burn . . . clean.* Cf. Tilley, H752, 'burn house to fright away the mice' (T. Adams, 1615); H757, 'set house on fire to roast eggs' (for which the earliest citation in *O.D.E.P.* is dated 1530); and H763, 'burn house to warm his hands' (Caxton, 1481).

34–PAGE **403**, 1. *like a wise father . . . of it.* No doubt the reader is intended to appreciate the irony of Pyrocles' using this simile in tendering advice to his own father.

PAGE **403**, 21–PAGE **408**, 7. *This . . . charge.* L. Challis in *S.P.* lxii (1965), 569–71, contrasts the arguments of Euarchus, based on reason, proceeding from the general to the particular, with Philanax's outburst; but it should be noted that Euarchus emphasizes (p. 404, 24–30) that judging well rests not on the exercise of reason in a vacuum, but on the application of the laws of a country to a particular case (though these laws derived from the exercise of reason in the first place).

PAGE **404**, 27–8. *out of them . . . came.* 'from the free play of reason and the knowledge of philosophy came the laws of Greece and the statutes of Arcadia'.

PAGE **405**, 24. *would.* The edition of 1621 reads *yet would*, which is an improvement, but not essential to the meaning.

26. (var.). *Wherein . . . loss.* By giving the princes an identical punishment, 93 harmonizes with the actual innocence of Pyrocles in this version; but either Sidney or the editors failed to alter the original separate punishment a few pages later (p. 408, 1–5). The removal of Euarchus's 'philosophy of marriage' as the 'root of humanity, the beginning and maintaining of living creatures' (p. 406, 2), was an incidental casualty rather than a deliberate elimination; his lofty view of 'right love' (p. 407, 2–5) is allowed to stand.

PAGE **406**, 20. *Europa.* Cf. Ovid, *Met.* ii. 833 ff.

26. *had rightly pitied.* The emendation in 13 seems necessary.

PAGE **407**, 14. *measure . . . law.* The use of *foot* (misread by Feuillerat in Cl as *force*) may be explained by *O.D.E.P.*, 'Measure yourself (not another) by your own foot' (Tilley, E217 and F567); Cf. Tilley, L202, 'To have (know) the length of one's foot'.

24–34. *Without . . . agreement.* Here Euarchus counters Musidorus's argument that he was merely the counsellor to a prince (p. 402, 9–13).

27. *simply.* 'as a simple private citizen'. *singly* in 93 is probably a compositor's misreading.

34–PAGE **408**, 5. *Thus . . . Dametas.* See note to p. 405, 26 (var.).

PAGE **408**, 27. *appassionate.* See note to p. 135, 9.

28–PAGE **409**, 7. *But first . . . directed him.* Musidorus's stratagem is described on p. 41, 22–30, but Kalodoulus is not named there, though he is in NA (*Works*, i. 116), where this passage from Book V is re-used—hence the cuts in 93 at this point.

PAGE **409**, 24–9 (var.). The alteration in 93 was made necessary by the revised version of Euarchus's journey at pp. 355–7.

PAGE **410**, 35–PAGE **411**, 4. *But Euarchus . . . his mind.* Euarchus's dilemma may be compared with that of Lucius Junius Brutus when the conspiracy of his sons to restore Tarquinius was revealed by a slave, and the traitors were condemned to death. Cf. the comment of Livy, ii. 5, 5–9, tr. Holland, E5^v–E6^r:

> Which suffering of theirs was the more notable, for that the father, by his place and virtue of his office, was bound and charged to see execution done upon his own children: and he who otherwise ought not to have been a spectator and looker-on, even he (such was his fortune) was forced of necessity to be the principal actor in this tragical execution.

In Heliodorus, Hydaspes soon yields to the pressure of the crowd to spare his daughter Chariclea.

PAGE **411**, 20. *lynx's eyes.* They were proverbially sharp. *Lynceus* in As shows the copyist's knowledge of the king of Argos, so named for his reputed ability to see through the earth. The manuscripts. indicate that the usual spelling was *linces*, hence the confusion with *princes* and *links*.

PAGE **412**, 29. *Howsoever . . . cruelty*. Fraunce, 9, quotes as an example of the 'metonymia of the adjunct'.

PAGE **413**, 30–1. *My blood . . . country*. Fraunce, 44, quotes as an example of symploce, 'when the same sound is repeated both in beginnings and endings'. Pyrocles piles on the agony with references to his deceased mother and the living mother of Musidorus. This is to emphasize the horrible dilemma of Euarchus, and Sidney does not intend the reader to accept Pyrocles' insinuation that all Euarchus cares about is his reputation as a just judge; see the aside at p. 414, 31–2.

PAGE **415**, 15–PAGE **416**, 8. *So it was . . . younger*. See note to p. 224, 1–11 for the love potion.

PAGE **416**, 10–35. *In which . . . justly*. See Introduction, p. lxii, for a discussion of the overruling of Euarchus's just sentence by Basilius.

16. *Cleophila*. 'or/Zelmane' is written in a later hand in the margin of St.

34–5. *so uncertain . . . justly*. Cf. Duplessis-Mornay, *A work concerning the trueness of the Christian religion*, trans. A. Golding (1587), pp. 193–4:

> Again, how often have judges condemned some man for a crime, whereof he hath been guiltless, and in the denial whereof he hath stood even upon the scaffold, and yet hath there confessed himself faulty in some other crime? . . . As for example, the judge condemneth them for conspiracy against the commonweal, whereas God condemneth them (perchance) for behaving themselves loosely in defending the commonweal.

PAGE **417**, 3–4. *Philanax . . . ever held*. I have treated this as an absolute; the insertion in As of *was*, making a separate sentence, is probably an intelligent scribal 'improvement'.

8–9 (var.). Clitophon, the son of Kalander, is added by 93 from NA.

15–18 (var.). 93 omits Amasis, who does not appear in NA, and substitutes Plexirtus, Helen, and Amphialus, who do. Greville, *Life*, 14–15, gives a rather different account of how Sidney would have continued the *Arcadia*.

20–1. *the strange . . . desire*. See note to p. 328, 2–21. Ringler thinks that some time between finishing OA and writing the opening of NA, where Strephon and Klaius lament the absence of their mistress, Sidney wrote the poem OP 4, telling how Strephon and Klaius first fell in love with Urania, and of their pursuit of her during a country game of barley-break.

GLOSSARY

A CONCORDANCE of Sidney's word usage must await the completion of satisfactory editions of all his writings. Here an attempt has been made to gloss words which are not immediately familiar, and words used in senses which are no longer the familiar ones. In the case of the latter, the occurrences of the words in their older senses only are given. Thus *salve*, 'salutation', will be found, but not *salve*, 'ointment, cure'. When a word such as *fact*, 'deed', occurs frequently, a page-and-line reference is given for one occurrence only, followed by 'etc.'. It emerges that, like Spenser, Sidney used a good many rustic and archaic words, especially in some of the eclogues. He was also something of an innovator, and to do justice to this aspect of his vocabulary, words which are still current usage are included when the first citation in *O.E.D.* is either from Sidney or from a later writer. Page-and-line references followed by 'n.' indicate that a note will be found in the Commentary. Page-and-line references followed by '(var.)' indicate that the word will be found in the variant readings at the foot of the page, and not in the text itself.

A

abroad *adv.* widely apart; stretched out 267, 28.

absented *pp. adj.* removed (from customary residence) 127, 1.

abuse *v.* deceive 85, 19.

accident *n.* event; happening (not necessarily bad) 155, 33, 286, 25.

accompanable *adj.* fit to go with as a companion 334, 29.

accord *n.* harmony 106, 25; *v.* make to harmonize with or proportionate to 189, 22, 312, 21; **accorded** *pp.* harmonized; made proportionate 57, 28, 229, 14, 293, 3.

activity *n.* skill, esp. in athletics 41, 18, 126, 32, 154, 34, 244, 19.

adamant *n.* loadstone; magnet 290, 27.

adherent *n.* that which is attached to as a circumstance 127, 29; *adj.* attached to as a circumstance 85, 32 n.

adusted *pp. adj.* choler adust *n.* medical state characterized by dryness of the body, heat, thirst, etc. 80, 1 n.

advantage *n.* chance; favourable opportunity 109, 16.

affect *n.* affection; emotion 170, 15, etc.; **affected** *pp. adj.* full of affection 54, 26, 274, 32; aimed at 323, 34; assumed;

put-on 113, 17, 357, 1; **affection** *n.* emotion 263, 25; **affectionated** *pp. adj.* passionate 185, 27 n.

after-live *v.* survive 299, 20 n.; **after-liver** *n.* 110, 4.

agreeable *adj.* consistent with 356, 2.

ai *interj.* the Greek cry of lament 345, 26 n.

aland *adv.* ashore 105, 6.

alarum *n.* alarm 106, 37, 126, 29.

all to- *used as an intensive* 186, 24.

allowance *n.* agreement; permission; acceptance 12, 32, etc.; **allowing** *adj.* agreeing; assenting 368, 8.

alonely *adv.* solely 199, 18.

ambassade *n.* message sent by an ambassador; ambassador and his train 57, 8 n., 218, 4, 345, 9, 364, 7.

annoyed *pp. adj.* full of grief and vexations 280, 28.

apostle's mantle *n.* long cloak 377, 3 n.

apparent *adj.* manifest; plainly seen 31, 13.

appassionate *adj.* full of passion 135, 9 n., 155, 35, 408, 27.

appeased *pp. adj.* calm and collected 362, 11.

apply *v.* accommodate to 89, 39 n.

appropriated *pp.* suited; made to fit with **89**, 13.

approved *pp. adj.* proved by experience **26**, 13, **224**, 11, **362**, 19.

arbitrage *n.* arbitration **154**, 12.

ardency *n.* ardour; warmth of feeling **155**, 1.

arrant *adj.* thorough-going; out-and-out **274**, 1; **arrantest** *superl.* **390**, 32.

artificial *adj.* artistic **376**, 12.

asclepiadics *n. pl.* asclepiads (quantitative verse form) **166**, 7 n.

askances *conj.* as though **114**, 33 [this is the latest citation in *O.E.D.*, the previous one is for 1430].

assistants *n. pl.* audience; those present at an event **141**, 16.

attaint *v.* condemn; infect **345**, 13, **356**, 12.

attend *v.* wait for **267**, 16.

attent *pp. adj.* intent; attentive to **190**, 23; **attentive** *adj.* listening carefully **225**, 1, **285**, 28, **353**, 25.

attractive *adj.* drawing **169**, 30.

auditor *n.* listener; disciple **42**, 17.

available *adj.* availing; advantageous **364**, 13, **389**, 9.

B

bait *n.* resting place **189**, 2 n., **214**, 21 n.; **baiting** place *n.* stopping place for refreshment and changing horses on a journey **5**, 5 n., **150**, 29.

bale *n.* ill fortune; unhappiness **252**, 24.

basilisk *n.* fabulous monster that kills by its glance **333**, 8 n.

bastinados *n. pl.* blows (seemingly not on the soles of the feet) **270**, 19-20 [the earliest citation in *O.E.D.* is from Holinshed (1577)].

beam *n.* scales; set it to the beam, weigh it in the balance **383**, 30.

beaten *pp. adj.* inured to; experienced **226**, 32.

become *v.* befit; suit **40**, 3, **210**, 35.

beholding *pres. p.* under obligation **378**, 8; holding the eyes; looking attractive **198**, 12 [the earliest citation in *O.E.D.* is from NA (*Works*, i. 87), 'my beauty was no more beholding to him than my harmony'].

behoveful *adj.* useful; necessary **185**, 32, **379**, 33.

beldam *n.* old woman; witch **30**, 13-14.

benamed *pp.* described as **250**, 5 n.

best *n.* best course **178**, 20, **183**, 13.

bested *pp.* beset; pressed **202**, 17.

bettering *n.* improvement **14**, 23 and 26; **betterness** *n.* superiority **295**, 29.

bewonder *v.* fill with amazement **186**, 24 n., **211**, 6.

bewray *v.* divulge **228**, 15, etc.

blabber *v.* blurt **290**, 2.

blaze *v.* emblazon; picture **110**, 29, **163**, 9, **164**, 5; **blazings** *n. pl.* advertisements **269**, 22.

blea *v.* baa **145**, 32, **256**, 25.

bless *v.* wound **142**, 6 n., **161**, 27.

blockish *adj.* obtuse **147**, 33.

blow point *n.* children's game **77**, 33 n.

bob *n.* and *v.* blow; hit **132**, 27 n.

book *n.* without book, by rote; from memory **277**, 29 n.

booth *n.* temporary dwelling place **254**, 24.

bootless *adj.* useless **283**, 3.

bore *pp.* born **255**, 12.

botch *n.* ulcer; boil **140**, 2 (var.).

bought *n.* curve; bend **241**, 9.

brabbler *n.* caviller about trifles **402**, 34.

brave *adj.* boastful **132**, 31 n., etc.; magnificent **199**, 4; **bravery** *n.* bravado **29**, 33.

brawl *n.* a kind of dance **57**, 32.

brickle *adj.* brittle **134**, 16.

brim *adj.* breme; fierce **76**, 28.

briny *adj.* salt **280**, 16 n.

burden *n.* bass or undersong **16**, 7.

bussing *pres. p.* kissing **251**, 7 n.

busy *adj.* meddlesome; officious **77**, 29.

by-word *n.* epithet of scorn **261**, 21.

C

caitiff *n.* despicable creature **388**, 1; *adj.* wretched; miserable **106**, 9, **341**, 13.

calmy *adj.* tranquil **336**, 18.

camisado *n.* night attack (orig. one in which the attackers wore nightshirts over their armour for mutual recognition) **69**, 55.

canker *n.* cancer **226**, 15.

cannibal *n.* **353**, 9 n.

capitulate *v.* specify; make conditions **316**, 20 [the earliest citation in *O.E.D.* is for 1580].

captive *v.* captivate; take prisoner **278**, 20; captiving *pres. p. adj.* capturing **325**, 9.

careful *adj.* full of cares; anxious **53**, 11, etc.; careless *adj.* without anxiety or cares **93**, 24.

carking *pres. p. adj.* causing anxiety **85**, 32.

casting *pres. p.* deliberating **193**, 4.

cates *n. pl.* choice victuals; delicacies **198**, 5.

causeful *adj.* having good cause; well grounded **72**, 21, etc.

chafe *n.* rage **32**, 8, etc.; chafing *pres. p.* raging **33**, 34.

charming *adj.* magical **195**, 19.

chase *n.* prey; that which is hunted **47**, 20; in chase, whilst pursuing **333**, 6.

chat *n.* talk **261**, 4 n.

chaw *v.* chew **260**, 12 n.

chiefer *comp. adj.* more important **9**, 37.

chumpish *adj.* sullen; grumpy **250**, 17 n.

Cimmerian *adj.* dark as the dwellings of the Cimmerii **343**, 18 n.

circumspect *adj.* attentive to all the circumstances **268**, 9.

cithern, cittern *n.* a sort of guitar, strung with wire, and played with a plectrum **214**, 15.

clampering *vbl. n.* clumsy disturbance of the peace **354**, 29.

clause *n.* close, final point **221**, 31.

clearing *vbl. n.* removal of suspicion of guilt **293**, 29; clearness *n.* innocence **291**, 17.

clerkly *adj.* learned **255**, 17.

coaly, colly *adj.* coal black **345**, 16.

cockered *pp. adj.* pampered **78**, 8.

cockles *n. pl.* hot cockles, a children's game **77**, 33 n.

cockling *n.* young one; child **78**, 8.

coinhabiters *n. pl.* dwellers in together **404**, 2.

colour *n.* rhetorical flourish; pretext **68**, 31, etc.; *v.* justify; supply a pretext for **184**, 15; colourable *adj.* plausible **233**, 30; coloured *pp. adj.* deceitful; plausible **352**, 29.

comfit *n.* sweetmeat **241**, 24.

commodity *n.* opportunity; advantage **119**, 17, **321**, 13, **356**, 15.

common *adj.* shared by all alike **258**, 7, **324**, 8.

compact *n.* combination; joining together **242**, 8 [*O.E.D.* cites 1590 and 1601 for similar meanings].

con *v.* con thank, acknowledge gratitude **77**, 20 n.

conceit *n.* idea; conception **4**, 17, etc.

concent *n.* harmony **15**, 24, **335**, 19, **337**, 33 [the earliest citation in *O.E.D.* is from Foxe's *Sermons* (1585); but it is frequently confused with *consent*, and is so spelt in the OA MSS.].

conclusion *n.* legal impediment or stoppage **348**, 14.

confection *n.* combination of objects **59**, 34.

conjoined *pp. adj.* connected; coherent **277**, 3.

consort *n.* agreement **388**, 11 n.; consorted *pp. adj.* tuned in harmony; agreeing **135**, 10, **211**, 3 [*O.E.D.* cites **135**, 10 for the specialized sense, and *Love's Labour's Lost* for the fig. use as in **211**, 3].

contemned *pp. adj.* despised **211**, 23.

contentation *n.* contentment **4**, 6, etc.

convoy *n.* channel; way **137**, 2 n.

corner *adj.* secret; sly **178**, 24 [this is the citation in *O.E.D.* under 15b fig.].

corrosive *n.* exacerbation of grief **57**, 11 n.

corse *n.* corpse **336**, 8 and 9.

couthe *v.* 3*rd pers. pl. past* knew **254**, 22 n.

coyed *pp.* appeased; coaxed **73**, 29.

cradle *adj.* youngest **334**, 17.

crapal *n.* toad stone **31**, 1 n.

craven *n.* coward **394**, 13 n.

crouch *n.* crutch **142**, 6 and 7 n.

crown *n.* poem composed of linked stanzas, where the last line of each stanza forms the first line of the next, and the last line of the whole sequence repeats the line that began it **331**, 3 n.

crud *n.* curd **191**, 23.

cry *n.* pack of people **274**, 7 [the earliest citation in *O.E.D.* 13†b is from *Hamlet* III. ii. 289, 'cry of players']; cryingly *adv.* with lamenting shouts **284**, 2.

cumber *n.* trouble; burden **98**, 1, etc.; *v.* trouble; be a burden **139**, 11, etc.; cumbersome *adj.* troublesome; burdensome **113**, 33, etc.; cumbrous *adj.* troublesome **260**, 27.

N n

cunning *n.* skill; knowledge 4, 19, etc.; *adj.* skilful 241, 10, etc.; **cunningest** *superl. adj.* most skilful 363, 18.

curbed *pp. adj.* bent; curved 142, 25.

curious *adj.* careful; carefully made 138, 22, etc.; **curiousest** *superl. adj.* most careful 402, 24; **curiously** *adv.* carefully; exquisitely 95, 29, etc.

currish *adj.* quarrelsome; mean-spirited 150, 8, 302, 18–19.

cyclops *n. pl.* 353, 9 n.

D

daintiness *n.* fastidiousness 178, 25.

damage *n.* loss; detriment; injury 175, 24.

dark *v.* darken 335, 15; **darkling** *adv.* in the dark 225, 20.

deadly *adj.* dying 278, 32.

debateful *adj.* contentious 279, 19.

deceit *n.* deception 223, 28.

deface *v.* destroy 130, 30, 136, 30; defame 78, 26, 145, 19, 149, 24.

defensive *n.* defence 277, 6.

delicacy *n.* luxury 179, 25.

demean *n.* demeanour 79, 6; **demeanour** *n.* behaviour 269, 22.

denizened *pp. adj.* naturalized 80, 33.

depart *n.* departure 335, 14; *v.* separate 297, 22; **departure** *n.* parting; separation 176, 9.

deprave *v.* vilify; defame 338, 19.

descrier *n.* discoverer 326, 24 [the earliest citation in *O.E.D.* is from Minsheu, *Spanish Dictionary* (1599)].

desireful *adj.* desirable 320, 10.

despaired *pp. adj.* cast into despair; without hope 141, 29.

despota *n.* despot; ruler 385, 1 n.

destinied *pp.* destined 382, 20.

determinate *adj.* resolute; determined 227, 29, etc.

dicker *n.* half a score 253, 15 n.

disaccustomed *pp. adj.* no longer used to 278, 21–2.

disannul *v.* cancel; annul 412, 2.

disastered *pp. adj.* stricken with disaster; ill starred 113, 1 n.

discomfort *v.* defeat the plans of 155, 16.

discontentation *n.* discontent; displeasure 141, 9, 265, 19 (var.).

discountenance *n.* abashment 265, 19; **discountenanced** *pp.* abashed 46, 22.

disdained *pp. adj.* affronted by; offended at 302, 18.

disgrace *n.* affront 178, 22; **disgracing** *pres. p. adj.* affronting 400, 26.

disguisement *n.* disguise 184, 25–6 [the earliest citation in *O.E.D.* is from NA (*Works*, i. 93)].

disjoined *pp. adj.* separated 383, 26.

disjunction *n.* separation 313, 16.

disparagement *n.* marriage to one of inferior rank 100, 33.

distrain *v.* compel by confiscation or seizure to perform a legal obligation 348, 6.

disuse *v.* cease to be accustomed to 40, 8.

diversified *pp. adj.* diverse; different 320, 24.

dividing *vbl. n.* separating 215, 27.

dizain *n.* poem in ten stanzas of ten lines each 331, 2 n.

downfall *n.* downpour 279, 20 n.

drivel *n.* drudge; foul slut 192, 16, 400, 32.

duello *n.* duel 146, 14 (var.).

E

ebon *adj.* black as ebony 238, 14 (var.) n.

efficacy *n.* power to produce effects 129, 14.

eft *adv.* moreover; again 143, 7.

emmet *n.* ant 85, 11.

enclosed *pp. adj.* kept in control and hidden 168, 9 [the earliest citation for the adjectival use in *O.E.D.* is for 1607].

engrieved *pp.* aggravated; exacerbated 382, 1.

ensue *v.* pursue 135, 26, etc.

entireness *n.* absolute devotion; friendship 41, 16 [the earliest citation in *O.E.D.* †2 is for 1599].

ermelin, ermion *n.* ermine 241, 28 n., 257, 19.

erst *adv.* before 251, 24, etc.

essential *adj.* actual; real (as opposed to 'imaginative', 'fancied', and 'opinionate') 134, 2, 266, 14, 361, 34.

estimation *n.* esteem; appreciation 59, 22, 63, 23, 68, 28–9.

event *n.* outcome consequence 88, 9, etc.

exigent *n.* occasion requiring immediate action 96, 8, 281, 16.

F

fact *n.* deed 65, 26, etc.

faintly *adv.* timidly 28, 35.

fairing *n.* complimentary gift 226, 13.

fantastical *adj.* imaginary 281, 17 n.

far-fet *adj.* far-fetched 45, 15, 194, 18.

fearful *adj.* full of fear 75, 22.

feeling *adj.* sympathetic; deeply felt 106, 8; touching 270, 4 n. **feelingly** *adv.* with feeling; on one's own pulses 108, 30.

fellowless *adj.* without fellow; peerless 290, 14.

fit *n.* paroxysm 259, 19.

fixed *pp.* rigid and immobile 279, 2 n.

flix *n.* flux; dysentery 33, 22.

foen *n. pl.* foes 76, 31, 258, 28.

fond *adj.* foolish 263, 9.

forcible *adj.* able to be taken by force 179, 6.

fore-appointed *pp. adj.* predestined 280, 22.

forefeeling *n.* anticipation 228, 22; **forefelt** *pp. adj.* felt in anticipation 226, 25.

foregoer *n.* forerunner; harbinger 328, 29.

fore-judging *pres. p. adj.* pre-judging 353, 25.

forepassed *pp. adj.* that had occurred previously 279, 15, 318, 26, 320, 18.

foresightful *adj.* foreseeing 134, 17.

foretaken *pp. adj.* taken previously 92, 16, 365, 15.

forlorn hope *n.* lit. 'lost troop', a picked body of men, detached to the front to begin the attack 135, 8.

forwasted *pp. adj.* wasted away 202, 10.

forworn *pp. adj.* ancient; grown old 189, 16.

framed *pp.* disposed 139, 1.

franzy *n.* frenzy 140, 15.

free-holding *pres. p. adj.* possessing the tenure of 280, 2–3.

fremd *adj.* unfriendly 261, 11 n.

freshly *adv.* vigorously 95, 12.

frisk *adj.* full of life and spirit 260, 11.

fugitive *adj.* fleeing 57, 1.

furmenty *n.* frumenty, dish made of hulled wheat boiled in milk, and seasoned with cinnamon, etc. 196, 4.

furniture *n.* equipment 233, 29, 289, 23.

G

galled *pp. adj.* (*fig.*) fretted; distressed 121, 23 (var.) n. [the earliest citation in *O.E.D.* is for 1601].

gan *v. used as an intensive*, did *rather than* began 258, 10, etc.

garboil *n.* confusion; tumult 327, 2, 416, 15.

gat *v.* arrived at 254, 24.

geometrical *adj.* that can be determined by scientific measurement 363, 31.

german *n.* cousin german, first cousin 9, 38.

ghastful *adj.* ghastly 18, 29; **ghastfulness** *n.* ghastliness 266, 24; **ghastly** *adv.* in a horrified way 91, 21.

gittern *n.* cithern (q.v.); a musical stringed instrument 132, 20.

glad *v.* make or become happy; rejoice 106, 32, etc.

glass *v.* see or look at the reflection of 150, 22, 191, 33; **glasses** *n. pl.* hand mirrors 3, 29.

gloire *n.* glory 259, 11 n.

glorious *adj.* boastful 136, 6; **gloriously** *adv.* boastfully 371, 27.

glut *n.* act of feeding to excess; gluttony 78, 28; **gluttonish** *adj.* voracious 307, 6 n.

goat-herd *adj.* 328, 23 n.

grateful *adj.* pleasing 84, 22, etc.

Grew *n.* Greek 77, 5.

H

halidom *n.* holy relic; by my halidom, a frequent oath 101, 32.

handless *adj.* incapable of action 392, 13–14 (var.) n.

handsel *n.* omen or token; earnest 289, 16.

harbour *n.* place of rest, refreshment, and entertainment 85, 27 n.

hard *adv.* hard by; close to 273, 1.

hardy *adj.* courageous 85, 16, 87, 29.

harness *n.* armour 165, 7; **harnished** *pp.* [an eye-rhyme for **varnished**] clad in armour 60, 13.

harquebus *n.* the common form of movable gun 41, 7.

hatch *v.* conceal 335, 28 n.

headily *adv.* impetuously 275, 32.

heartless *adj.* lacking courage 51, 26, 392, 13–14 (var.) n.

hent *pp.* seized **333, 23**.

hight *pp.* called **337, 32**.

historify *v.* relate the history of **59, 11 n**.

hoise *v.* raise (sail) by means of tackle, etc. **125, 25**.

hostry *n.* hostelry; inn **87, 27**.

humorist *n.* person governed by his humours; fantasist **166, 28**.

hurtless *adj.* harmless **130, 9**, etc.; hurtlessly *adv.* unhurtably **7, 23**.

I

imaginative *adj.* imaginary, fantastic **134, 2, 219, 5, 220, 16, 281, 17** (var.) n., **363, 10** (var.).

immodest *adj.* arrogant; impudent **393, 24 n**.

imp *n.* offspring **285, 2**.

impair *v.* grow worse **332, 29**; impairing *vbl. n.* worsening **14, 22**.

implied *pp.* accommodated to **90, 3 n**.

imported *pp.* concerned **374, 31**.

impostumed *pp. adj.* diseased; corrupted **234, 21** [the first citation in *O.E.D.* is for 1400, and the second from this passage].

impresa *n.* emblem; device **37, 15** and **18** (var.) n.

incaved *pp.* hollowed; bent inwards **241, 9** [this is the earliest citation in *O.E.D.*].

incirclet *n.* light circular curl or spiral **239, 5** [this is the earliest citation in *O.E.D.*].

indifferency *n.* lack of prejudice **396, 6**.

infortunate *adj.* inopportune; unlucky **202, 7, 217, 18** (var.); infortunateness *n.* **360, 30**; infortune *n.* misfortune; misadventure **105, 16**.

inhabiter *n.* dweller-in; inhabitant **329, 10**.

inheritrix *n.* heiress **154, 20**, etc.

inly *adj.* inward **342, 9**.

insolence *n.* pride and ambition **69, 23**.

interessed *pp.* interested; concerned **275, 33**.

interlude *n.* stage play **42, 26**.

intricate *adj.* perplexingly entangled **97, 17** [the earliest citation in *O.E.D.* is for 1579].

inward *adj.* secret **188, 29**.

iwis *adv.* indeed **143, 2**.

J

jarl *v.* quarrel **76, 27 n**.

jaundice *n.* black jaundice **33, 22**; yellow jaundice **365, 17 n**.

joyed *pp. adj.* gladdened; filled with joy **275, 10, 328, 25**.

jump *adj.* exact **255, 23**; jumply *adv.* exactly **362, 17**.

jurat *n.* sworn witness **73, 8**.

just *adv.* precisely **89, 13**.

K

keels *n. pl.* kayles, ninepins or skittles **77, 33 n**.

ken *v.* recognize **170, 21**.

kind *n.* nature **48, 32**, etc.; kindly *adj.* natural **208, 8**, etc.; *adv.* naturally; according to nature **19, 24**, etc.

L

lamentable *adj.* lamenting; plaintive; sorrowful **40, 2, 92, 27, 279, 25**.

launder *n.* woman who washes clothes; laundress **20, 21**.

lay *n.* lair **75, 24** [the earliest citation in *O.E.D.* 72 is from *Greene's Mourning Garment* (1590)].

learn *v.* show; teach **59, 12**.

let *n.* hindrance **103, 16**, etc.

license *v.* give leave of departure to **167, 19** [*O.E.D.* †2 cites for 1483, 1551, and then from NA (*Works*, i. 429), 'Amphialus licensed the gentleman…'].

lickerous *adj.* greedy for; eagerly desirous of **88, 20**; wanton; delightful **239, 31** (var.); lickerousness *n.* greedy desire **361, 14**.

lighten *v.* give light to **56, 31**; lightsome *adj.* bright **266, 15**.

loathsomely *adv.* with loathing **189, 8**.

lobbish *adj.* clownish **314, 23** [this is the latest citation in *O.E.D.*].

lour *n.* gloomy, sullen look **261, 15**.

lucklest *superl. adj.* most unlucky **261, 16**.

luxuriousness *n.* lecherousness **390, 32–3**.

lyra *n.* lyre, harp **165, 2** [this is the earliest citation in *O.E.D.*].

M

madding *vbl. n.* madness **270, 21**.

madrigal *n.* song of one stanza with long and short lines and varying rhyme scheme **207, 7 n**.

magistracy *n.* condition of being a ruler 385, 16.

main *adj.* mighty 13, 24; **mainly** *adv.* vehemently 17, 22.

make *n.* mate 286, 20.

malapert *adj.* impudent; presumptuous 75, 7.

manage *v.* perform the movements proper to a trained horse 31, 25.

mankind *adj.* masculine; virago-like 34, 21.

manwood *adj.* fierce like a man 78, 10 n.

marchpane *n.* marzipan 241, 24.

marting *pres. p. adj.* trading 170, 22.

masteries *n. pl.* trying of masteries, testing strength and skill in competitive feats 56, 5.

match *n.* wick or cord prepared for firing cannon, etc. 79, 3.

mate *n.* checkmate; defeat 142, 14; **mated** *pp. adj.* downcast; sorrowful 170, 31.

matter *v.* form matter; fester 58, 31.

maugre *prep.* in spite of 132, 21.

may-game *adj.* trivial 267, 22 [the earliest citation in *O.E.D.* 4 *attrib.* is for 1586].

meagre *adj.* spiteful; sour 261, 1, 271, 26.

meanness *n.* low estate 106, 22, 130, 25.

medals *n. pl.* 187, 20 n. and 27.

medley *n.* confusion 301, 3 n.

memorative *adj.* pertaining to the memory 373, 16 n.

mettle *n.* disposition; temperament 27, 28 n., 117, 23 n., 137, 20.

mew *n.* cage for a hawk 259, 2; *v.* put a hawk in a cage while moulting 220, 36.

mickle *adv.* much 78, 12, 251, 20, 255, 11.

mischief *n.* misfortune 139, 16; evil deed 202, 12.

miser *adj.* wretched 65, 30.

mismeaning *vbl. n.* evil intention 290, 22.

moanful *adj.* expressing grief 88, 13 [this is the earliest citation in *O.E.D.*], 181, 7, 283, 1.

mollified *pp.* softened 184, 2.

monarchal *adj.* ruled by a monarch 320, 5, 383, 13 [this is the earliest citation in *O.E.D.*].

moony *adj.* belonging to the moon 338, 15 n.

mortal *adj.* deadly 329, 32.

mote *v.* may 141, 28.

mould *n.* shape 62, 32, 80, 1.

mountainets *n. pl.* hillocks 37, 14 n.

mountebank *adj.* characteristic of an itinerant quack 393, 16 n.

mowing *pres. p.* pulling faces; grimacing 257, 27.

muddy *adj.* confused 85, 31, 186, 19.

muett *adj.* mute 137, 27 n.

mumping *pres. p.* muttering 270, 8 [this is the earliest citation in *O.E.D.* †1].

municipal *adj.* pertaining to the internal laws of a state 404, 27.

murrey *n.* and *adj.* purple-red colour of the mulberry 169, 5, 377, 6 n.

N

namely *adv.* particularly 78, 33.

nar *comp. adv.* nearer 77, 6.

ne *adv.* not 255, 13; nor 335, 31, 340, 6, 341, 34.

necessary *adj.* fated; unavoidable 279, 20.

next *adj.* nearest 156, 9.

nis *v.* is not 256, 14.

noised *pp. adj.* sounded 132, 33; **noisome** *adj.* harmful; noxious 278, 30, 330, 3.

noll *n.* head 270, 3.

not *v.* know not 256, 6.

O

occasion *n.* opportunity 9, 14, etc.

occurrents *n. pl.* events 410, 6.

opinionate *adj.* fancied; supposed 362, 1.

original *n.* origin 396, 5.

oughts *n. pl.* things of no consequence; noughts 161, 31.

ounce *n.* lynx 257, 10.

out *adj.* confused; lacking in judgement 77, 12.

overshot *pp. adj.* wide of the mark; mistaken or deceived 396, 12.

owe *v.* own 406, 11.

owly *adj.* having poor vision in daylight 373, 33.

P

pack *n.* gang; set of criminals 304, 12.

pain *n.* difficulty 78, 21; **painful** *adj.* taking trouble or pains 75, 31.

painted *pp. adj.* having the false colours of rhetoric 244, 2.

panic *adj.* showing groundless emotion such as was attributed to the influence of the god Pan 269, 19 (var.) n.

pantable *n.* pantofle; slipper 29, 32 n.

paragon *n.* touchstone; trial for comparison 26, 26 n.

pardie *interj.* by God 399, 13.

partage *n.* share 154, 4.

partakers *n. pl.* sharers 104, 31.

pass *v.* surpass 39, 31, etc.; alleviate 183, 30.

passenger *n.* traveller 8, 29, etc.

passionated *pp. adj.* activated by passion; made sorrowful 99, 19.

pastor *n.* shepherd 82, 25, etc.; pastorals *n. pl.* pastoral games and pastimes 44, 2 n., etc.

patrociny *n.* patronage 101, 8 (var.) n.

pattern *n.* model for comparison 26, 26 (var.) n., 106, 13.

patron *n.* pattern 106, 13 (var.).

peculiar *adj.* especial; particular to 385, 21.

pedant *n.* schoolmaster 343, 25 n.

peise *v.* weigh 59, 23.

pelf *n.* wealth 62, 11.

period *n.* end 279, 8.

pewing *pres. p.* (of a bird) crying plaintively 256, 29.

phaleuciacs *n. pl.* phaleucian hendecasyllables 165, 2 n.

pie *n.* magpie 58, 29, 78, 27 n.

pilled *adj.* (1) bereft of feathers; (2) plundered 78, 27 n.

pinching *pres. p. adj.* painful 171, 21.

pistle *n.* epistle 252, 13 n.

pitfall, pitfold *n.* small trap for catching birds 75, 23.

plain *v.* utter complaints 146, 29, etc.; plainfulness *n.* mournfulness; state of being full of complaints 151, 15; plaining *vbl. n.* complaining 346, 29; *adj.* 181, 27. plaintful *adj.* full of complaints 104, 31.

platform *n.* basis 367, 5.

plausible *adj.* willing; accepting 86, 5, 380, 26.

plum *adj.* plump 191, 18.

points *n. pl.* tagged laces for attaching hose to doublet 30, 10.

policied *pp. adj.* civilly organized 155, 31; policy *n.* system of government 256, 13; politic *adj.* political 363, 30.

pommel *n.* round, globe-shaped object 239, 29 n.

pomps *n. pl.* ceremonies 357, 1.

poor *adj.* incompetent 65, 9.

portraiture *n.* portrait; portrayal 181, 18.

prentice *n.* apprentice 208, 29.

presently *adv.* immediately 50, 13; presentness *n.* immediacy 363, 4–5.

prest *adj.* ready 337, 13.

pretend *v.* claim 362, 26; pretended *pp. adj.* purposed, designed 383, 12.

prevent *v.* forestall 260, 4.

prime *n.* first hour of morning 75, 25.

prize *n.* reward 175, 3 n.; play a prize, engage in a contest 206, 31.

proof *n.* experience 138, 14; prove *v.* experience; find 61, 18, etc.

provoking *pres. p. adj.* stirring up, calling forth (feeling and interest) 82, 20.

puddled *pp. adj.* confused; unclear 166, 28.

puling *pres. p.* crying 261, 2.

puppet *n.* doll; automaton 85, 19, 112, 18, 195, 21.

purgation *n.* purge (med.) 34, 5.

purled *pp. adj.* trimmed, either with gold thread or frills 26, 4.

purling *pres. p. adj.* murmuring 46, 5.

Q

quab *v.* tremble; palpitate 102, 21 n.

quaint *adj.* full of conceits; fanciful; cunning 58, 28, 108, 2 n.

queen-apple *n.* variety of red apple 238, 30 n.

queint *pp.* quenched 349, 11 n.

quick *adv.* alive 279, 13, 383, 23.

quitted *pp.* acquitted 366, 22.

R

race *n.* strong current 171, 15.

rampire *n.* rampart 165, 18, 190, 14, 370, 25.

rathe *adj.* early 144, 7.

ravening *n.* laying waste 4, 13; ravenous *adj.* seeking for prey 47, 5, 130, 25; ravin *n.* rapine; robbery 258, 19.

rayed *pp.* diseased 142, 1 n.

reasonable *adj.* having the power of reason 4, 30, 19, 14.

rebeck *n.* musical instrument with three strings 65, 7.

receipt *n.* reception 180, 33, etc.; receiver 222, 5.

recklessness *n.* neglect 248, 3.

reclaimed *pp. adj.* (of a hawk) reduced to obedience 153, 7.

recomfort *n.* solace, comfort 86, 23, 88, 4; **recomforted** *pp. adj.* comforted 168, 2 (var.).

recommend *v.* consign; commit 6, 13, etc.

record *v.* repeat quietly or sadly 29, 20, etc.

recovery *n.* remedy 344, 13.

red *v. past* advised 77, 9 n.; **rede** *n.* advice 255, 17.

refection *n.* recreation; refreshment 138, 31.

refelled *pp.* refuted; disproved 158, 4, 384, 22.

refrain *v.* restrain; hold back 146, 30, 348, 4.

regiment *n.* rule; government 388, 19.

rehearsal *n.* recital 159, 31, 303, 24 (var.).

reins *n. pl.* loins 43, 26, 74, 36.

relent *v.* soften; cause to relent 148, 15 [the earliest citation in *O.E.D.* †3b is from Spenser]; **relenting** *vbl. n.* slackening 13, 23.

remorsed *pp. adj.* affected with remorse 232, 3 [this is the earliest citation in *O.E.D.*].

renting *n.* rending; tearing 176, 17.

reprieval *n.* reprieve 203, 12 [this is the earliest citation in *O.E.D.*].

resolved *pp. adj.* resolute; settled 180, 10.

resound *n.* a returned or echoed sound 145, 29, 345, 3 [this is the earliest citation in *O.E.D.*].

reverence *n.* gesture of respect 33, 29, etc.

richess *n.* richness; precious quality 61, 4, 84, 22 n., 85, 15, 263, 16 (var.) n., 300, 25.

rine *n.* rind; bark 198, 21 n., 199, 17.

rosed *pp. adj.* redolent of roses 344, 9.

rouse *v.* (of a hawk) shake the feathers 221, 1.

rudeness *n.* uncouthness 31, 10.

runagate *n.* vagabond 65, 29.

S

sadder *comp. adj.* more serious; graver 245, 20; **saddest** *superl. adj.* most serious; gravest 77, 12.

salve *n.* salutation 289, 4 [the earliest citation in *O.E.D.* 4 is from Greene, *Mamillia* (*c.* 1580)].

sample *n.* example 260, 10.

satrapas *n.* satrap, governor of a province under the ancient Persian monarchy 68, 26.

say *n.* assay; foretaste 239, 35 n.

scape *n.* escape 143, 19.

scimitars *n.* a kind of sword 27, 15.

scope *n.* purpose; aim 104, 25, etc.

scrawling *pres. p.* crawling 309, 21.

scrip *n.* wallet; small bag 141, 33, 142, 1.

secret *n.* method or process hidden from all but the initiated 406, 17.

seech *v.* [an eye-rhyme for speech] seek 256, 31.

seigniory *n.* lordship; sovereignty 353, 17, 361, 32.

self-conceit *n.* good opinion of oneself 44, 20, 262, 19 [the earliest citation in *O.E.D.* is from Marlowe's *Faustus*].

self-fancy *n.* idea of pleasing oneself 278, 1.

self-liking *adj.* self-indulgent 179, 24.

selfness *n.* self-centredness; egoism 133, 34 n.

self-respect *n.* private, personal, or selfish end 153, 21 [the earliest citation in *O.E.D.* †1 is for 1613].

semblance *n.* appearance 377, 19.

sensible *adj.* sensitive 270, 10; of the senses 372, 27, 373, 16; **sensibly** *adv.* feelingly, with sensitivity 173, 11; **sensive** *adj.* having senses; sensitive 87, 12.

sentence *n.* wise saying; maxim 249, 9.

serene *n.* harmful dew of summer evenings 329, 32 n.

sestine *n.* sestina 284, 9 n., 328, 21 n., 349, 2 n.

several *adj.* separate 222, 2.

shepherdish *adj.* belonging to, or typical of, a shepherd 37, 8, 113, 16, 417, 18 [the earliest citation in *O.E.D.* is from NA (*Works*, i. 18)]; **shepherdry** *n.* business of a shepherd 168, 29 [the earliest citation in *O.E.D.* is for 1594].

shift *v.* change one's clothing 157, 35.

short *adj.* below standard 266, 21.

shrewdly *adv.* severely 30, 26; **shrewdness** *n.* shrewishness; severity 189, 27.

sicker *adv.* certainly 78, 23.

sieve *n.* small net for snaring birds 144, 10.

sightfulness *n.* power of seeing; ability to see 141, 2, 150, 32 [*O.E.D.* cites these two passages only].

silly *adj.* ignorant; simple 65, 9, etc.

singled *pp.* separated 58, 32.

singularity *n.* distinction due to superiority 38, 21.

skill *n.* knowledge 75, 26, etc.; *v.* know 258, 9; it skills not, it does not matter 232, 32–3; skill-less *adj.* without knowledge or understanding 72, 19, 255, 19.

skipjack *n.* pert, shallow-brained fellow 189, 19.

sleek *adj.* smooth 240, 23; sleekstone-like *adv.* in the manner of a slick or sleek stone used for smoothing or polishing 191, 24.

sleightly *adv.* cunningly; craftily 204, 35.

smackering *vbl. n.* inclination towards 100, 20 [this is the earliest citation in *O.E.D.*].

smirkly *adv.* simperingly 339, 26 [this is the earliest citation in *O.E.D.*].

snakish *adj.* venomous 134, 12; snaky *adj.* venomous; deceitful 166, 26, 167, 11, 280, 2 n., 389, 25.

sneb *v.* snub 77, 8 n.

sort *n.* way; manner 281, 30.

sotted *pp.* besotted; made foolish 184, 30, 290, 11.

sparefulness *n.* frugality 138, 24 [*O.E.D.* cites as sole authority].

spent *pp.* destroyed 333, 16.

spill *v.* destroy; spoil 152, 3, 347, 28.

spite *v.* act spitefully towards 339, 29.

splay *adj.* (of foot) broad, turned outward 30, 14.

spoil *n.* despoliation 78, 28.

sprent *pp.* sprinkled 150, 13 [the earliest citation in *O.E.D.* is from Spenser, *F.Q.*, II, xii. 45].

squeamish *adj.* averse, unwilling to do something 249, 14, 254, 14.

staff *n.* (*pl.* staves) stanza 169, 6 (var.) n.

stain *v.* deprive of lustre, usually in a musical connection 143, 24, etc. [the earliest citation in *O.E.D.* is from 191, 14].

stanza *n.* 169, 6 n.

stark *adv.* absolutely 35, 24.

starting *pres. p. adj.* causing one to start or be startled 120, 32.

stay *n.* stop; hindrance 211, 4, 265, 12; condition 338, 27.

stead *v.* succour; help 95, 4 [the earliest citation in *O.E.D.* is for 1582].

stepmother *adj.* cruel (unlike a true parent) 285, 3.

stomacher *n.* waistcoat 30, 9.

stone *n.* touchstone (for testing purity of metals) 147, 32.

store *n.* plenty 111, 2, etc.

stour *n.* time of turmoil 259, 19 n.

straight *adv.* immediately 259, 24, etc.

straitly *adv.* closely 119, 13 n.

stroke *v.* with adv. or similar extension, bring into a specified position 176, 6. [the earliest citation in *O.E.D.* 3 g is from Nashe, *The Unfortunate Traveller* (1594)].

stroy *v.* destroy 334, 5.

sublimed *pp.* elevated 274, 15.

suddenly *adv.* immediately 267, 28.

surfeit *adj.* excessive; intemperate 141, 6.

suspectful *adj.* suspicious 130, 26 [this is the earliest citation in *O.E.D.*].

swannish *adj.* pertaining to a swan 329, 15 [this is the earliest citation in *O.E.D.*].

swink *n.* toil; labour 257, 4.

sylvan *adj.* pertaining to woods 109, 26 [the earliest citation in *O.E.D.* is from Greene, *Mamillia* (*c.* 1580), followed by this passage].

T

table *n.* picture 64, 18, 305, 6; pair of tables, writing tablets 41, 26; table-talk, familiar conversation at meals [cf. *Defence of Poetry* (*Works*, iii. 12)] 127, 8.

tarantula *n.* tarantism; hysterical dancing disease, supposed to be caused by the bite of the tarantula spider 17, 11 n.

taster *n.* domestic official whose job it was to taste food and drink about to be served to his master, in order to detect poison, etc. 278, 27.

tell *v.* count 132, 33.

temper *n.* quality; nature 5, 32, etc.; tempered *pp. adj.* adjusted 4, 5, etc.

thee *v.* thrive; prosper 141, 28.

thilke *dem. pron.* these 255, 22.

tho *adv.* then 258, 28.

thralled *pp. adj.* captivated 103, 11.

througher *comp. adj.* of **through** (thorower 93) 292, 25.

tickled *pp. adj.* pleasurably excited 189, 14.

tie *v.* enforce 40, 9.

tine *n.* a very little time 145, 1.

tire *v.* (of a hawk) prey upon 182, 8.

torpedo *n.* electric ray or cramp fish 332, 33 n.

touch *v.* censure 78, 31; touched *pp. adj.* tainted 381, 2.

towardness *n.* advancement; furtherance 9, 26, etc.

trace *n.* track; path 135, 28.

train *v.* decoy; deceive; persuade 75, 24, etc.

travailed *pp. adj.* oppressed with cares 116, 29.

traversed *pp.* passed through; experienced 98, 1.

treen-dish *n.* wooden platter 142, 4.

trick *adj.* trim; handsome 249, 22 [this is the earliest citation in *O.E.D.*]; tricked *pp.* dressed 114, 1.

trim *adj.* (with irony) fine; pretty 211, 14, 394, 8.

trunk *n.* pipe used as speaking-tube or ear-trumpet 180, 22.

trussed *pp.* with the points attaching hose to doublet tied up 30, 10.

try *v.* experience 40, 4, etc.

tway, *n.* two 77, 6, 262, 30.

U

unaptness *adj.* lack of aptitude 54, 2.

unassayed *pp.* untested; unattempted 8, 24, 283, 3.

unbashed *pp. adj.* unabashed 129, 24 [see variants].

uncomfortable *adj.* lacking in comfort or consolation 100, 9.

uncouth *adj.* unnatural 5, 18.

undecent *adj.* unbecoming; indecent 277, 15.

undeserved *pp. adj.* unwarranted 233, 6.

uneath *adv.* scarcely 41, 33.

unendly *adj.* unending 342, 20 [this is the earliest citation in *O.E.D.*].

unentangled *pp. adj.* at liberty 336, 3.

unhap *n.* misfortune; misery 113, 27 n.

unharboured *pp.* dislodged; without refuge 204, 7.

unlikely *adj.* unseemly; unsuitable 98, 26, 100, 28.

unmeet *adj.* improper 128, 7.

unreachable *adj.* beyond the reach of man 371, 17 n.

unreadying *n.* undressing 225, 10 n.

unrefrained *adj.* unchecked 207, 28 [not in *O.E.D.*].

unsearchable *adj.* not to be searched 292, 12, 371, 17 (var.) n., 413, 19.

unsensible *adj.* without good sense 31, 10.

unstaid *adj.* instable 225, 18; **unstaidness** *n.* instability 16, 4.

unsurety *n.* incertainty; insecurity 230, 25.

untouched *pp. adj.* unviolated 233, 31.

untried *pp. adj.* unsmelted 31, 2.

untrussed *pp.* with the points attaching hose to doublet undone 30, 9.

unused *pp. adj.* unusual; unaccustomed 129, 24, 197, 32.

upbore *v. past* bore up 255, 30.

use *n.* accustomed practice 222, 9; used *pp.* accustomed 212, 20.

utmost *adj.* outermost 223, 32.

V

vagabonding *pres. p.* wandering about like vagabonds 307, 8.

vail *v.* vail bonnet *fig.*, yield; acknowledge submission 77, 19 [the earliest citation in *O.E.D.* is from Gosson (1579)].

vainness *n.* futility; vanity 203, 5.

varnished *pp.* embellished 60, 15.

veered *pp.* changed course or direction 323, 33 n.

vindicative *adj.* vindictive 287, 21.

viny *adj.* closely entwined 273, 10 n.

W

wanhope *n.* despair 107, 8.

warbled *pp. adj.* injured by warbles (swellings, generally on animals, caused by the larvae of gadflies) 33, 22.

warefulness *n.* watchfulness 138, 22 n.

waste *n.* destruction 78, 28; *pp.* destroyed 332, 7 n.

watered *adj.* filled with water 118, 19 n., 170, 26.

waymenting *n.* lamenting 62, 19, 286, 19 n.

weed *n.* dress; clothing 62, 5, etc.

welkin *n.* firmament 255, 1.

whereupon *adv.* upon which 127, 15.

whether *rel. pron.* which of two 46, 8, etc.

whilom *adv.* once 336, 15.

widowed *pp. adj.* having lost a husband 104, 19 n.

winy *adj.* drunken 127, 3, 128, 8.

without *prep.* outside; beyond 13, 12, etc.

witold *n.* cuckold 150, 4.

woned *pp.* inhabited 256, 8 n.

wormish *adj.* wretched 385, 33 [this is the earliest citation in *O.E.D.*].

wrack *n.* ruin; wreck 180, 29, etc.

wrought *pp. adj.* embroidered 37, 27.

wrying *pres. p.* twisting, contorting 100, 24.

Y

ycleped *pp.* called 255, 3.

yclothed *v. past* clothed 257, 9.

younker *n.* youngster; gay young man 141, 20.

ywroughten *pp. adj.* embroidered 142, 2.

INDEX OF CHARACTERS

INDEX OF OTHER NAMES

(*Mainly classical*)

INDEX OF PLACES

INDEX OF FIRST LINES OF POEMS

GENERAL INDEX TO INTRODUCTION AND COMMENTARY

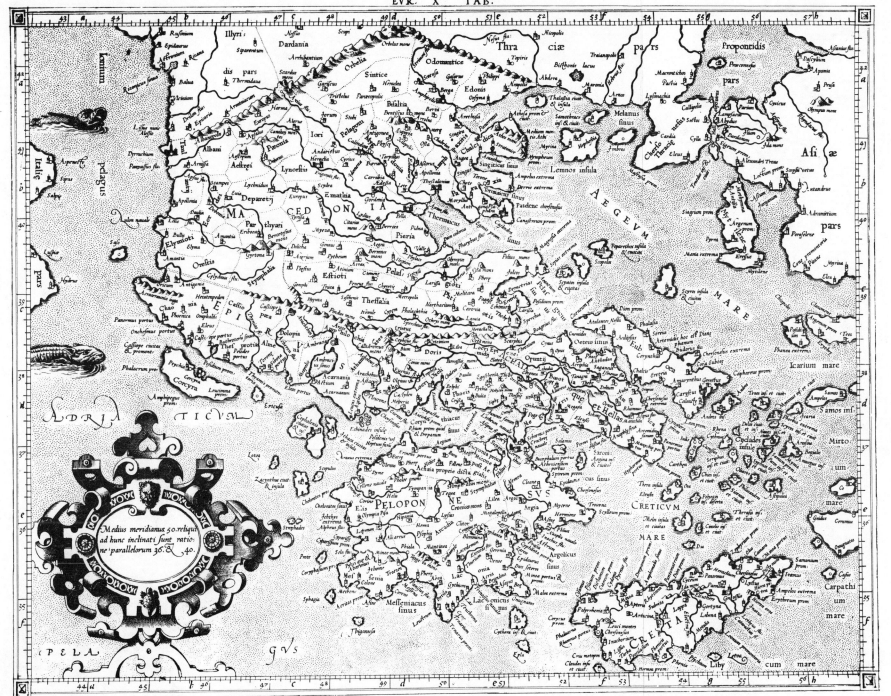

Mercator's Map X of Europe

Mercator's Map I of Asia